图解小学生英汉词典

LONGMAN ILLUSTRATED CHILDREN'S ENGLISH-CHINESE DICTIONARY

附送 活用词典练习

赵嘉文 编著 克里斯·福克斯 审订

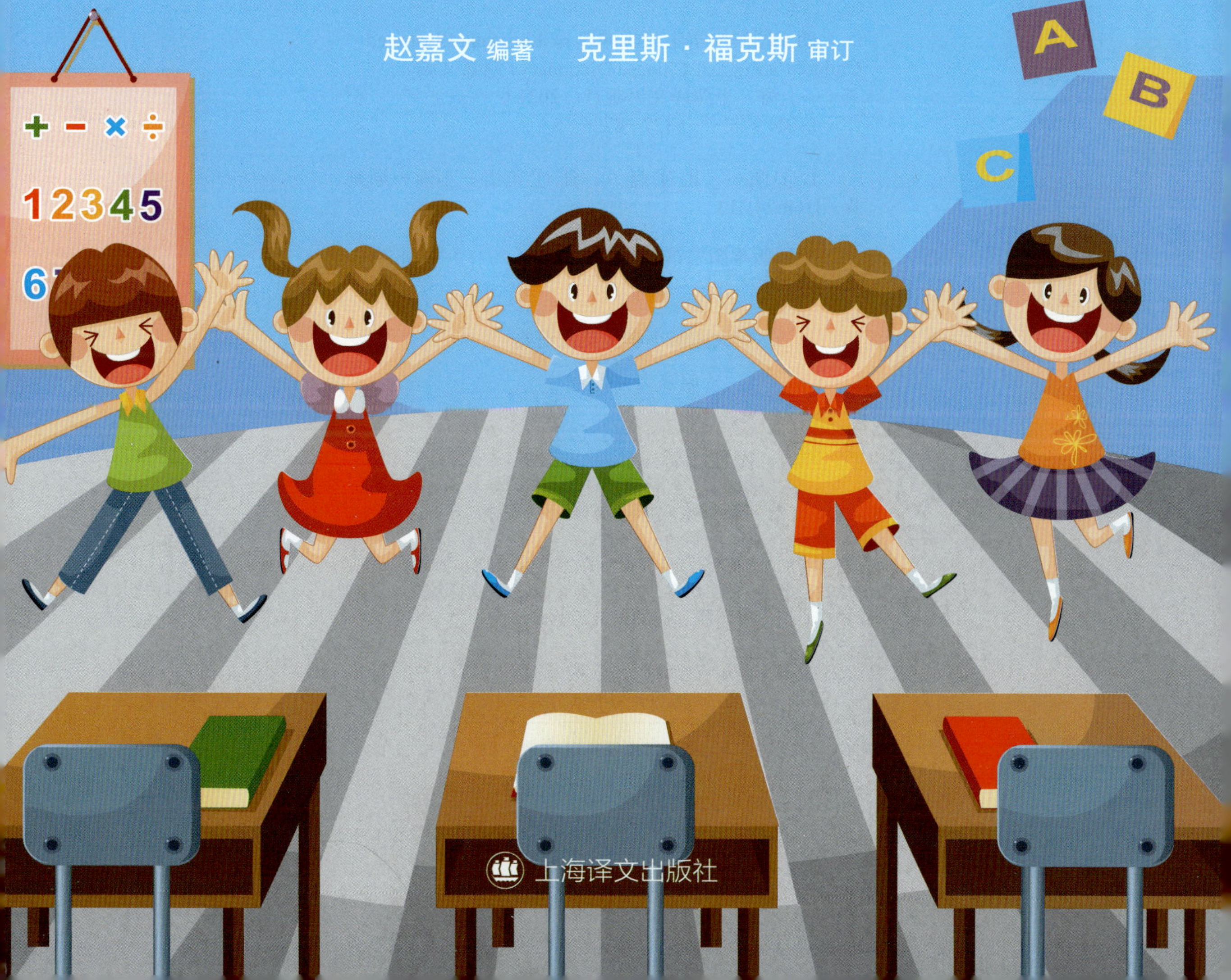

上海译文出版社

图字：09–2014–093 号

图书在版编目（CIP）数据

朗文图解小学生英汉词典 = Longman Illustrated Children's English-Chinese Dictionary / 赵嘉文编著 .—上海：上海译文出版社，2021.6
ISBN 978-7-5327-8726-5

Ⅰ. ①朗…　Ⅱ. ①赵…　Ⅲ. ①英语—小学—词典
Ⅳ. ①G624.313

中国版本图书馆 CIP 数据核字（2021）第 082925 号

朗文图解小学生英汉词典

赵嘉文　编著

上海译文出版社有限公司出版、发行
网址：www.yiwen.com.cn
200001　上海福建中路 193 号
浙江新华数码印务有限公司印刷

开本 787 × 1092　1/16　印张 25　字数 817,000
2021 年 6 月第 1 版　2021 年 6 月第 1 次印刷
印数：0,001–3,200 册

ISBN 978-7-5327-8726-5/H · 1517
定价：108 元

如有质量问题，请与承印厂质量科联系。T：0571-85155604

Contents 目录

Publisher and editorial team of the original version
原版工作人员名单

出版人 **Publisher**	黄娴 Isa Wong		
作者 **Author**	赵嘉文 Aman Chiu		
策划编辑 **Managing Editor**	王伟文 Wong Wai Man		
审订 **Reviser**	Chris Fox		
责任编辑 **Executive Editor**	梁洁莹 Crystal Leung		
编辑 **Editors**	谭乃英 Tam Laying	黄玉麟 Wong Yuk Lun	
	黄奇芳 Alice Wong	林耀辉 Andrew Lam	
照片编辑 **Photo Editor**	J.J. Mel Mohd Abdoh		
插图画师 **Illustrators**	甄淑明 Jessica Yan	钱惠卿 Chin Wai Heng	
	林美云 Gwen Lim	涂敏忠 Heymans Tho	
	Milch	罗衣 Roy Foo	陈素云 Sue Tan
平面设计 **Graphic Designers**	梁若基 Timothy Leung	张凤仪 Selina Cheung	
排版 **Pagemaking**	姚琍 Judy Yao		

To our readers 致读者

要培养自学英语的能力，一本有趣实用的英语词典是必不可少的。我们从培生引进的这本《朗文图解小学生英汉词典》是专为6—12岁儿童编写的工具书，旨在全面提升英语读写听说的能力。本词典的趣味和实用性体现于以下几点:

1. 精选**彩色照片和插图**约 1600 幅，图文并茂，既能提高学习兴趣，又能加深对词语的理解。
2. 收录 **5200 个词目和短语**，数量为同类型词典之冠。其中包括大量流行新词，例如 tablet computer（平板电脑）、USB drive（U盘），切合现今的学习需要。
3. **常用词**和小学生必须掌握的词汇，以星号突出，方便重点学习。
4. 特设**口语专栏**，包括“日常会话”、“教室里”、“餐厅里”等，内容都是活生生的英语口语。这不仅是本词典的特点，也是同类词典中少见或独创的。
5. 特设“**用法**”栏和“**注意**”栏，除了指出词语的正确用法，也分析学生常犯的错误，帮助他们分辨容易混淆的词语。
6. **附录**内容丰富，把英语知识呈现在生活化的情景中。

本词典附赠一本《**活用词典练习**》，帮助学生学习查阅词典的方法，学会善用词典，培养自学能力。

本词典的作者赵嘉文先生，在词典编写过程中精益求精，贯彻了其“寓教于乐”的宗旨。英国培生的词典专家 Chris Fox 先生审订了词典的正文，确保内容符合英语语用习惯。在此谨向两位致谢。

虽然我们在编辑的过程之中务求尽善尽美，但仍难免有错误或不足之处，尚请读者不吝指正。

要学好英语，必须从小培养查阅词典的好习惯。衷心希望本词典能成为儿童学习道路上的良师益友。

上海译文出版社

Acknowledgements 鸣谢

以下图片由王烨提供，谨此致谢！

9 (animal); 17 (bamboo); 20 (beak); 21 (beer); 32 (Buddha); 36 (cake); 39 (carnation); 40 (cart); 55 (container ship); 80 (drug); 81 (durian); 103 (folder); 122 (ham); 123 (handcuffs); 132 (hopscotch); 137 (ice skating); 154 (laptop); 162 (loaf); 164 (lotus); 175 (mobile phone); 176 (monitor); 178 (mouse); 190 (office); 191 (omelette); 200 (park); 203 (peach); 203 (paw); 204 (pedal); 218 (projector); 224 (quilt); 225 (rabbit);225 (radar); 226 (rap); 226 (rainbow); 227 (raw); 228 (recycle); 234 (river); 235 (roast); 236 (Rollerblade); 236 (roller skate); 237 (roundabout); 237 (rough); 239 (rusty); 241 (salmon); 241 (sampan); 242 (sashimi); 242 (satay); 242 (satellite);243 (scale); 243 (scanner); 243 (scarecrow); 245 (screwdriver); 245 (screen); 246 (sea lion); 246 (seahorse); 250 (sew); 252 (shirt); 254 (shrimp); 256 (silk); 262 (socket); 265 (soya bean); 267 (sponge); 268 (squash); 269 (squid); 269 (squirrel); 270 (starfruit); 270 (starfish); 276 (suck); 277 (sugarcane); 277 (sunbathe); 278 (sunshade);280 (swan); 280 (sweatshirt); 283 (tablet computer); 290 (theatre); 292 (thorn); 296 (toilet); 298 (touch screen); 299 (T-shirt); 302 (tracksuit); 303 (tug-of-war); 310 (USB drive); 318 (wastepaper basket); 319 (waterfall); 319 (water skiing); 322 (well); 323 (whale); 323 (wheelchair); 327 (windsurfing); 334 (yacht);335 (yoga); 335 (yoghurt); 336 (yo-yo); 337 (zebra)

How to use the dictionary 词典使用指南

词条的基本结构

星号标示英语书面语最常用的1000个词语及小学英语必须掌握的词语

释义

全书配有精美的彩色插图，有助加深对词目的理解

例句

词语搭配或动词短语以橙色显示

前面为国际音标（IPA），标示英国读音；后面为K.K.音标，标示美国读音

词性，包括：

adj 形	形容词
adv 副	副词
art 冠	冠词
conj 连	连接词
interj 感叹	感叹词
n 名	名词
num 数	数词
ordinal num 序数	序数
plural n 复数名词	复数名词
prep 介	介词
pron 代	代名词
v 动	动词

***home** /həʊm; hom/ *n* 名

the place where you live 家

I must go home now. 我现在必须回家了。

at home 在家里

Is your mother at home? 你的妈妈在家里吗？

Daily conversation 日常会话

make yourself at home 请随意（招呼客人时说的话）

"I'll get you a cup of tea. Make yourself at home." "我给你拿一杯茶，请随意。"

分列词条和多义词

swim[1] 和 swim[2] 的词性不同，分为两个词条

***swim[1]** /swɪm; swɪm/ *v* 动

swims, swimming, swam, swum

to move through water using your arms and legs 游泳；游水

They swam across the river. 他们游到了河的对岸。

swim[2] /swɪm; swɪm/ *n* 名

a period of time when you swim 游泳

Let's go for a swim. 我们去游泳吧。

***fly[1]** /flaɪ; flaɪ/ *v* 动

flies, flying, flew, flown

1. to move through the air 飞
   The birds are flying in the sky. 鸟儿在天空中飞。

2. to travel by plane 坐飞机
   We are flying to Bangkok tomorrow. 我们明天乘飞机去曼谷。

提供单词的不同词义

名词、动词和形容词的不同形式

***addition** /ə'dɪʃn; ə`dɪʃən/ *n* 名

没有复数的名词 → **无复数**

adding numbers together 加；加法

Let's do some simple addition. 我们来做一些简单的加法吧。

***address** /ə'dres; ə`drɛs/ *n* 名

显示不是加 s 构成复数形式的名词 → **复数**：***addresses***

the place where someone lives 地址

Please write the address on the envelope. 请在信封上写上地址。

***eat** /i:t; it/ *v* 动

eats, eating, ate, eaten ← 动词的不规则形式：顺序为现在式、现在分词、过去式和过去分词

to put food into your mouth and swallow it 吃

She is eating some cakes. 她在吃蛋糕。

***happy** /'hæpi; `hæpɪ/ *adj* 形

happier, happiest ← 形容词的比较级和最高级形式如果不是加 more 和 most 构成，逐一列出

feeling pleased 快乐的；愉快的

I'm happy because it's the start of the holidays. 我很开心，因为开始放假了。

反义 **sad, unhappy**

标签

attachment /ə'tætʃmənt; ə`tætʃmənt/ *n* 名

标示电脑用语 → 【电脑】a computer file sent with an email message（电邮的）附件

Can you download this email attachment for me? 可以帮我下载这个电邮附件吗？

***aeroplane** /'eərəpleɪn; `ɛrə͵plen/ *n* 名【英】 ← 标示英式英语和美式英语

美式：***airplane***

a flying machine with wings 飞机

Henry is playing with a toy aeroplane. 亨利正在玩玩具飞机。

同义 **plane**

airplane /'eəpleɪn; `ɛr͵plen/ *n* 名【美】

英式拼法的词条 → **英式** **aeroplane**

***beautiful** /ˈbjuːtɪfl; ˋbjutəfəl/
adj 形

1. nice to look at or listen to 美丽的；漂亮的
   Candy is a beautiful woman. 坎蒂是个美丽的女人。
   She has a beautiful voice. 她的嗓音很优美。

同义词 → **同义 pretty**

反义词 → **反义 ugly**

用法 形容男性一般不用 beautiful，而用 handsome。

2. very pleasant 美好的
   What a beautiful day! Let's go swimming. 今天天气多好！我们去游泳吧。

rug /rʌg; rʌg/ *n* 名

a piece of thick material that covers part of the floor 小地毯

My dog likes to sleep on the rug.
我的狗喜欢睡在小地毯上。

比较 carpet

cock /kɒk; kɑk/ *n* 名

a male chicken 公鸡

There are a lot of cocks on the farm.
农场里有很多公鸡。

另见 chicken, hen

与词目相关的词

也作/缩写

laptop /ˈlæptɒp; ˋlæpˌtɑp/ *n* 名

也作：***laptop computer*** ← 标示词目的其他写法

【电脑】a computer that you can carry with you 膝上型电脑；手提电脑

My father is working on his laptop.
爸爸正在用手提电脑工作。

同义 notebook

标示单词的缩写 →

***barbecue** /ˈbɑːbɪkjuː; ˋbarbɪˌkju/ *n* 名

缩写：***BBQ*** | 美式：***barbeque***

a meal cooked outside on a fire 烧烤野餐

We had a barbecue at the park yesterday. 我们昨天到公园烧烤。

BBQ /ˈbɑːbɪkjuː; ˋbarbɪˌkju/ *n* 名

the short form of **barbecue** ← 全称

☆barbecue 的缩写

"用法"栏和"注意"栏

介绍语法、拼法等知识，帮助你正确使用词语

***say** /seɪ; se/ *v* 动

says, saying, said, said

to speak or tell someone something 说；讲

"I'm very hungry!" he said. "我饿极了！"他说。

I don't understand what you said. 我不明白你说的话。

用法 say 不以人作宾语，例如不可以说 He said me something，要说 He said something to me。

***December** /dɪˈsembə; dɪˋsɛmbɚ/ *n* 名

缩写：***Dec.***

the twelfth month of the year 十二月

It is cold in December. 12 月时天气寒冷。

注意 开头的字母必须用大写。

***mail** /meɪl; mel/ *n* 名

无复数

letters and parcels that you send or receive 邮件；信件

We got a lot of mail last week. 上星期我们收到了很多邮件。

注意 发音和 male 相同。 ← "注意"栏也包括发音提示

口语例子

包括"In the classroom 教室里"、"Asking for directions 问路"、"At a restaurant 餐厅里"、"Greetings 问候"和"Daily conversation 日常会话"，帮助你活用英语

***aloud** /əˈlaʊd; əˋlaud/ *adv* 副

in a loud voice 大声地

The boys are crying aloud. 那些男孩在大声叫喊。

In the classroom 在教室里

"Paul, would you read the poem aloud to us?" "Sure." "保罗，请你给我们朗读这首诗吧。""好的。"

★a /ə; ɑ; *strong* 强读 eɪ; e/ *art* 冠

1. one 一个
   He bought a book and some pencils. 他买了一本书和几支铅笔。

2. each 每一
   I play basketball three times a week. 我每星期打三次篮球。

用法 a 和 an 用于单数可数名词之前，意思相当于中文的"一个"、"一张"、"一支"、"一只"、"一本"、"一辆"等等。

用 a 还是 an 看后面的词的读音而定，不看它开头的字母。

以下的词前面用 a:

1. 以非元音来起音的词（元音可见于书末的发音表），例如 a car（一辆汽车）和 a pig（一只猪）;
2. 以 u 字母开始而起音像 you 的词，例如 a university（一所大学）。

以下的词前面用 an:

1. 以元音来起音的词（元音可见于书末的发音表），例如 an egg（一只鸡蛋）;
2. 以 h 字母开始但 h 不发音的词，例如 an hour（一小时）和 an honest child（诚实的孩子）。

比较 **an, the**

另见 **article**

abbreviation /əˌbriːviˈeɪʃn; əˏbrivɪˋeʃən/ *n* 名

a shorter way of writing a word or name 缩写

"HK" is the abbreviation for "Hong Kong". HK 是 Hong Kong 的缩写。

ability /əˈbɪləti; əˋbɪlətɪ/ *n* 名

复数：***abilities***

the power to do something 能力；本领

This fish has the ability to jump above the water. 这种鱼能够跳出水面。

★able /ˈeɪbl; ˋebḷ/ *adj* 形

abler, ablest

can do something 能（做…）的；会…的

My dog is able to swim. 我的狗会游泳。

反义 **unable**

aboard[1] /əˈbɔːd; əˋbɔrd/ *prep* 介

on, in, or into (a bus, plane, ship or train) 上（巴士/飞机/船/火车）；在（巴士/飞机/船/火车）上

They went aboard the plane. 他们上了飞机。

aboard[2] /əˈbɔːd; əˋbɔrd/ *adv* 副

on, in, or into a bus, plane, ship or train 在巴士/飞机/船/火车上

Welcome aboard! 欢迎乘坐本巴士/飞机/船/火车！

★about[1] /əˈbaʊt; əˋbaʊt/ *prep* 介

having to do with 关于

Tell me about what happened. 告诉我发生了什么事。

This is a book about music. 这是一本关于音乐的书。

★about[2] /əˈbaʊt; əˋbaʊt/ *adv* 副

1. not exactly 大约
   I weigh about 30 kg. 我的体重约为 30 公斤。
2. in different places in the same area 四处；到处
   People are sitting about on the grass. 人们在草地四处坐着。

★about[3] /əˈbaʊt; əˋbaʊt/ *adj* 形

be about to do something

to be going to do something very soon 正要/即将做某事

The plane is about to take off. 飞机即将起飞。

★above /əˈbʌv; əˋbʌv/ *prep* 介

higher than; over 高于；在…上面

We flew above the clouds. 我们在云层上面飞行。

反义 **below**

abroad /əˈbrɔːd; əˋbrɔd/ *adv* 副

in or to another country 在国外；去国外

A

My brother is studying abroad. 我的哥哥在国外读书。

absent /ˈæbsənt; ˋæbsn̩t/ *adj* 形

not at your school or work 缺席的；不在的

Two students were absent today. 今天有两个学生缺席。

反义 **present**[1]

*__accept__ /əkˈsept; əkˋsɛpt/ *v* 动

to say yes to doing something 接受；答应

She invited me to the party, and I accepted. 她邀请我参加派对，我答应了。

反义 **refuse**

accident /ˈæksɪdənt; ˋæksədənt/ *n* 名

something that happens by mistake 意外

The woman was hurt in the road accident. 那个女人在交通事故中受伤。

*__according to__ /əˈkɔːdɪŋ tuː; əˋkɔrdɪŋ tu/ *prep* 介

said by someone or shown by something 根据；依照

According to the map, we are very close to the forest. 根据地图所示，我们离森林很近。

*__account__ /əˈkaʊnt; əˋkaʊnt/ *n* 名

an arrangement with a bank to look after your money for you 银行账户

We put our money in the bank account. 我们把钱存进银行账户里。

accurate /ˈækjʊrət; ˋækjərɪt/ *adj* 形

exactly correct 正确的；准确的

Is this clock accurate? 这只时钟准确吗?

accuse /əˈkjuːz; əˋkjuz/ *v* 动

accuses, accusing, accused, accused

to say someone has done something wrong 指责；控告

accuse someone of (doing) something 指责某人做某事

The teacher accused me of drawing on the wall. 老师指责我在墙上画东西。

ache[1] /eɪk; ek/ *v* 动

aches, aching, ached, ached

to hurt; be painful 疼痛；痛

My head is aching. 我头痛。

同义 **hurt**

ache[2] /eɪk; ek/ *n* 名

a continuous pain, especially one that is not very strong 疼痛；痛

The old man has an ache in his knee. 那位老人的膝盖痛。

*__achieve__ /əˈtʃiːv; əˋtʃiv/ *v* 动

achieves, achieving, achieved, achieved

to succeed in doing something 做成（某事）；达到（目标）

The students achieved good results in the exams. 那些学生在考试中取得了好成绩。

*__across__[1] /əˈkrɒs; əˋkrɔs/ *prep* 介

1. from one side to the other side of something 横过

   They built a bridge across the river. 他们在河上建了一座桥。

2. on the other side of something 在…对面

   The train station is across the road. 火车站就在马路对面。

Asking for directions 问路

"Excuse me. Where is the nearest post office?" "It's right across the street." "请问最近的邮局在哪儿？" "就在马路对面。"

*__across__[2] /əˈkrɒs; əˋkrɔs/ *adv* 副

from one side to the other side 到对面

Can you jump across? 你能跳到对面去吗?

*__act__[1] /ækt; ækt/ *v* 动

1. to do something 做

   The policemen acted quickly and caught the thief. 警察迅速行动，抓住了小偷。

2. to take a part in a play or film 扮演

   Paul acted the part of the prince in the play. 保罗在戏剧里扮演王子。

*__act__[2] /ækt; ækt/ *n* 名

a part of a play（戏剧的）一幕

The monster is killed in Act 2. 在第 2 幕怪兽被杀死了。

注意 开头的字母常用大写。

***action** /'ækʃn; `ækʃən/ *n* 名

a thing done 行动

Her quick action saved his life. 她行动敏捷，救了他的命。

active /'æktɪv; `æktɪv/ *adj* 形

1. moving around a lot 好动的；活跃的

   My grandfather is old but he is still very active. 我的祖父年纪很大，但精力充沛。

2. always ready to do things 主动的；积极的

   She is a good student and she is always active in helping her classmates. 她是一个好学生，经常主动帮助同学。

反义 **passive**

***activity** /æk'tɪvəti; æk`tɪvətɪ/ *n* 名

复数：***activities***

something you do 活动

She likes school activities. 她喜欢参加学校的活动。

actor /'æktə; `æktɚ/ *n* 名

a man or boy who acts in a play or film 男演员

His father is an actor. 他的爸爸是一名演员。

actress /'æktrɪs; `æktrɪs/ *n* 名

复数：***actresses***

a woman or girl who acts in a play or film 女演员

Lily is the best actress in the play. 莉莉是这出戏中最出色的女演员。

actual /'æktʃuəl; `æktʃuəl/ *adj* 形

real 真实的；实际的

Are those her actual words? 她真的是那么说的吗？

***actually** /'æktʃuəli; `æktʃuəlɪ/ *adv* 副

really 实际上

Do you actually believe in ghosts? 你真的相信有鬼吗？

***ad** /æd; æd/ *n* 名

the short form of **advertisement**☆ advertisement 的缩写

***add** /æd; æd/ *v* 动

1. to find the sum of numbers 加

   If you add 1 and 3 you get 4. 1 加 3 等于 4。

   1+3=4

2. to put two or more things together 增加；添加

   I added some salt to the soup. 我在汤里加了点盐。

***addition** /ə'dɪʃn; ə`dɪʃən/ *n* 名

无复数

adding numbers together 加；加法

Let's do some simple addition. 我们来做一些简单的加法吧。

***address** /ə'dres; ə`drɛs/ *n* 名

复数：***addresses***

the place where someone lives 地址

Please write the address on the envelope. 请在信封上写上地址。

adjective /'ædʒɪktɪv; `ædʒɪktɪv/ *n* 名

a word that tells you about someone or something. In the sentence "She is beautiful", "beautiful" is an adjective. 形容词（在 She is beautiful 这个句子中，beautiful 是个形容词。）

admire /əd'maɪə; əd`maɪr/ *v* 动

admires, admiring, admired, admired

to think a person or thing is very good 仰慕；赞赏

They admired my new coat. 他们赞赏我的新外衣。

***admit** /əd'mɪt; əd`mɪt/ *v* 动

admits, admitting, admitted, admitted

to agree that something bad is true or that you have done something wrong 承认

Mike admitted that he broke the vase. 迈克承认是他打破了花瓶。

反义 **deny**

***adult** /'ædʌlt; `ædʌlt/ *n* 名

a person who is not a child any more 成年人

Children can get in free but adults have to buy a ticket. 儿童可免费进场，成人则需要购票。

同义 **grown-up**

***adventure** /əd'ventʃə; əd`vɛntʃɚ/ *n* 名

an exciting thing that you do 冒险

The book is about the adventures of a boy called Harry Potter. 这本书是关于一个名叫哈利·波特的男孩的冒险。

adverb /'ædvɜːb; `ædvɝb/ *n* 名

a word that tells you how, when, or where. In the sentence "He ran quickly", "quickly" is an adverb. 副词（在 He ran quickly 这个句子中，quickly 是个副词。）

A

advertise /ˈædvətaɪz; ˋædvɚˏtaɪz/ *v* 动

advertises, advertising, advertised, advertised

to tell people about something, in order to persuade them to buy it or do it 登广告；做广告

Many companies advertise their products on TV. 很多公司在电视上做广告宣传他们的产品。

***advertisement** /ədˈvɜːtɪsmənt; ˏædvɚˋtaɪzmənt/ *n* 名

缩写：***ad***

a notice or a short film, that tries to persuade people to buy something or do something 广告

There are a lot of advertisements in the newspaper. 报纸上有很多广告。

***advice** /ədˈvaɪs; ədˋvaɪs/ *n* 名

无复数

something that you say that someone should do 劝告；建议

He gave me some good advice. 他给了我一些很好的建议。

***advise** /ədˈvaɪz; ədˋvaɪz/ *v* 动

advises, advising, advised, advised

to tell someone what they should do 劝告；建议

The doctor advised him to rest for a few days. 医生建议他休息几天。

***aeroplane** /ˈeərəpleɪn; ˋɛrəˏplen/ *n* 名【英】

美式：***airplane***

a flying machine with wings 飞机

Henry is playing with a toy aeroplane. 亨利正在玩玩具飞机。

同义 plane

affect /əˈfekt; əˋfɛkt/ *v* 动

to change or influence someone or something 影响

Smoking affects health. 吸烟影响健康。

比较 effect

afford /əˈfɔːd; əˋfɔrd/ *v* 动

to have enough money to buy something 负担得起

I can't afford to buy a new car. 我没钱买一辆新车。

用法 afford 只能用在主动句中。

***afraid** /əˈfreɪd; əˋfred/ *adj* 形

frightened 害怕的

I am not afraid of snakes. 我不怕蛇。

用法 不能用在名词之前，而且通常与 of 一起使用，即 afraid of。

***after**[1] /ˈɑːftə; ˋæftɚ/ *prep* 介

1. later than something（时间上）在…之后

   After breakfast I go to school. 我吃过早餐，然后上学去。

反义 before[1]

2. following someone or something 在…后面

   The dog is running after me. 那条狗在追我。

反义 before[1]

after school 放学后

Let's play basketball after school. 我们放学后一起去打篮球吧。

the day after tomorrow 后天

I'll see you the day after tomorrow. 我们后天再见吧。

***after**[2] /ˈɑːftə; ˋæftɚ/ *conj* 连

when you have done something, or when something has happened 在…之后

I watch TV after I have done my homework. 我做完作业后才看电视。

反义 before[2]

***after**[3] /ˈɑːftə; ˋæftɚ/ *adv* 副

later than something or someone 之后；以后

Peter came home first. Lily came home soon after. 彼得先回到家里，不久之后莉莉也回来了。

反义 before[3]

***afternoon** /ˌɑːftəˈnuːn; ˏæftɚˋnun/ *n* 名

the time between midday and evening 下午

I saw Ross yesterday afternoon. 昨天下午我看到了罗斯。

Greetings 问候

"Good afternoon. How are you today?" "Good afternoon. I'm fine, thank you. And you?" "下午好！你今天好吗？""下午好！我很好，谢谢。你呢？"

afterwards /ˈɑːftəwədz; ˋæftɚwɚdz/ *adv* 副【英】

美式：***afterward***

later 在…之后；然后

Last night we watched a movie first and had dinner afterwards. 昨晚我们先去看电影，然后吃晚饭。

***again** /əˈgen; əˋgɛn/ *adv* 副

once more 再次

The teacher asked me to do it again. 老师要我再做一次。

again and again 一再

They kept on trying again and again until they succeeded. 他们一再尝试，直到成功为止。

Daily conversation 日常会话

"Can you say that again? I didn't hear you." "All right." "可以再说一遍吗？我听不到呢。""好的。"

***against** /ə'genst; ə`gɛnst/ *prep* 介

1. not agreeing with something 反对
   Many people are against the idea of building a new airport. 很多人反对兴建新机场。
2. trying to defeat someone in a game or fight（比赛时）对抗
   Our school will play basketball against your school. 我们学校将与你们学校进行篮球比赛。
3. touching a surface 倚着；靠着
   Put the bicycle against the wall. 把自行车靠在墙上。

against the law/rules 违反法律/规则

It is against the school rules to run in the corridors. 在走廊追逐是违反校规的行为。

***age** /eɪdʒ; edʒ/ *n* 名

how old you are 年龄

Lily and Ross are the same age. 莉莉和罗斯同年。

agent /'eɪdʒənt; `edʒənt/ *n* 名

a person who does business for somebody else 代理人；经纪

He bought an air ticket to Paris from the agent. 他从代理人那里买了去巴黎的机票。

***ago** /ə'gəʊ; ə`go/ *adv* 副

in the past 以前

She left about ten minutes ago. 她大概10分钟前离开了。

用法 用 ago 时要与过去式连用，例如上句不可以说：She has left about ten minutes ago.

***agree** /ə'griː; ə`gri/ *v* 动

agrees, agreeing, agreed, agreed

to say yes to something 同意；赞成

Ross suggested having a party and we agreed. 罗斯提议开派对，我们都赞成。

agree with someone 同意某人

I agree with you. 我同意你。

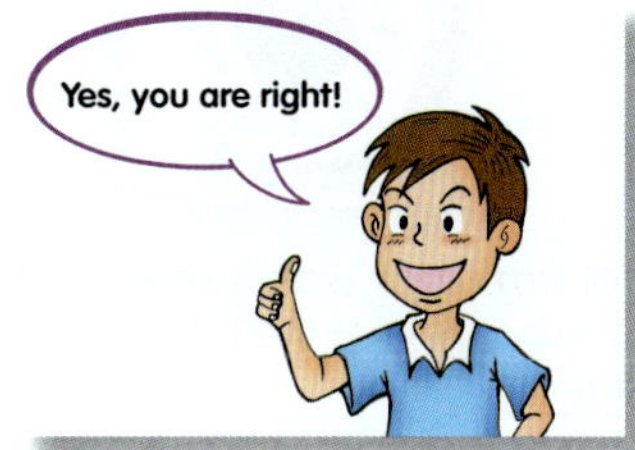

agree to something 赞同某事

He will not agree to the idea. 他不会赞成这个想法。

反义 disagree

agriculture /'ægrɪˌkʌltʃə; `ægrɪˌkʌltʃɚ/ *n* 名

无复数

growing things and keeping animals for food 农业

People in this village work in agriculture. 这个村子的居民以农业为生。

ahead /ə'hed; ə`hɛd/ *adv* 副

1. in front of someone or something 在前
   Be careful – there's a busy road ahead! 小心！前面的道路很繁忙！
2. in or for the future 在未来；预先；事前
   We need to plan ahead. 我们需要预先计划。

Daily conversation 日常会话

go ahead 请吧

"May I use your phone?" "Go ahead!" "我可以用你的电话吗？""请吧！"

aid /eɪd; ed/ *n* 名

无复数

help 帮助；救助

The government gives aid to poor people. 政府向贫穷的人提供援助。

aim[1] /eɪm; em/ *v* 动

to want to achieve something 目标是；打算

We aim to win. 我们的目标是要获胜。

aim[2] /eɪm; em/ *n* 名

something that you want or plan to do 目标

His aim is to get good results in the exam. 他的目标是在考试中取得好成绩。

同义 goal

***air** /eə; ɛr/ *n* 名

无复数

the gas that we breathe 空气

Let's go out for some fresh air. 我们到外边呼吸一下新鲜空气吧。

the air 空中；天空

The eagles are flying in the air. 鹰在空中飞翔。

by air 以航空件邮寄；乘飞机

Let's send the parcel by air. 我们按航空件把包裹寄出吧。

We went to Beijing by air. 我们乘飞机去北京。

air-conditioner /'eə kənˌdɪʃnə; `ɛr kənˌdɪʃənɚ/ *n* 名

a machine for cooling air 冷气机；空调

A

Turn off the air-conditioner. It's too cold. 把空调关掉吧，太冷了。

aircraft /ˈeəkrɑːft; ˋɛrˌkræft/ *n* 名

复数：*aircraft*

a plane or helicopter 飞行器（如飞机、直升飞机等）

The passengers are getting off the aircraft. 乘客正在下飞机。

air force, airforce /ˈeə fɔːs; ˋɛr fɔrs/ *n* 名

the people who use planes to fight for a country 空军

That country has a strong air force. 那个国家拥有强大的空军。

比较 **army, navy**

airline /ˈeəlaɪn; ˋɛrˌlaɪn/ *n* 名

a company that carries people by plane 航空公司

Cathay Pacific is a large airline in Hong Kong. 国泰航空是香港一家大规模的航空公司。

airmail /ˈeəmeɪl; ˋɛrˌmel/ *n* 名

无复数

letters or parcels sent by plane 航空邮件

He sent a letter by airmail. 他以航空件的形式把信寄出。

airplane /ˈeəpleɪn; ˋɛrˌplen/ *n* 名【美】

英式 **aeroplane**

***airport** /ˈeəpɔːt; ˋɛrˌpɔrt/ *n* 名

a place where planes land and take off 飞机场

Many planes land at the airport every day. 每天在这个机场降落的飞机很多。

***alarm** /əˈlɑːm; əˋlɑrm/ *n* 名

something such as a bell that warns you of danger 警报；警铃

Where's the fire alarm? 火警铃在哪儿？

alarm clock /əˈlɑːm ˌklɒk; əˋlɑrm ˌklɑk/ *n* 名

a clock that makes a noise to wake you up 闹钟

My alarm clock wakes me up at 7 a.m. every day. 我的闹钟每天早上7点把我叫醒。

***album** /ˈælbəm; ˋælbəm/ *n* 名

a book for photographs or stamps 相册；邮票簿

One of his birthday gifts is a stamp album. 他的生日礼物中有一本邮票簿。

alcohol /ˈælkəhɒl; ˋælkəˌhɔl/ *n* 名

something that can make you drunk 酒精

All wines contain alcohol. 所有的葡萄酒都含酒精。

alien /ˈeɪliən; ˋelɪən/ *n* 名

a being from another world 外星人；外太空生物

It has twelve pairs of legs! Isn't it an alien? 它有十二对脚！难道不是外太空生物吗？

alike /əˈlaɪk; əˋlaɪk/ *adj* 形

the same in some way 相似的；相同的

The two girls look alike. 这两个女孩长得很像。

用法 alike 不能用在名词之前。

alive /əˈlaɪv; əˋlaɪv/ *adj* 形

having life; living 活着的

His grandparents are still alive. 他的祖父母仍然健在。

用法 alive 不能用在名词之前。

反义 **dead**

***all[1]** /ɔːl; ɔl/ *adj* 形

the whole of something 全部的

He ate all the cake. 他把蛋糕吃光了。

***all[2]** /ɔːl; ɔl/ *pron* 代

everyone or everything 每个人；每样东西；全部

We all wanted to go to the beach. 我们全都想去海滩。

***all[3]** /ɔːl; ɔl/ *adv* 副

completely 完全

He forgot all about doing his homework. 他完全忘了要做功课。

all over 到处都是

There was mud all over the floor. 地板上到处都是泥浆。

(not) at all 根本（不）；丝毫（没有）

There was nothing to eat at all. 根本没有东西吃。

allow /əˈlaʊ; əˋlaʊ/ *v* 动

to let someone do something 容许；准许

My mother allowed me to go on a picnic last Saturday. 妈妈准许我上星期六去野餐。

反义 **forbid**

***all right[1]** /ˌɔːl ˈraɪt; ˌɔl ˋraɪt/ *adj* 形

1. good enough, but not very good 好的；不错的

   The film was all right, but it wasn't very exciting. 那部电影不错，但是不够刺激。

2. safe; not ill; not hurt 没事的；安全的；健康的

   Sam just had a cold but he is all

right now. 山姆只是感冒，现在没事了。

***all right²** /ˌɔ:l ˈraɪt; ˏɔl ˋraɪt/ *interj* 感叹

used when saying yes to someone 好的（用于口语，表示同意）

"Can I use your mobile phone?" "All right." "可以借用你的手机吗？" "好的，没问题。"

almond /ˈɑ:mənd; ˋɑmənd/ *n* 名

a kind of seed that you can eat 杏仁

This almond cake tastes good. 这个杏仁蛋糕很好吃。

***almost** /ˈɔ:lməust; ˋɔlˏmost/ *adv* 副

nearly 几乎；差不多

My grandfather is almost 100 years old. 我的祖父快 100 岁了。

***alone¹** /əˈləun; əˋlon/ *adj* 形

without anyone else 单独的；独自的

I was alone in the room. 我独自一人在房间里。

用法 alone 不能用在名词之前，而且多用于书面语，口语一般说 by yourself/on your own，例如 I was by myself。

***alone²** /əˈləun; əˋlon/ *adv* 副

not with other people 单独地；独自地

The old woman lives alone. 那老妇人一个人住。

***along** /əˈlɒŋ; əˋlɔŋ/ *prep* 介

from one end of a place towards the other 沿着

We walked along the beach. 我们沿着海滩走。

***aloud** /əˈlaud; əˋlaud/ *adv* 副

in a loud voice 大声地

The boys are crying aloud. 那些男孩在大声叫喊。

In the classroom 在教室里

"Paul, would you read the poem aloud to us?" "Sure." "保罗，请你给我们朗读这首诗吧。" "好的。"

alphabet /ˈælfəbet; ˋælfəˏbɛt/ *n* 名

a list of letters used to spell words 字母表

You can find all the 26 letters of the English alphabet on this page. 你可以在这页中找到英文字母表中所有 26 个字母。

alphabetical /ˌælfəˈbetɪkl; ˏælfəˋbɛtɪkl/ *adj* 形

in the order of the letters of the alphabet 按字母次序排列的

The words in this dictionary are in alphabetical order. 这本词典的单词是按字母顺序排列的。

***already** /ɔ:lˈredi; ɔlˋrɛdɪ/ *adv* 副

before now 已经

The film has already started. 电影已经开始了。

***also** /ˈɔ:lsəu; ˋɔlso/ *adv* 副

as well; too 也；又；同样

He speaks English and also a little Japanese. 他会说英语，还会说一点日语。

***although** /ɔ:lˈðəu; ɔlˋðo/ *conj* 连

even if; even so 虽然；尽管

Although he was ill, he went to school. 他虽然生病，但还是去上学了。

注意 although 和 but 不可出现在同一句中。

同义 **though**

***altogether** /ˌɔ:ltəˈgeðə; ˏɔltəˋgɛðɚ/ *adv* 副

including everyone or everything 总共

There are five people in the shop altogether. 店里共有 5 个人。

***always** /ˈɔ:lweɪz; ˋɔlwez/ *adv* 副

every time, or at all times 总是

I always get up at six o'clock. 我总是 6 点钟就起床。

am /əm; əm; *strong* 强读 æm; æm/ *v* 动

缩写：*'m*

a form of **be**, used with "I" ☆be 的一种形式，与 I 一起使用

I am happy. 我很高兴。

Am I good-looking? 我样子好看吗？

***a.m.** /ˌeɪ ˈem; ˏe ˋɛm/

in the morning; before midday 上午；午前

My father gets up at 8 a.m. 爸爸早上 8 点起床。

另见 **p.m.**

A

***amazing** /ə'meɪzɪŋ; ə`mezɪŋ/ *adj* 形

very surprising and exciting 令人吃惊的；了不起的

What an amazing story! 多么棒的一个故事啊！

ambition /æm'bɪʃn; æm`bɪʃən/ *n* 名

a strong wish to be successful 抱负；野心

His ambition is to be an astronaut! 他的志向是要成为宇航员！

ambulance /'æmbjələns; `æmbjələns/ *n* 名

a van that takes sick or injured people to hospital 救护车

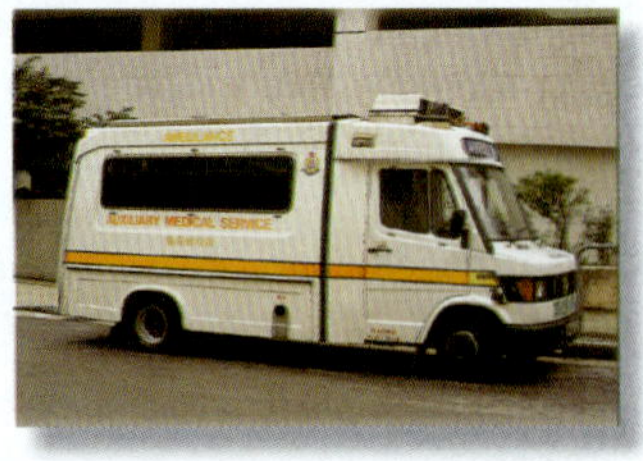

They carried the sick old woman into the ambulance. 他们把那个生病的老妇抬进救护车。

***among** /ə'mʌŋ; ə`mʌŋ/ *prep* 介

1. in the middle of 在…中
   The house is hidden among trees. 这座房子隐藏在树林中。
2. to each one of a group 给每个成员
   Tracy shared the chocolate among the class. 特蕾西把巧克力分给班里的同学。

用法 among 用于指在三个或以上的人或物之间，例如 Lily is standing among the boys（莉莉站在一群男孩之间）。在两个人或物之间一般用 between，例如 Lily is standing between Ben and Ross（莉莉站在本和罗斯两人之间）。

比较 **between**

***amount** /ə'maʊnt; ə`maʊnt/ *n* 名

how much of something there is 数量

The old woman has saved a small amount of money. 这个老妇人存了一小笔钱。

amuse /ə'mju:z; ə`mjuz/ *v* 动

amuses, amusing, amused, amused

to make someone laugh or smile 使人发笑

His stories are very funny and they always amuse me. 他的故事很有趣，总是使我发笑。

amusement park /ə'mju:zmənt ˌpɑ:k; ə`mjuzmənt ˌpɑrk/ *n* 名

a large park where people can have fun 游乐场；游乐园

We had a nice day at the amusement park. 我们在游乐场度过了愉快的一天。

amusing /ə'mju:zɪŋ; ə`mjuzɪŋ/ *adj* 形

funny and making you laugh 有趣的，使人发笑的

This is an amusing story. 这是一个有趣的故事。

同义 **funny**

***an** /ən; ən; *strong* 强读 æn; æn/ *art* 冠

one 一个［只、张、本等］

I want an orange. 我要一个橙子。

用法 an 和 a 一样，用于单数可数名词之前。an 放在以元音来起音的词前面（元音可见于书末的发音表），或者以 h 字母开始但 h 不发音的词前面，以代替 a。详见 a 条。

比较 **a, the**

另见 **article**

ancestor /'ænsəstə; `ænsɛstɚ/ *n* 名

someone in your family who lived a long time ago 祖先

My ancestors came from Shanghai. 我的祖先来自上海。

ancient /'eɪnʃənt; `enʃənt/ *adj* 形

very old 古代的；古老的

There are many ancient buildings in Beijing. 北京有许多古老的建筑物。

反义 **modern**

***and** /ənd; ənd; *strong* 强读 ænd; ænd/ *conj* 连

a word used to join words in a sentence or two parts of a sentence 和；又；与

I have a cat and two dogs. 我有一只猫和两条狗。

She came in and sat down. 她走进来，然后坐下。

用法 and 用于连接两个词语或句子的两个部分。

angel /'eɪndʒəl; `endʒəl/ *n* 名

a servant of God 天使

All angels have wings. 所有的天使都有翅膀。

anger /ˈæŋgə; ˋæŋgɚ/ *n* 名

无复数

a strong feeling which makes you want to shout at people or hurt them 愤怒

She cannot control her anger. 她怒不可遏。

angle /ˈæŋgl; ˋæŋgl̩/ *n* 名

the corner where two lines meet 角；角度

These two lines form an angle of 90°. 这两条线组成了一个直角。

***angrily** /ˈæŋgrəli; ˋæŋgrɪlɪ/ *adv* 副

in an angry way 生气地；愤怒地

"Go away!" he shouted angrily. "走开！"他愤怒地喊道。

***angry** /ˈæŋgri; ˋæŋgrɪ/ *adj* 形

angrier, angriest

feeling that you want to shout at someone or hurt someone 生气的；愤怒的

When he is angry, his face turns bright red. 他生气的时候总是涨红了脸。

angry about something 为某事生气

Lily was angry about losing the money. 莉莉因为丢了钱而生气。

angry with someone 生某人的气

Ada was angry with Paul because he lied to her. 爱达对保罗非常生气，因为保罗向她撒谎。

***animal** /ˈænɪml; ˋænəml̩/ *n* 名

something living that is not a plant 动物

We can see many animals in the zoo. 我们在动物园可以见到很多动物。

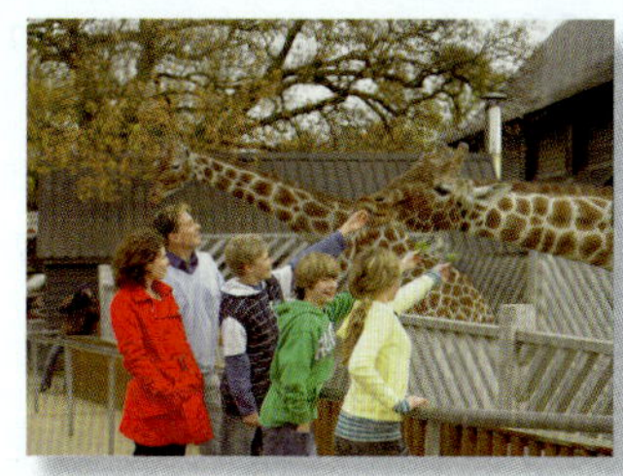

***ankle** /ˈæŋkl; ˋæŋkl̩/ *n* 名

the part of your body that joins your foot to your leg 脚踝

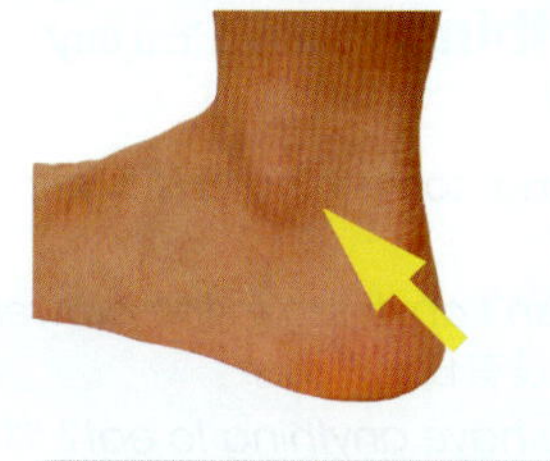

Ben hurt his ankle when he was playing badminton. 本打羽毛球时扭伤了脚踝。

annoy /əˈnɔɪ; əˋnɔɪ/ *v* 动

to make someone a little angry 使人生气

The children annoyed the teacher because they were noisy. 那些孩子很顽皮，所以把老师惹怒了。

annoyed /əˈnɔɪd; əˋnɔɪd/ *adj* 形

feeling a little angry 生气的

He was annoyed because he missed his train. 他没赶上火车，所以很生气。

annoying /əˈnɔɪ·ɪŋ; əˋnɔɪ·ɪŋ/ *adj* 形

making you angry 使人生气的；使人烦恼的

The noise was annoying. 那噪音真烦人。

annual /ˈænjuəl; ˋænjuəl/ *adj* 形

happening every year or once a year 每年的

She invited me to go to the annual party. 她邀请我参加一年一度的舞会。

***another** /əˈnʌðə; əˋnʌðɚ/ *adj* 形

1. one more 再一；又一

   Let's play another game. 我们再玩一次吧。

2. a different one 另一个

   I don't like this one. Do you have another one? 我不喜欢这一件，你有另外一件吗？

one another 互相

We greeted one another. 我们互相问好。

同义 **each other**（见 **each²**）

***answer¹** /ˈɑːnsə; ˋænsɚ/ *v* 动

to reply to a question 回答

The teacher asked Sally to answer the question. 老师要求莎莉回答问题。

answer back 顶嘴；无礼回答

Don't answer back. It's rude! 不要顶嘴，那是不礼貌的！

同义 **reply¹**

反义 **ask**

> **In the classroom 在教室里**
>
> *"Can you answer my question, John?" "Sure."* "约翰，你能回答我的问题吗？""当然。"

***answer²** /ˈɑːnsə; ˋænsɚ/ *n* 名

what you say or write to a question 答案

Please write down your answers. 请把你的答案写下来。

同义 **reply²**

***ant** /ænt; ænt/ *n* 名

a tiny insect 蚂蚁

A

Ants live in nests under the ground. 蚂蚁住在地下的巢穴里。

***anxious** /'æŋkʃəs; `æŋkʃəs/ *adj* 形

worried 不安的；担心的

Candy was anxious the day before the exam. 坎蒂在考试前夕很不安。

***any[1]** /'eni; `ɛnɪ/ *adj* 形

used in questions or negative sentences to mean "one or some" 任何的（用在疑问句或否定句）

There isn't any tea. 没有茶了。

比较 **some[1]**

Daily conversation 日常会话

"Do you have any T-shirts?" "Yes. Over there." "你们有T恤吗？""有的，在那儿。"

***any[2]** /'eni; `ɛnɪ/ *pron* 代

used in questions or negative sentences to mean "one or some" 任何一个；任何一些（用在疑问句或否定句）

My brother wanted some sweets but there isn't any left. 我的弟弟想吃糖，但糖已经被吃光了。

比较 **some[2]**

any[3] /'eni; `ɛnɪ/ *adv* 副

much, more or a small amount 一点；一些

Are you feeling any better? 你觉得好一点了吗？

any longer 再长一点时间

We've to go. We can't stay any longer. 我们要走了，不能再待着了。

any more, anymore 不再

Helen does not go to our school anymore. 海伦已不在我们的学校上学了。

***anybody** /'eniˌbɒdi; `ɛnɪˌbadɪ/, **anyone** /'eniwʌn; `ɛnɪˌwʌn/ *pron* 代

any person 任何人

I did not see anybody. 我没有看见谁。

Has anyone seen my school bag? 有没有人见过我的书包？

用法 在疑问句或否定句中常用 anybody 或 anyone。在肯定句中则常用 somebody 或 someone，例如 There's somebody over there（那里有人）。

***anything** /'eniθɪŋ; `ɛnɪˌθɪŋ/ *pron* 代

any thing; something 任何东西；一些东西

There isn't anything in the drawer. 抽屉里没有任何东西。

Do you have anything to eat? 你有吃的东西吗？

用法 在疑问句或否定句中常用 anything。在肯定句中则常用 something，例如 I want something to eat（我想吃点东西）。

anyway /'eniweɪ; `ɛnɪˌwe/ *adv* 副

in any case 无论如何；不管怎样

The doll is expensive but I'll buy it anyway. 那个玩具娃娃很贵，但我还是要买它。

anywhere /'eniweə; `ɛnɪˌhwɛr/ *adv* 副

in, at or to any place 无论哪里；任何地方

I don't want to go anywhere today. 今天我任何地方都不想去。

用法 在疑问句或否定句中常用 anywhere。在肯定句中则常用 somewhere，例如 I want to go somewhere warm for the trip（我想去暖和的地方旅行）。

apart /ə'pɑ:t; ə`part/ *adv* 副

separated by a distance or time 相距；相隔

The school and the park are just 100 metres apart. 学校和公园只相距100米。

apartment /ə'pɑ:tmənt; ə`partmənt/ *n* 名【美】

英式 **flat**

ape /eɪp; ep/ *n* 名

a large monkey without a tail 猿

Apes have long arms. 猿的手臂很长。

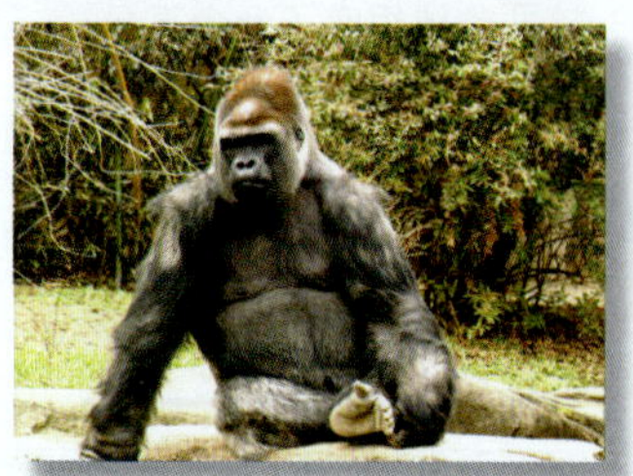

apologize /ə'pɒlədʒaɪz; ə`pɑləˌdʒaɪz/ *v* 动

apologizes, apologizing, apologized, apologized

也作：***apologise***【英】

to say you are sorry 道歉；认错

I apologized to her for being late. 我因迟到而向她道歉。

apology /ə'pɒlədʒi; ə`pɑlədʒɪ/ *n* 名

复数：***apologies***

something you say or write to show that you are sorry 道歉

Please accept my apologies. 请接受我的道歉。

apostrophe /ə'pɒstrəfi; ə`pɑstrəfɪ/ *n* 名

the sign used to show that letters have been left out or used with "s" to show that something belongs to someone (') 撇号；省字号

另见 附录：Punctuation 标点符号

***appear** /ə'pɪə; ə`pɪr/ *v* 动

1. to seem 好像；似乎

The bird appears friendly, but it may bite you. 那只鸟看上去很友善，但它也可能会啄你。

2. to come into view 出现；露出

   The dog suddenly appears in the doorway. 那只狗突然出现在门前。

反义 **disappear**

appearance /əˈpɪərəns; əˋpɪrəns/ *n* 名

the way you look 外表；外貌

Her appearance has changed since I last saw her. 自从我上次见到她后，她的外表改变了。

appetite /ˈæpɪtaɪt; ˋæpəˌtaɪt/ *n* 名

无复数

the feeling that you want to eat something 胃口

I don't have much appetite today. 我今天没什么胃口。

lose your appetite 丧失食欲

I lost my appetite when I was ill. 我生病的时候什么都不想吃。

***apple** /ˈæpl; ˋæpl/ *n* 名

a round hard fruit that is usually red or green 苹果

My parrot likes to eat apples. 我的鹦鹉喜欢吃苹果。

apple pie 苹果馅饼；苹果派

My mother has made an apple pie. 妈妈做了一个苹果馅饼。

***apply** /əˈplaɪ; əˋplaɪ/ *v* 动

applies, applying, applied, applied

to ask for something 申请

He applied for a job in a bank. 他申请了银行里的工作。

***April** /ˈeɪprəl; ˋeprəl/ *n* 名

缩写：***Apr.***

the fourth month of the year 四月

Easter is usually in April. 复活节通常在 4 月。

注意 开头的字母必须用大写。

apron /ˈeɪprən; ˋeprən/ *n* 名

a cloth you put over your clothes to keep them clean 围裙

My mother wears an apron when she cooks. 妈妈在烧菜时穿着围裙。

aquarium /əˈkweəriəm; əˋkwɛrɪəm/ *n* 名

复数：***aquariums/aquaria***

a glass container or a building that has fish and other sea animals in it 水族馆

Let's look at the sharks in the aquarium. 我们到水族馆去看鲨鱼吧。

are /ə; ɚ, *strong* 强读 ɑː; ɑr/ *v* 动

缩写：***'re***

a form of **be**, used with "we", "you", and "they" ☆be 的一种形式，与 we，you 和 they 一起使用

We are Chinese. 我们是中国人。

Are you sleepy? 你困吗？

Who are they? 他们是谁？

***area** /ˈeəriə; ˋɛrɪə/ *n* 名

1. the size of a surface 面积

   What's the area of the park? 这个公园的面积有多大？

2. a place 地区；地方

   There aren't any supermarkets in this area. 这个地区没有超市。

***aren't** /ɑːnt; ɑrnt/

the short form of "**are not**" ☆are not 的缩写

We aren't going to the party. 我们不去参加聚会了。

***argue** /ˈɑːgjuː; ˋɑrgju/ *v* 动

argues, arguing, argued, argued

to not agree, often speaking loudly and angrily 争论；争吵

My sisters are always arguing about something. 我的姊妹们经常为一些事吵架。

argue with someone 与某人争论/争吵

My father is arguing with the waiter about the bill. 父亲正为账单跟服务员争论。

A

***argument** /ˈɑːgjumənt; ˋargjəmənt/ *n* 名

a quarrel 争论；争辩

Peter had an argument with Ross yesterday so they do not talk to each other today. 彼得昨天和罗斯吵了一架，所以他们今天不跟对方说话。

arithmetic /əˈrɪθmətɪk; əˋrɪθməˌtɪk/ *n* 名

无复数

adding, multiplying etc numbers 算术

She is not very good at arithmetic. 她的算术不太好。

***arm** /ɑːm; ɑrm/ *n* 名

the part of your body between your shoulder and your hand 手臂

My father has strong arms. 我爸爸的手臂很有力。

***armchair** /ˈɑːmtʃeə; ˋarmˌtʃɛr/ *n* 名

a comfortable chair with sides to rest your arms on 扶手椅

My grandmother was sitting in the armchair. 我的祖母坐在扶手椅上。

***army** /ˈɑːmi; ˋarmɪ/ *n* 名

复数：*armies*

a large group of soldiers who fight on land 军队；陆军

The army attacked the city. 军队攻打了这个城市。

比较 **air force, navy**

***around**[1] /əˈraʊnd; əˋraʊnd/ *prep* 介

1. on all sides of something 围着；环绕

   The whole family sits around the table at dinner. 晚饭时全家人围坐在桌子旁。
2. moving in a circle 旋转；绕着

   The earth moves around the sun. 地球绕着太阳转。
3. in many different places 到处；各处

   The harbour has ships from all around the world. 来自世界各地的船只停泊在港口。

***around**[2] /əˈraʊnd; əˋraʊnd/ *adv* 副

1. moving in a circle 旋转；绕着

   The wheels slowly started to turn around. 轮子慢慢地旋转起来。
2. in different places 各处；四处

   On my first day at the school, one of the teachers showed me around. 在我上学的第一天，一位老师带我在学校四处走走看看。

arrange /əˈreɪndʒ; əˋrendʒ/ *v* 动

arranges, arranging, arranged, arranged

1. to put something in order 排列

   The girl is arranging her dolls on the shelf. 那女孩把她的玩具娃娃在架子上排好。

2. to make plans for something 安排

   Let's arrange a birthday party for Paul! 我们为保罗安排一个生日派对吧！

arrangement /əˈreɪndʒmənt; əˋrendʒmənt/ *n* 名

a plan that something will happen 安排

They have made all the arrangements for the party. 他们已为派对做好一切安排。

***arrest** /əˈrest; əˋrɛst/ *v* 动

to catch someone 拘捕

The police arrested the thief. 警察拘捕了小偷。

arrival /əˈraɪvl; əˋraɪvl̩/ *n* 名

无复数

when someone or something gets to a place 到达

Sam met us on his arrival in Hong Kong. 山姆到达香港后与我们见面。

***arrive** /əˈraɪv; əˋraɪv/ *v* 动

arrives, arriving, arrived, arrived

to get to a place 到达

The train will arrive at this station at 5 p.m. 火车将在下午 5 点到达这个车站。

arrow /ˈærəʊ; ˋæro/ *n* 名

1. a stick with a sharp point, used as a weapon 箭

   He shot an arrow at the bird. 他一箭射向那只鸟。
2. a sign that points the way 箭头

A

This arrow points to the exit. 箭头指向出口。

***art** /ɑ:t; ɑrt/ *n* 名

无复数

the skill of drawing, painting, etc 艺术；美术

Keith loves art. 基斯热爱艺术。

article /ˈɑ:tɪkl; ˋɑrtɪkḷ/ *n* 名

the words **a**, **an** and **the** 冠词

用法 冠词是置于名词之前的词，说明该名词所指称的事物是否特定。英语中有三个冠词：a、an、the。如名词所指称的事物只是一般而不是特定的，用 a 或 an。如名词所指称的事物是特定的，则用 the。

另见 **a, an, the**

artist /ˈɑ:tɪst; ˋɑrtɪst/ *n* 名

someone who is good at drawing, painting, etc 艺术家；画家

The artist is painting a picture. 那位画家在画一幅画。

***as¹** /əz; əz; *strong* 强读 æz; æz/ *conj* 连

1. when; while 正当；在…的同时
   I sang as I ran. 我边跑边唱。
2. because 因为
   Paul can't go to school as he is ill. 保罗因为生病而不能上学。

as if, as though 好像；仿佛

It looks as if it is going to rain. 天看起来好像快要下雨了。

as usual 照常；像往常一样

I got up early in the morning as usual. 我像平常一样很早起床。

***as²** /əz; əz; *strong* 强读 æz; æz/ *adv* 副

used when comparing two people, things, etc 用于比较两个人、两件物件等

as…as… 像…一样…

Ivan is as tall as Henry. 伊凡和亨利一样高。

ash /æʃ; æʃ/ *n* 名

复数：***ashes***

the powder left after something has been burnt 灰

The palace was burnt to ashes. 那座宫殿已烧成灰烬。

***ashamed** /əˈʃeɪmd; əˋʃemd/ *adj* 形

feeling bad about something you have done 惭愧的；羞愧的

He was ashamed that he had lied. 他因为说谎而感到羞愧。

aside /əˈsaɪd; əˋsaɪd/ *adv* 副

to or towards one side 向一边；到一边

He moved aside to let them pass. 他站到一边让他们通过。

***ask** /ɑ:sk; æsk/ *v* 动

to say a question 发问；问

"What's your name?" she asked. "你叫什么名字？" 她问道。

ask someone for something 向…要…

I asked my mother for some sweets. 我向妈妈要了一些糖果。

ask someone to 请（某人）；要（某人）

Paul asked me to go to his birthday party. 保罗邀请我参加他的生日派对。

反义 **answer¹, reply¹**

***asleep** /əˈsli:p; əˋslip/ *adj* 形

sleeping 睡着的

Keep quiet! The baby is asleep. 保持安静！婴儿睡着了。

fall asleep 入睡

I fell asleep on the sofa. 我在沙发上睡着了。

用法 asleep 不能用在名词之前。

反义 **awake**

***assembly** /əˈsembli; əˋsɛmblɪ/ *n* 名

复数：***assemblies***

a meeting 集会

We have an assembly in the school hall every morning. 我们每天早上在学校礼堂举行集会。

assistant /əˈsɪstənt; əˋsɪstənt/ *n* 名

1. someone who sells things in a shop 店员；伙计
   He asked the shop assistant about the price of the toy train. 他向店员询问那辆玩具火车的价钱。

2. someone who helps a person in the job 助手
   He is the doctor's assistant. 他是医生的助手。

astronaut /ˈæstrənɔ:t; ˋæstrəˌnɔt/ *n* 名

a person who travels in space 太空人；宇航员

A

The astronaut is walking on the moon. 宇航员正在月球上面漫步。

***at** /ət; ət; *strong* 强读 æt; æt/ *prep* 介

1. in a particular place 在（某地）
   I'm at home now. 我现在在家里。
2. used about the time when something happens 在（某时）
   I'll see you at 9 o'clock. 我会在9点跟你见面。
3. towards someone or something 向；对着
   She looked up at the sky. 她抬头看天。

at first 最初
At first I didn't like him, but now we're good friends. 起初我不喜欢他，但现在我们是好朋友了。
at last 最后；终于
The rain stopped at last. 雨终于停了。
at once 立刻；马上
Please come at once! 请马上来！
at the same time 同时
They arrived at the same time. 他们同时到达。

ate /eɪt; et/ *v* 动
the past tense of **eat** ☆eat 的过去式

athlete /'æθliːt; `æθlit/ *n* 名
a person who is good at sports 运动员

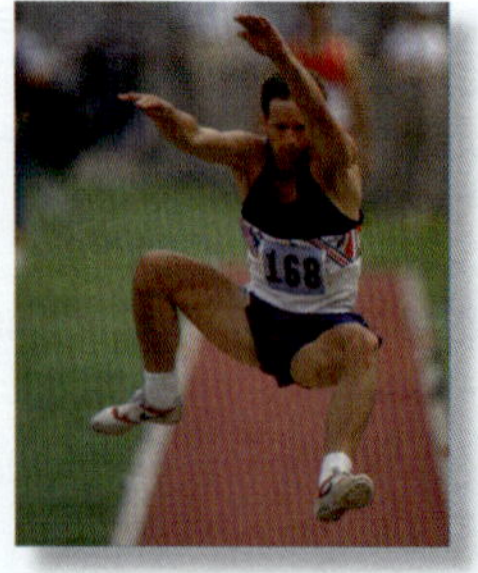

Henry wants to be an athlete. 亨利希望成为运动员。

athletics /æθ'letɪks; æθ`lɛtɪks/ *n* 名
无复数
sports like running and jumping 田径运动
Agnes is a member of the athletics club. 艾格尼丝是田径学会的会员。

atlas /'ætləs; `ætləs/ *n* 名
复数：***atlases***
a book of maps 地图集；地图册
Can you look up Shanghai in the atlas? 你能在地图册上找出上海吗？

attachment /ə'tætʃmənt; ə`tætʃmənt/ *n* 名
【电脑】a computer file sent with an email message（电邮的）附件
Can you download this email attachment for me? 可以帮我下载这个电子邮件的附件吗？

attack[1] /ə'tæk; ə`tæk/ *v* 动
to start fighting or hurting someone 攻击；袭击
Suddenly, the lion attacked the zoo-keeper. 突然，狮子袭击了动物园管理员。

attack[2] /ə'tæk; ə`tæk/ *n* 名
an attempt to hurt someone, or to get control of a place by force 攻击；袭击
The attack on the island failed. 向该岛发动的进攻失败了。

attempt[1] /ə'tempt; ə`tɛmpt/ *v* 动
to try to do something 尝试；试图
They attempted to swim across the harbour. 他们尝试游过这个海港。

***attempt**[2] /ə'tempt; ə`tɛmpt/ *n* 名
If you make an attempt to do something, you try to do it 尝试；努力
He made an attempt to climb the mountain. 他试图爬上山。

attend /ə'tend; ə`tɛnd/ *v* 动
to go to a meeting, class etc 参加；出席
She attended the meeting. 她参加了会议。

***attention** /ə'tenʃn; ə`tɛnʃən/ *n* 名
无复数
when you carefully listen to, think about or watch someone or something 留心；专心
We should give attention to details. 我们必须留心细节。

> **In the classroom 在教室里**
> *"Can I have your attention, please?"* "请大家注意一下！"

***attract** /ə'trækt; ə`trækt/ *v* 动
to make people interested 吸引
The show attracts a big audience every night. 这个表演每晚都吸引来大批观众。

attractive /ə'træktɪv; ə`træktɪv/ *adj* 形
beautiful and nice to look at 吸引的；动人的
She is an attractive woman with long hair. 这个女人有一头长发，样子漂亮。

***audience** /'ɔːdiəns; `ɔdɪəns/ *n* 名
无复数
all the people watching or listening to something 观众；听众

The audience clapped loudly. 观众大声鼓掌。

***August** /'ɔ:gəst; `ɔgəst/ *n* 名

缩写：***Aug.***

the eighth month of the year 八月

My brother was born in August. 我的兄弟在 8 月出生。

注意 开头的字母必须用大写。

***aunt** /ɑ:nt; ænt/ *n* 名

the sister of your mother or father, or the wife of your uncle 姨妈；姑妈；婶婶；伯母；舅母

My aunt is a nurse. 我的姨妈是护士。

author /'ɔ:θə; `ɔθɚ/ *n* 名

a person who writes books etc 作者

She is the author of this book. 她是这本书的作者。

automatic /ˌɔ:tə'mætɪk; ˌɔtə`mætɪk/ *adj* 形

working by itself 自动的

You don't have to open the door because it is automatic. 你不用开门，因为这是自动门。

***autumn** /'ɔ:təm; `ɔtəm/ *n* 名【英】

美式：***fall***

the season between summer and winter 秋天；秋季

In autumn, leaves fall from the trees. 在秋天，树叶从树上落下来。

avenue /'ævənju:; `ævəˌnu/ *n* 名

a wide street, usually with trees on both sides 林荫道；大道

I often take a walk with my dog along this avenue. 我经常和我的狗沿着这条林荫大道散步。

***average** /'ævərɪdʒ; `ævərɪdʒ/ *adj* 形

found by adding several amounts together and dividing the total by the number of amounts 平均的

The average age of the students in this class is ten. 这个班学生的平均年龄是 10 岁。

***avoid** /ə'vɔɪd; ə`vɔɪd/ *v* 动

to stay away from a person, place or thing 避免；避开

He wanted to avoid me so he didn't come to the party. 他想避免和我碰面，所以没来参加聚会。

***awake** /ə'weɪk; ə`wek/ *adj* 形

not sleeping 醒的；没睡的

He was awake the whole night. 他整晚没有睡。

用法 awake 不能用在名词之前。

反义 **asleep**

***award[1]** /ə'wɔ:d; ə`wɔrd/ *v* 动

to give someone a prize for doing something well 奖赏（某人）

The school awarded Paul two books. 学校奖励给保罗两本书。

***award[2]** /ə'wɔ:d; ə`wɔrd/ *n* 名

a prize given to someone for doing something well 奖赏

Henry won the award for Best Actor. 亨利赢得了最佳男演员奖。

***away** /ə'weɪ; ə`we/ *adv* 副

1. to another place 到别处

   Go away! 走开！

   She turned round and walked away. 她转身就走开了。

2. not at home or at work 不在家；不在工作岗位

   My parents are away from home. 我的父母现在不在家。

***awful** /'ɔ:fl; `ɔfl̩/ *adj* 形

very bad 糟透了的；可怕的

The weather was awful. 天气十分恶劣。

awfully /'ɔ:fli; `ɔfl̩ɪ/ *adv* 副

very 十分；非常

It's awfully cold today. 今天冷得很厉害。

axe /æks; æks/ *n* 名

a tool for cutting wood 斧头

The firefighter broke the door down with an axe. 消防员用斧头劈开这扇门。

B

***baby** /ˈbeɪbi; ˋbebɪ/ *n* 名

复数：***babies***

a very young child 婴儿

The baby is crying. 这个婴儿在哭。

***back[1]** /bæk; bæk/ *n* 名

1. the part of your body that is behind you 背部
   His back is aching. 他背痛。
2. （无复数）the part of something that is farthest from the front 后面
   I always sit at the back of the classroom. 我总是坐在教室后排。

反义 **front[1]**

***back[2]** /bæk; bæk/ *adv* 副

in the place where someone or something was before 回原处

Please go back to your seat. 请回到你的座位上。

Daily conversation 日常会话

"I'm sorry. Stanley went out a few minutes ago." "When will he be back?" "Around five." "对不起，史丹利几分钟前出去了。""他什么时候回来呢？""大概5点。"

background /ˈbækgraʊnd; ˋbækˌgraʊnd/ *n* 名

the back part of a picture or photo, behind the main things or people （图画或照片的）背景

There are three tall trees in the background of the photo. 这照片的背景里有3棵大树。

***backpack** /ˈbækpæk; ˋbækˌpæk/ *n* 名

a bag that you carry on your back 背包；背囊

This backpack is very heavy. 这背囊很重。

backup /ˈbækʌp; ˋbækˌʌp/ *n* 名

【电脑】an extra copy of a file（档案的）备份

Mr Brown makes a backup of his files every day. 布朗先生每天都会给文件做个备份。

***backwards** /ˈbækwədz; ˋbækwɚdz/ *adv* 副【英】

美式：***backward***

to a place that is behind you 向后；向后退

The boy took a step backwards to let the old man pass. 那男孩向后退一步，让路给老人。

反义 **forward**

***bacon** /ˈbeɪkən; ˋbekən/ *n* 名

无复数

thin slices of salted or smoked meat from a pig 腌/熏猪肉；烟肉；培根

Do you want bacon or ham for your breakfast? 你早餐要吃熏肉片还是火腿?

***bad** /bæd; bæd/ *adj* 形

worse, worst

1. not good or not nice 不好的；坏的
   Eating too many sweets is bad for your teeth. 吃太多糖果对牙齿不好。

   反义 **good**
2. not able to do something well 差的；不擅长的
   I am bad at singing. 我不擅长唱歌。

   反义 **good**

badge /bædʒ; bædʒ/ *n* 名

something you fix to your clothes or uniform 徽章

We wear the school badge on our shirts. 我们在衬衫上佩戴校徽。

badly /ˈbædli; ˋbædlɪ/ *adv* 副

worse, worst

1. not well; in a bad way 不好；差
   The man treats his dog badly. 那个男人待他的狗很差。

   反义 **well**
2. very much 非常
   Those poor people badly need help. 这些穷人非常需要帮助。

badminton /ˈbædmɪntən; ˋbædmɪntən/ *n* 名

无复数

a game in which you use a racket to hit a small object with feathers 羽毛球（运动）

Badminton is my favourite sport. 羽毛球是我最喜爱的运动。

***bag** /bæg; bæg/ *n* 名

something you use for carrying or storing things 袋；包

My school bag is heavy. 我的书包很重。

B

Daily conversation 日常会话

"Do you need a bag?" "No, thank you." "你需要袋子吗？""不用了，谢谢。"

baggage /ˈbæɡɪdʒ; ˋbæɡɪdʒ/ *n* 名

无复数

bags that you carry when you travel 行李

She hasn't got much baggage with her. 她没带很多行李。

用法 baggage 没有复数形式，不可与 many 和 few 一起使用。如要说明数量，必须用量词，例如 a piece of baggage（一件行李）和 two pieces of baggage（两件行李）。

同义 **luggage**

***bake** /beɪk; bek/ *v* 动

bakes, baking, baked, baked

to cook in an oven 烘；烤

My mother is baking some cookies for us. 妈妈正在给我们烤曲奇饼。

baker /ˈbeɪkə; ˋbekɚ/ *n* 名

a person who makes bread and cakes 面包师；糕点师

Sally's uncle is a baker. 莎莉的叔叔是个面包师。

bakery /ˈbeɪkəri; ˋbekərɪ/ *n* 名

复数：***bakeries***

a shop that sells bread and cakes 面包店

They bought some cakes at the bakery. 他们在面包店买了一些蛋糕。

***balcony** /ˈbælkəni; ˋbælkənɪ/ *n* 名

复数：***balconies***

a place above the ground on the outside of a building 露台；阳台

I can see the harbour from my balcony. 我从露台可看见海港。

***ball** /bɔːl; bɔl/ *n* 名

a round thing used in games 球

My cat likes to play with a ball. 我的猫喜欢玩球。

ballet /ˈbæleɪ; ˋbæle/ *n* 名

无复数

a kind of dancing that tells a story 芭蕾舞

They went to a ballet last Saturday. 他们上星期六看了一场芭蕾舞演出。

***balloon** /bəˈluːn; bəˋlun/ *n* 名

a small rubber bag that is filled with air 气球

The clown is giving out balloons to the children. 那小丑正在给小朋友送气球。

ballpoint pen /ˌbɔːlpɔɪnt ˈpen; ˌbɔlpɔɪnt ˋpen / *n* 名

也作：***ballpoint***

a pen with a small metal ball at the point 圆珠笔；原子笔

You should use a ballpoint pen in the test. 你在测验时必须使用圆珠笔。

bamboo /ˌbæmˈbuː; bæmˋbu/ *n* 名

无复数

a tall plant with long hard stems 竹

Pandas like to eat bamboo. 熊猫喜欢吃竹子。

***banana** /bəˈnɑːnə; bəˋnænə/ *n* 名

a long curved fruit with yellow skin 香蕉

Monkeys like to eat bananas. 猴子喜欢吃香蕉。

***band** /bænd; bænd/ *n* 名

1. a narrow piece of cloth, plastic, rubber, etc 带子；箍带

   Tracy uses a rubber band to tie her hair back. 翠西用橡皮筋把头发扎到脑后。

2. a group of people who play music together 乐队

   The band is playing on the stage. 乐队正在台上演奏。

bandage /ˈbændɪdʒ; ˋbændɪdʒ/ *n* 名

a piece of cloth used to cover a wound 绷带

The nurse is putting a bandage round his elbow. 护士正在用绷带包扎他的肘部。

***bang**[1] /bæŋ; bæŋ/ *n* 名

a sudden loud noise 砰然巨响

The box fell onto the floor with a

loud bang. 砰的一声，箱子掉到地上。

***bang²** /bæŋ; bæŋ/ *v* 动

to hit something with a loud noise 用力敲打

Don't bang the table with your spoon. 别用汤匙砰砰地敲打桌子。

***bank** /bæŋk; bæŋk/ *n* 名

1. a place where people keep their money 银行

He went to the bank to get some money. 他去银行取钱。

2. the side of a river or lake 河岸；堤岸；湖畔

She takes a walk along the river bank every evening. 她每天傍晚都会沿着河岸散步。

banknote, bank note

/ˈbæŋknəʊt; ˋbæŋkˏnot/ *n* 名【英】

美式：***bill***

a piece of paper money 纸币；钞票

He likes to collect old banknotes. 他喜欢收集旧纸币。

同义 **note¹**

banquet /ˈbæŋkwɪt; ˋbæŋkwɪt/ *n* 名

a large formal meal for an important event 宴会

The government held a big banquet for a visit by the president. 政府为到访的总统举行盛大的宴会。

***bar** /bɑː; bar/ *n* 名

1. a piece of soap, chocolate, or metal 棒；条；块

The girl is eating a chocolate bar. 那女孩在吃一块巧克力。

2. a place where people go to drink alcohol 酒吧

Sam likes to go to the bar after work. 山姆下班后喜欢去酒吧。

***barbecue** /ˈbɑːbɪkjuː; ˋbarbɪˏkju/ *n* 名

缩写：***BBQ*** | 美式：***barbeque***

a meal cooked outside on a fire 烧烤野餐

We had a barbecue at the park yesterday. 我们昨天到公园烧烤。

barber /ˈbɑːbə; ˋbarbɚ/ *n* 名

someone whose job is to cut men's hair 理发师

The barber cut my hair short. 理发师把我的头发剪短了。

the barber's 理发店

I went to the barber's to have my hair cut. 我去了理发店剪发。

barefoot /ˈbeəfʊt; ˋbɛrˏfut/ *adv* 副

without shoes 赤足地

The children went barefoot on the beach. 小孩在沙滩上赤着脚走。

bargain¹ /ˈbɑːgɪn; ˋbargɪn/ *n* 名

something that is cheap and much less than the usual price 便宜货；减价品

This teddy bear was expensive but now it is a bargain at only 10 dollars. 这只玩具熊本来很贵，现在是减价品，只售 10 元。

bargain² /ˈbɑːgɪn; ˋbargɪn/ *v* 动

to try to get the best price when you are buying or selling 讲价；议价

She bargained with the salesman. 她和售货员讨价还价。

***bark¹** /bɑːk; bark/ *v* 动

if a dog barks, it makes a loud noise 吠

The dog barked at the man. 狗对着那个人吠。

***bark²** /bɑːk; bark/ *n* 名

1. a loud noise made by a dog 狗吠

   The dog gave a loud bark. 那条狗大声地叫。

2. (无复数) the outside part of a tree 树皮

   The bark of this tree is very thick. 这棵树的树皮非常厚。

baseball /ˈbeɪsbɔːl; ˋbesˏbɔl/ *n* 名

1. (无复数) a game played with a bat and a ball, in which you have to run around the field 棒球(运动)

Can you play baseball? 你会打棒球吗？

2. the ball used in a game of baseball 棒球

   A baseball is smaller than a basketball. 棒球比篮球小。

***basic** /ˈbeɪsɪk; ˋbesɪk/ *adj* 形

simple and most necessary 基本的；基础的

Mrs Smith is studying basic Chinese. 史密斯太太正在学基础汉语。

***basin** /ˈbeɪsn; ˋbesn̩/ *n* 名【英】

a large bowl fixed to the wall for washing your hands and face 洗手盆；洗脸盆

There is a basin in the corner of the bathroom. 在浴室的角落有一个洗脸盆。

***basket** /ˈbɑːskɪt; ˋbæskɪt/ *n* 名

a light container for holding or carrying things 篮子

She took away two apples from the basket. 她从篮子里拿走两个苹果。

***basketball** /ˈbɑːskɪtbɔːl; ˋbæskɪtˏbɔl/ *n* 名

1. （无复数）a game played by two teams in which a large ball is thrown into a net 篮球（运动）

   We play basketball every Friday. 我们每个星期五都打篮球。

2. the ball used in a game of basketball 篮球

   I shot the basketball into the basket. 我把篮球投进篮框。

***bat** /bæt; bæt/ *n* 名

1. a small animal like a mouse with wings 蝙蝠

   Bats come out at night. 蝙蝠晚上出来。

2. a piece of wood used to hit a ball in some games 球拍；球板；球棒

   May I borrow your table tennis bats? 我可以借用你的乒乓球拍吗？

***bath**[1] /bɑːθ; bæθ/ *n* 名

1. 【英】（美式：***bathtub***）a thing that you sit in to wash yourself 浴缸

   I washed my dog in the bath. 我把狗放在浴缸里给它洗澡。

2. if you have a bath, you wash your body in a bath 洗澡

   I am very dirty. I need a bath now. 我脏极了，现在要洗个澡。

have a bath, take a bath 洗澡

I take a bath every night. 我每天晚上都洗澡。

***bath**[2] /bɑːθ; bæθ/ *v* 动【英】

美式：***bathe***

to wash yourself or someone in a bath 给…洗澡

She is bathing her baby in the bathroom. 她在浴室给婴儿洗澡。

***bathroom** /ˈbɑːθrʊm; ˋbæθˏrum/ *n* 名

a room where you can wash yourself, or a room with a toilet 浴室；洗手间

There are two bathrooms in our flat. 我们的住所里有两个浴室。

另见 附录：Inside a flat 住所里

bathtub /ˈbɑːθtʌb; ˋbæθˏtʌb/ *n* 名【美】

英式 **bath**[1]

***battery** /ˈbætəri; ˋbætərɪ/ *n* 名

复数：***batteries***

a thing that gives electricity 电池

The toy car needs two small batteries. 这辆玩具汽车需用两节小电池。

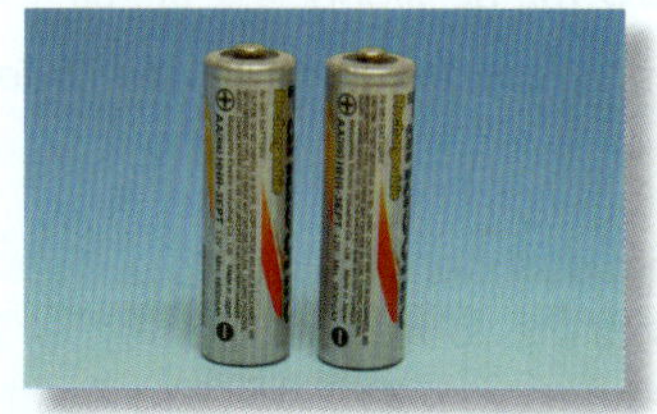

***battle** /ˈbætl; ˋbætl̩/ *n* 名

a fight between armies, ships, or planes 战斗；战役

The soldiers fought bravely in the battle. 士兵在战役中英勇奋战。

比较 **war**

bauhinia /bəʊˈhɪnɪə; boˋhɪnɪə/ *n* 名

无复数

a flowering plant 洋紫荆

B

B

There is a white bauhinia flower on the flag of Hong Kong. 香港的区旗上有一朵白色的洋紫荆花。

bay /beɪ; be/ *n* 名

a curved area of sea with land next to it 海湾

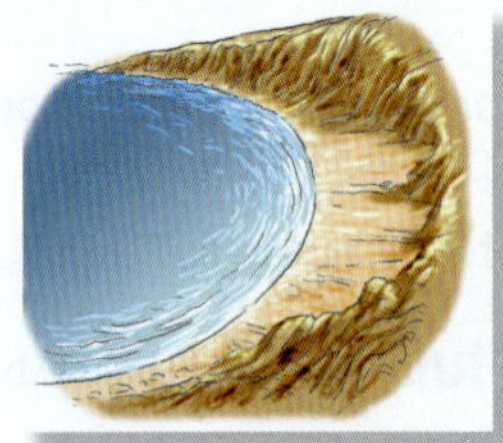

I can see a beautiful bay from the window. 我从窗户望去可以看见美丽的海湾。

BBQ /ˈbɑːbɪkjuː; ˋbɑrbɪˏkju/ *n* 名

the short form of **barbecue** ☆barbecue 的缩写

***be** /bi; bɪ; *strong* 强读 biː; bi/ *v* 动

am/is/are, being, was/were, been

used to tell something about people or things 是；在；发生

I am a student. 我是个学生。

What are you doing? 你在做什么？

He was born in 2005. 他于 2005 年出生。

另见 **am, are, been, being[1], is, was, were**

***beach** /biːtʃ; bitʃ/ *n* 名

复数：***beaches***

a sandy area beside the sea 滩；海滩

The children are playing on the beach. 那些孩子正在沙滩上玩耍。

beach umbrella 太阳伞

It's very hot. We need a beach umbrella. 太热了，我们需要太阳伞。

bead /biːd; bid/ *n* 名

a small ball with a hole through the middle 有孔小珠；珠子

She was wearing a string of beads around her neck. 她在颈上戴着一串珠子。

beak /biːk; bik/ *n* 名

the hard part of a bird's mouth 鸟嘴

This bird has a very long beak. 这只鸟有很长的嘴。

***bean** /biːn; bin/ *n* 名

a small seed eaten as food 豆

There are some green beans in the soup. 这碗汤里有些青豆。

bean curd 豆腐

Tracy likes to eat fried bean curd. 翠西喜欢吃煎豆腐。

bean sprout 豆芽；豆芽菜

The cook put some bean sprouts in the noodles. 厨师在面里放了一些豆芽。

***bear** /beə; bɛr/ *n* 名

a large furry wild animal 熊

I saw some bears at the zoo. 我在动物园里看到几头熊。

beard /bɪəd; bɪrd/ *n* 名

hair on a man's face below his mouth 胡子

Santa Claus has a long white beard. 圣诞老人留着长长的白胡子。

***beat** /biːt; bit/ *v* 动

beats, beating, beat, beaten

1. to defeat someone in a game or fight 打败；胜过

   She beat me at swimming. 她游泳赢了我。

2. to hit someone or something many times 打；敲

   Ross was beating his drums. 罗斯在打鼓。

beaten /ˈbiːtn; ˋbitn̩/ *v* 动

the past participle of **beat** ☆beat 的过去分词

***beautiful** /ˈbjuːtɪfl; ˋbjutəfəl/ *adj* 形

1. nice to look at or listen to 美丽的；漂亮的

   Candy is a beautiful woman. 坎蒂是个美丽的女人。

   She has a beautiful voice. 她的嗓音很优美。

同义 **pretty**

反义 **ugly**

用法 形容男性一般不用 beautiful，而用 handsome。

2. very pleasant 美好的

   What a beautiful day! Let's go swimming. 今天天气多好！我们去游泳吧。

beautifully /ˈbjuːtɪfli; ˋbjutəfəlɪ/ *adv* 副

very well 美丽地；美妙地

She sings beautifully. 她唱得好听极了。

became /bɪˈkeɪm; bɪˋkem/ *v* 动

the past tense of **become** ☆become 的过去式

***because[1]** /bɪˈkɒz; bɪˋkɔz/ *conj* 连

used when you are giving a reason for something 因为

Philip did not go to school

because he was ill. 菲利浦没有上学，因为他病了。

***because²** /bɪˈkɒz; bɪˋkɔz/ *prep* 介

used when you are giving a reason for something

because of something or someone 因为；由于

We stayed at home because of the typhoon. 因为台风侵袭，我们留在家里。

***become** /bɪˈkʌm; bɪˋkʌm/ *v* 动

becomes, becoming, became, become

to change into, or grow to be something 变成；成为

I want to become a pilot when I grow up. 我长大后想成为一名飞行员。

***bed** /bed; bɛd/ *n* 名

something you sleep on 床

My cat sleeps on my bed in the daytime. 我的猫白天睡在我的床上。

go to bed 睡觉

I usually go to bed at ten thirty. 我通常晚上十点半睡觉。

make the bed 整理床铺

My brother helped me to make the bed. 弟弟帮我铺好床。

Daily conversation 日常会话

"It's 11 o'clock now. It's time for bed." "Okay, I will go to bed now." "现在 11 点了，该去睡觉了。" "好的，我现在就去睡觉。"

***bedroom** /ˈbedrʊm; ˋbɛd͵rum/ *n* 名

a room for sleeping in 卧室

My sister and I share a bedroom. 我和姐姐共用一间卧室。

另见 附录：Inside a flat 住所里

***bee** /biː; bi/ *n* 名

a small flying insect that makes honey 蜜蜂

I saw some bees in the garden. 我在花园看到一些蜜蜂。

***beef** /biːf; bif/ *n* 名

无复数

the meat from a cow or bull 牛肉

We often eat beef. 我们经常吃牛肉。

been /biːn; bɪn/ *v* 动

1. the past participle of **be** ☆be 的过去分词

   I have been sick for two days. 我已经病了两天了。

2. **have been to a place**

   if you have been to a place, you have visited it 去过；曾到过某地

   We have been to London. 我们去过伦敦。

beer /bɪə; bɪr/ *n* 名

无复数

a brown drink with alcohol in it 啤酒

Chris likes to drink beer. 克里斯喜欢喝啤酒。

beetle /ˈbiːtl; ˋbitl/ *n* 名

an insect with a hard back 甲虫

There is a beetle on the leaf. 树叶上有一只甲虫。

***before¹** /bɪˈfɔː; bɪˋfɔr/ *prep* 介

1. earlier than something 在…之前

   I always finish my homework before dinner. 我总是在吃晚饭前做完作业。

   反义 after¹

2. in front of 在…前面

   My dog is running before me. 我的狗跑在我前面。

   反义 after¹

***before²** /bɪˈfɔː; bɪˋfɔr/ *conj* 连

earlier than something 在…之前

Sally usually watches TV before she goes to bed. 莎莉睡觉前通常会看看电视。

反义 after²

***before³** /bɪˈfɔː; bɪˋfɔr/ *adv* 副

at an earlier time; in the past 以前

I have never seen a shark before. 我以前从未见过鲨鱼。

反义 after³

beg /beg; bɛg/ *v* 动

begs, begging, begged, begged

to ask for food, money or other things 恳求；乞求

The man was begging for food. 那人在讨饭吃。

Daily conversation 日常会话

I beg your pardon 请原谅；请再说一遍

"It is 9 o'clock now." "I beg your pardon?" "I said it's 9 o'clock now". "现在是9点。""你可以再说一遍吗？""我刚才说现在是9点。"

"That is my pencil." "I beg your pardon, I thought that was mine" "那是我的铅笔。""对不起，我以为那是我的。"

began /bɪ'gæn; bɪ`gæn/ *v* 动

the past tense of **begin** ☆begin 的过去式

beggar /'begə; `bɛgɚ/ *n* 名

someone who lives by asking people for money or food 乞丐

Aunt Susan gave the beggar some money. 苏珊阿姨给了那个乞丐一些钱。

*begin /bɪ'gin; bɪ`gɪn/ *v* 动

begins, beginning, began, begun

to start 开始

School begins at 8 a.m. 学校在早上8点开始上课。

反义 **end², finish**

beginner /bɪ'gɪnə; bɪ`gɪnɚ/ *n* 名

a person who is starting to learn or do something 初学者

This tennis class is for beginners. 这个网球班是给初学者上的。

beginning /bɪ'gɪnɪŋ; bɪ`gɪnɪŋ/ *n* 名

无复数

the first part of something 开始；起点

It rained a lot at the beginning of this month. 这个月初下了很多雨。

反义 **end¹**

begun /bɪ'gʌn; bɪ`gʌn/ *v* 动

the past participle of **begin** ☆begin 的过去分词

behave /bɪ'heɪv; bɪ`hev/ *v* 动

behaves, behaving, behaved, behaved

to speak or do things in a particular way 表现；举动

The boy always behaves badly. 这个小男孩总是很顽皮。

In the classroom 在教室里

behave yourself 守规矩点

"Children, behave yourselves!" "孩子们，请守规矩点！"

*behaviour /bɪ'heɪvjə; bɪ`hevjɚ/ *n* 名【英】

无复数｜美式：***behavior***

the way someone behaves 行为

Paul won a prize for good behaviour. 保罗因品行优良而得奖。

同义 **conduct**

*behind¹ /bɪ'haɪnd; bɪ`haɪnd/ *prep* 介

at the back of someone or something 在…后面

The dog ran behind Simon. 狗在西蒙的后面跑。

反义 **in front of**

*behind² /bɪ'haɪnd; bɪ`haɪnd/ *adv* 副

1. at the back of someone or something 在后面
   My mother went in front and I walked behind. 妈妈在前面走，我跟在后面。
2. in the same place, after people have left somewhere 在原处
   The teacher asked me to stay behind after school. 老师叫我放学后留下。

being¹ /'biːɪŋ; `biɪŋ/ *v* 动

the present participle of **be** ☆be 的现在分词

It is great being here with you. 很高兴能和你一起在这儿。

being² /'biːɪŋ; `biɪŋ/ *n* 名

a living thing 生物

This film is about beings from outer space. 这部电影是关于外太空生物的。

human being 人类

Are there human beings on Mars? 火星上有人类吗？

***believe** /bɪˈliːv; bɪˋliv/ *v* 动

believes, believing, believed, believed

to think something is true 信；相信

I don't believe what he said. 我不相信他说的话。

believe in someone or something 相信…的存在；信仰

Many people believe in God. 很多人信仰上帝。

***bell** /bel; bɛl/ *n* 名

a metal thing that rings 钟；铃

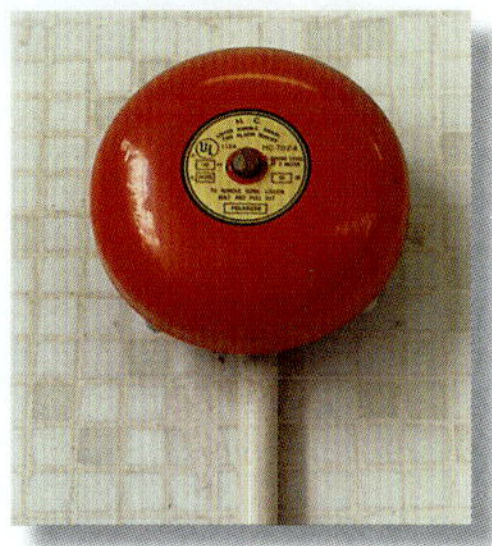

The bell is ringing. It is time for recess. 铃响了，休息时间到了。

***belong** /bɪˈlɒŋ; bəˋlɔŋ/ *v* 动

to be in the right place 该在

Does this chair belong here? 这椅子该放在这儿吗?

belong to someone 属于

This dictionary belongs to me. 这本词典是我的。

belong to something 是…的一部分；是…的成员

We all belong to the school choir. 我们都是校内合唱团的成员。

belongings /bɪˈlɒŋɪŋz; bɪˋlɔŋɪŋz/ *plural n* 复数名词

the things you own 财物；所有物

Please take all your belongings with you when you leave. 离开时请带走你的所有随身物品。

***below** /bɪˈləʊ; bɪˋlo/ *prep* 介

1. under 在…下面

   She lives in the flat below ours. 她住在我们楼下的单元。

2. less than 少于；低于

   Children below twelve years old cannot watch this film. 12 岁以下的儿童不得观看这部电影。

反义 **above**

***belt** /belt; bɛlt/ *n* 名

something that you wear round your waist 皮带；腰带

He wore a belt round his waist. 他的腰间系着一条皮带。

safety belt, seat belt 安全带

Remember to wear a seat belt! 记得系上安全带啊!

***bench** /bentʃ; bɛntʃ/ *n* 名

复数：***benches***

a long seat for two or more people 长椅

We sat on the bench in the park and talked. 我们坐在公园的长椅上聊天。

***bend** /bend; bɛnd/ *v* 动

bends, bending, bent, bent

to make a curve 弄弯；弄曲

The man is bending the iron bar. 那个男人在弄弯那根铁棒。

bend down, bend over 弯腰；俯身

He bent down to take off his shoes. 他弯下腰脱鞋。

beneath /bɪˈniːθ; bɪˋniθ/ *prep* 介

under or below 在…之下

The river flows beneath the bridge. 河从桥下流过。

bent /bent; bɛnt/ *v* 动

the past tense and past participle of **bend** ☆bend 的过去式和过去分词

berry /ˈberi; ˋbɛrɪ/ *n* 名

复数：***berries***

a small soft fruit with small seeds 莓；浆果

The children are picking berries in the field. 那些孩子正在田里采浆果。

***beside** /bɪˈsaɪd; bɪˋsaɪd/ *prep* 介

next to 在…旁边；在…侧

There is a tree beside the house. 屋子旁有一棵树。

besides /bɪˈsaɪdz; bɪˋsaɪdz/ *prep* 介

also; in addition to 除…之外

No one else knows besides you and

B

me. 除了你和我之外，没有其他人知道了。

***best**[1] /best; bɛst/ *adj* 形（*good* 的最高级）

better than anything else or anyone else 最好的

Tracy is my best friend. 翠西是我最好的朋友。

反义 **worst**[1]

***best**[2] /best; bɛst/ *adv* 副（*well* 的最高级）

in a way that is better than any other 最好地

Sally speaks English best in our class. 在我班里，莎莉的英语讲得最好。

反义 **worst**[2]

***best**[3] /best; bɛst/ *n* 名

无复数

someone or something that is better than any other 最好的人或物

Which camera is the best? 哪个相机是最好的呢？

do your best 尽力；尽量

I will do my best to help you. 我会尽力帮助你。

反义 **worst**[3]

***better**[1] /ˈbetə; ˋbɛtɚ/ *adj* 形（*good* 的比较级）

1. more good 较好的；更好的

   Lily's drawing is better than Candy's. 莉莉的画比坎蒂的好看。

反义 **worse**[1]

2. less ill 健康好转的

   Henry had a cold, but he is better now. 亨利患上了感冒，但现在好多了。

反义 **worse**[1]

***better**[2] /ˈbetə; ˋbɛtɚ/ *adv* 副（*well* 的比较级）

in a better way 更好地

Paul can sing better than me. 保罗唱歌比我好。

反义 **worse**[2]

Daily conversation 日常会话

had better 最好；应该（用于建议）

You'd (= You had) better go home now. 你该回家了。

***between** /bɪˈtwiːn; bɪˋtwin/ *prep* 介

1. in the middle of 在…中间

   The girl walked between her father and mother. 那女孩走在她父母的中间。

2. used to say which people or things get or have something that is shared 在…（和…）之间分享或共用

   She divided the cake between her two children. 她把蛋糕分给两个孩子。

用法 谈及两个人或两种东西用 between，如 between her two children, between Ann and Ben。谈及三个人或三种或以上的东西则用 among。

比较 **among**

3. in the period from one time to another（时间）由…至

   The library is open between 10 a.m. and 6 p.m. 图书馆从上午 10 点开放至下午 6 点。

beware /bɪˈweə; bɪˋwɛr/ *v* 动

be careful 当心；提防

Beware of pickpockets! 提防扒手！

注意 beware 用于提醒他人当心某事，没有词形变化。

beyond /bɪˈjɒnd; bɪˋjand/ *prep* 介

further than; on the far side of 越过…的范围；在…的那一边

Don't park your car beyond this line. 停车不要超越这条线。

***bicycle** /ˈbaɪsɪkl; ˋbaɪsɪkḷ/ *n* 名

a vehicle with two wheels that you ride 自行车；脚踏车；单车

The girl is riding a bicycle. 那个女孩在骑自行车。

同义 **bike**

***big** /bɪg; bɪg/ *adj* 形

bigger, biggest

large in size 大的

My parents bought a big birthday cake for me. 我的父母给我买了一个很大的生日蛋糕。

同义 **large**

反义 **little**[1], **small**

bike /baɪk; baɪk/ *n* 名

a bicycle 自行车；脚踏车；单车

Can you ride a bike? 你会骑自行车吗？

同义 **bicycle**

B

***bill** /bɪl; bɪl/ *n* 名

1. a piece of paper that tells you how much to pay 账单
   How much is the water bill? 这水费单是多少钱？

At a restaurant 餐厅里
"Can I have the bill, please?" "Yes, of course." "请结账。" "好的。"

2. 【美】纸币 英式 **banknote, note**

***bin** /bɪn; bɪn/ *n* 名

a container for rubbish 垃圾箱
Please put the rubbish in the bin. 请把垃圾放进垃圾箱里。

同义 **dustbin**

***bird** /bɜːd; bɝd/ *n* 名

an animal with feathers and wings 鸟
A lot of birds are flying in the sky. 很多鸟儿正在天空中飞。

***birth** /bɜːθ; bɝθ/ *n* 名

无复数
the time when someone is born 出生
What is your date of birth? 你的出生日期是什么?
give birth to someone 生育
Lily gave birth to twins. 莉莉生了双胞胎。

***birthday** /ˈbɜːθdeɪ; ˋbɝθˏde/ *n* 名

the day when you were born 生日
My birthday is on 2 March. 我的生日在 3 月 2 日。

***biscuit** /ˈbɪskɪt; ˋbɪskɪt/ *n* 名【英】

美式：***cookie***
a thin, flat cake 饼干
I ate some biscuits after I came home. 我回家后吃了几块饼干。

bit¹ /bɪt; bɪt/ *v* 动

the past tense of **bite**☆bite 的过去式

***bit²** /bɪt; bɪt/ *n* 名

a small piece or amount 小片；一点；少许
We fed the fish with tiny bits of bread. 我们用面包屑来喂鱼。
a bit, a little bit 有点儿；稍微
I felt a bit tired. 我觉得有点儿累。
bit by bit 一点一点地；慢慢地
We climbed up the hill bit by bit. 我们慢慢地爬上山。

***bite** /baɪt; baɪt/ *v* 动

bites, biting, bit, bitten
to cut food or hurt someone with your teeth 咬
Peter was bitten by a dog yesterday. 彼得昨天被狗咬了。
bite into something 咬
She bit into the apple. 她咬了一口苹果。

bitten /ˈbɪtn; ˋbɪtn̩/ *v* 动

the past participle of **bite**☆bite 的过去分词

***bitter** /ˈbɪtə; ˋbɪtɚ/ *adj* 形

with a strong taste which is not sweet 有苦味的
I don't like the medicine – it has a very bitter taste. 我不喜欢这药，它太苦了。

***black¹** /blæk; blæk/ *adj* 形

blacker, blackest
having the darkest colour 黑色的
She wore a pair of black shoes to school. 她穿着一双黑鞋子去上学。

***black²** /blæk; blæk/ *n* 名

the dark colour of night 黑色
They are all dressed in black. 他们都穿着黑色的服装。

***blackboard** /ˈblækbɔːd; ˋblækˏbɔrd/ *n* 名

a board that you write on with chalk 黑板
The teacher is standing in front of the blackboard. 老师站在黑板的前面。

***blame** /bleɪm; blem/ *v* 动

blames, blaming, blamed, blamed
to say that someone caused something bad 责怪；指责
It was not his fault. Don't blame him. 这不是他的错，别责怪他。
blame someone for something
I blamed him for the mess. 我责怪他弄得一塌糊涂。

blank /blæŋk; blæŋk/ *n* 名

an empty space 空白；空格
Fill in the blanks with the correct words. 把正确的词语填入空格内。

***blanket** /ˈblæŋkɪt; ˋblæŋkɪt/ *n* 名

a thick, warm cloth used to cover the body 毯子
It is cold. I need a blanket to keep me warm. 天气冷了，我需要盖一条毯子保暖。

blazer /ˈbleɪzə; ˋblezɚ/ *n* 名

a short coat; a jacket 短外衣；夹克上衣
My school blazer is blue in colour. 我的校服短外衣是蓝色的。

bled /bled; blɛd/ *v* 动

the past tense and past participle of **bleed**☆bleed 的过去式和过去分词

bleed /bliːd; blid/ *v* 动

bleeds, bleeding, bled, bled

to have blood coming out 流血；出血

I just cut my finger and it is still bleeding. 我刚刚不小心切到手指，现在还在流血。

blew /bluː; blu/ *v* 动

the past tense of **blow**☆blow 的过去式

blind¹ /blaɪnd; blaɪnd/ *adj* 形

not able to see 盲的；瞎的

The old man is blind. 这个老人是盲人。

blind² /blaɪnd; blaɪnd/ *n* 名

something you put on a window to keep out the sun 窗帘

We closed the blinds because it was too bright outside. 外面太亮了，所以我们把窗帘拉上了。

比较 **curtain**

***block¹** /blɒk; blɑk/ *n* 名

1. a large solid piece of something, usually with straight sides 一块

   The statue is made of a big block of ice. 那雕像由一个大冰块雕成。

2. a large building 大楼；大厦

   My father works in a large office block. 爸爸在一座大型办公楼内工作。

***block²** /blɒk; blɑk/ *v* 动

to stop someone or something from getting through 阻塞；封锁

The police blocked the road because there was a fire. 由于发生火灾，警察封锁了这条路。

blog /blɒg; blɑg/ *n* 名

【电脑】your own website where you write your diary 博客

Mike writes in his blog every day. 迈克每天都写博客。

***blood** /blʌd; blʌd/ *n* 名

无复数

the red liquid inside your body 血；血液

He lost a lot of blood in the accident. 他在事故中流了很多血。

blouse /blaʊz; blaʊs/ *n* 名

复数：*blouses*

a shirt for women or girls 女式衬衫

She is wearing a yellow blouse today. 她今天穿着黄色的衬衫。

***blow¹** /bləʊ; blo/ *v* 动

blows, blowing, blew, blown

1. if the wind blows, it makes the air move（风）吹

   The wind blew his balloon away! 风把他的气球吹走了！

2. to send air out from your mouth（用口）吹气

   He blew on his tea to cool it down. 他把茶吹凉。

blow out 吹熄

She blew out the candles. 她吹熄了蜡烛。

blow up 给…充气

He is blowing up the balloon. 他正在给气球吹气。

blow your nose 擤鼻子

He had a cold so he blew his nose. 他患了感冒，所以擤鼻涕。

***blow²** /bləʊ; blo/ *n* 名

a hard hit 重击；打击

The thief received a blow on the head and fainted. 小偷被击中了头，然后就晕了。

blown /bləʊn; blon/ *v* 动

the past participle of **blow**☆blow 的过去分词

***blue¹** /bluː; blu/ *adj* 形

having the colour of a clear sky 蓝的；蓝色的

He is wearing a blue cap. 他戴着一顶蓝色的帽子。

***blue²** /bluː; blu/ *n* 名

the colour of a clear sky 蓝；蓝色

My favourite colour is blue. 我最喜欢的颜色是蓝色。

blunt /blʌnt; blʌnt/ *adj* 形

blunter, bluntest

not sharp 钝的

This knife is blunt and I can't use it to cut the meat. 这把刀钝了，我不能用它切肉。

反义 sharp

***board** /bɔːd; bɔrd/ *n* 名

a flat, thin piece of something, often wood 板；木板

The teacher wrote on the board. 老师在黑板上写字。

on board 在巴士/飞机/船/火车上

The plane took off after all the passengers went on board. 所有乘客都登机后，飞机便起飞了。

boast /bəʊst; bost/ *v* 动

to talk too proudly about yourself 自夸；自吹自擂

He boasted that he could swim across the river. 他自夸能游过这条河。

***boat** /bəʊt; bot/ *n* 名

a small, open ship 小船

There are some boats on the lake. 湖上有几只小船。

***body** /ˈbɒdi; ˋbadɪ/ *n* 名

复数：***bodies***

all of you, including your chest, legs, and arms（人或动物的）身体

Exercise is good for the body. 运动对身体有益。

另见 **附录**：The body 身体

***boil** /bɔɪl; bɔɪl/ *v* 动

to make a liquid very hot 煮沸；烧开

She boiled some water to make coffee. 她烧了点开水冲咖啡。

bold /bəʊld; bold/ *adj* 形

bolder, boldest

1. brave and confident 勇敢的；无畏的

   He was bold and said the truth. 他很勇敢地说出真相。
2. 【电脑】printed in thick type 黑体的；粗体的

   The answers are in bold type. 答案以粗体字显示。

bomb /bɒm; bam/ *n* 名

a weapon that explodes with a loud noise 炸弹

The police found a bomb in a car. 警方在一辆汽车里找到一枚炸弹。

***bone** /bəʊn; bon/ *n* 名

a hard, white part inside the body 骨头

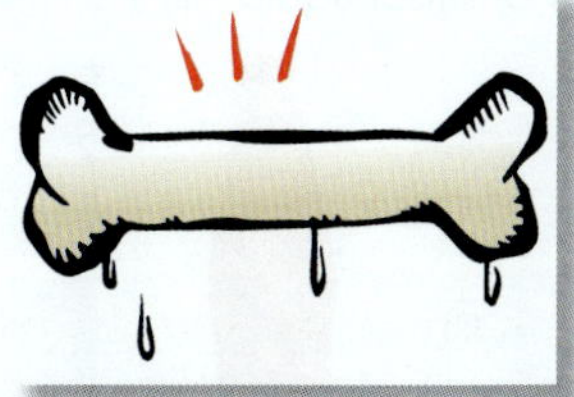

My dog is chewing a bone. 我的狗正在咬一根骨头。

***book¹** /bʊk; bʊk/ *n* 名

an object that has pages and a cover 书本；簿

She is reading a story book. 她在读一本故事书。

***book²** /bʊk; bʊk/ *v* 动

to ask for a table in a restaurant, a seat in a theatre etc before you need it 预定；登记

I have booked three tickets for the film tonight. 今晚看电影，我已经订了三张票。

At a restaurant 餐厅里

"I'd like to book a table for dinner tonight." "Certainly. May I have your name please?" "我想预定晚饭的座位。" "没问题。请问您贵姓？"

bookcase /ˈbʊk-keɪs; ˋbʊk͵kes/ *n* 名

a piece of furniture for keeping books 书架；书柜

He put the books on the bookcase. 他把书放到书架上。

bookshop /ˈbʊkʃɒp; ˋbʊk͵ʃap/ *n* 名【英】

美式：***bookstore***

a shop that sells books 书店

You can buy a dictionary in this bookshop. 你可以在这家书店买到字典。

boot¹ /buːt; but/ *n* 名

a kind of shoe that covers your foot and part of your leg 靴子；长靴

I like wearing my boots in winter. 在冬天，我喜欢穿靴子。

boot² /buːt; but/ *v* 动

也作：***boot up***

【电脑】to turn on your computer 启动（电脑）

I could not boot up my computer. 我不能启动电脑。

B

booth /buːð; buθ/ *n* 名

a small place where you can buy things, play games, etc 摊位

I always buy snacks from this booth. 我常常在这个摊子买小吃。

phone booth 电话亭

There is a phone booth beside our school. 在我们学校的旁边有一个电话亭。

***bored** /bɔːd; bɔrd/ *adj* 形

tired and not interested 无聊的；厌烦的

I am bored. Let's go to the cinema. 我觉得很无聊，我们去看电影吧。

用法 bored 用来形容你对事物的感受。

比较 boring

***boring** /ˈbɔːrɪŋ; ˋbɔrɪŋ/ *adj* 形

not interesting; long and tiring 令人厌烦的；沉闷的；乏味的

This film is very boring. 这部电影很沉闷。

用法 boring 用来形容事物。

同义 dull

反义 interesting

比较 bored

***born** /bɔːn; bɔrn/ *adj* 形

if a baby is born, it comes out of its mother's body 出生的

Jane was born in 2005. 简是在 2005 年出生的。

***borrow** /ˈbɒrəʊ; ˋbɑro/ *v* 动

to use something that belongs to another person and give it back later（向别人）借

May I borrow your rubber? 我可以借用你的橡皮擦吗？

borrow from someone or something

I borrow books from the library once a week. 我每星期会到图书馆借一次书。

用法 向别人借东西用 borrow，把东西借给别人用 lend。

比较 lend

boss /bɒs; bɔs/ *n* 名

复数：***bosses***

the person who tells other people what to do 上司；老板

Mr Smith is the boss of this company. 史密斯先生是这家公司的老板。

比较 employer

***both1** /bəʊθ; boθ/ *adj* 形

used to talk about two people, things etc together 双方的；两者的

Both girls have brown hair. 两个女孩的头发都是棕色的。

***both2** /bəʊθ; boθ/ *pron* 代

the two people or things together 双方；两者

I like the toy plane and the toy car. Can I buy both? 我喜欢那架玩具飞机也喜欢那辆玩具车。可以两个都买吗？

both of 两个都

Both of us like to play badminton. 我们两个都喜欢打羽毛球。

***bottle** /ˈbɒtl; ˋbɑtl̩/ *n* 名

a glass or plastic container for water or other liquids 瓶子

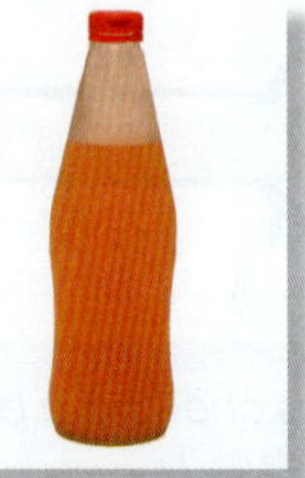

Ross drank a bottle of orange juice. 罗斯喝了一瓶橙汁。

***bottom** /ˈbɒtəm; ˋbɑtəm/ *n* 名

1. the lowest part 底部

   There were some coins at the bottom of the pool. 水池底有几枚硬币。

   反义 top1

2. the part of the body that you sit on 臀部；屁股

   She fell on her bottom. 她摔倒时屁股着地。

bought /bɔːt; bɔt/ *v* 动

the past tense and past participle of **buy** ☆ buy 的过去式和过去分词

bounce /baʊns; baʊns/ *v* 动

bounces, bouncing, bounced, bounced

to move up and down or to make something do this（使）弹跳；（使）反弹

Peter bounced the ball for a few times before he passed it to Ross. 彼得让球弹了数次，然后才传给罗斯。

bow1 /baʊ; baʊ/ *v* 动

to bend forward to show respect 鞠躬；弯腰

We bowed to the principal. 我们都向校长鞠躬。

bow2 /baʊ; baʊ/ *n* 名

the action of bending the top part of your body forward 鞠躬；弯腰

The clown made a bow to the audience. 小丑向观众鞠了个躬。

bow3 /bəʊ; bo/ *n* 名

1. a weapon used to shoot arrows 弓

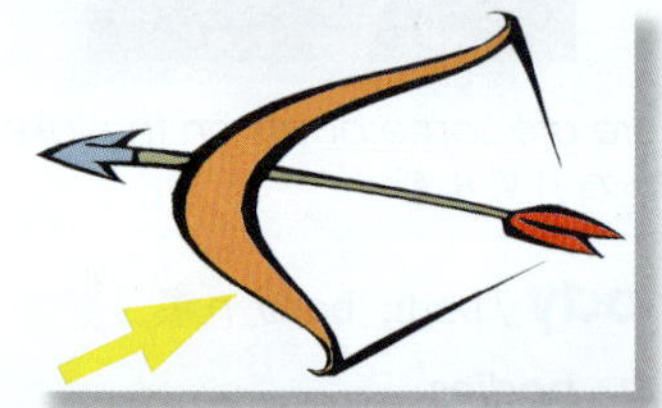

The hunter shot the deer with a bow and arrow. 猎人用弓箭射中了鹿。

2. a kind of knot to tie something 蝴蝶结

I tied the ribbon in a bow. 我把丝带打成蝴蝶结。

***bowl** /bəʊl; bol/ *n* 名

a deep, round dish 碗

I ate a bowl of noodles for lunch today. 我今天午餐时吃了一碗面。

bowling /'bəʊlɪŋ; `bolɪŋ/ *n* 名

无复数

a game where you try to knock down bottle-shaped objects with a ball 保龄球（运动）

I went bowling with my father last Sunday. 我上星期日和爸爸去打保龄球。

***box** /bɒks; bɑks/ *n* 名

复数：*boxes*

a square or rectangular container 箱子；盒子

This box is made of wood. 这个箱子是木制的。

boxer /'bɒksə; `bɑksɚ/ *n* 名

someone who does boxing 拳击手

The boxer was hurt in the match. 拳击手在比赛中受伤了。

boxing /'bɒksɪŋ; `bɑksɪŋ/ *n* 名

无复数

a sport in which you hit the other person with your fists 拳击运动；拳术

Mike is good at boxing. 迈克擅长拳击。

***boy** /bɔɪ; bɔɪ/ *n* 名

a male child 男孩；儿子

Mr Brown has two boys and one girl. 布朗先生有两个儿子和一个女儿。

bracelet /'breɪslət; `breslɪt/ *n* 名

a ring or a chain that you wear round your wrist 手镯

My grandmother has a gold bracelet. 我的祖母有一只金手镯。

bracket /'brækɪt; `brækɪt/ *n* 名

one of a pair of marks you put around words ( ) 括弧；括号

另见 **附录**：Punctuation 标点符号

***brain** /breɪn; bren/ *n* 名

the thing in your head that you use for thinking and controlling your body 脑；大脑

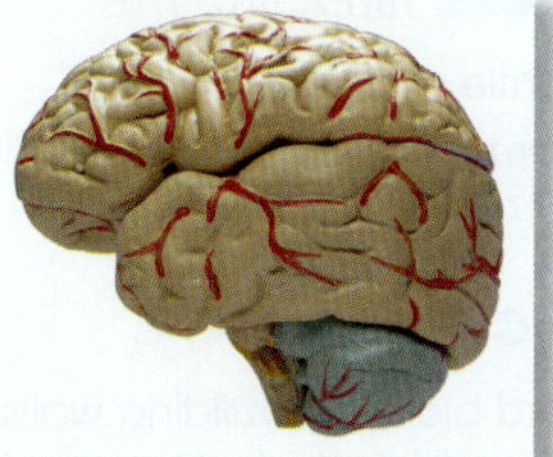

The brain controls the body. 大脑控制身体。

***branch** /brɑːntʃ; bræntʃ/ *n* 名

复数：*branches*

a part of a tree that grows out from the trunk 树枝

A parrot is sitting on a branch. 有一只鹦鹉停在树枝上。

brand /brænd; brænd/ *n* 名

something that is made by a company and has a name 牌子；商标

What is your favourite brand of chocolate? 你最喜欢什么牌子的巧克力?

***brave** /breɪv; brev/ *adj* 形

braver, bravest

not afraid or showing fear 勇敢的

The brave firefighter saved the old woman from the fire. 勇敢的消防员从大火中救出了老妇。

反义 **cowardly**

bravely /'breɪvli; `brevlɪ/ *adv* 副

in a brave way 勇敢地

He bravely jumped in the water to rescue his dog. 他勇敢地跳进水里救了他的狗。

bravery /'breɪvəri; `brevərɪ/ *n* 名

无复数

doing dangerous things without feeling afraid 勇敢

Henry got a medal for his bravery. 亨利因勇敢获得了奖章。

同义 **courage**

B

***bread** /bred; brɛd/ *n* 名

无复数

a type of food made from flour 面包

I have bread for breakfast every day. 我每天早餐都吃面包。

用法 如要表示数量，必须用量词，例如 a piece of bread（一块面包），a loaf of bread（一条面包），和 a slice of bread（一片面包）。

***break[1]** /breɪk; brek/ *v* 动

breaks, breaking, broke, broken

1. to make something separate into pieces 打碎；打破
   Who broke the window? 谁打破了窗户？
2. to separate into pieces 摔破；破碎
   The vase fell on the floor and broke. 花瓶掉在地上，摔碎了。

break down 发生故障

The bus broke down on the way to school. 校巴在上学途中坏了。

break into something 闯入

A burglar broke into our flat last night. 昨晚窃贼闯进了我们家里。

break out 突然发生

The fire broke out when they were asleep. 他们睡觉时突然起火了。

break[2] /breɪk; brek/ *n* 名

1. a short time for rest 小休
   I am very tired and want to have a break. 我很累了，想休息一会。
2. 【英】（无复数）（美式：***recess***）a period of time between lessons when students can rest 小憩
   I often go to the canteen at break. 我经常在食堂小憩。

***breakfast** /ˈbrekfəst; ˋbrɛkfəst/ *n* 名

the first meal of the day 早餐

I had bread and milk for breakfast today. 我今天早餐吃面包和牛奶。

***breath** /breθ; brɛθ/ *n* 名

air that goes into or out of your nose and mouth 吸入的气；呼出的气

I took a breath before I jumped into the pool. 我吸了一口气，然后跳进水池。

hold your breath 屏住气

How long can you hold your breath? 你能屏住气多长时间？

out of breath 上气不接下气；喘不过气

I was out of breath after running for the bus. 我气喘吁吁地追赶公共汽车。

***breathe** /bri:ð; brið/ *v* 动

breathes, breathing, breathed, breathed

to take air into and out of your nose and mouth 呼吸

The doctor asked the patient to breathe slowly. 医生叫病人慢慢呼吸。

breeze /bri:z; briz/ *n* 名

a gentle wind 微风

A warm breeze was blowing. 暖和的微风吹拂着。

***brick** /brɪk; brɪk/ *n* 名

a hard block for building walls and houses 砖；砖块

The old building was made of bricks. 这座旧建筑物是用砖造的。

bride /braɪd; braɪd/ *n* 名

a woman who is getting married 新娘

The bride is wearing a white wedding dress. 新娘穿着一件白色的婚纱。

bridegroom /ˈbraɪdgru:m; ˋbraɪdˏgrum/ *n* 名

a man who is getting married 新郎

The bridegroom gave the bride a kiss. 新郎给了新娘一个吻。

***bridge** /brɪdʒ; brɪdʒ/ *n* 名

something built over a river, road etc so that people or vehicles can cross it 桥

There is a bridge over the river. 河上有一座桥。

***bright** /braɪt; braɪt/ *adj* 形

brighter, brightest

1. shining with a lot of light, or full of light 明亮的；（天气）晴朗的
   Today is a bright day. 今天天气晴朗。

反义 **dark**

2. clever 聪明的；伶俐的
   Paul is a bright boy. 保罗是个聪明的男孩。

brightly /ˈbraɪtli; ˋbraɪtlɪ/ *adv* 副

in a bright way 明亮地
The sun shone brightly today. 今天阳光灿烂。

***brilliant** /ˈbrɪljənt; ˋbrɪljənt/ *adj* 形

very clever; very good 非常聪明的；好极的
She is a brilliant athlete. 她是一个很出色的运动员。

***bring** /brɪŋ; brɪŋ/ *v* 动

brings, bringing, brought, brought
to take someone or something with you to a place 带来；拿来
Can I bring my sister to the party? 我可以带我妹妹来参加派对吗?

***broad** /brɔːd; brɔd/ *adj* 形

broader, broadest
wide 宽阔的；广阔的
We saw a broad river in front of us. 我们看见前面有一条宽阔的河流。

反义 **narrow**

broccoli /ˈbrɒkəli; ˋbrɑkəlɪ/ *n* 名

a green vegetable with a thick stem 西兰花

My father cooked some chicken with broccoli. 爸爸做了一道西兰花炖鸡。

broke /brəʊk; brok/ *v* 动

the past tense of **break** ☆break 的过去式

broken[1] /ˈbrəʊkən; ˋbrokən/ *v* 动

the past participle of **break** ☆break 的过去分词

***broken**[2] /ˈbrəʊkən; ˋbrokən/ *adj* 形

1. in pieces 破裂的；破碎的
   The plate is broken. 这个盘子碎了。
2. not working 坏了的
   Can you repair this broken camera? 你能修好这台坏了的照相机吗？

broom /bruːm; brum/ *n* 名

a brush with a long handle for cleaning the floor 扫帚

Lily is sweeping the floor with a broom. 莉莉正在用扫帚扫地。

***brother** /ˈbrʌðə; ˋbrʌðɚ/ *n* 名

a boy or man who has the same parents as you 哥哥；弟弟；兄弟
Candy's brother is older than her. 坎蒂的哥哥比她年长。

brought /brɔːt; brɔt/ *v* 动

the past tense and past participle of **bring** ☆bring 的过去式和过去分词

***brown**[1] /braʊn; braʊn/ *adj* 形

having the colour of coffee or wood 棕色的；褐色的
The doll has brown hair. 这个玩具娃娃的头发是棕色的。

***brown**[2] /braʊn; braʊn/ *n* 名

the colour of coffee or wood 棕色；褐色
She likes to dress in brown. 她喜欢穿褐色的衣服。

browse /braʊz; braʊz/ *v* 动

browses, browsing, browsed, browsed
【电脑】to look for information on a computer or on the Internet 浏览
Paul often browses the Internet. 保罗常常上网浏览。

browser /ˈbraʊzə; ˋbraʊzɚ/ *n* 名

也作：***web browser***
【电脑】a program that you use to find information on the Internet 浏览器
Which browser do you use? 你用哪个浏览器呢?

bruise /bruːz; bruz/ *n* 名

a dark mark on your skin where you have been hurt 淤伤；伤痕
He has a lot of bruises on his arms and legs. 他的手臂和双腿有多处淤伤。

B

***brush[1]** /brʌʃ; brʌʃ/ *n* 名

复数：***brushes***

a thing you use for cleaning or painting 刷子；画笔

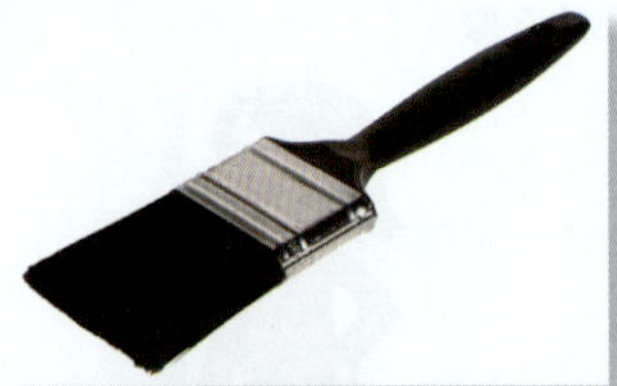

She is painting the door with a brush. 她正用刷子给门上漆。

***brush[2]** /brʌʃ; brʌʃ/ *v* 动

brushes, brushing, brushed, brushed

to clean something with a brush 刷

I brush my teeth before going to bed every day. 我每天睡觉前都会刷牙。

***bubble** /ˈbʌbl; ˋbʌbl̩/ *n* 名

a ball of air in liquid 气泡；泡沫

There are many bubbles in the soft drink. 汽水里有很多气泡。

***bucket** /ˈbʌkɪt; ˋbʌkɪt/ *n* 名

a container with a handle used for carrying liquids 提桶；水桶

They poured a bucket of water over me! 他们把一桶水泼在我身上了！

bud /bʌd; bʌd/ *n* 名

a young flower or leaf before it opens 花蕾；苞；芽

New buds appear on the trees in spring. 树木在春天长出新芽。

Buddha /ˈbʊdə; ˋbʊdə/ *n* 名

1. （无复数）the man whose teachings form Buddhism 佛
2. a picture or statue of Buddha 佛像

I can see the big Buddha far away. 我能看见远处的大佛。

Buddhism /ˈbʊdɪzəm; ˋbʊdɪzəm/ *n* 名

无复数

the religion based on the teachings of Buddha 佛教

Buddhist /ˈbʊdɪst; ˋbʊdɪst/ *n* 名

someone who believes in Buddhism 佛教徒

Some Buddhists do not eat meat. 有些佛教徒不吃肉类。

buffalo /ˈbʌfələʊ; ˋbʌfəˌlo/ *n* 名

复数：***buffaloes***

a large animal with horns 水牛

There are two buffaloes in the fields. 田里有两只水牛。

buffet /ˈbʊfeɪ; bəˋfe/ *n* 名

a meal where you serve yourself different dishes on a table and go somewhere else to eat 自助餐

The children ate a lot at the buffet. 那些孩子大吃了一顿自助餐。

bug /bʌg; bʌg/ *n* 名

a small insect 小虫子

Look! There's a bug on your hair! 看！你头发上有条小虫子！

***build** /bɪld; bɪld/ *v* 动

builds, building, built, built

to make something such as a house, a road, or a wall 建筑；建造

The birds are building a nest in the tree. 鸟儿正在树上筑巢。

builder /ˈbɪldə; ˋbɪldɚ/ *n* 名

someone who builds and repairs buildings 建筑工人；建造商

The builders are repairing the old house. 那些建筑工人正在修补旧房屋。

***building** /ˈbɪldɪŋ; ˋbɪldɪŋ/ *n* 名

a place that has a roof and walls 建筑物；房屋

There are many tall buildings in the city. 城市里有许多高楼大厦。

built /bɪlt; bɪlt/ *v* 动

the past tense and past participle of **build** ☆build 的过去式和过去分词

bulb /bʌlb; bʌlb/ *n* 名

也作：***light bulb***

the glass part of a light that produces light 灯泡

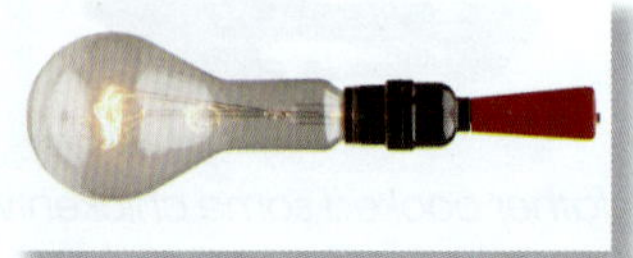

This bulb is hot! 这个灯泡很烫手！

***bull** /bʊl; bʊl/ *n* 名

a male cow 公牛

A cowboy is riding on the bull. 一个牛仔骑在公牛背上。

另见 **cow, ox**

bullet /ˈbʊlɪt; ˋbʊlɪt/ *n* 名

a thing that you fire from a gun 子弹

The man was killed by a bullet. 那个男人是被子弹打死的。

bump[1] /bʌmp; bʌmp/ *v* 动

to hit something 碰撞

Paul bumped into the wall and hit his head. 保罗撞到了墙上，把头撞伤了。

bump into someone 碰见某人；遇见某人

I bumped into my class teacher in the supermarket. 我在超级市场碰见我的班主任。

bump[2] /bʌmp; bʌmp/ *n* 名

a swelling on your body（碰撞造成的）肿块

Paul had a bump on his forehead. 保罗的额头上起了一个肿块。

*bun /bʌn; bʌn/ *n* 名

a small round kind of bread 小圆面包

The cook uses buns to make hamburgers. 厨师用小圆面包做汉堡包。

*bunch /bʌntʃ; bʌntʃ/ *n* 名

复数：***bunches***

a group of flowers, fruit, keys etc 串；束

They gave their mother a bunch of flowers. 他们给母亲一束花。

bundle /ˈbʌndl; ˋbʌndl̩/ *n* 名

a group of things tied together 一包；一捆

He tied up all the old newspapers into a bundle. 他把所有的旧报纸束成了一捆。

*burger /ˈbɜːgə; ˋbɝgɚ/ *n* 名

a flat round piece of chopped meat that is cooked and eaten between slices of a bun 汉堡包

Mike loves to eat burgers and fries. 迈克喜欢吃汉堡包和薯条。

同义 **hamburger**

burglar /ˈbɜːglə; ˋbɝglɚ/ *n* 名

someone who steals from a building（入屋行窃的）小偷；窃贼

The burglar broke into her flat and stole all her jewellery. 窃贼破门入屋，偷走了她所有的珠宝首饰。

burglary /ˈbɜːgləri; ˋbɝglərɪ/ *n* 名

复数：***burglaries***

the crime of stealing things from a building 盗窃；入屋行窃

A lot of burglaries happened in this area last year. 去年这个地区发生了许多宗盗窃案。

burn /bɜːn; bɝn/ *v* 动

burns, burning, burnt/burned, burnt/burned

1. if something burns, it gets very hot and produces heat and light 燃烧

   Dry wood burns very easily. 干柴很容易燃烧。

2. to destroy something using heat 焚烧；烧毁

   She burnt all the letters. 她把所有的信都烧了。

3. to hurt someone with fire 烧伤；烫伤

   He has burnt his face. 他烫伤了脸。

burnt /bɜːnt; bɝnt/ *v* 动

the past tense and past participle of **burn** ☆burn 的过去式和过去分词

*burst /bɜːst; bɝst/ *v* 动

bursts, bursting, burst, burst

to break open suddenly, often with a loud noise 破裂；爆裂

Stop blowing! The balloon is going to burst. 别再吹气了！气球快要破了。

burst into tears 突然哭起来

She burst into tears because the ending of the story was very sad. 那故事的结局很悲伤，她不禁哭了起来。

burst out laughing/crying 突然放声大笑/大哭

We burst out laughing when we heard the joke. 我们听到笑话哈哈大笑。

*bury /'beri; `bɛrɪ/ *v* 动

buries, burying, buried, buried

to put something in the ground and cover it with earth 掩蔽；埋藏

The dog buried the bone. 那只狗把骨头埋了起来。

*bus /bʌs; bʌs/ *n* 名

复数：***buses***

a large vehicle with many seats 公共汽车；巴士

I go to school by bus. 我坐公共汽车上学。

bus station/stop 公交车站

We should get off at the next bus stop. 我们应在下一个公交车站下车。

*bush /bʊʃ; bʊʃ/ *n* 名

复数：***bushes***

a plant with a lot of thin branches 矮树；灌木

I saw a snake in the bush. 我看到矮树丛里有一条蛇。

busily /'bɪzɪli; `bɪzəlɪ/ *adv* 副

in a busy way 忙碌地

She was working busily in the shop. 她正在店里忙着工作。

business /'bɪznəs; `bɪznɪs/ *n* 名

1. the work of buying and selling things 生意；买卖

   His father works in the food business. 他的父亲从事食品生意。

2. a company that buys and sells things 公司；企业

   The two brothers started their own business. 那对兄弟成立了自己的公司。

*busy /'bɪzi; `bɪzɪ/ *adj* 形

busier, busiest

1. having a lot of things to do 忙碌的

   I am busy doing my homework. 我正忙着做功课。

2. full of people or vehicles 繁忙的；热闹的

   This road is very busy on Sundays. 这条街道在星期日非常繁忙。

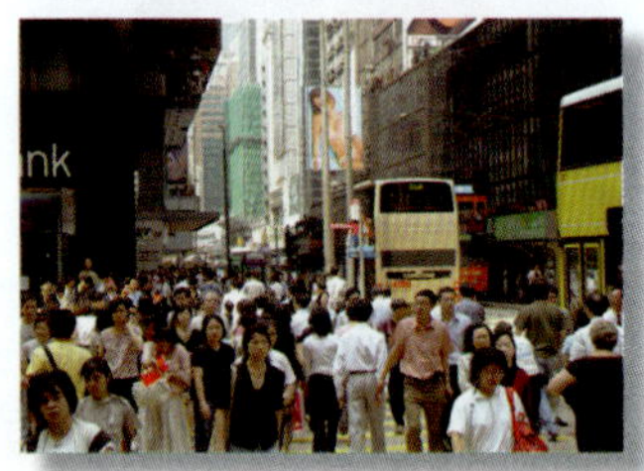

Daily conversation 日常会话

"Hello. Is Mr Brown there?" "I'm sorry he's busy now. Can you phone later?" "喂，布朗先生在吗？""他现在很忙，你待会再打电话过来，好吗？"

*but /bət; bət; *strong* 强读 bʌt; bʌt/ *conj* 连

a word you use to show although one thing is true, something opposite is also true 但；可是；不过

They are poor but happy. 他们虽然穷，但活得开心。

butcher /'bʊtʃə; `bʊtʃɚ/ *n* 名

someone who cuts and sells meat 肉食商；肉贩；屠夫

The butcher is cutting some meat. 肉贩在切肉。

the butcher's 肉店

My mother bought some beef at the butcher's. 妈妈在肉店买了些牛肉。

*butter /'bʌtə; `bʌtɚ/ *n* 名

无复数

a soft yellow food made from milk 黄油；牛油

She put some butter on her bread. 她在面包上涂了一些黄油。

*butterfly /'bʌtəflaɪ; `bʌtɚˌflaɪ/ *n* 名

复数：***butterflies***

an insect with large colourful wings 蝴蝶

There are a lot of butterflies in the park. 公园里有很多蝴蝶。

***button** /ˈbʌtn; ˋbʌtn̩/ *n* 名

1. a small round thing used for fastening clothes 钮扣

A button has come off my coat. 我外套上的一颗钮扣掉了。

2. a round thing that you press to start or stop a machine 按钮

Press this button and the robot will move. 按下这个按钮，机器人就会动起来。

***buy** /baɪ; baɪ/ *v* 动

buys, buying, bought, bought

to get something by paying money for it 购买

She bought some fish for dinner. 她买了几条鱼做晚餐。

反义 **sell**

buzz /bʌz; bʌz/ *v* 动

if a bee buzzes, it makes a continuous low sound（蜜蜂）发出嗡嗡声

Some bees are buzzing among the flowers. 蜜蜂在花丛中嗡嗡叫。

***by** /baɪ; baɪ/ *prep* 介

1. near or beside 靠近；在旁边

She is sitting by the window. 她坐在窗旁。

2. using a way of travelling 乘；坐

I go to school by bus every day. 我每天坐公共汽车上学。

3. before; no later than 不迟于

Please come here by five o'clock. 请在 5 点前来到这儿。

4. used to show who or what does something 被；由

He was bitten by a snake. 他被一条蛇咬了。

***bye** /baɪ; baɪ/, **bye-bye** /baɪ ˈbaɪ; baɪ ˋbaɪ/ *interj* 感叹

a short word for **goodbye** 再见

Bye! See you tomorrow. 再见！明天见。

cabbage /ˈkæbɪdʒ; ˋkæbɪdʒ/ *n* 名

a large, round vegetable with thick, green leaves 卷心菜；洋白菜；花椰菜

Cabbage is one of my favourite vegetables. 卷心菜是我最喜欢的一种蔬菜。

cable car /ˈkeɪbl kɑː; ˋkebl̩ kɑr/ *n* 名

a type of car that moves along a wire and takes people up and down a mountain 登山缆车；吊车

At Ocean Park, we can take a ride on the cable car. 我们在海洋公园可以坐登山缆车。

***café** /ˈkæfeɪ; kæˋfe/ *n* 名

a small restaurant 小餐馆；咖啡馆

We had dinner in a café. 我们在一家小餐馆吃晚餐。

注意 café 来自法语，请注意 é 的写法。

cage /keɪdʒ; kedʒ/ *n* 名

a box made of metal or wooden bars for keeping animals or birds 笼

There is a bird in the cage. 笼子里有一只鸟。

***cake** /keɪk; kek/ *n* 名

a kind of sweet food made of flour, butter, eggs and sugar 蛋糕

We gave Alice a big birthday cake. 我们送给爱丽丝一个很大的生日蛋糕。

注意 一个蛋糕、两个蛋糕是 a cake, two cakes，但一片蛋糕、两片蛋糕是 a piece of cake, two pieces of cake。

a cake　　a piece of cake

calculator /ˈkælkjʊleɪtə; ˋkælkjəˌletɚ/ *n* 名

a machine that you use to add, divide, etc 计算器

I used a calculator to add the numbers. 我用计算器把这些数字加起来。

***calendar** /ˈkæləndə; ˋkæləndɚ/ *n* 名

1. something that shows the days, weeks and months of a year 日历；月历
   There is a calendar on the wall. 墙上挂着一份月历。
2. 【美】日记簿 英式 **diary**

calf /kɑːf; kæf/ *n* 名

复数：***calves***

a young cow 小牛

The calf is learning to walk. 小牛正在学走路。

***call[1]** /kɔːl; kɔl/ *v* 动

1. to shout 大声叫唤；呼唤
   Someone was calling my name. 有人在叫我的名字。
2. to telephone someone 打电话
   I called you this morning but you were not at home. 我今天早上打过电话给你，但你不在家。
3. to give someone a name 称…为；把…叫做；给…取名为
   They called their baby Anna. 他们给婴儿取名为安娜。

call someone back 给某人回电话

Call me back when you can. 你方便的话就给我回个电话。

Daily conversation 日常会话

"What's your name?" "My name is Donald. You can call me Don." "你叫什么名字？" "我叫 Donald。你可以叫我 Don。"

***call[2]** /kɔːl; kɔl/ *n* 名

a phone call（一次）电话

Please give me a call when you get to the airport. 你到机场时请打电话给我。

calm /kɑːm; kɑm/ *adj* 形

calmer, calmest

1. not worried or excited 镇定的；沉着的

   You should keep calm in a fire. 起火时，你应该保持镇定。

2. (of a sea or a river) with no big waves（水面）平静的

   The sea is calm because there is no wind. 海面很平静，因为没有风。

反义 **rough**

calmly /ˈkɑːmli; ˋkɑmlɪ/ *adv* 副

in a calm way 镇定地；沉着地

We left the classroom calmly when the fire alarm rang. 火警铃响起时，我们镇定地离开教室。

calves /kɑːvz; kævz/ *n* 名

the plural of **calf** ☆calf 的复数形式

came /keɪm; kem/ *v* 动

the past tense of **come** ☆come 的过去式

camel /ˈkæml; ˋkæml̩/ *n* 名

a large animal that lives in the desert 骆驼

Camels are useful animals in the desert. 在沙漠里，骆驼是很有用的动物。

***camera** /ˈkæmərə; ˋkæmərə/ *n* 名

a machine for taking photographs 照相机；摄影机

I took some pictures of my dog with my camera. 我用照相机给我的狗拍了几张照片。

***camp[1]** /kæmp; kæmp/ *n* 名

an outdoor area where people stay in a tent for a short time 营地

It's getting late – let's get back to camp. 时间不早了，我们回营地吧。

***camp[2]** /kæmp; kæmp/ *v* 动

to stay in a tent for a short time 露营；野营

They camped in a country park. 他们在郊野公园露营。

***can[1]** /kən; kən; *strong* 强读 kæn; kæn/ *v* 动

could

1. to be able to do something 能够；会

   My cat can jump over the wall. 我的猫能跳过这堵墙。

2. to be allowed to do something 可以

   You can go now. 你现在可以走了。

***can[2]** /kæn; kæn/ *n* 名

a metal container 罐头；金属罐

We had a few cans of fruit juice. 我们喝了几罐果汁。

***cancel** /ˈkænsl; ˋkænsl̩/ *v* 动

cancels, cancelling, cancelled, cancelled

to decide that a planned event will not happen 取消

The match was cancelled. 球赛被取消了。

cancer /ˈkænsə; ˋkænsɚ/ *n* 名

a serious illness in which bad cells grow in the body 癌症

Smoking causes lung cancer. 吸烟导致肺癌。

***candle** /ˈkændl; ˋkændl̩/ *n* 名

a stick of wax that you burn to give light 蜡烛

There were ten candles on her birthday cake. 她的生日蛋糕上有 10 支蜡烛。

candy /ˈkændi; ˋkændɪ/ *n* 名【美】

复数：***candies*** | 英式：***sweet***

a sweet food made from sugar or chocolate 糖果

These candies are very sweet. 这些糖果很甜。

***cannot** /ˈkænət; ˋkænɑt/ *v* 动

缩写：***can't***

1. to be unable to do something 不能够；不会

   My brother cannot swim. 我的弟弟不会游泳。

2. to not be allowed to do something 不可以

   You cannot stay here. 你不可以留在这儿。

C

***can't** /kɑːnt; kænt/

the short form of **cannot** ☆ cannot 的缩写

I can't go out because I haven't finished my homework. 我不能出去，因为没有做完功课。

***canteen** /kæn'tiːn; kæn`tin/ *n* 名

a place in a school or factory where meals are sold 食堂；餐厅

They often have lunch in the school canteen. 他们经常在学校食堂吃午餐。

***cap** /kæp; kæp/ *n* 名

1. a soft, flat hat with a part that sticks out in front（有帽舌的）便帽；软帽

He wears a cap every day. 他每天都戴着一顶便帽。

比较 **hat**

2. a cover on the end or top of a bottle, jar, pen, etc 盖子

   Please put the cap back on the bottle. 请盖上瓶盖。

capable /'keɪpəbl; `kepəbl̩/ *adj* 形

able to do things well 有才能的

She is a very capable businesswoman. 她是个能干的商人。

capable of something 有能力做某事

Henry is capable of looking after himself. 亨利能照顾自己。

***capital** /'kæpɪtl; `kæpətl̩/ *n* 名

1. the city where a country has its government 首都

   Tokyo is the capital of Japan. 东京是日本的首都。

2. a large letter of the alphabet 大写字母

   You begin a sentence with a capital. 句子的第一个字母要大写。

captain /'kæptɪn; `kæptɪn/ *n* 名

1. the leader of a team 队长；组长

   Chris is the captain of our basketball team. 克里斯是我们篮球队的队长。

2. someone who controls a ship or plane 船长；机长

   He is the captain of this plane. 他是这架飞机的机长。

capture /'kæptʃə; `kæptʃɚ/ *v* 动

captures, capturing, captured, captured

to catch or hold a person or animal 俘虏；捕获

The hunters captured a tiger. 猎人捕获了一只老虎。

***car** /kɑː; kɑr/ *n* 名

a machine on wheels that carries people 汽车

May is driving a car. 梅正在开车。

***card** /kɑːd; kɑrd/ *n* 名

a piece of hard paper that shows information or you use to send someone a message 卡片；贺卡

I received a lot of cards last Christmas. 去年圣诞节我收到很多贺卡。

cardboard /'kɑːdbɔːd; `kɑrd͵bɔrd/ *n* 名

无复数

thick, hard paper used for making boxes 硬纸板

This fruit box is made of cardboard. 这个水果箱是用硬纸板做的。

cardigan /'kɑːdɪgən; `kɑrdɪgən/ *n* 名

a piece of clothing made of wool that has long sleeves and buttons in front 开襟羊毛衣；开襟毛线衫

She is wearing a green cardigan. 她穿着一件绿色的开襟羊毛衣。

***care[1]** /keə; kɛr/ *n* 名

无复数

1. the process of looking after someone or something 照顾；看护

   A baby needs a lot of care. 婴儿需要悉心照顾。

   take care of someone 照料某人

   I took care of my younger sister when my mother went to work. 当妈妈上班后，我照顾妹妹。

2. trying to do something well and carefully 小心；谨慎

   The students drew the pictures with great care. 学生非常仔细地画画。

Daily conversation 日常会话

"Take care! See you tomorrow!" "You, too!" "保重！明天见！""保重！明天见！"

***care[2]** /keə; kɛr/ *v* 动

cares, caring, cared, cared

to be interested in, or worried about someone or something because you think they are important 关心；在乎；介意

You are a good friend and I care about you. 你是我的好朋友，所以我关心你。

***careful** /ˈkeəfl; ˋkɛrfəl/ *adj* 形

taking care so that you do not make a mistake or miss anything 小心的；谨慎的

Iris is a careful driver. 艾丽丝是个谨慎的司机。

反义 **careless**

carefully /ˈkeəfəli; ˋkɛrfəlɪ/ *adv* 副

in a careful way 小心地；谨慎地

Cross the road carefully! 过马路要小心！

反义 **carelessly**

In the classroom 在教室里

"Children, listen carefully before you answer the questions." "Okay." "小朋友，在回答问题之前，请仔细听。""知道了。"

***careless** /ˈkeələs; ˋkɛrlɪs/ *adj* 形

not taking care 粗心的；大意的

He was careless and made a lot of mistakes in the exam. 他很粗心，在考试时犯了很多错误。

反义 **careful**

carelessly /ˈkeələsli; ˋkɛrlɪslɪ/ *adv* 副

in a careless way 粗心地；大意地

I carelessly left my bag on the bus. 我不小心把包落在公交车上了。

反义 **carefully**

cargo /ˈkɑːgəʊ; ˋkɑrgo/ *n* 名

复数：***cargoes/cargos***

all the things carried in a ship, plane or train 货物

The ship was carrying a cargo of oil. 那艘船装载了一批油。

carnation /kɑːˈneɪʃn; kɑrˋneʃən/ *n* 名

a white, pink, or red flower that smells sweet 康乃馨

Tracy bought some carnations for her mother. 翠西给她妈妈送了几枝康乃馨。

carol /ˈkærəl; ˋkærəl/ *n* 名

a song that people sing at Christmas 圣诞颂歌

Can you sing the carol "Silent Night"? 你会唱《平安夜》这首圣诞颂歌吗？

car park /ˈkɑː pɑːk; ˋkɑr pɑrk/ *n* 名

a place where drivers stop their cars and leave for some time 停车场

Harry parked his car in the car park. 哈利把车停在停车场里。

carpet /ˈkɑːpɪt; ˋkɑrpɪt/ *n* 名

a thick cover for the floor 地毯

We have just put new carpets in our house. 我们家里刚铺好新的地毯。

比较 **rug**

carriage /ˈkærɪdʒ; ˋkærɪdʒ/ *n* 名

one of the parts of a train where people sit 火车车厢

This train has eight carriages. 这列车有 8 节车厢。

carried /ˈkærid; ˋkærɪd/ *v* 动

the past tense and past participle of **carry** ☆carry 的过去式和过去分词

***carrot** /ˈkærət; ˋkærət/ *n* 名

a long, hard, orange vegetable 胡萝卜

I sometimes feed carrots to my rabbit. 我有时喂我的兔子吃胡萝卜。

C

C

***carry** /ˈkæri; ˋkærɪ/ *v* 动

carries, carrying, carried, carried

to hold something and take it somewhere 携带；提

She is carrying a basket of fruit. 她提着一篮水果。

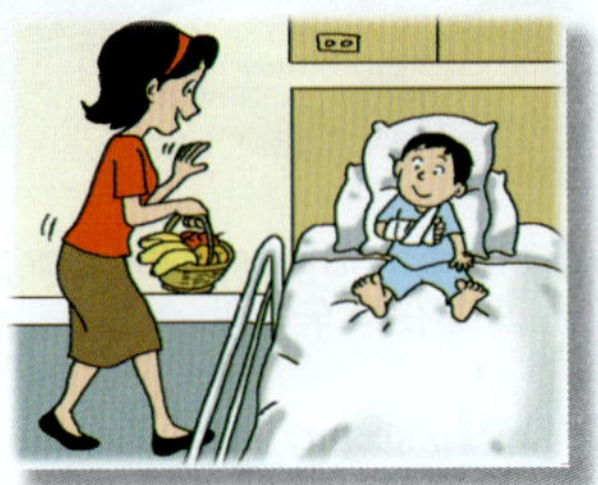

carry on 继续

Carry on with your work. 继续做你的工作吧。

cart /kɑ:t; kɑrt/ *n* 名

a vehicle with wheels usually pulled by a horse or pushed by a person 马车；手推车

The horse was pulling a cart. 那匹马拉着一辆车。

carton /ˈkɑ:tn; ˋkɑrtn̩/ *n* 名

a strong paper or plastic box for holding food or drinks 纸盒；塑料盒

I bought a carton of milk this afternoon. 我今天下午买了一盒牛奶。

***cartoon** /kɑ:ˈtu:n; kɑrˋtun/ *n* 名

1. a story or film made of drawings 动画；卡通片

   We like to watch Walt Disney cartoons. 我们喜欢看迪士尼卡通片。

2. a funny drawing 漫画

   Ben is good at drawing cartoons. 本的漫画画得非常好。

***case** /keɪs; kes/ *n* 名

1. a box or container 箱；盒

   She put all the old clothes in a big case. 她把所有的旧衣服放进一个大箱子里。

2. a particular situation 情况；情形

   In this case we should be more careful. 在这种情况下，我们应加倍小心。

in any case 无论如何；不管怎样

It may be cloudy. In any case, we are having a picnic tomorrow. 明天可能多云，但不管怎样我们都会去野餐。

in case 以防；如果

Take an umbrella with you in case it rains. 带着雨伞吧，以防下雨。

cash /kæʃ; kæʃ/ *n* 名

无复数

money 现金

Do you have any cash? 你有现金吗？

***cashier** /kæˈʃɪə; kæˋʃɪr/ *n* 名

someone who takes in or pays out money in a shop or bank 出纳员；收款员

My aunt is a cashier in a supermarket. 我的阿姨在超市里当收银员。

castle /ˈkɑ:sl; ˋkæsl̩/ *n* 名

a strong building with thick walls, built in the past for keeping people safe 城堡；堡垒

There is an old castle on the hill. 山丘上有一座旧城堡。

***cat** /kæt; kæt/ *n* 名

an animal with soft fur and a long tail, which people keep as a pet or for catching mice 猫

Mrs Smith has a cat. 史密斯太太养了一只猫。

***catch** /kætʃ; kætʃ/ *v* 动

catches, catching, caught, caught

1. to get hold of something moving through the air 捕捉；接住

   I caught the ball. 我把球接住了。

2. to stop someone you are chasing 捕获

   The policeman caught the thief. 警察抓住了小偷。

catch a cold 着凉；患上感冒

Lily caught a bad cold. 莉莉患了重感冒。

catch the bus, train, etc 搭乘公共汽车、火车等

We must catch the first train. 我们一定要赶上第一班火车。

catch up 赶上；追上

Don't walk so fast. I can't catch up with you. 别走那么快，我跟不上了。

***caterpillar** /ˈkætəˌpɪlə; ˋkætɚˌpɪlɚ/ *n* 名

a long, thin insect with many legs that turns into a butterfly or another flying insect 毛虫

The caterpillar will soon become a butterfly. 毛毛虫很快就会变成蝴蝶了。

cattle /ˈkætl; ˋkætl̩/ *plural n* 复数名词

cows and bulls kept on a farm 牛；牛群

This farmer keeps some cattle. 这个农夫养了几头牛。

catty /ˈkæti; ˋkætɪ/ *n* 名

复数：***catties***

a Chinese unit for measuring weight 斤

My mother bought a catty of beef. 妈妈买了一斤牛肉。

另见 **tael**

caught /kɔːt; kɔt/ *v* 动

the past tense and past participle of **catch** ☆catch 的过去式和过去分词

cauliflower /ˈkɒlɪˌflaʊə; ˋkɔləˌflaʊɚ/ *n* 名

a large, round, white vegetable with leaves on the outside 花椰菜；椰菜花

Cauliflower is my favourite vegetable. 花椰菜是我最喜爱的蔬菜。

***cause**[1] /kɔːz; kɔz/ *n* 名

the reason that something happens 原因

Nobody knows the cause of the accident. 没有人知道那次事故的原因。

同义 **reason**

***cause**[2] /kɔːz; kɔz/ *v* 动

causes, causing, caused, caused

to make something happen 导致；造成

What caused the fire? 是什么导致了这场火灾？

***cave** /keɪv; kev/ *n* 名

a large hole under the ground or in the side of a hill 地洞；洞穴

They found some treasure in the cave. 他们在洞穴里找到了一些宝藏。

CD /ˌsiː ˈdiː; ˏsi ˋdi/ *n* 名

a disc with music or information stored on it 激光唱片；（电脑）光碟（compact disc 的缩写）

I like all the CDs of this singer. 这位歌手所有的唱片我都喜欢。

CD player 激光唱机

My CD player is not working. 我的激光唱机坏了。

CD-ROM /ˌsiː diː ˈrɒm; ˏsi di ˋram/ *n* 名

【电脑】a CD with text or pictures that can be read by a computer 只读光碟；只读光盘

The teacher saved the information onto a CD-ROM. 老师把资料储存在只读光碟内。

***ceiling** /ˈsiːlɪŋ; ˋsilɪŋ/ *n* 名

the upper surface inside a room 天花板

Our living room has a very low ceiling. 我们客厅的天花板很低。

***celebrate** /ˈseləbreɪt; ˋsɛləˌbret/ *v* 动

celebrates, celebrating, celebrated, celebrated

to do something enjoyable on a special day 庆祝

We are celebrating our grandfather's birthday today. 今天我们庆祝爷爷的生日。

***celebration** /ˌseləˈbreɪʃn; ˏsɛləˋbreʃən/ *n* 名

a special meal or party when you celebrate something 庆祝活动

We had a big celebration at New Year. 我们在新年举行大型的庆祝活动。

cell /sel; sɛl/ *n* 名

a smallest part of a plant or an animal that can exist on its own 细胞

There are many different types of cells in your body. 身体内有很多种细胞。

cello /ˈtʃeləʊ; ˋtʃɛlo/ *n* 名

a musical instrument like a large violin 大提琴

I can play the cello. 我会拉大提琴。

cellphone /'selfəʊn; `sɛlfon/ *n* 名【美】

英式 **mobile phone**

cent /sent; sɛnt/ *n* 名

a unit of money. There are 100 cents in a dollar. 一分钱（¢）（货币单位）

This pen costs five dollars fifty cents. 这支笔价值 5 元 5 角。

注意 10 cents 即一角钱。

center /'sentə; `sɛntɚ/ *n* 名【美】

英式 **centre**

***centimetre** /'sentɪˌmiːtə; `sɛntəˌmitɚ/ *n* 名【英】

缩写：***cm*** ｜美式：***centimeter***

a unit of length. There are 100 centimetres in a metre. 厘米；公分

This ruler is 30 centimetres long. 这把尺长 30 厘米。

另见 附录：Weights and measures 度量单位

***central** /'sentrəl; `sɛntrəl/ *adj* 形

in the middle of something 中心的；中央的

There is a castle in the central part of the amusement park. 游乐场的中心地带有一座城堡。

***centre** /'sentə; `sɛntɚ/ *n* 名【英】

美式：***center***

1. the middle of something 中心；中央

Our school is in the centre of the city. 我们的学校在城市的中心。

2. a place where people go to do a particular activity（某种活动的）中心

We went to the shopping centre yesterday. 我们昨天到购物中心去了。

century /'sentʃəri; `sɛntʃərɪ/ *n* 名

复数：***centuries***

a period of 100 years 一世纪；一百年

We are living in the 21st century. 我们生活在 21 世纪。

***cereal** /'sɪəriəl; `sɪrɪəl/ *n* 名

food made from grain, which you usually eat with milk for breakfast 谷类食品

I had cereal with milk this morning. 今天早上我吃了谷类食物和牛奶。

***ceremony** /'serəməni; `sɛrəˌmonɪ/ *n* 名

复数：***ceremonies***

a public event, usually on a special occasion 典礼；仪式

The principal gave out awards at the ceremony. 校长在典礼上颁发奖项。

***certain** /'sɜːtn; `sɝtn̩/ *adj* 形

completely sure 肯定的；确定的

I am certain that she is at home now. 我肯定她这个时候在家。

同义 **sure**

***certainly** /'sɜːtnli; `sɝtn̩lɪ/ *adv* 副

definitely 一定；必定

I will certainly work hard for the exam. 我一定会努力准备考试。

certificate /sə'tɪfɪkət; sɚ`tɪfəkɪt/ *n* 名

a document saying you have achieved something 证书

I got a certificate when I finished the class. 我完成课程后获得了一张证书。

chain /tʃeɪn; tʃen/ *n* 名

a line of metal rings joined together 链子

This chain is made of gold. 这是一条金链子。

***chair** /tʃeə; tʃɛr/ *n* 名

a piece of furniture for you to sit on 椅子

She sat on a chair and ate her dinner. 她坐在椅子上吃晚餐。

chairman /'tʃeəmən; `tʃɛrmən/ *n* 名

复数：***chairmen***

the man who is in charge of a meeting, a committee, a company, etc（男性）主席

Henry is the chairman of this company. 亨利是这家公司的主席。

chairperson /'tʃeəˌpɜːsn; `tʃɛrˌpɝsn̩/ *n* 名

复数：***chairpersons***

the person who is in charge of a meeting, a committee, a company, etc 主席

Mary is the chairperson of our class club. 玛丽是我们班会的主席。

chairwoman /'tʃeəˌwʊmən; `tʃɛrˌwʊmən/ *n* 名

复数：***chairwomen***

the woman who is in charge of a meeting, a committee, a company, etc 女主席

The chairwoman was writing a report. 女主席在写报告。

chalk /tʃɔːk; tʃɔk/ *n* 名

a small stick used for writing on a

blackboard 粉笔

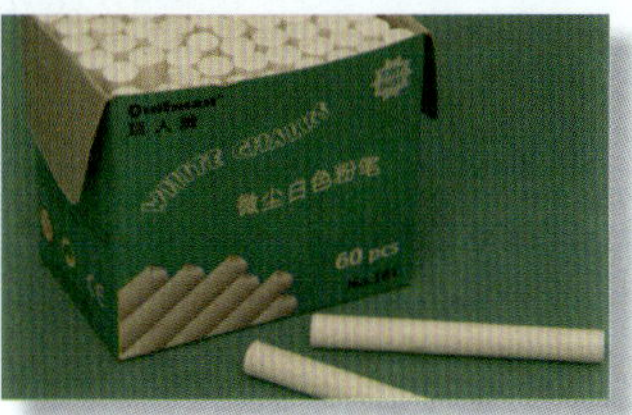

There is a box of chalks on the desk. 书桌上有一盒粉笔。

champion /ˈtʃæmpiən; ˋtʃæmpɪən/ *n* 名

a person or a team that has won a competition 冠军

Mike is the school table tennis champion. 迈克是学校里的乒乓球冠军。

***chance** /tʃɑːns; tʃæns/ *n* 名

1. the possibility that something will happen 机会；可能性
   There is little chance of rain. 大概不会下雨的。
2. a time when something may be done 机会
   We will have a chance to go to Rome this summer. 我们将有机会在这个夏天去罗马。

同义 **opportunity**

***change¹** /tʃeɪndʒ; tʃendʒ/ *v* 动

changes, changing, changed, changed

1. to become different, or to make something different 改变；变化
   She has changed a lot this year. 今年她改变了很多。
2. to replace something with something new or different 更换
   Paul changed the light bulb. 保罗更换了灯泡。
3. to put on different clothes 换衣服
   Please wait a moment while I change. 请等一会儿，让我换一下衣服。
4. to leave one bus, train or plane, and get in another one 换车；中途转车
   To get to Kowloon Tong from Central, you have to change at Mong Kok. 从中环到九龙塘，你得在旺角换车。

***change²** /tʃeɪndʒ; tʃendʒ/ *n* 名

1. something that has changed 改变；变动；变化
   We made some changes to our plan. 我们对计划作出了一些改变。
2. （无复数）coins; the money that you get back when you pay more than the cost of something 零钱；找回的钱
   I gave her 10 dollars and she gave me 50 cents change. 我给了她 10 元，她找给我 5 毛钱。

changing room /ˈtʃeɪndʒɪŋ ruːm; ˋtʃendʒɪŋ rum/ *n* 名

a room where people change their clothes 更衣室

There are changing rooms at the beach. 这个海滩设有更衣室。

channel /ˈtʃænl; ˋtʃænl̩/ *n* 名

a radio or television station and its programme（电台/电视）频道

Sometimes I watch the English TV channels. 有时候我会看英语电视频道。

***chapter** /ˈtʃæptə; ˋtʃæptɚ/ *n* 名

a part of a book 章

This book has twenty chapters. 这本书有 20 章。

***character** /ˈkærəktə; ˋkærɪktɚ/ *n* 名

1. what someone is like 性格
   He has a strong character. 他性格坚强。
2. a letter, sign or mark used in writing, printing or on a computer 字；符号
   Mrs Smith can write Chinese characters. 史密斯太太会写汉字。
3. a person in a book, film or play 角色；人物
   Which character do you like best in this film? 你最喜欢这部电影中的哪一个角色？

***charge¹** /tʃɑːdʒ; tʃardʒ/ *n* 名

1. the money you pay for something 费用；价钱
   There is a charge of $5 for adults to enter the park. 成人进入这个公园需付入场费 5 元。
2. （无复数）**be in charge (of something)** having control on something or someone 主管；负责
   The principal is in charge of the school. 校长负责管理学校。

charge² /tʃɑːdʒ; tʃardʒ/ *v* 动

charges, charging, charged, charged

to ask for a particular amount of money for something 收费

How much do you charge for a haircut? 理发要多少钱？

charity /ˈtʃærəti; ˋtʃærətɪ/ *n* 名

复数：***charities***

an organization that helps people, especially poor or sick people 慈善机构；慈善团体

Mark works for a charity. 马克在慈善机构里工作。

charming /ˈtʃɑːmɪŋ; ˋtʃarmɪŋ/ *adj* 形

very attractive and pleasing 迷人的；有吸引力的

Mike is very charming. Everyone likes him. 迈克很有吸引力，所有人都喜欢他。

C

***chart** /tʃɑːt; tʃɑrt/ *n* 名

a picture or graph with information 图表

The weather chart shows that next Tuesday will be sunny. 天气图显示下星期二天晴。

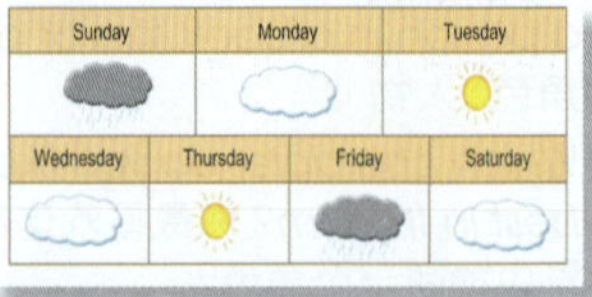

***chase** /tʃeɪs; tʃes/ *v* 动

chases, chasing, chased, chased

to run after someone or something to catch them 追赶

The dog is chasing a rabbit. 这只狗在追赶一只兔子。

***chat**[1] /tʃæt; tʃæt/ *v* 动

chats, chatting, chatted, chatted

to talk in a friendly way 闲谈；聊天

They are chatting about their holidays. 他们在聊他们的假期。

***chat**[2] /tʃæt; tʃæt/ *n* 名

a friendly talk 闲谈；聊天

I had a chat with Candy yesterday. 我昨天和坎蒂闲谈。

***cheap** /tʃiːp; tʃip/ *adj* 形

cheaper, cheapest

not costing much money 便宜的；廉价的

The pencil is cheaper than the pen. 铅笔比钢笔便宜。

同义 **inexpensive**

反义 **dear, expensive**

cheaply /ˈtʃiːpli; ˋtʃiplɪ/ *adv* 副

for a low price 以低廉的价格；便宜地

You can buy vegetables cheaply in the market. 在这个市场买蔬菜很便宜。

***cheat** /tʃiːt; tʃit/ *v* 动

to do something which is not fair, honest or against rules 欺骗；作弊

Students should not cheat in exams. 学生不该在考试中作弊。

***check**[1] /tʃek; tʃɛk/ *v* 动

to make sure that something is correct or good 检查；核对

He checked his answers and found two mistakes. 他核对自己的答案，发现了两个错误。

check in（在酒店、机场等地方）办理登记手续

We checked in at the hotel. 我们在酒店办理入住登记手续。

check out 办理（酒店）退房手续

You have to check out before noon. 你必须在中午之前办理退房手续。

check[2] /tʃek; tʃɛk/ *n* 名【美】

英式 **cheque**

cheek /tʃiːk; tʃik/ *n* 名

the part of the face under the eye 面颊；脸蛋

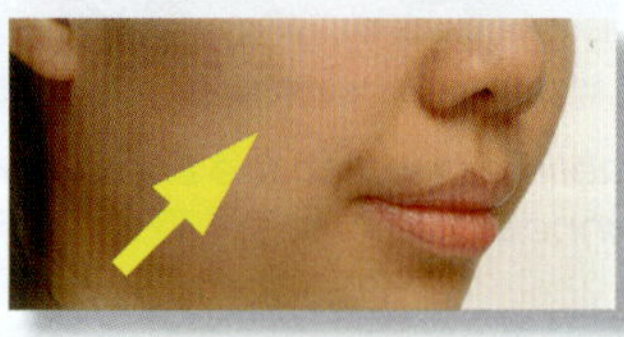

The baby has lovely pink cheeks. 这个宝宝有张可爱的红脸蛋。

***cheer**[1] /tʃɪə; tʃɪr/ *v* 动

1. to shout because you are happy 喝彩；欢呼
   We all cheered when our team won. 我们的队获胜了，大家都欢呼喝彩。
2. to become happier or to make someone feel happier（使）高兴起来；（使）振作起来

cheer up 开心起来；振作起来

Cheer up! Don't worry too much. 开心些！别太担心。

cheer someone up 使某人高兴；使某人振作

Anita is not happy. Let's cheer her up. 安妮塔不高兴，我们来逗她开心吧。

***cheer**[2] /tʃɪə; tʃɪr/ *n* 名

a shout of joy 喝彩；欢呼

The crowd gave loud cheers. 群众高声欢呼。

***cheerful** /ˈtʃɪəfl; ˋtʃɪrfəl/ *adj* 形

happy 高兴的；快乐的

John looks very cheerful today. 约翰今天看来很高兴。

cheerfully /ˈtʃɪəfəli; ˋtʃɪrfəlɪ/ *adv* 副

in a happy way 高兴地；快乐地

The children were all waiting cheerfully for their presents. 那些孩子兴奋地等待着礼物。

***cheese** /tʃiːz; tʃiz/ *n* 名

无复数

a hard food made from milk 干酪；芝士

I added some cheese to my sandwich. 我在三明治里加了些干酪。

chef /ʃef; ʃɛf/ *n* 名

a cook who works in a restaurant, especially the most important cook 厨师；主厨

Paul's father is a chef in a hotel. 保罗的父亲是酒店的主厨。

比较 **cook**[2]

cheque /tʃek; tʃɛk/ *n* 名【英】

美式：*check*

a piece of paper from the bank that you use instead of money to pay for things 支票

You may pay in cash or by cheque. 你可以用现金或支票付款。

***cherry** /ˈtʃeri; ˋtʃɛrɪ/ *n* 名

复数：***cherries***

a small, round, red or black fruit 樱桃

There are a lot of cherries on top of the cake. 那个蛋糕上面有许多樱桃。

***chess** /tʃes; tʃɛs/ *n* 名

无复数

a game that two people play by moving pieces on a special board. You win by capturing the other person's king. 国际象棋

Mike is very good at chess. 迈克擅长下国际象棋。

Chinese chess 中国象棋

Mr Brown likes playing Chinese chess. 布朗先生喜欢下象棋。

chest /tʃest; tʃɛst/ *n* 名

the front of your body between your shoulders and your stomach 胸部；胸膛

He has a wound in his chest. 他的胸部有一处伤口。

chew /tʃu:; tʃu/ *v* 动

to bite something many times in the mouth 咀嚼

The dog is chewing a bone. 狗在嚼一块骨头。

chewing gum /ˈtʃu:ɪŋ gʌm; ˋtʃuɪŋ gʌm/ *n* 名

无复数

a sweet that you chew but do not swallow 口香糖；香口胶

You cannot take chewing gum to school. 你不能带口香糖上学。

***chicken** /ˈtʃɪkɪn; ˋtʃɪkɪn/ *n* 名

1. a bird that you keep for its meat and eggs 鸡

My uncle keeps a lot of chickens on his farm. 叔叔在农场里养了很多鸡。

2. (无复数) meat from a chicken 鸡肉

Angela likes to eat chicken. 安琪拉喜欢吃鸡。

另见 **cock, hen**

***chief** /tʃi:f; tʃif/ *adj* 形

the most important 主要的；最重要的

Rice is the chief crop in China. 稻米是中国主要的农作物。

同义 **main**

***child** /tʃaɪld; tʃaɪld/ *n* 名

复数：***children***

a boy or girl 孩子；儿童

He is the only child in the family. 他是家中的独生子。

childhood /ˈtʃaɪldhʊd; ˋtʃaɪld͵hʊd/ *n* 名

无复数

the time when you are a child 童年

I had a very happy childhood. 我有一个非常快乐的童年。

***children** /ˈtʃɪldrən; ˋtʃɪldrən/ *n* 名

the plural of **child** ☆child 的复数形式

chilli /ˈtʃɪli; ˋtʃɪlɪ/ *n* 名【英】

复数：***chillies*** | 美式：***chili***

a small, thin, red or green vegetable that tastes hot 辣椒

My mother cooked a dish of chicken with chillies. 妈妈烧了一盘辣子鸡。

***chime** /tʃaɪm; tʃaɪm/ *v* 动

chimes, chiming, chimed, chimed

to ring (钟、铃)鸣响

The church bell chimes every morning and evening. 教堂的钟每天早晚都会响。

chimney /ˈtʃɪmni; ˋtʃɪmnɪ/ *n* 名

a tall pipe that lets smoke out of a

C

building 烟囱
Santa Claus goes into houses through the chimney. 圣诞老人从烟囱爬进屋内。

chin /tʃɪn; tʃɪn/ *n* 名
the part of your face below your mouth 下巴

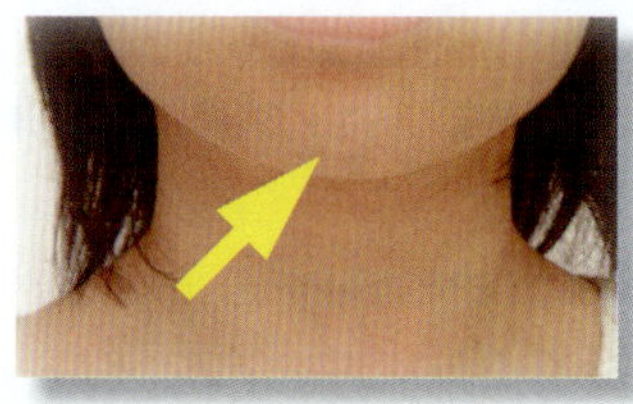

He has a long beard on his chin. 他的下巴留着长胡子。

***Chinese**[1] /ˌtʃaɪˈniːz; ˌtʃaɪˋniz/ *n* 名
无复数
1. the language used in China 中文；汉语
   Mrs Brown can speak Chinese. 布朗太太会说中文。
2. **the Chinese** people from China 中国人
   Fireworks were invented by the Chinese a long time ago. 中国人在许多年前发明了烟花。

注意 开头的字母必须用大写。

***Chinese**[2] /ˌtʃaɪˈniːz; ˌtʃaɪˋniz/ *adj* 形
from or about China 中国的
He drinks Chinese tea every day. 他每天都喝中国茶。

注意 开头的字母必须用大写。

Chinese New Year /ˌtʃaɪˈniːz njuː jɪə; ˌtʃaɪˋniz nu jɪr/ *n* 名
无复数
a Chinese festival at the beginning of spring 农历新年；春节
People visit their relatives at Chinese New Year. 人们在农历新年时给亲戚拜年。

***chip** /tʃɪp; tʃɪp/ *n* 名
1. 【英】(美式：**French fry**) a long piece of fried potato 炸薯条
   They are eating hamburgers and chips. 他们在吃汉堡包和炸薯条。
2. 【美】薯片 **英式** **crisp**

***chocolate** /ˈtʃɒklət; ˋtʃɑkəlɪt/ *n* 名
a sweet, brown food 巧克力
My aunt gave me a box of chocolates. 阿姨给了我一盒巧克力。

***choice** /tʃɔɪs; tʃɔɪs/ *n* 名
1. a chance to choose between different things or people 选择
   You have a choice of coffee or tea. 你可以选咖啡或茶。
2. a person or thing that you choose 被选中的人或物
   I like your choice of colours. 我喜欢你选的颜色。

***choir** /kwaɪə; kwaɪr/ *n* 名
a group of people who sing together 合唱团
Kitty joined the school choir last year. 吉蒂去年参加了学校的合唱团。

***choose** /tʃuːz; tʃuz/ *v* 动
chooses, choosing, chose, chosen
to decide which one you want 选择；挑选
He chose a book from the shelf. 他从书架上挑选了一本书。

***chop** /tʃɒp; tʃɑp/ *v* 动
chops, chopping, chopped, chopped
to cut something into pieces 砍；切
She is chopping onions. 她在切洋葱。

chopper /ˈtʃɒpə; ˋtʃɑpɚ/ *n* 名
a large knife for cutting food 菜刀；切肉刀
My father is cutting up the meat with a chopper. 爸爸正在用菜刀切肉。

chopstick /ˈtʃɒp-stɪk; ˋtʃɑpˏstɪk/ *n* 名
one of a pair of thin sticks for eating 筷子

Mr Brown doesn't know how to use chopsticks. 布朗先生不会用筷子。

注意 常用复数。

chose /tʃəʊz; tʃoz/ *v* 动
the past tense of **choose** ☆choose 的过去式

chosen /ˈtʃəʊzn; ˋtʃozn̩/ *v* 动
the past participle of **choose** ☆choose 的过去分词

Christian /ˈkrɪstʃən; ˋkrɪstʃən/ *n* 名
someone who follows the teachings

of Jesus Christ 基督徒
Helen is a Christian. 海伦是个基督徒。

Christianity /ˌkrɪstɪˈænɪtɪ; ˏkrɪstʃɪˋænətɪ/ *n* 名
the religion based on the teachings of Jesus Christ 基督教

***Christmas** /ˈkrɪsməs; ˋkrɪsməs/ *n* 名
无复数 | 缩写：*Xmas*
a festival on 25 December 圣诞节
I received a lot of presents last Christmas. 去年圣诞节我收到了很多礼物。

***church** /tʃɜːtʃ; tʃɝtʃ/ *n* 名
复数：*churches*
a building where people pray 教堂

Our school is opposite the church. 我们的学校在教堂对面。

cigarette /ˌsɪɡəˈret; ˏsɪɡəˋrɛt/ *n* 名
a thin paper tube filled with tobacco for smoking 香烟

Children are not allowed to buy cigarettes. 儿童不准购买香烟。

***cinema** /ˈsɪnəmə; ˋsɪnəmə/ *n* 名
a building where you watch films 电影院

I will wait for you at the cinema. 我在电影院等你。
go to the cinema 看电影
I went to the cinema last night. 昨晚我去看电影。
比较 theatre

Daily conversation 日常会话
"What's on at the cinema?" "Kung Fu Panda." "什么电影在上映？" "《功夫熊猫》。"

***circle¹** /ˈsɜːkl; ˋsɝkl̩/ *n* 名
a round shape 圆形；圆圈
She drew a circle on the blackboard. 她在黑板上画了一个圆圈。

***circle²** /ˈsɜːkl; ˋsɝkl̩/ *v* 动
circles, circling, circled, circled
to draw a circle round something 在…周围画圆圈；圈出
Circle the correct answers. 把正确的答案圈出来。

***circus** /ˈsɜːkəs; ˋsɝkəs/ *n* 名
复数：*circuses*
a group of people and animals that perform a show in a big tent 马戏团

I like the clowns at this circus. 我喜欢这个马戏团的小丑。

***citizen** /ˈsɪtɪzən; ˋsɪtəzn̩/ *n* 名
a person who belongs to a country or lives in a town, city or country 公民；市民
Joan is an American citizen. 琼是美国公民。

***city** /ˈsɪti; ˋsɪtɪ/ *n* 名
复数：*cities*
a large important town 城市
New York is a famous city. 纽约是个著名的城市。

***clap** /klæp; klæp/ *v* 动
claps, clapping, clapped, clapped
to hit one hand with the other 拍手；鼓掌
The audience clapped at the end of the concert. 观众在音乐会结束时鼓掌。

***class** /klɑːs; klæs/ *n* 名
复数：*classes*
a group of people who learn together 班；班级
They are in the same class. 他们在同一个班里上课。

classmate /ˈklɑːsmeɪt; ˋklæsˏmet/ *n* 名
someone who is in the same class as you 同学
Tracy and Ross are my classmates. 翠西和罗斯是我的同学。

***classroom** /ˈklɑːsrʊm; ˋklæsˏrum/ *n* 名
a room in a school in which you have lessons 教室
There are thirty pupils in the classroom. 教室里有 30 个学生。

claw /klɔː; klɔ/ *n* 名
a sharp curved nail of an animal or bird 爪

Cats have sharp claws. 猫的爪子很锋利。

clay /kleɪ; kle/ *n* 名

无复数

soft sticky earth for making pots, bricks, etc 黏土

These cups are made from clay. 这些杯子是用黏土制成的。

***clean**[1] /kliːn; klin/ *adj* 形

cleaner, cleanest

not dirty 清洁的；干净的

We must keep the classroom clean. 我们必须保持教室清洁。

反义 **dirty**

***clean**[2] /kliːn; klin/ *v* 动

to remove dirt from something 把…弄干净

She is cleaning the floor. 她在打扫地板。

clean up 整理干净；收拾

You must clean up your bedroom. 你必须收拾好你的卧室。

***clear**[1] /klɪə; klɪr/ *adj* 形

clearer, clearest

1. easy to see, hear or understand 清晰的；清楚的

   The teacher's explanation was very clear. 老师的解释很清楚。
2. with nothing in the way 畅顺的

   The roads are usually clear in the early morning. 清晨道路通常畅顺无阻。

***clear**[2] /klɪə; klɪr/ *v* 动

to take something away from a place 清除

He cleared the rubbish from the kitchen. 他清理了厨房里的垃圾。

clear up 整理；收拾

Can you help me clear up the room? 可以请你帮忙收拾房间吗？

clearly /ˈklɪəli; ˋklɪrlɪ/ *adv* 副

in a clear way 清晰地

Candy speaks very clearly. 坎蒂说话很清晰。

clerk /klɑːk; klɝk/ *n* 名

a person whose job is to keep files in an office 文员；文书人员

His brother is a clerk in a bank. 他的哥哥在银行做文员。

***clever** /ˈklevə; ˋklɛvɚ/ *adj* 形

cleverer, cleverest

good at learning and understanding things 聪明的；机敏的

He is clever and hard-working so he always gets good results in exams. 他既聪明又用功，所以总在考试中取得好成绩。

同义 **smart**

反义 **foolish, silly, stupid**

click /klɪk; klɪk/ *v* 动

【电脑】to select something using a mouse 按鼠标；点击

Click here to send your email. 点击这里，把电子邮件发出去。

cliff /klɪf; klɪf/ *n* 名

a steep rocky hill, often next to the sea 悬崖；峭壁

Don't stand close to the edge of the cliff. 不要靠近悬崖边。

climate /ˈklaɪmət; ˋklaɪmɪt/ *n* 名

the usual weather of a place 气候

Most penguins live in a cold climate. 大多数企鹅在气候寒冷的地方生活。

***climb** /klaɪm; klaɪm/ *v* 动

to go up 爬；攀

They climbed the stairs to the third floor. 他们爬楼梯到三楼。

climb up 爬；攀

The man climbed up the tree. 那个人爬上了树。

climbing frame /ˈklaɪmɪŋ ˌfreɪm; ˋklaɪmɪŋ ˌfrem/ *n* 名

a large thing made of bars for children to climb on 儿童玩的攀登架

There is a climbing frame in the park. 公园里有一座攀登架。

***clinic** /ˈklɪnɪk; ˋklɪnɪk/ *n* 名

a place where sick people go to see a doctor 诊所

There are a lot of patients in the clinic. 诊所里有很多病人。

***clip** /klɪp; klɪp/ *n* 名

a small metal or plastic object for holding things together 夹子；回形针

I use a clip to hold the test papers together. 我用回形针把考卷夹住。

***clock** /klɒk; klɑk/ *n* 名

a machine that shows you the time 时钟

There is a clock on the wall. 墙上挂了一个钟。

***close[1]** /kləʊz; kloz/ *v* 动

closes, closing, closed, closed

1. to shut 关闭

   Close the door, please. 请把门关上。

反义 **open[2]**

2. to stop doing business 关门；停止营业

   The shop closes at 10 p.m. 商店晚上 10 点关门。

同义 **shut[1]**

反义 **open[2]**

***close[2]** /kləʊs; klos/ *adj* 形

closer, closest

1. near 接近的

   Our school is close to the church. 我们的学校邻近教堂。

2. liking each other 亲密的

   Ada and Amy are close friends. 爱达和艾美是亲密的朋友。

***close[3]** /kləʊs; klos/ *adv* 副

near 接近

Sally and Candy sat close together. 莎莉和坎蒂紧挨着坐在一起。

close to 接近

George lives close to the school. 乔治住在学校附近。

closed /kləʊzd; klozd/ *adj* 形

1. not open 关闭的；闭着的

   You must keep your eyes closed when you play this game. 玩这个游戏时，必须闭上眼睛。

同义 **shut[2]**

反义 **open[1]**

2. not open to the public 关闭的；不营业的

   The library is closed on Wednesdays. 这个图书馆逢星期三闭馆。

反义 **open[1]**

closely /ˈkləʊsli; ˋkloslɪ/ *adv* 副

in a close manner 贴近地；贴紧地；仔细地

The dog followed me closely. 那条狗紧紧地跟着我走。

***cloth** /klɒθ; klɔθ/ *n* 名

1. （无复数）materials for making clothes 衣料；布匹

   He used the cloth to make some clothes. 他用那匹布做了一些衣服。

2. a piece of material you use for cleaning things 一块布

   She cleaned the window with a cloth. 她用一块布抹窗户。

***clothes** /kləʊðz; kloz/ *plural n* 复数名词

things that you wear 衣服

My mother bought some new clothes for me. 妈妈给我买了一些新衣服。

clothing /ˈkləʊðɪŋ; ˋkloðɪŋ/ *n* 名

无复数

clothes 衣服

We wear warm clothing in winter. 我们冬天时穿保暖的衣服。

***cloud** /klaʊd; klaʊd/ *n* 名

a white or grey shape in the sky 云

There are clouds in the sky. 天空中有云。

***cloudy** /ˈklaʊdi; ˋklaʊdɪ/ *adj* 形

cloudier, cloudiest

full of clouds 多云的；阴天的

It's cloudy today. 今天多云。

***clown** /klaʊn; klaʊn/ *n* 名

a person who wears colourful clothes and does silly things to make people laugh 小丑

The clown looks very funny. 那小丑的样子十分滑稽。

C

***club** /klʌb; klʌb/ *n* 名

a group of people who do something they are interested in together 社团；俱乐部

I am a member of the drama club at school. 我是学校戏剧社的会员。

clubhouse /'klʌbhaʊs; `klʌb͵haʊs/ *n* 名

a building where a club meets 俱乐部会所

There are two restaurants in the clubhouse. 俱乐部会所内有两家餐厅。

***clue** /kluː; klu/ *n* 名

something that helps you answer a question 线索；提示

The question looks difficult. Can you give me a clue? 这个问题好像很难，可以给我个提示吗?

cm

the short form of **centimetre**☆ centimetre 的缩写

***coach** /kəʊtʃ; kotʃ/ *n* 名

复数：***coaches***

1. someone who teaches a sport or skill 教练

 He is a football coach. 他是足球教练。

2. 【英】(美式：***bus***) a bus for long journeys 长途汽车

 We went to the country park by coach. 我们乘长途汽车去郊野公园。

coal /kəʊl; kol/ *n* 名

无复数

a black material that is burnt to give heat 煤；煤块

They put some coal on the fire. 他们把煤放进火里。

coast /kəʊst; kost/ *n* 名

the land by the sea 海岸；海滨

The village is on the coast. 村庄坐落在海滨。

***coat** /kəʊt; kot/ *n* 名

a piece of clothing that you wear over your other clothes to keep you warm 外衣；外套

It is cold outside. Put on your coat. 外面冷，你要穿上外套。

cobweb /'kɒbweb; `kɑb͵wɛb/ *n* 名

a thin net made by a spider 蜘蛛网

The old house is full of cobwebs. 这老房子里到处都是蜘蛛网。

cock /kɒk; kɑk/ *n* 名

a male chicken 公鸡

There are a lot of cocks on the farm. 农场里有很多公鸡。

另见 **chicken, hen**

cockroach /'kɒkrəʊtʃ; `kɑk͵rotʃ/ *n* 名

复数：***cockroaches***

a large flat brown insect that lives in dirty houses 蟑螂

Cockroaches spread germs. 蟑螂传播细菌。

coconut /'kəʊkənʌt; `kokənʌt/ *n* 名

a kind of big brown nut 椰子

Sally opened the coconut with a knife. 莎莉用刀把椰子劈开。

code /kəʊd; kod/ *n* 名

a number of words or signs that mean other words 密码；代号

Do you understand this code? 你知道这个密码的意思吗?

***coffee** /'kɒfi; `kɔfɪ/ *n* 名

无复数

a kind of brown drink 咖啡

Would you like tea or coffee? 你要茶还是咖啡?

coffin /'kɒfɪn; `kɔfɪn/ *n* 名

a long box used to bury a dead person 棺材

They buried the coffin. 他们把棺材埋了。

***coin** /kɔɪn; kɔɪn/ *n* 名

a round piece of metal, used as

money 硬币；辅币
He likes to collect old coins. 他喜欢收集旧硬币。

***cold[1]** /kəʊld; kold/ *adj* 形

colder, coldest

not warm or hot 冷的

It is cold in winter. 冬天天气寒冷。

反义 **hot**

***cold[2]** /kəʊld; kold/ *n* 名

an illness that makes you sneeze and cough 伤风；感冒
I have a bad cold. 我得了重感冒。

collar /ˈkɒlə; ˋkɑlɚ/ *n* 名

the part of a shirt or jacket that goes around your neck 衣领
The collar of my shirt is dirty. 我衬衫的衣领脏了。

***collect** /kəˈlekt; kəˋlɛkt/ *v* 动

1. to put things together in one place 集中；收集
   He collected all his toys and put them in a big box. 他把玩具收拾起来，放在一个大箱子里。
2. to get things and keep them together, because you like them 收藏；搜集
   Mary collects stamps. 玛丽搜集邮票。

In the classroom 在教室里

"Colin, please collect the exercise books for me and put them on my desk." "Yes, of course." "科林，请你帮我收一下练习册，然后放在我的桌子上。" "好的。"

***collection** /kəˈlekʃn; kəˋlɛkʃən/ *n* 名

a group of similar things that are kept together 收藏品
The museum has a collection of valuable paintings. 这座博物馆内有珍贵的藏画。

colon /ˈkəʊlən; ˋkolən/ *n* 名

the sign you use in writing before giving an example, a list, etc (:) 冒号

另见 附录：Punctuation 标点符号

***colour[1]** /ˈkʌlə; ˋkʌlɚ/ *n* 名【英】

美式：***color***

red, green, yellow, blue, etc 颜色
Which colour do you like best? 你最喜欢什么颜色？

***colour[2]** /ˈkʌlə; ˋkʌlɚ/ *v* 动【英】

美式：***color***

to give something a particular colour 涂上颜色；着色
He coloured the wall green. 他把墙壁刷成绿色。

***colourful** /ˈkʌləfl; ˋkʌlɚfəl/ *adj* 形【英】

美式：***colorful***

having bright colours or many different colours 颜色鲜艳的；色彩缤纷的
The flowers are very colourful. 那些花朵鲜艳夺目。

column /ˈkɒləm; ˋkɑləm/ *n* 名

a line of numbers or words written under each other 列
The teacher asked us to add up the numbers in each column. 老师叫我们把每列的数字加起来。

***comb[1]** /kəʊm; kom/ *n* 名

a thing that you use to make your hair tidy 梳子
She carries a comb in her handbag. 她的手提包里有一把梳子。

***comb[2]** /kəʊm; kom/ *v* 动

to use a comb to make your hair tidy 梳理
Tracy combs her hair every morning. 翠西每天早上梳头发。

combine /kəmˈbaɪn; kəmˋbaɪn/ *v* 动

combines, combining, combined, combined

to become one thing, or to join things together 结合；联合
The two towns have combined to become a large city. 两个城镇已合并成为一个大城市。

***come** /kʌm; kʌm/ *v* 动

comes, coming, came, come

to move to or towards a place, especially the place where you are now 来；过来
Come here, please. 请过来。

come from somewhere 来自某地；出生于某地
Mr Brown comes from America. 布朗先生来自美国。

come in/into (somewhere) 进来；进入
The door opened and they came in. 门开了，他们走进来。

come on 快点
Come on! The train is about to leave. 快点吧！火车快开了。

反义 **go**

comedy /ˈkɒmədi; ˋkɑmədɪ/ *n* 名

复数：***comedies***

a funny film, play, etc 喜剧

The film is a comedy about the adventure of a group of toys. 这部

C

喜剧电影是关于一群玩具的冒险故事。

另见 **tragedy**

***comfortable** /ˈkʌmftəbl; ˋkʌmfətəbl/ *adj* 形

1. a comfortable bed, chair, or place is nice to sit on, lie on, or be in 舒适的；舒服的
   I have a comfortable bed. 我有一张舒适的床。
2. if you are comfortable, you do not have any unpleasant feelings 舒适的；舒服的
   Are you comfortable in that chair? 你坐在那张椅子上觉得舒适吗？

反义 **uncomfortable**

***comic** /ˈkɒmɪk; ˋkamɪk/ *n* 名

a book with pictures that tell a story 连环漫画书

This comic is very funny. 这本漫画书十分有趣。

comma /ˈkɒmə; ˋkamə/ *n* 名

the sign you use to show a short stop in a sentence (,) 逗号

另见 附录：Punctuation 标点符号

comment /ˈkɒment; ˋkamɛnt/ *n* 名

what a person says about something 意见；评论

The teacher made some comments on my homework. 老师对我的作业给了些意见。

***committee** /kəˈmɪti; kəˋmɪtɪ/ *n* 名

a group of people who plan and arrange things 委员会

Ross is a member of the Sports Committee. 罗斯是体育委员会的成员。

***common** /ˈkɒmən; ˋkamən/ *adj* 形

commoner, commonest

found in many places or happening often 平常的；常见的；普遍的

The teacher told us about some common English mistakes. 老师告诉我们一些常见的英语错误。

同义 **usual**

反义 **rare, unusual**

communicate /kəˈmjuːnɪkeɪt; kəˋmjunəˏket/ *v* 动

communicates, communicating, communicated, communicated

to speak or write to someone 沟通；交流；交谈

Family members should communicate with each other. 家庭成员之间应互相沟通。

***communication** /kəˌmjuːnɪˈkeɪʃn; kəˏmjunəˋkeʃən/ *n* 名

speaking or writing to someone 沟通；交流；通讯

They use email for communication. 他们用电子邮件来交流。

compact disc /ˌkɒmpækt ˈdɪsk; kəmˏpækt ˋdɪsk/ *n* 名

另见 **CD**

***company** /ˈkʌmpəni; ˋkʌmpənɪ/ *n* 名

1. （复数：***companies***） an organization that sells things or services to make money 公司
   Mr Brown's company sells computers. 布朗先生的公司销售电脑。
2. （无复数） being with someone and not alone 陪伴
   I enjoy my grandfather's company. 我喜欢和爷爷在一起。

***compare** /kəmˈpeə; kəmˋpɛr/ *v* 动

compares, comparing, compared, compared

to see how similar or different two things are 比较

She compared the two hats and bought the pink one. 她比较了两顶帽子后，买了粉红色的那一顶。

compass /ˈkʌmpəs; ˋkʌmpəs/ *n* 名

1. （复数：***compasses***） a thing that shows directions, with a needle that points north 指南针；罗盘

   We used a compass to find our way down the mountain. 我们用指南针找到了下山的路。
2. （也作：***compasses***） a thing for drawing circles 圆规

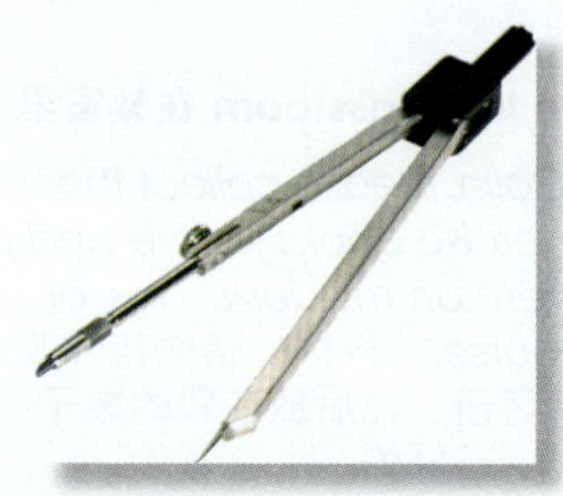

I use a pair of compasses to draw circles. 我用圆规来画圆圈。

compete /kəm'pi:t; kəm`pit/ *v* 动

competes, competing, competed, competed

to try to win 比赛；竞争

The children are competing in the race. 那些孩子在比赛。

***competition** /ˌkɒmpə'tɪʃn; ˌkɑmpə`tɪʃən/ *n* 名

an event in which people or teams try to be the winner 比赛；竞赛

Mike won the swimming competition. 迈克在游泳比赛中胜出了。

competitor /kəm'petɪtə; kəm`pɛtətɚ/ *n* 名

a person who takes part in a competition 参赛者；竞争对手

He is a very strong competitor. 他是个实力很强的竞争对手。

***complain** /kəm'pleɪn; kəm`plen/ *v* 动

to say that you are angry or not happy about something or someone 投诉；抱怨

I complained to the teacher because Gordon pulled my hair. 戈登拉扯我的头发，所以我向老师告状。

complain about something 抱怨某事

He is complaining about the noise. 他在抱怨声音太吵。

complaint /kəm'pleɪnt; kəm`plent/ *n* 名

something that you say when you are angry or not happy about something or someone 投诉；抱怨

The train company has received many complaints because its trains are dirty. 这家铁路公司接到很多投诉，因为它的车厢不干净。

***complete**[1] /kəm'pli:t; kəm`plit/ *adj* 形

full; having no parts missing 完全的；完整的

Please answer in complete sentences. 请用完整的句子回答。

***complete**[2] /kəm'pli:t; kəm`plit/ *v* 动

completes, completing, completed, completed

to finish 完成

I will complete my homework tonight. 今晚我要完成功课。

completely /kəm'pli:tli; kəm`plitlɪ/ *adv* 副

totally 完全地；完整地

You are completely wrong. 你完全错了。

complicated /'kɒmplɪkeɪtɪd; `kɑmpləˌketɪd/ *adj* 形

difficult to understand; having many parts 复杂的

This is a complicated question. 这个问题很复杂。

***composition** /ˌkɒmpə'zɪʃn; ˌkɑmpə`zɪʃən/ *n* 名

a piece of writing that you do at school 作文；文章

We write an English composition every week. 我们每星期写一篇英语作文。

comprehension /ˌkɒmprɪ'henʃn; ˌkɑmprɪ`hɛnʃən/ *n* 名

无复数

1. your ability to understand 理解（力）

   I have no comprehension of the life of a farmer a hundred years ago. 我完全不理解 100 年前的农民生活。

2. an exercise to see if you understand written or spoken language（阅读/听力）理解练习

   We had a reading comprehension test this morning. 我们今天早上进行了阅读理解测验。

***computer** /kəm'pju:tə; kəm`pjutɚ/ *n* 名

a machine that stores information, which you use for doing things such as writing, playing games, or using the Internet 电脑

Today, most people know how to use computers. 现在大多数人都会使用电脑。

***concert** /'kɒnsət; `kɑnsɝt/ *n* 名

a performance of music 音乐会

My sister is playing the violin at the concert. 姐姐正在音乐会上演奏小提琴。

***condition** /kən'dɪʃn; kən`dɪʃən/ *n* 名

1. **conditions**（复数名词）the situation in which someone lives or works 环境

   She lives in crowded conditions. 她居住的环境很拥挤。

2. （无复数）how good or bad someone or something is 状况；状态

in (a) good / poor condition 状态良好/情况不好

The car was in good condition. 这辆车的性能良好。

conduct /'kɒndʌkt; `kɑndʌkt/ *n* 名

无复数

the way you behave 品行；表现

Sally is a good student and received a prize for good conduct. 莎莉是个好学生，因品行优良而得奖。

同义 **behaviour**

conductor /kən'dʌktə; kən`dʌktɚ/ *n* 名

a person who shows a group of people how to sing or play music（合唱团或乐队的）指挥

Paul is the conductor of our school orchestra. 保罗是我们学校管弦乐团的指挥。

cone /kəʊn; kon/ *n* 名

a container of ice cream that you can eat 冰淇淋蛋筒

Would you like your ice cream in a cone or a cup? 你的冰淇淋放在蛋筒里还是杯子里?

***confidence** /'kɒnfɪdəns; `kɑnfədəns/ *n* 名

无复数

a feeling that you can do things well 自信心

The boy is very shy and does not have confidence. 这男孩很害羞，没有自信心。

***confident** /'kɒnfɪdənt; `kɑnfədənt/ *adj* 形

sure that you can do things well 自信的；有信心的

Tracy was very confident of getting a good result in English dictation. 翠西自信能在英文听写中取得好成绩。

congee /'kɒndʒi; `kɑndʒi/ *n* 名

无复数

rice boiled in a lot of water 粥；稀饭

Mary was ill and her mother cooked her some congee for dinner. 玛丽病了，所以她的妈妈给她煮了稀饭当晚餐。

***congratulations** /kənˌgrætʃʊ'leɪʃnz; kənˌgrætʃə`leʃənz/ *plural n* 复数名词

words said to someone for their good work or good luck 祝贺；恭喜

Congratulations on winning the prize! 恭喜你得奖!

conjunction /kən'dʒʌŋkʃn; kən`dʒʌŋkʃən/ *n* 名

a word such as "and" or "but" that connects parts of sentence 连词

connect /kə'nekt; kə`nɛkt/ *v* 动

to join things or places together 连接；连结

The bridge connects the two cities. 这座大桥把这两个城市连接起来。

conquer /'kɒŋkə; `kɑŋkɚ/ *v* 动

to defeat an enemy 征服；打败

Finally, the king conquered the country. 那位国王终于征服了那个国家。

***consider** /kən'sɪdə; kən`sɪdɚ/ *v* 动

to think about something carefully 考虑；细想

My father is considering buying a car. 我的爸爸在考虑买一辆汽车。

consist /kən'sɪst; kən`sɪst/ *v* 动

to be made of 由…组成；包括

consist of something 由某事物组成

My lunch consisted of rice, vegetables and beef. 我的午餐包括饭、蔬菜和牛肉。

consonant /'kɒnsənənt; `kɑnsənənt/ *n* 名

a letter or the sound of a letter that is not a vowel, for example, "b" and "c" 辅音字母；辅音

另见 书末的发音表

比较 **vowel**

***contain** /kən'teɪn; kən`ten/ *v* 动

to have something inside 包含；装有

What does that bottle contain? 那个瓶子里装着什么？

container /kən'teɪnə; kən`tenə/ *n* 名

a box, bottle, etc that you put things in 容器

Don't leave food in an open container. 不要用没有盖子的容器装食物。

container ship /kən'teɪnə ʃɪp; kən`tenə ʃɪp/ *n* 名

a ship that carries goods 集装箱船

A container ship can carry a lot of heavy goods. 集装箱船能载很多重物。

contented /kən'tentɪd; kən`tentɪd/ *adj* 形

happy; pleased 满足的；满意的

My grandfather was contented with his life in the village. 祖父很满意乡村的生活。

contents /'kɒntents; `kantɛnts/ *plural n* 复数名词

1. the things inside something（某物里）装着的东西；内含物

   All the contents of her school bag dropped out. 她书包里的所有东西都掉出来了。

2. the things that are written in a book, letter, etc（信、书等的）内容

   You should not tell anyone about the contents of this letter. 你不应该把这封信的内容告诉任何人。

table of contents 目录

The table of contents of this book is on page 1. 本书的目录在第一页。

contest /'kɒntest; `kantɛst/ *n* 名

a competition 比赛；竞赛

My sister won the dancing contest. 我的姐姐赢了舞蹈比赛。

continent /'kɒntɪnənt; `kantənənt/ *n* 名

a large piece of land such as Asia, Africa and Europe 大洲；大陆

Asia is the largest continent in the world. 亚洲是世界上最大的洲。

***continue** /kən'tɪnju:; kən`tɪnju/ *v* 动

continues, continuing, continued, continued

1. to keep happening 连续不断；持续

   The rain continued all night. 雨下了整整一夜。

2. to start again after you have stopped（停顿后）继续；重新开始

   We continued our lessons after lunch. 午饭以后，我们继续上课。

continuous /kən'tɪnjʊəs; kən`tɪnjʊəs/ *adj* 形

continuing to happen 持续的；不间断的

There was a continuous pain in his knee. 他的膝盖持续疼痛。

***control[1]** /kən'trəʊl; kən`trol/ *n* 名 **无复数**

power over someone or something 控制

A teacher should have control of the class during lessons. 一个老师必须能在课堂上管好学生。

out of control 不受控制；失控

The car went out of control and hit a tree. 汽车失控，撞到一棵树上。

***control[2]** /kən'trəʊl; kən`trol/ *v* 动

controls, controlling, controlled, controlled

to make someone or something do what you want 控制

He controlled his toy plane very well. 他对玩具飞机操纵自如。

convenient /kən'vi:niənt; kən`vinjənt/ *adj* 形

1. easy to use 方便的；便利的

   Email is a convenient way of sending photos to friends. 用电子邮件把照片传给朋友十分方便。

   反义 inconvenient

2. easy to get to 附近的；近而方便的

   The supermarket is convenient. You can get there in five minutes. 超市就在附近，5 分钟就到了。

反义 inconvenient

C

conversation /ˌkɒnvəˈseɪʃn; ˌkɑnvɚˋseʃən/ *n* 名

a talk between two or more people 谈话；交谈

Peter and Lily had a long conversation about their pets. 彼得和莉莉谈他们的宠物谈了很久。

***cook[1]** /kʊk; kuk/ *v* 动

to prepare food for eating using heat 烹调；煮

My mother is cooking beef soup. 妈妈正在煮牛肉汤。

***cook[2]** /kʊk; kuk/ *n* 名

someone who cooks 厨师

My uncle is a cook in a restaurant. 我的叔叔在餐厅当厨师。

比较 **chef**

cooker /ˈkʊkə; ˋkukɚ/ *n* 名

the thing you use for cooking 锅；炉具

Mrs Smith cooked the rice in her new rice cooker. 史密斯太太用新饭锅煮饭。

cookery /ˈkʊkəri; ˋkukərɪ/ *n* 名

无复数

the skill or activity of cooking 烹调法；烹饪

Lily studied cookery at school. 莉莉在学校学过烹饪。

***cookie** /ˈkʊki; ˋkukɪ/ *n* 名【美】

英式：**biscuit**

a small flat sweet cake 小甜饼；曲奇饼

I had some cookies for breakfast this morning. 我今天早餐吃了小甜饼。

cooking /ˈkʊkɪŋ; ˋkukɪŋ/ *n* 名

无复数

making food; the way you cook 烹饪；做饭

I do all the cooking at home. 在家里，我负责做饭。

***cool** /kuːl; kul/ *adj* 形

cooler, coolest

a little cold 凉快的

The weather is cool in autumn. 秋天天气凉爽。

反义 **warm**

cooperate /kəʊˈɒpəreɪt; koˋɑpəret/ *v* 动

cooperates, cooperating, cooperated, cooperated

to work together 合作

All students should cooperate to keep the school clean. 所有学生应同心协力保持校园清洁。

cooperation /kəʊˌɒpəˈreɪʃn; koˏɑpəˋreʃən/ *n* 名

无复数

working together 合作

Thank you for your cooperation. 谢谢你的合作。

copy[1] /ˈkɒpi; ˋkɑpɪ/ *v* 动

copies, copying, copied, copied

to do something that is exactly the same as another thing 抄；复制

Copy the sentences on the blackboard into your notebook. 把黑板上的句子抄在笔记本上。

copy[2] /ˈkɒpi; ˋkɑpɪ/ *n* 名

复数：***copies***

a thing made to be like another thing 复印件；复制品；副本

Please bring a copy of your birth certificate. 请带一份你的出生证明复印件。

coral /ˈkɒrəl; ˋkɔrəl/ *n* 名

无复数

a thing you find under the sea, which looks like a plant, but is made from the hard bones of small sea animals 珊瑚

Coral is very colourful. 珊瑚色彩缤纷。

cork /kɔːk; kɔrk/ *n* 名

a thing you put in the top of a bottle to close it 软木塞

I pulled the cork out of the bottle. 我拔出瓶子的软木塞。

corn /kɔːn; kɔrn/ *n* 名

无复数

1. 【英】the seeds of plants such as wheat 谷物
   People use corn to make flour. 人们用谷物来做面粉。
2. 【美】甜玉米 英式 **sweetcorn**

***corner** /ˈkɔːnə; ˋkɔrnɚ/ *n* 名

the place where two lines, streets or walls meet 角；角落；拐角处

There is a desk in the corner of the room. 这个房间的角落放了一张书桌。

Asking for directions 问路

"Where's the museum?" "It's on the corner of these two streets." "博物馆在哪里？" "在这两条街的拐角处。"

cornflakes /ˈkɔːnfleɪks; ˋkɔrnˏfleks/ *plural n* 复数名词

a breakfast food that is usually eaten with milk and sugar 玉米片

I usually have cornflakes for breakfast. 我早餐通常吃玉米片。

***correct**[1] /kəˈrekt; kəˋrɛkt/ *adj* 形

not wrong 正确的；对的

All your answers are correct. 你所有的答案都正确。

同义 **right**[1]

反义 **incorrect, wrong**[1]

In the classroom 在教室里

"What does 4 times 150 equal?" "600." "Correct!" "4 乘 150 等于多少？" "600。" "正确！"

***correct**[2] /kəˈrekt; kəˋrɛkt/ *v* 动

to change something so that it is right and without any mistakes 改正；更正

Please correct these mistakes. 请更正这些错误。

correction /kəˈrekʃn; kəˋrɛkʃən/ *n* 名

a change that corrects a mistake 改正；修改

The teacher made corrections to my composition. 老师修改了我的作文。

correctly /kəˈrektli; kəˋrɛktlɪ/ *adv* 副

in the right way 正确地

Paul answered the question correctly. 保罗答对了问题。

***corridor** /ˈkɒrɪdɔː; ˋkɔrədə/ *n* 名

a long narrow passage in a building or train 走廊；通道

Our classroom is at the end of the corridor. 我们的教室在走廊的尽头。

***cost**[1] /kɒst; kɔst/ *n* 名

the money you pay to buy or do something 价钱；费用

The cost of food is increasing. 食物的价格越来越高。

***cost**[2] /kɒst; kɔst/ *v* 动

costs, costing, cost, cost

to have a particular price 价值

That dress costs $200. 那条连衣裙要 200 元。

costume /ˈkɒstjuːm; ˋkɑstum/ *n* 名

clothes that you wear in a film, play, etc 戏服；服装

We wore colourful costumes in the play. 我们演话剧时穿上五颜六色的戏服。

cot /kɒt; kɑt/ *n* 名【英】

a bed with high sides for a baby 婴儿床

Mrs Smith put her baby into a cot. 史密斯太太把她的宝宝放进婴儿床。

cottage /ˈkɒtɪdʒ; ˋkɑtɪdʒ/ *n* 名

a small house, usually in the countryside 农舍；村舍

They live in a comfortable cottage. 他们住在一间舒适的农舍里。

***cotton** /ˈkɒtn; ˋkɑtn̩/ *n* 名

无复数

1. light cloth made from a plant 棉布
   This shirt is made of cotton. 这件衬衫是棉布做的。
2. a plant grown in warm regions that can be used for making clothes 棉
   His grandfather worked in the cotton fields. 他的祖父在棉花田里工作。

cotton wool 药棉

C

Wipe the blood away with a piece of cotton wool! 用药棉把血抹掉！

***cough[1]** /kɒf; kɔf/ *v* 动

to make a sudden sound as you force air out of your throat 咳嗽

He has got a cold and keeps coughing all the time. 他得了感冒，整天不停咳嗽。

***cough[2]** /kɒf; kɔf/ *n* 名

1. an illness that makes you cough a lot 咳嗽
   Susan had a fever and a cough. 苏珊发烧咳嗽。
2. a sudden sound you make in your throat 咳嗽（声）
   The boys stop talking after the coach gave a little cough. 那些男孩听到教练轻咳一声后，全都安静下来。

***could** /kəd; kəd; *strong* 强读 kʊd; kud/ *v* 动

1. the past tense of **can** ☆can 的过去式
2. used as a polite way of asking someone to do something for you 能够；可以（用于有礼貌地请求别人帮忙）
   Could you open the door, please? 你可以开一下门吗？

couldn't /ˈkʊdnt; ˋkudnt/

the short form of "**could not**" ☆could not 的缩写

Yesterday I couldn't go to school because I was ill. 我昨天生病了，所以没能去上课。

***count** /kaʊnt; kaunt/ *v* 动

1. to say numbers in order（按顺序）数
   Count from one to ten and then open your eyes. 从 1 数到 10，然后睁开眼睛。
2. to find the total number of something 点算
   The man is counting the money. 那人在数钱。

count on someone 依靠某人

You can count on me. I'll help you. 你可以依靠我，我会帮忙的。

counter /ˈkaʊntə; ˋkauntɚ/ *n* 名

a long table in a bank, shop, etc（银行、商店等的）柜台

I put the food on the counter. 我把食物放在柜台上。

***country** /ˈkʌntri; ˋkʌntrɪ/ *n* 名

1. （复数：***countries***） a place with one government 国家
   Russia is the largest country in the world. 俄罗斯是世界上最大的国家。
2. **the country**（无复数） land that is not in a town or city 郊外；乡间
   Sam lives in the country. 山姆住在乡间。

同义 **countryside**

***countryside** /ˈkʌntrisaɪd; ˋkʌntrɪˌsaɪd/ *n* 名

无复数

the land away from towns and cities 乡间；农村

We went for a walk in the countryside. 我们到乡间散步。

同义 **the country**（见 **country**）

couple /ˈkʌpl; ˋkʌpl̩/ *n* 名

1. two people or things 一双；一对
   My grandparents are a happy couple. 我的祖父母是幸福的一对。
2. （无复数） a few 几个
   I need to ask you a couple more questions. 我还要问你几个问题。

a couple of something 几个

I stayed at my aunt's home for a couple of days. 我在姑妈家里住了几天。

***coupon** /ˈkuːpɒn; ˋkupan/ *n* 名

a small piece of paper you use to buy something at a lower price or to get something free 优惠券；赠券

Collect ten coupons for a free teddy bear. 集齐 10 张优惠券可免费换取玩具熊 1 只。

courage /ˈkʌrɪdʒ; ˋkɝɪdʒ/ *n* 名

无复数

the ability to do something dangerous or difficult without being afraid 勇气

I didn't have the courage to jump into the river. 我没有勇气跳进河里去。

同义 **bravery**

***course** /kɔːs; kɔrs/ *n* 名

a set of lessons 课程

They are doing a painting course. 他们在上绘画课。

Daily conversation 日常会话

of course 当然（表示坚决与肯定）

"Do you know how to use a computer?" "Of course I know!" "你会用电脑吗？" "当然了！"

***court** /kɔːt; kɔrt/ *n* 名

1. a place where judges and lawyers work 法庭；法院

   Everyone stood up when the judge came into the court. 法官出庭时，法庭内每个人都站了起来。

2. an area where you play games such as basketball or tennis（篮球、网球等）球场；场地

   We were playing on the basketball court. 我们在篮球场上玩耍。

***cousin** /ˈkʌzn; ˋkʌzn̩/ *n* 名

the child of your uncle or aunt 堂兄弟；堂姊妹；表兄弟；表姊妹

I went swimming with my cousins last Sunday. 我上周日和几个表亲一起去游泳。

***cover[1]** /ˈkʌvə; ˋkʌvɚ/ *v* 动

to put something over something else 覆盖；遮掩

Cover the table with a cloth. 在桌面上铺一块布。

cover[2] /ˈkʌvə; ˋkʌvɚ/ *n* 名

1. something put over or on top of something else 罩；套

   My mother is changing the cushion covers. 妈妈在更换坐垫套。

2. the outside of a book or magazine（书刊的）封面

   This book has a colourful cover. 这本书的封面色彩丰富。

***cow** /kaʊ; kaʊ/ *n* 名

a large female animal which gives milk 母牛；乳牛

Cows eat grass. 母牛吃草。

另见 **bull, ox**

coward /ˈkaʊəd; ˋkaʊɚd/ *n* 名

a person who is not brave enough to do something 懦夫；胆小的人

He was a coward so he ran away. 他是个懦夫，所以跑开了。

cowardly /ˈkaʊədli; ˋkaʊɚdlɪ/ *adj* 形

showing that you have no courage 懦弱的；胆小的

He was cowardly and did not shout for help. 他很胆小，没有大声呼救。

反义 **brave**

CPU /siː piː ˈjuː; ˌsi pi ˋju/ *n* 名

【电脑】the part of a computer that controls all the other parts of it 中央处理器

The CPU is the most important part of a computer. 中央处理器是电脑最重要的部分。

另见 **附录**：The computer world 电脑世界

***crab** /kræb; kræb/ *n* 名

a sea animal with a hard shell and ten legs 蟹

The children caught some crabs on the beach. 孩子们在沙滩上捉了一些螃蟹。

crack /kræk; kræk/ *v* 动

to break, making thin lines on the surface 破裂；打裂

The plate fell to the floor and cracked. 碟子掉到地板上碎了。

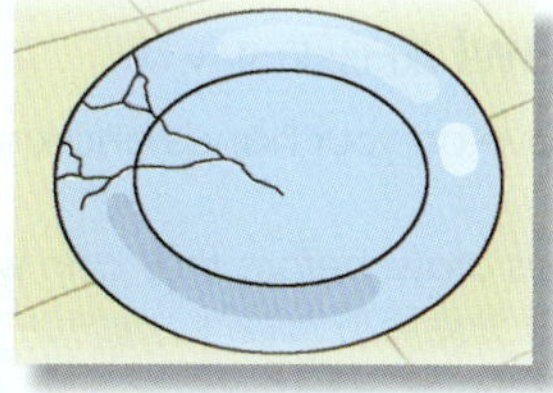

craft /krɑːft; kræft/ *n* 名

a job or activity in which you make things with your hands 手艺；工艺

Making lanterns is a traditional craft. 制作灯笼是一项传统手艺。

crane /kreɪn; kren/ *n* 名

a machine with a long arm used to lift and move heavy things 起重机

They lifted the car with a crane. 他们用起重机把车子吊起。

***crash¹** /kræʃ; kræʃ/ *n* 名

复数：***crashes***

1. an accident in which a car, a train, etc hits something 相撞；坠毁；失事

   Two men died in the car crash. 两个男人在撞车事故中死去。
2. a loud noise 巨响；碰撞声

   The vase fell to the floor with a crash. 花瓶哗啦一声掉到地板上。

***crash²** /kræʃ; kræʃ/ *v* 动

crashes, crashing, crashed, crashed

1. to hit something, used for a car, a train, etc 相撞

   The van crashed into the taxi. 小型货车撞上了出租车。
2. (of a computer) to stop working （电脑）死机

   His old computer crashes all the time. 他那台旧电脑老是死机。

***crawl** /krɔːl; krɔl/ *v* 动

to move on your hands and knees 爬行

Babies crawl before they can walk. 婴儿在会走路前先爬行。

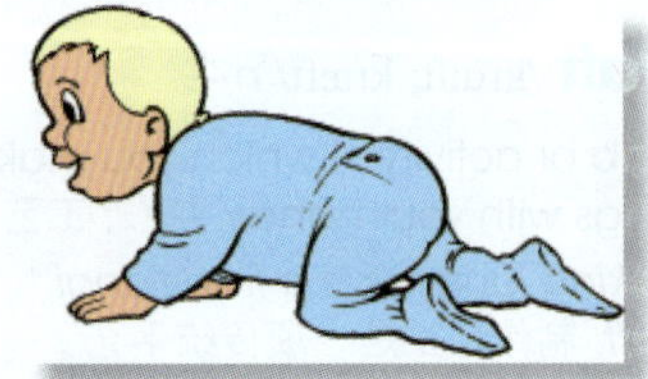

***crayon** /ˈkreɪən; ˋkreən/ *n* 名

a stick of coloured wax for drawing 彩色蜡笔

She drew a rainbow with crayons. 她用彩色蜡笔画了一道彩虹。

***crazy** /ˈkreɪzi; ˋkrezɪ/ *adj* 形

crazier, craziest

silly or strange 疯狂的；愚蠢的

That story sounds completely crazy! 那故事真的很疯狂！

crazy about someone or something 对某事/人着迷；非常喜爱某事/人

He is crazy about computer games. 他沉迷于电脑游戏。

cream /kriːm; krim/ *n* 名

无复数

1. the part of milk with the most fat in it 奶油

   We put strawberries and cream on the cake. 我们在蛋糕上加了草莓和奶油。
2. a thick liquid that you put on your skin 乳霜

   Tracy always puts face cream on her face after a bath. 翠西洗澡后总会在脸上涂面霜。

***create** /kriˈeɪt; krɪˋet/ *v* 动

creates, creating, created, created

to make something new 创造；创作

JK Rowling created the Harry Potter stories. 罗琳创作了哈利波特的故事。

***creative** /kriˈeɪtɪv; krɪˋetɪv/ *adj* 形

good at making new and interesting things 有创意的

Lily is very creative and she is good at drawing. 莉莉很有创意，擅长绘画。

***creature** /ˈkriːtʃə; ˋkritʃɚ/ *n* 名

a living thing 生物

There are a lot of interesting creatures living in the sea. 海里有很多有趣的生物。

credit card /ˈkredɪt ˌkɑːd; ˋkrɛdɪt ˌkɑrd/ *n* 名

a small plastic card that you can use to buy things and pay for them later 信用卡

She bought a watch with her credit card. 她用信用卡买了一只手表。

> **Daily conversation 日常会话**
>
> *"Do you want to pay in cash or by credit card?" "I'll pay by credit card."* "你要用现金还是信用卡付款呢？" "信用卡吧。"

crew /kruː; kru/ *n* 名

all the people who work on a ship, plane, etc （全体）船员；机组人员

The crew of the plane were very helpful. 机组人员很愿意帮忙。

cricket /ˈkrɪkɪt; ˋkrɪkɪt/ *n* 名

1. an insect which makes a loud noise and jumps 蟋蟀

   The two crickets are fighting. 那两只蟋蟀正在打架。
2. （无复数） a game played with a bat and a ball, by two teams of 11 people 板球（运动）

   Ross likes to play cricket. 罗斯喜欢打板球。

cried /kraɪd; kraɪd/ *v* 动

the past tense and past participle of **cry** ☆cry 的过去式和过去分词

cries /kraɪz; kraɪz/ *v* 动

a form of **cry** ☆cry 的另一种现在式，与主语 he，she 和 it 一起使用

crime /kraɪm; kraɪm/ *n* 名

something that is against the law 罪行；罪恶

Killing people is a serious crime. 杀人是严重罪行。

*crisp /krɪsp; krɪsp/ *n* 名【英】

美式：***chip***

a very thin piece of fried potato that you eat cold 炸马铃薯片；炸薯片

Potato crisps contain a lot of salt. 炸薯片含有很多盐。

*crocodile /ˈkrɒkədaɪl; ˋkrɑkəˏdaɪl/ *n* 名

a large river animal with sharp teeth, short legs and a long tail 鳄鱼

The zoo keeps two crocodiles in the pool. 动物园在水池里养了两条鳄鱼。

crooked /ˈkrʊkɪd; ˋkrʊkɪd/ *adj* 形

not straight 弯曲的

We walked along a crooked path. 我们沿着弯弯曲曲的小径走。

反义 **straight[1]**

crop /krɒp; krɑp/ *n* 名

a plant grown in large amounts for food 农作物

Farmers usually plant their crops in spring. 农民通常在春天种植农作物。

*cross[1] /krɒs; krɔs/ *n* 名

复数：***crosses***

a mark or shape that looks like an "X" or a "+" 交叉号；十字形

The teacher put a cross next to the wrong answer. 老师在错的答案旁打了一个叉。

*cross[2] /krɒs; krɔs/ *v* 动

crosses, crossing, crossed, crossed

1. to go from one side to the other 横过；穿过

   Look carefully before you cross the street. 要先看清楚四周的情况再过马路。

2. **cross out** to draw a line through something that you have written, usually because it is wrong 划掉；删去

   Cross out the wrong words in the sentence. 把句子中错误的词划掉。

crossing /ˈkrɒsɪŋ; ˋkrɔsɪŋ/ *n* 名

a place where you can safely cross a road, river, etc 人行横道；行人过路处

You should cross the road at the crossing. 你应该在人行横道过马路。

crossroads /ˈkrɒsrəʊdz; ˋkrɔsˏrodz/ *n* 名

复数：***crossroads***

a place where two roads go across each other 十字路口

There was an accident at the crossroads. 在十字路口发生了一起交通事故。

crossword /ˈkrɒswɜːd; ˋkrɔsˏwɝd/ *n* 名

也作：***crossword puzzle***

a game in which you fill in blank squares with letters to form words 填字游戏；纵横字谜

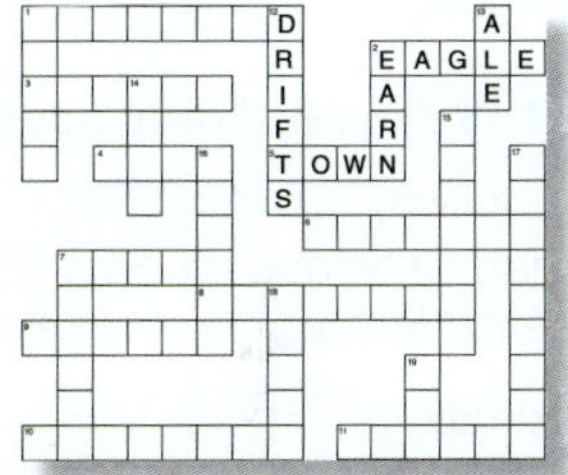

This crossword is too difficult for us. 这个填字游戏对我们来说太难了。

crow /krəʊ; kro/ *n* 名

a big, black bird 乌鸦

Some crows are flying in the sky. 天空中有几只乌鸦在飞。

*crowd /kraʊd; kraʊd/ *n* 名

a lot of people together in the same place 人群；群众

There was a crowd in front of the cinema. 人群挤在戏院门前。

*crowded /ˈkraʊdɪd; ˋkraʊdɪd/ *adj* 形

full of people 拥挤的

The shop was very crowded. 商店里挤满了人。

C

crown /kraʊn; kraʊn/ *n* 名

a special hat worn by a king or queen 王冠

There are many jewels on the crown. 王冠上有很多宝石。

***cruel** /'kru:əl; `kruəl/ *adj* 形

crueller, cruellest

very unkind and trying to hurt people or animals 残忍的；残暴的

Don't be cruel to animals. 不要虐待动物。

反义 kind[2]

cruelly /'kru:əli; `kruəlɪ/ *adv* 副

in a cruel way 残忍地；残暴地

The man hit his dog cruelly. 那个男人残暴地打他的狗。

反义 kindly

cruelty /'kru:əlti; `kruəltɪ/ *n* 名

无复数

cruel behaviour 残忍；虐待

The dogs were treated with great cruelty. 那些狗被严重虐待。

crumb /krʌm; krʌm/ *n* 名

a small bit of bread, biscuit or cake 面包屑；饼干碎

The dog is eating the bread crumbs on the floor. 那只狗在吃地上的面包屑。

crush /krʌʃ; krʌʃ/ *v* 动

crushes, crushing, crushed, crushed

to make something flat or break it into pieces 压；压碎

He fell and crushed the box. 他摔了一跤，压扁了盒子。

crutch /krʌtʃ; krʌtʃ/ *n* 名

复数：***crutches***

a long stick that helps you walk T 字形拐杖

on crutches 拄着 T 字形拐杖

He was on crutches because he had a broken leg. 他拄着 T 字形拐杖走路，因为他把腿摔断了。

***cry[1]** /kraɪ; kraɪ/ *v* 动

cries, crying, cried, cried

1. to produce tears from your eyes 哭

   The baby cried loudly because he was hungry. 婴儿饿了，所以大哭起来。

2. to shout 叫喊；呼叫

   "Help!" she cried. "救命啊！" 她呼叫。

***cry[2]** /kraɪ; kraɪ/ *n* 名

1. （复数：***cries***）a shout 叫喊；呼叫

   I heard a cry for help. 我听到呼救声。

2. （无复数）a period of time when you produce tears from your eyes 哭

   Her eyes are red because she just had a cry. 她的眼睛红红的，因为刚哭了一场。

crystal /'krɪstl; `krɪstḷ/ *n* 名

a precious rock that looks like ice 水晶

This crystal lamp is beautiful. 这盏水晶灯十分美丽。

cube /kju:b; kjub/ *n* 名

a solid thing with six square sides 立方体

This box is a cube. 这个箱子是立方体。

***cucumber** /'kju:kʌmbə; `kjukʌmbɚ/ *n* 名

a long, green vegetable 黄瓜；青瓜

She cut up a cucumber for the salad. 她把黄瓜切碎来做沙拉。

cuff /kʌf; kʌf/ *n* 名

the end of a sleeve 袖口

The cuffs of the shirt are dirty. 这件衬衫的袖口很脏。

cunning /ˈkʌnɪŋ; ˋkʌnɪŋ/ *adj* 形

clever, especially at tricks 狡猾的；狡诈的

The fox in the story is cunning. 故事中的狐狸很狡猾。

***cup** /kʌp; kʌp/ *n* 名

1. a small container for drinking tea, coffee, etc 杯子

There are five new cups in the cupboard. 碗柜里有 5 只新杯子。

比较 **mug**

2. the amount of a drink in a cup 一杯（份量）

He had a cup of coffee this morning. 今天早上他喝了一杯咖啡。

比较 **mug**

***cupboard** /ˈkʌbəd; ˋkʌbɚd/ *n* 名

a piece of furniture with doors, for keeping things in 橱柜；碗柜

She put the bowls in the cupboard. 她把碗放进碗柜里。

cure[1] /kjʊə; kjur/ *n* 名

a way of making an illness go away completely 药物；疗法

Doctors are trying to find a cure for cancer. 医生正在试图寻找癌症的治疗方法。

cure[2] /kjʊə; kjur/ *v* 动

cures, curing, cured, cured

to make an illness go away completely, or make a sick person completely better 医治；治好

Her fever was completely cured. 她的发烧被治好了。

curiosity /ˌkjʊəriˈɒsəti; ˌkjurɪˋɑsətɪ/ *n* 名

无复数

a strong wish to know about something because it seems interesting and unusual 好奇心

The children had never seen a kangaroo before and they looked at it with great curiosity. 那些孩子从未见过袋鼠，所以充满好奇地看它。

***curious** /ˈkjʊəriəs; ˋkjurɪəs/ *adj* 形

wanting to know about something 好奇的

Children are curious about everything. 儿童对所有事物都感到好奇。

curl[1] /kɜːl; kɝl/ *v* 动

to bend or move into a round or curved shape 弄卷；使卷曲

My cat often curls into a ball when it sleeps. 我的猫睡觉时总是会蜷成一团。

curl[2] /kɜːl; kɝl/ *n* 名

a piece of hair that forms a round shape 鬈发

The girl has beautiful curls. 那个女孩有一头漂亮的鬈发。

***curly** /ˈkɜːli; ˋkɝlɪ/ *adj* 形

curlier, curliest

having curls 卷曲的；鬈曲的

My aunt has long curly hair. 我的阿姨有一头鬈发。

***curry** /ˈkʌri; ˋkɝɪ/ *n* 名

复数：*curries*

a spicy dish from India 咖喱

This chicken curry is very hot. 这道咖喱鸡很辣。

cursor /ˈkɜːsə; ˋkɝsɚ/ *n* 名

【电脑】a small arrow or hand on a computer screen, which you can move to select or start working on something（电脑屏幕上的）光标

The cursor moves when you move the mouse. 当你移动鼠标时，光标便会移动。

***curtain** /ˈkɜːtn; ˋkɝtn̩/ *n* 名

a piece of cloth that hangs across a window 窗帘

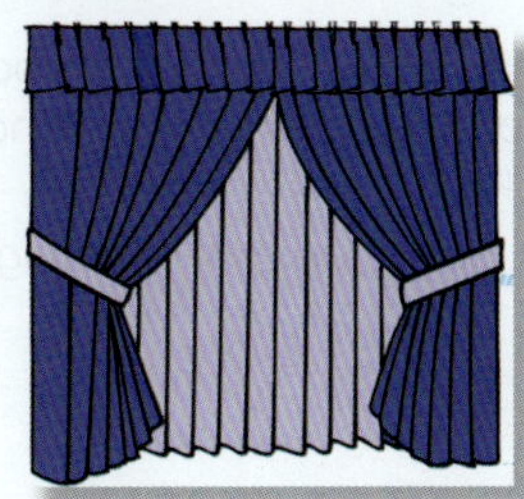

C

The curtains in our living room are purple. 我们客厅里的窗帘是紫色的。

比较 **blind²**

C

curve /kɜːv; kɝv/ *n* 名

a line or surface that bends gradually 曲线；弯曲处

The river has a lot of curves. 这条河很曲折。

curved /kɜːvd; kɝvd/ *adj* 形

having a round shape 弯曲的

The curved path leads to the peak. 这条弯曲的小径通往山顶。

*cushion /ˈkʊʃn; ˋkʊʃən/ *n* 名

a cloth bag filled with something soft to sit on 软垫；坐垫

There are two cushions on the sofa. 沙发上有两个软垫。

custom /ˈkʌstəm; ˋkʌstəm/ *n* 名

something that people in a society often do because it is traditional 习俗；风俗

When did the custom of eating mooncakes begin? 吃月饼这个习俗是什么时候开始的呢？

*customer /ˈkʌstəmə; ˋkʌstəmɚ/ *n* 名

someone who buys things from a shop 顾客

He is very polite to his customers. 他对顾客很有礼貌。

*cut¹ /kʌt; kʌt/ *v* 动

cuts, cutting, cut, cut

to break or divide something into pieces with a knife, scissors, etc 切；割；剪

I cut the cake into eight pieces. 我把蛋糕切成 8 块。

cut and paste【电脑】剪切和粘贴

The students learnt how to cut and paste sentences on a computer. 学生学习如何在电脑上剪切和粘贴句子。

cut down 砍倒

He cut down the tree with an axe. 他用斧头把树砍倒。

cut out 剪下

He cut the picture out of the magazine. 他从杂志上剪下图片。

cut up 切碎

Mrs Smith cut up the food for her baby. 史密斯太太把食物切碎给她的宝宝吃。

*cut² /kʌt; kʌt/ *n* 名

a wound made by a knife, scissors, etc（割伤的）伤口

There is a cut on his finger. 他的手指上有一个伤口。

cute /kjuːt; kjut/ *adj* 形

cuter, cutest

pretty and attractive 可爱的；逗人喜爱的

What a cute little girl! 多么可爱的小女孩啊！

cycle /ˈsaɪkl; ˋsaɪkḷ/ *v* 动

cycles, cycling, cycled, cycled

to ride a bicycle 骑自行车；骑脚踏车

It is dangerous to cycle on a busy street. 在繁忙的街上骑自行车很危险。

cycling /ˈsaɪklɪŋ; ˋsaɪklɪŋ/ *n* 名

无复数

the activity of riding a bicycle 骑自行车；骑脚踏车

Cycling is a good exercise. 骑自行车是很好的运动。

***dad** /dæd; dæd/, **daddy** /ˈdædi; ˋdædɪ/ *n* 名

复数：***daddies***

father 爸爸

My dad is a manager. 我爸爸是个经理。

Daddy is going to work now. 爸爸现在要去上班了。

用法 dad 和 daddy 常用于口语，father 常用于比较正式的场合或书面语。

比较 **father**

dagger /ˈdægə; ˋdægɚ/ *n* 名

a short sharp knife 短剑；匕首

The robber had a dagger. 那个劫匪有一把匕首。

daily[1] /ˈdeɪli; ˋdelɪ/ *adj* 形

happening every day 每天的

The programme is about people's daily lives. 这个节目是关于人们的日常生活的。

daily[2] /ˈdeɪli; ˋdelɪ/ *adv* 副

every day 每天

The library is open daily from 10 a.m. to 8 p.m. 图书馆每天从上午 10 点开放至晚上 8 点。

dairy /ˈdeəri; ˋdɛrɪ/ *n* 名

复数：***dairies***

a place on a farm where people keep cows for milk and produce butter and cheese 牛奶场

Milk, butter and cheese are made in dairies. 牛奶、牛油和干酪都是在牛奶场制造的。

daisy /ˈdeɪzi; ˋdezɪ/ *n* 名

复数：***daisies***

a small white flower with a yellow centre 雏菊（花）

Sally wore a daisy in her hair. 莎莉在头发上插了一朵雏菊。

dam /dæm; dæm/ *n* 名

a high wall built across a river to stop the water from flowing 水坝

The workers are building a dam. 工人正在建造水坝。

***damage**[1] /ˈdæmɪdʒ; ˋdæmɪdʒ/ *n* 名

无复数

the harm that something does 毁坏；损伤

The storm caused a lot of damage to the city. 暴风雨对该城市造成了重大破坏。

***damage**[2] /ˈdæmɪdʒ; ˋdæmɪdʒ/ *v* 动

damages, damaging, damaged, damaged

to harm or hurt something or someone 损坏；损害

The plane was damaged in the accident. 飞机在意外中撞坏了。

damp /dæmp; dæmp/ *adj* 形

damper, dampest

a bit wet 潮湿的

My mother used a damp cloth to clean the windows. 我妈妈用湿布擦窗户。

同义 **humid, wet**

反义 **dry**[1]

***dance**[1] /dɑːns; dæns/ *v* 动

dances, dancing, danced, danced

to move to music 跳舞

They are dancing happily. 他们快乐地跳舞。

***dance**[2] /dɑːns; dæns/ *n* 名

a special way of moving to music 舞蹈

I learnt a dance at school today. 我今天在学校学了一支舞。

dancer /ˈdɑːnsə; ˋdænsɚ/ *n* 名

a person who dances 舞蹈演员；舞蹈家

My sister is a very good dancer. 我的妹妹是个出色的舞蹈演员。

dancing /ˈdɑːnsɪŋ; ˋdænsɪŋ/ *n* 名

无复数

the activity of moving your body to music 舞蹈

Do you like dancing? 你喜欢跳舞吗？

danger /ˈdeɪndʒə; ˋdendʒɚ/ *n* 名

无复数

a situation in which something very bad could happen to someone or something 危险

The sign reads "Danger"! 那个告示上写着“危险”！

out of danger 脱离危险

The patient is out of danger. 那位病人脱离危险了。

同义 **risk**[1]

反义 **safety**

D

D

***dangerous** /ˈdeɪndʒərəs; ˋdendʒərəs/ *adj* 形

likely to hurt or kill someone or to damage something 危险的

Tigers are dangerous animals. 老虎是危险的动物。

反义 **safe**[1]

dangerously /ˈdeɪndʒərəsli; ˋdendʒərəslɪ/ *adv* 副

in a dangerous way 危险地

Peter often drives dangerously. 彼得驾车时常常不顾安全。

反义 **safely**

dare /deə; dɛr/ *v* 动

dares, daring, dared, dared

to be brave enough to do something 敢；胆敢

He broke the vase but he didn't dare tell his parents. 他打破了花瓶，但不敢告诉父母。

daren't /deənt; dɛrnt/

the short form of "**dare not**" ☆dare not 的缩写

We daren't go into the cave. 我们不敢走进山洞里。

***dark**[1] /dɑːk; dɑrk/ *adj* 形

darker, darkest

1. with little or no light 暗的；黑暗的

   It is too dark to read here. 这里太暗了，不能看书。

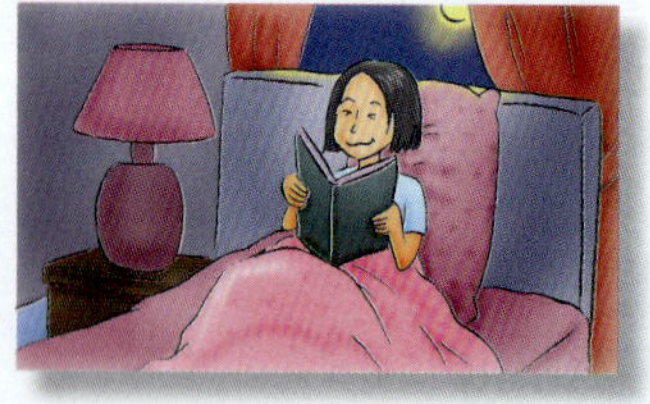

反义 **bright**

2. of a colour that is almost black 深色的

   Lily likes light green, but Ross likes dark blue. 莉莉喜欢浅绿色，而罗斯就喜欢深蓝色。

反义 **light**[2]

***dark**[2] /dɑːk; dɑrk/ *n* 名

无复数

when there is no light 黑暗

My sister is afraid of the dark. 我的妹妹怕黑。

after dark 天黑后

Bats come out after dark. 蝙蝠在天黑以后出来活动。

before dark 天黑前

We arrived there before dark. 我们在天黑前到达了那里。

darkness /ˈdɑːknəs; ˋdɑrknɪs/ *n* 名

无复数

when there is no light 黑暗

The cave was in darkness. 山洞里一片漆黑。

darling /ˈdɑːlɪŋ; ˋdɑrlɪŋ/ *n* 名

a word you use for someone you love 亲爱的（人）

Mr Brown calls his daughter "darling". 布朗先生叫女儿"亲爱的"。

Daily conversation 日常会话

"Darling, I miss you so much." "I miss you too." "亲爱的，我很想你！" "我也很想你！"

dash /dæʃ; dæʃ/ *n* 名

复数：***dashes***

a sign you write to separate two parts of a sentence (—) 破折号

另见 附录：Punctuation 标点符号

data /ˈdeɪtə; ˋdetə/ *n* 名

无复数

【电脑】information stored on a computer 数据；资料

The new computer can store a lot of data. 这台新的电脑可以储存大量的数据。

***date** /deɪt; det/ *n* 名

a day of the month or year 日期

Write down your date of birth. 写下你的出生日期。

比较 **day**

In the classroom 在课室里

"What's the date today?" "It's the 8th of January." "今天是几月几日？" "今天是1月8日。"

***daughter** /ˈdɔːtə; ˋdɔtɚ/ *n* 名

a female child 女儿

They have two sons and a daughter. 他们有两个儿子和一个女儿。

另见 **son**

dawn /dɔːn; dɔn/ *n* 名

无复数

the time of the day when the sun rises 黎明；破晓

My grandparents usually get up at dawn. 我的祖父母通常在黎明时分起床。

***day** /deɪ; de/ *n* 名

1. a period of 24 hours 一天；一日

   Sarah read the book in five days. 莎拉花了5天把这本书看完了。

比较 **date**

2. the time when it is light 白天；日间

   We can't see stars in the day. 白天看不见星星。

反义 **night**

one day 过去某一天；将来某一天

One day last month, we went to the amusement park. 上个月的某一天我们去了游乐场。

the other day 几天前；不久前

I saw Mary the other day. 几天前我遇见了玛丽。

Daily conversation 日常会话
"What day is it today?" "It's Friday." "今天是星期几？" "星期五。"

daydream /'deɪdriːm; `deˌdrim/ v 动

to think about something nice which makes you forget about the present 幻想；做白日梦
Lily is daydreaming about the summer holidays. 莉莉在幻想着放暑假。

daytime /'deɪtaɪm; `deˌtaɪm/ n 名

无复数
the time when it is light 白天；日间
Cats often sleep in the daytime. 猫常在白天睡觉。

*dead /ded; dɛd/ adj 形

not living any more 死去的
The snake is dead. 那条蛇死了。
反义 **alive, live², living**

deaf /def; dɛf/ adj 形

not able to hear anything 聋的
He cannot hear you because he is deaf. 他听不见你说什么，因为他耳聋。

用法 deaf 用于形容人，所以应该说 He is deaf，不应该说 His ears are deaf。

*dear /dɪə; dɪr/ adj 形

dearer, dearest
1. much loved 心爱的；亲爱的
   Sarah is my dearest friend. 莎拉是我最亲爱的朋友。

2. a word used to start a letter 亲爱的（用于书信的开头）
   Dear Tracy 亲爱的翠西
3. 【英】expensive 昂贵的
   I don't want to buy this skirt because it is too dear. 我不想买这条裙子，因为它太贵了。

同义 **expensive**
反义 **cheap, inexpensive**

death /deθ; dɛθ/ n 名

无复数
the end of life 死亡；逝世
His death made us sad. 他的死使我们难过。

*December /dɪ'sembə; dɪ`sɛmbɚ/ n 名

缩写：*Dec.*
the twelfth month of the year 十二月
It is cold in December. 十二月天气寒冷。
注意 开头的字母必须用大写。

*decide /dɪ'saɪd; dɪ`saɪd/ v 动

decides, deciding, decided, decided
to choose what you will do after thinking carefully 决定；决心
Lily decided to buy a doll for her sister. 莉莉决定买一个玩具娃娃给她的妹妹。

decimal /'desɪml; `dɛsəml̩/ n 名

a number less than one 小数
"Half" is written as 0.5 in decimals. "一半" 写成小数是 0.5。

*decision /dɪ'sɪʒn; dɪ`sɪʒən/ n 名

a choice that you make after careful thinking 决定
I think your decision is right. 我认为你的决定是对的。

D

deck /dek; dɛk/ n 名

the floor on a ship or bus（船的）甲板；（公共汽车、船的）一层
We watched the waves from the deck. 我们在甲板上看海浪。

*decorate /'dekəreɪt; `dɛkəˌret/ v 动

decorates, decorating, decorated, decorated
1. to paint the inside walls of a room or put special paper on them 装修；粉刷；贴墙纸
   Lily decorated her bedroom in light blue. 莉莉把她的卧室粉刷成浅蓝色。
2. to make something look more pretty by adding things to it 装饰；点缀；布置
   The girls are decorating the Christmas tree. 那些女孩正在装饰圣诞树。

decoration /dekə'reɪʃn; dɛkə`reʃən/ n 名

a thing you put on something to make it look pretty 装饰品
We made some New Year decorations. 我们做了些贺年装饰品。

decrease¹ /dɪ'kriːs; dɪ`kris/ v 动

decreases, decreasing, decreased, decreased

to become less, or to make something become less 减少

The number of trees is decreasing. 树木的数量正在减少。

反义 increase¹

D

decrease² /ˈdi:kri:s; ˋdikris/ *n* 名

when something decreases 减少

There was a decrease in the number of traffic accidents last year. 去年交通事故的数量减少了。

反义 increase²

***deep** /di:p; dip/ *adj* 形

deeper, deepest

measuring a long way down to the bottom 深的

This lake is very deep. 这个湖很深。

反义 shallow

deep-fried /ˌdi:p ˈfraɪd; ˏdip ˋfraɪd/ *adj* 形

cooked in a lot of hot oil 油炸的

Paul had deep-fried chicken for lunch. 保罗午饭时吃炸鸡。

***deer** /dɪə; dɪr/ *n* 名

复数：*deer*

a large animal that has horns and can run very fast 鹿

The horns of a male deer look like tree branches. 雄鹿的角看起来像树枝一样。

defeat /dɪˈfi:t; dɪˋfit/ *v* 动

to beat someone in a game, competition or battle 打败

The soldiers defeated their enemies. 那些士兵打败了敌人。

defend /dɪˈfend; dɪˋfɛnd/ *v* 动

to protect someone or something by fighting 保护；保卫

The bird was defending its eggs. 那只鸟保护着自己生下的蛋。

definite /ˈdefɪnət; ˋdɛfənɪt/ *adj* 形

sure; certain; not going to change 明确的；肯定的

Please give me a definite answer. 请给我明确的答复。

definitely /ˈdefɪnətli; ˋdɛfənɪtlɪ/ *adv* 副

certainly 明确地；肯定地

I am definitely taller than you. 我肯定比你高。

Daily conversation 日常会话

"Are we going to the beach tomorrow?" "Definitely!" "我们明天会去沙滩吗？" "那肯定！"

***degree** /dɪˈgri:; dɪˋgri/ *n* 名

a unit for measuring temperature or angles 度；度数

The temperature now is 32 degrees. 现在的气温是 32 度。

delay¹ /dɪˈleɪ; dɪˋle/ *n* 名

a situation in which something happens later than you expected 延误；耽误

The train company apologized for the delay. 火车公司为延误而道歉。

delay² /dɪˈleɪ; dɪˋle/ *v* 动

to make something slow or late 延误

The bad weather delayed the plane by one hour. 恶劣的天气使飞机误点了一小时。

delete /dɪˈli:t; dɪˋlit/ *v* 动

deletes, deleting, deleted, deleted

to remove information from a computer or something that has been written 删除；删去

Henry deleted some files on his computer. 亨利从电脑中删除了几份文件。

***delicious** /dɪˈlɪʃəs; dɪˋlɪʃəs/ *adj* 形

very good to eat 美味的；可口的

We had a delicious dinner. 我们吃了一顿美味的晚餐。

同义 tasty

At a restaurant 餐厅里

"How is the food?" "It's delicious!" "食物的味道如何？" "很美味！"

delighted /dɪˈlaɪtɪd; dɪˋlaɪtɪd/ *adj* 形

very happy 欢喜的；高兴的

图解小学生英汉词典

LONGMAN ILLUSTRATED CHILDREN'S ENGLISH-CHINESE DICTIONARY

活用词典练习

上海译文出版社

目 录

1. 如何查找单词

本词典收录4400个单词，按字母表顺序排列：

A B C D E F G H I J K L M N O P Q R S T U V W X Y Z

a b c d e f g h i j k l m n o p q r s t u v w x y z

即以 a 开头的单词排在最前面，以 z 开头的单词则排在最后。

例如 woman 以 w 开头，apple 以 a 开头，mother 以 m 开头，因此这三个词在词典中的顺序是：apple、mother、woman。

练习 1a. 按顺序在字母下面写上1、2、3等：

r	q	g	a	x	o	k	d
___	___	___	1	___	___	___	___

如果两个单词开头的字母相同但第二个字母不相同（如 **a**pple 和 **a**nt），则第二个字母（即 p 和 n）决定它们的顺序，因此 ant 在 apple 前面。如果两个单词的头两个字母都相同（如 **an**y 和 **an**other），则第三个字母（即 y 和 o）决定它们的顺序，以此类推。

练习 1b. 把下列单词按字母顺序排列出来：

duck	doll	die	dark	different
door	drive	difference	diet	dad

1. *dad*　　2. ______　　3. ______　　4. ______　　5. ______

6. ______　　7. ______　　8. ______　　9. ______　　10. ______

2. 词性标签

学习一个新词，要知道它的词性是什么，才能恰当地运用。

英文单词依其在句子中的功能分为各种词性，例如名词用于表示人、地点、动物或事物的名称，形容词用于描写人或物，动词用于说明某人或某物做什么。本词典以下列缩写标示各词性：

词性		缩写	例子
adjective	形容词	*adj* 形	short, smart, stupid, tall
adverb	副词	*adv* 副	quickly, quite, slowly, very
article	冠词	*art* 冠	a, an, the
conjunction	连接词	*conj* 连	and, but, if, or, when
interjection	感叹词	*interj* 感叹	bye, oh
noun	名词	*n* 名	bird, boy, bus, hair, man
number	数词	*num* 数	one, two, three
ordinal number	序数	*ordinal num* 序数	first, second, sixteenth
plural noun	复数名词	*plural n* 复数名词	pyjamas, scissors, trousers
preposition	介词	*prep* 介	at, for, in, of, on
pronoun	代名词	*pron* 代	she, some, we, you
verb	动词	*v* 动	drink, eat, jump, speak, walk

练习 2a. 在词典中查找下列单词的词性，答案可多于一个。

1. fish 例：名，动　　2. brown ______
3. each ______　　4. new ______
5. play ______　　6. plus ______
7. really ______　　8. secret ______
9. third ______　　10. under ______

3. 名词

a. 可数名词

可数名词前面可以加上 a 或 an，或以复数形式使用 。大部分可数名词都在词尾加上 s 以构成复数，如 cat 的复数是 cats 。

有些可数名词的复数不是在词尾加上 s 构成，如 church 的复数是 churches 、 woman 的复数是 women 、sheep 的复数仍旧是 sheep。本词典标明这些不规则的复数形式。

***church** /tʃɜːtʃ; tʃɝtʃ/ *n* 名
复数:***churches***
a building where people pray 教堂
Our school is opposite the church. 我们的学校在教堂对面。

***woman** /ˈwʊmən; ˋwʊmən/ *n* 名
复数:***women***
an adult female person 女人;妇女
A woman is crossing the road. 一个女人正在过马路。

***sheep** /ʃiːp; ʃip/ *n* 名
复数:***sheep***
a farm animal that you keep for its meat and wool 羊;绵羊
These sheep produce very soft wool. 这些绵羊的羊毛很柔软。

练习 3a. 在词典中查找下列名词的复数形式:

1. watch ____________
2. enemy ____________
3. foot ____________
4. fruit ____________
5. wife ____________
6. quiz ____________
7. ox ____________
8. potato ____________
9. leaf ____________
10. goose ____________

b. 不可数名词

不可数名词前面不能加 a 或 an,没有复数形式,如 cash 。本词典注明没有复数的名词,例如:

baggage /ˈbægɪdʒ; ˋbægɪdʒ/ *n* 名
无复数
bags that you carry when you travel 行李
She hasn't got much baggage with her. 她没带很多行李。

用法 baggage 没有复数形式,不可与 many 和 few 一起使用。如要说明数量,必须用量词,例如 a piece of baggage(一件行李)和 two pieces of baggage(两件行李)。

同义 **luggage**

练习 3b. 在词典中查找下列单词,圈出没有复数的名词。

aircraft	air	ash	money	half
shelf	furniture	rain	salad	weather

4. 动词的形式

动词有不同的形式以显示各种时态,有些动词在词尾加上 ing 构成现在分词;加上 ed 构成过去式或过去分词,例如 play:

She is **playing** the piano now.(现在分词)
She **played** the piano yesterday.(过去式)
She has **played** the piano already.(过去分词)

有些动词的时态变化较大。例如 drive：

He is **driving** to work now.（现在分词）
He **drove** to work yesterday.（过去式）
He has **driven** to work every day this week.（过去分词）

有些动词若与 he, she 或 it 同用，要在词尾加上 es 构成现在式，例如 go：

She **goes** to school on foot.（现在式）

本词典标明这些不规则的动词形式。

练习 4. 在词典中查找正确的动词形式来填空。

1. We ________________ (go) to Rome last year.
2. Candy ________________ (wear) a red dress yesterday.
3. Keep quiet! The baby is ________________ (sleep) now.
4. My grandmother has never ________________ (fly) before.
5. My teacher ________________ (teach) me a song yesterday.
6. They have just ________________ (move) to a new town.

5. 词性和一词多义

某些单词包含两个或以上的意思，例如 bank 既可作“银行”，又可作“河岸”；empty 既可作“空的”，又可作“倒空”。在本词典中，这些单词以两种方式排列。词性相同的不同意思，分项列于单词下，如：

***bank** /bæŋk; bæŋk/ *n* 名

1. a place where people keep their money 银行
   He went to the bank to get some money. 他去银行取钱。
2. the side of a river or lake 河岸；堤岸；湖畔
   She takes a walk along the river bank every evening. 她每天傍晚都会沿着河岸散步。

如果一个单词有不同词性，本词典以独立词条列出每个词性，例如：

***empty[1]** /'empti; `ɛmptɪ/ *adj* 形
emptier, emptiest
having nothing or no people inside 空的
The drawer is empty. 这个抽屉是空的。
反义 **full**

***empty[2]** /'empti; `ɛmptɪ/ *v* 动
empties, emptying, emptied, emptied
to take everything out of something 把里面的东西全部取出；倒空
Lily empties the bin every night. 莉莉每晚都会倒空垃圾筒。
反义 **fill**

练习 5. 在词典中查找下列粗体的单词，并在横线上以中文写出其意思：

1. The **earth** goes round the sun. ______________
   She planted some seeds in the **earth**. ______________
2. Can whales live on **land**? ______________
   The plane **landed** at the airport. ______________
3. The red **sign** means "stop". ______________
   He **signed** the cheque. ______________

6. 同义词和反义词

我们在说话或写作时，若反复使用同一个单词，会让人觉得单调乏味。如果我们能够巧用同义词和反义词，便可以更明确、更生动地表达感情和观点。

本词典在某些词条的末尾会标示出同义词或反义词，例如：

> ***big** /bɪg; bɪg/ *adj* 形
> ***bigger, biggest***
> large in size 大的
> *My parents bought a big birthday cake for me.* 我的父母给我买了一个大生日蛋糕。
> 同义 **large**
> 反义 **little**[1]**, small**

练习 6a. 在词典中查找下列单词的同义词，并写在横线上。

1. scare ______________
2. opportunity ______________
3. mistake ______________
4. prison ______________

练习 6b. 在词典中查找下列单词的反义词，并写在横线上。

1. clean ______________
2. pretty ______________
3. quickly ______________
4. war ______________

7. 动词短语

动词短语由一个动词加一个副词或介词构成，并有特定的意思。例如动词 get on 解作“上车”，get off 解作“下车”， get up 则有“起床”的意思。

在本词典中，动词下列出由其构成的动词短语，以橙色字标出，例如 give 下的 give away，give back， give in， give out， give up。

give something away 赠送；捐赠
We gave away our old clothes to charity. 我们把旧衣服捐赠给了慈善机构。

give something back 归还；送回
I will give you back the book tomorrow. 我明天会把书还给你。

give in 屈服；投降；让步
John and Colin argued for a long time. At last, John gave in. 约翰和科林争论了很久。最后约翰让步了。

give something out 分发
The teacher is giving out the exam papers. 老师在分发试卷。

give something up 停止做某事
Sam has given up smoking. 山姆已经戒烟了。

give up 放弃
Don't give up. You've finished most of the work. 别放弃。你已经完成了大部分的工作。

练习 7. 在词典中查找正确的副词或介词填空：

1. The word was wrong, so I crossed it ________________ .
2. I often mix ________________ the twins in my class.
3. It was cold. So I put ________________ a coat before I went out.
4. I ran ________________ Mrs Walker in the supermarket.

8. 短语和惯用语

短语和惯用语由几个单词组成，以表达一个特定的意思，例如 make a face 意思是“做鬼脸”。

make a face 做鬼脸
The clown made a face at us.
小丑对我们做了个鬼脸。

在本词典中，短语和惯用语以橙色字标出，例如 on foot 在 foot 下列出、 at the moment 在 moment 下列出。

on foot 步行

I go to school on foot. 我走路上学。

at any moment 随时

It may rain at any moment. 随时可能下雨。

at the moment 现在；此刻

He is busy at the moment. 他现在很忙。

练习 8. 在词典中查找下列短语或惯用语，并在横线上以中文写出其意思：

1. in a second ________________
2. have a temperature ________________
3. free of charge ________________
4. take place ________________

"用法"栏详细讲解单词的用法。例如：

***bread** /bred; brɛd/ *n* 名

无复数

a type of food made from flour

面包

I have bread for breakfast every day. 我每天早餐都吃面包。

用法 如要表示数量，必须用量词，例如 a piece of bread（一块面包），a loaf of bread（一条面包）和 a slice of bread（一片面包）。

"注意"栏说明单词的使用范围、发音、学生的常犯错误等，并指示如何正确使用单词。例如：

***pupil** /pju:pl; `pjupl/ *n* 名

a child who is studying at a school

（小）学生；学童

Our school has 700 pupils. 我们的学校有 700 名学生。

注意 pupil 一般指小学生，中学生或大学生是 student。

练习 9. 查找有关的"用法"栏或"注意"栏，以解答下列问题：

1. 哪个单词的发音与 tale 相同？

____

2. "She is an afraid girl." 这句话错在哪里？（见 afraid 词条）

____

3. "His ears are deaf." 这句话错在哪里？（见 deaf 词条）

____

4. 形容一部刺激的电影，该用 excited 还是 exciting？为什么呢？

____

5. 形容一个人很高，该用 high 还是 tall？为什么呢？

____

10. 例句的用途

例句用来展示单词的含义，说明单词的用法，例如：

***break**[1] /breɪk; brek/ *v* 动

breaks, breaking, broke, broken

1. to make something separate into pieces 打碎；打破
   Who broke the window? 谁打破了窗户？
2. to separate into pieces 摔破；破碎
   The vase fell on the floor and broke. 花瓶掉在地上，摔碎了。

以上例句说明 break 既可作"打碎"，后接宾语 window，又可作"破碎"，后面没有宾语。

例句也可说明单词的搭配关系，例如：

***ride**[1] /raɪd; raɪd/ *v* 动

rides, riding, rode, ridden

to travel on a bicycle or an animal such as a horse, or in a bus, car, etc
骑；乘
My mother and I enjoy riding a bicycle. 妈妈和我都喜欢骑自行车。

以上例句说明 ride 可与 a bicycle 搭配组成词组，解作"骑自行车"。

练习 10. 在词典中查找下列单词，并写出可以与它们搭配的词语：

1. ________________ alarm
2. ________________ noodles
3. diamond ________________
4. ________________ jokes
5. ________________ the lift

11. 纵横字谜

以下的提示都取自本词典中的释义。试根据释义想出单词，填入适当的格子里。（提示：每个单词都与身体有关，除正文外，也可参考附录：Parts of the body 身体部位。）

横
1. the soft part in your mouth that you use for tasting and speaking
2. the part of your face for eating and speaking
3. one of the two soft parts around your mouth
4. one of the two parts in your face that you use to see
5. the part of the face under the eye
6. the top part of your face above the eyes and below your hair

纵
7. one of the hard, white things in your mouth that you use for biting food
8. **the line of hair above your eye**
9. the thin, thread-like things that grow on the head and body of a person
10. the part of your face below your mouth
11. one of the two parts on the sides of your head with which you hear sounds
12. the part of your face you use to breathe and smell

答案

练习 1a.　1. a　2. d　3. g　4. k　5. o　6. q　7. r　8. x

练习 1b.　1. dad　2. dark　3. die　4. diet　5. difference　6. different　7. doll　8. door　9. drive　10. duck

练习 2.　2. 形，名　3. 形，代　4. 形　5. 动，名　6. 介　7. 副　8. 名，形　9. 序数　10. 介，副

练习 3a.　1. watches　2. enemies　3. feet　4. fruit/fruits　5. wives　6. quizzes　7. oxen　8. potatoes　9. leaves　10. geese

练习 3b.　air, money, furniture, rain, weather

练习 4.　1. went　2. wore　3. sleeping　4. flown　5. taught　6. moved

练习 5.　1. 地球，泥土　2. 陆地，降落　3. 符号，签名

练习 6a.　1. frighten　2. chance　3. error　4. jail

练习 6b.　1. dirty　2. ugly　3. slowly　4. peace

练习 7.　1. out　2. up　3. on　4. into

练习 8.　1. 一会儿，片刻　2. 发烧　3. 免费　4. 发生，进行

练习 9.　1. tail

2. afraid 不能用在名词之前

3. deaf 用于形容人，因此不能说 His ears are deaf, 而要说 He is deaf。

4. exciting (excited 用来形容人的感受，exciting 用来形容事物)

5. tall (high 不可以用来形容人，若要形容人长得高，应用 tall)

练习 10.　1. (fire) alarm　2. (fried) noodles　3. diamond (ring)　4. (funny) jokes　5. (take) the lift

练习 11.

		[1]T[7]	O	N	G	U	E[11]	
		O					A	
	[2]M	O	U	T	H[9]		R	
		T			A			N[12]
		H		[3]L	I	P		O
			[8]E		R			S
			Y			[4]E	Y	E
[5]C	H	E	E	K				
			B		C[10]			
	[6]F	O	R	E	H	E	A	D
			O		I			
			W		N			

He was delighted to see his friends. 他很高兴见到他的朋友们。

同义 **pleased**

deliver /dɪˈlɪvə; dɪˋlɪvɚ/ *v* 动

to take something to a particular place or person 递送

They will deliver the pizza to your home. 他们会把披萨送到你家 。

delivery /dɪˈlɪvəri; dɪˋlɪvərɪ/ *n* 名

复数：***deliveries***

bringing something to a particular place or person 递送；运送

This supermarket offers free delivery. 这家超市免费送货。

demand /dɪˈmɑːnd; dɪˋmænd/ *v* 动

to ask for something strongly 要求

The angry man demanded to speak to the manager. 那个气愤的人要求跟经理谈话。

democracy /dɪˈmɒkrəsi; dɪˋmɑkrəsɪ/ *n* 名

无复数

a system in which all the people can vote to choose the people who represent them in the government 民主政体；民主制度

In some places, people are still fighting for democracy. 在一些地方，人们仍在争取建立民主政体。

demonstrate /ˈdemənstreɪt; ˋdɛmənˏstret/ *v* 动

demonstrates, demonstrating, demonstrated, demonstrated

to show, usually by doing something 示范；演示

She demonstrated how to use a life jacket. 她示范如何使用救生衣。

dense /dens; dɛns/ *adj* 形

denser, densest

thick; having a lot of people or things close together 稠密的

We walked through the dense jungle. 我们步行穿过密林。

***dentist** /ˈdentɪst; ˋdɛntɪst/ *n* 名

someone who treats your teeth 牙医

The dentist said I had a bad tooth. 牙医说我有一颗蛀牙。

deny /dɪˈnaɪ; dɪˋnaɪ/ *v* 动

denies, denying, denied, denied

to say that something is not true or you have not done something 否认

The thief denied that he had stolen the jewellery. 那小偷否认偷了珠宝。

反义 **admit**

depart /dɪˈpɑːt; dɪˋpart/ *v* 动

to leave 离开；出发

The plane departed at 2 p.m. 飞机在下午 2 点起飞了。

***department** /dɪˈpɑːtmənt; dɪˋpartmənt/ *n* 名

a part of a government, shop, company etc 部门

Mrs Smith works in the sales department. 史密斯太太在销售部工作。

department store /dɪˈpɑːtmənt ˌstɔː; dɪˋpartmənt ˏstɔr/ *n* 名

a large shop that sells different types of things 百货公司

My mother bought a vase in a department store. 妈妈在百货商店买了一个花瓶。

***depend** /dɪˈpend; dɪˋpɛnd/ *v* 动

1. to trust 倚靠；依赖

   We cannot always depend on others. 我们不能总是依赖别人。

2. to be decided by 看…而定

D

It depends on the weather. 这要看天气而定。

用法 通常与 on 连用，即 depend on。

Daily conversation 日常会话

"Will you go to the cinema?" "It depends." "你会去看电影吗？" "那得看情况。"

D

depth /depθ; dɛpθ/ *n* 名

how deep something is 深度

The depth of this pool is only one metre. 这个水池只有一米深。

*describe /dɪ'skraɪb; dɪ`skraɪb/ *v* 动

describes, describing, described, described

to talk or write about what something is like 形容；描述

The boy is describing the animals at the zoo. 那个男孩在描述动物园里的动物。

In the classroom 在教室里

"What do you see in the picture, Lily? Can you describe them?" "I see..." "莉莉，你在图中看见什么？可以描述一下吗？" "我看见…"

desert /'dezət; `dɛzɚt/ *n* 名

a hot and dry place that is covered by sand 沙漠

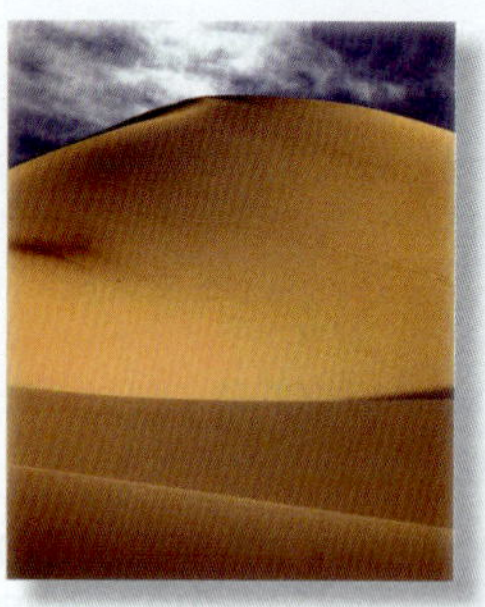

Very few plants grow in the desert. 沙漠里很少有植物生长。

deserve /dɪ'zɜ:v; dɪ`zɝv/ *v* 动

deserves, deserving, deserved, deserved

to be good or bad enough for something 该得；应得

His work deserves good marks. 他的作业该得高分。

*design¹ /dɪ'zaɪn; dɪ`zaɪn/ *n* 名

1. a pattern or shape 设计；图案

   The designs on this scarf are beautiful. 这条围巾的图案很漂亮。

2. the way that something is made 设计

   I like the design of the new school. 我喜欢这所新学校的设计。

*design² /dɪ'zaɪn; dɪ`zaɪn/ *v* 动

to make a pattern or decide how something will be made 设计

Sally designed the clothes for the actors. 莎莉为演员设计服装。

designer /dɪ'zaɪnə; dɪ`zaɪnɚ/ *n* 名

a person who decides how something will look when it is made 设计者；设计师

She wants to be a fashion designer. 她想成为一名时装设计师。

*desk /desk; dɛsk/ *n* 名

a table that you sit at to write and work 书桌；办公桌

This desk is made of wood. 这张书桌是木制的。

另见 table

desktop computer /ˌdesktɒp kəm'pju:tə; ˏdɛsktɑp kəm`pjutɚ/ *n* 名

缩写：*desktop*

【电脑】a computer used on a desk 台式电脑

This new desktop computer is fast. 这台新的台式电脑速度很快。

另见 **附录**：The computer world 电脑世界

*dessert /dɪ'zɜ:t; dɪ`zɝt/ *n* 名

something sweet that you eat at the end of a meal 餐后甜点

I had mango pudding for dessert. 我的餐后甜点是芒果布丁。

destination /ˌdestɪ'neɪʃn; ˏdɛstə`neʃən/ *n* 名

the place you are going to 目的地

The destination of the plane is London. 这架飞机的目的地是伦敦。

destroy /dɪ'strɔɪ; dɪ`strɔɪ/ *v* 动

to damage something completely 破坏；毁灭

The earthquake destroyed a lot of houses. 地震破坏了许多房子。

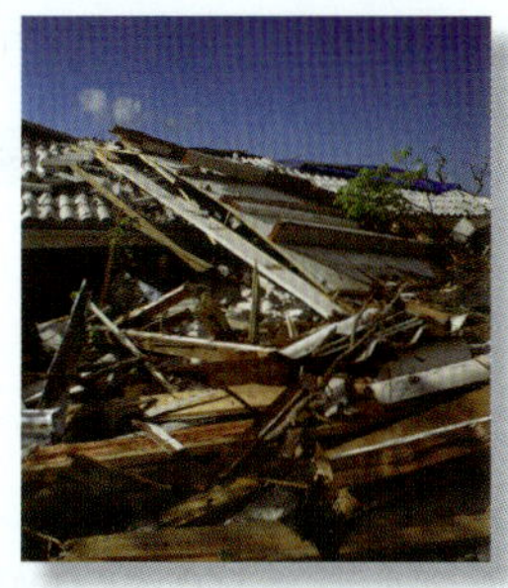

***detail** /dɪ:teɪl; dɪ`tel/ *n* 名

a small point or fact 详情；细节

Please tell me the details of your plan. 请告诉我你计划的细节。

in detail 详细地

I told him my plan in detail. 我详细地把计划告诉了他。

detective /dɪ'tektɪv; dɪ`tɛktɪv/ *n* 名

a person who finds out information about crime 侦探

The story is about a detective. 这故事是关于一名侦探的。

detergent /dɪ'tɜ:dʒənt; dɪ`tɝdʒənt/ *n* 名

a liquid or powder for washing clothes, dishes, etc 清洁剂；洗衣粉

Susan used detergent to wash the dishes. 苏珊用清洁剂来洗碗碟。

determined /dɪ'tɜ:mɪnd; dɪ`tɝmɪnd/ *adj* 形

wanting to do something very much 坚决的；有决心的

The team is determined to win the basketball competition. 这支球队决心在篮球赛中取胜。

***develop** /dɪ'veləp; dɪ`vɛləp/ *v* 动

to grow or become bigger and better 成长；发展

The small village has developed into a big city. 小乡村已发展成为大城市。

devil /'devl; `dɛvl̩/ *n* 名

an evil spirit 魔鬼；恶魔

Do you believe in devils? 你相信有魔鬼吗？

dew /dju:; du/ *n* 名

无复数

small drops of water that form on the ground, plants, etc at night 露水；露珠

There was dew on the grass this morning. 今天早晨，草叶上满是露水。

diagonal /daɪ'ægənl; daɪ`ægənl̩/ *adj* 形

going from corner to corner, across the middle 对角线的

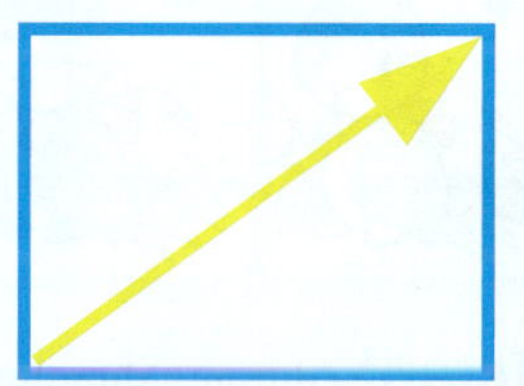

He drew a diagonal line on the paper. 他在纸上画了一条对角线。

***dial** /'daɪəl; `daɪəl/ *v* 动

dials, dialling, dialled, dialled

to press the buttons on the telephone to call someone 拨电话；打电话

In an emergency, dial 110 for help. 紧急时，拨 110 求助。

diameter /daɪ'æmɪtə; daɪ`æmətɚ/ *n* 名

a line across a circle, passing through the centre, or the length of this line 直径

The diameter of the tree trunk is one metre. 那棵树干的直径是一米。

diamond /'daɪəmənd; `daɪəmənd/ *n* 名

1. a hard, bright jewel 钻石

   Mrs Smith has a beautiful diamond ring. 史密斯太太有一枚漂亮的钻石戒指。

2. a shape like this "◆" 菱形

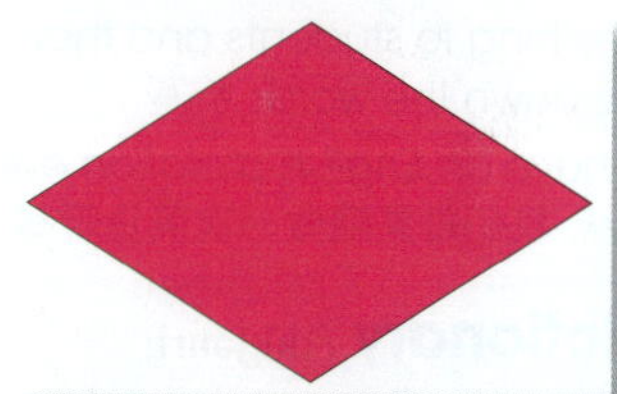

She drew a red diamond on the paper. 她在纸上画了个红色的菱形。

***diary** /'daɪəri; `daɪərɪ/ *n* 名

复数：***diaries***

1. a book in which you write down the things that happen to you each day 日记本

   I wrote my dream in my diary. 我把梦写在日记中。

2. 【英】(美式：***calendar***) a book in which you can write down things you have to do in the future 记事本

   I wrote the date of the meeting in my diary. 我在记事本上记下了开会的日期。

D

dice¹ /daɪs; daɪs/ *n* 名

复数：***dice***

a small cube, with 1-6 spots on each side, that you use in games 骰子

He threw a pair of dice and got seven in total. 他掷了一对骰子，总共是7点。

dice² /daɪs; daɪs/ *v* 动

dices, dicing, diced, diced

to cut food into small square pieces （把食物）切成小块

She diced the carrots. 她把胡萝卜切成小块。

***dictation** /dɪkˈteɪʃn; dɪkˋteʃən/ *n* 名

a test in which a teacher reads something to students and they write down the words 听写

We have an English dictation every week. 我们每星期做一次英语听写。

***dictionary** /ˈdɪkʃənri; ˋdɪkʃənˏɛrɪ/ *n* 名

复数：***dictionaries***

a book which tells you the meanings of words 字典；词典

I often look up words in a dictionary. 我经常查词典。

did /dɪd; dɪd/ *v* 动

the past tense of **do** ☆ do 的过去式

didn't /ˈdɪdnt; ˋdɪdn̩t/

the short form of "**did not**" ☆ did not 的缩写

Candy didn't come to school yesterday. 坎蒂昨天没有上学。

***die** /daɪ; daɪ/ *v* 动

dies, dying, died, died

to stop living 死

Luckily no people died in the fire. 很幸运没有人在火灾中死去。

die of 死于（疾病）

She died of cancer. 她死于癌症。

反义 **live¹**

***diet** /ˈdaɪət; ˋdaɪət/ *n* 名

the food that a person usually eats 日常饮食

It is important to have a healthy diet. 健康饮食是很重要的。

on a diet （为减肥而）节食

Peter is overweight so he is on a diet. 彼得体重超重，所以正在节食。

***difference** /ˈdɪfrəns; ˋdɪfərəns/ *n* 名

how something is not the same 不同之处；差别

Can you find the differences between these two pictures? 你能找出这两幅图片的不同之处吗？

***different** /ˈdɪfrənt; ˋdɪfərənt/ *adj* 形

not the same 不同的；有分别的

These flowers have different colours. 这些花的颜色不同。

反义 **same¹, similar**

***difficult** /ˈdɪfɪklt; ˋdɪfəˏkʌlt/ *adj* 形

not easy; hard 不容易的；困难的

The exam was very difficult. 这次考试很难。

反义 **easy, simple**

***difficulty** /ˈdɪfɪklti; ˋdɪfəˏkʌltɪ/ *n* 名

复数：***difficulties***

a problem 困难

Ben had difficulties doing his homework. 本做作业时遇到了困难。

注意 若在 difficulty 后使用动词，必须用动词的 -ing 形式。

***dig** /dɪg; dɪg/ *v* 动

digs, digging, dug, dug

to move soil, snow, etc using your hands or a tool 挖；掘

The gardener dug a hole in the garden to plant a tree. 园丁在花园挖了一个洞来植树。

dim sum /ˌdɪm ˈsʌm; ˏdɪm ˋsʌm/ *n* 名

无复数

Chinese foods cooked in steam or hot oil 中式点心

Nancy likes dim sum very much. 南茜非常喜欢吃中式点心。

dining room /ˈdaɪnɪŋ ruːm; ˋdaɪnɪŋ rum/ *n* 名

a room for eating meals 饭厅

We are having dinner in the dining room. 我们正在饭厅吃晚餐。

***dinner** /ˈdɪnə; ˋdɪnɚ/ *n* 名

the main meal of the day, usually in the evening 正餐；晚餐

My mother is busy cooking dinner. 妈妈正忙着做晚饭。

dinosaur /ˈdaɪnəsɔː; ˋdaɪnəˏsɔr/ *n* 名

a very large animal that lived long ago 恐龙

Dinosaurs lived millions of years ago. 恐龙活在几千万年前。

direct /daɪˈrekt; dəˋrɛkt/ *adj* 形

going straight from one place to another 直接的

This is the most direct way to our school. 这是通往我们学校最近的路。

***direction** /daɪˈrekʃn; dəˋrɛkʃən/ *n* 名

1. the way someone or something moves or faces 方向

   The robber ran away in that direction. 劫匪朝那个方向逃跑了。

2. **directions**（复数名词）the way to get to a place or to do something（如何去某地的）指示；（如何做某事的）指南；说明

   Read the directions on the box carefully. 要仔细阅读盒子上的说明。

Asking for directions 问路

"Could you give me directions to the train station?" "Just go down this street. It's on your left." "请你告诉我怎样去火车站好吗？""沿这条路一直走，火车站就在左边。"

director /daɪˈrektə; dəˋrɛktɚ/ *n* 名

someone who tells other people what to do in a film or play 导演

Mike is the director of our school play. 迈克是我们学校戏剧的导演。

dirt /dɜːt; dɝt/ *n* 名

无复数

something that makes thing dirty, for example, dust 污垢

There is some dirt on your face. 你的脸上有一些污点。

***dirty** /ˈdɜːti; ˋdɝtɪ/ *adj* 形

dirtier, dirtiest

not clean 肮脏的；不洁的

We put all the dirty clothes in a basket. 我们把所有的脏衣服放在一个篮子里。

反义 **clean**[1]

disabled /dɪsˈeɪbld; dɪsˋebḷd/ *adj* 形

a disabled person is unable to use part of their body, or has difficulty using it 残疾的；伤残的

We should help disabled people. 我们应帮助伤残人士。

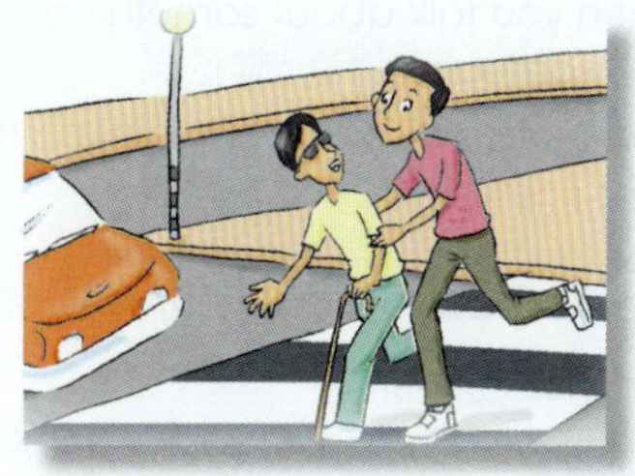

disagree /ˌdɪsəˈgriː; ˏdɪsəˋgri/ *v* 动

disagrees, disagreeing, disagreed, disagreed

to have a different opinion about something 意见不合；不同意

Although Lily and Mary are good friends, they disagree sometimes. 虽然莉莉和玛丽是好朋友，但是有时也会意见不合。

disagree (with someone) on something 对（某事情）意见不一致

Ross disagreed with Peter on a lot of things. 罗斯和彼得对于很多事的意见不一致。

反义 **agree**

disappear /ˌdɪsəˈpɪə; ˏdɪsəˋpɪr/ *v* 动

if something disappears, you cannot see it anymore 消失；失踪

My dog ran into the crowd and disappeared. 我的狗跑到人群中，消失不见了。

反义 **appear**

***disappointed** /ˌdɪsəˈpɔɪntɪd; ˏdɪsəˋpɔɪntɪd/ *adj* 形

feeling sad because you wanted something better 失望的

The boys were disappointed because they lost the game. 那些男孩输了球赛，所以他们很失望。

用法 disappointed 用来形容人的感受。

比较 **disappointing**

disappointing /ˌdɪsəˈpɔɪntɪŋ; ˏdɪsəˋpɔɪntɪŋ/ *adj* 形

making you sad because you wanted something better 令人失望的

It is really a disappointing film. 这真是一部令人失望的电影。

用法 disappointing 用来形容事物。

比较 **disappointed**

disaster /dɪ'zɑ:stə; dɪ`zæstɚ/ *n* 名

a terrible event in which many people are hurt or die, or a lot of things are damaged 灾难；灾祸

100 people died in the disaster. 100 人在灾难中丧生。

disc /dɪsk; dɪsk/ *n* 名【英】

美式：***disk***

【电脑】a round flat object you use in your computer 磁盘

You can save the information on a disc. 你可以将资料储存在磁盘里。

disco /'dɪskəʊ; `dɪsko/ *n* 名

a place where people dance to pop music 迪斯科舞厅

Last Sunday they went to the disco to dance. 他们上星期日去了迪斯科舞厅跳舞。

discount /'dɪskaʊnt; `dɪskaʊnt/ *n* 名

money taken off the usual price of something 折扣

There is a 30% discount on all the toys. 所有玩具都打七折。

注意 英语中的 30% discount（或 30% off）即中文的七折，而 15% discount（或 15% off）即八五折，依此类推。

***discover** /dɪs'kʌvə; dɪs`kʌvɚ/ *v* 动

to find out or learn about something 发现

They discovered some gold coins in the cave. 他们在山洞里发现了一些金币。

比较 **invent**

discovery /dɪs'kʌvəri; dɪs`kʌvərɪ/ *n* 名

复数：***discoveries***

something that someone finds out about for the first time 被发现的事物

Many discoveries in science have changed our lives. 科学上很多的发现都改变了我们的生活。

***discuss** /dɪ'skʌs; dɪ`skʌs/ *v* 动

discusses, discussing, discussed, discussed

to talk about something with someone 讨论

They were discussing their exam. 他们在谈论考试的事情。

discuss something with someone 与（某人）讨论（某事）

The teacher discussed the problem with the students. 老师与学生讨论问题。

用法 不可后接 about，例如不能说 discuss about their exam。

***discussion** /dɪ'skʌʃn; dɪ`skʌʃən/ *n* 名

when you talk about something with someone 讨论；谈论

They had a discussion in class. 他们进行了课堂讨论。

***disease** /dɪ'zi:z; dɪ`ziz/ *n* 名

an illness 疾病

He suffers from heart disease. 他患了心脏病。

***dish** /dɪʃ; dɪʃ/ *n* 名

复数：***dishes***

1. a container for food 盘子；碟子
   Please put the dirty dishes in the sink. 请把脏盘子放在水槽里。
2. food cooked in a particular way 菜肴；一道菜
   What is your favourite dish? 你最爱吃哪一道菜？

do the dishes 洗碗碟

Let me do the dishes. 我来洗碗碟吧。

dishonest /dɪs'ɒnɪst; dɪs`ɑnɪst/ *adj* 形

telling lies very often or cheating people 不诚实的

Nobody likes dishonest children. 没有人喜欢不诚实的孩子。

反义 **honest**

dishwasher /'dɪʃˌwɒʃə; `dɪʃˏwɑʃɚ/ *n* 名

a machine that washes dishes 洗碗机

There is a dishwasher in the kitchen. 厨房里有一台洗碗机。

dislike /dɪs'laɪk; dɪs`laɪk/ *v* 动

dislikes, disliking, disliked, disliked

to not like someone or something 不喜欢；讨厌

I dislike rude people. 我不喜欢粗鲁无礼的人。

反义 like[1]

dismiss /dɪsˈmɪs; dɪsˋmɪs/ *v* 动

dismisses, dismissing, dismissed, dismissed

to tell someone that they can leave 解散

The teacher dismissed the class when the bell rang. 铃声一响，老师就宣布下课了。

disobedient /ˌdɪsəˈbiːdiənt; ˏdɪsəˋbidɪənt/ *adj* 形

not doing what you are told to do 不服从的；不听话的

Henry is sometimes disobedient to his parents. 亨利有时候不听他父母的话。

反义 obedient

display /dɪˈspleɪ; dɪˋsple/ *v* 动

to show something to many people 展出；陈列

Our drawings were displayed at the school hall. 我们的图画在学校的礼堂里展出过。

distance /ˈdɪstəns; ˋdɪstəns/ *n* 名

the space between two places or things 距离

The distance between the two houses is 50 metres. 这两座房子之间的距离是 50 米。

distant /ˈdɪstənt; ˋdɪstənt/ *adj* 形

far away 遥远的

The stars are distant from us. 星星距离我们十分遥远。

***district** /ˈdɪstrɪkt; ˋdɪstrɪkt/ *n* 名

a part of a city or country 地区；区域

There are many factories in this district. 这个地区工厂林立。

disturb /dɪˈstɜːb; dɪˋstɝb/ *v* 动

to stop someone from working, thinking etc 打扰；妨碍

Don't disturb him. He is asleep. 别打扰他，他睡着了。

ditch /dɪtʃ; dɪtʃ/ *n* 名

复数：***ditches***

a narrow place for water to run away 沟渠

Our ball fell into the ditch. 我们的球掉进沟渠里了。

dive /daɪv; daɪv/ *v* 动

dives, diving, dived, dived

to jump into water with your arms and head first 跳水

They dived into the pool. 他们跳入水池。

***divide** /dɪˈvaɪd; dəˋvaɪd/ *v* 动

divides, dividing, divided, divided

1. to separate something into two or more parts 分开

   I divided the cake into six pieces. 我把蛋糕分成 6 块。
2. to find out how many times a number contains another number（数学中）除

   Twelve divided by three is four. 12 除以 3 等于 4。

***division** /dɪˈvɪʒn; dəˋvɪʒən/ *n* 名

无复数

dividing one number by another 除法

Our teacher taught us how to do division. 老师教我们除法。

dizzy /ˈdɪzi; ˋdɪzɪ/ *adj* 形

dizzier, dizziest

feeling as if you are going to fall 头晕的

I felt dizzy when I looked down from the peak. 我从山顶向下望时感到头晕目眩。

***do** /duː; du/ *v* 动

does, doing, did, done

1. to perform an action 做

   What are you doing? 你在做什么？

   I have nothing to do now. 我现在没有事情可做。
2. a word used with "not" before another verb or to ask a question 辅助动词（用于否定或疑问）

Do you like dogs? 你喜欢狗吗？
I do not like dogs. 我不喜欢狗。

dock /dɒk; dɑk/ *n* 名

a place where ships stay 码头；船坞

The ships stopped at the dock. 船只停泊在码头。

***doctor** /ˈdɒktə; ˋdɑktɚ/ *n* 名

someone who treats sick people 医生

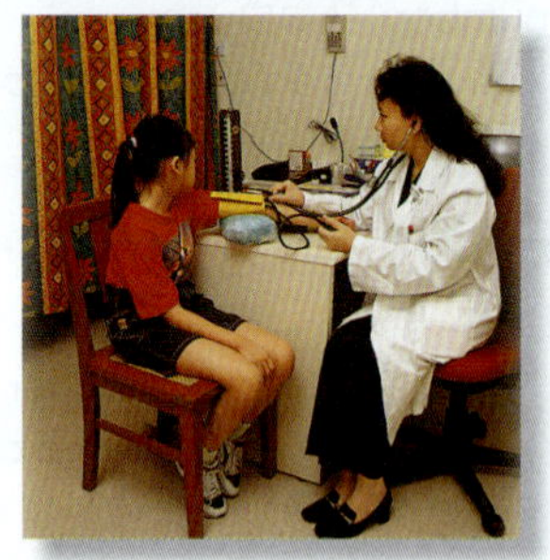

I was sick yesterday so I went to the doctor. 我昨天病了，于是去看医生。

document /ˈdɒkjumənt; ˋdɑkjəmənt/ *n* 名

【电脑】a piece of written work that is saved on a computer 文件
Save this document. 保存这个文件。

does /dəz; dəz; *strong* 强读 dʌz; dʌz/ *v* 动

a form of **do** ☆do 的另一种现在式，与主语 he、she 和 it 同用
Does he like swimming? 他喜欢游泳吗?

doesn't /ˈdʌznt; ˋdʌznt/

the short form of "**does not**" ☆does not 的缩写
Henry doesn't like swimming. 亨利不喜欢游泳。

***dog** /dɒg; dɔg/ *n* 名

an animal with four legs that is often kept as a pet 狗
Mike takes his dog to the park every day. 迈克每天都带他的狗去公园。

***doll** /dɒl; dɑl/ *n* 名

a toy that looks like a person 玩具娃娃

She has many dolls. 她有很多玩具娃娃。

***dollar** /ˈdɒlə; ˋdɑlɚ/ *n* 名

the unit of money used in Hong Kong, the United States etc ($)（货币单位）元
That pencil box costs twenty dollars. 那个铅笔盒卖 20 元。

dolphin /ˈdɒlfɪn; ˋdɑlfɪn/ *n* 名

a large sea animal, sometimes taught to do tricks in shows 海豚

We went to Ocean Park to see the dolphins. 我们去海洋公园看海豚。

***donate** /dəʊˈneɪt; ˋdonet/ *v* 动

donates, donating, donated, donated
to give money, food, etc to a person or charity 捐赠；捐献
Everyone donates money to help the poor. 大家都捐钱来帮助穷人。
donate blood 献血
Susan donates blood once a year. 苏珊每年献血一次。

donation /dəʊˈneɪʃn; doˋneʃən/ *n* 名

something you give to a person or charity 捐赠品；捐款
Mr Lee made a donation to the temple. 李先生捐了一笔钱给寺庙。

done /dʌn; dʌn/ *v* 动

the past participle of **do** ☆do 的过去分词

donkey /ˈdɒŋki; ˋdɑŋkɪ/ *n* 名

an animal like a small horse with long ears 驴

Donkeys can carry very heavy goods. 驴子能驮很重的货物。

don't /dəʊnt; dont/ *v* 动

the short form of "**do not**" ☆do not 的缩写
Don't do it again! 不要再这样做了！

***door** /dɔː; dɔr/ *n* 名

a piece of wood, metal etc that is used to close the entrance to a building, room, etc 门

She opened the door and went into the classroom. 她开了门，走进教室。

dot /dɒt; dɑt/ *n* 名

a small, round mark 点；圆点

I like the dots on the dress. 我喜欢这条裙子上的圆点。

double[1] /ˈdʌbl; ˋdʌbl̩/ *adj* 形

1. with two things that are the same or similar 出现两次的；双的

   Don't park the car on double yellow lines. 不得在双黄线上停车。

2. twice as big, twice as much etc as something else 两倍的

   The new phone costs double the price of the old one. 新电话的价钱是旧电话的两倍。

double[2] /ˈdʌbl; ˋdʌbl̩/ *n* 名

无复数

something that is twice as big, twice as much etc as something else 两倍；双倍

They got paid double for working at the Chinese New Year holiday. 他们在农历新年工作，所以获得双倍薪水。

double[3] /ˈdʌbl; ˋdʌbl̩/ *v* 动

doubles, doubling, doubled, doubled

to become twice as big, or make something twice as big 是…的两倍；使加倍

The city doubled in size. 这个城市的面积增加了一倍。

dough /dəʊ; do/ *n* 名

无复数

a mixture of flour, water etc that is used to make bread, cakes etc 生面团

The cook is using the dough to make biscuits. 厨师正在用生面团做饼干。

dove /dʌv; dʌv/ *n* 名

a white bird often used as a sign of peace 鸽

There are many doves in the square. 广场上有很多鸽子。

*down[1] /daʊn; daʊn/ *adv* 副

1. to or towards a lower place or position 由上而下地；向低处

   Please sit down. 请坐下。

They are running down from the hill. 他们正从山上跑下来 。

反义 **up[1]**

2. to or at a lower amount or level 减少；减弱

   Can you turn down the volume, please? 请把音量调低一些，可以吗？

反义 **up[1]**

*down[2] /daʊn; daʊn/ *prep* 介

to or towards a lower place or position; moving along a road, river, etc 向下；沿着

They walked down the beach. 他们沿着海滩走。

> **Asking for directions 问路**
>
> *"How do you get to the bank?" "Go down this street and you'll see it."* "该怎么去银行呢？" "沿着这条街往前走，你就会见到了。"

反义 **up[2]**

*down[3] /daʊn; daʊn/ *adj* 形

1. sad 情绪低落的；沮丧的

   What's the matter with Lily? She looks a bit down. 莉莉怎么了？她看起来不太开心。

2. 【电脑】not working 停机的；死机的

   My computer was down. 我的电脑死机了。

download /ˌdaʊnˈləʊd; ˋdaʊnˏlod/ *v* 动

【电脑】to get information or programs from the Internet 下载（数据或电脑程序）

You can download this program from the Internet. 你可以从互联网上下载这个电脑程序。

反义 **upload**

*downstairs /ˌdaʊnˈsteəz; ˏdaʊnˋstɛrz/ *adv* 副

on or to a lower level of a building 到楼下；在楼下

My cat is coming downstairs. 我的猫正走下楼。

反义 **upstairs**

doze /dəʊz; doz/ *v* 动

dozes, dozing, dozed, dozed

D

to sleep for a very short time 打瞌睡；打盹

Sam was dozing in front of the television. 山姆在电视机前打盹儿。

dozen /ˈdʌzn; ˋdʌzn̩/ *n* 名

复数：***dozen/dozens***

twelve 一打；十二个

My mother bought a dozen eggs. 妈妈买了一打鸡蛋。

Dr /ˈdɒktə; ˋdɑktɚ/ *n* 名

the short form of **doctor** 医生（doctor 的缩写）

I was sick and went to see Dr Li yesterday. 我昨天病了，所以去看李医生。

用法 只可用于医生的姓名前。

注意 开头的字母必须用大写。

drag /dræg; dræg/ *v* 动

drags, dragging, dragged, dragged

to pull something heavy along the ground 拖；用力拉

He is dragging a desk into his bedroom. 他正把一张书桌拖进卧室里。

drag and drop【电脑】拖放

Drag and drop the file into the recycle bin. 把文件拖放到回收站里。

dragon /ˈdrægən; ˋdrægən/ *n* 名

an animal in stories that looks like a giant lizard with wings and claws 龙

In the story, the dragon can make rain or storms. 在个这故事里，龙会呼风唤雨。

dragon boat 龙舟；龙船

There are dragon boat races every year. 每年都举行龙舟竞赛。

dragon dance 舞龙

Sam took part in the dragon dance. 山姆参加了舞龙。

dragonfly /ˈdrægənflaɪ; ˋdrægənˏflaɪ/ *n* 名

复数：***dragonflies***

an insect that has a long body and two pairs of wings 蜻蜓

Some dragonflies are flying near the river. 几只蜻蜓在河边飞。

drain /dreɪn; dren/ *n* 名

a pipe that takes away dirty water 排水管；排水渠

A drain takes the dirty water away from our house. 排水渠把我们房子的脏水排走。

drama /ˈdrɑːmə; ˋdrɑmə/ *n* 名

a play for the theatre, television, etc 戏剧

Henry watched a drama last night. 亨利昨晚看了一出戏剧。

TV drama 电视剧

My mother likes to watch TV dramas. 妈妈喜欢看电视剧。

drank /dræŋk; dræŋk/ *v* 动

the past tense of **drink** ☆drink 的过去式

***draw**[1] /drɔː; drɔ/ *v* 动

draws, drawing, drew, drawn

1. to make a picture with a pencil, pen, etc 画

   I drew a picture in the art lesson. 我上美术课时画了一幅画。

比较 **paint**[2]

2. to take something out 抽出；拿出

   To play the game, each person draws five cards. 玩游戏时，每人抽 5 张纸牌。

3. to finish a game without any side winning 打成平局；不分胜负

   My class drew with the school team. 我班与校队打成平局。

***draw**[2] /drɔː; drɔ/ *n* 名

a game that ends with no one winning 和局；平局

The football match was a draw. 足球比赛踢成了平局。

***drawer** /drɔː; drɔr/ *n* 名

a part of a desk, a cupboard etc that is like a box for keeping things in 抽屉

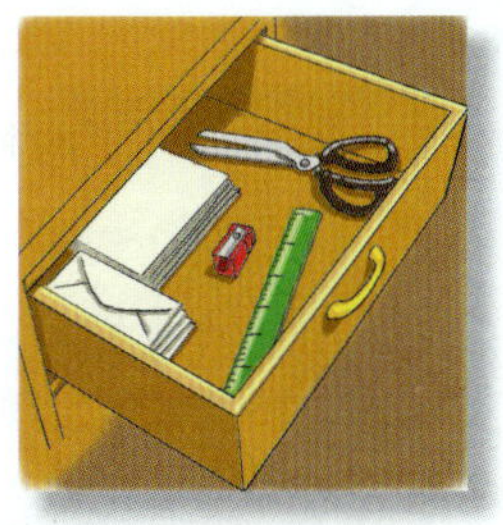

The scissors are in the drawer. 剪刀在抽屉里。

drawing /drɔːɪŋ; drɔɪŋ/ *n* 名

a picture that you draw 图画

The teacher posted my drawing on the board. 老师把我的图画贴在板上。

drawn /drɔːn; drɔn/ *v* 动

the past participle of **draw** ☆draw 的过去分词

***dream**[1] /driːm; drim/ *n* 名

1. something that happens in your mind when you are asleep 梦

I had a strange dream last night. 我昨晚做了一个奇怪的梦。

2. something that you hope will happen 梦想

Her dream is to travel around the world. 她的梦想是环游世界。

***dream**[2] /driːm; drim/ *v* 动

dreams, dreaming, dreamt/ dreamed, dreamt/dreamed

to have a dream 做梦

Jack dreamt he was in his old school. 杰克梦见自己回到从前的学校。

dreamt /dremt; drɛmt/ *v* 动

the past tense and past participle of **dream** ☆dream 的过去式和过去分词

***dress**[1] /dres; drɛs/ *n* 名

复数：***dresses***

a piece of clothing for a woman or girl that covers the body and part of the legs 连衣裙

She is wearing a blue dress. 她穿着一条蓝色的连衣裙。

比较 **skirt**

***dress**[2] /dres; drɛs/ *v* 动

dresses, dressing, dressed, dressed

to put clothes on yourself or another person 穿衣服；给…穿衣服

Shirley is dressing her baby. 雪莉在给她的婴儿穿衣服。

get dressed 穿好衣服

Get dressed quickly or you will be late! 赶快穿好衣服，否则你就会迟到了！

drew /druː; dru/ *v* 动

the past tense of **draw** ☆draw 的过去式

dried /draɪd; draɪd/ *v* 动

the past tense and past participle of **dry** ☆dry 的过去式和过去分词

***drink**[1] /drɪŋk; drɪŋk/ *v* 动

drinks, drinking, drank, drunk

to take liquid into your mouth and swallow it 喝

Sally drinks a glass of milk every morning. 莎莉每天早上都喝一杯牛奶。

Daily conversation 日常会话

"What will you have to drink?" *"Orange juice will be fine."* "你要喝点什么呢？" "橙汁就可以了。"

***drink**[2] /drɪŋk; drɪŋk/ *n* 名

liquid for drinking 饮料；饮品

Paul bought some drinks from the shop. 保罗从商店里买了一些饮品。

Daily conversation 日常会话

"Would you like to have a drink?" *"Hot milk, please."* "你要点一杯饮品吗？" "热牛奶，谢谢。"

drip /drɪp; drɪp/ *v* 动

drips, dripping, dripped, dripped

to fall in drops, or to produce water in drops 滴下；滴出

The tap is dripping. 水龙头在滴水。

***drive** /draɪv; draɪv/ *v* 动

drives, driving, drove, driven

to make a car, bus, etc move 驾驶

Can you drive? 你会开车吗？

driven /ˈdrɪvn; ˋdrɪvən/ *v* 动

the past participle of **drive** ☆drive 的过去分词

***driver** /ˈdraɪvə; ˋdraɪvɚ/ *n* 名

someone who drives a car, bus, etc 司机

My uncle is a bus driver. 我的叔叔是个公交车司机。

D

D

***drop[1]** /drɒp; drɑp/ *v* 动

drops, dropping, dropped, dropped

1. to fall 跌下；落下
   An apple dropped to the ground. 一个苹果掉到了地上。
2. to let something fall 掉下
   She dropped her cup and broke it. 她摔破了杯子。

***drop[2]** /drɒp; drɑp/ *n* 名

a small amount of liquid 滴；点
There are some drops of water on the leaves. 叶子上有一些水珠。

drought /draʊt; draʊt/ *n* 名

a long period of dry weather, with little or no rain 干旱；旱灾
Most of the crops died in the drought. 旱灾期间大部分的农作物都死了。

drove /drəʊv; drov/ *v* 动

the past tense of **drive** ☆drive 的过去式

drown /draʊn; draʊn/ *v* 动

to die in water because you cannot breathe 淹死；溺死
The ship sank and many passengers drowned in the sea. 那艘船沉没了，很多乘客在海中溺亡。

***drug** /drʌg; drʌg/ *n* 名

1. a medicine 药物
   This drug can cure a headache. 这种药物可以治疗头痛。
2. something illegal that people take to make themselves happy, excited, etc 毒品
   Say "No" to drugs! 对毒品说“不”！

***drum** /drʌm; drʌm/ *n* 名

a musical instrument that you hit with your hands or a stick 鼓

The boy was banging on a drum and making a lot of noise. 那个男孩在打鼓，发出很吵的声音。

drumstick /ˈdrʌmstɪk; ˋdrʌmstɪk/ *n* 名

the lower part of the leg of a chicken or other bird that is eaten as food（鸡或禽类的）腿下段
James likes to eat fried drumsticks. 詹姆斯喜欢吃炸鸡腿。

drunk[1] /drʌŋk; drʌŋk/ *v* 动

the past participle of **drink** ☆drink 的过去分词

drunk[2] /drʌŋk; drʌŋk/ *adj* 形

having had too much alcohol and unable to control your behaviour 喝醉的
Sam was drunk. 山姆喝醉了。

用法 不能用于名词前。

drunken /ˈdrʌŋkən; ˋdrʌŋkən/ *adj* 形

a drunken person has drunk too much alcohol 酒醉的
The drunken men were laughing loudly. 那几个醉汉在大笑。

用法 只用于名词前。

***dry[1]** /draɪ; draɪ/ *adj* 形

drier, driest

not wet 干的；干燥的
The earth is dry because it has not rained for a long time. 土地很干，因为很久没有下雨了。

反义 **damp, humid**

***dry[2]** /draɪ; draɪ/ *v* 动

dries, drying, dried, dried

to take away water from something 弄干
He dried his hair with a towel. 他用毛巾擦干头发。

***duck** /dʌk; dʌk/ *n* 名

a bird with short legs that swims on water 鸭

There are many ducks in the pond. 池塘里有很多鸭子。

duckling /ˈdʌklɪŋ; ˋdʌklɪŋ/ *n* 名

a young duck 小鸭
The ducklings are following their mother. 那些小鸭跟在鸭妈妈的后面。

dug /dʌg; dʌg/ *v* 动

the past tense and past participle of **dig** ☆dig 的过去式和过去分词

dull /dʌl; dʌl/ *adj* 形

duller, dullest

1. not interesting or exciting 沉闷的；乏味的
   That film was very dull. 那部电影非常沉闷。

同义 **boring**

反义 interesting

2. not bright 阴沉的；灰暗的
   Today is a dull day. 今天阴天。

dumb /dʌm; dʌm/ *adj* 形

not able to speak 哑的

The man was deaf and dumb. 那人又聋又哑。

注意 这个字有冒犯意味。

dumpling /ˈdʌmplɪŋ; ˋdʌmplɪŋ/ *n* 名

a piece of dough that you cook with meat or vegetables 饺子

She is making some dumplings. 她正在包饺子。

rice dumpling 粽子

People eat rice dumplings at the Dragon Boat Festival. 人们在端午节吃粽子。

durian /ˈdʊərɪən; ˋdʊrɪən/ *n* 名

a kind of fruit with a hard shell and strong smell 榴莲

Peter doesn't like the smell of durians. 彼得不喜欢榴莲的气味。

***during** /ˈdjʊərɪŋ; ˋdʊrɪŋ/ *prep* 介

1. at some point in a period of time 在（一段时间中的）某个时候
   I learnt swimming during the summer. 我在暑假时学游泳。
2. from the beginning to the end of a period of time 在…期间
   The hotels are all full during the summer. 在暑假期间，所有酒店都客满。

***dust¹** /dʌst; dʌst/ *n* 名

无复数

very small and dry pieces of dirt 灰尘；尘埃

The window is covered with dust. 窗口布满了灰尘。

***dust²** /dʌst; dʌst/ *v* 动

to take away the dirt 拭去灰尘

She is dusting the furniture. 她在打扫家具上的灰尘。

dustbin /ˈdʌstbɪn; ˋdʌstˌbɪn/ *n* 名

a container for rubbish 垃圾箱；垃圾筒

Throw the old newspapers in the dustbin. 把旧报纸扔进垃圾箱里。

同义 bin

duster /ˈdʌstə; ˋdʌstɚ/ *n* 名

a cloth for removing dust from furniture 抹布；（除尘的）掸子

She cleaned the chair with a duster. 她用抹布擦椅子。

***duty** /ˈdjuːti; ˋdutɪ/ *n* 名

复数：*duties*

something that you must do 责任；本分

It is our duty to keep the school clean. 保持学校清洁是我们的责任。

on/off duty 值班/下班

The nurse is on duty tonight. She will go off duty next morning. 这位护士今晚值班，明天早上下班。

DVD /ˌdiː viː ˈdiː; ˌdi vi ˋdi/ *n* 名

复数：*DVDs*

a disc that is like a CD but can store much more information 数码影碟；数字多功能光盘；数码光碟

We watched the DVD of "Alice in Wonderland" yesterday. 我们昨天看了《爱丽丝梦游仙境》的数码影碟。

DVD player 数码影碟机

Mr Brown put the DVD in the DVD player and started watching the movie. 布朗先生把数码影碟放在影碟机中，开始看电影。

dwarf /dwɔːf; dwɔrf/ *n* 名

复数：*dwarfs/dwarves*

a creature in stories that looks like a small person 侏儒；小矮人

Snow White makes friends with seven dwarfs in the story. 在故事中，白雪公主和七个小矮人做朋友。

dye /daɪ; daɪ/ *v* 动

dyes, dyeing, dyed, dyed

to change the colour of your hair or clothes 染；把…染色

Susan wanted to dye her hair brown. 苏珊想把头发染成褐色。

注意 发音与 die 相同。

dying /ˈdaɪ-ɪŋ; ˋdaɪ-ɪŋ/ *v* 动

the present participle of **die** ☆die 的现在分词

E

***each¹** /iːtʃ; itʃ/ *adj* 形

every one of two or more 每个；各个

Each child has an apple. 每个小孩都有一个苹果。

用法 each 后用单数名词，后接单数动词。

同义 **every**

***each²** /iːtʃ; itʃ/ *pron* 代

every one of two or more 每个；各个

The apples cost $4 each. 苹果每个4元。

The students each have a pen. 学生们每人都有一支笔。

用法 若 each 用于复数名词后，其后用复数动词。

each of 每人；每个

Mrs Smith gave each of the children a toy. 史密斯太太给孩子们每人一个玩具。

each other 彼此；互相

Harry and Mike often help each other. 哈利和迈克经常互相帮助。

同义 **one another**（见 **another**）

eager /ˈiːgə; ˋigɚ/ *adj* 形

wanting something very much 渴望的；急切的

I am eager to know the results of the exam. 我急于知道考试成绩。

eagle /ˈiːgl; ˋigl/ *n* 名

a large bird that eats small animals 鹰

Some eagles live in mountains. 有些鹰住在高山上。

***ear** /ɪə; ɪr/ *n* 名

one of the two parts on the sides of your head with which you hear sounds 耳朵

Rabbits have long ears. 兔子的耳朵很长。

***early¹** /ˈɜːli; ˋɝlɪ/ *adj* 形

earlier, earliest

1. at or near the beginning of a period of time 早的；初期的

   They went swimming in the early morning. 他们一大早就去游泳。

反义 **late¹**

2. happening before the usual or expected time 提早的；提前的

   The train was three minutes early. 火车早到了 3 分钟。

反义 **late¹**

***early²** /ˈɜːli; ˋɝlɪ/ *adv* 副

1. at or near the beginning of a period of time 早；初期

   I get up early every day. 我每天都起得很早。

反义 **late²**

2. before the usual or expected time 提早；提前

   We arrived early and had to wait outside the cinema. 我们提早到了，所以要在电影院门口等候。

反义 **late²**

***earn** /ɜːn; ɝn/ *v* 动

to get money for the work you do 赚钱

He earns a lot of money. 他赚的钱很多。

***earring** /ˈɪərɪŋ; ˋɪrˌrɪŋ/ *n* 名

a piece of jewellery that you wear on your ear 耳环

She is wearing a pair of pearl earrings. 她戴着一对珍珠耳环。

***earth** /ɜːθ; ɝθ/ *n* 名

无复数

1. （也作：***Earth***）the planet that we live on 地球；世界

The earth moves round the sun. 地球绕着太阳转。

用法 可与 the 或 on 同用。若与 on 同用，在 earth 前面不用加 the，即 on earth，指世界上，如 Mount Everest is the highest mountain on earth.（珠穆朗玛峰是世界上最高的山。）

2. soil 泥土；土壤

She filled the pot with earth. 她把花盆装满泥土。

earthquake /ˈɜːθˌkweɪk; ˋɝθˌkwek/ *n* 名

a strong shaking of the ground 地震
Many people died in the earthquake. 很多人在地震中死去。

earthworm /ˈɜːθwɜːm; ˋɝθˌwɝm/ *n* 名
a long, soft worm that lives in the soil 蚯蚓
Some birds eat earthworms. 有些鸟吃蚯蚓。

***easily** /ˈiːzɪli; ˋizɪlɪ/ *adv* 副
without difficulty 容易地；轻易地
Paul finished his homework easily. 保罗轻而易举地把功课做完了。

east[1] /iːst; ist/ *n* 名
无复数 | 缩写：*E*
the direction from which the sun rises 东方；东面

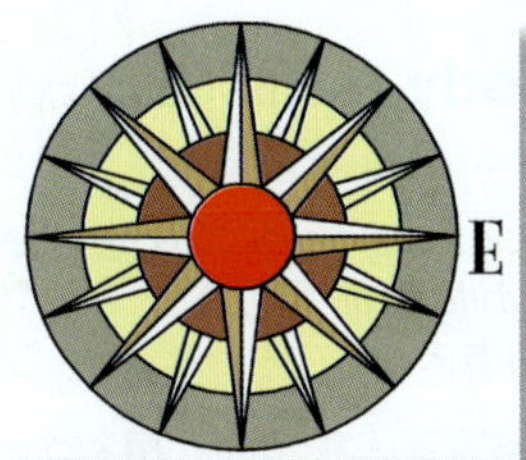

The sun rises in the east. 太阳从东方升起。

east[2] /iːst; ist/ *adj* 形
in the east or facing the east 东方的；东面的；向东的
There is a temple on the east side of the street. 这条街的东边有一间寺庙。

east[3] /iːst; ist/ *adv* 副
towards the east 向东
The plane is flying east. 飞机向东飞行。

***Easter** /ˈiːstə; ˋistɚ/ *n* 名
a Christian festival in spring, when Christians remember Jesus Christ's death and his return to life 复活节
I will have a holiday at Easter. 我在复活节休假。

eastern /ˈiːstən; ˋistɚn/ *adj* 形
in or from the east of a country or place 东方的；东部的
The storm is moving to the eastern part of China. 暴风雨正向着中国东部移动。

***easy** /ˈiːzi; ˋizɪ/ *adj* 形
easier, easiest
not difficult 容易的
The test was easy and many students got full marks. 这次测验很容易，很多学生都得了满分。
同义 simple
反义 difficult, hard[1]

***eat** /iːt; it/ *v* 动
eats, eating, ate, eaten
to put food into your mouth and swallow it 吃
She is eating some cakes. 她在吃蛋糕。

eaten /ˈiːtn; ˋitn̩/ *v* 动
the past participle of **eat** ☆eat 的过去分词

edge /edʒ; ɛdʒ/ *n* 名
the part furthest from the middle 边缘
Be careful! Don't stand near the edge of the pool. 小心！别站在水池边上。

editor /ˈedɪtə; ˋɛdɪtɚ/ *n* 名
someone who decides what to include in books, newspapers, etc and checks them before they are printed 编辑
She is a magazine editor. 她是杂志编辑。

***educate** /ˈedjʊkeɪt; ˋɛdʒəˌket/ *v* 动
educates, educating, educated, educated
to teach 教育；教导
The government should educate young people to protect the environment. 政府应教导年轻人保护环境。

***education** /ˌedjʊˈkeɪʃn; ˌɛdʒəˋkeʃən/ *n* 名
无复数
teaching and learning 教育
Our school gives us good education. 我们的学校给我们提供良好的教育。

eel /iːl; il/ *n* 名
a long fish that looks like a snake 鳗；鳝

Do you eat eels? 你吃鳗鱼吗?

***effect** /ɪˈfekt; əˋfɛkt/ *n* 名
a result 效果；影响
Cutting down trees can have a bad effect on the environment. 砍伐树木可能会对环境造成不良的影响。
比较 affect

efficient /ɪˈfɪʃnt; əˋfɪʃənt/ *adj* 形
doing things well and quickly without wasting time, money or energy 效率高的；能干的

Machines are more efficient than humans and they can do things much more quickly. 机器比人类更有效率，能更快完成工作。

***effort** /ˈefət; ˋɛfɚt/ *n* 名

the energy that you need to do something 努力；尽力

Henry has put a lot of effort into his work. 亨利很努力地工作。

E

e.g. /ˌiː ˈdʒiː; ˌi ˋdʒi/

the short form of "**for example**" 例如（for example 的缩写）

You should eat more fruit, e.g. apples, oranges and pears. 你应该多吃一点水果，例如苹果、橙、梨子。

***egg** /eg; ɛg/ *n* 名

1. a round object that contains a baby bird, fish, turtle, etc, before it is born 蛋；卵
   The fish lays its eggs at the bottom of the river. 鱼在河床上产卵。
2. a round object with a shell which comes from a female bird such as a chicken and is eaten as food（食用的）蛋

I ate an egg for breakfast. 我吃了一个鸡蛋作早餐。

***eight** /eɪt; et/ *num* 数

the number 8 八

Susan is eight years old. 苏珊 8 岁。

***eighteen** /ˌeɪˈtiːn; eˋtin/ *num* 数

the number 18 十八

Two times nine is eighteen. 2 乘以 9 等于 18。

eighteenth /eɪˈtiːnθ; eˋtinθ/ *ordinal num* 序数

18th in order 第十八（的）

We live on the eighteenth floor of this building. 我们住在这幢大楼的 18 楼。

eighth /eɪtθ; etθ/ *ordinal num* 序数

8th in order 第八（的）

August is the eighth month of a year. 8 月是一年里的第 8 个月份。

eightieth /ˈeɪtiəθ; ˋetɪɪθ/ *ordinal num* 序数

80th in order 第八十（的）

It's my grandmother's eightieth birthday today. 今天是我祖母的 80 岁生日。

***eighty** /ˈeɪti; ˋetɪ/ *num* 数

the number 80 八十

The old man is over eighty years old. 那老人年过八十。

***either[1]** /ˈaɪðə; ˋiðɚ/ *pron* 代

one or the other of two people or things（两者中的）任何一个

There's ice cream and cake. You can have either. 这里有冰淇淋和蛋糕，你可以任选一种。

另见 **neither[1]**

***either[2]** /ˈaɪðə; ˋiðɚ/ *conj* 连

either ... or ...

used to show two different people or things that you can choose …或者…

You can have either tea or coffee. 你可以喝茶或咖啡。

另见 **neither[2]**

***elbow** /ˈelbəʊ; ˋɛlˌbo/ *n* 名

the part in the middle of your arm, where it bends 肘

Ben hurt his elbow while playing badminton. 本打羽毛球时伤了手肘。

elder[1] /ˈeldə; ˋɛldɚ/ *adj* 形

older 较年长的

Ross has two elder brothers. 罗斯有两个哥哥。

用法 只用于名词前（如上例），常用于指家庭成员。此外，并不能与 than 连用，例如不能说 He is elder than me。若要比较年龄，要用 older，如 He is older than me.（他比我年长）。

反义 **younger**

elder[2] /ˈeldə; ˋɛldɚ/ *n* 名

someone who is older than you 长者；长辈

Children should respect their elders. 小孩应尊敬长辈。

***elderly** /ˈeldəli; ˋɛldɚlɪ/ *adj* 形

old 年长的；年老的

The doctor is an elderly gentleman with white hair. 那位医生是一个满头白发的老人。

用法 形容某人年纪大，用 elderly 比用 old 有礼貌。

***eldest** /ˈeldɪst; ˋɛldɪst/ *adj* 形

the oldest in a group 年纪最大的；最年长的

Her eldest son is a doctor. 她的长子是个医生。

反义 **youngest**

elect /iˈlekt; ɪˋlɛkt/ *v* 动

to choose someone for a job by voting for him or her 选举

We elected Mike as class monitor. 我们选迈克做班长。

electric /iˈlektrɪk; ɪˋlɛktrɪk/ *adj* 形

using or involving power from electricity 电的；电动的

People didn't have electric lights in

the past and they had to use candles. 从前人们没有电灯，只能用蜡烛。

electricity /iˌlekˈtrɪsəti; ɪˌlɛkˋtrɪsətɪ/ *n* 名

无复数

the power for light, heat, machines, etc 电；电力

Electricity is very important in modern life. 电力在现代化生活中非常重要。

***elephant** /ˈelɪfənt; ˋɛləfənt/ *n* 名

a large grey animal with a long nose (called a trunk) 象

There are two elephants in the zoo. 动物园里有两头大象。

***eleven** /iˈlevn; ɪˋlɛvən/ *num* 数

the number 11 十一

Lily is eleven years old. 莉莉今年 11 岁。

***eleventh** /iˈlevnθ; ɪˋlɛvənθ/ *ordinal num* 序数

11th in order 第十一（的）

Today is the eleventh of May. 今天是 5 月 11 日。

***else** /els; ɛls/ *adv* 副

1. other; different 其他；别的
   I don't like coffee. Can I have something else? 我不喜欢喝咖啡，我可以点别的吗？
2. more 另外；还有
   What else do you need? 你还需要什么？

***email¹** /ˈiː meɪl; ˋi mel/ *n* 名

也作：***electronic mail***

【电脑】a message that you send to others with a computer over the Internet 电邮；电子邮件

I received an email from Ross yesterday. 昨天我收到罗斯的一封电子邮件。

***email²** /ˈiː meɪl; ˋi mel/ *v* 动

【电脑】to send someone an email 给…发送电子邮件

I'll email you tomorrow. 我明天会给你发个电子邮件。

***embarrassed** /ɪmˈbærəst; ɪmˋbærəst/ *adj* 形

feeling silly or shy in front of other people 感到尴尬的；难为情的

He felt embarrassed when he was late for school this morning. 他今天早上上学迟到，感到很难为情。

emergency /iˈmɜːdʒənsi; ɪˋmɝdʒənsɪ/ *n* 名

复数：***emergencies***

a sudden and dangerous event which needs you to do something quickly 紧急事件；突发事件

In an emergency, press this button for help. 如遇紧急情况，请按这个按钮求救。

emigrate /ˈemɪgreɪt; ˋɛməˌgret/ *v* 动

emigrates, emigrating, emigrated, emigrated

to leave your own country and go to live in another country 移居（外国）

My uncle emigrated to Canada ten years ago. 叔叔十年前移居加拿大。

emperor /ˈempərə; ˋɛmpərɚ/ *n* 名

a man who rules a big country or many countries 皇帝

Who was the first emperor of China? 谁是中国的第一位皇帝？

empire /ˈempaɪə; ˋɛmpaɪr/ *n* 名

a group of countries that are controlled by one government 帝国

The British Empire was once the largest empire in the world. 大英帝国曾是世界上最大的帝国。

employ /ɪmˈplɔɪ; ɪmˋplɔɪ/ *v* 动

to give someone a job 雇用；聘用

The school employed two new teachers this year. 学校今年聘用了两位新老师。

E

E

employee /ɪm'plɔɪ-iː; ɪm`plɔɪ·i/ *n* 名

a person who receives money to work for someone else 雇员

Their employees work five days a week. 他们的雇员每星期工作5天。

employer /ɪm'plɔɪə; ɪm`plɔɪə/ *n* 名

a person or company that pays someone to work for them 雇主

Mr Brown is a very good employer. 布朗先生是个很好的雇主。

***empty**¹ /'empti; `ɛmptɪ/ *adj* 形

emptier, emptiest

having nothing or no people inside 空的

The drawer is empty. 这个抽屉是空的。

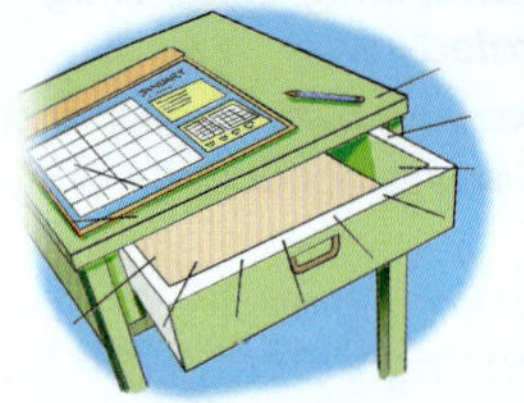

反义 full

***empty**² /'empti; `ɛmptɪ/ *v* 动

empties, emptying, emptied, emptied

to take everything out of something 把里面的东西全部取出；倒空

Lily empties the bin every night. 莉莉每晚都会倒空垃圾筒。

反义 fill

***encourage** /ɪn'kʌrɪdʒ; ɪn`kɜɪdʒ/ *v* 动

encourages, encouraging, encouraged, encouraged

to make someone more determined, hopeful, or confident so that they will do something 鼓励；激励

Miss Chen always encourages us to read more English books. 陈老师总是鼓励我们多看一些英文书。

***end**¹ /end; ɛnd/ *n* 名

the furthest or last part of something 尽头；末端；结束

The summer holiday has come to an end. 暑假结束了。

in the end 终于；最后

In the end, we got to the top of the hill. 我们终于抵达山顶。

反义 beginning

Asking for directions 问路

"Can you tell me how to get to the church?" "Go to the end of the street and turn right. You can't miss it." "我要去教堂该怎么走呢？""一直走到街道的尽头，然后转右。你准会找到的。"

***end**² /end; ɛnd/ *v* 动

to finish 结束；终止

All of the audience clapped their hands when the play ended. 话剧结束时，所有观众都鼓掌。

反义 begin, start¹

***ending** /'endɪŋ; `ɛndɪŋ/ *n* 名

the end of a story, film, or play 结局；结尾

The story has a sad ending. 这个故事的结局很悲伤。

enemy /'enəmi; `ɛnəmɪ/ *n* 名

复数：***enemies***

someone who hates you 仇人；敌人

Cats and mice are enemies. 猫和老鼠是仇敌。

反义 friend

***energy** /'enədʒi; `ɛnədʒɪ/ *n* 名

无复数

1. strength that you need to do things that use effort 精力；力量

   I haven't got any energy after running for 2 hours. 我跑了两小时，已经没有气力了。

2. power that is used for making things work or producing heat 能源；能量

   We switch off the lights to save energy. 我们关上电灯，节约能源。

***engine** /'endʒɪn; `ɛndʒən/ *n* 名

a machine which makes things work or move 引擎；发动机

Oliver couldn't start the engine of his car. 奥利弗大法启动汽车引擎。

engineer /ˌendʒɪ'nɪə; ˏɛndʒə`nɪr/ *n* 名

someone who designs and builds machines, roads, etc 工程师

Candy's father is an engineer. 坎蒂的爸爸是工程师。

***English**¹ /'ɪŋglɪʃ; `ɪŋglɪʃ/ *n* 名

无复数

1. the language used in England, the United States, etc 英语；英文

   I can speak Chinese and English. 我会说汉语和英语。

2. **the English** people from England 英国人

   The English like tea. 英国人喜欢喝茶。

注意 开头的字母必须用大写。

In the classroom 在教室里

"How do you say that in English?" "An apple." "那个用英语怎么说？" "An apple。"

English² /'ɪŋglɪʃ; `ɪŋglɪʃ/ *adj* 形

coming from England 英国的；英语的

She likes reading English books. 她喜欢看英文书。

注意 开头的字母必须大写。

***enjoy** /ɪn'dʒɔɪ; ɪn`dʒɔɪ/ *v* 动

to like doing something 享受；喜爱

We enjoyed the dinner very much. 我们非常享受那顿晚餐。

enjoy doing something 喜欢做（某事）；享受…的乐趣

I enjoy listening to music. 我喜欢听音乐。

enjoy yourself 过得愉快；玩得开心

Did you enjoy yourself in the party? 你在派对中玩得开心吗?

***enjoyable** /ɪn'dʒɔɪəbl; ɪn`dʒɔɪəbl/ *adj* 形

making someone happy 令人快乐的

We had an enjoyable holiday. 我们度过了愉快的假期。

enlarge /ɪn'lɑ:dʒ; ɪn`lardʒ/ *v* 动

enlarges, enlarging, enlarged, enlarged

to make something bigger 扩大；增大

I enlarged the photograph. 我把这幅照片放大了。

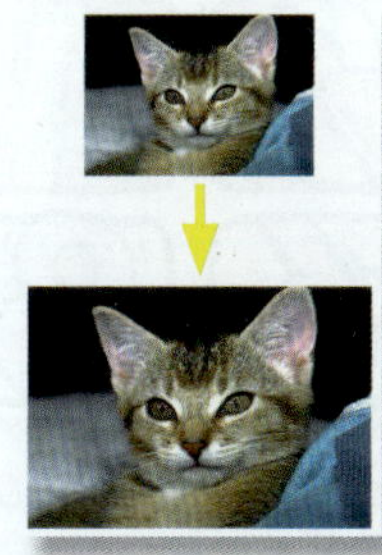

enormous /i'nɔ:məs; ɪ`nɔrməs/ *adj* 形

very big 巨大的

The monster has an enormous nose. 这只怪兽有个巨大的鼻子。

同义 huge

反义 tiny

***enough[1]** /ɪ'nʌf; ɪ`nʌf/ *adj* 形

as much or as many as you need 足够的；充足的

There is enough food for me! 这儿有足够的食物给我吃！

***enough[2]** /ɪ'nʌf; ɪ`nʌf/ *adv* 副

as good, old, big, warm, etc as you need 足够；充足

You haven't brought a coat with you. Are you warm enough? 你没有带外套，够暖和吗?

***enter** /'entə; `ɛntɚ/ *v* 动

to go or come into a place 进入

The principal entered the hall. 校长走进礼堂。

用法 多用于正式场合，一般场合用 go into 或 come into。

entertain /ˌentə'teɪn; ˌɛntɚ`ten/ *v* 动

to make people laugh or interest them by singing, telling stories, etc 提供娱乐；使快乐

Sam did some magic to entertain us. 山姆表演魔术来娱乐我们。

***entertainment** /ˌentə'teɪnmənt; ˌɛntɚ`tenmənt/ *n* 名

无复数

things that people can watch or do in order to enjoy themselves 娱乐

There are lots of things you can do for entertainment in Shanghai. 在上海你可以找到很多娱乐节目。

entire /ɪn'taɪə; ɪn`taɪr/ *adj* 形

whole or complete 整个的；全部的

I've read the entire book. 我看完了整本书。

***entrance** /'entrəns; `ɛntrəns/ *n* 名

the door or gate where you go into a place 入口；门口

I waited for my friends at the entrance to the zoo. 我在动物园门口等朋友。

反义 exit

entry /'entri; `ɛntrɪ/ *n* 名

无复数

going into a place 进入

The road sign says "No Entry". 路牌上写着"禁止进入"。

***envelope** /'envələup; `ɛnvəˌlop/ *n* 名

a paper cover for a letter 信封

Don't forget to stick a stamp on the envelope. 别忘了在信封上贴邮票。

envious /'enviəs; `ɛnvɪəs/ *adj* 形

wanting something that someone else has 羡慕的

The other boys were envious of Chris because he got good results in his exams. 那些男孩很羡慕克里斯，因为他在考试中取得了好成绩。

比较 jealous

***environment** /ɪn'vaɪrənmənt; ɪn`vaɪrənmənt/ *n* 名

无复数

the world you live in 环境

We need to protect the environment. 我们要保护环境。

***equal¹** /'i:kwəl; \`ikwəl/ *adj* 形

same 相等的；相同的

I cut the cake into six equal pieces. 我把蛋糕切成 6 等块。

E

***equal²** /'i:kwəl; \`ikwəl/ *v* 动

equals, equalling, equalled, equalled

to be the same as 等于

Four plus six equals ten. 4 加 6 等于 10。

equator /ɪ'kweɪtə; ɪ\`kwetə/ *n* 名

无复数

the line on maps around the middle of the Earth 赤道

The areas near the equator are very hot. 赤道附近的地区非常热。

用法 常与 the 一起使用，即 the equator。

***equipment** /ɪ'kwɪpmənt; ɪ\`kwɪpmənt/ *n* 名

无复数

the things you need for a particular purpose or job 设备；器材

Our school bought some new sports equipment. 我们的学校购买了一批新的运动器材。

eraser /ɪ'reɪzə; ɪ\`resə/ *n* 名【美】

英式 **rubber**

error /'erə; \`ɛrə/ *n* 名

a mistake 错误

There are some errors in your answers. 你的答案有几个错误。

***escalator** /'eskəleɪtə; \`ɛskə͵letə/ *n* 名

a set of moving stairs 自动扶梯

Let's take the escalator to the fifth floor. 我们乘自动扶梯去 5 楼吧。

比较 **lift²**

***escape** /ɪ'skeɪp; ə\`skep/ *v* 动

escapes, escaping, escaped, escaped

to get away from somewhere or someone 逃走；逃脱

A monkey escaped from the cage. 有只猴子从笼子里逃跑了。

***especially** /ɪ'speʃli; ə\`spɛʃəlɪ/ *adv* 副

more than others, or more than usual 尤其；特别

I love animals, especially dogs. 我喜爱动物，尤其是狗。

***essay** /'eseɪ; \`ɛse/ *n* 名

a short piece of writing 文章；短文

I write an essay every week. 我每周写一篇短文。

***estate** /ɪ'steɪt; ə\`stet/ *n* 名【英】

an area where a group of similar buildings are built in a planned way 社区；住宅区；工业区

Mike and I live on the same estate. 迈克和我住在同一个住宅区。

etc. /et 'setrə; ͵ɛt \`sɛtərə/ *adv* 副

也作：*etc*【英】

and other things 等等

The shop sells apples, pears, oranges, etc. 这家店铺卖苹果、梨子、橙子等。

eve /i:v; iv/ *n* 名

the night or day before an important day 前夕；前一天

We went to a party on Christmas Eve. 我们在平安夜那天参加了一个派对。

用法 如指节日的前夕，常作 Eve，例如 New Year's Eve（除夕）。

***even¹** /'i:vn; \`ivən/ *adv* 副

used to say that something is surprising or unusual 甚至；即使

The question is easy. Even a child can solve it. 这个问题很简单，即使小孩也能解答。

even if/though 即使；就算

Even if you don't agree, I will do it. 即使你不同意，我还是会做。

***even²** /'i:vn; \`ivən/ *adj* 形

an even number is one that you can divide by two 双数的；偶数的

2, 4, 6 and 8 are all even numbers. 2、4、6 和 8 都是偶数。

反义 **odd**

***evening** /'i:vnɪŋ; \`ivnɪŋ/ *n* 名

the part of the night between the

end of the afternoon and the time you go to sleep 傍晚；晚上

We'll go to the cinema this evening. 我们今晚会去看电影。

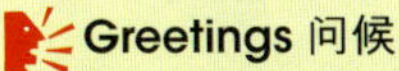

Greetings 问候

"Good evening. How are you doing?" "Fine. How about you?" "晚上好，你好吗？" "很好，你呢？"

*event /ɪˈvent; ɪˋvɛnt/ *n* 名

something that happens, especially something important 事件

Sports Day is an important event in our school. 运动会是我校的一大盛事。

eventually /ɪˈventʃuəli; ɪˋvɛntʃuəlɪ/ *adv* 副

after a lot of other things have happened 最后；终于

The school team won the football competition eventually. 最后，校队赢了足球比赛。

*ever /ˈevə; ˋɛvɚ/ *adv* 副

at any time 曾经；在任何时候

Have you ever been to London? 你去过伦敦吗?

ever since 自从

They have been friends ever since they were children. 他们从小就一直是朋友。

*every /ˈevri; ˋɛvrɪ/ *adj* 形

each one of a group of things or people 每一（个）

He has read every book in the bookcase. 他读过书架上的每一本书。

every day 每天

I get up very early every day. 我每天都很早起床。

比较 everyday

every other day 每隔一天

Tracy goes to the library every other day. 翠西每隔一天就去图书馆一次。

用法 在 every 后必定用单数名词，后接单数动词。

同义 each[1]

*everybody /ˈevribɒdi; ˋɛvrɪˏbadɪ/, everyone /ˈevriwʌn; ˋɛvrɪˏwʌn/ *pron* 代

every person 每个人；大家

Everyone likes the pandas in the zoo. 大家都喜欢动物园里的大熊猫。

用法 后接单数动词。

Greetings 问候

"Good morning, everybody!" "Good morning, Mrs Smith!" "各位早安！" "史密斯太太早安！"

everyday /ˌevriˈdeɪ; ˋɛvrɪˏde/ *adj* 形

ordinary or usual 平常的；日常的

Computers are part of everyday life. 电脑是日常生活的一部分。

注意 不要将 everyday 与 every day 混淆。everyday 是形容词，用于名词前，而 every day 是指"每天"。

比较 every day（见 every）

*everything /ˈevriθɪŋ; ˋɛvrɪˏθɪŋ/ *pron* 代

all of a group of things 一切；所有东西；每样事物

Is everything ready for the picnic? 去野餐的所有东西都准备好了吗?

用法 与单数动词同用。

*everywhere /ˈevriweə; ˋɛvrɪˏwɛr/ *adv* 副

in or to every part of a place 处处；到处

Ronald is looking everywhere for his school bag. 罗纳德正到处找他的书包。

evil /ˈiːvl; ˋivḷ/ *adj* 形

doing very bad or cruel things 邪恶的

In the story, the queen is an evil person. 在这故事里，王后是个邪恶的人。

exact /ɪɡˈzækt; ɪɡˋzækt/ *adj* 形

completely correct in every way 准确的；确切的

Please write down the exact number of words in your composition on the last page. 请在最后一页写上作文中的准确字数。

*exactly /ɪɡˈzæktli; ɪɡˋzæktlɪ/ *adv* 副

no earlier or later than a time, or no more or less than a number, age, or amount 准确地；确切地；不多不少地

The plane arrived at exactly 8 o'clock. 飞机 8 点整到达。

Daily conversation 日常会话

"So you think we should cancel the picnic?" "Exactly." "你的意思是我们应该取消野餐？" "正是。"

*exam /ɪɡˈzæm; ɪɡˋzæm/ *n* 名

the short form of **examination** 考试（examination 的缩写）

When will we know the exam results? 我们什么时候会知道考试结果?

*examination /ɪɡˌzæmɪˈneɪʃn; ɪɡˏzæməˋneʃən/ *n* 名

缩写：*exam*

a test about a subject 考试

He is taking an examination now. 他正在考试。

E

examine /ɪg'zæmɪn; ɪg`zæmɪn/ *v* 动

examines, examining, examined, examined

to look at something carefully 检查；检验

The vet examined the dog carefully. 兽医仔细地替那只狗做检查。

***example** /ɪg'zɑ:mpl; ɪg`zæmpl̩/ *n* 名

something you mention, to explain the kind of thing you are talking about 例子

The teacher asked me to give an example. 老师要我举个例子。

for example 例如；举例来说（**缩写：e.g.**）

Some animals, for example cows and sheep, eat grass. 有些动物吃草，例如牛和羊。

In the classroom 在教室里

"I'm sorry I don't understand." "Okay. Let me give you an example." "对不起，我不明白。" "好的，我来举个例子吧。"

***excellent** /'eksələnt; `ɛksl̩ənt/ *adj* 形

very good 优秀的；卓越的；杰出的

Lily's exam results were excellent. 莉莉的考试成绩优异。

同义 **outstanding**

In the classroom 在教室里

"You got all the answers correct. Excellent!" "Thank you." "你的答案全对。非常好！" "谢谢。"

except /ɪk'sept; ɪk`sɛpt/ *prep* 介

but not; apart from 除…以外

The library is open every day except Wednesday. 除星期三外，图书馆每天都开放。

***exchange** /ɪks'tʃeɪndʒ; ɪks`tʃendʒ/ *v* 动

exchanges, exchanging, exchanged, exchanged

to give in return for something else 交换；调换

We exchanged presents at the party. 我们在派对上交换礼物。

***excited** /ɪk'saɪtɪd; ɪk`saɪtɪd/ *adj* 形

feeling very happy, especially because something good has happened or is going to happen 兴奋的；激动的

I'm excited because my parents are taking me to Ocean Park this Sunday. 父母星期天会和我到海洋公园，所以我非常兴奋。

用法 excited 用来形容人的感受。

比较 **exciting**

***exciting** /ɪk'saɪtɪŋ; ɪk`saɪtɪŋ/ *adj* 形

making you feel very happy or interested 刺激的；令人兴奋的

The football match was very exciting. 那场足球比赛非常刺激。

用法 exciting 用来形容事物。

比较 **excited**

exclamation mark /ˌekskləˈmeɪʃn ˌmɑ:k; ˏɛkskləˋmeʃən ˏmɑrk/ *n* 名

the sign used at the end of a sentence to show surprise or anger (!) 感叹号

另见 **附录**：Punctuation 标点符号

***excuse[1]** /ɪk'skju:s; ɪk`skjus/ *n* 名

a reason you give for doing something wrong 借口；理由

He made excuses for being late this morning. 他为早上迟到的事找借口。

***excuse[2]** /ɪk'skju:z; ɪk`skjuz/ *v* 动

excuses, excusing, excused, excused

to forgive someone 原谅

Please excuse me for leaving early. 请原谅我要早退。

Daily conversation 日常会话

excuse me 请问；对不起（用于提问或道歉）

"Excuse me, where is the washroom?" "It's over there." "请问洗手间在哪儿？" "就在那儿。"

***exercise[1]** /'eksəsaɪz; `ɛksɚˏsaɪz/ *n* 名

1. activity that you do to make your body strong and healthy 运动；锻炼

Swimming is good exercise. 游

泳是很好的运动。

2. a piece of work you do to help you learn something 练习
   I have some math exercises to do today. 我今天要完成一些数学练习。

In the classroom 在教室里
"Now, please do Exercise 8 on page 30." "Okay." "请完成第 30 页的练习 8。" "好。"

***exercise²** /'eksəsaɪz; `ɛksɚˏsaɪz/ *v* 动

exercises, exercising, exercised, exercised

to do activities to make your body strong and healthy 做运动
You should exercise regularly. 你应该定时做运动。

exercise book /'eksəsaɪz ˌbʊk; `ɛksɚsaɪz ˏbʊk/ *n* 名

a book that students use to do their work for school 练习簿
Write all your answers in the exercise book. 把所有答案写在练习簿上。

exhausted /ɪɡ'zɔːstɪd; ɪɡ`zɔstɪd/ *adj* 形

very tired 筋疲力尽的

They were exhausted after walking all day. 他们走了一整天，感到筋疲力尽。

exhibition /ˌeksɪ'bɪʃn; ˏɛksə`bɪʃən/ *n* 名

a show where people can look at pictures or objects 展览
We went to see an exhibition of Chinese paintings at the museum. 我们到博物馆看国画展览。

***exist** /ɪɡ'zɪst; ɪɡ`zɪst/ *v* 动

if something exists, it is present in the world 存在
Dinosaurs do not exist now. 恐龙不再存在了。

***exit** /'eksɪt; `ɛɡzət/ *n* 名

a door or gate that you go through to leave a place 出口；通道
My classmates and I left the school hall by the nearest exit. 我和同学从最近的出口离开礼堂。

emergency/fire exit 紧急出口/消防通道
There is an emergency exit at the end of the corridor. 走廊的尽头有一个紧急出口。

反义 **entrance**

***expect** /ɪk'spekt; ɪk`spɛkt/ *v* 动

to think that something will happen 预期；预料
I expect it will rain this afternoon. 我以为今天下午会下雨。

***expensive** /ɪk'spensɪv; ɪk`spɛnsɪv/ *adj* 形

costing a lot of money 昂贵的
Mr Brown does not have enough money to buy that expensive watch. 布朗先生没有足够的钱买那只昂贵的手表。

同义 **dear**

反义 **cheap, inexpensive**

***experience** /ɪk'spɪəriəns; ɪk`spɪrɪəns/ *n* 名

1. （无复数）skill or knowledge you get from doing something 经验
   She is a teacher with many years of experience. 她是一位有多年教学经验的老师。

2. something that has happened to you 经历
   The school picnic was a happy experience for me. 我觉得这次学校旅行是一次开心的经历。

***experiment** /ɪk'sperɪmənt; ɪk`spɛrəmənt/ *n* 名

a test to see what happens, or to see if something is true 实验；试验

We did an experiment in the science lesson today. 我们今天上科学课时做了一个实验。

***explain** /ɪk'spleɪn; ɪk`splen/ *v* 动

1. to make something easy to understand 解释（某事使它易于理解）；说明
   The teacher explained the meaning of the poem to the students. 老师向学生解释这首诗的含义。
2. to say why you did something or why something happened 解释（做某事的理由、某事发生的原因等）；说明
   Henry explained why he was late. 亨利解释他迟到的原因。

In the classroom 在教室里
"I'm sorry I don't understand." "Okay. Let me explain." "对不起，我不明白。" "好的。我来解释一下吧。"

E

explode /ɪk'spləʊd; ɪkˋsplod/ *v* 动

explodes, exploding, exploded, exploded

to burst or make something burst loudly and dangerously 爆炸

A bomb exploded on a train and many passengers were hurt. 一枚炸弹在火车上爆炸，很多乘客受了伤。

***explore** /ɪk'splɔː; ɪkˋsplɔr/ *v* 动

explores, exploring, explored, explored

to travel around a place in order to find out more about it 探索；考察

There are lots of interesting places to explore in Beijing. 北京有很多有趣的地方让人去探索。

explorer /ɪk'splɔːrə; ɪkˋsplɔrə/ *n* 名

a person who travels to a place that people do not know much about, in order to find out more about it 探险家

Columbus was a famous explorer. 哥伦布是著名的探险家。

***express[1]** /ɪk'spres; ɪkˋsprɛs/ *v* 动

expresses, expressing, expressed, expressed

to say or show your feeling, thought, etc by words, actions, etc 表达；表示

The students expressed their opinions in class. 学生在课堂上表达了意见。

***express[2]** /ɪk'spres; ɪkˋsprɛs/ *n* 名

复数：***expresses***

a fast train or bus that only stops at a few places（火车或公共汽车的）快车

We took the express to the airport. 我们乘快车去机场。

expression /ɪk'spreʃn; ɪkˋsprɛʃən/ *n* 名

1. a word, or group of words 词语；表达方式

   "Shut up!" is a very rude expression. "闭嘴！"是非常粗鲁的话。

2. the look on your face 表情

The expression on his face was funny. 他脸上的表情很好笑。

***extra[1]** /'ekstrə; ˋɛkstrə/ *adj* 形

more than usual 额外的；附加的

Peter will need extra time to finish his homework because he is sick today. 彼得今天病了，需要额外的时间来完成作业。

***extra[2]** /'ekstrə; ˋɛkstrə/ *adv* 副

more than usual 额外地；附加地

You have to pay two dollars extra for cold drinks. 如果你要冷饮，需要多付2元。

extraordinary /ɪk'strɔːdnəri; ɪkˋstrɔrdṇɛrɪ/ *adj* 形

1. very unusual or strange 不寻常的；奇特的

   The birds fly thousands of miles every year. How extraordinary! 这些鸟儿每年飞数千英里，真令人惊奇！

   反义 **ordinary**

2. much better than usual 极好的；非凡的

   Candy has an extraordinary memory. 坎蒂拥有非凡的记忆力。

   反义 **ordinary**

***extremely** /ɪk'striːmli; ɪkˋstrimlɪ/ *adv* 副

very 非常；极度

Mr Brown was extremely busy today. 布朗先生今天非常忙碌。

***eye** /aɪ; aɪ/ *n* 名

one of the two parts in your face that you use to see 眼睛

Rabbits have red eyes. 兔子的眼睛是红色的。

eyebrow /'aɪbraʊ; ˋaɪˌbraʊ/ *n* 名

the line of hair above your eye 眉毛

Charles has thick eyebrows. 查尔斯的眉毛浓密。

eyelash /'aɪlæʃ; ˋaɪˌlæʃ/ *n* 名

复数：***eyelashes***

one of the hairs that grow along the edges of your eyes 眼睫毛

Her eyelashes are long and beautiful. 她的睫毛又长又漂亮。

fable /ˈfeɪbl; ˋfebl̩/ *n* 名

a short story, usually about animals, that teaches you something 寓言

Have you ever read a fable called "The Boy Who Cried Wolf"? 你有没有读过一则叫做《狼来了》的寓言？

***face**[1] /feɪs; fes/ *n* 名

the front part of your head 面部；脸

I wash my face every morning. 我每天早上洗脸。

make a face 做鬼脸

The clown made a face at us. 小丑对我们做了个鬼脸。

***face**[2] /feɪs; fes/ *v* 动

faces, facing, faced, faced

to point towards something 面向；朝

The balcony faces the sea. 阳台面向着大海。

facilities /fəˈsɪlətiz; fəˋsɪlətɪz/ *plural n* 复数名词

rooms, equipment, etc that are used for a special activity 设施；设备

My school has very good sports facilities. 我校有很好的运动设施。

***fact** /fækt; fækt/ *n* 名

something that is true 事实；真相

It is a fact that the sun rises in the east. 太阳从东方升起，这是事实。

in fact 事实上；其实

I don't like swimming. In fact, I hate it. 我不喜欢游泳，事实上我讨厌游泳。

***factor** /ˈfæktə; ˋfæktɚ/ *n* 名

1. one of several things that cause something 因素；要素

   The disease is caused by a number of factors. 这个病是由几个因素导致的。
2. a number that divides into another number exactly（数学）因子；因数

   2 and 5 are factors of 10. 2 和 5 都是 10 的因子。

***factory** /ˈfæktri; ˋfæktərɪ/ *n* 名

复数：***factories***

a place where people make things with machines 工厂

Alan works in a toy factory. 艾伦在玩具工厂上班。

fade /feɪd; fed/ *v* 动

fades, fading, faded, faded

to lose colour or to become less bright 褪色；失去光泽

The colour of the cloth has faded. 这块布料褪色了。

***fail** /feɪl; fel/ *v* 动

1. to not pass a test or an exam（测验或考试）不及格

   Ben failed the exam. 本考试不及格。

   反义 **pass**[1]
2. to not succeed 失败；未能

   The bus broke down on the road and Sally failed to arrive on time. 公共汽车在途中坏了，所以莎莉未能准时到达。

   反义 **succeed**

faint[1] /feɪnt; fent/ *adj* 形

fainter, faintest

not strong; not clear 微弱的；模糊的

We heard a faint sound in the dark. 我们听到黑暗中传来微弱的声音。

faint[2] /feɪnt; fent/ *v* 动

to suddenly lose the feeling that you are awake and fall down 晕倒

The beggar fainted because he was hungry. 那个乞丐因饥饿而晕倒了。

fair /feə; fɛr/ *adj* 形

fairer, fairest

1. treating everyone equally 公平的

   Why do you give her more chocolates? It's not fair! 为什么你给她的巧克力多？这样不公平！

   反义 **unfair**
2. good, but not very good 尚可的；一般的

   His Chinese is very good but his English is only fair. 他的中文很好，但英文只是一般水平。

注意 发音与 fare 相同。

F

fairly /ˈfeəli; ˋfɛrlɪ/ *adv* 副

more than a little, but less than very 相当；颇

Your school results are fairly good this term. 你这个学期的成绩不错。

同义 **quite**

fairy /ˈfeəri; ˋfɛrɪ/ *n* 名

复数：*fairies*

(in stories) a small person with wings who has magic powers 神仙；小仙子

In the story, the fairies made the girl's wishes come true. 在故事中，神仙让小女孩愿望成真。

fairy tale 童话

Our teacher told us a fairy tale today. 老师今天给我们讲了一个童话。

faithful /ˈfeɪθfl; ˋfeθfəl/ *adj* 形

loyal to someone and continuing to support them 忠诚的；忠实的

Mary is a faithful friend. 玛丽是一位忠实的朋友。

***fall[1]** /fɔːl; fɔl/ *v* 动

falls, falling, fell, fallen

to drop or go down from a higher position to a lower position 落下；跌落；倒下

Some apples fell to the ground. 一些苹果掉落在地上。

fall behind 落后；跟不上

You are falling behind with your school work and you need to work harder. 你跟不上学校的进度，所以应该再努力一些。

fall down 摔下

The man fell down the stairs. 那个人从楼梯上摔了下来。

fall over 跌倒

I fell over because the floor was very slippery. 地面很湿滑，所以我跌倒了。

fall to pieces 破碎

The vase fell to pieces. 花瓶摔碎了。

fall[2] /fɔːl; fɔl/ *n* 名【美】

英式 **autumn**

fallen /fɔːlən; fɔlən/ *v* 动

the past participle of **fall[1]** ☆fall[1] 的过去分词

***false** /fɔːls; fɔls/ *adj* 形

1. not true or correct 不正确的；错误的

   Please put a cross next to the false sentences. 请在错误的句子旁打叉。

2. not real 假的；不真实的

   My grandfather has false teeth. 爷爷镶了假牙。

familiar /fəˈmɪliə; fəˋmɪljə/ *adj* 形

well-known to you 熟悉的

I heard a familiar voice. 我听到一个熟悉的声音。

***family** /ˈfæmli; ˋfæməlɪ/ *n* 名

复数：*families*

a group of people which includes parents and their children 家庭；家人

Mr Brown works in Hong Kong, but his family is in Canada. 布朗先生在香港工作，但他的家人在加拿大。

family name 姓氏

Could you tell me your family name? 请问你贵姓？

family tree 家谱

Can you draw your family tree? 你能把你的家谱画出来吗？

***famous** /ˈfeɪməs; ˋfeməs/ *adj* 形

known by many people 著名的

Mount Fuji is a famous mountain in Japan. 富士山是日本的一座名山。

famous for 以…闻名

That restaurant is famous for its desserts. 那家餐厅以甜品闻名。

***fan** /fæn; fæn/ *n* 名

1. something that moves the air to make you cooler 扇；风扇

   He turned on the electric fan. 他开了电风扇。

2. someone who likes a famous person, sports team, etc very much 歌迷；影迷；球迷

   Roger is a fan of Bruce Lee. 罗杰是李小龙的影迷。

fancy /ˈfænsi; ˋfænsɪ/ *v* 动【英】

fancies, fancying, fancied, fancied

to want something or want to do something 想要

It's hot today. I fancy a swim. 今天很热，我想去游泳。

***fantastic** /fænˈtæstɪk; fænˋtæstɪk/ *adj* 形

very good, enjoyable, etc 极好的

We had a fantastic holiday! 我们过了一个很棒的假期！

同义 great

Daily conversation 日常会话
"I've won the first prize!" "Fantastic!" "我得了第一名！""太棒了！"

***far[1]** /fɑː; fɑr/ *adv* 副

farther/further, farthest/furthest

1. a long distance 远
   Jack lives far from school. 杰克住得离学校很远。

反义 near[2]

2. very much 非常；十分
   He runs far faster than I do. 他远比我跑得快。

by far 显然；…得多
He is by far the best boxer. 他显然是最出色的拳击手。

far away 遥远的
Mars is far away from Earth. 火星离地球很远。

so far 到目前为止；直到现在
So far you have done well. 到目前为止，你做得不错。

***far[2]** /fɑː; fɑr/ *adj* 形

farther/further, farthest/furthest

a long distance from a place 远的；遥远的
The park isn't far from here. We can walk there. 公园离这儿不远，我们可以走路过去。

反义 near[3]

***fare** /feə; fɛr/ *n* 名

money you pay to travel on a bus, train, etc 票价；车费
What is the bus fare to the airport? 到机场的公共汽车费是多少？

注意 发音与 fair 相同。

比较 fee

***farm** /fɑːm; fɑrm/ *n* 名

a place where people grow food or keep animals 农场

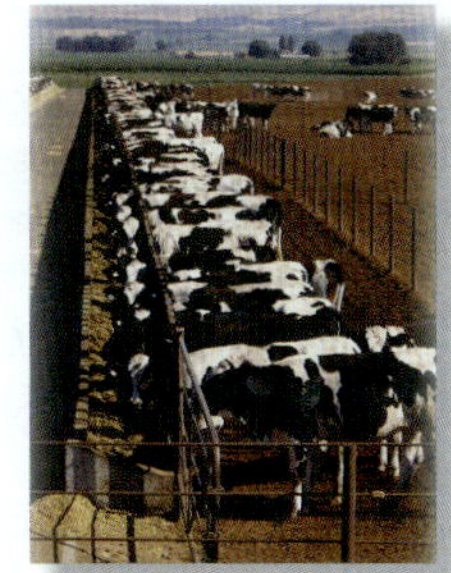

I stayed on my uncle's farm during summer holidays. 暑假时我住在伯伯的农场上。

farmer /ˈfɑːmə; ˋfɑrmɚ/ *n* 名

a person who owns or works on a farm 农场主人；农夫

My mother buys vegetables from local farmers. 妈妈向本地农夫那里买蔬菜。

farther[1] /ˈfɑːðə; ˋfɑrðɚ/, **further** /ˈfɜːðə; ˋfɝðɚ/ *adv* 副（*far*[1] 的比较级）

at or to a greater distance 更远地
How much farther do we have to walk? 我们还要走多远？

farther[2] /ˈfɑːðə; ˋfɑrðɚ/, **further** /ˈfɜːðə; ˋfɝðɚ/ *adj* 形（*far*[2] 的比较级）

at a greater distance 更远的
The restaurant is at the farther end of the road. 餐厅在这条路的较远处。

用法 只可用于名词前。

farthest[1] /ˈfɑːðɪst; ˋfɑrðɪst/, **furthest** /ˈfɜːðɪst; ˋfɝðɪst/ *adv* 副（*far*[1] 的最高级）

at or to the greatest distance 最远地
Annie jumped the farthest in the competition. 安妮在比赛中跳得最远。

farthest[2] /ˈfɑːðɪst; ˋfɑrðɪst/, **furthest** /ˈfɜːðɪst; ˋfɝðɪst/ *adj* 形（*far*[2] 的最高级）

at the greatest distance 最远的
The farthest destination of his trip is the North Pole. 他旅行最远的目的地是北极。

***fashion** /ˈfæʃn; ˋfæʃən/ *n* 名

the popular way of dressing or doing something 时装；潮流
This shop sells new fashions. 这家商店卖流行时装。

***fast[1]** /fɑːst; fæst/ *adj* 形

faster, fastest

1. moving or doing something quickly 快的；迅速的
   This is a fast horse. 这是一匹快马。

反义 slow

2. if a clock or watch is fast, it shows a time that is later than the real time（钟、表）偏快的
   Your watch is five minutes fast. 你的表快了 5 分钟。

反义 slow

Daily conversation 日常会话
"What's the fastest way to get to the airport?" "By taxi!" "怎样去机场最快？""坐计程车吧！"

***fast[2]** /fɑːst; fæst/ *adv* 副

quickly 快速地
Don't drive too fast. 车不要开得太快。

反义 slowly

fasten /ˈfɑːsn; ˋfæsn̩/ *v* 动

to join together two sides of something so that it is closed 系紧；扣上
Please fasten your seat belt. 请系上安全带。

fast food / ˈfɑːst fuːd; ˋfæst fud/ *n* 名

无复数

F

food such as burgers and chips that is quick to cook and can be taken away with you 快餐
My doctor told me not to eat too much fast food. 医生叫我不要吃太多快餐。
fast food shop 快餐店
We had our lunch at a fast food shop. 我们在快餐店吃午饭。

***fat** /fæt; fæt/ *adj* 形
fatter, fattest
if a person is fat, he or she weighs too much 肥胖的
You will get fat if you eat too much. 你吃太多的话就会发胖。
反义 **skinny, slim, thin**

***father** /ˈfɑːðə; ˋfɑðɚ/ *n* 名
a male parent 父亲；爸爸
The boy looks like his father. 那个男孩长得像他的父亲。
用法 father 常用于比较正式的场合或书面语。
比较 **dad, daddy**

Father Christmas /ˌfɑːðə ˈkrɪsməs; ˌfɑðɚ ˋkrɪsməs/ *n* 名【英】
an old man who wears red clothes and is said to bring presents to children at Christmas 圣诞老人
Darren acted the part of Father Christmas in the play. 达伦在戏剧里扮演圣诞老人。

同义 **Santa Claus**

fault /fɔːlt; fɔlt/ *n* 名
something wrong with a machine, or with someone's character（机器的）故障；（人的）缺点
The problem was caused by a fault in the ship's engine. 这个问题是船的引擎故障导致的。
be someone's fault 过失；责任
Don't blame Joe. It's not his fault. 不要责备乔，那不是他的错。

favor /ˈfeɪvə; ˋfevɚ/ *n* 名【美】
英式 **favour**

favorite /ˈfeɪvrət; ˋfevərɪt/ *adj* 形【美】
英式 **favourite**

favour /ˈfeɪvə; ˋfevɚ/ *n* 名【英】
美式：***favor***
something that you do to help someone 恩惠；帮忙
Can you do me a favour? 可以请你帮个忙吗？

***favourite** /ˈfeɪvrət; ˋfevərɪt/ *adj* 形【英】
美式：***favorite***
your favourite thing or person is the one that you like the most 最喜爱的
My favourite food is chocolate. 我最喜爱的食物是巧克力。

Daily conversation 日常会话
"Who's your favourite singer?" "I'm a fan of Justin Bieber." "你最喜欢的歌手是谁？""我是贾斯汀·比伯的歌迷。"

***fear¹** /fɪə; fɪr/ *n* 名
the feeling of being afraid of something or someone 害怕；惧怕
Angela has a great fear of spiders. 安琪拉非常害怕蜘蛛。

fear² /fɪə; fɪr/ *v* 动
to be afraid of someone or something 害怕；惧怕
We feared that we would get lost in the forest. 我们非常担心会在森林迷路。

feast /fiːst; fist/ *n* 名
a large meal of good food for many people to celebrate something 盛宴；宴会

The king held a feast in his palace. 国王在王宫里举行了一场盛宴。

***feather** /ˈfeðə; ˋfɛðɚ/ *n* 名
one of the light, soft things that covers a bird's body 羽毛
The parrot has very beautiful feathers. 那只鹦鹉的羽毛非常漂亮。

***February** /ˈfebruəri; ˋfɛbruˌɛrɪ/ *n* 名
复数：***Februaries*** | 缩写：***Feb.***
the second month of the year 二月
Mike's birthday is in February. 迈克的生日在 2 月。
注意 开头的字母必须用大写。

fed /fed; fɛd/ *v* 动
the past tense and past participle of **feed** ☆feed 的过去式和过去分词

fee /fi:; fi/ *n* 名

money paid to a school, a doctor, a lawyer, etc 费用；酬金

It's a good school, but the fees are very high. 这是一所好学校，但学费很昂贵。

比较 **fare**

***feed** /fi:d; fid/ *v* 动

feeds, feeding, fed, fed

to give food to a person or an animal 喂；饲养

I feed my cat twice a day. 我每天喂两次猫。

***feel** /fi:l; fil/ *v* 动

feels, feeling, felt, felt

1. to have a particular feeling 觉得；感到

   I closed the windows because I felt cold. 我觉得冷，所以关上了窗。

2. to give you a particular feeling when you touch something 触摸；感觉

   My cat's fur feels soft. 我那只猫的毛摸起来很柔软。

feel like something 想要某物；想做某事

The little girl felt like crying. 那个小女孩想要哭。

> **Daily conversation 日常会话**
>
> *"You look pale. Are you okay?" "I feel sick."* "你看来很苍白，没事吧？" "我觉得恶心。"

***feeling** /ˈfi:lɪŋ; ˋfilɪŋ/ *n* 名

something that you feel, such as anger or happiness 感觉；感情

Your words have hurt her feelings. 你的话伤害了她的感情。

feet /fi:t; fit/ *n* 名

the plural of **foot** ☆foot 的复数形式

fell /fel; fɛl/ *v* 动

the past tense of **fall**[1] ☆fall[1] 的过去式

felt /felt; fɛlt/ *v* 动

the past tense and past participle of **feel** ☆feel 的过去式和过去分词

***female** /ˈfi:meɪl; ˋfi͵mel/ *adj* 形

relating to women or girls, or the sex that can produce babies or eggs 女性的；雌性的；母的

Mrs Smith has a female dog. 史密斯太太养了一条母狗。

反义 **male**

***fence** /fens; fɛns/ *n* 名

a thing like a wall that is made of wood or wire and is put around an area of land 篱笆；围栏

George built a fence round the garden. 乔治在花园四周筑了篱笆。

***ferry** /ˈferi; ˋfɛrɪ/ *n* 名

复数：***ferries***

a boat that takes people, vehicles, or goods across an area of water 渡船；渡轮

You can take the ferry across the harbour. 你可以乘渡轮过海港。

***festival** /ˈfestɪvl; ˋfɛstəvl̩/ *n* 名

a day or time when people celebrate something 节日；节庆

Chinese New Year is the most important festival to Chinese people. 农历新年是中国人最重要的节日。

fetch /fetʃ; fɛtʃ/ *v* 动

fetches, fetching, fetched, fetched

to go and get someone or something and bring them back 拿来；取回

Please fetch me my school bag. 请替我把书包拿过来。

fetch someone from something 去某处接某人

Mrs Smith fetched her children from school. 史密斯太太去学校把孩子接回家。

***fever** /ˈfi:və; ˋfivɚ/ *n* 名

a body temperature that is higher than normal, usually caused by illness 发烧

Frank had a high fever last night. 法兰克昨晚发高烧。

***few**[1] /fju:; fju/ *adj* 形

fewer, fewest

1. not many people or things 不多的；很少的

   Few people like snakes. 很少有人喜欢蛇。

   反义 **many**[1]

   比较 **little**[1]

2. **a few** a small number of people or things; some 一些；几个

   I will be away from Hong Kong for a few days. 我会离开香港几天。

用法 few 和 a few 与复数名词一起使用。

F

***few²** /fjuː; fju/ *pron* 代

1. not many people or things 不多；很少
   His stories are very interesting, but few are true. 他说的故事很有趣，但很少是真实的。
2. **a few** a small number of people or things; some 一些；几个
   He has written many books but only a few are popular. 他写了很多本书，但只有几本畅销。

F

***field** /fiːld; fild/ *n* 名

1. a piece of land used for keeping animals or growing crops 田地；田野

   The farmers are working in the field. 农民正在田里工作。
2. an open area where people play ball games 运动场
   The boys were playing on the football field. 那些男孩在足球场上踢球。

fierce /fɪəs; fɪrs/ *adj* 形

fiercer, fiercest

looking angry or ready to attack 凶猛的；凶恶的
Gordon keeps a fierce dog. 戈登养了一条恶狗。

***fifteen** /ˌfɪfˈtiːn; ˌfɪfˋtin/ *num* 数

the number 15 十五
Five and ten equals fifteen. 5 加 10 等于 15。

fifteenth /ˌfɪfˈtiːnθ; ˌfɪfˋtinθ/ *ordinal num* 序数

15th in order 第十五（的）
We live on the fifteenth floor. 我们住在 15 楼。

fifth /fɪfθ; fɪfθ/ *ordinal num* 序数

5th in order 第五（的）
May is the fifth month of the year. 5 月是一年的第 5 个月。

fiftieth /ˈfɪftiəθ; ˋfɪftɪɪθ/ *ordinal num* 序数

50th in order 第五十（的）
Today is May's fiftieth birthday. 今天是梅的 50 岁生日。

***fifty** /ˈfɪfti; ˋfɪftɪ/ *num* 数

the number 50 五十
There are fifty members in the swimming club. 游泳俱乐部有 50 名会员。
fifty-fifty 均等的；一半的
He has a fifty-fifty chance of winning. 他获胜的机率是百分之五十。

***fight** /faɪt; faɪt/ *v* 动

fights, fighting, fought, fought

to try to hurt someone by hitting or kicking them 打架
The two cocks are fighting. 那两只公鸡在打架。

***figure** /ˈfɪgə; ˋfɪgjɚ/ *n* 名

a written number such as 2, 4, 6, or 9 数字
She has a very good job and she earns a six figure salary. 她有一份好工作，薪金达六位数字。

***file** /faɪl; faɪl/ *n* 名

1. a box or folded piece of thick paper for keeping papers in order 文件夹；文件箱
   I put all the worksheets in a file. 我把所有工作表放入一个文件夹。
2. 【电脑】a computer document 档案；文件
   Please email the file to me. 请把那份文件发电子邮件给我。

***fill** /fɪl; fɪl/ *v* 动

也作：***fill up***

to make something full or to become full of something 填满；盛满
He filled the glass with milk. 他在杯子里倒满了牛奶。
fill in/out 填写
Please fill in the form. 请填写这份表格。

反义 **empty²**

***film** /fɪlm; fɪlm/ *n* 名【英】

美式：***movie***

moving pictures shown on television or at a cinema 电影；影片
We saw a film about animals. 我们看了一部关于动物的电影。
film star 电影明星
Candy wants to become a film star. 坎蒂想当电影明星。

***final** /ˈfaɪnl; ˋfaɪnḷ/ *adj* 形

being or happening at the end of something; last 最后的；最终的
We had our final exam today. 我们今天期末考试。

***finally** /ˈfaɪnəli; ˋfaɪnḷɪ/ *adv* 副

1. after a long time 终于；最终
   I finally finished my homework. 我终于完成了我的作业。
2. used to talk about the last thing in a list 最后
   Finally, I would like to thank my teachers for their help. 最后，我要感谢老师们给我的帮助。

同义 **lastly**

***find** /faɪnd; faɪnd/ *v* 动

finds, finding, found, found

1. to see or get something after looking for it, especially something you have lost 找到；发现
   I can't find my train ticket! 我找不到我的火车票了！

反义 **lose**

2. to discover something that you did not expect 碰见；（偶然）发现

   I found a pencil bag in the corridor. 我在走廊找到了一个笔袋。

3. to discover or learn something 发现；找出

   Sophie finally found a solution to the problem. 苏菲终于找到了问题的答案。

find out 查明；查出

We have found out that you were lying. 我们查出你在说谎。

*fine /faɪn; faɪn/ *adj* 形

finer, finest

1. very good; very nice 很好的；优秀的

   She is a fine actress. 她是一个优秀的演员。

2. sunny and not raining 晴朗的

   The weather is fine today. 今天天气很好。

Daily conversation 日常会话

"How are you?" "Fine, thanks." "你好吗？""很好，谢谢。"

*finger /ˈfɪŋgə; ˋfɪŋgɚ/ *n* 名

any of the five long thin parts of your hand 手指

She pressed the button with her finger. 她用手指按键。

*finish /ˈfɪnɪʃ; ˋfɪnɪʃ/ *v* 动

finishes, finishing, finished, finished

1. to do all of something 完成；做完

   I always finish my homework before dinner. 我总是在晚饭前完成功课。

2. to come to the end 结束

   The football match finished at five o'clock. 足球比赛在5点结束。

反义 **begin, start**[1]

3. to eat or drink something completely so that there is nothing left 吃光；喝光

   She has finished her lunch. 她吃完午餐了。

*fire[1] /faɪə; faɪr/ *n* 名

1. the flames, light and heat from something burning 火

   Children shouldn't play with fire. 儿童不应该玩火。

2. flames and heat that destroy things 火灾

   There was a fire here yesterday. 昨天这里失火了。

catch fire 着火

Dry wood catches fire easily. 干柴很容易着火。

on fire 着火

The house is on fire! 房子着火了！

fire[2] /faɪə; faɪr/ *v* 动

fires, firing, fired, fired

to shoot with a gun 射击；开枪

The policeman fired his gun into the air. 那个警察朝天开枪。

fire engine /ˈfaɪər ˌendʒɪn; ˋfaɪr ˏɛndʒən/ *n* 名

a large truck that carries firefighters and their equipment to a fire 消防车

The fire engines came five minutes after I called 119. 我打了119之后5分钟消防车就来了。

fire extinguisher /ˈfaɪər ɪkˌstɪŋgwɪʃə; ˋfaɪr ɪkˏstɪŋgwɪʃɚ/ *n* 名

a thing for stopping a small fire 灭火器

There is a fire extinguisher on each floor of the school. 学校各层都放了灭火器。

firefighter /ˈfaɪəˌfaɪtə; ˋfaɪrˏfaɪtɚ/ *n* 名

someone whose job is to stop fires 消防员

The firefighters put out the fire quickly. 消防员很快就把火扑灭了。

firefly /ˈfaɪəflaɪ; ˋfaɪrˏflaɪ/ *n* 名

复数：***fireflies***

an insect that shines in the dark 萤火虫

We saw some fireflies near the pond. 我们在池塘边看见了萤火虫。

fire station /ˈfaɪə ˌsteɪʃn; ˋfaɪr ˏsteʃən/ *n* 名

a building where firefighters wait with their fire engines until they are needed 消防局
My class visited a fire station today. 我的班级今天参观了消防局。

*__firework__ /'faɪəwɜ:k; `faɪr͵wɝk/ *n* 名

a thing that makes very loud noises and colourful lights when it explodes 烟花；烟火

Where is the best place to see the fireworks? 哪里是观赏烟花的最佳位置？

firm[1] /fɜ:m; fɝm/ *adj* 形

firmer, firmest

if something is firm, it does not feel soft when you press it 结实的
The tomatoes are fresh and firm. 这些番茄又新鲜又硬。

*__firm__[2] /fɜ:m; fɝm/ *n* 名

a company 公司；商号
My uncle works at a trading firm. 我的舅舅在一家贸易公司工作。

*__first__[1] /fɜ:st; fɝst/ *ordinal num* 序数

number one in order 第一（的）
Steve was the first person to get to the top of the mountain. 史蒂夫是第一个抵达山顶的人。

for the first time 第一次；头一次
I saw a shark for the first time in my life. 我有生以来第一次看见鲨鱼。

反义 **last**[1]

*__first__[2] /fɜ:st; fɝst/ *adv* 副

before anything else; at the beginning 首先；起初
First I got up, and then I brushed my teeth. 我先起床，然后刷牙。

at first 最初
At first, I didn't like her. 起初我不喜欢她。

first of all 首先；第一
First of all, listen to the CD carefully. Then answer the questions in the exercise book. 请先细心听 CD，然后回答练习册中的问题。

反义 **last**[2]

first aid /ˌfɜ:st 'eɪd; ˏfɝst `ed/ *n* 名

无复数

quick help given to someone who is hurt or suddenly becomes ill 急救
Henry knows how to give first aid. 亨利懂得急救。

first name /'fɜ:st neɪm; `fɝst nem/ *n* 名

the name that comes before an English family name 名字
What is your first name, Mr Brown? 布朗先生，请问你叫什么名字？

另见 **family name**（见 **family**），**last name, surname**

*__fish__[1] /fɪʃ; fɪʃ/ *n* 名

复数：***fish/fishes***

an animal that lives in water 鱼；鱼类
There are lots of fish in the sea. 海里有很多鱼。

用法 复数一般用 fish，但指不同品种的鱼类时可用 fishes。

fish[2] /fɪʃ; fɪʃ/ *v* 动

fishes, fishing, fished, fished

to try to catch fish 钓鱼；捕鱼
Sam is fishing by the river. 山姆在河边钓鱼。

fisherman /'fɪʃəmən; `fɪʃɚmən/ *n* 名

复数：***fishermen***

someone who catches fish 渔人
The fishermen go out to fish early in the morning. 渔夫一大早就出海捕鱼。

fishing /'fɪʃɪŋ; `fɪʃɪŋ/ *n* 名

无复数

the sport or job of catching fish 钓鱼；捕鱼

Dad goes fishing once a month. 爸爸每个月钓一次鱼。

fist /fɪst; fɪst/ *n* 名

the hand with the fingers closed tightly 拳头

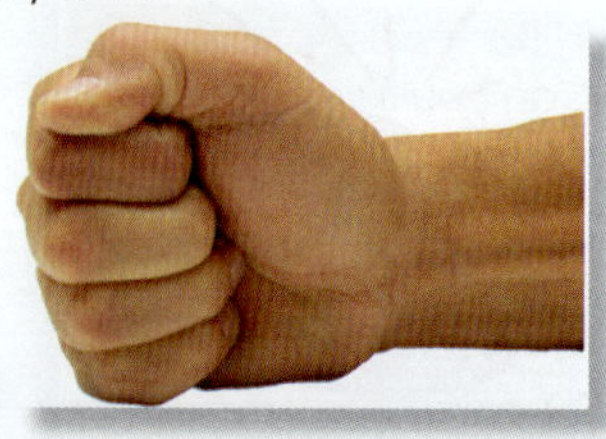

Bill hit me with his fists. 比尔用拳头打了我。

***fit¹** /fɪt; fɪt/ *adj* 形

fitter, fittest

1. healthy and strong 强壮的；健康的
   She is very fit because she swims every day. 她身体很健康，因为每天都游泳。
2. suitable or good enough for someone or something 适合的；恰当的
   This TV programme is not fit for children. 这个电视节目不适合儿童观看。

***fit²** /fɪt; fɪt/ *v* 动

fits, fitting, fitted, fitted

to be the right size and shape or suitable for someone or something 合身；适合

This T-shirt doesn't fit me. 这件 T 恤我穿起来不合身。

***five** /faɪv; faɪv/ *num* 数

the number 5 五

There are five classrooms on each floor. 每层有 5 个教室。

fix /fɪks; fɪks/ *v* 动

fixes, fixing, fixed, fixed

1. to mend 修理
   Can you fix my watch? 你能修好我的手表吗？
2. to fasten something to something else so that it cannot move 固定；安装
   My father fixed the mirror to the wall. 爸爸把镜子固定在墙上。
3. to arrange 安排
   We have fixed the date for the picnic. 我们定好了野餐的日期。

***flag** /flæg; flæg/ *n* 名

a piece of cloth with a special design that represents a country or group 旗；旗帜

The flag of Hong Kong has a flower in the centre. 香港区旗中间有一朵花。

flame /fleɪm; flem/ *n* 名

bright burning gas from something that is on fire 火焰

I saw flames coming out of the house. 我看见火焰从房子里冒出来。

in flames 熊熊燃烧；熊熊烈火

The whole building was in flames. 整座大楼被火海淹没。

flap /flæp; flæp/ *v* 动

flaps, flapping, flapped, flapped

if a bird flaps its wings it moves them up and down to fly（鸟）振翼；拍（翅膀）

The birds flapped their wings to fly. 鸟儿拍打翅膀飞起来。

***flash¹** /flæʃ; flæʃ/ *n* 名

复数：***flashes***

a sudden bright light that shines for a short time 闪光

There was a flash of lightning. 那里有一道闪电 。

flash² /flæʃ; flæʃ/ *v* 动

flashes, flashing, flashed, flashed

to give out a sudden bright light for a short time 发出闪光；闪亮

A light flashed and then disappeared. 一道光闪了一下就消失了。

flask /flɑːsk; flæsk/ *n* 名

a special bottle for keeping liquids either hot or cold 保温瓶

She poured out a cup of hot tea from the flask. 她从保温瓶中倒了一杯热茶。

***flat¹** /flæt; flæt/ *adj* 形

flatter, flattest

having no part higher than another; not hilly 平的；平坦的

They built their houses on flat land. 他们在平地上建房子。

反义 **steep**

***flat²** /flæt; flæt/ *n* 名【英】

美式：***apartment***

a set of rooms for people to live in 一套房子；（居住）单位

There are eight flats on each floor. 每层楼有 8 套房子。

***flavour** /ˈfleɪvə; ˋflevɚ/ *n* 名【英】

美式：***flavor***

the taste of a food or drink 味道

This shop sells 20 flavours of ice cream. 这家店卖 20 种口味的冰淇淋。

flew /fluː; flu/ *v* 动

F

the past tense of **fly**[1] ☆fly[1] 的过去式

flies[1] /flaɪz; flaɪz/ *v* 动

a form of **fly**[1] ☆fly[1] 的另一种现在式，与主语 he、she 和 it 一起使用

flies[2] /flaɪz; flaɪz/ *n* 名

the plural of **fly**[2] ☆fly[2] 的复数形式

flight /flaɪt; flaɪt/ *n* 名

a journey by plane 航程；航班

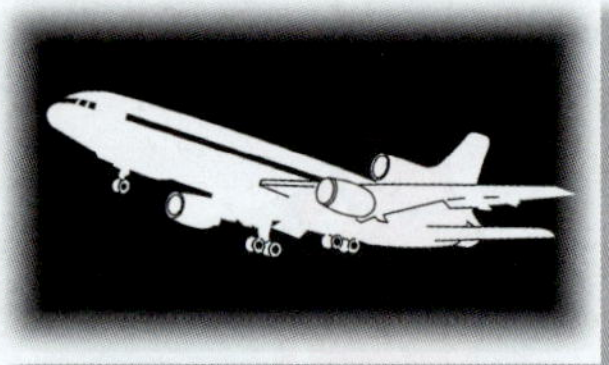

How long is the flight from London to Paris? 从伦敦飞往巴黎的航程需要多久？

***float** /fləʊt; flot/ *v* 动

to stay or move slowly on top of a liquid or in the air 浮；漂；飘浮

There is a flower floating in the pool. 一朵花浮在池面上。

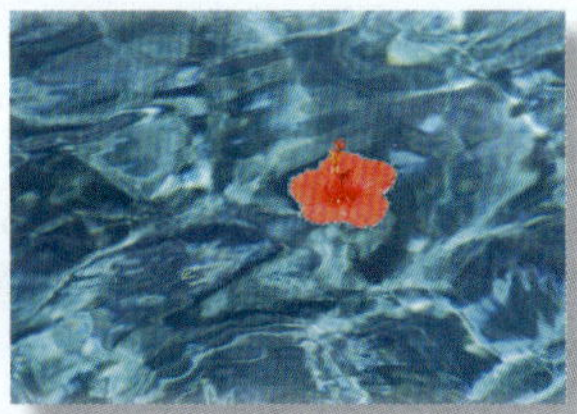

反义 **sink**[2]

flood[1] /flʌd; flʌd/ *n* 名

a lot of water covering a place that is usually dry 水灾；洪水

The floods destroyed many houses. 洪水冲毁了许多房屋。

flood[2] /flʌd; flʌd/ *v* 动

to cover with a lot of water, or to become covered with water 淹没

The fields were flooded after the storm. 暴风雨过后，田地被淹没了。

***floor** /flɔː; flɔr/ *n* 名

1. the part of a building that you stand on 地板

   The baby is crawling on the floor. 婴儿在地板上爬行。

比较 **ground**

2. a level in a building 层

   There are sixty floors in this building. 这座大楼有 60 层。

florist /ˈflɒrɪst; ˋflɔrɪst/ *n* 名

也作：***florist's***

a shop that sells flowers 花店

He bought a bunch of roses at the florist. 他在花店买了一束玫瑰。

***flour** /ˈflaʊə; flaʊr/ *n* 名

无复数

powder that is made from grain and used for making bread, cake, etc 面粉

We use flour to make bread. 我们用面粉做面包。

***flow** /fləʊ; flo/ *v* 动

if a liquid flows, it moves without stopping 流；流动

The water is flowing into the sea. 水正流入大海。

***flower** /ˈflaʊə; ˋflaʊɚ/ *n* 名

the coloured part of a plant where the seed or fruit develops 花

I put some flowers in the vase. 我把几朵花插进花瓶里。

flown /fləʊn; flon/ *v* 动

the past participle of **fly**[1] ☆fly[1] 的过去分词

flu /fluː; flu/ *n* 名

无复数

an illness, like a very bad cold with a fever 流行性感冒

Susan didn't come to school because she had the flu. 苏珊没来上学，因为她患了流感。

flush /flʌʃ; flʌʃ/ *v* 动

flushes, flushing, flushed, flushed

1. to become red in the face, especially because you are ashamed or angry 脸红

   Connie flushed when she heard these words. 康妮听到这些话，脸红了。

2. to clean a toilet by making water go through it 冲洗（厕所）

   Flush the toilet after using it. 用后请冲厕。

flute /fluːt; flut/ *n* 名

a musical instrument that looks like a pipe 长笛

Helen is learning how to play the flute. 海伦在学吹长笛。

*fly[1] /flaɪ; flaɪ/ *v* 动

flies, flying, flew, flown

1. to move through the air 飞

   The birds are flying in the sky. 鸟儿在天空中飞。

2. to travel by plane 坐飞机

   We are flying to Bangkok tomorrow. 我们明天乘飞机去曼谷。

*fly[2] /flaɪ; flaɪ/ *n* 名

复数：***flies***

a small insect with wings 苍蝇

Don't let the flies touch the food! 不要让苍蝇碰到食物！

flying saucer /ˌflaɪ-ɪŋ ˈsɔːsə; ˌflaɪɪŋ ˋsɔsɚ/ *n* 名

a round flying object that comes from space 飞碟；不明飞行物

Some people believe in flying saucers. 有些人相信有飞碟。

同义 UFO

flyover /ˈflaɪəʊvə; ˋflaɪˌovɚ/ *n* 名

a bridge that takes one road over another road 天桥；立交桥

There was a traffic jam on the flyover. 天桥上交通堵塞。

比较 footbridge

fog /fɒg; fag/ *n* 名

thick cloud near the ground which is difficult to see through 雾

We got lost in the fog. 我们在雾中迷路了。

foggy /ˈfɒgi; ˋfagɪ/ *adj* 形

foggier, foggiest

full of fog 有雾的

Tomorrow will be foggy. 明天会有雾。

*fold /fəʊld; fold/ *v* 动

to bend one part of something over another part 折叠

I folded the letter and put it in the envelope. 我把信折好放进信封里。

fold something up 把东西折叠

Fold your clothes up. 把你的衣服叠好。

fold your arms 双臂交叉放在胸前

He folded his arms and looked at me. 他把手臂交叉放在胸前，看着我。

folder /ˈfəʊldə; ˋfoldɚ/ *n* 名

1. a container for keeping loose papers 文件夹

   I put the drawings in a folder. 我把画放进文件夹里。

2. 【电脑】a group of files stored on a computer 资料夹；文件夹

   I deleted the folder on the computer. 我把电脑中的这个文件夹删除了。

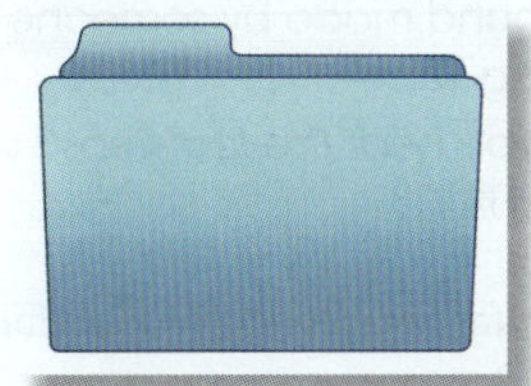

*follow /ˈfɒləʊ; ˋfalo/ *v* 动

1. to walk, drive etc a short distance behind someone or something 跟随

   My dog loves to follow me everywhere. 我的狗喜欢跟着我四处跑。

2. to understand something or someone 明白

   Am I speaking too fast? Can you follow me? 我会不会说得太快？明白我在说什么吗？

3. to accept instructions, etc and do what someone has asked you to do 跟着做；服从

   Please follow the instructions carefully when you use the oven. 请小心按指示使用烤炉。

as follows 如下

The answers to the questions are as follows. 这些问题的答案如下。

fond /fɒnd; fand/ *adj* 形

fonder, fondest

1. **be fond of someone or (doing) something**

   liking something or someone a lot 很喜欢（某人或做某事）

   Maggie is very fond of music. 玛姬非常喜欢音乐。

2. showing that you like someone a lot 温柔的；深情的

   The father gave his daughter a fond look. 那父亲温柔地看着他的女儿。

用法 只可用于名词前。

font /fɒnt; fant/ *n* 名

【电脑】a set of letters and symbols

F

of a particular design and size, used in printing or on computers 字体
You can use different fonts when you type. 你可以用不同的字体来打字。

Hello ***Hello***
HELLO *Hello*

F

***food** /fuːd; fud/ *n* 名
无复数
things that people or animals eat 食物；食品
Mrs White likes Chinese food. 怀特太太喜欢吃中餐。

***fool** /fuːl; ful/ *n* 名
a silly person 笨人；傻瓜
You are a fool. How can you believe him? 你是个傻瓜。怎么能相信他呢?
make a fool of someone 愚弄某人
Don't try to make a fool of me! 别想愚弄我!

foolish /ˈfuːlɪʃ; ˋfulɪʃ/ *adj* 形
stupid or silly 笨的；愚蠢的
It was a foolish mistake. 那是一个愚蠢的错误。
反义 clever

***foot** /fʊt; fut/ *n* 名
复数：*feet*
1. the part of your body below the ankle that you stand on 足；脚
   My feet ached after I went hiking last Sunday. 我上星期日远足后，双脚很痛。
2. a unit of length. There are 12 inches in a foot. 英尺
   David is five feet tall. 大卫的身高是5英尺。

on foot 步行
I go to school on foot. 我走路上学。

***football** /ˈfʊtbɔːl; ˋfutˌbɔl/ *n* 名
1. （无复数）a ball game where two teams of players try to kick a ball into the other team's goal 足球运动
   Mike plays football on Saturdays. 迈克逢星期六踢足球。
2. a ball used in a football game 足球

Steven kicked the football into the goal. 史蒂芬把足球踢进了球门。

footbridge /ˈfʊtˌbrɪdʒ; ˋfutˌbrɪdʒ/ *n* 名
a bridge for people to walk on 人行桥
We can cross the road on a footbridge. 我们可以从人行桥过马路。
比较 flyover

footpath /ˈfʊtpɑːθ; ˋfutˌpæθ/ *n* 名
a narrow path for people to walk on, especially in the countryside 小径
This footpath leads to the beach. 这条小径通往海滩。

footprint /ˈfʊtˌprɪnt; ˋfutˌprɪnt/ *n* 名
the mark made by a foot or shoe 足迹；脚印
We left footprints in the sand. 我们在沙子上留下了足迹。

footstep /ˈfʊtstep; ˋfutˌstɛp/ *n* 名
the sound made by someone walking 脚步声
Can you hear the footsteps? 你能听到脚步声吗?

***for** /fə; fɚ; *strong* 强读 fɔː; fɔr/ *prep* 介
1. used to say who should get something 给
   This letter is for you. 这封信是给你的。
2. used to say the purpose of something 用来
   This brush is for cleaning shoes. 这把刷子是用来刷鞋的。
3. used to say a length of time 达（表示动作或情况持续的时间）
   My aunt has lived in Australia for ten years. 我的阿姨在澳洲住了10年。
4. used to say the price of something 以…的价钱；值
   I bought the shoes for $250. 我花了250元买了这双鞋子。
5. meaning 表示
   What is the German word for "food"? 德语"食物"怎么讲?
6. because of something 由于；因为
   He was punished for bad behaviour. 他因为顽皮受到处罚。

forbade /fəˈbæd; fɚˋbed/ *v* 动
the past tense of **forbid** ☆forbid 的过去式

forbid /fəˈbɪd; fɚˋbɪd/ *v* 动
forbids, forbidding, forbade, forbidden
to tell someone that they must not do something 禁止；不许
The law forbids smoking in restaurants. 法例禁止在餐厅中吸烟。

用法 多用于书面语，口语一般用 not let，例如 They didn't let her go to the party.

反义 allow

forbidden /fəˈbɪdn; fɚˋbɪdn̩/ *v* 动
the past participle of **forbid** ☆forbid 的过去分词

***force¹** /fɔːs; fɔrs/ *n* 名
无复数
the strength or power of something 力量

A bomb exploded with great force. 一个炸弹猛烈爆炸了。

***force²** /fɔːs; fɔrs/ *v* 动

forces, forcing, forced, forced

to make someone do something they do not want to do 强迫；迫使

I forced myself to get up early this morning because I had to catch the first train. 今天早上我强迫自己起床，因为要赶上第一班火车。

forecast /ˈfɔːkɑːst; ˋfɔrˌkæst/ *n* 名

something that says what is likely to happen, based on the information you have now 预测；预报

I hope the weather forecast is right. 我希望天气预报准确。

forehead /ˈfɔːhed; ˋfɔrɪd/ *n* 名

the top part of your face above the eyes and below your hair 前额

That man has a wide forehead. 那个男人的前额很宽。

***foreign** /ˈfɒrən; ˋfɔrɪn/ *adj* 形

from or relating to other countries 外国的；外来的

Harry can speak a number of foreign languages. 哈利会讲几种外语。

反义 **local**

foreigner /ˈfɒrənə; ˋfɔrɪnɚ/ *n* 名

someone who comes from another country 外国人

A lot of foreigners live in Shanghai. 有很多外国人在上海居住。

***forest** /ˈfɒrɪst; ˋfɔrɪst/ *n* 名

a piece of land where a lot of trees grow together 森林

There was a fire in the forest. 森林里发生了火灾。

***forever** /fərˈevə; fɚˋɛvɚ/ *adv* 副

for your whole life; always 永远地

"I will love you forever," he said to his wife. 他对妻子说："我永远爱你。"

forgave /fəˈgeɪv; fɚˋgev/ *v* 动

the past tense of **forgive** ☆forgive 的过去式

***forget** /fəˈget; fɚˋgɛt/ *v* 动

forgets, forgetting, forgot, forgotten

to not remember something or do something 忘记

I forgot to bring my homework to school. 我忘了带作业去学校。

反义 **remember**

> **Daily conversation 日常会话**
> **don't forget** 别忘记（用作提醒）
> *Don't forget the keys!* 别忘了带钥匙！

forgetful /fəˈgetfl; fɚˋgɛtfəl/ *adj* 形

often forgetting things 健忘的；没记性的

My grandmother is very forgetful. 我的祖母很健忘。

***forgive** /fəˈgɪv; fɚˋgɪv/ *v* 动

forgives, forgiving, forgave, forgiven

to stop being angry with someone who has hurt you 原谅；宽恕

He was very rude. I can't forgive him. 他太没礼貌了，我不能原谅他。

forgiven /fəˈgɪvn; fɚˋgɪvən/ *v* 动

the past participle of **forgive** ☆forgive 的过去分词

forgot /fəˈgɒt; fɚˋgɑt/ *v* 动

the past tense of **forget** ☆forget 的过去式

forgotten /fəˈgɒtn; fɚˋgɑtn̩/ *v* 动

the past participle of **forget** ☆forget 的过去分词

***fork** /fɔːk; fɔrk/ *n* 名

a thing with points for picking up food 叉子

Iris ate her steak with a knife and fork. 艾丽丝用刀叉吃牛排。

***form¹** /fɔːm; fɔrm/ *n* 名

1. a class in a school 级；班
   My cousin, Oscar, is in Form 1. 我的表哥奥斯卡在读初一。
2. a piece of paper where you write information 表格
   Please fill in this form. 请填好这张表格。
3. a way of writing or saying a word 字的形式
   "Color" is the American form of "colour". color 是 colour 的美式拼法。

***form²** /fɔːm; fɔrm/ *v* 动

1. to make something 组成；制作
   Use these ten letters to form five English words. 用这 10 个字母组成 5 个英文单词。
2. to start to exist somewhere 形成；产生；出现
   Ice began to form on the window. 窗户上开始出现冰花。

fort /fɔːt; fɔrt/ *n* 名

a castle 堡垒

Many tourists visit this old fort. 许多游客来这座古堡参观。

F

F

fortieth /ˈfɔːtiəθ; ˋfɔrtɪɪθ/ *ordinal num* 序数

40th in order 第四十（的）

They live on the fortieth floor of the building. 他们住在这座大厦的 40 楼。

fortnight /ˈfɔːtnaɪt; ˋfɔrtnaɪt/ *n* 名

two weeks 两星期；十四天

Mabel will go to New York for a fortnight. 梅布尔将去纽约两星期。

fortunate /ˈfɔːtʃənət; ˋfɔrtʃənɪt/ *adj* 形

lucky 幸运的

Paul is fortunate to have many good friends. 保罗有很多好朋友，真是幸运。

fortune /ˈfɔːtʃən; ˋfɔrtʃən/ *n* 名

1. （无复数）luck 运气；幸运

   Connie had the good fortune to win a prize. 康妮运气好，中了奖。
2. a large amount of money 一大笔钱

   He made a fortune in his business. 他做生意赚了一大笔钱。

tell someone's fortune 替人算命

The man said he could tell my fortune. 那个人说他可以给我算命。

***forty** /ˈfɔːti; ˋfɔrtɪ/ *num* 数

the number 40 四十

The drama club has forty members. 戏剧社有 40 个会员。

注意 这个词的拼法中没有 u，不要写成 fourty。

***forward** /ˈfɔːwəd; ˋfɔrwəd/ *adv* 副

也作：*forwards*

1. towards the front 向前

   Lily walked forward to the blackboard. 莉莉向前走到黑板处。

反义 **backwards**

2. towards the future 向将来

   I always look forward but don't forget the past. 我经常向前看，但也不会忘记过去。

look forward to (doing) something 期待；盼望（做）某事

I'm looking forward to the Christmas holidays. 我很盼望圣诞假期的到来。

fought /fɔːt; fɔt/ *v* 动

the past tense and past participle of **fight**☆fight 的过去式和过去分词

found /faʊnd; faʊnd/ *v* 动

the past tense and past participle of **find**☆find 的过去式和过去分词

***fountain** /ˈfaʊntɪn; ˋfaʊntn̩/ *n* 名

a structure that pumps water into the air 喷泉；喷水池

We took pictures in front of the fountain. 我们在喷水池前拍照。

***four** /fɔː; fɔr/ *num* 数

the number 4 四

Our dog is four years old. 我们的狗 4 岁了。

***fourteen** /fɔːˈtiːn; ˌfɔrˋtin/ *num* 数

the number 14 十四

There were fourteen passengers on the tram. 电车上有 14 名乘客。

fourteenth /fɔːˈtiːnθ; ˌfɔrˋtinθ/ *ordinal num* 序数

14th in order 第十四（的）

Jack's office is on the fourteenth floor. 杰克的办公室在 14 楼。

fourth /fɔːθ; fɔrθ/ *ordinal num* 序数

4th in order 第四（的）

Lawrence came fourth in the competition. 劳伦斯在比赛中得了第 4 名。

***fox** /fɒks; fɑks/ *n* 名

复数：*foxes*

a wild animal like a dog with a thick tail 狐狸

A fox killed this chicken last night. 昨晚一只狐狸杀死了这只鸡。

fraction /ˈfrækʃn; ˋfrækʃən/ *n* 名

a part of a whole number（数学）分数

The fraction "one half" can be written as 1/2 or 0.5. 分数“二分之一”可以写成 1/2 或 0.5。

***frame** /freɪm; frem/ *n* 名

a wood or metal structure which surrounds the edge of a picture, window, etc 相框；框架

I put a picture of my family in a photo frame. 我把全家福放在一个相框里。

***free[1]** /friː; fri/ *adj* 形

1. not costing money 免费的

   They got two free film tickets. 他们获得了两张免费的电影票。
2. allowed to do what you want and not controlled by anyone 自由的；不受约束的

   We are free to play in the PE lesson. 我们在体育课可以自由玩耍。
3. not busy 空闲的；有空的

   I am free after dinner tonight. 今天我吃完晚饭后有空。

free of charge 免费

Drinks are free of charge. 饮料免费。

free time 空闲时间；闲暇

I like reading in my free time. 我喜欢在闲暇时看书。

Daily conversation 日常会话
"Are you free this afternoon?" "Yes, I am." "你今天下午有空吗？" "有空。"

***free²** /friː; fri/ *v* 动
frees, freeing, freed, freed
to let someone leave a prison; to let an animal leave a cage 释放；使自由
They freed the monkeys from the cages. 他们把猴子从笼里放了出来。

freedom /ˈfriːdəm; ˋfridəm/ *n* 名
无复数
being able to do what you like 自由
Everybody loves freedom. 人人都爱自由。

freeze /friːz; friz/ *v* 动
freezes, freezing, froze, frozen
to become cold and hard because the temperature is low 结冰；凝固
It's so cold that the lake has frozen. 天气冷得湖都结了冰。
反义 **melt**

freezer /ˈfriːzə; ˋfrizɚ/ *n* 名
a large piece of equipment for storing frozen food 冰柜
She put the ice cream in the freezer. 她把冰淇淋放在冰柜里。

另见 **fridge, refrigerator**

French fry /ˌfrentʃ ˈfraɪ; ˏfrɛntʃ ˋfraɪ/ *n* 名【美】
也作：***fry*** | 复数：***French fries***
英式：***chip***
a long thin piece of fried potato 炸薯条
I had a hamburger and some French fries. 我吃了一个汉堡包和一些炸薯条。

frequently /ˈfriːkwəntli; ˋfrikwəntlɪ/ *adv* 副
often 经常地；频繁地
The buses run frequently in the morning. 早上公共汽车的班次很频繁。

***fresh** /freʃ; frɛʃ/ *adj* 形
fresher, freshest
1. recently made and not frozen 新鲜的
   Fresh food is good for our health. 新鲜食物对我们的健康有益。
2. clean 清新的
   The air in the park is fresh. 公园的空气清新。

***Friday** /ˈfraɪdeɪ; ˋfraɪdɪ/ *n* 名
缩写：***Fri.***
the day between Thursday and Saturday 星期五
This Friday is a public holiday. 这个星期五是公共假期。
注意 开头的字母必须用大写。

fridge /frɪdʒ; frɪdʒ/ *n* 名
a piece of equipment for keeping food and drinks cold 冰箱
Paul put the vegetables in the fridge. 保罗把蔬菜放进冰箱里。
同义 **refrigerator**
另见 **freezer**

fried¹ /fraɪd; fraɪd/ *v* 动
the past tense and past participle of **fry** ☆fry 的过去式和过去分词

fried² /fraɪd; fraɪd/ *adj* 形
cooked in hot oil 油煎的；油炸的
I had fried eggs for breakfast. 我早餐吃煎蛋。

***friend** /frend; frɛnd/ *n* 名
someone who you know well and like 朋友
Angela and Ellen are good friends. 安琪拉和艾伦是好朋友。
make friends 交朋友
We made friends with the new classmates. 我们和新同学交朋友。

反义 **enemy**

friendly /ˈfrendli; ˋfrɛndlɪ/ *adj* 形
friendlier, friendliest
behaving in a kind way towards someone 友善的；亲切的
The waiters of this restaurant are very friendly. 这家餐馆的服务生待客很亲切。
同义 **nice**
反义 **unfriendly**

friendship /ˈfrendʃɪp; ˋfrɛndʃɪp/ *n* 名
a relationship between friends 友谊；友情
Their friendship began last year. 他们的友谊始于去年。

fries /fraɪz; fraɪz/ *v* 动
a form of **fry** ☆fry 的另一种现在式，与主语 he、she 和 it 一起使用

frighten /ˈfraɪtn; ˋfraɪtn̩/ *v* 动
to make someone suddenly feel afraid 使害怕；使惊吓

F

The loud noise frightened us. 巨大的声响吓了我们一跳。

同义 **scare**

***frightened** /ˈfraɪtnd; ˋfraɪtṇd/ *adj* 形

feeling afraid 受惊的；害怕的

Don't be frightened to tell the truth. 别害怕说真话。

frightened of something 害怕（某物）

Lily is frightened of cockroaches. 莉莉很怕蟑螂。

用法 frightened 用来形容人的感受。

比较 **frightening**

F

***frightening** /ˈfraɪtn-ɪŋ; ˋfraɪtṇɪŋ/ *adj* 形

making someone feel afraid 使人害怕的；吓人的

The forest was very dark and frightening. 森林很黑暗，令人害怕。

用法 frightening 用来形容事物。

比较 **frightened**

***frog** /frɒg; frag/ *n* 名

a small animal that lives near water, has large eyes and long legs for jumping 青蛙

Some frogs are swimming in the pond. 几只青蛙在池塘里游泳。

***from** /frəm; frəm; *strong* 强读 frɒm; fram/ *prep* 介

1. starting at 从（某时候）开始
   The concert was from 7 p.m. to 9 p.m. 音乐会从晚上 7 点到 9 点。
2. coming from 从（某地方）来
   These pineapples come from Thailand. 这些菠萝产自泰国。
3. sent or given by someone 来自（某人）
   This present is from Fanny. 这份礼物是芬妮送的。
4. used to say how far away something is 距离（多远）
   The railway station is not far from my home. 火车站离我家不远。
5. using; out of 用…制成
   Paper is made from wood. 纸是用木材制成的。

from ... on 从（某时候）起

From now on, Mr Jones will be our English teacher. 从现在起，琼斯先生就是我们的英语老师。

***front[1]** /frʌnt; frʌnt/ *n* 名

无复数

1. the part that is furthest forward 最前面；最前部
   Lucy sits at the front of the class. 露西坐在教室的前面。

反义 **back[1]**

2. the surface or side that faces forward 前面；前部
   They decorated the front of the house with lights at Christmas. 在圣诞节时，他们用灯泡装饰了屋子的前面。

in front of someone/something 在（某人或某物的）前面

Henry is sitting in front of me. 亨利坐在我的前面。

***front[2]** /frʌnt; frʌnt/ *adj* 形

at, in, or on the front of something 前面的；前部的

One of his front teeth fell off. 他的一颗门牙掉落了。

front door 前门

The snake came in through the front door. 那条蛇从前门进来。

frown /fraʊn; fraʊn/ *v* 动

to move your eyebrows in a way that shows you are angry or worried 皱眉

He frowned when I asked the question. 我提出问题，他眉头一皱。

froze /frəʊz; froz/ *v* 动

the past tense of **freeze** ☆freeze 的过去式

frozen[1] /ˈfrəʊzn; ˋfrozṇ/ *v* 动

the past participle of **freeze** ☆freeze 的过去分词

frozen[2] /ˈfrəʊzn; ˋfrozṇ/ *adj* 形

1. frozen food is stored at a very low temperature（食物）冷冻的
   Danny cooked dinner using frozen meat. 丹尼用冷冻肉来做晚饭。
2. if water is frozen, it has changed to ice 结冰的

The river was frozen. 河结冰了。

***fruit** /fruːt; frut/ *n* 名

复数：***fruit/fruits***

1. a type of sweet food that grows on trees or plants, for example an apple or a strawberry 水果
   We should eat fruit every day. 我们每天都应吃水果。
2. the part of a tree or plant that has its seeds 果实
   The fruit of the tree is poisonous. 这种树的果实有毒。

fry /fraɪ; fraɪ/ *v* 动

fries, frying, fried, fried

to cook in hot oil 煎；炸；炒

She fried the fish in a pan. 她用平底锅来煎鱼。

fuel /ˈfjuːəl; ˋfjuəl/ *n* 名

something that burns and gives heat, power or light 燃料

Coal, oil and gas are fuels. 煤、油和煤气都是燃料。

***full** /fʊl; fʊl/ *adj* 形

1. having as much as possible inside 满的
   The bottle is full. 瓶子满了。

反义 **empty[1]**

2. complete 完整的；详尽的
   Write down your full name and class number on the test paper. 请在考卷上写上你的全名和学号。
3. having eaten so much food that you cannot eat any more 吃饱了的
   I'm full. I can't eat any more. 我饱了，再也吃不下了。

反义 **hungry**

full of something 充满

The house was full of smoke. 屋子里满是烟。

full stop /ˌfʊl ˈstɒp; ˏfʊl ˋstɑp/ *n* 名

the sign you use to end a sentence (.) 句号；句点

另见 **附录**：Punctuation 标点符号

***fun** /fʌn; fʌn/ *n* 名

无复数

a happy or joyful time 乐趣；好玩的事

The party was good fun. 那派对很好玩。

have fun 玩得开心

We had fun in the park. 我们在公园里玩得很开心。

make fun of someone/something 嘲弄；取笑

They all made fun of her thick glasses. 他们都拿她的厚眼镜来开玩笑。

***function** /ˈfʌŋkʃən; ˋfʌŋkʃən/ *n* 名

the purpose that something is used for 功能；作用

This machine has many functions. 这部机器有很多功能。

funeral /ˈfjuːnrəl; ˋfjunərəl/ *n* 名

a ceremony for burying or burning a dead person 葬礼

Many people attended the funeral. 很多人参加了葬礼。

funny /ˈfʌni; ˋfʌnɪ/ *adj* 形

funnier, funniest

making you laugh 有趣的；滑稽的

The clown is very funny. 那个小丑很滑稽。

fur /fɜː; fɝ/ *n* 名

无复数

the soft hair that covers the bodies of some animals（动物身上的）软毛

My cat has soft fur. 我的猫有柔软的毛。

furious /ˈfjʊəriəs; ˋfjʊrɪəs/ *adj* 形

very angry 大怒的；极其愤怒的

My brother broke my toy train so I was furious with him. 哥哥弄坏了我的玩具火车，所以我很生气。

furniture /ˈfɜːnɪtʃə; ˋfɝnɪtʃɚ/ *n* 名

无复数

tables, chairs, beds, desks etc used in a home or an office 家具

The furniture in the room is beautiful. 房间里的家具很漂亮。

注意 如要表示家具的数量，需要用量词 piece，如 a piece of furniture、two pieces of furniture。

further[1] /ˈfɜːðə; ˋfɝðɚ/ *adv* 副

另见 **farther[1]**

further[2] /ˈfɜːðə; ˋfɝðɚ/ *adj* 形

另见 **farther[2]**

F

furthest[1] /ˈfɜːðɪst; ˋfɝðɪst/ *adv* 副

另见 farthest[1]

furthest[2] /ˈfɜːðɪst; ˋfɝðɪst/ *adj* 形

另见 farthest[2]

***future** /ˈfjuːtʃə; ˋfjutʃə/ *n* 名

无复数

the time that is after the present 将来；未来

We should make plans for the future. 我们应该为未来做计划。

in future 今后

Please be more careful in future. 今后请你小心些。

反义 past[3]

g

the short form of **gram** ☆gram 的缩写

gain /geɪn; gen/ *v* 动

to get something you want or need 获得；赢得

I gained some valuable experience from the competition. 我在比赛中得到了宝贵的经验。

gala /ˈgɑːlə; ˋgelə/ *n* 名【英】

a sports event, especially in swimming 运动会（尤指游泳比赛）

My school holds a swimming gala once a year. 我的学校每年举行一次水上运动会。

gallery /ˈgæləri; ˋgælərɪ/ *n* 名

复数：***galleries***

a building or room for displaying art 美术馆；画廊

Annie likes visiting art galleries and museums. 安妮喜欢参观画廊和博物馆。

gallop /ˈgæləp; ˋgæləp/ *v* 动

if a horse gallops, it runs very fast, with all four feet leaving the ground together（马）疾跑；奔驰

Those horses are galloping. 那些马在奔驰。

gamble /ˈgæmbl; ˋgæmbḷ/ *v* 动

gambles, gambling, gambled, gambled

to risk money on a game, race, etc in the hope of winning more money 赌博

Children should not gamble. 儿童不应该赌博。

***game** /geɪm; gem/ *n* 名

an activity that has rules, in which you play against other people 游戏

The children are enjoying the game. 孩子玩游戏玩得很开心。

gang /gæŋ; gæŋ/ *n* 名

a group of people who spend time together and usually do bad things（尤指做坏事的）一帮人

The gang of robbers ran away in a car. 这帮劫匪坐汽车逃跑了。

gap /gæp; gæp/ *n* 名

a space between two things or two parts of something 裂缝；缺口

My sister has a gap between her two front teeth. 妹妹的两颗门牙中间有条缝隙。

garage /ˈgærɑːʒ; gəˋrɑʒ/ *n* 名

1. a place where you keep your car 车库

   My father parked the car in the garage. 爸爸把车停放在车库里。

2. a place where cars are repaired 汽车修理厂

   After the accident, we sent the car to the garage for repair. 事故发生后，我们把车子送到修车厂修理。

***garden** /ˈgɑːdn; ˋgɑrdṇ/ *n* 名

a piece of land around your house where you grow plants 花园

There are many flowers in the garden. 花园里有很多花。

gardener /ˈgɑːdnə; ˋgɑrdṇə/ *n* 名

someone who works in a garden 园丁

The gardener is watering the flowers. 园丁正在给花浇水。

***garlic** /ˈgɑːlɪk; ˋgɑrlɪk/ *n* 名

无复数

a vegetable with a strong taste, used in cooking 蒜；大蒜；蒜头

My mother cooked the vegetable with garlic. 妈妈把蒜和蔬菜一起做。

G

***gas** /gæs; gæs/ *n* 名

1. （复数：***gases***）something like air that is not liquid or solid 气体；气
   Air is made up of several kinds of gases. 空气是由几种气体组成的。
2. （无复数）something like air that is used for cooking or heating 煤气
   Turn off the gas when you have finished cooking. 你烧完饭后要关掉煤气。
3. 【美】（无复数）（英式：***petrol***）a liquid that you put into a car to make it go 汽油
   Andy stopped the car to get some gas. 安迪把汽车停下来加汽油。

***gate** /geɪt; get/ *n* 名

a door in a fence or outside wall that you can open and close 大门；闸门

The school gates open at 7 a.m.
学校上午 7 点开门。

***gather** /ˈgæðə; ˋgæðɚ/ *v* 动

1. to come together in one place 集合；聚集
   All the students gathered in the school hall. 全体学生在学校礼堂里集合。
2. to bring things together 收集
   Mary gathered her books and put them in her bag. 玛丽收拾书本放进袋子里。

gave /geɪv; gev/ *v* 动

the past tense of **give**☆give 的过去式

geese /giːs; gis/ *n* 名

the plural of **goose**☆goose 的复数形式

***general[1]** /ˈdʒenrəl; ˋdʒɛnərəl/ *adj* 形

including the main parts of something, not its details 总体的；普遍的

Their general opinion of the new teacher is good. 他们对新老师的总体评价不错。

in general 大致上；通常

In general, his schoolwork is very good. 他的功课通常都很好。

general[2] /ˈdʒenrəl; ˋdʒɛnərəl/ *n* 名

a very important officer in the army or air force 将军；上将

He is a four-star general. 他是一名四星上将。

***generally** /ˈdʒenrəli; ˋdʒɛnərəlɪ/ *adv* 副

usually 一般；通常

They generally play badminton on Sundays. 他们通常星期天打羽毛球。

***generous** /ˈdʒenrəs; ˋdʒɛnərəs/ *adj* 形

willing to give money or help 慷慨的；大方的

Winnie is very generous with her money. 威妮用钱很大方。

genius /ˈdʒiːniəs; ˋdʒinjəs/ *n* 名

复数：***geniuses***

someone who is very clever or good at something 天才

Newton was a genius. 牛顿是一个天才。

***gentle** /ˈdʒentl; ˋdʒɛntl̩/ *adj* 形

gentler, gentlest

1. kind and careful not to hurt someone or something 温柔的；温和的
   She is very gentle with her cat. 她温柔地对待她的猫。

2. not strong 柔和的；轻柔的
   There is a gentle wind blowing. 和风轻轻吹着。

gentleman /ˈdʒentlmən; ˋdʒɛntl̩mən/ *n* 名

复数：***gentlemen***

1. a polite word for a man 先生（对男士的客气称呼）
   Good morning, ladies and gentlemen. 女士们，先生们，早安。

另见 **lady**

2. a man who is polite and kind to other people 绅士；彬彬有礼的人
   Mr Brown is a real gentleman. 布朗先生是个真正的绅士。

geography /dʒiˈɒgrəfi; dʒiˋɑgrəfɪ/ *n* 名

无复数

a subject in which you learn about the Earth, its climate, rivers, mountains, rocks, etc 地理（学）

Geography is an interesting subject. 地理是一门有趣的学科。

germ /dʒɜːm; dʒɝm/ *n* 名

a very small living thing which makes you ill 病菌；细菌

Flies spread germs. 苍蝇传播病菌。

***get** /get; gɛt/ *v* 动

gets, getting, got, got

1. to obtain or buy something 取得；买
   Can you get some bread from the supermarket? 你到超市买点面包好吗？

2. to be given something 获得；收到
 Lily got a prize in the cooking competition. 莉莉在烹饪比赛中得了奖。
3. to go and bring back something or someone 拿来；带来
 Please get me some water. 请拿些水给我。
4. to become 变成；变得
 The weather is getting cooler. 天气正逐渐转凉。
5. to arrive at a place 到达
 Call me when you get to your aunt's home. 你到阿姨家就打电话给我。

get along/on with someone 和某人相处融洽
I get along well with all my classmates. 我和所有同学相处融洽。

get away (from someone or somewhere) 逃跑；逃脱
I tied my dog here, but it got away! 我把狗拴在这里，可是它逃跑了！

get back 回来；回家
Dad will get back soon. 爸爸很快就会回来了。

get on/off 上/下（公共汽车、火车、飞机等）
We got on the bus. 我们上了公共汽车。

get up 起床
I get up early every day. 我每天都很早起床。

ghost /gəʊst; gost/ *n* 名
the form of a dead person that some people believe they can see 鬼；鬼魂
Sally dreamt that she saw a ghost. 莎莉梦见了鬼。

giant[1] /'dʒaɪənt; `dʒaɪənt/ *adj* 形
very big 巨大的
The hunter caught a giant snake in the forest. 那猎人在森林中捕获了一条巨蛇。

giant[2] /'dʒaɪənt; `dʒaɪənt/ *n* 名
a very big man in stories 巨人
The giant lifted up the elephant easily. 巨人轻易地举起了大象。

***gift** /gɪft; gɪft/ *n* 名
a present 礼物
This teddy bear is my birthday gift. 这玩具熊是我的生日礼物。

giggle /'gɪgl; `gɪgḷ/ *v* 动
giggles, giggling, giggled, giggled
to laugh quietly in a silly way 傻笑；咯咯地笑
The joke was funny, and we could not stop giggling. 那个笑话很有趣，我们听了咯咯地笑个不停。

ginger /'dʒɪndʒə; `dʒɪndʒɚ/ *n* 名
无复数
a root with a hot taste, often used in cooking 姜
The cook steamed the fish with some ginger. 厨师蒸鱼时放了一些姜。

***giraffe** /dʒə'rɑːf; dʒə`ræf/ *n* 名
a tall animal with a very long neck 长颈鹿
The giraffe is eating the leaves on the tree. 那只长颈鹿在吃树上的叶子。

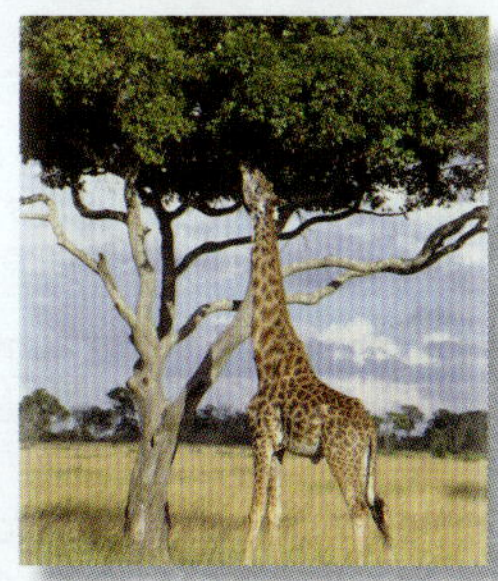

***girl** /gɜːl; gɝl/ *n* 名
a female child 女孩
The girl danced very well. 那个女孩跳舞跳得很好。

***give** /gɪv; gɪv/ *v* 动
gives, giving, gave, given
1. to let someone have something 给；给予
 Santa Claus gave each of us a present. 圣诞老人给我们每人一份礼物。

反义 **receive**

2. to do something 做（某个动作）
 Alice gave a big smile. 爱丽丝满面笑容。

give something away 赠送；捐赠
We gave away our old clothes to charity. 我们把旧衣服捐赠给了慈善机构。

give something back 归还；送回
I will give you back the book tomorrow. 我明天会把书还给你。

give in 屈服；投降；让步
John and Colin argued for a long time. At last, John gave in. 约翰和科林争论了很久。最后约翰让步了。

give something out 分发
The teacher is giving out the exam papers. 老师在分发试卷。

give something up 停止做某事
Sam has given up smoking. 山姆已经戒烟了。

give up 放弃
Don't give up. You've finished most of the work. 别放弃。你已经完成了大部分的工作。

***glad** /glæd; glæd/ *adj* 形
gladder, gladdest
pleased; happy 高兴的；欢喜的
I am glad to see you. 我很高兴和你见面。

G

glance /glɑːns; glæns/ *n* 名

a quick look 匆匆一看

I took a glance at the letterbox before going into the lift. 我乘电梯前，匆匆看了看信箱。

***glass** /glɑːs; glæs/ *n* 名

1. （无复数）a clear, hard material that you can see through and is used for making windows, bottles, etc 玻璃
   Cinderella's shoes are made of glass. 灰姑娘的鞋子是用玻璃做的。
2. （复数：***glasses***）a small container used for drinking 玻璃杯
   There are five glasses in the cupboard. 碗柜里有5只玻璃杯。
3. （复数：***glasses***）the amount of a drink in a glass 一杯（的份量）
   I had a glass of milk this morning. 今天早上我喝了一杯牛奶。
4. **glasses**（复数名词）something you wear over your eyes to help you see better or protect your eyes 眼镜
   My grandmother wears glasses when she reads the newspaper. 祖母看报纸时，总戴上眼镜。

glide /glaɪd; glaɪd/ *v* 动

glides, gliding, glided, glided

to move smoothly and quietly 滑行；滑动

Polly glided over the ice. 波莉在冰上滑行。

globe /gləʊb; glob/ *n* 名

1. a round object that has the map of the world on it 地球仪

   Can you find Asia on the globe? 你能在地球仪上找出亚洲吗？
2. **the globe**（无复数）the world 地球；世界
   I want to travel all over the globe. 我想周游世界。

glossary /ˈglɒsəri; ˋglɑsərɪ/ *n* 名

复数：***glossaries***

a list of words and their meanings, usually at the end of a book 词汇表

This is a glossary of computer words. 这是电脑用语的词汇表。

***glove** /glʌv; glʌv/ *n* 名

a piece of clothing that you wear on your hand 手套

My mother always wears a pair of gloves when she washes the dishes. 妈妈洗碗时总戴上一副手套。

glove puppet（套在手上操纵的）布袋木偶

The teacher showed us how to make a glove puppet today. 今天老师教我们制作布袋木偶。

比较 **mitten**

glow /gləʊ; glo/ *v* 动

to shine 发光

The cat's eyes glowed in the dark. 猫的眼睛在黑暗中发光。

***glue** /gluː; glu/ *n* 名

无复数

something that is used to stick things together 胶；胶水

I made a kite with paper and glue. 我用纸和胶水做了一个风筝。

***go** /gəʊ; go/ *v* 动

goes, going, went, gone

1. to move from one place to another or travel somewhere 去（某处）
   I went to the park last Sunday. 我上星期日去了那个公园。

反义 **come**

2. to travel somewhere to do something 去做（某事）；去进行（某活动）
   Jack goes swimming every morning. 杰克每天早上都去游泳。
3. to leave a place 离开；出发
   It's getting late. I should go now. 很晚了。我得走了。
4. to reach 通往
   This path goes to the seaside. 这条小径通往海滨。

be going to 将要；快要

The concert is going to start soon. 音乐会快要开始了。

go away 离开（某处）；出外（度假）

They usually go away at the Chinese New Year. 他们通常在新年时出外度假。

go back 回去

Let's go back home now. 我们现在回家吧。

go on 发生；继续

What's going on here? 这里发生了什么事?

Please go on with your work. 请继续做你的事。

go out 外出；熄灭

He went out for a walk after dinner. 他晚饭后外出散步。

The candle went out. 蜡烛熄灭了。

*goal /gəʊl; gol/ *n* 名

1. something that you want to do in the future 目标

   I always set goals for myself at the beginning of each year. 我每年初都会为自己定下目标。

同义 aim²

2. an area where the ball must enter to get a point in football and other sports 球门

   Roger kicked the ball into the goal. 罗杰把球踢进了球门。

3. a point that a team gets when the ball goes into the goal 进球得分

   We beat them by five goals to three. 我们以五比三赢了他们。

*goat /gəʊt; got/ *n* 名

an animal with horns and long hair under its chin 山羊

Goats can climb trees. 山羊会爬树。

goblin /ˈgɒblɪn; ˋgɑblɪn/ *n* 名

a small, ugly creature in stories that enjoys tricking people or causing trouble 小妖精；小妖怪

The goblin played tricks on the children. 小妖精捉弄了那些孩子。

*god /gɒd; gɑd/ *n* 名

1. **God**（无复数）the being that created the universe and rules over it, according to Christians and people of other religions 上帝；主

   He believes in God. 他信仰上帝。

注意 G 字要用大写，不与 the 连用。

2. a male being that people believe controls the world 神

   There are a lot of different gods in Chinese legends. 中国传说中有各式各样的神。

Daily conversation 日常会话

Oh God/My God! 天哪！（表示惊讶、恐惧、生气等）

"Oh God! Why did you do that?" "天哪！你为何那样做？"

注意 说 Oh God 或者 My God 可能会冒犯别人。

goddess /ˈgɒdes; ˋgɑdɪs/ *n* 名

复数：*goddesses*

a female being that people believe controls the world 女神

Venus is the goddess of love. 维纳斯是爱的女神。

goes /gəʊz; goz/ *v* 动

a form of **go** ☆go 的另一种现在式，与主语 he、she 和 it 一起使用

goggles /ˈgɒglz; ˋgɑglz/ *plural n* 复数名词

a pair of large, round glasses that you wear to protect your eyes 护目镜；防水镜；泳镜

I wear my goggles when I swim. 我游泳的时候会戴一副泳镜。

going /ˈgəʊɪŋ; ˋgoɪŋ/ *v* 动

the present participle of **go** ☆go 的现在分词

*gold¹ /gəʊld; gold/ *n* 名

无复数

a shiny, yellow metal that costs a lot of money 金；黄金

This bracelet is made of gold. 这只手镯是金子做的。

*gold² /gəʊld; gold/ *adj* 形

made of gold or having the colour of gold 黄金的；金色的

My mother has a beautiful gold chain. 妈妈有一条漂亮的金项链。

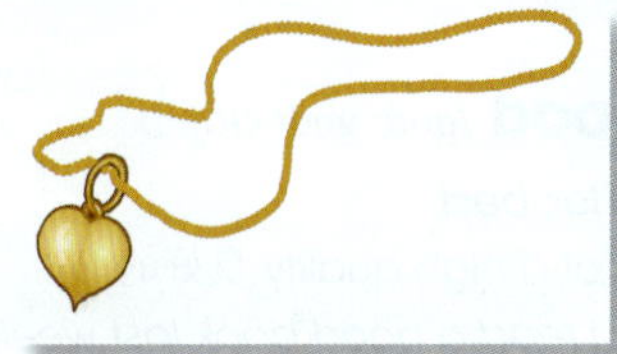

*golden /ˈgəʊldən; ˋgoldn̩/ *adj* 形

made of gold or having the colour of gold 金制的；金色的；金黄色的

Tony has golden hair. 托尼有一头金发。

goldfish /ˈgəʊldfɪʃ; ˋgold͵fɪʃ/ *n* 名

复数：*goldfish*

a small, gold or orange fish often kept as a pet 金鱼

We keep a tank of goldfish in the living room. 我们在客厅里养了一缸金鱼。

G

G

golf /gɒlf; gɑlf/ *n* 名

无复数

a game in which you use a long, thin stick to hit a small ball into holes in the ground 高尔夫球（运动）

Jenny is good at playing golf. 珍妮擅长打高尔夫球。

gone /gɒn; gɔn/ *v* 动

the past participle of **go** ☆go 的过去分词

***good** /gʊd; gʊd/ *adj* 形

better, best

1. of a high quality 良好的

   I read a good book last week. 上星期我读了一本好书。

反义 **bad**

2. happy and enjoyable 愉快的；开心的

   We had a good time at the party. 我们在派对上玩得很开心。

3. able to do something well 熟练的；擅长的

   Helen is a good dancer. 海伦擅长跳舞。

反义 **bad**

4. useful or suitable 有用的；有益的；合适的

   Fruit and vegetables are good for your health. 水果和蔬菜对健康有益。

反义 **bad**

5. if children are good they behave well（孩子）乖的；守规矩的

   Are you a good child? 你是个乖孩子吗？

反义 **naughty**

6. kind 善良的；好心的

   He is a good man who always helps others. 他是个好人，常常帮助其他人。

反义 **bad**

good afternoon（问候语）午安；下午好

Good afternoon everyone. 各位下午好。

good at something 擅长于（某事）

Ben is very good at chess. 本精通棋艺。

good evening（问候语）晚上好

Good evening, ladies and gentlemen! 女士们，先生们，晚上好！

good morning（问候语）早安；早上好

Miss Lee came into the classroom and said, "Good morning, class." 李老师走进教室说："同学们早上好。"

good night 晚安（晚上分别时或临睡前的用语）

Good night. Sleep well. 晚安。好好睡吧。

> **Daily conversation 日常会话**
>
> *"Let's go swimming this afternoon." "Good idea!"*
> "我们下午去游泳吧！""好主意！"

***goodbye** /gʊd'baɪ; gʊd`baɪ/ *interj* 感叹

也作：***bye***

used when you are leaving someone or when someone is leaving 再见

Goodbye Amy! See you tomorrow. 再见，艾米！明天见。

good-looking /gʊd 'lʊkɪŋ; gʊd `lʊkɪŋ/ *adj* 形

having an attractive face（人）好看的；漂亮的

She's a good-looking girl. 她是个漂亮的女孩。

反义 **ugly**

goodness /'gʊdnəs; `gʊdnɪs/ *n* 名

无复数

a word you use when you are surprised 天啊；哎呀（用于口语，表示惊讶）

My goodness! I lost my wallet! 天啊！我的钱包丢了！

goods /gʊdz; gʊdz/ *plural n* 复数名词

things that are produced to be sold 商品

That shop sells expensive goods. 那家商店销售昂贵的商品。

goose /gu:s; gus/ *n* 名

复数：***geese***

a large bird that looks like a duck 鹅

The geese are drinking water. 那些鹅在喝水。

gorilla /gə'rɪlə; gə`rɪlə/ *n* 名

an animal that is like a monkey but is much larger 大猩猩

Some gorillas live in this forest. 有些大猩猩住在这个森林里。

got /ɡɒt; ɡɑt/ *v* 动

the past tense and past participle of **get** ☆get 的过去式和过去分词

govern /ˈɡʌvn; ˋɡʌvɚn/ *v* 动

to control a country and make important decisions about it 治理；统治

The president governed the country for four years. 这位总统统治了国家 4 年。

***government** /ˈɡʌvnmənt; ˋɡʌvɚnmənt/ *n* 名

a group of people who control a country 政府

The government has planned to build more schools. 政府已计划兴建更多学校。

grab /ɡræb; ɡræb/ *v* 动

grabs, grabbing, grabbed, grabbed

to take and hold something or someone suddenly or rudely 抓住；抢夺

The thief grabbed my handbag and ran away. 那小偷抢了我的手提包就逃跑了。

graceful /ˈɡreɪsfl; ˋɡresfəl/ *adj* 形

moving in a smooth, attractive way or having an attractive shape 优美的；优雅的

The dancers moved in a graceful way. 舞蹈演员的舞姿优美。

***grade** /ɡreɪd; ɡred/ *n* 名

a mark in a test or exam 成绩；分数

Henry got good grades in his exams. 亨利在考试中取得了好成绩。

同义 **mark**[1]

gradual /ˈɡrædʒuəl; ˋɡrædʒuəl/ *adj* 形

happening or changing slowly over a long period of time 逐渐的；逐步的

The change was gradual. I didn't notice it. 变化是逐渐发生的。我没注意到。

gradually /ˈɡrædʒuəli; ˋɡrædʒuəlɪ/ *adv* 副

slowly, over a long period of time 逐渐地；逐步地

The rain gradually stopped. 雨逐渐停了。

反义 **suddenly**

grain /ɡreɪn; ɡren/ *n* 名

1. （无复数）the seeds from food plants which can be eaten, such as rice or wheat 谷物；粮食

   They used the grain to make flour for making bread. 他们用谷物制造面粉做面包。
2. a seed of rice, wheat etc 谷粒

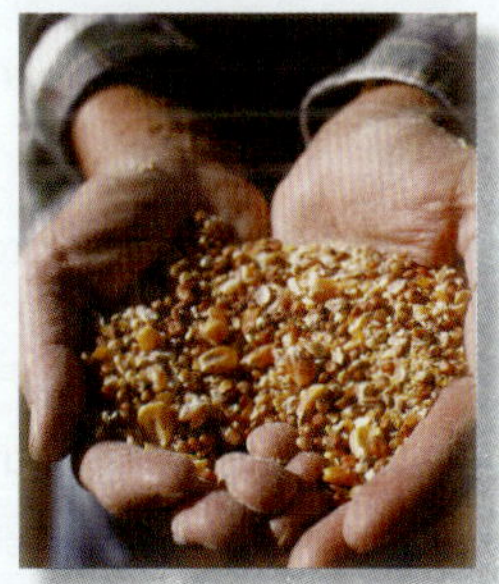

A few grains of rice are in the bowl. 碗里有几粒米。

gram /ɡræm; ɡræm/ *n* 名

也作：***gramme*** ｜ 缩写：***g***

a unit of weight. There are 1000 grams in a kilogram. 克（重量单位）

The bag of sugar weighs 500 grams. 这包糖重 500 克。

另见 附录：Weights and measures 度量单位

grammar /ˈɡræmə; ˋɡræmɚ/ *n* 名

无复数

the rules by which words are put together into sentences 语法；文法

Mrs Smith thinks that Chinese grammar is very difficult. 史密斯太太认为中文语法很难。

grand /ɡrænd; ɡrænd/ *adj* 形

grander, grandest

very big and special 壮丽的；富丽堂皇的

The museum looks very grand. 那家博物馆看上去很富丽堂皇。

grandad, granddad /ˈɡrændæd; ˋɡrænˌdæd/ *n* 名

grandfather 爷爷；外公

Grandad is old but he is still strong. 虽然外公年纪大，但仍然很硬朗。

用法 常用于口语中。

grandchild /ˈɡræntʃaɪld; ˋɡrændˌtʃaɪld/ *n* 名

复数：***grandchildren***

the child of your son or daughter 孙子；孙女；外孙子；外孙女

She has ten grandchildren. 她有10个孙儿女。

***granddaughter** /ˈgrænˌdɔːtə; ˋgrænˏdɔtɚ/ *n* 名

the daughter of your son or daughter 孙女；外孙女

Mrs Green's granddaughter visited her last Sunday. 格林太太的孙女上星期日探望了她。

***grandfather** /ˈgrændˌfɑːðə; ˋgrændˏfɑðɚ/ *n* 名

the father of your father or mother 祖父；外祖父

That man is Tom's grandfather. 那是汤姆的祖父。

用法 用于比较正式的场合或书面语中。

grandma /ˈgrænmɑː; ˋgrænmɑ/ *n* 名

grandmother 奶奶；外婆

Grandma likes hiking. 奶奶喜欢远足。

用法 常用于口语中。

***grandmother** /ˈgrænˌmʌðə; ˋgrændˏmʌðɚ/ *n* 名

the mother of your father or mother 祖母；外祖母

My grandmother lives with us. 祖母和我们住在一起。

用法 用于比较正式的场合或书面语中。

grandpa /ˈgrænpɑː; ˋgrænpɑ/ *n* 名

a grandfather 爷爷；外公

Grandpa does exercise in the park every morning. 爷爷每天早上去公园做运动。

用法 常用于口语中。

grandparent /ˈgrænˌpeərənt; ˋgrændˏpɛrənt/ *n* 名

the father or mother of your father or mother 祖父（母）；外祖父（母）

My grandparents love me very much. 祖父母很疼我。

***grandson** /ˈgrænsʌn; ˋgrændˏsʌn/ *n* 名

the son of your son or daughter 孙子；外孙

He always plays with his grandson. 他经常和孙子玩耍。

granny, grannie /ˈgræni; ˋgrænɪ/ *n* 名

复数：***grannies***

a grandmother 奶奶；外婆

Who takes care of your granny? 谁照顾你的外婆？

用法 常用于口语中。

***grape** /greɪp; grep/ *n* 名

a small, round, green or purple fruit used for making wine 葡萄

There is a bunch of grapes on the table. 桌子上有一串葡萄。

grapefruit /ˈgreɪpfruːt; ˋgrepˏfrut/ *n* 名

复数：***grapefruit/grapefruits***

a large, round, yellow fruit that is sour 葡萄柚；西柚

I put grapefruit in my salad. 我在沙拉里放了葡萄柚。

graph /grɑːf; græf/ *n* 名

a picture that uses a line or lines to show the relationship between two or more numbers 图表；曲线图

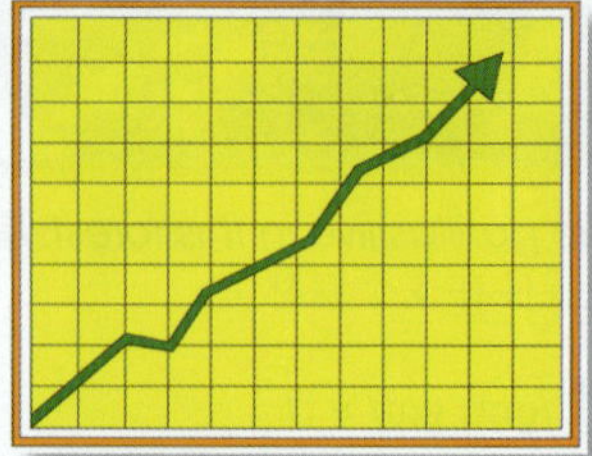

This graph shows that house prices are increasing quickly. 这张图表显示房价上涨得很快。

***grass** /grɑːs; græs/ *n* 名

无复数

a green plant with thin leaves that grows in gardens and fields 草

Keep off the grass! 别践踏草地！

grasshopper /ˈgrɑːsˌhɒpə; ˋgræsˏhɑpɚ/ *n* 名

an insect that can jump very high and makes a short loud sound 蚱蜢

Grasshoppers like to eat grass and leaves. 蚱蜢喜欢吃草和树叶。

grateful /ˈgreɪtfl; ˋgretfəl/ *adj* 形

feeling that you want to thank someone for helping you 感激的

I am very grateful for your help. 我非常感谢你的帮忙。

***grave** /greɪv; grev/ *n* 名

a place in the ground where a dead person is buried 坟墓；坟地

She put some flowers on the grave. 她在墓上放了一些花。

***great** /greɪt; gret/ *adj* 形

greater, greatest

1. a lot of or very large 很多的；大量的；大的
   She takes great care of her children. 她照顾儿女无微不至。
2. important or special 重要的；伟大的
   The Sports Day is a great day for our school. 运动会是我们学校的重要日子。
3. very good 极好的
   It's great to see you here! 在这儿看到你，实在太好了！

Daily conversation 日常会话
"Let's go to the cinema!" "That's great!" "我们去看电影吧！" "好极了！"

greedily /ˈgriːdɪli; ˋgridɪlɪ/ *adv* 副

in a greedy way 贪心地；贪婪地
Peter was hungry and he ate the bread greedily. 彼得很饿，狼吞虎咽地把面包吃了。

***greedy** /ˈgriːdi; ˋgridɪ/ *adj* 形

greedier, greediest

wanting to have more than you need 贪心的；贪婪的
The greedy child took away all the burgers. 那贪心的孩子拿走了所有汉堡包。

***green[1]** /griːn; grin/ *adj* 形

greener, greenest

1. having the colour of leaves and grass 绿色的
   The traffic lights have turned green. 交通灯已转绿了。
2. good for the environment 环保的；与环保有关的
   My mother prefers to buy green products. 妈妈喜欢购买环保产品。

***green[2]** /griːn; grin/ *n* 名

the colour of leaves and grass 绿色
The girl was dressed in green. 那个女孩穿着绿色衣服。

greet /griːt; grit/ *v* 动

to say hello to someone or welcome them when you meet them 打招呼；问候

He is polite and always greets everyone with a smile. 他待人有礼，总是微笑着跟人打招呼。

greeting /ˈgriːtɪŋ; ˋgritɪŋ/ *n* 名

what you say or do when you meet someone 问候；招呼
They shook hands and exchanged greetings. 他们互相握手问候。

grew /gruː; gru/ *v* 动

the past tense of **grow** ☆grow 的过去式

***grey[1]** /greɪ; gre/ *adj* 形【英】

greyer, greyest

美式：***gray***

having the colour of a cloudy sky, between black and white 灰色的；灰白色的
The old man has grey hair. 那位老人的头发是灰白色的。

***grey[2]** /greɪ; gre/ *n* 名【英】

美式：***gray***

the colour of a cloudy sky, between black and white 灰色；灰白色
I am knitting a sweater in grey. 我在织一件灰色的毛衣。

grill /grɪl; grɪl/ *v* 动

to cook food under or over direct heat 烧烤

They are grilling steaks. 他们正在烤牛排。

grin[1] /grɪn; grɪn/ *v* 动

grins, grinning, grinned, grinned

to give a big smile and show your teeth 露齿而笑；咧嘴而笑

She grinned when she heard the joke. 她听到笑话时咧开嘴笑了。

另见 **smile¹, laugh**

G

grin² /grɪn; grɪn/ *n* 名

a big smile in which you show your teeth 露齿笑；咧嘴笑

Ada gave a big grin when she saw her baby. 艾达见到她的宝宝时咧嘴笑了。

另见 **smile², laughter**

grip /grɪp; grɪp/ *v* 动

grips, gripping, gripped, gripped

to hold something tightly 紧握；抓牢

My grandmother gripped my hand when we crossed the road. 过马路时，外婆紧握着我的手。

grocer /ˈgrəʊsə; ˋgrosɚ/ *n* 名

someone who sells food and other things used in the home 杂货商；杂货店店员

The grocer sells rice, oil, salt and sugar. 这个杂货商卖米、油、盐和糖。

grocer's 杂货店

I bought some apples from the grocer's. 我在这家杂货店里买了几个苹果。

grocery /ˈgrəʊsəri; ˋgrosərɪ/ *n* 名

1. **groceries**（复数名词）food or other things sold by a grocer or a supermarket 食品杂货

   I usually buy groceries at a supermarket. 我通常到超市买食品杂货。

2. （复数：***groceries***）（也作：***grocery store***）a shop that sells food or other things used in the home 杂货店

   That grocery sells food at low prices. 那家杂货店的食品价格便宜。

*ground /graʊnd; graʊnd/ *n* 名

1. （无复数）the part of the earth that you walk on 地面；地

   The dog is lying on the ground. 那只狗趴在地上。

比较 **floor**

2. an area of land for a particular activity（某种活动的）场地

   The football ground was wet after the rain. 下雨后，足球场湿了。

*group /gruːp; grup/ *n* 名

a number of people or things together 组；群

The teacher divided us into three groups. 老师把我们分成了三组。

*grow /grəʊ; gro/ *v* 动

grows, growing, grew, grown

1. to become bigger or taller 成长；发育；长大

   My sister has grown a lot recently. 我的妹妹近期长高了很多。

2. to become 逐渐变得；逐渐成为

   The sky grew dark. 天色逐渐变暗。

3. to plant and look after flowers, trees, etc 种植；栽培

   Grace grew some roses in the garden. 格蕾丝在花园里种了一些玫瑰花。

grow up 成长；长大

When I grow up, I want to be a teacher. 我长大后想当教师。

*grown-up /ˌgrəʊn ˈʌp; ˌgron ˋʌp/ *n* 名

a man or woman, who is not a child 大人；成年人

A child should take the lift with a grown-up. 小孩子应该和大人一起乘电梯。

用法 主要为儿童所用。

同义 **adult**

*growth /grəʊθ; groθ/ *n* 名

无复数

an increase in amount, size or number 增大；增多

There has been a gradual growth in the population. 人口逐渐增加。

grumble /ˈgrʌmbl; ˋgrʌmbl̩/ *v* 动

grumbles, grumbling, grumbled, grumbled

to complain about someone or something in an unhappy way 抱怨；发牢骚

They grumbled about having too

much homework. 他们抱怨作业太多。

guard¹ /gɑːd; gɑrd/ *n* 名

someone who protects a building or a person 警卫；守卫
There were two guards at the entrance of the building. 两个守卫站在大楼的入口。

guard² /gɑːd; gɑrd/ *v* 动

to protect a building or a person by staying near them 守卫；护卫
The policemen are guarding the palace. 警察守卫着王宫。

guava /ˈgwɑːvə; ˋgwɑvə/ *n* 名

a green or yellow fruit that is pink or white inside and has many seeds 番石榴
She put some guavas in the fruit salad. 她在水果沙拉中放了一些番石榴。

***guess¹** /ges; gɛs/ *v* 动

guesses, guessing, guessed, guessed
to give an answer, when you are not sure if you are right 猜想；猜测
Can you guess my name? 你能猜到我的名字吗？

***guess²** /ges; gɛs/ *n* 名

复数：*guesses*
an answer that you think is right but are not sure about 猜测
Where is the ball? Make a guess! 球在哪里？猜猜看！

***guest** /gest; gɛst/ *n* 名

someone who is invited to your home or to a special event such as a party 客人；宾客
Oscar has invited some guests for dinner tonight. 奥斯卡邀请了一些客人今晚来吃晚饭。

比较 host

***guide¹** /gaɪd; gaɪd/ *n* 名

1. someone who takes you to an interesting place and tells you about it 导游
   The guide took the tourists to the Great Wall. 导游带游客去了长城。
2. a book that teaches you about something 指南；手册
   This is a guide for new parents. 这是给新手父母的一本指南。
3. （也作：***Guide***）a member of a club for girls 女童子军
   The Guides go camping every year. 女童子军每年都去露营。

另见 scout

***guide²** /gaɪd; gaɪd/ *v* 动

guides, guiding, guided, guided
to take someone to a place or show someone the direction to a place 带路；带领
A policeman guided us to the hotel. 一个警察带领我们到酒店。

guilty /ˈgɪlti; ˋgɪltɪ/ *adj* 形

guiltier, guiltiest
feeling ashamed and unhappy because you have done something wrong 内疚的；羞愧的
Andy felt guilty because he told a lie. 安迪因为说谎感到内疚。

***guitar** /gɪˈtɑː; gɪˋtɑr/ *n* 名

a musical instrument with strings that you play with your fingers 吉他
Paul is playing the guitar. 保罗正在弹吉他。

gum /gʌm; gʌm/ *n* 名

1. the pink part inside your mouth that holds your teeth 牙龈；齿龈
   You may hurt your gums if you brush too hard. 如果刷牙时太用力，你会损伤齿龈。
2. （无复数）（**也作：*chewing gum***）a sweet that you chew but do not swallow 口香糖
   She blew bubbles with a piece of gum. 她用一块口香糖吹泡泡。

***gun** /gʌn; gʌn/ *n* 名

a weapon for shooting bullets 枪

He went hunting with a gun. 他带着枪去打猎。

***gym** /dʒɪm; dʒɪm/ *n* 名

1. （也作：***gymnasium***）a hall or room with equipment for doing exercise 体育馆；健身房
   Nick often goes to the gym to keep fit. 尼克经常到健身房健身。
2. （无复数）exercises that you do indoors, especially at school 体操
   The students did gym in the PE lesson. 学生在体育课时做体操。

gymnastics /dʒɪmˈnæstɪks; dʒɪmˋnæstɪks/ *n* 名

无复数
indoor exercises that make you strong 体操
Gymnastics can help you to stay healthy. 体操能帮助你保持身体健康。

G

***habit** /ˈhæbɪt; ˋhæbɪt/ *n* 名

something that you usually do 习惯
Smoking is a bad habit. 抽烟是个坏习惯。

get into/in the habit of doing something 养成（做某事的）习惯
I have got into the habit of doing exercise. 我养成了做运动的习惯。

had /həd; həd; *strong* 强读 hæd; hæd/ *v* 动

the past tense and past participle of **have** ☆ have 的过去式和过去分词

hadn't /ˈhædnt; ˋhædnt/

the short form of "**had not**" ☆ had not 的缩写
Henry said he hadn't been to China before. 亨利说他从没去过中国。

***hair** /heə; hɛr/ *n* 名

1. （无复数）the thin, thread-like things that grow on the head and body of a person or an animal 头发；毛
   I comb my hair every morning. 我每天早上都梳头。
2. one of the thin, thread-like things that grow on the head and body of a person or an animal 一根头发；一根毛
   There is a hair in my glass of water. 我这杯水里有一根头发。

haircut /ˈheəkʌt; ˋhɛrˏkʌt/ *n* 名

if you have a haircut, someone cuts your hair 理发
Do I need a haircut? 我该去理发吗？

hairdresser /ˈheəˌdresə; ˋhɛrˏdrɛsɚ/ *n* 名

a person who cuts and shapes hair 理发师；发型师
The hairdresser cut my hair short. 发型师把我的头发剪短。

hairdryer /ˈheəˌdraɪə; ˋhɛrˏdraɪɚ/ *n* 名

a machine used for drying hair 吹风机
I dried my hair with a hairdryer. 我用吹风机来吹干头发。

***half** /hɑːf; hæf/ *n* 名

复数：***halves***
one of two equal parts of something 一半；半数
Half of ten is five. 10 的一半是 5。

in half 分成两半
I cut the pear in half. 我把梨子切成两半。

halfway /ˌhɑːfˈweɪ; ˌhæfˋwe/ *adv* 副

at the middle point between two things; in the middle of a period of time 半途；中间
I met my aunt halfway home. 我在回家的半路上遇到了阿姨。

***hall** /hɔːl; hɔl/ *n* 名

a large room or building for meetings or other events 会堂；礼堂
The concert took place in the school hall. 音乐会在学校礼堂举行。

Halloween /ˌhæləʊˈiːn; ˌhæloˋin/ *n* 名

也作：***Hallowe'en***
the night of 31 October, when children dress as ghosts, witches, etc 万圣节（10 月 31 日夜晚）
They held a party to celebrate Halloween. 他们举行派对庆祝万圣节。

***ham** /hæm; hæm/ *n* 名

meat from a pig's leg that has had salt added to stop it going bad 火腿

I put two slices of ham in my noodles. 我在面里放了两片火腿。

***hamburger** /ˈhæmbɜːgə; ˋhæmbɝgɚ/ *n* 名

a flat round piece of chopped beef that is cooked and eaten between two pieces of bread 汉堡包

I had a hamburger and French fries

for lunch today. 我今天午餐吃汉堡包和薯条。

同义 **burger**

***hammer** /ˈhæmə; ˋhæmɚ/ *n* 名

a tool used for hitting nails or breaking things 锤子

The worker is hitting nails into the wall with a hammer. 那个工人用锤子把钉子敲进墙里。

hamster /ˈhæmstə; ˋhæmstɚ/ *n* 名

a small animal like a mouse, often kept as a pet 仓鼠

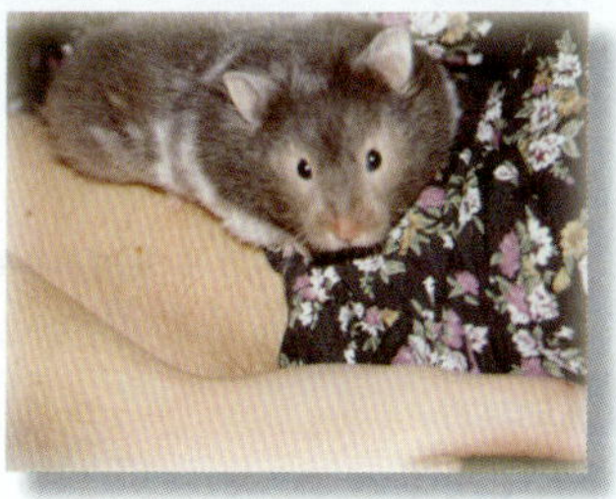

Ivan keeps three hamsters. 伊万养了三只仓鼠。

***hand¹** /hænd; hænd/ *n* 名

1. the part of your body at the end of your arm, including your fingers and thumb 手
   I always wash my hands before a meal. 我吃饭前都会洗手。
2. **a hand** help 帮助（某人）
   Can you give me a hand? 你能帮我一个忙吗？

by hand 用手

This hat is made by hand. 这顶帽子是手工做的。

hand in hand 手牵手

Annie and Connie walked hand in hand. 安妮和康妮手牵着手走着。

shake hands with someone 与某人握手

The singer shook hands with her fans. 那位歌手与她的歌迷握手。

***hand²** /hænd; hænd/ *v* 动

to give something to someone with your hand 递；交给

Lily handed the dictionary to me. 莉莉把词典递给我。

hand in 提交；上交

Time's up! Please hand in your exam papers. 时间到了！请交试卷。

hand out 分发；散发

The monitor handed out the exercise books. 班长分发了练习册。

Daily conversation 日常会话

"Can you hand me the phone, please?" "Sure." "请你把电话递给我好吗？" "好的。"

***handbag** /ˈhændbæg; ˋhændˌbæg/ *n* 名

a small bag for money, keys, etc that is usually used by women 手袋

My sister always has a mirror in her handbag. 我姐姐的手袋里总有一面镜子。

handcuffs /ˈhændkʌfs; ˋhændˌkʌfs/ *plural n* 复数名词

two metal rings used for holding the wrists of a prisoner together 手铐

The policeman caught the thief and put handcuffs on him. 警察抓到了小偷，给他戴上手铐。

handful /ˈhændfʊl; ˋhændˌfʊl/ *n* 名

an amount of something that you can hold in your hand 一把

The boy is holding a handful of popcorn. 那男孩手上拿着一把爆米花。

handicapped /ˈhændikæpt; ˋhændɪˌkæpt/ *adj* 形

not able to use a part of your body or mind because it has been injured or damaged 残疾的

He built a school for handicapped children. 他为残疾儿童建了一座学校。

注意 有人认为这是冒犯的用语。

handicraft /ˈhændikrɑːft; ˋhændɪˌkræft/ *n* 名

也作：***craft***

an activity such as sewing that requires skilful use of your hands 手工艺

Nick taught handicrafts at a summer class last year. 尼克去年在暑期班教手工。

用法 一般用复数。

***handkerchief** /ˈhæŋkətʃɪf; ˋhæŋkɚtʃɪf/ *n* 名

a piece of cloth for drying your eyes or nose 手帕

She wiped her tears with a handkerchief. 她用手帕擦干眼泪。

handle¹ /ˈhændl; ˋhændḷ/ *n* 名

the part that you use to hold or pull something 柄；把手

Michael turned the handle and opened the door. 迈克尔转动把手，打开了门。

handle² /ˈhændl; ˋhændḷ/ *v* 动

handles, handling, handled, handled

to hold or touch something 触；摸；拿
The vase is made of glass. Handle it carefully. 这个是玻璃花瓶。拿着要小心。

handlebars /ˈhændlbɑːz; ˋhændl͵barz/ *plural n* 复数名词
the parts of a bicycle or motorcycle that you hold and use to control it （自行车或摩托车的）把手

You must hold onto the handlebars while you are riding a bicycle. 当你骑自行车时，一定要握着把手。

***handsome** /ˈhænsəm; ˋhænsəm/ *adj* 形
good-looking — usually used about men 英俊的（常用于男性）
Peter is a handsome man. 彼得是个英俊的男子。
反义 **ugly**

handwriting /ˈhændˌraɪtɪŋ; ˋhænd͵raɪtɪŋ/ *n* 名
无复数
1. a person's particular way of writing 笔迹；书法
   Your handwriting is difficult to read. 你写的字很难看得懂。
2. writing that someone does by hand 手写的文字
   I had handwriting classes in kindergarten. 我在幼儿园上过写字课。

***hang** /hæŋ; hæŋ/ *v* 动
hangs, hanging, hung, hung
to fasten something at the top so that the top part is fixed and the lower part is free to move 挂；吊；悬
She hung the towels on the hook. 她把毛巾挂在钩上。

Daily conversation 日常会话
Hang on! 等一下！
"Hang on! I'll be back in a minute." "Okay." "等一下！我马上就回来。""好的。"

hanger /ˈhæŋə; ˋhæŋə/ *n* 名
something used for hanging clothes 衣架
Susan hangs her coat on a hanger. 苏珊把大衣挂在衣架上。

***happen** /ˈhæpən; ˋhæpən/ *v* 动
to take place, usually without being planned 发生
The car accident happened in the early morning. 车祸是在清晨发生的。

happily /ˈhæpɪli; ˋhæpɪlɪ/ *adv* 副
in a happy way 快乐地；愉快地
The children were playing happily in the park. 孩子们在公园里玩得很开心。
反义 **unhappily**

happiness /ˈhæpinəs; ˋhæpɪnɪs/ *n* 名
无复数
the feeling of being happy 快乐；幸福
Money can't buy happiness. 金钱不能够买到快乐。

***happy** /ˈhæpi; ˋhæpɪ/ *adj* 形
happier, happiest
feeling pleased 快乐的；愉快的
I'm happy because it's the start of the holidays. 我很开心，因为开始放假了。
反义 **sad, unhappy**

***harbour** /ˈhɑːbə; ˋharbə/ *n* 名
美式：***harbor***
an area of water where ships can stay safely 港口；海港

There are a lot of ships in the harbour. 海港里停了很多船只。

***hard[1]** /hɑːd; hard/ *adj* 形
harder, hardest
1. difficult to bend, break or cut 坚硬的；坚固的
   I don't like hard sweets. 我不喜欢硬糖。
   反义 **soft**
2. difficult to do or understand 艰难的；困难的
   The questions in the test were very hard. 测验的题目很难。
   反义 **easy**

***hard[2]** /hɑːd; hard/ *adv* 副
harder, hardest
with a lot of effort 努力地；费力地
Ann worked hard and got good results in the exam. 安很用功，在考试中取得了好成绩。

hard copy /ˌhɑːd ˈkɒpɪ; ͵hard ˋkapɪ/ *n* 名
复数：***hard copies***
【电脑】a piece of paper with information from a computer printed on it（从电脑打印的）打印本；硬拷贝
You should hand in a hard copy of the composition to the teacher. 你要把作文的打印本交给老师。

hard disk /ˌhɑːd ˈdɪsk; ͵hard ˋdɪsk/ *n* 名
【电脑】the part of a computer that

stores information 硬盘

You can save the data on the hard disk. 你可以将数据存储在硬盘里。

hardware /'hɑ:dweə; `hard͵wɛr/ *n* 名

无复数

【电脑】the parts of a computer, not including programs 硬件

Hardware includes things like a computer keyboard or a mouse. 电脑硬件包括键盘和鼠标等组件。

比较 **software**

hard-working /ˌhɑ:d 'wɜ:kɪŋ; ˏhard `wɝkɪŋ/ *adj* 形

working with a lot of effort 努力工作的；勤奋的

Jenny is hard-working and does revision after school every day. 珍妮很勤奋，每天回家都会温习功课。

反义 **lazy**

hare /heə; hɛr/ *n* 名

a wild animal with long ears that looks like a large rabbit 野兔

A hare can run very fast. 野兔可以跑得很快。

注意 发音与 hair 相同。

harm¹ /hɑ:m; harm/ *n* 名

无复数

damage or injury 伤害；损害

Eating too many sweets will do you harm. 吃太多糖对你有害处。

harm² /hɑ:m; harm/ *v* 动

to hurt someone or damage something 伤害；损伤

The dog is very gentle and he won't harm you. 这只狗很友善，不会伤害你。

harmful /'hɑ:mfəl; `harmfəl/ *adj* 形

causing harm 有害的；伤人的

Smoking is harmful to health. 吸烟危害健康。

harvest /'hɑ:vɪst; `harvɪst/ *n* 名

1. the time when crops are gathered 收获；收割

The farmers were busy with the harvest. 农民忙着收割。

2. the amount of crops that are gathered 收成；收获量

They had a good harvest last year. 他们去年的收成很好。

***has** / həz; həz; *strong* 强读 hæz; hæz/ *v* 动

a form of **have** ☆ have 的另一种现在式，与主语 he、she 和 it 一起使用

hasn't /'hæznt; `hæzn̩t/ *v* 动

the short form of "**has not**" ☆ has not 的缩写

Henry hasn't had his dinner yet. 亨利还没有吃晚饭。

***hat** /hæt; hæt/ *n* 名

something you wear on your head 帽子

She is wearing a hat with flowers on it. 她戴了一顶带花的帽子。

比较 **cap**

***hate** /heɪt; het/ *v* 动

hates, hating, hated, hated

to dislike someone or something very much 憎恨；讨厌；厌恶

I hate mosquitoes because they bite. 我讨厌蚊子，因为它们会叮人。

反义 **love¹**

***have** /v, əv, həv; v, əv, həv; *strong* 强读 hæv; hæv/ *v* 动

has, having, had, had

1. used to describe what someone or something looks like 有；具有

   She has long hair and beautiful eyes. 她有一头长发和漂亮的眼睛。

用法 这用法没有进行式。

2. to own, hold or keep something 有；拥有

   The two girls have a lot of dolls. 那两个女孩有很多玩具娃娃。

用法 这一用法没有进行式。在日常对话有时候会用 have got 来代替 have，以上的例子可说成 The two girls have got a lot of dolls。

3. to become ill 患（病）

   Anna has a bad cold. 安娜患了重感冒。

H

用法 这用法没有进行式。在日常对话有时候会用 have got 来代替 have，以上的例子可说成 Anna's got a bad cold。

4. to eat or drink 吃；喝
   I had fried noodles for lunch. 我午餐吃炒面。
5. used together with the past participle to say that something happened in the past 已经（与过去分词连用，表示某动作已完成）
   I have finished my homework. 我已经做完功课了。

have to/have got to 必须；不得不
We have to leave now or we will miss the train. 我们必须立刻离开，否则会赶不上火车。

H

haven't /'hævnt; `hævn̩t/

the short form of "**have not**" ☆have not 的缩写
We haven't been to New York before. 我们从未去过纽约。

hawker /'hɔ:kə; `hɔkɚ/ *n* 名

someone who sells goods in the street 小贩
The hawker is selling oranges. 那个小贩在卖橙子。

*he /ɪ, hɪ; ɪ, hɪ; *strong* 强读 hi:; hi/ *pron* 代

a man, boy or male animal that has already been mentioned or is known about 他
This is George. He is my classmate. 这是乔治。他是我的同学。

*head /hed; hɛd/ *n* 名

1. the top part of your body above your neck that has your brain, eyes, ears, mouth, etc 头
   She put her head out of the window. 她把头伸出窗外。
2. your mind or brain 头脑；脑筋
   Please use your head, Thomas! 托马斯，请动动脑筋！
3. the leader or most important person in a group 主管；领导人
   His mother is the head of the company. 他的母亲是这家公司的主管。

from head to foot/toe 从头到脚；全身
I was wet from head to toe in the rain. 我在雨中全身湿透了。

*headache /'hedeɪk; `hɛd͵ek/ *n* 名

a pain in the head 头痛
Susan has a bad headache. 苏珊头痛得厉害。

heading /'hedɪŋ; `hɛdɪŋ/ *n* 名

words at the top of a piece of writing as a title 标题；题目
The heading of this essay is "My School". 这篇文章的标题是《我的学校》。

headphones /'hedfəʊnz; `hɛd͵fonz/ *plural n* 复数名词

a piece of equipment that you wear over your ears to listen to music, the radio, etc 耳机

Ross is listening to the songs on headphones. 罗斯正在用耳机听歌。

heal /hi:l; hil/ *v* 动

to become healthy again; to make something healthy again 痊愈
The cut on his head has healed. 他头上的伤口已痊愈。

注意 发音和 heel 相同。

health /helθ; hɛlθ/ *n* 名

无复数

the condition of your body 健康（情况）
Fruit and vegetables are good for your health. 水果和蔬菜对身体有益。

in good/bad/poor health 身体健康/不健康
The doctor said my grandmother was in good health. 医生说我的祖母很健康。

*healthy /'helθi; `hɛlθɪ/ *adj* 形

healthier, healthiest

well and fit; not ill 健康的；健壮的
They are healthy because they do exercise every day. 他们每天都运动，所以身体很健康。

反义 **ill, sick, unhealthy**

heap /hi:p; hip/ *n* 名

an untidy pile of things 堆
There was a heap of old clothes in the corner. 角落里有一堆旧衣服。

*hear /hɪə; hɪr/ *v* 动

hears, hearing, heard, heard

1. to know that someone or something is making a sound, using your ears 听见；听到
   I heard a noise when I was reading. 我阅读时听到吵闹声。
2. to listen to someone or something 听；聆听
   Did you hear the news on the radio? 你有没有在电台听到这条新闻？

hear about/of someone or something 听说过某人/某事物
I have never heard of the place. 我从未听说过这个地方。

hear from someone 听到某人的消息
I haven't heard from him for a long time. 我很久没听到他的消息了。

注意 发音和 here 相同。

比较 **listen**

***heart** /hɑːt; hɑrt/ *n* 名

1. the part of your body that moves blood around your body 心脏；心

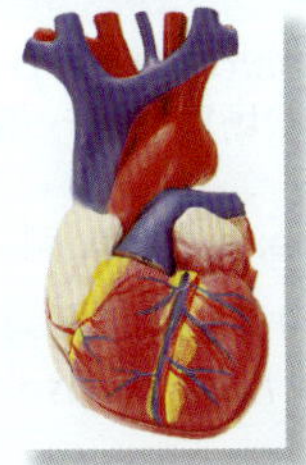

I am very nervous. My heart is beating fast! 我很紧张。心跳得很快！

2. your feelings or your character 心地；感情

She had a kind heart and was always helping people. 她心地善良，常常帮助他人。

by heart 熟记；背诵

We learnt the poem by heart. 我们把这首诗记熟了。

heat¹ /hiːt; hit/ *n* 名

无复数

the quality of being hot 热；高温

The sun gives us light and heat. 太阳给我们光和热。

heat² /hiːt; hit/ *v* 动

to make something hot 加热

I am heating some soup. 我在把汤加热。

heater /ˈhiːtə; ˋhitɚ/ *n* 名

a thing that makes air or water hotter 暖炉；加热器

It is cold today so we have turned on the heater. 今天很冷，所以我们开了暖炉。

heaven /ˈhevn; ˋhɛvən/ *n* 名

无复数

a place where God is believed to live and where good people go when they die 天堂；天国

Some people believe that there are angels in heaven. 有些人相信天堂里住着天使。

比较 **hell**

heavily /ˈhevɪli; ˋhɛvɪlɪ/ *adv* 副

very much 大量地

It was raining heavily. 雨下得很大。

***heavy** /ˈhevi; ˋhɛvɪ/ *adj* 形

heavier, heaviest

1. weighing a lot 重的；沉重的

There are a lot of books in my school bag so it is very heavy. 我的书包里有很多书，所以很重。

反义 **light²**

2. great in amount or high in level 大量的；严重的

The floods were caused by the heavy rain. 暴雨导致这场水灾。

反义 **light²**

he'd /iːd, hiːd; ɪd, hɪd; *strong* 强读 hiːd; hid/

1. the short form of "**he had**" ☆he had 的缩写

He said he'd seen a UFO before. 他说他见过不明飞行物。

2. the short form of "**he would**" ☆he would 的缩写

He'd like a burger and fries. 他想吃汉堡包和薯条。

hedge /hedʒ; hɛdʒ/ *n* 名

a line of bushes or small trees growing close together 树篱

The hedges are cut into animal shapes. 树篱被修剪成动物形状。

heel /hiːl; hil/ *n* 名

1. the back part of your foot 脚跟

The new shoes hurt my heels. 这双新鞋弄痛了我的脚跟。

2. the bottom part of a shoe that is under your heel 鞋后跟

She likes to wear shoes with high heels. 她喜欢穿高跟鞋。

height /haɪt; haɪt/ *n* 名

how tall something is 高；高度

Sally is the same height as her brother. 莎莉与她的弟弟一样高。

held /held; hɛld/ *v* 动

the past tense and past participle of **hold** ☆hold 的过去式和过去分词

H

helicopter /ˈhelɪkɒptə; ˋhɛlɪˌkɑptɚ/ *n* 名

an aircraft that can fly straight up and down 直升机

The helicopter took him to a hospital. 直升机送他去医院。

he'll /iːl, hiːl; ɪl, hɪl; *strong* 强读 hiːl; hil/

the short form of "**he will**" ☆he will 的缩写

He'll go to Shanghai next week. 他下星期会去上海。

hell /hel; hɛl/ *n* 名

无复数

the place where bad people are believed to go to after they die 地狱

He thinks the robber will be punished in hell. 他认为这个强盗将下地狱。

比较 **heaven**

***hello** /həˈləʊ; həˋlo/ *interj* 感叹

used when you meet someone or start a telephone conversation 嗨；喂

Hello, Sally! 嗨，莎莉！

另见 hi

Daily conversation 日常会话

"Hello. May I speak to Annie, please?" "One moment please." "喂，请问安妮在吗？""请稍等。"

helmet /ˈhelmɪt; ˋhɛlmɪt/ *n* 名

a hard hat that protects your head 头盔；安全帽

You should wear a helmet when you ride a bicycle. 当你骑自行车时，应戴上头盔。

***help[1]** /help; hɛlp/ *v* 动

to do something for someone 帮助；帮忙

My mother sent me to help him. 我妈妈让我去帮助他。

can't help (doing) something 忍不住；禁不住

I couldn't help laughing when I heard the joke. 我听到这个笑话时，不禁笑了出来。

Help! 救命啊！

Help! The house is on fire! 救命啊！房子着火啦！

help someone (to) do something 帮某人做某事

I helped my mother to tidy the living room. 我帮妈妈收拾客厅。

help yourself to something 自己取（食物）

Please help yourself to the food. 请随便吃。

***help[2]** /help; hɛlp/ *n* 名

无复数

things you do for someone 帮助；帮忙

Thank you very much for your help. 非常谢谢你的帮助。

helpful /ˈhelpfl; ˋhɛlpfəl/ *adj* 形

willing to help 乐于助人的

The man in the shop was very helpful. 那家店铺里的男人非常乐于助人。

反义 unhelpful

***hen** /hen; hɛn/ *n* 名

a female chicken 母鸡

The hen laid two eggs yesterday. 这只母鸡昨天生了两个蛋。

另见 chicken, cock

***her[1]** /ə, hə; ɚ, hɚ; *strong* 强读 hɜː; hɝ/ *pron* 代

a word used for a woman, girl or female animal that has already been mentioned or is known about 她

I saw her at the supermarket. 我在超市遇见了她。

***her[2]** /ə, hə; ɚ, hɚ; *strong* 强读 hɜː; hɝ/ *adj* 形

belonging to a woman, girl or female animal that has already been mentioned or is known about 她的

This is her dictionary. 这是她的字典。

herd /hɜːd; hɝd/ *n* 名

a group of animals of the same kind 牧群；兽群

He kept a herd of sheep on his farm. 他在农场里养了一群羊。

***here** /hɪə; hɪr/ *adv* 副

in, at or to this place 在这里；到这里

Come over here, please. 请到这里来。

here and there 各处；到处

Birds are singing here and there in the park. 公园里鸟儿到处鸣叫。

比较 there[1]

Daily conversation 日常会话

here it is 这是你要的东西（用于指示）

"Have you seen my jacket?" "Here it is, hanging on the door." "你见过我的外套吗？""就在这里，挂在门上。"

here you are（把东西给别人时说）这是给你的

"May I borrow your pen?" "Sure, here you are." "我可以借用你的笔吗？""可以，拿去吧。"

hero /ˈhɪərəʊ; ˋhɪro/ *n* 名

复数：*heroes*

a man who does something very brave 英雄

The hero killed the monster. 英雄把怪兽杀了。

heroine /ˈherəʊɪn; ˋhɛro·ɪn/ *n* 名

a woman who does something very brave 女英雄

The heroine saved the child from the robber. 女英雄从强盗手中救出了小孩。

hers /hɜːz; hɝz/ *pron* 代

used to refer to something that belongs to a woman, girl or female animal that has already been mentioned 她的（东西）

This dictionary is hers, not mine. 这本词典是她的，不是我的。

***herself** /ə'self; ɚ`sɛlf; *strong* 强读 hə'self; hɚ`sɛlf / *pron* 代

the same woman or girl that the sentence is about 她自己；她本人

She hurt herself when she fell down. 她跌倒时受了伤。

by herself 她独自；一个人

The woman lives by herself. 那个女人独自居住。

he's /iz, hiz; ɪz, hɪz; *strong* 强读 hi:z; hiz/

1. the short form of "**he is**" ☆he is 的缩写

   This is Sam. He's a doctor. 这是山姆，他是医生。

2. the short form of "**he has**" ☆he has 的缩写

   He's gone home. 他回家去了。

hey /heɪ; he/ *interj* 感叹

used to get attention or to express surprise, anger, etc 喂；嘿；嗨

Hey! What's that? 喂！那是什么？

hi /haɪ; haɪ/ *interj* 感叹

used as a greeting 喂；嗨

Hi Maggie, how are you? 嗨，玛姬，你好吗？

用法 hi 是比 hello 更为随便的用语。

另见 **hello**

hid /hɪd; hɪd/ *v* 动

the past tense of **hide** ☆hide 的过去式

hidden /'hɪdn; `hɪdn̩/ *v* 动

the past participle of **hide** ☆hide 的过去分词

***hide** /haɪd; haɪd/ *v* 动

hides, hiding, hid, hidden

1. to put something somewhere that no one knows 把…藏起来

   My dog hid the bone in the garden. 我的狗把骨头藏在花园里。

2. to be in a place where no one can see or find you 躲藏

   The thief is hiding under the bed. 小偷躲在床底下。

***hide-and-seek** /ˌhaɪd ənd 'si:k; ˌhaɪd ənd `sik/ *n* 名

无复数

a children's game in which one child shuts his or her eyes while the other children hide, and tries to find them 捉迷藏

We played hide-and-seek in the park. 我们在公园里玩捉迷藏。

***high** /haɪ; haɪ/ *adj* 形

higher, highest

1. having a great distance from the bottom to the top or being far from the ground 高的

   Which is the highest building in Shanghai? 上海哪一座大厦最高？

用法 不可以用来形容人。若要形容人，应用 tall。

反义 **low**

比较 **tall**

2. greater than normal in amount, number, size or level（比平常）高的；超乎寻常的

   The price of land is very high. 土地的价格很高。

反义 **low**

highway /'haɪweɪ; `haɪˌwe/ *n* 名

a main road 公路

This highway joins the two cities. 这条公路连接两个城市。

hijack /'haɪdʒæk; `haɪˌdʒæk/ *v* 动

to take control of a plane, bus, etc in a violent way 劫机；劫车

Three men hijacked the plane. 三名男子劫持了飞机。

hiking /'haɪkɪŋ; `haɪkɪŋ/ *n* 名

无复数

the activity of taking long walks in the countryside 远足；徒步旅行

We are going hiking this Sunday. 这个星期天我们会去远足。

***hill** /hɪl; hɪl/ *n* 名

a small mountain 小山；山丘

They walked to the top of the hill. 他们走到了山顶上。

hilly /'hɪli; `hɪlɪ/ *adj* 形

hillier, hilliest

having a lot of hills 多山丘的

Running in a hilly area takes a lot of

H

energy. 在丘陵地区跑步很费力气。

***him** /ɪm; ɪm; *strong* 强读 hɪm; hɪm/ *pron* 代

a word used for a man, boy or male animal that has already been mentioned or is known about 他

His name is Daniel but I call him Danny. 他的名字是丹尼尔，但我叫他丹尼。

***himself** /ɪm'self; ɪm`sɛlf; *strong* 强读 hɪm'self; hɪm`sɛlf/ *pron* 代

the same man or boy that the sentence is about 他自己；他本人

He cut himself with the scissors. 他用剪刀割伤了自己。

by himself 他独自；一个人

He moved the table by himself. 他一个人搬动了那张桌子。

H

hint /hɪnt; hɪnt/ *n* 名

something that you say or do to help someone to guess an answer or do something 暗示；提示

I don't know the answer. Can you give me a hint? 我不知道答案。可以给我一点提示吗？

hip /hɪp; hɪp/ *n* 名

the part of your body between the top of your legs and your waist 臀部

This exercise makes your hips stronger. 这种运动有助于加强臀部肌肉。

另见 附录：The body 身体

hippopotamus

/ˌhɪpə'pɒtəməs; ˌhɪpə`pɑtəməs/ *n* 名

复数：***hippopotamuses/ hippopotami*** ｜ 也作：***hippo***

a large, grey animal from Africa that lives near rivers 河马

Angela first saw hippopotamuses at the zoo. 安琪拉在动物园第一次看见河马。

hire /'haɪə; haɪr/ *v* 动

hires, hiring, hired, hired

to pay for using something or getting someone's help 租用；雇用

He hired a car when he went to Japan. 他去日本时，租了一辆汽车。

***his**[1] /ɪz; ɪz; *strong* 强读 hɪz; hɪz/ *adj* 形

belonging to a man, boy or male animal that has already been mentioned 他的

I did not call Peter because I lost his phone number. 我没打电话给彼得，因为我遗失了他的电话号码。

***his**[2] /ɪz; ɪz; *strong* 强读 hɪz; hɪz/ *pron* 代

used to refer to something that belongs to a man, boy or male animal that has already been mentioned 他的（东西）

This toy car is his, not mine. 这辆玩具车是他的，不是我的。

hiss /hɪs; hɪs/ *v* 动

hisses, hissing, hissed, hissed

to make a long "s" sound 发出嘶嘶声

The snake hissed at the monkey. 蛇向猴子发出嘶嘶声。

***history** /'hɪstri; `hɪstrɪ/ *n* 名

无复数

1. all the things that happened in the past 历史

   This is a book about Chinese history. 这是一本有关中国历史的书。
2. the study of things that happened in the past 历史科；历史学

   He is studying history at university. 他在大学攻读历史学。

***hit** /hɪt; hɪt/ *v* 动

hits, hitting, hit, hit

to touch someone or something quickly and with force 打；击

Annie hit him with her book. 安妮用书打他。

***hobby** /'hɒbi; `hɑbɪ/ *n* 名

复数：***hobbies***

an activity that you enjoy doing when you are free 爱好；爱好

Henry's hobby is making models. 亨利的爱好是制作模型。

同义 interest

Daily conversation 日常会话

"What are your hobbies?" "I like reading a lot." "你有什么爱好？""我很喜欢读书。"

hoist /hɔɪst; hɔɪst/ *v* 动

to lift or raise something with a rope 升起；扯起

A policeman is hoisting the flag. 一名警察正在升旗。

***hold** /həʊld; hold/ *v* 动

holds, holding, held, held

1. to have something in your hand, arms, etc 拿住；握住

   The robber was holding a gun. 劫匪手上拿着枪。

2. to have something inside 容纳；装下
   Our school hall can hold 500 people. 我们学校的礼堂可容纳500人。
3. to have a meeting, competition, etc 举行；举办
   We held our class meeting yesterday. 我们昨天开班会。

Daily conversation 日常会话
hold on 等等
"Hold on, please. She's coming." "请等等，她就来了。"

***hole** /həʊl; hol/ *n* 名

an empty space in something 洞；孔
The mouse went into the house through a small hole. 老鼠从小洞窜进屋里。

***holiday** /ˈhɒlədeɪ; ˋhɑləˏde/ *n* 名
【英】
美式：***vacation***
a period of time when you do not go to work or school 假期；假日
A lot of students love the summer holidays. 很多学生都喜欢暑假。
on holiday 在休假
Angela will be on holiday next week. 安琪拉下星期休假。

hollow /ˈhɒləʊ; ˋhɑlo/ *adj* 形

having an empty space inside 空心的；中空的
He cut down the hollow tree. 他砍了那棵空心树。

holy /ˈhəʊli; ˋholɪ/ *adj* 形
holier, holiest
connected with God and religion 神圣的；有关神的；有关宗教的
The Bible is the holy book of the Christians.《圣经》是基督徒的经典。

***home** /həʊm; hom/ *n* 名

the place where you live 家

I must go home now. 我现在必须回家了。
at home 在家里
Is your mother at home? 你的妈妈在家里吗？

Daily conversation 日常会话
make yourself at home 请随便（招呼客人时说的话）
"I'll get you a cup of tea. Make yourself at home." "我给你拿一杯茶。请随意。"

homeless /ˈhəʊmləs; ˋhomləs/ *adj* 形

having no home 无家可归的
The homeless man slept in the park last night. 那个无家可归的人昨晚在公园里露宿。

homepage, home page /ˈhəʊmpeɪdʒ; ˋhomˏpedʒ/ *n* 名
【电脑】the main page of a website 主页；首页
Click here to go back to the homepage. 点击这里回到主页。

***homework** /ˈhəʊmwɜːk; ˋhomˏwɝk/ *n* 名
无复数
work that teachers ask students to do at home 功课；家庭作业
I have a lot of homework today. 我今天有很多功课。

比较 **schoolwork**

***honest** /ˈɒnɪst; ˋɑnɪst/ *adj* 形

someone who is honest does not lie, steal or cheat 诚实的
Everyone likes Ivy because she is honest. 所有人都喜欢艾薇，因为她很诚实。
反义 **dishonest**

honesty /ˈɒnɪsti; ˋɑnɪstɪ/ *n* 名
无复数
the quality of being honest 诚实
I like your honesty. 我欣赏你的诚实。

***honey** /ˈhʌni; ˋhʌnɪ/ *n* 名
无复数
sweet sticky liquid that bees make and is used as food 蜂蜜

He put honey in the tea. 他在茶中加蜂蜜。

hoof /huːf; hʊf/ *n* 名
复数：***hoofs/hooves***

H

the hard part of the foot of a horse, cow, etc 蹄

A horse has four hooves. 马有四蹄。

hook /hʊk; hʊk/ *n* 名

a curved piece of plastic or metal for holding things or catching fish 钩

Roger hung his coat on the hook. 罗杰把他的外套挂在钩上。

***hop** /hɒp; hɑp/ *v* 动

hops, hopping, hopped, hopped

to move by jumping（人）单脚跳；（动物）跳跃

The grasshopper hopped onto my hand. 蚱蜢跳到了我的手上。

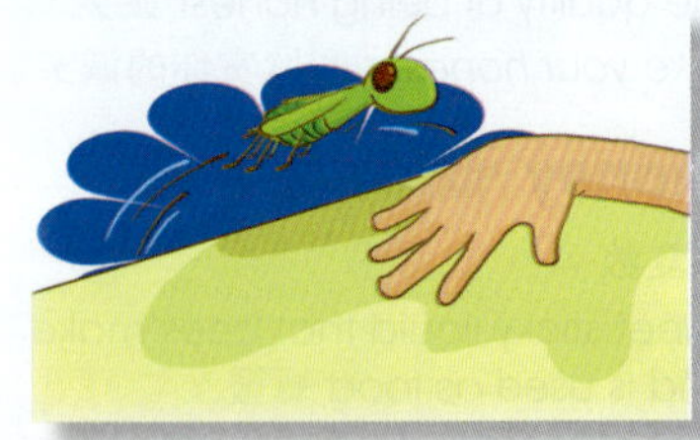

用法 用 hop 描述人的动作时，指单脚跳，但指动物时，例如：青蛙、兔子、鸟类等，则为双脚或四只脚一起跳。

***hope¹** /həʊp; hop/ *v* 动

hopes, hoping, hoped, hoped

to want something to happen or to be true and believe that it is possible 希望；期望

I hope it will be sunny on Sunday. 我希望星期日天气晴朗。

比较 wish¹

***hope²** /həʊp; hop/ *n* 名

1. a feeling that something you want will happen 希望；期望
   I have two hopes for the future. 我对未来抱有两个希望。
2. a chance that something good will happen 机会；可能性
   Is there any hope that our team will win? 我们的球队有可能赢吗？

hopscotch /ˈhɒpskɒtʃ; ˋhɑpˌskɑtʃ/ *n* 名

无复数

a children's game in which squares are drawn on the ground and children jump from one square to another 跳房子游戏；跳飞机

We play hopscotch during recess every day. 我们每天休息时都玩跳房子。

horizon /həˈraɪzn; həˋraɪzn̩/ *n* 名

the horizon（无复数）the line where the sky seems to meet the land or sea 地平线

The sun is setting on the horizon. 太阳落在地平线上。

horizontal /ˌhɒrɪˈzɒntl; ˌhɑrəˋzɑntl̩/ *adj* 形

flat and parallel to the ground 水平的

He drew a horizontal line on the blackboard. 他在黑板上画了一条水平线。

反义 vertical

horn /hɔːn; hɔrn/ *n* 名

1. the hard pointed part that grows in pair on the head of cows, goats, etc（动物的）角
   The comb is made of ox horn. 这把梳子是用牛角做的。
2. something in a vehicle that is used to make a loud sound（汽车的）喇叭
   The driver blew his horn at the dog. 司机对着狗按喇叭。

3. a musical instrument that you blow into 号（乐器）
   Amy is playing the horn. 艾米正在吹号。

***horrible** /ˈhɒrəbl; ˋhɔrəbl̩/ *adj* 形

very bad or unpleasant 可怕的；糟糕的

I didn't sleep well last night because I had a horrible dream. 我昨晚睡得不好，因为我做了一个可怕的梦。

同义 terrible

horror /ˈhɒrə; ˋhɔrɚ/ *n* 名

无复数

a strong feeling of fear and shock 惊恐；震惊

They cried out in horror when they saw the snake. 他们见到那条蛇时，惊恐得叫了起来。

***horse** /hɔːs; hɔrs/ *n* 名

a large animal that people use for riding on or for carrying things 马

I have never ridden a horse. 我从未骑过马。

hose /həʊz; hoz/ *n* 名

a long plastic or rubber pipe that you use to put water onto fires, gardens, etc 软管；胶管

My father washed the car with a hose. 爸爸用胶管冲洗汽车。

***hospital** /ˈhɒspɪtl; ˋhɑspɪtl/ *n* 名

a place where sick people are given care and treated by doctors and nurses 医院

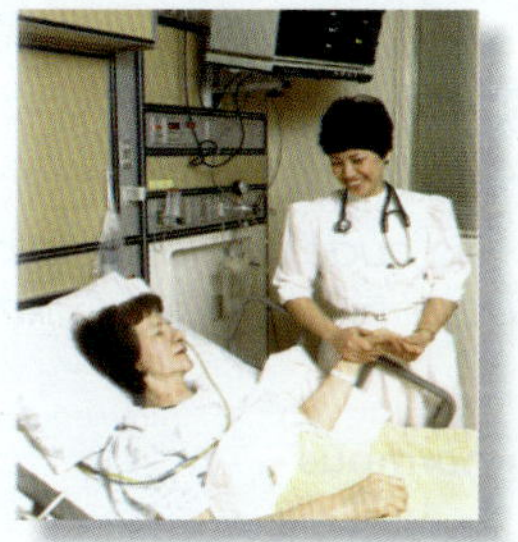

Jack went to hospital yesterday because he broke his leg. 杰克昨天进了医院，因为他摔断了腿。

in hospital 住医院

Candy's grandfather is in hospital now. 坎蒂的祖父正在住院。

host /həʊst; host/ *n* 名

someone who invites guests to a party, meal, etc 主人

The host greeted the guests at the entrance. 主人在入口迎接宾客。

比较 **guest**

hostel /ˈhɒstl; ˋhɑstl/ *n* 名

a cheap place where people can stay and eat 客栈

They stayed in a hostel when they were in Singapore. 他们去新加坡时住在客栈里。

***hot** /hɒt; hɑt/ *adj* 形

hotter, hottest

1. having a high temperature 热的；烫的

   It is very hot today. 今天很热。

反义 **cold**[1]

2. used to describe food that produces a burning feeling in your mouth 辣的

   These chillies are too hot for me. 我觉得这些辣椒太辣了。

同义 **spicy**

***hot dog** /ˌhɒt ˈdɒg; ˌhɑt ˋdɑg/ *n* 名

a cooked sausage in a bread roll 热狗

I like hot dogs more than hamburgers. 比起汉堡包，我更喜欢吃热狗。

***hotel** /həʊˈtel; hoˋtɛl/ *n* 名

a building which has rooms that you can pay to stay in 旅馆；酒店

When we went to Rome, we stayed in a good hotel. 我们去罗马时，住在一家很好的酒店里。

hotpot /ˈhɒtpɒt; ˋhɑtˌpɑt/ *n* 名

a meal with meat and vegetables cooked in a pot 火锅

We often have hotpot in winter. 我们在冬天里经常吃火锅。

***hour** /ˈaʊə; aʊr/ *n* 名

60 minutes 小时

There are 24 hours in a day. 一天有24小时。

half an hour 半个小时

It took me half an hour to finish my homework. 我花了半小时把功课做好。

注意 发音和 our 相同。

另见 **附录**：Time 时间

***house** /haʊz; haʊz/ *n* 名

a building that people live in 房屋；住宅

There are three bedrooms in the house. 这所房子有三间睡房。

***housewife** /ˈhaʊswaɪf; ˋhaʊsˌwaɪf/ *n* 名

复数：***housewives***

a woman who stays at home to take care of her family 家庭主妇

My mother is a good housewife. 妈妈是个很好的家庭主妇。

housework /ˈhaʊswɜːk; ˋhaʊsˌwɝk/ *n* 名

无复数

the work of cleaning the house 家务

I often help my mother do the housework. 我经常帮妈妈做家务。

housing estate /ˈhaʊzɪŋ ɪˌsteɪt; ˋhaʊzɪŋ əˏstet/ *n* 名

an area with a large number of houses or flats built at the same time 住宅区

Ben and Henry live on the same housing estate. 本和亨利住在同一个住宅区里。

hovercraft /ˈhɒvəkrɑːft; ˋhʌvɚˏkræft/ *n* 名

复数：***hovercraft/hovercrafts***

a vehicle that can move over land or water 气垫船

We went to that island by hovercraft. 我们坐气垫船去那个岛。

另见 **hydrofoil, jetfoil**

***how** /haʊ; haʊ/ *adv* 副

1. in what way 怎样；如何

   How do you get to school? 你怎样去上学呢？

2. used in greetings 好吗?（问候别人时用）

   How is your grandmother? 你的祖母好吗？

Daily conversation 日常会话

"How do you do?" "你好。"（初次见面的问候语，用于正式场合，回答时同样用 How do you do?）

"How are you?" "I'm fine, thanks." "你好吗？" "很好，谢谢。"（较随便的用语）

3. used in questions about time, amount, size, etc 多少；多大（用于问句中）

   how long 多久

   How long should I wait? 我要等多久？

   how many 多少（用于可数名词）

   How many brothers and sisters do you have? 你有几个兄弟姐妹？

   how much 多少（用于不可数名词）；多少钱

   How much salt is in the bag? 袋子里有多少盐？

   How much is the pen? 这支笔多少钱？

   how old 年龄多大

   How old is your youngest brother? 你最小的弟弟今年几岁？

4. used to make something you say stronger 多么（用作强调）

   How beautiful! 多么漂亮啊！

Daily conversation 日常会话

how about (doing) something? …好吗？…行吗？怎么样？（用于建议）

How about going to the beach? 去海滩好吗？

how about ...? 怎么样？（用于询问别人意见）

I don't like watching TV. How about you? 我不爱看电视。你呢？

how come ...? 怎么会…呢？为什么…呢？

How come you didn't know that? 你怎么会不知道那件事呢？

Asking for directions 问路

"How do I get to the train station?" "Go straight down this street. It's on your right." "去火车站该怎样走呢？" "沿这条街走下去，火车站就在你的右边。"

***however** /haʊˈevə; haʊˋɛvɚ/ *adv* 副

1. used to say something that seems surprising or different from what you have just said 但是；不过

   I said sorry to Lily. However, she was still very angry. 我已经向莉莉道歉，但是她仍然很生气。

2. in whatever way 无论如何；不管怎样

   However hard the work is, we will not give up. 无论这工作有多困难，我们都不会放弃。

***hug[1]** /hʌg; hʌg/ *v* 动

hugs, hugging, hugged, hugged

to hold someone or something tightly with your arms to show that you like or love them 拥抱

Candy is hugging her teddy bear. 坎蒂紧抱着她的玩具熊。

***hug[2]** /hʌg; hʌg/ *n* 名

the action of holding someone or something tightly with your arms to show that you like or love them 拥抱

Give me a hug! 抱我一下！

***huge** /hjuːdʒ; hjudʒ/ *adj* 形

very big 巨大的；庞大的

There is a huge garden in front of the house. 房子前面有一个很大的花园。

同义 **enormous**

反义 **tiny**

***human** /ˈhjuːmən; ˋhjumən/ *n* 名

也作：***human being***

a person 人

He was the only human on the island. 他是岛上唯一的人。

humid /ˈhjuːmɪd; ˋhjumɪd/ *adj* 形

wet（天气）潮湿的

Hong Kong is humid in the summer. 香港的夏天很潮湿。

同义 **damp**

反义 **dry**[1]

humidity /hjuˈmɪdəti; hjuˋmɪdətɪ/ *n* 名

无复数

the amount of water in the air 湿度

The humidity is high today. 今天的湿度很高。

***hundred** /ˈhʌndrəd; ˋhʌndrəd/ *num* 数

the number 100 一百

There are three hundred students in the hall. 礼堂里有 300 名学生。

用法 如要说出具体数目，如 200 名学生，hundred 不作复数，后面不加 of，应写成 two hundred students; 如要说“数百”，hundred 便要用复数和后接 of，例如 hundreds of students。

hundredth /ˈhʌndrədθ; ˋhʌndrədθ/ *ordinal num* 序数

100th in order 第一百（的）

He is the hundredth athlete to finish the race. 他是第一百位完成比赛的运动员。

hung /hʌŋ; hʌŋ/ *v* 动

the past tense and past participle of **hang** ☆hang 的过去式和过去分词

hunger /ˈhʌŋgə; ˋhʌŋgɚ/ *n* 名

无复数

the feeling that you want to eat 饥饿

Her hunger woke her up. 她饿醒了。

***hungry** /ˈhʌŋgri; ˋhʌŋgrɪ/ *adj* 形

hungrier, hungriest

wanting to eat something 饥饿的

Do you have anything to eat? I'm hungry. 你有东西可以吃吗？我饿了。

反义 **full**

比较 **thirsty**

***hunt** /hʌnt; hʌnt/ *v* 动

to chase and kill animals or birds 打猎；猎杀

The men hunted in the forest. 那些人在森林里打猎。

hunter /ˈhʌntə; ˋhʌntɚ/ *n* 名

a person who hunts animals or birds 猎人

The hunter is going to kill the bird. 那个猎人要杀死那只鸟。

hurray /hʊˈreɪ; hʊˋre/ *interj* 感叹

也作：***hooray/hurrah***

a word you shout when you are happy or excited（欢呼声）好哇

We've won! Hurray! 我们赢了！好哇！

hurricane /ˈhʌrɪkən; ˋhɝɪˏken/ *n* 名

a big storm with strong winds that can cause a lot of damage 飓风

The hurricane destroyed a lot of houses. 飓风摧毁了很多房屋。

注意 特别指大西洋西部的飓风。

***hurry**[1] /ˈhʌri; ˋhɝɪ/ *v* 动

hurries, hurrying, hurried, hurried

to go somewhere or do something more quickly than usual 赶快；匆忙

She hurried to catch her train. 她急匆匆地赶火车。

同义 **rush**

Daily conversation 日常会话

Hurry up! 快点！

"Hurry up or we'll be late." “快点！要不然我们会迟到的。”

***hurry**[2] /ˈhʌri; ˋhɝɪ/ *n* 名

无复数

doing things or moving more quickly than usual 匆忙；赶时间

What is the hurry? We have plenty of time. 为什么这样着急？我们时间多得很。

in a hurry 匆忙地

She left in a hurry. 她匆忙地离开了。

***hurt** /hɜːt; hɝt/ *v* 动

hurts, hurting, hurt, hurt

1. if part of your body hurts, it feels painful（身体）感到疼痛

   My neck hurts badly. 我的脖子痛得很厉害。

   同义 **ache**[1]

2. to injure yourself or someone 弄伤

   Mike hurt his leg while he was playing football. 迈克在踢足球时弄伤了腿。

   同义 **injure**

***husband** /ˈhʌzbənd; ˋhʌzbənd/ *n* 名

the man that a woman is married to 丈夫

Her husband is a teacher. 她的丈夫是名教师。

另见 **wife**

hut /hʌt; hʌt/ *n* 名

a small house that has only one or two rooms 小屋

They live in a hut on the hill. 他们住在山丘上的小屋里。

hydrofoil /'haɪdrəʊfɔɪl; `haɪdrə͵fɔɪl/ *n* 名

a large boat that rises above the surface of water when it moves very fast 水翼船

We can go to Macau by hydrofoil. 我们可乘水翼船到澳门。

另见 **hovercraft, jetfoil**

hymn /hɪm; hɪm/ *n* 名

a song that praises God 圣歌

The boys are singing hymns in the church. 男孩们正在教堂里唱圣歌。

注意 发音与 him 相同。

hyphen /'haɪfn; `haɪfən/ *n* 名

a sign that joins two words or parts of a word (-) 连字符

另见 附录 : Punctuation 标点符号

***I** /aɪ; aɪ/ *pron* 代

the person who is speaking 我

Paul and I are classmates. 保罗和我是同学。

注意 必须用大写。

***ice** /aɪs; aɪs/ *n* 名

无复数

frozen water 冰；冰块

I put some ice in my apple juice. 我在苹果汁里放了些冰块。

***ice cream** /ˌaɪs ˈkriːm; ˏaɪs ˋkrim/ *n* 名

无复数

a soft, sweet food which is very cold 冰淇淋；雪糕

I like to eat ice cream on a hot day. 我喜欢在大热天吃冰淇淋。

ice lolly /ˈaɪs ˌlɒli; ˋaɪs ˏlɑlɪ/ *n* 名

复数：***ice lollies***

a piece of sweet-tasting ice on a stick 冰棍；冰棒；雪糕

I put the ice lollies in the fridge. 我把冰棍放进了冰箱里。

ice skating /ˈaɪs skeɪtɪŋ; ˋaɪs sketɪŋ/ *n* 名

无复数

moving or dancing on ice 滑冰；溜冰

Sally loves ice skating very much. 莎莉十分喜爱溜冰。

I'd /aɪd; aɪd/

1. the short form of "**I had**" ☆I had 的缩写

   I thought I'd lost my umbrella. 我想我已把雨伞弄丢了。

2. the short form of "**I would**" ☆I would 的缩写

   I'd like a ham sandwich and a cup of tea, please. 我想来一份火腿三明治和一杯茶。

ID card /ˌaɪ ˈdiː kɑːd; ˏaɪ ˋdi kɑrd/ *n* 名

the short form of **identity card** ☆identity card 的缩写

***idea** /aɪˈdɪə; aɪˋdɪə/ *n* 名

a plan or suggestion 主意；想法

I have an idea. Let's go swimming! 我有一个主意，我们去游泳吧！

Daily conversation 日常会话

I have no idea 我不知道

"How old is Miss Jones?" "I've no idea." "琼斯小姐几岁了？""我不知道。"

identity card /aɪˈdentɪti kɑːd; aɪˋdɛntətɪ kɑrd/ *n* 名

缩写：***ID card***

a special card which says who someone is 身份证

I always carry my identity card. 我总是随身携带身份证。

***if** /ɪf; ɪf/ *conj* 连

1. used to talk about something that might happen 如果；假如

   You can come with me if you like. 如果你愿意的话，可以和我一起去。

2. whether 是否；会不会

   I don't know if Henry will come. 我不知道亨利会不会来。

Daily conversation 日常会话

If I were you 如果我是你（用于提出建议）

"If I were you, I would not do that." "如果我是你，我不会那样做。"

ignore /ɪgˈnɔː; ɪgˋnɔr/ *v* 动

ignores, ignoring, ignored, ignored

to pay no attention to 不理会；忽视

I said "hello" to Miranda, but she ignored me. 我跟米兰达说"嗨"，但她没理会我。

***ill** /ɪl; ɪl/ *adj* 形

not feeling well 生病的

My aunt can't go to work today because she is ill. 我的阿姨病了，今天不能去上班。

同义 **sick**

反义 **healthy, well**[1]

I'll /aɪl; aɪl/

the short form of "**I will**" or "**I shall**" ☆I will 或 I shall 的缩写

I'll see Lily this afternoon. 今天下午我会与莉莉见面。

illegal /ɪ'li:gl; ɪ`ligḷ/ *adj* 形

against the law 违法的；非法的

It is illegal to take drugs. 吸毒是违法的。

反义 **legal**

illness /'ɪlnəs; `ɪlnɪs/ *n* 名

复数：***illnesses***

a disease, or the condition of being ill 疾病；患病

He had a serious illness. 他患了重病。

I'm /aɪm; aɪm/

the short form of "**I am**" ☆I am 的缩写

I'm reading a book now. 我正在看书。

imagination /ɪˌmædʒɪ'neɪʃn; ɪˌmædʒə`neʃən/ *n* 名

the ability to think of things that are not real 想象；想象力

The writer has a good imagination. 这位作家的想象力很丰富。

*imagine /ɪ'mædʒɪn; ɪ`mædʒɪn/ *v* 动

imagines, imagining, imagined, imagined

to think of things that are not real 想象；设想

Can you imagine what it is like to live on the moon? 你能想象在月球上生活的情景吗？

*immediately /ɪ'mi:diətli; ɪ`midɪɪtlɪ/ *adv* 副

at once 马上；立即

I went home immediately after school. 放学后我马上回家。

impatient /ɪm'peɪʃnt; ɪm`peʃənt/ *adj* 形

a little angry because something happens too slowly 不耐烦的

Don't be so impatient! The shop will open soon. 别那么不耐烦！商店快开门了。

反义 **patient**[2]

impatiently /ɪm'peɪʃntli; ɪm`peʃəntlɪ/ *adv* 副

not wanting to wait because something is happening too slowly 不耐烦地

I waited impatiently for the train. 我不耐烦地等火车来。

反义 **patiently**

impolite /ˌɪmpə'laɪt; ˌɪmpə`laɪt/ *adj* 形

rude; not having good manners 不礼貌的；粗鲁的

It is impolite to talk in class. 上课时讲话是没礼貌的。

反义 **polite**

*important /ɪm'pɔ:tənt; ɪm`pɔrtṇt/ *adj* 形

1. if something is important, it is very necessary or it has a big effect 重要的；意义重大的

   It is important to be honest. 诚实是很重要的。

反义 **unimportant**

2. having power or influence（人）有权力的；有影响力的

   Mr Harris is an important man in the company. 哈里斯先生是公司内的重要人物。

反义 **unimportant**

impossible /ɪm'pɒsəbl; ɪm`pɑsəbḷ/ *adj* 形

cannot happen or be done 不可能的

It is impossible for a cat to fly. 猫是不可能飞的。

反义 **possible**

*improve /ɪm'pru:v; ɪm`pruv/ *v* 动

improves, improving, improved, improved

1. to become better 进步；变好

   Grandma's health is improving. 祖母的健康状况在逐渐改善。

2. to make something better 改良；改进

   I want to improve my English. 我想提高我的英语水平。

***in[1]** /ɪn; ɪn/ *prep* 介

1. used to show where someone or something is 在…里面
   Robert put his toys in a box. 罗伯特把他的玩具放在箱子里。

2. used to say when something happens 在（某月、某年等）
   My birthday is in August. 我的生日在 8 月。

***in[2]** /ɪn; ɪn/ *adv* 副

1. inside a place or thing 在里面
   Terry opened the door and went in. 泰瑞打开门走进去。

反义 **out**

2. at home or in the place where you work 在家；在工作的地方
   I called you but you were not in. 我给你打过电话，但是你不在家。

反义 **out**

Daily conversation 日常会话
"Hello, may I speak to Colin?" "Sorry, he hasn't come in yet." "你好，请问科林在吗？" "对不起，他还没来上班。"

inch /ɪntʃ; ɪntʃ/ *n* 名

复数：***inches***

a unit of length. There are 12 inches in a foot. 英寸；寸
Nick is five feet and seven inches tall. 尼克的身高是 5 英尺 7 英寸。

***include** /ɪn'klu:d; ɪn`klud/ *v* 动

includes, including, included, included

to have something or someone as a part 包括；算入
The price of the air ticket includes a meal. 机票的价钱包括一餐的费用。

inconvenient /ˌɪnkən'vi:niənt; ˏɪnkən`vinjənt/ *adj* 形

causing trouble or difficulty 不方便的
It's an inconvenient time for me. 那个时间我不太方便。

反义 **convenient**

incorrect /ˌɪnkə'rekt; ˏɪnkə`rɛkt/ *adj* 形

not correct 不正确的；错的
Your answer is incorrect. Please do it again. 你的答案错了，请重做。

同义 **wrong[1]**

反义 **correct[1], right[1]**

***increase[1]** /ɪn'kri:s; ɪn`kris/ *v* 动

increases, increasing, increased, increased

to become or make something become more in number or size 增加；增大
The price of food increased a lot last year. 去年食物的价格上涨了不少。

反义 **decrease[1]**

***increase[2]** /'ɪnkri:s; `ɪnkris/ *n* 名

a situation in which something gets bigger in number or size 增加；增大

There was an increase in the price of food. 食物的价格上涨了。

反义 **decrease[2]**

***indeed** /ɪn'di:d; ɪn`did/ *adv* 副

a word you use to make what you are saying stronger 实在；的确
I love my parents very much indeed. 我实在很爱我的父母。

independent /ˌɪndi'pendənt; ˏɪndɪ`pɛndənt/ *adj* 形

able to look after yourself, without having to ask people for help 独立的；自主的
Jenny is a very independent girl who can take care of herself. 珍妮是个独立的女孩，能够照顾自己。

indoor /'ɪndɔ:; `ɪnˏdɔr/ *adj* 形

played or done inside a building 室内的
Let's play indoor games. 我们玩室内游戏吧。

反义 **outdoor**

indoors /ˌɪn'dɔ:z; ˏɪn`dɔrz/ *adv* 副

inside a building 在室内
I stayed indoors with my cat all day. 我和猫儿整天待在屋内。

反义 **outdoors**

***industry** /'ɪndəstri; `ɪndəstrɪ/ *n* 名

1. （无复数）the activity of making things in factories 工业
   A lot of people here work in industry. 在这里许多人从事工业。
2. （复数：***industries***）a particular type of work 行业
   Irene works in the tourist industry. 艾琳从事旅游业。

inexpensive /ˌɪnɪkˈspensɪv; ˏɪnɪkˋspɛnsɪv/ *adj* 形

low in price 便宜的；不贵的

This restaurant is inexpensive, but the food is good. 这家餐馆并不贵，但食物不错。

同义 cheap

反义 dear, expensive

***influence**[1] /ˈɪnfluəns; ˋɪnfluəns/ *n* 名

the power to affect someone or something 影响；影响力

That TV programme has a bad influence on teenagers. 那个电视节目对青少年有不良影响。

influence[2] /ˈɪnfluəns; ˋɪnfluəns/ *v* 动

influences, influencing, influenced, influenced

to have an effect on someone or something 影响；对…起作用

What influenced you to become a teacher? 你是受了什么影响而当教师的？

***information** /ˌɪnfəˈmeɪʃn; ˏɪnfəˋmeʃən/ *n* 名

无复数

facts about someone or something 消息；信息；资料

You can get a lot of information from the Internet. 你可以从互联网获得许多信息。

注意 information 是不可数名词，如要表示一项、两项信息，用 a piece of information、two pieces of information 等。

***ingredient** /ɪnˈgriːdiənt; ɪnˋgridɪənt/ *n* 名

one of the things that you use when you are cooking（烹饪的）材料；配料

Flour and eggs are the main ingredients of bread. 面粉和鸡蛋是面包的主要成分。

inhabitant /ɪnˈhæbɪtənt; ɪnˋhæbətənt/ *n* 名

someone who lives in a particular place 居民

Hong Kong has more than seven million inhabitants. 香港有超过 700 万居民。

initial /ɪˈnɪʃl; ɪˋnɪʃəl/ *n* 名

the first letter of a person's name（姓名的）首字母

His name is Bill Brown, so his initials are BB. 他叫 Bill Brown，所以他姓名的首字母是 BB。

injection /ɪnˈdʒekʃn; ɪnˋdʒɛkʃən/ *n* 名

putting a drug into someone's body with a needle 注射

The nurse gave her an injection. 护士给她打了一针。

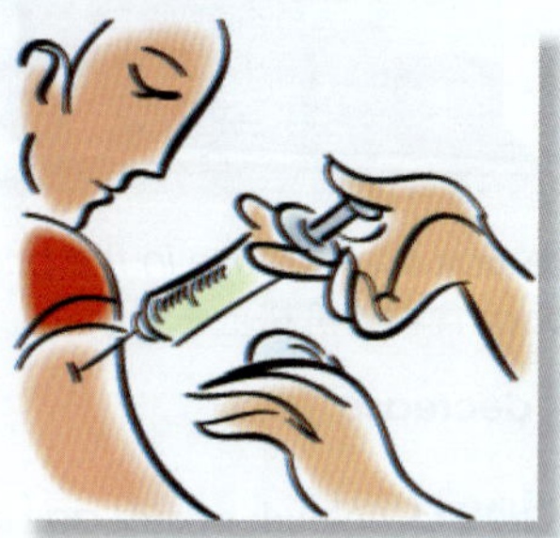

injure /ˈɪndʒə; ˋɪndʒə/ *v* 动

injures, injuring, injured, injured

to hurt someone 伤害；弄伤

Five people were injured in the car accident. 5 人在车祸中受伤。

同义 hurt

injury /ˈɪndʒəri; ˋɪndʒərɪ/ *n* 名

复数：***injuries***

damage to part of your body 受伤处；损伤

He fell and had serious injuries. 他摔倒了，受了重伤。

***ink** /ɪŋk; ɪŋk/ *n* 名

无复数

a liquid for writing or printing（书写用的）墨水；（印刷用的）油墨

My printer has run out of ink. 我的打印机已经没有油墨了。

inn /ɪn; ɪn/ *n* 名

a small hotel 小旅馆；客栈

They stayed at an inn by the sea. 他们住在海边的一家小旅馆。

innocent /ˈɪnəsənt; ˋɪnəsn̩t/ *adj* 形

not having done something wrong 清白的；无辜的

In fact, this prisoner was innocent. 这个囚犯实际上是清白的。

input /ˈɪnpʊt; ˋɪnpʊt/ *v* 动

inputs, inputting, input/inputted, input/inputted

【电脑】to put information into a computer（向电脑）输入（信息）

I input the data into my computer. 我把数据输入电脑。

***insect** /ˈɪnsekt; ˋɪnsɛkt/ *n* 名

a very small animal that has six legs and no bones 昆虫

Ants and mosquitoes are insects. 蚂蚁和蚊子都是昆虫。

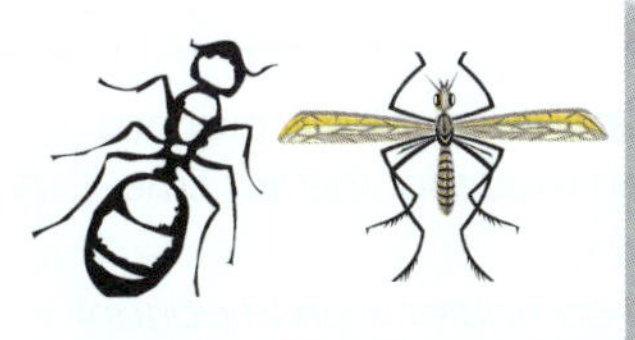

***inside[1]** /ˌɪnˈsaɪd; ˋɪnˋsaɪd/ *n* 名

无复数

the part within 里面；内部

The inside of the house was very dark. 房子里面十分黑暗。

反义 **outside[1]**

***inside[2]** /ˌɪnˈsaɪd; ˋɪnˋsaɪd/ *adv* 副

in or into something 在里面；往里面

I opened the door and looked inside. 我打开门，往里面看。

反义 **outside[2]**

***inside[3]** / ɪnˈsaɪd; ɪnˋsaɪd/ *prep* 介

in or into something 在…里面

He put the coins inside his pocket. 他把硬币放进口袋里。

反义 **outside[3]**

inspector /ɪnˈspektə; ɪnˋspɛktɚ/ *n* 名

1. someone who checks if something is right or going well 视察员；检查员

   An inspector came to our school this morning. 今天早上有一位督察员到我们的学校视察。

2. a police officer of middle rank 督察（中级警官）

   Paul's father is a police inspector. 保罗的爸爸是一名警务督察。

inspire /ɪnˈspaɪə; ɪnˋspaɪr/ *v* 动

inspires, inspiring, inspired, inspired

to make someone want to do something 启发；给…灵感

His wife inspired him to write this song. 他的妻子给了他写这首歌的灵感。

instant noodles /ˈɪnstənt ˌnuːdlz; ˋɪnstənt ˌnudl̩z/ *plural n* 复数名词

noodles that are quick and easy to prepare 即食面；方便面

I know how to cook instant noodles. 我知道怎样煮方便面。

***instead** /ɪnˈsted; ɪnˋstɛd/ *adv* 副

in the place of someone or something 代替

If I can't go, my brother will go instead. 我不能去的话，哥哥会代我去。

instead of 代替；而不是

Now I can walk to school instead of taking the school bus. 现在我可以步行上学而不用搭校车。

instruction /ɪnˈstrʌkʃn; ɪnˋstrʌkʃən/ *n* 名

information that tells you how to do or use something 用法说明；指示

Read the instructions before you use the tool. 使用工具前先阅读说明书。

***instrument** /ˈɪnstrəmənt; ˋɪnstrəmənt/ *n* 名

1. a tool for doing a special job 工具；仪器

   The doctor used different instruments to treat the patient. 那位医生用了不同工具为病人治疗。

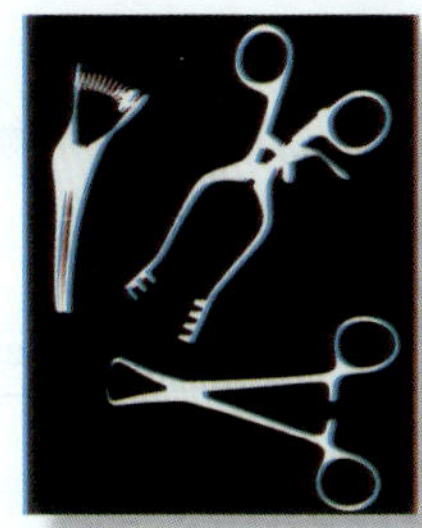

2. an object for playing music 乐器

   What instruments can you play? 你会演奏什么乐器？

***intend** /ɪnˈtend; ɪnˋtɛnd/ *v* 动

to plan to do something 计划；打算

They intend to go to Australia this summer. 他们计划在今年夏天去澳洲。

***interest** /ˈɪntrəst; ˋɪntərɪst/ *n* 名

1. （无复数）wanting to know more about someone or something 兴趣

   Lily has no interest in sport. 莉莉对体育运动没有兴趣。

2. something you enjoy doing 爱好；嗜好

   My interests are drawing and dancing. 我的爱好是画画和跳舞。

同义 **hobby**

***interested** /ˈɪntrəstɪd; ˋɪntərɪstɪd/ *adj* 形

wanting to do something or know more about it 感兴趣的

I am very interested in English. 我对英语很感兴趣。

用法 interested 用来形容人的感受。

比较 **interesting**

***interesting** /ˈɪntrəstɪŋ; ˋɪntərɪstɪŋ/ *adj* 形

making you want to pay attention 有趣的；令人感兴趣的

That is a very interesting book. 那是一本很有趣的书。

I

反义 **boring, dull**

用法 interesting 用来形容事物。

比较 **interested**

***international** /ˌɪntəˈnæʃnəl; ˏɪntəˋnæʃənl/ *adj* 形

for or by many countries 国际的

Are you interested in international news? 你会留意国际新闻吗？

Internet /ˈɪntənet; ˋɪntəˏnɛt/ *n* 名

无复数

the Internet【电脑】a system that connects computers all over the world so that people can share information 互联网

I heard about it on the Internet. 我从互联网上得知这个消息。

interrupt /ˌɪntəˈrʌpt; ˏɪntəˋrʌpt/ *v* 动

to stop someone while they are talking or doing something 打断；打扰

I don't want to interrupt him when he is working. 他工作时我不想打扰他。

***interview¹** /ˈɪntəvjuː; ˋɪntəˏvju/ *n* 名

a meeting in which a person asks someone questions 面试；访问

He has a job interview this afternoon. 今天下午他要参加求职面试。

***interview²** /ˈɪntəvjuː; ˋɪntəˏvju/ *v* 动

to find out about someone by asking questions 采访；访问

David is interviewing the principal. 大卫正在访问校长。

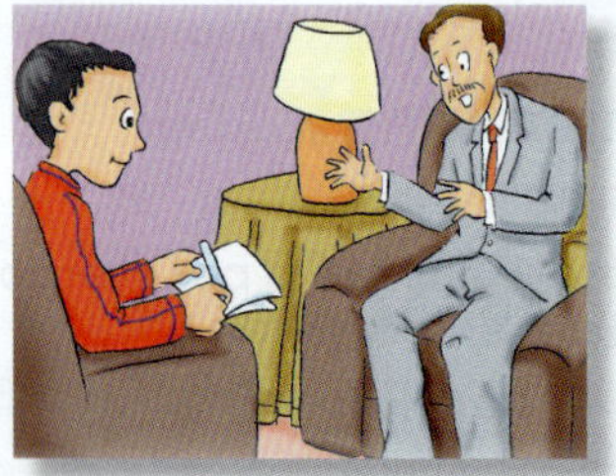

***into** /ˈɪntə, ˈɪntuː; ˋɪntə, ˋɪntu/ *prep* 介

1. towards the inside of something 进入

   We jumped into the pool. 我们跳入了水池中。

2. used to show how things change 变成；成为

   My mother cut the tomatoes into small pieces. 妈妈把番茄切成小块。

***introduce** /ˌɪntrəˈdjuːs; ˏɪntrəˋdjus/ *v* 动

introduces, introducing, introduced, introduced

to tell someone another person's name when they first meet 介绍

I introduced Rose to my parents. 我把罗丝介绍给父母认识。

invade /ɪnˈveɪd; ɪnˋved/ *v* 动

invades, invading, invaded, invaded

to attack a place or country 侵略

Japan invaded China in 1931. 日本在1931年入侵中国。

invent /ɪnˈvent; ɪnˋvɛnt/ *v* 动

to think of and make something for the first time 发明；创造

Do you know who invented the light bulb? 你知道是谁发明了电灯泡吗？

比较 **discover**

invention /ɪnˈvenʃn; ɪnˋvɛnʃən/ *n* 名

a machine, tool, etc that has been made for the first time 发明（物）

The computer is an important invention. 电脑是一项重要的发明。

inventor /ɪnˈventə; ɪnˋvɛntɚ/ *n* 名

someone who thinks of and makes something for the first time 发明者；创造者

Thomas Edison was the inventor of the light bulb. 托马斯·爱迪生是电灯泡的发明者。

inverted commas /ɪnˌvɜːtɪd ˈkɒməz; ɪnˏvɝtɪd ˋkɑməz/ *plural n* 复数名词

a pair of signs used in writing to show what someone said or wrote (' '), (" ") 引号

同义 **quotation marks**

另见 附录：Punctuation 标点符号

I

investigate /ɪn'vestɪgeɪt; ɪn`vɛstəˌget/ *v* 动

investigates, investigating, investigated, investigated

to try to find out about a crime, an accident, etc 调查

The police are investigating the car accident. 警方正在调查那起交通事故。

invisible /ɪn'vɪzəbl; ɪn`vɪzəbl̩/ *adj* 形

unable to be seen 看不见的；隐形的

In the film, the boy can make himself invisible. 在这部电影里，那个男孩能使自己隐形。

反义 **visible**

invitation /ˌɪnvɪ'teɪʃn; ˌɪnvə`teʃən/ *n* 名

asking for someone to go somewhere or do something 邀请

I received an invitation to the party. 我收到了派对的邀请。

***invite** /ɪn'vaɪt; ɪn`vaɪt/ *v* 动

invites, inviting, invited, invited

to ask someone to go somewhere or do something 邀请

Joanna invited me to her birthday party. 乔安娜邀请我参加她的生日派对。

inwards /'ɪnwədz; `ɪnwɚdz/ *adv* 副【英】

美式：***inward***

towards the middle 向内；往内

The door opens inwards. 这扇门向内开。

反义 **outwards**

***iron**[1] /'aɪən; `aɪɚn/ *n* 名

1. （无复数）a common metal that is very useful 铁

   The school gates are made of iron. 学校闸门是铁造的。

2. a thing that you use to make clothes smooth 熨斗

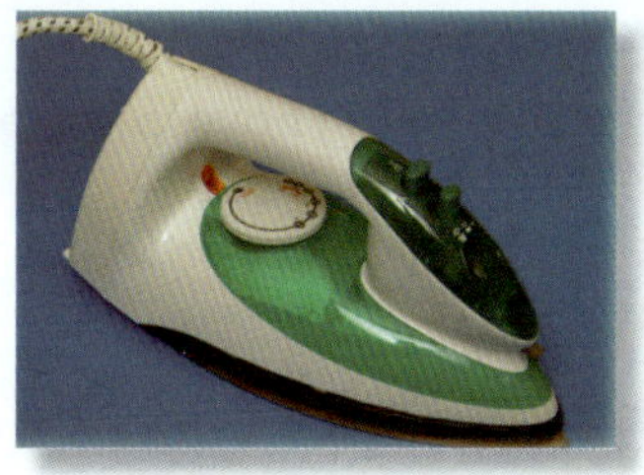

Be careful, the iron is hot. 当心，熨斗很热。

***iron**[2] /'aɪən; `aɪɚn/ *v* 动

to make clothes smooth with an iron 熨平

I ironed my school uniform myself. 我自己熨了校服。

is /s, z, əz; s, z, əz; *strong* 强读 ɪz; ɪz/ *v* 动

a form of **be** ☆ be 的一种现在式，与主语 he、she 和 it 一起使用

Mrs Smith is from England. 史密斯太太是英国人。

***island** /'aɪlənd; `aɪlənd/ *n* 名

a piece of land with sea all round it 岛；岛屿

There are many islands in the Philippines. 菲律宾有很多岛。

isn't /'ɪznt; `ɪznt̩/

the short form of "**is not**" ☆ is not 的缩写

It's a beautiful day, isn't it? 天气真好，不是吗？

***it** /ɪt; ɪt/ *pron* 代

1. a thing or an animal that has been mentioned 它；它

   Look at the cat! It has blue eyes. 看那只猫！它的眼睛是蓝色的。

2. used to talk about the weather, time, date, etc 指天气、时间、日期等

   It is very cold today. 今天很冷。

italics /ɪ'tælɪks; ɪ`tælɪks/ *plural n* 复数名词

【电脑】printed letters that lean to the right 斜体；斜体字

This sentence is in italics. 这个句子是用斜体字显示的。

itch /ɪtʃ; ɪtʃ/ *v* 动

itches, itching, itched, itched

if your skin itches, it makes you want to rub it 发痒

The mosquito bites are making my skin itch. 蚊子咬的地方让我的皮肤很痒。

it'd /'ɪtəd; `ɪtəd/

1. the short form of "**it would**" ☆ it would 的缩写

   It'd be good to see you again. 能再跟你见面就好了。

2. the short form of "**it had**" ☆ it had 的缩写

   It'd taken me two hours to make this model car. 我花了两小时来制作这辆模型车。

it'll /'ɪtl; `ɪtl̩/

the short form of "**it will**" ☆ it will 的缩写

It'll be dark very soon. 很快就会天黑了。

it's /ɪts; ɪts/

1. the short form of "**it is**" ☆ it is 的缩写

   It's going to rain. 快下雨了。

2. the short form of "**it has**" ☆ it has 的缩写

   It's stopped raining. 雨已经停了。

注意 不要与 its（它的；它的）混淆。

***its** /ɪts; ɪts/ *adj* 形

belonging to a thing or an animal

I

that has been mentioned 它的；它的

The dog broke its leg. 那只狗的腿摔断了。

注意 不要与 it's (= it is/it has) 混淆。

***itself** /ɪtˈself; ɪtˋsɛlf/ *pron* 代

the same thing or animal that the sentence is about 它自己；它自己

The elephant is washing itself in the river. 这只大象在河里洗澡。

I've /aɪv; aɪv/

the short form of "**I have**" ☆I have 的缩写

I've been waiting for two hours. 我已经等了两个小时了。

ivory /ˈaɪvəri; ˋaɪvərɪ/ *n* 名

无复数

the hard, white material from the long teeth of an elephant 象牙

These chopsticks are made of ivory. 这双筷子是象牙做的。

I

***jacket** /ˈdʒækɪt; ˋdʒækɪt/ *n* 名

a short, light coat 外套；短上衣

He is wearing a white jacket. 他穿着一件白色外套。

jade /dʒeɪd; dʒed/ *n* 名

无复数

a hard, green stone used for making jewellery 翡翠；玉

This ring is made of jade. 这枚戒指是用翡翠做的。

jail /dʒeɪl; dʒel/ *n* 名

a prison 监狱；监牢

The thief was sent to jail for one year. 那个小偷被判监禁一年。

***jam** /dʒæm; dʒæm/ *n* 名

1. a sweet food made of fruit and sugar 果酱

I put some jam on the biscuit. 我在饼干上涂了一些果酱。

2. a situation when it is difficult to move because there are too many cars or things 堵塞

We were late because there had been a traffic jam. 因为交通阻塞，我们迟到了。

***January** /ˈdʒænjuəri; ˋdʒænjuˏɛrɪ/ *n* 名

复数：***Januaries*** | **缩写**：***Jan.***

the first month of the year 一月

Nancy was born in January. 南茜是在 1 月出生的。

注意 开头的字母必须用大写。

***jar** /dʒɑː; dʒɑr/ *n* 名

a glass or plastic container used for storing food 玻璃瓶；广口瓶

I put the biscuits in a jar. 我把饼干放进瓶子里。

jaw /dʒɔː; dʒɔ/ *n* 名

one of the parts of your face which contains your teeth 颌；颚

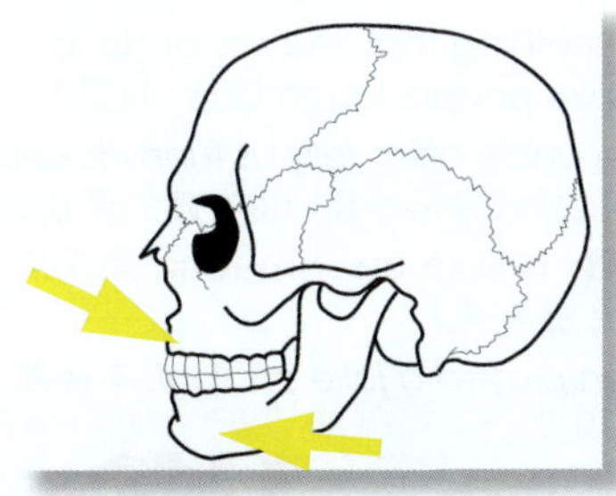

Simon hurt his lower jaw while playing football. 西蒙踢足球时弄伤了下颌。

jealous /ˈdʒeləs; ˋdʒɛləs/ *adj* 形

feeling angry or unhappy because you want something that someone else has 嫉妒的；妒忌的

I was jealous of Henry's new toy. 我很妒忌亨利有新玩具。

比较 **envious**

***jeans** /dʒiːnz; dʒinz/ *plural n* 复数名词

trousers made of strong, thick cotton 牛仔裤

Angela was wearing a pair of blue jeans. 安琪拉穿着一条蓝色牛仔裤。

Jell-O, jello /ˈdʒeləʊ; ˋdʒɛlo/ *n* 名【美】

无复数

英式 **jelly**

***jelly** /ˈdʒeli; ˋdʒɛlɪ/ *n* 名【英】

复数：***jellies*** | **美式**：***Jell-O, jello***

a soft, sweet food made with fruit juice and sugar 果冻

I have several kinds of jelly. Which one would you like? 我有几种不同的果冻，你要吃哪一种？

jellyfish /ˈdʒelifɪʃ; ˋdʒɛlɪˏfɪʃ/ *n* 名

复数：***jellyfish/jellyfishes***

a soft sea animal that can sting 水母；海蜇

Jellyfish are beautiful but can be dangerous. 水母样子漂亮，但可能有危险性。

Jesus Christ /ˌdʒiːzəs ˈkraɪst; ˏdʒizəs ˋkraɪst/ *n* 名

a man whose life and teachings form the Christian religion 耶稣基督

J

jet /dʒet; dʒɛt/ *n* 名

a fast plane with a powerful engine 喷气式飞机；喷射机

Some jets can fly faster than the speed of sound. 有些喷射机的飞行速度比音速还要快。

比较 **jumbo jet**

jetfoil /ˈdʒetfɔɪl; ˋdʒɛtfɔɪl/ *n* 名

a fast boat with a powerful engine 水翼喷射船

The jetfoil got to Macau in an hour. 一小时后水翼喷射船到达澳门。

另见 **hovercraft, hydrofoil**

jewel /ˈdʒuːəl; ˋdʒuəl/ *n* 名

a valuable stone 宝石

There are many jewels in the crown. 王冠上有许多宝石。

jewellery /ˈdʒuːəlri; ˋdʒuəlrɪ/ *n* 名【英】

无复数 | 美式：***jewelry***

things like rings, necklaces, etc 珠宝；首饰

She put all her jewellery in a box. 她把所有的珠宝饰物放在盒子里。

***job** /dʒɒb; dʒɑb/ *n* 名

1. work that you do for money 职业；工作

   He got a job as a waiter. 他找到了一份服务员的工作。

2. something that you have to do 一件工作；任务

   Cooking is not an easy job. 做饭不是一件容易的事。

***jog** /dʒɒg; dʒɑg/ *v* 动

jogs, jogging, jogged, jogged

to run slowly for exercise 慢跑

She jogs in the park every morning. 她每天早晨在公园里慢跑。

***join** /dʒɔɪn; dʒɔɪn/ *v* 动

1. to bring two or more things together 连接；结合

   A railway joins these two cities. 一条铁路把这两座城市连接起来。

2. to become a member of a group 参加；加入

   I joined the choir last month. 我上个月加入了合唱团。

Daily conversation 日常会话

"We're going to the beach. Would you like to join us?" "Sure!" "我们去海滩玩，你也一起来好吗？""好的！"

***joke¹** /dʒəʊk; dʒok/ *n* 名

something that you say or do to make people laugh 笑话；玩笑

My uncle often tells us funny jokes. 我的叔叔常常给我们讲有趣的笑话。

play a joke on someone 戏弄某人；捉弄某人

Ben played a joke on Paul. 本捉弄了保罗。

***joke²** /dʒəʊk; dʒok/ *v* 动

jokes, joking, joked, joked

to say or do something that makes people laugh 说笑话；开玩笑

You must be joking! 你一定是在开玩笑！

joss stick /ˈdʒɒs ˌstɪk; ˋdʒɑs ˏstɪk/ *n* 名

a thin stick that people usually burn in temples（祭祀用的）香

My grandmother burns some joss sticks every day. 祖母每天都烧香。

***journey** /ˈdʒɜːni; ˋdʒɝnɪ/ *n* 名

when you travel from one place to another 旅程；旅行

The journey to the city takes five hours. 去这个城市需要 5 小时。

joy /dʒɔɪ; dʒɔɪ/ *n* 名

无复数

happiness and pleasure 喜悦；欢欣

He was full of joy when he heard the good news. 他听到那个好消息时满心欢喜。

judge /dʒʌdʒ; dʒʌdʒ/ *n* 名

1. someone who makes decisions in a court 法官

   The judge sent the robber to

prison for five years. 法官判这名劫匪监禁 5 年。

2. someone who decides the winners of a competition 评判

   Miss Hall was the judge of the singing contest. 霍尔小姐是那次歌唱比赛的评判。

judo /ˈdʒuːdəʊ; ˋdʒudo/ *n* 名

无复数

a Japanese sport in which two people fight and try to throw each other onto the ground to win 柔道

Derek takes a judo class every Saturday. 德里克每星期六上柔道课。

比较 **karate, kung fu**

jug /dʒʌg; dʒʌg/ *n* 名

a container with a handle, for holding and pouring liquids（有柄带嘴的）壶

Max filled the jug with water. 麦克斯把壶注满水。

***juice** /dʒuːs; dʒus/ *n* 名

无复数

the liquid from fruit or vegetables 果汁；蔬菜汁

Henry likes mango juice. 亨利喜欢喝芒果汁。

juicy /ˈdʒuːsi; ˋdʒusɪ/ *adj* 形

juicier, juiciest

full of juice 多汁的

The tomatoes were big and juicy. 那些番茄又大又多汁。

***July** /dʒuˈlaɪ; dʒʊˋlaɪ/ *n* 名

复数：*Julies* | **缩写：*Jul.***

the seventh month of the year 七月

It is quite hot in July. 7 月的天气相当热。

注意 开头的字母必须用大写。

jumbo jet /ˈdʒʌmbəʊ dʒet; ˋdʒʌmbo ˏdʒɛt/ *n* 名

a very large plane which can carry a lot of people 大型喷气式客机

Mr Miller went to Paris on a jumbo jet. 米勒先生乘坐大型喷气式客机去巴黎。

比较 **jet**

***jump** /dʒʌmp; dʒʌmp/ *v* 动

to move off the ground quickly by pushing yourself with your legs 跳；跳跃

The monkey jumped onto the elephant's back. 猴子跳到大象的背上。

***June** /dʒuːn; dʒun/ *n* 名

缩写：*Jun.*

the sixth month of the year 六月

1 June is International Children's Day. 6 月 1 日是国际儿童节。

注意 开头的字母必须用大写。

jungle /ˈdʒʌŋgl; ˋdʒʌŋgl/ *n* 名

a thick forest in a hot country 热带丛林；密林

There are many wild animals in the jungle. 热带丛林中有很多野生动物。

junk /dʒʌŋk; dʒʌŋk/ *n* 名

1. （无复数）old things that you do not want 废旧的东西；垃圾

   Your room is full of junk! 你的房间全是杂物！

2. a Chinese boat with sails 中国帆船

The fishermen lived on a junk. 渔民以前住在帆船上。

junk food /ˈdʒʌŋk fuːd; ˋdʒʌŋk fud/ *n* 名

无复数

J

food that is not healthy 垃圾食品
Eating too much junk food is bad for your health. 吃太多垃圾食品对健康不好。

***just** /dʒʌst; dʒʌst/ *adv* 副

1. only 只是；仅仅
   I came here just to say hello to you. 我来这里只想和你打个招呼。
2. a very short time ago 刚才；刚刚
   We just had lunch half an hour ago. 我们在半小时前刚吃过午餐。
3. exactly 正好；恰好
   Grace looks just like her mother. 格蕾丝和她妈妈长得一模一样。

just about 几乎；差不多
Just about everyone has left. 差不多所有人都走了。

just as 正当…的时候
She called just as I was going to bed. 我正要去睡觉的时候，她打电话来。

Daily conversation 日常会话

just a minute/second/moment 等一下

"May I speak to Dr Brown?" "Just a minute, please. I'll get him for you." "请问布朗医生在吗？""请稍等，我去请他来。"

J

kangaroo /ˌkæŋgəˈruː; ˌkæŋgəˋru/ *n* 名

a large animal from Australia which can jump a long way 袋鼠

We saw many kangaroos in Australia. 我们在澳洲看到了很多袋鼠。

karaoke /ˌkæriˈəʊki; ˌkɑrəˋokɪ/ *n* 名

无复数

the activity of singing songs while a machine is playing music 卡拉 OK

We sang karaoke at home yesterday. 我们昨天在家里唱卡拉 OK。

karate /kəˈrɑːti; kəˋrɑtɪ/ *n* 名

无复数

a Japanese sport in which you fight using your hands and feet 空手道

My brother is learning karate. 我的弟弟在学空手道。

比较 **judo, kung fu**

keen /kiːn; kin/ *adj* 形

keener, keenest

wanting to do something very much 渴望的；热衷的

William is keen to join the swimming competition. 威廉渴望参加游泳比赛。

keen on 喜爱；热衷于

Lily is keen on playing the piano. 莉莉喜爱弹钢琴。

***keep** /kiːp; kip/ *v* 动

keeps, keeping, kept, kept

1. to have something and not give it back 保留；保存

   You can keep this book. I don't need it. 这本书你可以留着，我不需要了。

2. to put something in a particular place 收藏；存放

   I keep all my toys in a big box. 我把所有玩具都放在一个大箱子里。

3. to stay in a particular condition or position 保持（某种状态）

   Please keep quiet! 请保持安静！

4. to make someone or something stay in a particular condition or position 使（某人或某物）保持（某种状态）

   You should keep your room tidy. 你应该保持房间整洁。

keep a secret 保守秘密

Can you keep a secret? 你能保守秘密吗？

keep away 躲开；回避

Keep away from the fire! 远离火堆！

keep (on) doing something 继续做某事；不断做某事

I tried to stop him but he kept on walking. 我想让他停下来，但他一直往前走。

kept /kept; kɛpt/ *v* 动

the past tense and past participle of **keep**☆keep 的过去式和过去分词

ketchup /ˈketʃəp; ˋkɛtʃəp/ *n* 名

无复数

a thick, sweet, red sauce made from tomatoes 番茄酱；茄汁

Would you please hand me the ketchup? 请你把番茄酱递给我好吗？

***kettle** /ˈketl; ˋkɛtl̩/ *n* 名

a pot with a lid and a handle, used for boiling water（烧水用的）水壶

She boiled some water in a kettle. 她用水壶来烧些水。

K

***key** /kiː; ki/ *n* 名

a thing for locking and unlocking doors, boxes, etc 钥匙

My father is looking for his keys. 我的爸爸在找钥匙。

keyboard /ˈkiːbɔːd; ˋkiˌbɔrd/ *n* 名

a set of buttons on a computer, piano, etc（电脑、钢琴等的）键盘

My keyboard has Chinese characters on it. 我的键盘上有汉字。

另见 **附录**：The computer world 电脑世界

kg

the short form of **kilogram**☆kilogram 的缩写

***kick¹** /kɪk; kɪk/ *v* 动

to hit something with your foot 踢

I kicked the ball to him. 我把球踢给他。

kick² /kɪk; kɪk/ *n* 名

the action of hitting something with your foot 踢

The naughty boy gave the dog a kick. 那个顽皮的男孩踢了那只狗一下。

***kid** /kɪd; kɪd/ *n* 名

a child 小孩

The kids were playing hide-and-seek. 孩子们在玩捉迷藏。

用法 kid 常用于口语中，较正式的说法是 child。

kidnap /ˈkɪdnæp; ˋkɪdnæp/ *v* 动

kidnaps, kidnapping, kidnapped, kidnapped

to take someone away and hide them, especially in order to get money from their family 绑架；诱拐

They kidnapped the young prince. 他们绑架了那位年幼的王子。

kidnapper /ˈkɪdnæpə; ˋkɪdnæpɚ/ *n* 名

someone who takes a person away and asks for money 绑匪

The kidnappers asked for ten million dollars! 绑匪要求一千万赎金！

***kill** /kɪl; kɪl/ *v* 动

to make a person, an animal or a plant die 杀死

Dennis killed the cockroach. 丹尼斯把蟑螂杀死了。

kill time 消磨时间；打发时间

We killed time by playing computer games. 我们玩电脑游戏来消磨时间。

kilogram /ˈkɪləgræm; ˋkɪləˏgræm/ *n* 名

也作：***kilogramme***【英】｜缩写：***kg***

a unit of weight. There are 1000 grams in a kilogram. 公斤；千克

This bag of rice weighs 10 kilograms. 这包米重 10 公斤。

另见 附录：Weights and measures 量度单位

kilometre /kɪˈlɒmɪtə; kəˋlɑːmətɚ/ *n* 名【英】

缩写：***km***｜美式：***kilometer***

a unit of length. There are 1000 metres in a kilometre. 公里；千米

Mr Brown is driving at 80 kilometres per hour. 布朗先生以每小时 80 公里的速度驾驶。

另见 附录：Weights and measures 度量单位

***kind¹** /kaɪnd; kaɪnd/ *n* 名

a type of person or thing 种类；类型

Many kinds of animals live on this island. 许多种动物在这个岛上栖息。

kind of 有点；有一些

I feel kind of sleepy. 我觉得有点困。

用法 kind of 用于非正式的场合。

同义 **sort, type¹**

***kind²** /kaɪnd; kaɪnd/ *adj* 形

kinder, kindest

helpful, friendly, and nice to other people 仁慈的；和蔼的

Mrs Moore is a very kind person. 摩尔太太很仁慈。

反义 **cruel, unkind**

kindergarten /ˈkɪndəˌgɑːtn; ˋkɪndɚˏgɑrtn̩/ *n* 名

a school for very young children 幼儿园

Susan goes to kindergarten. 苏珊上幼儿园。

同义 **nursery school**

kindly /ˈkaɪndli; ˋkaɪndlɪ/ *adv* 副

in a nice, helpful and good way 仁慈地；友善地；亲切地

My parents treat everyone kindly. 我的父母对每个人都很友善。

kindness /ˈkaɪndnəs; ˋkaɪndnɪs/ *n* 名

无复数

being nice, helpful and good 仁慈；好心；好意

Thank you very much for your kindness. 非常感谢你的好意。

***king** /kɪŋ; kɪŋ/ *n* 名

a man who is the ruler of a country. When he dies, his son or someone else in his family becomes the ruler. 国王

The king lives in a palace. 国王住在王宫里。

另见 **queen**

kingdom /ˈkɪŋdəm; ˋkɪŋdəm/ *n* 名

a country ruled by a king or queen 王国

The king ruled a large kingdom. 国王统治一个庞大的王国。

***kiss[1]** /kɪs; kɪs/ *v* 动

kisses, kissing, kissed, kissed

to touch someone with your lips, especially to show that you love them 吻；亲吻

Mrs White kissed her daughter. 怀特太太吻了她的女儿。

kiss someone goodbye/goodnight 向某人吻别/亲亲某人说晚安

Dad kissed mum goodbye. 爸爸和妈妈吻别。

***kiss[2]** /kɪs; kɪs/ *n* 名

复数：***kisses***

a touch with your lips 吻；亲吻

The Prince gave Sleeping Beauty a kiss. 王子亲了睡美人一下。

***kitchen** /ˈkɪtʃən; ˋkɪtʃɪn/ *n* 名

a room where you cook food 厨房

We always keep the kitchen clean. 我们一向保持厨房清洁。

另见 附录：Inside a flat 住所里

***kite** /kaɪt; kaɪt/ *n* 名

a toy that flies in the air and is usually made of paper 风筝

The boys are flying kites in the park. 那些男孩正在公园里放风筝。

***kitten** /ˈkɪtn; ˋkɪtn̩/ *n* 名

a young cat 小猫

The kitten was playing with a ball. 那只小猫在玩球。

km

the short form of **kilometre** ☆kilometre 的缩写

***knee** /niː; ni/ *n* 名

the part in the middle of your leg where it bends 膝；膝盖

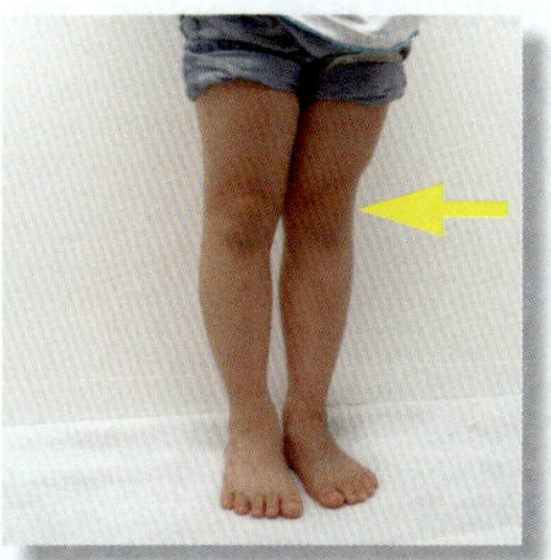

The baby crawled on her hands and knees. 宝宝手膝并用地爬着。

kneel /niːl; nil/ *v* 动

kneels, kneeling, knelt, knelt

to bend your legs and rest on your knees 跪下

She knelt down and prayed. 她跪下来祷告。

knelt /nelt; nɛlt/ *v* 动

the past tense and past participle of **kneel** ☆kneel 的过去式和过去分词

knew /njuː; nju/ *v* 动

the past tense of **know** ☆know 的过去式

***knife** /naɪf; naɪf/ *n* 名

复数：***knives***

a tool used for cutting, which has a handle and a sharp edge 刀

The thief carried a sharp knife. 那个小偷手持一把锋利的刀。

***knit** /nɪt; nɪt/ *v* 动

knits, knitting, knitted/knit, knitted/knit

to make clothes with two long needles and wool 编织

She is knitting a sweater. 她在织毛衣。

K

***knock¹** /nɒk; nɑk/ *v* 动

1. to make a noise by hitting a door, window, etc 敲（门、窗等）
   Mr Wilson knocked and went into the room. 威尔逊先生敲敲门，然后走进房间。

2. to hit something so that it moves or falls 撞倒；碰倒
   He knocked over the vase on the table. 他把桌上的花瓶碰倒了。

knock someone down 撞倒某人
The old man was knocked down by a car. 那个老人被一辆汽车撞倒了。
knock something down 拆除某物
They knocked down the old building. 他们把那座旧楼拆掉了。

knock² /nɒk; nɑk/ *n* 名

the sound made by hitting a hard surface 敲击声
Did you hear a knock at the door? 你听见敲门声了吗？

knot /nɒt; nɑt/ *n* 名

a part made by tying one or more pieces of string, rope, etc together （绳子等的）结
She tied her scarf with a knot. 她把围巾打了一个结。

注意 发音和 not 相同。

***know** /nəʊ; no/ *v* 动

knows, knowing, knew, known

1. to have information about something in your mind 知道
   I know her phone number. 我知道她的电话号码。
2. to have a skill in something 懂得
   Eric knows how to cook Italian food. 埃里克会烧意大利菜。
3. to understand something 明白
   I don't know what you mean. Can you say it again? 我不明白你的意思，你能再说一遍吗？
4. to have met someone before 相识
   I know your brother well. 我和你哥哥很熟。

注意 发音和 no 相同。

***knowledge** /ˈnɒlɪdʒ; ˋnɑlɪdʒ/ *n* 名

无复数
the things that someone knows about a subject 知识；学问
We have very little knowledge about this new disease. 我们对这种新疾病的了解很少。

known /nəʊn; non/ *v* 动

the past participle of **know** ☆know 的过去分词

koala /kəʊˈɑːlə; koˋɑlə/ *n* 名

也作：***koala bear***
an animal from Australia which looks like a small bear 树袋熊；无尾熊

Koalas sleep for many hours every day. 树袋熊每天睡很多小时。

kung fu /ˌkʌŋ ˈfuː; ˌkʌŋ ˋfu/ *n* 名

无复数
a Chinese sport in which you fight using your hands and feet 功夫
Mr Green likes to watch kung fu movies. 格林先生喜欢看功夫片。

比较 **judo, karate**

***label** /ˈleɪbl; ˋlebḷ/ *n* 名

a notice on something that gives information about it 标签

The label tells you how to wash the sweater. 这个标签说明了如何清洗毛衣。

比较 **sticker**

laboratory /ləˈbɒrətəri; ˋlæbrəˌtorɪ/ *n* 名

复数：***laboratories*** | 也作：***lab***

a room or building for doing tests and experiments 实验室

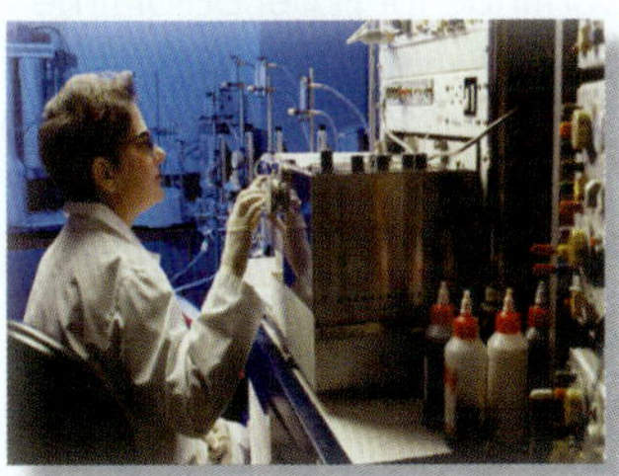

The blood was tested in a laboratory. 在实验室里进行了血液试验。

***ladder** /ˈlædə; ˋlædɚ/ *n* 名

a thing with steps for climbing up and down 梯子

My sister is painting the wall on a ladder. 姐姐在梯子上粉刷墙壁。

ladle /ˈleɪdl; ˋledḷ/ *n* 名

a big spoon with a long handle 长柄勺；汤勺

She used a ladle to stir the soup. 她用长柄勺来拌汤。

***lady** /ˈleɪdi; ˋledɪ/ *n* 名

复数：***ladies***

a polite word for a woman 女士（对女子的尊称）

Who's that lady? 那位女士是谁？

另见 **gentleman**

laid /leɪd; led/ *v* 动

the past tense and past participle of **lay**[1] ☆lay[1] 的过去式和过去分词

lain /leɪn; len/ *v* 动

the past participle of **lie**[1] ☆lie[1] 的过去分词

***lake** /leɪk; lek/ *n* 名

a very large pool of water with land all around it 湖

They crossed the lake by boat. 他们乘船到湖的另一边。

***lamb** /læm; læm/ *n* 名

a young sheep 小羊；羔羊

She is feeding the lambs on the farm. 她在农场喂小羊。

lame /leɪm; lem/ *adj* 形

not able to walk well because you have hurt your leg or it is weak 跛的；不便行走的

He is lame in his left leg. 他的左腿是跛的。

***lamp** /læmp; læmp/ *n* 名

something that gives light 灯

I switched off the lamp and went to bed. 我关了灯，上床睡觉。

***land[1]** /lænd; lænd/ *n* 名

无复数

1. the dry part of the earth 陆地
   Most snakes live on land. 大多数蛇在陆地上生活。
2. an area of ground 土地
   The land around Shanghai is very flat. 上海周围的土地很平坦。

land[2] /lænd; lænd/ *v* 动

to come down from the air onto the ground 着陆；降落

The plane landed at the airport this morning. 今天早上飞机在机场降落。

landslide /ˈlændslaɪd; ˋlændˌslaɪd/ *n* 名

a large amount of rocks and earth falling from a hill, etc 山崩；山泥倾泻

L

The landslide was caused by heavy rain. 这次山崩是由大雨引起的。

lane /leɪn; len/ *n* 名

1. a narrow road 小巷；小路
   I like to walk along the country lanes. 我喜欢沿着乡间小路散步。
2. one part of a road for cars to drive on（马路上的）车道；行车线
   The new road has four lanes. 这条新马路有 4 条车道。

***language** /ˈlæŋgwɪdʒ; ˋlæŋgwɪdʒ/ *n* 名

the words that we use in speaking and writing 语言
The guide can speak five languages. 这名导游会说 5 种语言。

L

***lantern** /ˈlæntən; ˋlæntən/ *n* 名

a light in a glass or paper container, often with a handle so that you can carry it 提灯；灯笼

We brought the lantern when we went camping. 我们去露营时带了提灯。

lap /læp; læp/ *n* 名

the top part of your legs, when you are sitting down（人坐着时的）大腿部
The girl has a basket on her lap. 那个女孩的大腿上有个篮子。

laptop /ˈlæptɒp; ˋlæpˌtɑp/ *n* 名

也作：***laptop computer***
【电脑】a computer that you can carry with you 膝上型电脑；手提电脑

My father is working on his laptop. 爸爸正在用手提电脑工作。

同义 **notebook**

***large** /lɑːdʒ; lardʒ/ *adj* 形

larger, largest
big 大的
An elephant is a very large animal. 大象是体形庞大的动物。

反义 **little[1], small**

***last[1]** /lɑːst; læst/ *adj* 形

1. closest before now; most recent 上一个的；最近的
   I visited my aunt last night. 我昨晚去探访阿姨。
2. coming after all the others 最后的；末尾的
   Andy was the last one to come in. 安迪是最后一个进来的。

反义 **first[1]**

***last[2]** /lɑːst; læst/ *adv* 副

1. most recently before now 上一次；最近
   When did you last see Annie? 你上次是什么时候见到安妮的？
2. after all the others 最后；最末
   She came last at the race. 她在赛跑中得了最后一名。

反义 **first[2]**

***last[3]** /lɑːst; læst/ *v* 动

to continue for a period of time 持续；延续
The rain lasted for two days. 雨持续下了两天。

lastly /ˈlɑːstli; ˋlæstlɪ/ *adv* 副

after everything else 最后
Lastly, let me thank you all again. 最后，让我再一次谢谢大家。

同义 **finally**

last name /lɑːst neɪm; ˋlæst nem/ *n* 名

your family name 姓氏
His first name is Andy, but I don't know his last name. 他的名字是安迪，但我不知道他的姓氏。

同义 **surname**

另见 **first name**

***late[1]** /leɪt; let/ *adj* 形

later, latest

1. coming after the usual or expected time 迟的；晚的
   Julie was late for school today.

茱莉今天上学迟到了。

反义 **early[1], punctual**

2. near the end of a period of time 晚期的；后期的

The school picnic is in late April. 学校郊游在 4 月底举行。

反义 **early[1]**

*late²

/leɪt; let/ *adv* 副

1. after the usual or expected time 迟；晚

The concert started half an hour late. 音乐会晚了半小时开始。

反义 **early[2]**

2. near the end of a period of time （时间上）接近末尾

Henry came home late at night. 亨利夜深时分才回家。

反义 **early[2]**

*later

/ˈleɪtə; ˋletɚ/ *adv* 副

after some time 以后；后来

I'm not hungry now. I'll have lunch later. 我现在不饿。晚一点再吃午餐。

later on 稍后；以后

Let's talk about this problem later on. 我们稍后再谈这个问题。

Daily conversation 日常会话

"Hello. May I speak to Mr Robinson?" "I'm sorry. He's busy now. Can you phone back later?" "你好，请问罗宾逊先生在吗？""对不起，他现在很忙，你稍后再来电好吗？"

*laugh

/lɑːf; læf/ *v* 动

to make a sound when you are happy or think something is funny 笑；发笑

The clown made us laugh. 那个小丑逗得我们哈哈大笑。

另见 **grin[1], smile[1]**

laughter

/ˈlɑːftə; ˋlæftɚ/ *n* 名

无复数

when someone laughs or the sound of laughing 笑；笑声

Her laughter made me happy. 她的笑声令我快乐。

另见 **grin[2], smile[2]**

laundry

/ˈlɔːndri; ˋlɔndrɪ/ *n* 名

无复数

clothes, sheets, towels, etc that are going to be washed, or that have been washed 待洗的衣服；刚洗好的衣服

My father is hanging out the laundry. 爸爸把洗好的衣服挂起来晾干。

lavatory

/ˈlævətəri; ˋlævəˌtɔrɪ/ *n* 名

复数：*lavatories*

a toilet 厕所；洗手间

Where's the lavatory, please? 请问洗手间在哪里？

注意 lavatory 是正式的说法。

*law

/lɔː; lɔ/ *n* 名

a rule or set of rules that everyone in a country must obey 法律

Stealing is against the law. 盗窃是违法的。

lawn

/lɔːn; lɔn/ *n* 名

a piece of land with short grass on it 草坪；草地

We had a picnic on the lawn. 我们在草坪上野餐。

*lawyer

/ˈlɔːjə; ˋlɔjɚ/ *n* 名

someone who gives advice to other people about the law 律师

Shirley's father has a good job. He is a lawyer. 雪莉的爸爸有份很好的职业。他是律师。

*lay¹

/leɪ; le/ *v* 动

lays, laying, laid, laid

1. to put someone or something on a surface carefully 放置；平放

Jack laid the picture on the desk. 杰克把图画放在书桌上。

比较 **lie[1]**

2. if a bird, an insect, etc lays eggs, it makes them and sends them out of its body 生蛋；产卵

The hen laid three eggs today. 这只母鸡今天下了 3 个蛋。

lay²

/leɪ; le/ *v* 动

the past tense of **lie[1]** ☆lie[1] 的过去式

L

*lazy

/ˈleɪzi; ˋlezɪ/ *adj* 形

lazier, laziest

not willing to work 懒惰的

Connie is clever but sometimes lazy. 康妮很聪明，但有时候很懒惰。

反义 **hard-working**

lb

the short form of **pound** ☆pound 的缩写

*lead

/liːd; lid/ *v* 动

leads, leading, led, led

1. to show someone how to go somewhere by going there in front of them 带领

The waitress led us to our table. 女服务员带我们到餐桌那里。

2. to go to a place 通往
   This path leads to the beach. 这条小径通往海滩。
3. to be in charge of something 领导；指挥
   He has led the country for ten years. 他领导这个国家 10 年了。

***leader** /ˈliːdə; ˋlidɚ/ *n* 名

someone who leads a team, country, etc 领袖；首领

Robert is our team leader. 罗伯特是我们的队长。

***leaf** /liːf; lif/ *n* 名

复数：***leaves***

a flat, green part of a plant 叶子；树叶

Leaves start falling in autumn. 树叶秋天开始掉落。

leaflet /ˈliːflət; ˋliflət/ *n* 名

a piece of paper printed with information on something 传单

She was giving out leaflets about the exhibition. 她在派发有关那个展览的传单。

L

leak /liːk; lik/ *v* 动

to have holes where water or gas passes in or out 漏；渗

The tent is leaking. 帐篷在漏水。

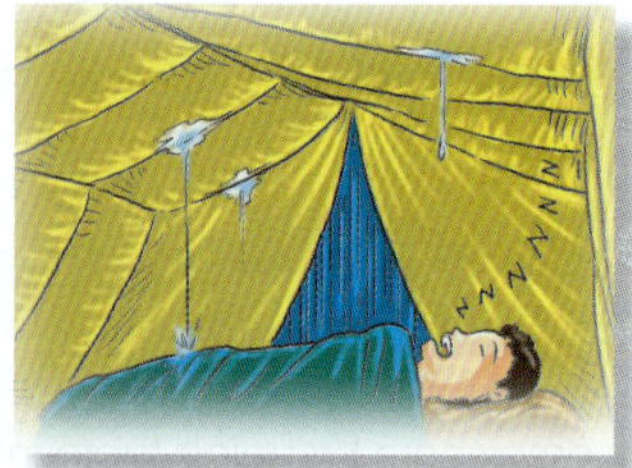

***lean** /liːn; lin/ *v* 动

leans, leaning, leaned/leant, leaned/leant

1. to move your body forwards, backwards or to the side 屈身；倾斜（身体）
   He leaned forward to listen to the radio. 他向前屈身听收音机。
2. to put your body or a thing against something 斜靠；靠着
   I leaned my bicycle against the wall. 我把自行车靠在墙上。

leap /liːp; lip/ *v* 动

leaps, leaping, leaped/leapt, leaped/leapt

to jump 跳；跳跃

Paul leapt across the stream. 保罗跳过了小溪。

***learn** /lɜːn; lɝn/ *v* 动

learns, learning, learned/learnt, learned/learnt

1. to get knowledge of something or skill in something 学习；学会
   I am learning to play the piano. 我在学弹钢琴。
2. to make yourself remember something by repeating it many times 熟记；记住
   I learnt this song and sang it to her. 我记熟了这首歌，唱给她听。

***least[1]** /liːst; list/ *adj* 形

having the smallest amount 最少的

This light bulb uses the least electricity. 这种电灯泡耗电最少。

at least 至少；起码

We need at least four people to play this game. 玩这个游戏至少需要 4 个人。

***least[2]** /liːst; list/ *adv* 副（*little[2]* 的最高级）

less than anything or anyone else 最少

The subject I like least is mathematics. 我最不喜欢的学科是数学。

反义 **most[1]**

***leather** /ˈleðə; ˋlɛðɚ/ *n* 名

无复数

animal skin used for making clothes, shoes, bags, etc 皮革

This jacket is made of leather. 这件外套是皮制的。

***leave** /liːv; liv/ *v* 动

leaves, leaving, left, left

1. to go away 离开
   The teacher has just left the classroom. 老师刚刚离开了教室。
2. to put something somewhere 把…放在
   Please leave the books on my desk. 请把书放在我的桌子上。
3. **be left/have (something) left** to remain after the rest has been taken away or used 留下；余下
   There are five sweets left. 还剩 5 颗糖。

leave someone alone 不打扰某人

Please leave me alone! 请让我一个人静一下！

leave something behind 忘了带东西；把东西留在原处

Oh no! I left my wallet behind. 糟糕！我忘了拿钱包！

leave something out 遗漏；不包括

Don't leave out an "r" in "embarrassed". 别忘记在 embarrassed 中有两个“r”。

led /led; lɛd/ *v* 动

the past tense and past participle of **lead** ☆lead 的过去式和过去分词

left[1] /left; lɛft/ *v* 动

the past tense and past participle of **leave** ☆leave 的过去式和过去分词

***left**[2] /left; lɛft/ *n* 名

无复数

the opposite of right 左边；左方

The school is on the left of the road. 学校在马路的左边。

反义 **right**[2]

***left**[3] /left; lɛft/ *adj* 形

on the opposite of right 左边的；左方的

Lily writes with her left hand. 莉莉用左手写字。

反义 **right**[1]

***left**[4] /left; lɛft/ *adv* 副

towards the opposite of right 向左边；往左方

Turn left at the next street. 在下一个街口向左拐。

反义 **right**[3]

> **Asking for directions 问路**
> *"Where's the church?" "Go down the street. Turn left at the corner and you'll find it."* "教堂在哪里？""沿这条街一直走，在街角向左转就到了。"

leftovers /ˈleftˌəuvəz; ˋlɛftˌovɚz/ *plural n* 复数名词

food that has not been eaten at the end of a meal 剩余的饭菜

Put the leftovers in the fridge. 把剩余的食物放进冰箱。

***leg** /leg; lɛg/ *n* 名

1. a part of the body of a person or an animal that is used for walking 腿

   Eric has broken his leg. 埃里克摔断了腿。

2. a part of a table, chair, etc that it stands on（桌椅等的）腿；脚

   This coffee table has only three legs. 这咖啡桌只有三条腿。

***legal** /ˈliːgl; ˋligl̩/ *adj* 形

allowed by law 合法的；法定的

Is it legal to download music from the Internet? 从互联网下载音乐是否合法?

反义 **illegal**

legend /ˈledʒənd; ˋlɛdʒənd/ *n* 名

a story about people or events in the past that may not be true 传说；传奇

My grandfather told me an old Chinese legend. 我的爷爷给我讲了一个古老的中国传说。

leisure /ˈleʒə; ˋliʒɚ/ *n* 名

无复数

time when you are not working or studying and can do things you enjoy 空闲；闲暇

We play basketball in our leisure time. 我们有空的时候会打篮球。

***lemon** /ˈlemən; ˋlɛmən/ *n* 名

a yellow fruit that tastes sour 柠檬

I cut the lemon into slices. 我把柠檬切成片。

lemonade /ˌleməˈneɪd; ˌlɛmənˋed/ *n* 名

a sweet drink with lemon juice 柠檬水；柠檬汽水

Matthew drank a glass of lemonade after school. 马修放学后喝了一杯柠檬水。

***lend** /lend; lɛnd/ *v* 动

lends, lending, lent, lent

to let someone use something that belongs to you for a short time 借出；借给

I lent the DVD to Max yesterday. 昨天我把那张数码影碟借给麦克斯了。

比较 **borrow**

> **Daily conversation 日常会话**
> *"Can you lend me your bicycle for a few days?" "All right."* "你把你的自行车借给我几天好吗？""好的。"

length /leŋθ; lɛŋθ/ *n* 名

无复数

how long something is 长度

The length of this bridge is 500 metres. 这座桥长 500 米。

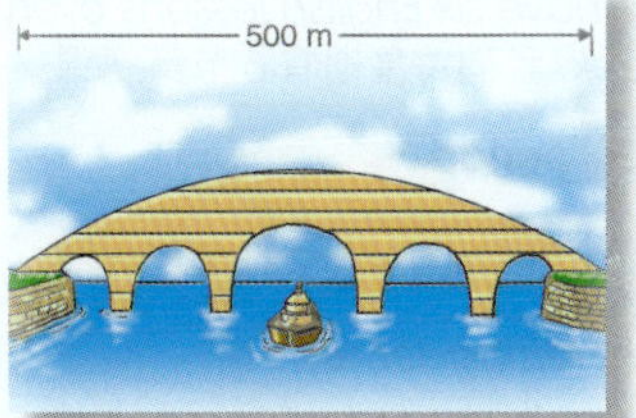

lent /lent; lɛnt/ *v* 动

the past tense and past participle of **lend** ☆lend 的过去式和过去分词

L

leopard /ˈlepəd; ˋlɛpəd/ *n* 名

a large, wild animal that has yellow fur and black spots 豹

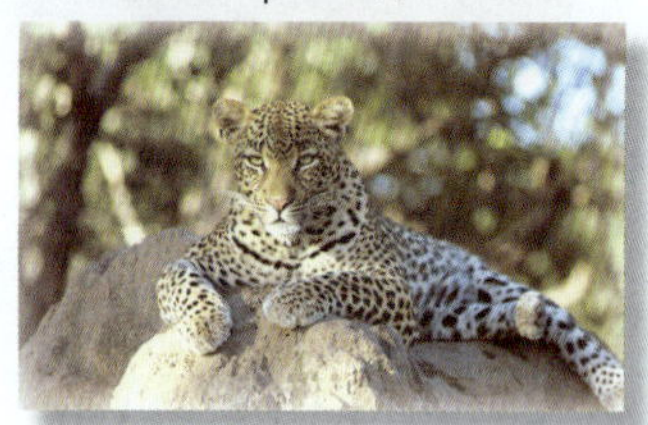

Leopards run very fast. 豹跑得很快。

***less**[1]* /les; lɛs/ *adv* 副（*little*² 的比较级）

not as much as something else 较少

He is looking for a less expensive place to live. 他在找比较便宜的住处。

反义 **more**[1]

***less**[2]* /les; lɛs/ *adj* 形

a smaller amount 较少的

The doctor told Gary to eat less sugar. 医生叫加里少摄入糖。

用法 less 用于不可数名词，例如 I have less money than Ben（我有的钱比本少）。可数名词则用 fewer，例如 I have fewer books than Ben（我有的书比本少）。

反义 **more**[2]

***lesson** /ˈlesn; ˋlɛsn̩/ *n* 名

a period of time when you learn something with a teacher 课

We have six English lessons every week. 我们每星期有 6 节英语课。

同义 **period**

***let** /let; lɛt/ *v* 动

lets, letting, let, let

to say that someone can do something 让；允许

My mother let me go to the party. 妈妈让我去参加派对。

let go 放手；松开

Hold the rope and don't let go! 抓住绳子，不要放开！

let someone know 让某人知道；告诉某人

Please let me know if you need help. 如果需要帮忙请告诉我。

用法 let 后接的动词不带 to，例如 Let him do it（让他去做吧）。

Daily conversation 日常会话

let's（= let us）让我们

"It's five o'clock. Let's go home." "All right." "现在 5 点了。我们回家吧。""好的。"

let's see/let me see 让我想想

"When are we going shopping, Mum?" "Let me see, what about tomorrow?" "妈妈，我们什么时候去买东西？""让我想想，明天怎么样？"

***letter** /ˈletə; ˋlɛtɚ/ *n* 名

1. one of the signs used in writing 字母
   There are 26 letters in the English alphabet. 英语字母表里有 26 个字母。
2. a piece of writing that you send to someone by post 信；信件

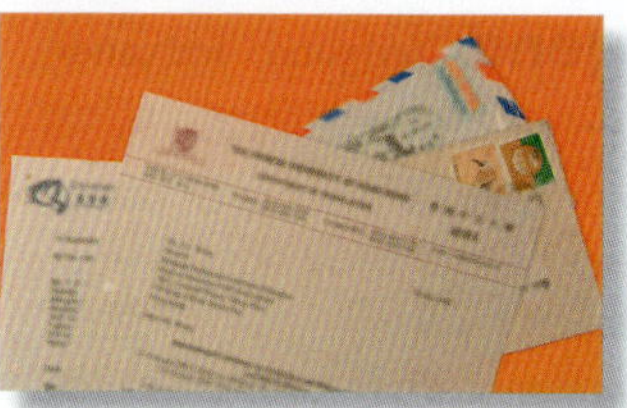

I am writing a letter to a friend. 我在给朋友写信。

letterbox /ˈletəbɒks; ˋlɛtɚˌbɑks/ *n* 名【英】

复数：***letterboxes*** | 美式：***mailbox***

a hole or box where you receive or post letters 信箱；邮筒

There is a postcard in our letterbox. 我们的信箱内有一张明信片。

lettuce /ˈletɪs; ˋlɛtɪs/ *n* 名

a vegetable with thin green leaves that is used in salads 莴苣；生菜

My mother made a salad with lettuce. 妈妈用生菜做沙拉。

注意 表示一种蔬菜时，lettuce 是不可数名词。当表示一个一个的莴苣时，lettuce 则是可数名词。

***level** /ˈlevl; ˋlɛvl̩/ *n* 名

1. the size, number or amount of something 程度；水平
   This computer game has three levels of difficulty. 这个电脑游戏有三个级别的难度。
2. the height of something above or below something else 高度
   The water level in the lake has risen after the heavy rain. 大雨后湖水水位上升了。

librarian /laɪˈbreəriən; laɪˋbrɛrɪən/ *n* 名

someone who works in a library 图书馆管理员

The librarian helped me find the book. 图书馆管理员帮我找到了那本书。

***library** /ˈlaɪbrəri; ˋlaɪˌbrɛrɪ/ *n* 名

复数：***libraries***

a place where you can borrow books 图书馆

I borrowed two books from the library. 我从图书馆借了两本书。

licence /ˈlaɪsns; ˋlaɪsn̩s/ *n* 名【英】

美式：***license***

something that shows you are allowed to do something by law 执照；许可证

You can't drive without a driving licence. 没有驾驶执照你不可以开车。

lick /lɪk; lɪk/ *v* 动

to touch something with your tongue 舔；舔食

The cat is licking its feet. 这只猫在舔自己的脚。

***lid** /lɪd; lɪd/ *n* 名

a cover for a box, pan, etc 盖子

Take the lid off the pan. 把锅盖拿起。

***lie¹** /laɪ; laɪ/ *v* 动

lies, lying, lay, lain

to rest with your body flat 躺卧

The man is lying on the beach. 那个男人躺在海滩上。

比较 **lay¹**

***lie²** /laɪ; laɪ/ *v* 动

lies, lying, lied, lied

to say something that is not true 说谎

I never lie to my teachers. 我从不向我的老师说谎。

***lie³** /laɪ; laɪ/ *n* 名

something you say that is not true 谎言；谎话

Don't tell lies. 别说谎。

反义 **truth**

***life** /laɪf; laɪf/ *n* 名

复数：***lives***

1. the period of time when someone is alive 生命

   He had a long life. 他很长寿。

2. （无复数）the way you live your life 生活

   She enjoys family life. 她很享受家庭生活。

3. （无复数）living things 生物

   Is there life on Mars? 火星上有没有生物？

lifeboat /ˈlaɪfbəʊt; ˋlaɪfˏbot/ *n* 名

a boat used to save people at sea 救生艇

A lifeboat saved three people last night. 一艘救生艇昨晚救了三个人。

lifeguard /ˈlaɪfgɑːd; ˋlaɪfˏgɑrd/ *n* 名

someone who works at a beach or swimming pool and helps swimmers that are in danger 救生员

The lifeguard saved the girl. 救生员救了那个女孩。

lift¹ /lɪft; lɪft/ *v* 动

to move something to a higher position 举起；抬起

She lifted her baby from the bed. 她把宝宝从床上抱起来。

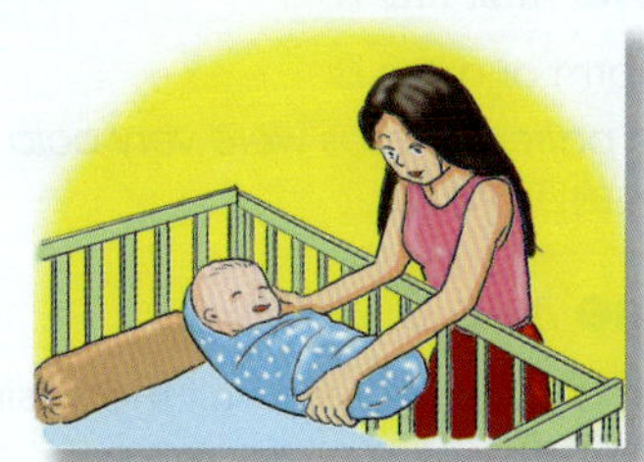

***lift²** /lɪft; lɪft/ *n* 名【英】

美式：***elevator***

a machine that takes people up and down in a building 电梯；升降机

We took the lift to the sixth floor. 我们乘电梯到6楼。

比较 **escalator**

***light¹** /laɪt; laɪt/ *n* 名

1. （无复数）the energy from the sun, a lamp, etc that helps you see 光

   There is a lot of light in this room. 这个房间里很明亮。

2. a thing that helps you see, which uses electricity 电灯

   Turn off the lights when you leave. 你离开时要关灯。

***light²** /laɪt; laɪt/ *adj* 形

lighter, lightest

1. pale in colour 浅色的

   I wore a light green T-shirt. 我穿了一件浅绿色的T恤。

反义 **dark¹**

2. not weighing much 轻的；不重的

   The cat is lighter than the rabbit. 这只猫比这只兔子轻。

反义 **heavy**

3. full of light 明亮的

   The living room is light and comfortable. 客厅明亮舒适。

4. not very strong or very much 轻柔的；少量的

   There was a light shower yesterday. 昨天下了一场小雨。

反义 **heavy**

L

***light³** /laɪt; laɪt/ *v* 动

lights, lighting, lighted/lit, lighted/lit

to make something start burning 点（火）；点燃

I lit seven candles. 我点了 7 支蜡烛。

lighter /ˈlaɪtə; ˋlaɪtɚ/ *n* 名

a small object that makes something burn 打火机

He lit a cigarette with a lighter. 他用打火机点了一支香烟。

lighthouse /ˈlaɪthaʊs; ˋlaɪtˏhaʊs/ *n* 名

a tall building that gives out bright light to help ships move safely 灯塔

There is a lighthouse near the entrance to the harbour. 海港入口附近有一座灯塔。

lightly /ˈlaɪtli; ˋlaɪtlɪ/ *adv* 副

using only a small amount of something 轻柔地；轻轻地；少许

She kissed her son lightly on the cheek. 她轻轻地吻了儿子的面颊。

lightning /ˈlaɪtnɪŋ; ˋlaɪtnɪŋ/ *n* 名

无复数

a bright flash of light in the sky 闪电

I saw lightning and then I heard thunder. 我看到闪电，然后听到雷声。

比较 **thunder**

Light Rail Transit /laɪt reɪl ˈtrænsɪt; laɪt rel ˋtrænsɪt/ *n* 名

缩写：***LRT***

a kind of railway transport in some cities 轻轨

My uncle goes to work by Light Rail Transit. 我的舅舅乘轻轨上班。

***like¹** /laɪk; laɪk/ *v* 动

likes, liking, liked, liked

to think that someone or something is nice 喜欢；喜爱

Molly likes to sing. 茉莉喜欢唱歌。

反义 **dislike**

***like²** /laɪk; laɪk/ *prep* 介

similar to 像；相似

He looks like his father. 他长得很像他爸爸。

***likely** /ˈlaɪkli; ˋlaɪklɪ/ *adj* 形

if something is likely, it will probably happen 很可能的

It is likely to rain today. 今天很可能会下雨。

lily /ˈlɪli; ˋlɪlɪ/ *n* 名

复数：***lilies***

a plant with bell-shaped flowers 百合花

There are a lot of lilies in her garden. 她的花园里有很多百合。

limb /lɪm; lɪm/ *n* 名

an arm or a leg 肢

The patient's limbs were very cold. 病人的四肢冰凉。

lime /laɪm; laɪm/ *n* 名

a small, round, green fruit that tastes sour 酸橙；青柠

Cut the lime into slices. 把酸橙切成薄片。

***line** /laɪn; laɪn/ *n* 名

1. a long, narrow mark 线

   Stand behind the yellow line when you are waiting for the train. 等火车时不要超越黄线。

2. a row of people or things 一排；一行

   There is a long line of people at the bus stop. 公共汽车站排了一条长龙。

3. a long piece of rope or string that you use for doing something（有某种用途的）绳；线

   I hung the clothes on the washing line. 我把衣服挂在晾衣绳上。

link /lɪŋk; lɪŋk/ *v* 动

to join two things together 连接

Draw a line to link the two points. 画一条线连接两点。

***lion** /ˈlaɪən; ˋlaɪən/ *n* 名

a big, dangerous wild animal with pale brown fur 狮子

We went to the zoo to see the lions. 我们去动物园看狮子。

lion dance /ˈlaɪən ˌdɑːns; ˋlaɪən ˌdæns/ *n* 名

a traditional Chinese dance in which people wear special clothes and move like a lion 舞狮

L

People believe that lion dances can bring good luck. 人们相信舞狮能带来好运。

***lip** /lɪp; lɪp/ *n* 名

one of the two soft parts around your mouth 嘴唇

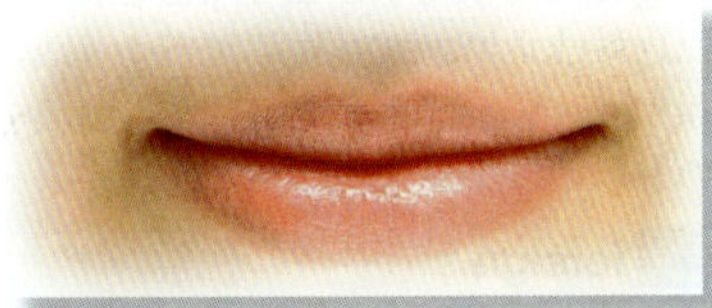

Amy has beautiful lips. 艾米的嘴唇很漂亮。

lipstick /ˈlɪpstɪk; ˋlɪpˌstɪk/ *n* 名

a thing that women put on their lips to make them colourful 口红；唇膏

She wears bright red lipstick. 她涂着鲜红的唇膏。

liquid /ˈlɪkwɪd; ˋlɪkwɪd/ *n* 名

something such as water, which flows easily and is not a solid or a gas 液体

He mixed the liquids in a glass. 他把液体在杯中混合。

***list** /lɪst; lɪst/ *n* 名

a set of things, names, etc written on a piece of paper 名单；清单

My mother is making a shopping list. 妈妈正在列一张购物清单。

***listen** /ˈlɪsn; ˋlɪsn̩/ *v* 动

to pay attention to what you are hearing 听；聆听

Listen carefully to the question before you give your answer. 在作答之前，先仔细听问题。

用法 listen 后多接 to。

注意 listen 是“留心地听”，而 hear 是“听到”，即不管是否愿意都听见了。

比较 hear

lit /lɪt; lɪt/ *v* 动

the past tense and past participle of **light³** ☆light³ 的过去式和过去分词

litre /ˈliːtə; ˋlitɚ/ *n* 名

美式：*liter*

a unit for measuring liquid 升；公升

This bottle holds one litre. 这个瓶子的容量是一升。

***litter** /ˈlɪtə; ˋlɪtɚ/ *n* 名

无复数

waste paper, bottles, etc that are left in public places 垃圾

Joe is helping to pick up the litter. 乔在帮忙把垃圾捡起来。

litter bin 垃圾箱

Put all the waste paper in the litter bin. 把所有废纸扔进垃圾箱里。

同义 rubbish

***little¹** /ˈlɪtl; ˋlɪtl̩/ *adj* 形

1. small 小的

   They are carrying their little babies. 她们抱着自己的小宝宝。

反义 big, large

2. not much 不多的；很少的

   I have got very little money left. 我没剩下多少钱。

用法 little 与不可数名词同用。

反义 much²

比较 few¹

a little 一点；少量

My grandfather knows a little English. 我的爷爷会一点英语。

a little bit 一点点；少量

I put a little bit of sugar in the tea. 我在茶里放了一点糖。

a little while 一会儿

Can you wait a little while? 你可以等一会儿吗?

Daily conversation 日常会话

"Would you like some more tea?" "Just a little, thanks." “你想再喝点茶吗？”“一点点就够了，谢谢。”

***little²** /ˈlɪtl; ˋlɪtl̩/ *adv* 副

less, least

not much 少；不多

Sam is very tired because he slept very little last night. 山姆很累，因为他昨晚睡得很少。

反义 much¹

***live¹** /lɪv; lɪv/ *v* 动

lives, living, lived, lived

1. to have your home in a place 居住

   Winnie lives in Beijing. 威妮住在北京。

2. to stay alive 生存；活着

   We need air to live. 我们生存需要空气。

反义 die

live on 以…为主食；靠…过活

Sheep live on grass. 羊靠吃青草维持生命。

***live²** /laɪv; laɪv/ *adj* 形

1. not dead 活着的

L

He has never seen a live lion. 他从未见过活的狮子。

同义 **living**

反义 **dead**

2. watched by people who are present 现场的

We watched a live performance last Saturday. 我们上星期六看了一场现场表演。

liver /ˈlɪvə; ˋlɪvɚ/ *n* 名

the part of your body that cleans your blood 肝；肝脏

Fruit and vegetables are good for your liver. 水果和蔬菜有益于肝脏健康。

living /ˈlɪvɪŋ; ˋlɪvɪŋ/ *adj* 形

alive 活着的

After her parents died, she had no living relatives. 她在父母死后已没有亲人在世了。

同义 **live²**

反义 **dead**

living room /ˈlɪvɪŋ ruːm; ˋlɪvɪŋ rum/ *n* 名

a room in a house where you sit and relax 客厅；起居室

We watch TV in the living room. 我们在客厅里看电视。

同义 **sitting room**

另见 **附录**：Inside a flat 住所里

lizard /ˈlɪzəd; ˋlɪzɚd/ *n* 名

a small animal with thick skin, four legs and a long tail 蜥蜴

There is a lizard on the wall. 墙上有只蜥蜴。

load¹ /ləʊd; lod/ *n* 名

things that are carried by a vehicle, person, etc 负载物；装载物

The lorry is carrying a load of fruit. 这辆货车载着一车水果。

load² /ləʊd; lod/ *v* 动

to put things onto or into a vehicle 装载；装货

Mr Brown loaded his luggage into his car. 布朗先生把行李装进汽车里。

反义 **unload**

*loaf /ləʊf; lof/ *n* 名

复数：***loaves***

bread that is baked in a long or round shape and can be cut into slices 一条面包

My father bought a loaf of bread. 我爸爸买了一条面包。

用法 bread 是不可数名词。一整条的面包叫作 a loaf of bread，一片的面包则是 a slice of bread。

lobby /ˈlɒbi; ˋlɑbɪ/ *n* 名

复数：***lobbies***

an area inside the entrance of a building 大厅；大堂

Let's wait at the hotel lobby. 我们在酒店大堂等候吧。

lobster /ˈlɒbstə; ˋlɑbstɚ/ *n* 名

a sea animal with a hard shell, eight legs and two large claws 龙虾

Lobsters turn red when they are cooked. 龙虾熟了就变成红色。

*local /ˈləʊkl; ˋlokl̩/ *adj* 形

near where you live, or in the place you are talking about 本地的；当地的

They are watching the local news on TV. 他们在看电视上的本地新闻。

反义 **foreign**

location /ləʊˈkeɪʃn; loˋkeʃən/ *n* 名

a place or position 地点；位置

Her shop is in a good location. 她的商店地点很好。

*lock¹ /lɒk; lɑk/ *n* 名

something you use to keep a door, a box, etc closed 锁

He used the key to open the lock. 他用那把钥匙开了锁。

*lock² /lɒk; lɑk/ *v* 动

to close a door, a box, etc with a key 锁上

She locked the door and went out. 她锁好门后出去了。

反义 **unlock**

locker /ˈlɒkə; ˋlɑkɚ/ *n* 名

a small cupboard with a lock for keeping things in 锁柜；寄物柜

I put the books in my locker. 我把书放在寄物柜内。

log¹ /lɒg; lɔg/ *n* 名

a thick piece of wood from a tree 原木

Let's put some logs on the fire. 我们往火里放些木柴吧。

log² /lɒg; lɔg/ *v* 动

logs, logging, logged, logged

log in/on 登入(电脑系统)

You need a password to log in to the computer. 你需要密码来登入这台电脑。

log out/off 登出(电脑系统)

Remember to log out after using the computer. 用完电脑后记得要退出。

***lonely** /ˈləʊnli; ˋlonlɪ/ *adj* 形

lonelier, loneliest

sad because you are alone 孤独的；寂寞的

Lisa felt very lonely without her family. 家人不在，丽莎感到很寂寞。

用法 lonely 是孤单的意思，alone 则指单独。名词前可以用 lonely，例如 a lonely person(一个孤独的人)，但不可以用 alone。

***long¹** /lɒŋ; lɔŋ/ *adj* 形

longer, longest

1. measuring a large length or distance(长度或距离)长的

   The puppet has a long nose. 这个木偶的鼻子很长。

反义 short

2. lasting a large amount of time 长时间的

   The film is very long. 这部电影很长。

反义 short

***long²** /lɒŋ; lɔŋ/ *adv* 副

for a large amount of time 长时间；长期

It won't take you long to finish the work. 完成这项工作不会花你很长时间。

as/so long as 只要；假如

You can watch TV as long as you have finished your homework. 只要你做完功课，就可以看电视。

long ago 很久以前

This school was built long ago. 这所学校在很久以前就建立了。

Daily conversation 日常会话

so long 再见

"So long! Take care." "You too." "再见！保重。" "你也保重。"

***look¹** /lʊk; lʊk/ *v* 动

1. to point your eyes towards something so that you can see it 看；瞧

   Look at the bird in the sky! 看看天上的鸟！

2. to seem 看来

   He looked very tired. 他看来很累。

look after 照顾

Mrs Smith looks after the baby. 史密斯太太照顾这个宝宝。

look for 寻找

I am looking for a book. 我在找一本书。

look forward to 盼望；期待

We are looking forward to the summer holidays. 我们期待着暑假的来临。

look out 小心；当心

Look out! There's a snake behind you! 小心！你后面有条蛇！

look up 查阅

Look up these words in the dictionary. 在词典中查这些词。

***look²** /lʊk; lʊk/ *n* 名

looking at something 看；瞧

Let me have a look at the photos. 让我看一看那些相片。

***loose** /luːs; lus/ *adj* 形

looser, loosest

1. not fixed to something 松动的；不牢固的

   Two buttons of my shirt are loose. 我的衬衫上有两颗钮扣松了。

2. not fitting closely 宽松的

   These shoes are too loose for me. 这双鞋子我穿太大了。

反义 tight

loosen /ˈluːsn; ˋlusn̩/ *v* 动

to make something less tight 放松；松开

Sam loosened his tie. 山姆松开了领带。

反义 tighten

***lorry** /ˈlɒri; ˋlɔrɪ/ *n* 名

复数：*lorries*

a big vehicle for carrying things 货车；卡车

There is a lorry parked outside the school. 有一辆货车停在学校外面。

同义 truck

L

***lose** /luːz; luz/ *v* 动

loses, losing, lost, lost

1. to be unable to find someone or something 遗失；丢失

   Kitty lost her umbrella. 吉蒂丢了雨伞。

反义 find

2. to not win a competition or game 输掉

   Our team lost the game. 我们的球队在比赛中输了。

反义 win

lose your way 迷路

We lost our way in the forest. 我们在森林里迷路了。

***loss** /lɒs; lɔs/ *n* 名

复数：*losses*

a situation in which you do not have someone or something any more 损失；遗失

If he leaves, it will be a great loss to the company. 如果他离开，对那家公司将是重大的损失。

L

lost[1] /lɒst; lɔst/ *v* 动

the past tense and past participle of **lose** ☆lose 的过去式和过去分词

lost[2] /lɒst; lɔst/ *adj* 形

not knowing where you are 迷路的

The little boy got lost in the park. 这个小男孩在公园里迷了路。

***lot** /lɒt; lɑt/ *n* 名

a large number or amount 大量；许多

My brother eats a lot. 我的弟弟食量很大。

a lot of/lots of 很多

There are a lot of cars on the road. 路上有很多车辆。

用法 a lot of 后可以接可数名词，例如 There are a lot of people（有很多人）；也可以接不可数名词，例如 He has a lot of money（他有很多钱）。

lotus /ˈləʊtəs; ˋlotəs/ *n* 名

复数：*lotuses*

a water plant with big flowers and leaves 莲花；荷花

The lotuses in the pond are very beautiful. 池塘中的莲花很漂亮。

***loud** /laʊd; laʊd/ *adj* 形

louder, loudest

making a lot of noise 大声的；响亮的

The music is too loud. 音乐声太大了。

反义 soft

In the classroom 在教室里

"Would you please speak louder?" "OK." "请你大声一点，好吗？" "好的。"

loudspeaker /ˌlaʊdˈspiːkə; ˋlaʊdˋspikɚ/ *n* 名

something that makes sound louder 扩音器；喇叭

Miss Evans called the names through a loudspeaker. 伊万斯小姐通过扩音器喊出名字。

lounge /laʊndʒ; laʊndʒ/ *n* 名

a room in a hotel or airport where you can sit, wait for the plane, etc 休息室；（机场的）候机室

Mr Anderson is reading a book in the lounge. 安德森先生在休息室里看书。

***love[1]** /lʌv; lʌv/ *v* 动

loves, loving, loved, loved

to like someone or something very much 爱；喜爱

Connie loves animals. 康妮很爱动物。

反义 hate

***love[2]** /lʌv; lʌv/ *n* 名

无复数

the feeling of liking someone or something very much 爱

A mother's love for her children is great. 母亲对孩子的爱是伟大的。

lovely /ˈlʌvli; ˋlʌvlɪ/ *adj* 形

lovelier, loveliest

beautiful; attractive 美丽的；可爱的；迷人的

This is a lovely skirt. 这条裙子真漂亮。

***low** /ləʊ; lo/ *adj* 形

lower, lowest

1. not high or far above the ground 低的；矮的

   The houses in the countryside are very low. 乡村的房屋都很矮。

反义 high

2. small in number or amount（数量）少的

   The price of food in this country is low. 这个国家的食物很便宜。

反义 high

3. not loud 轻声的；低声的

   Michael spoke to me in a low voice. 迈克尔低声对我说话。

loyal /ˈlɔɪəl; ˋlɔɪəl/ *adj* 形

showing support to someone or something 忠心的；忠实的

The dog is loyal to its owner. 那只狗对主人忠心耿耿。

LRT /el ɑː ˈtiː; ɛl ɑr ˋti/ *n* 名

另见 **Light Rail Transit**

***luck** /lʌk; lʌk/ *n* 名

无复数

the good or bad things that happen to you by chance 运气

I wish you good luck! 我祝你好运！

同义 **fortune**

luckily /ˈlʌkili; ˋlʌkılı/ *adv* 副

as a result of good luck 幸运地；幸而

Luckily, I found my purse. 幸好我找到了钱包。

lucky /ˈlʌki; ˋlʌkı/ *adj* 形

luckier, luckiest

having good luck 幸运的；运气好的

I was lucky to buy the last ticket. 我很幸运，买到了最后一张票。

同义 **fortunate**

反义 **unlucky**

lucky money /ˈlʌki mʌni; ˋlʌkı mʌnı/ *n* 名

无复数

the money that people give children during the Chinese New Year 红包

Henry got a lot of lucky money from his relatives. 亨利收到了很多亲戚给的红包。

***luggage** /ˈlʌɡɪdʒ; ˋlʌɡɪdʒ/ *n* 名

无复数

bags and cases that you take when you travel 行李

We put our luggage in the train. 我们把行李放进火车里。

用法 luggage 是不可数名词，如要表示一件、两件行李，用 a piece of luggage、two pieces of luggage 等。

同义 **baggage**

***lunch** /lʌntʃ; lʌntʃ/ *n* 名

复数：***lunches***

a meal that you eat in the middle of the day 午餐；午饭

We usually have lunch at 1 p.m. 我们通常在下午 1 点吃午餐。

lunch box 午餐盒

My mother prepares a lunch box for me every day. 我的妈妈每天为我准备一个饭盒。

lung /lʌŋ; lʌŋ/ *n* 名

one of the two parts in your chest that you use for breathing 肺

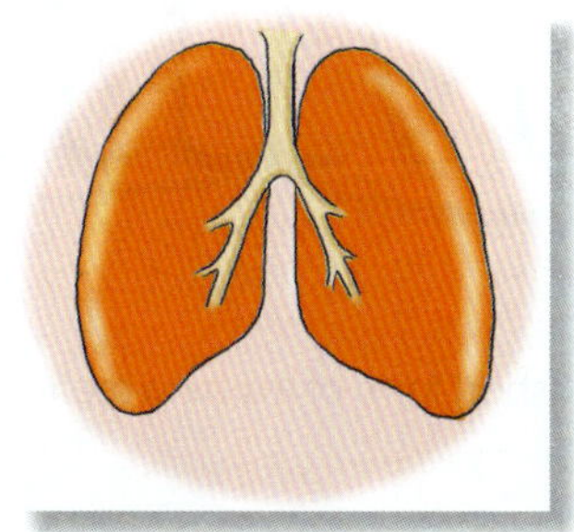

Smoking can cause lung cancer. 吸烟可能导致肺癌。

lychee /ˈlaɪtʃiː; ˋlaɪtʃi/ *n* 名

a small fruit that is red on the outside and white on the inside 荔枝

These lychees are sweet and fresh. 这些荔枝又甜又新鲜。

lying /ˈlaɪ-ɪŋ; ˋlaɪ-ɪŋ/ *v* 动

the present participle of **lie** ☆lie 的现在分词

L

m

the short form of **metre** ☆metre 的缩写

***machine** /məˈʃiːn; məˋʃin/ *n* 名

a piece of equipment with moving parts that helps you do a job 机器；机械

This machine is used to make bread. 这台机器是用来做面包的。

***mad** /mæd; mæd/ *adj* 形

madder, maddest

1. very silly; stupid 傻的；愚蠢的

   You're mad to go to swim in a storm. 暴风雨中还要去游泳，你真是疯了。

2. angry 生气的；愤怒的

   Mum was mad with me because I broke the vase. 我打碎了花瓶，妈妈很生气。

madam /ˈmædəm; ˋmædəm/ *n* 名

无复数

a polite way of speaking or writing to a woman 女士；夫人；小姐

May I help you, madam? 女士，有什么可以帮忙吗?

用法 对女子的尊称，常用于商店里服务员对女顾客的称呼。

另见 **sir**

made /meɪd; med/ *v* 动

the past tense and past participle of **make** ☆make 的过去式和过去分词

注意 发音和 maid 相同。

***magazine** /ˌmægəˈziːn; ˋmægəzin/ *n* 名

a thin book with stories and pictures that you can buy every week or month 杂志；期刊

Henry likes reading sports magazines. 亨利喜欢看体育杂志。

***magic** /ˈmædʒɪk; ˋmædʒɪk/ *n* 名

无复数

1. a special power used to do strange things 魔法；法术

   She turned the prince into a frog by magic. 她用魔法把王子变成了一只青蛙。

2. clever tricks that someone does to entertain people 魔术

   Philip can do magic. 菲利普会变魔术。

magician /məˈdʒɪʃn; məˋdʒɪʃən/ *n* 名

someone who does clever tricks to entertain people 魔术师

The magician pulled a rabbit out of his hat! 魔术师从他的帽子里掏出了一只兔子！

magnet /ˈmægnɪt; ˋmægnɪt/ *n* 名

a piece of iron that makes metal objects move towards it 磁铁；磁石

The magnet picked up the nails. 磁铁把那些铁钉吸了起来。

mahjong /ˌmɑːˈdʒɒŋ; maˋʒɑŋ/ *n* 名

无复数

a game played by four people with small pieces of wood or other material on a table 麻将；麻雀

My mother likes to play mahjong. 我的妈妈喜欢打麻将。

maid /meɪd; med/ *n* 名

a woman who works in someone's house 女仆；女佣

Our maid cooks for us every day. 我家的女佣每天为我们做饭。

注意 发音和 made 相同。

***mail** /meɪl; mel/ *n* 名

无复数

letters and parcels that you send or receive 邮件；信件

We got a lot of mail last week. 上星期我们收到了很多邮件。

注意 发音和 male 相同。

mailbox /ˈmeɪlbɒks; ˋmelˏbɑks/ *n* 名

复数：***mailboxes***

1. 【美】信箱 英式 **letterbox**
2. 【美】邮箱；邮筒 英式 **letterbox, postbox**
3. 【电脑】a place on a computer

M

where you get your email messages 电子邮箱
There are five new emails in my mailbox. 我的电子邮箱内有 5 封新邮件。

***main** /meɪn; men/ *adj* 形
the most important 主要的
Sally wrote down the main points of the speech. 莎莉把演讲的要点写了下来。

mainly /ˈmeɪnli; ˋmenlɪ/ *adv* 副
mostly 主要地；大部分
Tigers live mainly in Asia. 老虎主要在亚洲生活。

***major** /ˈmeɪdʒə; ˋmedʒɚ/ *adj* 形
very important or large 主要的；重要的；较大的
Hong Kong is a major city in Asia. 香港是亚洲的主要城市。

反义 **minor**

***make** /meɪk; mek/ *v* 动
makes, making, made, made

1. to produce something 做（某物）；制造
   Mrs Walker is making a cake. 沃克太太在做蛋糕。
2. to do something 做（某事）；作出
   He made a mistake. 他犯了一个错误。
3. to cause someone to do something or cause something to happen 使；引起
   She always makes me laugh. 她总是让我发笑。

be made from 用…做（材料发生变化时用）
Paper is made from wood. 纸是用木材制造的。
be made of 用…做（材料没有发生明显变化时用）
This chair is made of wood. 这张椅子是木头做的。
make the bed 整理床铺
I make my bed every morning. 我每天早上都会整理床铺。
make up 编造；捏造
He made up a story to cheat me. 他编了个故事来骗我。

Daily conversation 日常会话
make it 能参加；能出席
"Are you going to the party tomorrow?" "I'm sorry. I can't make it." "你参加明天的聚会吗？" "对不起，我不能来。"

make-up /ˈmeɪk ʌp; ˋmek ʌp/ *n* 名
无复数
something you put on the face to make you look better 化妆品

Helen was putting on her make-up in front of the mirror. 海伦正在镜子前化妆。

***male** /meɪl; mel/ *adj* 形
belonging to the sex that cannot have babies 男性的；雄性的
Many people think that football is a male sport. 很多人认为足球是一项男性运动。

注意 发音和 mail 相同。

反义 **female**

***mall** /mɔːl; mɔl/ *n* 名
也作：***shopping mall***
a large building that has many shops, restaurants, etc inside it 购物中心；商场
The mall is very crowded on Sundays. 那个商场星期天很拥挤。

同义 **shopping centre**

***man** /mæn; mæn/ *n* 名
复数：*men*

1. an adult male person 男人
   The men are drinking beer. 那些男人在喝啤酒。
2. （无复数）all humans; people 人类（总称）
   Man cannot live without air. 没有空气，人类无法生存。

***manage** /ˈmænɪdʒ; ˋmænɪdʒ/ *v* 动
manages, managing, managed, managed

1. to be able to do something difficult 努力应付（困难）；设法完成
   We managed to get there before 5 p.m. 我们争取在下午 5 点之前到那儿。
2. to control a company, business, etc 管理；经营
   Mr Thompson manages a large company. 汤普森先生管理一家大公司。

***manager** /ˈmænɪdʒə; ˋmænɪdʒɚ/ *n* 名
someone who controls a company, a shop, a restaurant, etc 经理
Sandra's father is a bank manager. 珊德拉的爸爸是银行经理。

***mango** /ˈmæŋgəʊ; ˋmæŋgo/ *n* 名
复数：*mangoes*
a sweet, yellow fruit with a large seed 芒果

My favourite dessert is mango pudding. 我最喜爱的甜点是芒果布丁。

man-made /ˌmæn ˈmeɪd; ˌmæn ˋmed/ *adj* 形
made by people 人造的；人工的
They are building a man-made

M

island here. 他们正在这里建造一个人工岛。

反义 **natural**

manner /ˈmænə; ˋmænɚ/ *n* 名

1. （无复数）the way you do something; the way you behave towards other people 方式；态度
   Fiona has a friendly manner. 菲安娜对人态度友善。
2. **manners**（复数名词）polite ways of behaving when you are with other people 礼貌；规矩
   We should have good manners all the time. 我们应始终保持礼貌。

manufacture /ˌmænjuˈfæktʃə; ˌmænjəˋfæktʃɚ/ *v* 动

manufactures, manufacturing, manufactured, manufactured

to make things in large numbers in a factory 制造；生产

These cars are manufactured in a local factory. 这些汽车在本地的一家工厂制造。

M

***many**[1] /ˈmeni; ˋmɛnɪ/ *adj* 形

more, most

a lot of 许多

There weren't many children in the playground. 游乐场里的孩子不是很多。

用法 many 多用于否定句或问句，与可数名词一起使用，例如 many books、many people 等。

反义 **few**[1]

比较 **much**[2]

***many**[2] /ˈmeni; ˋmɛnɪ/ *pron* 代

a large number of people or things 许多（人或物）

Many of the workers are female. 工人中有很多是女性。

***map** /mæp; mæp/ *n* 名

a drawing of a country, town, area, etc 地图

There is a world map on the wall. 墙上有一张世界地图。

marble /ˈmɑːbl; ˋmɑrbl̩/ *n* 名

a small glass ball that you use in a game 弹珠；弹子

The children were playing with marbles. 孩子们在玩弹珠。

***March** /mɑːtʃ; mɑrtʃ/ *n* 名

复数：***Marches*** | 缩写：***Mar.***

the third month of the year 三月

Paul's birthday is on the third of March. 保罗的生日是 3 月 3 日。

注意 开头的字母必须用大写。

***march** /mɑːtʃ; mɑrtʃ/ *v* 动

marches, marching, marched, marched

to walk like soldiers 齐步行走；行进

The Boy Scouts are marching in the playground. 男童子军在操场练习行进。

margarine /ˌmɑːdʒəˈriːn; ˋmɑrdʒərɪn/ *n* 名

无复数

a soft food like butter that you put on bread or use for cooking 人造黄油；人造牛油

I put some margarine on my bread. 我在面包上涂些人造牛油。

***mark**[1] /mɑːk; mɑrk/ *n* 名

1. a small dirty area on something 污迹；痕迹
   There are dirty marks on my shoes. 我的鞋子上有些污迹。
2. a number or letter that shows how good your work is 分数；成绩
   Betsy often gets good marks in English. 贝特西的英语常常拿到高分。

同义 **grade**

3. a written or printed symbol on something 符号；标记
   This mark shows that the sweater is made of pure wool. 这个标记表明毛衣是用纯羊毛织的。

***mark**[2] /mɑːk; mɑrk/ *v* 动

to give a number or letter on schoolwork to show how good it is 评分；批阅

Our teacher was marking our test papers. 老师在批改我们的试卷。

***market** /ˈmɑːkɪt; ˋmɑrkɪt/ *n* 名

a place where people buy and sell things 市场

My mother sells vegetables in the market. 我的妈妈在市场上卖菜。

marriage /ˈmærɪdʒ; ˋmærɪdʒ/ *n* 名

the relationship between a husband and wife 婚姻

Mr and Mrs Roberts have a happy marriage. 罗伯茨先生和太太的婚姻很美满。

married /ˈmærid; ˋmærɪd/ *adj* 形

having a husband or wife 已婚的

Gordon is a married man with two daughters. 戈登已婚，有两个女儿。

get married 结婚

Nora got married last Christmas. 诺拉在去年圣诞节结婚。

反义 single

***marry** /ˈmæri; ˋmærɪ/ *v* 动

marries, marrying, married, married

to become someone's husband or wife（和…）结婚；娶；嫁

Samuel wants to marry Vanessa. 塞缪尔想和瓦内莎结婚。

marsh /mɑːʃ; mɑrʃ/ *n* 名

复数：***marshes***

a piece of low land that is wet and soft 沼泽；湿地

Some birds live in marshes. 有些鸟类在湿地上栖息。

marshmallow /ˌmɑːʃˈmæləʊ; ˋmɑrʃˌmɛlo/ *n* 名

a very soft and light sweet 棉花糖

I love hot chocolate with marshmallows. 我喜欢喝热巧克力加棉花糖。

***marvellous** /ˈmɑːvləs; ˋmɑrvḷəs/ *adj* 形【英】

美式：***marvelous***

very good; great 极好的；了不起的

The play was marvellous! I enjoyed it very much. 那出戏剧棒极了！我很喜欢。

***mask** /mɑːsk; mæsk/ *n* 名

something that covers all or part of your face 面具；口罩

If you have flu, wear a mask. 患流感时要戴口罩。

Mass Transit Railway /mæs ˈtrænsɪt ˈreɪlweɪ; mæs ˋtrænsɪt ˋrelwe/ *n* 名

缩写：***MTR***

a kind of railway transport in Hong Kong（香港）地铁

Dick goes to school by MTR. 狄克坐地铁上学。

注意 地下铁路在不同国家有不同的叫法，例如英国叫 underground，美国则叫 subway。

master /ˈmɑːstə; ˋmæstɚ/ *n* 名

1. someone who controls others 主人

   The dog always follows its master. 那只狗总是跟着它的主人。

2. someone who is very good at doing something 能手；擅长…的人

   Walter is a chess master. 华特是棋艺高手。

***mat** /mæt; mæt/ *n* 名

a small piece of cloth that covers part of a floor 脚垫

Wipe your feet on the mat before you come in. 进屋前在脚垫上蹭蹭脚。

***match¹** /mætʃ; mætʃ/ *n* 名

复数：***matches***

1. a small wooden stick that you use to light a fire 火柴

   Don't play with matches. It's dangerous! 不要玩火柴，这很危险！

2. a game or competition 比赛

   Our team won the football match. 我们的球队赢了这场足球比赛。

***match²** /mætʃ; mætʃ/ *v* 动

matches, matching, matched, matched

1. to put similar things together 配对

   Match the photos with the names. 把照片和名称配对。

2. to look good together 相配；相称

   Lily's shoes match her dress very well. 莉莉的鞋子和连衣裙十分相配。

M

***material** /məˈtɪəriəl; məˋtɪrɪəl/ *n* 名

1. the things that you use to make or do something 材料；原料

   Wood and stone are building materials. 木材和石头是建筑材料。

2. cloth that you use for making clothes, curtains, etc 布料

   Wool is a good material for making clothes. 羊毛是制作衣服的好料子。

mathematics /ˌmæθəˈmætɪks; ˌmæθəˋmætɪks/ *n* 名

无复数 | 也作：***maths***【英】，***math***【美】

the study of numbers, shapes, etc 数学

Bill is good at mathematics. 比尔的数学很好。

maths /mæθs; mæθs/ *n* 名【英】

另见 **mathematics**

***matter**[1] /'mætə; `mætɚ/ *n* 名

something that you have to think about 事情

There is an important matter I'd like to discuss with you. 我有件重要的事想跟你谈谈。

no matter 不管；无论

No matter what happens, keep calm. 不论发生什么事，都要保持镇定。

> **Daily conversation 日常会话**
> **What's the matter?** 怎么啦？
> *"What's the matter with Winnie? She looks angry." "I have no idea."* "威妮怎么了？她看来很生气。" "我不知道。"

***matter**[2] /'mætə; `mætɚ/ *v* 动

to be important 重要；要紧

Health matters to all of us. 健康对我们每个人都重要。

> **Daily conversation 日常会话**
> *"Sorry, I'm late." "It doesn't matter."* "对不起，我迟到了。" "不要紧。"

mattress /'mætrəs; `mætrɪs/ *n* 名

复数：*mattresses*

the large, soft and thick part of a bed 床垫

This mattress is really comfortable to sleep on. 睡在这张床垫上真舒服。

***May** /meɪ; me/ *n* 名

the fifth month of the year 五月

We went to Singapore last May. 去年 5 月我们去了新加坡。

注意 开头的字母必须用大写。

***may** /meɪ; me/ *v* 动

might

1. if something may happen, it is possible that it will happen, but this is not certain 可能；也许
   We may go to the museum next week. 我们下星期可能会去博物馆。
2. to be allowed to do something 可以（表示允许）
   You may go now. 你现在可以走了。

> **Daily conversation 日常会话**
> **May I...?** 我可以…吗？
> *"May I go to the washroom?" "Sure."* "我可以去洗手间吗？" "当然可以。"

***maybe** /'meɪbi; `mebɪ/ *adv* 副

used to say that something may happen or may be true 也许；可能

Maybe you are right. 也许你是对的。

同义 **perhaps, possibly**

> **Daily conversation 日常会话**
> *"Are you going hiking with us?" "Maybe — I don't know yet."* "你跟我们一起去远足吗？" "可能吧，我还不知道。"

MB, Mb

the short form of **megabyte**

☆megabyte 的缩写

***me** /mi; mɪ; *strong* 强读 miː; mi/ *pron* 代

the person who is speaking 我

Please give me that book. 请把那本书给我。

> **Daily conversation 日常会话**
> *"I want to go swimming." "Me too."* "我想去游泳。" "我也想去。"

***meal** /miːl; mil/ *n* 名

an occasion when you eat food, for example breakfast, lunch or dinner 一顿饭；一餐

We usually have three meals a day. 我们通常一日吃三餐。

***mean**[1] /miːn; min/ *v* 动

means, meaning, meant, meant

1. to say something in other words 意思是；指
   Can I borrow your dictionary? I want to find what this word means. 我能借用一下你的词典吗？我想知道这个词是什么意思。
2. to be the same as 表示
   The red light means "Stop". 红灯表示"停步"。
3. to plan or want to do something 打算；故意
   He didn't mean to push you. 他不是故意推你的。

mean[2] /miːn; min/ *adj* 形

meaner, meanest

unkind; cruel 不友善的；刻薄的

Snow White's stepmother was a mean woman. 白雪公主的继母是个刻薄的女人。

***meaning** /'miːnɪŋ; `minɪŋ/ *n* 名

what something means 意思；意义

Can you tell me the meaning of this word? 你能告诉我这个词的意思吗?

meant /ment; mɛnt/ *v* 动

the past tense and past participle of **mean**[1] ☆mean[1] 的过去式和过去分词

meanwhile /'miːnwaɪl; `minˌwaɪl/ *adv* 副

while something else is happening 在此期间；同时

Lily watched TV. Meanwhile, I checked my email. 莉莉在看电视。与此同时，我在查阅电子邮件。

measles /ˈmiːzlz; ˋmizḷz/ *n* 名

无复数

a disease that causes fever and red spots on your face and body 麻疹

Wayne got measles and had to rest at home. 韦恩得了麻疹，要留在家里休息。

***measure¹** /ˈmeʒə; ˋmɛʒɚ/ *v* 动

measures, measuring, measured, measured

to find out the size, weight or amount of something 度量；计量

I measure my height every month. 我每个月都量一下身高。

measure² /ˈmeʒə; ˋmɛʒɚ/ *n* 名

1. a way of showing size, weight or amount 度量单位

   A kilogram is a measure of weight. 公斤是重量单位。

2. an action that you take to solve a problem 措施；办法

   We must take measures to stop shoplifting. 我们必须采取措施杜绝商店盗窃案 。

measurement /ˈmeʒəmənt; ˋmɛʒɚmənt/ *n* 名

the length, height, etc of something 尺寸；大小

The tailor took my measurements. 裁缝给我量了尺寸。

另见 **附录**：Weights and measures 度量单位

***meat** /miːt; mit/ *n* 名

无复数

food that comes from parts of animals and birds, for example beef and chicken 肉；肉类

Eating too much meat is not good for our health. 吃太多肉对我们的健康不好。

注意 发音和 meet 相同。

mechanic /mɪˈkænɪk; mɪˋkænɪk/ *n* 名

someone who repairs machines 机械工；技工

William is a car mechanic. 威廉是汽车技工。

***medal** /ˈmedl; ˋmɛdḷ/ *n* 名

a flat piece of metal that is given as a prize 奖牌；勋章

Ronald won a medal in the swimming competition. 罗纳德在游泳比赛中赢得了一枚奖牌。

***medicine** /ˈmedsn; ˋmɛdəsṇ/ *n* 名

something you eat or drink when you are ill, to help you get better 药；药水

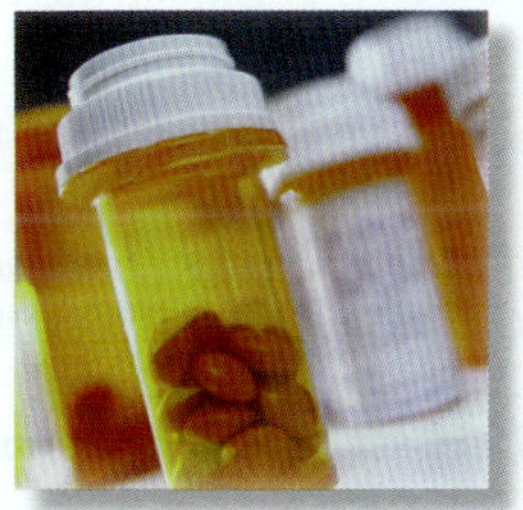

I felt better after taking the medicine. 我吃过药后感觉好多了。

***medium** /ˈmiːdiəm; ˋmidɪəm/ *adj* 形

of middle size or amount 中等的；中号的

My father is of medium height. 我的爸爸身材中等。

At a restaurant 餐厅里

"Would you like something to drink?" "A medium orange juice, please." "你要什么喝的吗？" "请给我中杯橙汁。"

***meet** /miːt; mit/ *v* 动

meets, meeting, met, met

1. to go to a place with someone else that you have arranged 会面；碰头

   Let's meet at the bus stop. 我们在公共汽车站等吧。

2. to see someone in the same place at the same time without planning 遇见；碰到

   I met Paula in the supermarket yesterday. 昨天我在超市遇见了保拉。

Greetings 问候

"Paul, this is Bruce." "Nice to meet you." "保罗，这位是布鲁斯。" "很高兴认识你。"

***meeting** /ˈmiːtɪŋ; ˋmitɪŋ/ *n* 名

an occasion when people come together to talk about something 会议

We will have a class meeting next Monday. 我们下星期一要开班会。

megabyte /ˈmegəbaɪt; ˋmɛgəbaɪt/ *n* 名

缩写：*MB, Mb*

【电脑】a unit for measuring computer information 兆；百万位元（电脑存储单位）

The size of the file is 50 megabytes. 这个文件的大小是 50 兆 。

***melon** /ˈmelən; ˋmɛlən/ *n* 名

a large, round, juicy fruit with a hard skin and a lot of seeds 甜瓜；香瓜

I cut the melon into slices. 我把瓜切成几片。

***melt** /melt; mɛlt/ *v* 动

to become liquid because of heat 融化；熔化

The ice cream is melting. 冰淇淋正在渐渐融化。

M

反义 **freeze**

***member** /'membə; `mɛmbɚ/ *n* 名

someone who belongs to a club or group 会员；成员

We are all members of the choir. 我们都是合唱团的成员。

***memory** /'meməri; `mɛmərɪ/ *n* 名

复数：*memories*

1. the ability to remember things 记忆力；记性

   Michael has a good memory. 迈克尔记性很好。

2. something that you remember 记忆；回忆

   I have a lot of happy memories of my childhood. 我有许多美好的童年回忆。

men /men; mɛn/ *n* 名

the plural of **man** ☆man 的复数形式

mend /mend; mɛnd/ *v* 动

to repair something that is broken 修补；修理

Uncle Frank mended my shoes. 法兰克叔叔修好了我的鞋子。

***mention** /'menʃn; `mɛnʃən/ *v* 动

to speak or write about something in a few words 提到；说到

Tony mentioned you on the phone. 托尼在电话里提起你。

Daily conversation 日常会话

don't mention it 不用客气

"Thank you very much for your help." "Don't mention it." "非常感谢你的帮忙。" "不客气。"

***menu** /'menju:; `mɛnju/ *n* 名

1. a list of food or drinks that you can order in a restaurant 菜单

   Can we have the menu, please? 请给我们菜单好吗？

2. 【电脑】a list of choices shown on a computer 菜单

   Click here to read the menu. 点击这里可以看到菜单。

meow /mi'aʊ; mɪ`aʊ/ *v* 动【美】

英式 **miaow**

merchant /'mɜ:tʃənt; `mɝtʃənt/ *n* 名

someone who buys and sells things 商人

The merchants brought back silk from China. 商人从中国带回丝绸。

mermaid /'mɜ:meɪd; `mɝmed/ *n* 名

a woman in stories who has a fish's tail and lives in the sea 美人鱼

Celia is reading a story about mermaids. 西莉亚在看一个美人鱼的故事。

merry /'meri; `mɛrɪ/ *adj* 形

merrier, merriest

happy; cheerful 快乐的；愉快的

Wish you all a Merry Christmas! 祝各位圣诞快乐！

***merry-go-round** /'meri gəʊ ˌraʊnd; `mɛrɪ go ˌraʊnd/ *n* 名

1. a big machine that you can ride on while it turns round and round 旋转木马

   We went to the amusement park to ride on the merry-go-round. 我们去游乐场坐旋转木马。

   同义 **roundabout**

2. 【美】旋转台 英式 **roundabout**

mess /mes; mɛs/ *n* 名

无复数

if a place is in a mess, it is dirty and untidy 凌乱；杂乱

Mabel's room is always in a mess. 美宝的房间总是乱七八糟的。

***message** /'mesɪdʒ; `mɛsɪdʒ/ *n* 名

words that one person sends to another 信息；口信；留言

Did you get my message? 你收到我的信息了吗？

M

messenger /ˈmesndʒə; ˋmɛsn̩dʒɚ/ *n* 名

someone who brings a message to another person 信差；送信人

A messenger brought me a letter. 信差给我送来一封信。

messy /ˈmesi; ˋmɛsɪ/ *adj* 形

messier, messiest

dirty or untidy 脏的；凌乱的

Clear up your messy room now! 立即把你脏乱的房间收拾干净！

met /met; mɛt/ *v* 动

the past tense and past participle of **meet** ☆meet 的过去式和过去分词

***metal** /ˈmetl; ˋmɛtl̩/ *n* 名

a hard material like iron, gold, etc 金属

The box is made of metal. 这个箱子是金属制的。

***method** /ˈmeθəd; ˋmɛθəd/ *n* 名

a way of doing something 方法；办法

Her new method of teaching English is fun. 她教英语的新方法很有趣。

metre /ˈmiːtə; ˋmitɚ/ *n* 名【英】

缩写：***m*** | 美式：***meter***

a unit of length. There are 100 centimetres in a metre. 米；公尺

The swimming pool is 50 metres long. 这个游泳池长 50 米。

另见 附录：Weights and measures 度量单位

miaow /miˈaʊ; mɪˋaʊ/ *v* 动【英】

美式：***meow***

if a cat miaows, it makes a crying sound（猫）喵喵叫

A cat was miaowing outside the door. 有只猫在门外喵喵叫。

mice /maɪs; maɪs/ *n* 名

the plural of **mouse (1)** ☆mouse (1) 的复数形式

***microphone** /ˈmaɪkrəfəʊn; ˋmaɪkrəˌfon/ *n* 名

something used to record sounds or make sounds louder 麦克风；话筒

The teacher is speaking through the microphone. 老师正在用麦克风讲话。

***microwave** /ˈmaɪkrəweɪv; ˋmaɪkrəˌwev/ *n* 名

也作：***microwave oven***

an oven that cooks food quickly 微波炉

Heat the sandwich in the microwave for two minutes. 把三明治放进微波炉加热两分钟。

Mid-Autumn Festival /mɪd ɔːtəm ˈfestɪvl; mɪd ɔtəm ˋfɛstəvl̩/ *n* 名

a Chinese festival on the 15th day of the eighth month in the Chinese calendar 中秋节

We enjoy watching the moon at the Mid-Autumn Festival. 中秋节时我们喜欢赏月。

midday /ˌmɪdˈdeɪ; ˋmɪdˌde/ *n* 名

无复数

12 o'clock in the middle of the day 中午；正午

The children have lunch at midday. 孩子们在中午吃午餐。

同义 **noon**

***middle**[1] /ˈmɪdl; ˋmɪdl̩/ *n* 名

无复数

the part in the centre 中间；中央

There is a pond in the middle of the park. 公园中央有一个池塘。

***middle**[2] /ˈmɪdl; ˋmɪdl̩/ *adj* 形

of the part in the centre 中间的；中央的

She opened the middle door and walked in. 她打开中间的门走了进去。

midnight /ˈmɪdnaɪt; ˋmɪdˌnaɪt/ *n* 名

无复数

12 o'clock at night 午夜

This park closes at midnight. 这个公园午夜关门。

***might** /maɪt; maɪt/ *v* 动

1. the past tense of **may** ☆may 的过去式
2. used to show that something is possible but not certain 可能；也许

   I think he might be lying. 我想他可能在说谎。

***mile** /maɪl; maɪl/ *n* 名

a unit of distance. There are 1609 metres in a mile. 英里

The hotel is 10 miles from the airport. 这家酒店距离机场 10 英里。

另见 附录：Weights and measures 度量单位

***milk** /mɪlk; mɪlk/ *n* 名

无复数

a white liquid that comes from female animals for feeding their babies 奶

M

Jimmy drinks a bottle of milk every morning. 吉米每天早上都喝一瓶牛奶。

milk shake /mɪlk ˈʃeɪk; mɪlk ˋʃek/ *n* 名

a cold drink made of milk, ice cream, chocolate, etc 泡沫牛奶；奶昔

Doris drank a chocolate milk shake. 多莉丝喝了一杯巧克力奶昔。

millimetre /ˈmɪlɪˌmiːtə; ˋmɪləˌmitɚ/ *n* 名【英】

缩写：***mm*** | 美式：***millimeter***

a unit of length. There are 1000 millimetres in a metre. 毫米

This line is 100 millimetres long. 这条线长 100 毫米。

另见 **附录**：Weights and measures 度量单位

million /ˈmiljən; ˋmɪljən/ *num* 数

the number 1,000,000 一百万

More than seven million people live in Hong Kong. 有七百多万人在香港居住。

M

millionaire /ˌmɪljəˈneə; ˏmɪljəˋnɛr/ *n* 名

someone who has at least a million dollars 百万富翁；富豪

The millionaire lives in a very big house. 那个富翁住在很大的房子里。

millionth /ˈmiljənθ; ˋmɪljənθ/ *ordinal num* 序数

1,000,000th in order 第一百万（的）

She is the millionth visitor of the theme park. 她是这个主题公园的第一百万名访客。

***mind**[1] /maɪnd; maɪnd/ *n* 名

the part of your brain used for thinking; your thoughts 头脑；思想

The problem stayed in my mind for a long time. 这个问题留在我的脑海里很长时间。

change your mind 改变主意

Monica changed her mind again and again. 莫妮卡一再改变主意。

keep something in mind 记住某事

I'll keep your advice in mind. 我会记住你的劝告。

make up your mind 下定决心；拿定主意

Stella made up her mind to study abroad. 史黛拉决定到国外留学。

***mind**[2] /maɪnd; maɪnd/ *v* 动

1. to be annoyed or worried about something 介意
   He didn't help me but I didn't mind. 他没帮我，但是我不介意。
2. to notice; to be careful of 注意；小心
   Please mind the gap between the platform and the train. 请小心月台与列车之间的空隙。

Daily conversation 日常会话

never mind 不要紧；没关系

"I'm sorry!" "Never mind." "对不起！" "不要紧。"

do/would you mind...? 你介意…吗？

"Do you mind if I come a little late?" "No, I don't." "我晚一点才到没问题吗？" "没问题。"

***mine** /maɪn; maɪn/ *pron* 代

something that belongs to me 我的（东西）

This doll is mine. 这个玩具娃娃是我的。

***mineral** /ˈmɪnərəl; ˋmɪnərəl/ *n* 名

a natural material from under the ground 矿物

This country sells a lot of minerals to other countries. 这个国家把许多矿物卖给其他国家。

***minibus** /ˈmɪnibʌs; ˋmɪnɪbʌs/ *n* 名

复数：***minibuses***

a small bus 小型公共汽车；中巴

I go to the cinema by minibus. 我乘中巴去电影院。

minor /ˈmaɪnə; ˋmaɪnɚ/ *adj* 形

not very important 次要的；不太重要的

There are some minor changes in our plan. 我们的计划有些小小的变动。

反义 **major**

minus /ˈmaɪnəs; ˋmaɪnəs/ *prep* 介

less 减；减去

15 minus 8 equals 7. 15 减 8 等于 7。

反义 **plus**

***minute** /ˈmɪnɪt; ˋmɪnɪt/ *n* 名

a unit of time. There are 60 minutes in an hour. 分；分钟

I'll be home in ten minutes. 10 分钟后我就到家了。

It's five minutes to nine. 现在是 8 点 55 分。

in a minute 立刻；马上

I'll come in a minute. 我马上就来。

just a minute 稍等一会

Just a minute! Where is the other sock? 等一下！另一只袜子在哪里?

另见 **附录**：Time 时间

***mirror** /ˈmɪrə; ˋmɪrɚ/ *n* 名

a piece of glass that you use to look at yourself 镜子

There is a mirror in the bathroom. 浴室里有一面镜子。

misbehave /ˌmɪsbɪˈheɪv; ˏmɪsbɪˋhev/ *v* 动

misbehaves, misbehaving, misbehaved, misbehaved

to behave badly 行为不端；调皮捣蛋

The boys were punished because they misbehaved. 那些男孩因行为不端而受罚。

mischievous /ˈmɪstʃɪvəs; ˋmɪstʃɪvəs/ *adj* 形

behaving badly 顽皮的；淘气的

The mischievous monkey threw fruit at us. 那只顽皮的猴子向我们扔水果。

miserable /ˈmɪzərəbəl; ˋmɪzərəbl̩/ *adj* 形

very unhappy 痛苦的；悲惨的

He is miserable because he failed the exam. 他感到很悲哀，因为考试不及格。

***Miss** /mɪs; mɪs/ *n* 名

1. a title for a woman who is not married 小姐

   Miss Evans is an American. 伊万斯小姐是美国人。

注意 开头的字母必须用大写。

比较 **Mrs, Ms**

2. 【英】a word that children use at school when they speak to or talk about a female teacher （女性）老师

   Good afternoon, Miss. 老师，下午好。

注意 开头的字母必须用大写。

另见 **sir**

***miss** /mɪs; mɪs/ *v* 动

misses, missing, missed, missed

1. to feel sad when someone is not there 怀念；思念

   I miss you so much! 我非常想念你！

2. to be too late for something 赶不上；错过

   Hurry up or you'll miss the last train! 快点，要不然你会错过最后一班火车！

3. to fail to hit or catch something 未击中；接不住

   He tried to hit the ball but he missed it. 他尝试击球，可没有击中。

missing /ˈmɪsɪŋ; ˋmɪsɪŋ/ *adj* 形

lost; gone 丢失的；失去的

I still can't find my missing book. 我还是找不到丢失的书。

mist /mɪst; mɪst/ *n* 名

thin cloud near the ground 薄雾

The mountain was covered in mist. 山笼罩在薄雾中。

***mistake** /mɪˈsteɪk; məˋstek/ *n* 名

something that is wrong 错误

I made three spelling mistakes in my essay. 我的文章有三个拼写错误。

by mistake 错误地

She took my umbrella by mistake. 她拿错了我的伞。

同义 **error**

mitten /ˈmɪtn; ˋmɪtn̩/ *n* 名

a kind of glove, with two different parts to cover your thumb and other fingers 连指手套

I often wear mittens in the winter. 我在冬天经常戴连指手套。

比较 **glove**

***mix** /mɪks; mɪks/ *v* 动

mixes, mixing, mixed, mixed

to put different things together 混合；搅拌

Mix the flour and butter together. 把面粉和黄油搅拌在一起。

mix up 混淆；弄乱

We always mix up the twin sisters in our class. 我们总是分不清班上那对双胞胎姐妹。

mixture /ˈmɪkstʃə; ˋmɪkstʃɚ/ *n* 名

something made by putting different things together 混合物

Pour the mixture of flour and eggs into the pan. 把拌好的面粉和鸡蛋倒进平底锅里。

mm

the short form of **millimetre**☆ millimetre 的缩写

mobile phone /ˌməʊbaɪl ˈfəʊn; ˏmobl̩ ˋfon/ *n* 名【英】

美式：***cellphone***

a telephone that you can carry with you 移动电话；手机

Matthew was talking on his mobile phone. 马修在打手机。

***model** /ˈmɒdl; ˋmɑdl̩/ *n* 名

1. a small copy of something 模型

   Keith is making a model of a ship. 凯斯在制作一艘船的模型。

2. someone who wears new clothes at a special show or for photos 模特儿

   Her sister is a fashion model. 她姐姐是一名时装模特儿。

***modern** /ˈmɒdn; ˋmɑdɚn/ *adj* 形

of the present time 现代的；当代的

Modern science develops quickly. 现代科学发展迅速。

***moment** /ˈməʊmənt; ˋmomənt/ *n* 名

M

a very short period of time 片刻；瞬间；一会儿

Please wait here for a moment. 请在这里等一会儿。

at any moment 随时

It may rain at any moment. 随时可能下雨。

at the moment 现在；此刻

He is busy at the moment. 他现在很忙。

Daily conversation 日常会话

"Could I speak to Mr Moore?" "Just a moment, please." "请问摩尔先生在吗？" "请稍等。"

monastery /ˈmɒnəstri; ˋmɑnəsˌtɛrɪ/ *n* 名

复数：***monasteries***

a place where monks live 修道院

We visited a monastery when we were in Europe. 我们去欧洲时参观了一座修道院。

***Monday** /ˈmʌndi; ˋmʌndɪ/ *n* 名

缩写：***Mon.***

the day between Sunday and Tuesday 星期一

We have a school assembly every Monday. 我们学校每星期一都有集会。

注意 开头的字母必须用大写。

***money** /ˈmʌni; ˋmʌnɪ/ *n* 名

无复数

coins and paper notes that you use to buy things 钱

He doesn't have enough money to buy the jeans. 他没有足够的钱买这条牛仔裤。

make money 赚钱；盈利

Amy has a good job and makes a lot of money. 艾米有一份好工作，赚很多钱。

***monitor** /ˈmɒnɪtə; ˋmɑnətə/ *n* 名

1. a student who is chosen to help teachers in class 班长
   Raymond is the monitor of our class. 雷蒙德是我们的班长。
2. 【电脑】a screen which is part of a computer 电脑显示器

Don't stare at the monitor for too long. 不要盯着显示器看太久。

monk /mʌŋk; mʌŋk/ *n* 名

a man who lives away from his family because of his religion 僧人；僧侣

Some monks live in temples. 一些僧人住在寺庙里。

***monkey** /ˈmʌŋki; ˋmʌŋkɪ/ *n* 名

an animal that has a long tail and climbs trees 猴子

Monkeys are clever animals. 猴子是聪明的动物。

***monster** /ˈmɒnstə; ˋmɑnstə/ *n* 名

a horrible creature in stories 怪物；怪兽

The monster has only one eye. 那只怪物只有一只眼睛。

***month** /mʌnθ; mʌnθ/ *n* 名

one of the twelve periods of time into which a year is divided 月；月份

I started working last month. 我上个月开始工作了。

monthly[1] /ˈmʌnθli; ˋmʌnθlɪ/ *adj* 形

happening once a month 每月（一次）的

My mother reads a monthly magazine. 我的妈妈阅读一份月刊。

monthly[2] /ˈmʌnθli; ˋmʌnθlɪ/ *adv* 副

once a month 每月（一次）

I get paid monthly. 我按月领薪水。

moo /muː; mu/ *v* 动

to make the sound of a cow（牛）哞哞叫

The cow is mooing. 母牛在哞哞叫。

mood /muːd; mud/ *n* 名

the way you feel 心情；情绪

Ada is in a bad mood today. 艾达今天心情不好。

***moon** /muːn; mun/ *n* 名

无复数

the big, round object that shines in the sky at night 月亮；月球

The moon is very bright tonight. 今晚的月亮很亮。

***mooncake** /ˈmuːnkeɪk; ˋmunkek/ *n* 名

a special cake you eat during the Mid-Autumn Festival 月饼

I shared a mooncake with my sister. 我和妹妹分享了一个月饼。

moonlight /ˈmuːnlaɪt; ˋmun͵laɪt/ *n* 名

无复数

the light from the moon 月光

We like to walk in the moonlight. 我们喜欢在月光下漫步。

比较 **sunlight**

mop /mɒp; mɑp/ *n* 名

a long stick with thick strings or sponge on one end, used to wash the floor 拖把

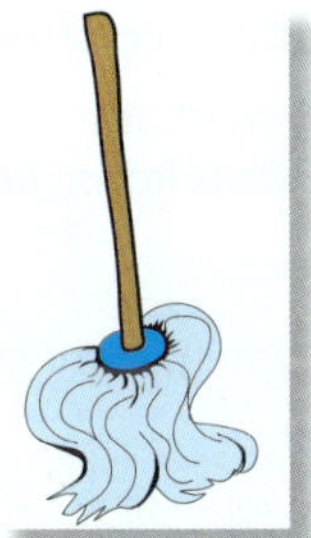

He cleaned the floor with a mop. 他用拖把拖地板。

***more[1]** /mɔː; mɔr/ *adv* 副（*much[1]* 的比较级）

to a higher level 更；更加

This book is more expensive than that one. 这本书比那本书贵。

more and more 越来越

The exams are getting more and more difficult. 考试越来越难了。

once more 再一次

Can you read the story once more? 你能把这个故事再读一遍吗？

反义 **less[1]**

***more[2]** /mɔː; mɔr/ *adj* 形（*many[1]* 和 *much[2]* 的比较级）

having a larger amount or number 更多的

He knows more words than I do. 他认识的单词比我多。

反义 **less[2]**

***morning** /ˈmɔːnɪŋ; ˋmɔrnɪŋ/ *n* 名

the early part of the day before noon 上午；早上

Our school starts at eight o'clock in the morning. 我们学校上午8点开始上课。

Greetings 问候

"Good morning, Gary." "Good morning, Maggie." "早安，加里。""早安，玛姬。"

***mosquito** /məˈskiːtəʊ; məˋskito/ *n* 名

复数：*mosquitoes/mosquitos*

a small, flying insect that bites and sucks blood 蚊子

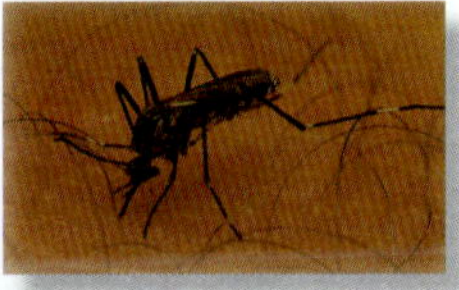

I often get bitten by mosquitoes. 我常常被蚊子叮。

***most[1]** /məʊst; most/ *adv* 副（*much[1]* 的最高级）

to the highest level 最

This is the most beautiful garden in the town. 这是镇上最美丽的花园。

反义 **least[2]**

***most[2]** /məʊst; most/ *adj* 形（*many[1]* 和 *much[2]* 的最高级）

almost all 大多数；大部分

Most people like flowers. 大多数人都喜欢花。

mostly /ˈməʊstli; ˋmostlɪ/ *adv* 副

mainly or almost all 主要地；大部分；多半

My classmates are mostly Chinese. 我的同学大部分是中国人。

moth /mɒθ; mɔθ/ *n* 名

an insect that flies at night and looks like a butterfly 蛾

Some moths are flying under the lamp. 一些蛾子在灯下飞来飞去。

***mother** /ˈmʌðə; ˋmʌðɚ/ *n* 名

a female parent 母亲；妈妈

His mother takes him to school. 他的妈妈带他上学。

用法 mother 多用于比较正式的场合或书面语中，mum 多用于口语，mummy 多用于儿语。

比较 **mum, mummy**

motor /ˈməʊtə; ˋmotɚ/ *n* 名

an engine that makes something move 发动机；马达

The motor made a loud noise. 那台发动机声响很大。

motorcycle /ˈməʊtə͵saɪkl; ˋmotɚ͵saɪkl/ *n* 名

也作：*motorbike*

a vehicle with two wheels moved by an engine 摩托车

Bill goes to work by motorcycle. 比尔骑摩托车上班。

***mountain** /ˈmaʊntɪn; ˋmaʊntn̩/ *n* 名

a very high hill 高山

He is the first person to climb this mountain. 他是登上这座山的第一个人。

M

***mouse** /maʊs; maus/ *n* 名

1. （复数：***mice***）a small animal with short fur and a long tail 老鼠

The mouse is eating the cheese. 老鼠在吃奶酪。

比较 **rat**

2. （复数：***mouses***）【电脑】a small tool you move with your hand to make a computer work 鼠标

Move the mouse over the words to hear them spoken. 把鼠标移动到单词上就能听到发音。

mouse pad 鼠标垫

This mouse pad is made of rubber. 这个鼠标垫是用橡胶做的。

moustache /məˈstɑːʃ; ˋmʌstæʃ/ *n* 名

hair that grows above a man's mouth 髭；小胡子

The man has a moustache. 这个男人留着小胡子。

***mouth** /maʊθ; maʊθ/ *n* 名

the part of your face for eating and speaking 嘴；口

The baby put its finger in its mouth. 婴儿把手指放在嘴里。

mouthful /ˈmaʊθfʊl; ˋmaʊθˏfʊl/ *n* 名

the amount of food or drink that you put in your mouth at one time 一口（食物或饮料）

I took a mouthful of the tea and found it very hot. 我喝了一口茶，觉得很烫。

***move** /muːv; muv/ *v* 动

moves, moving, moved, moved

1. to go from one place to another or change the position of something（使）移动；搬动

   I moved the table to another room. 我把桌子移到了另一个房间。

2. to go and live in another home 搬家

   My uncle will move to a new flat next week. 我的叔叔下星期会搬进新的住所。

***movement** /ˈmuːvmənt; ˋmuvmənt/ *n* 名

a change of position 移动；动作

Jack was watching the movement of the leaves in the wind. 杰克在看风中树叶的动静。

***movie** /ˈmuːvi; ˋmuvɪ/ *n* 名【美】

英式：***film***

moving pictures shown on television or at a cinema 电影；影片

Let's watch a movie this Saturday. 这个星期六我们去看电影吧。

MP3 /ˌem piː ˈθriː; ˏɛm pi ˋθri/ *n* 名

【电脑】a form of music you can put on a computer ☆MP3 档案（一种音乐档案）

I listen to MP3 music when I am on a bus. 我坐公共汽车时听 MP3 音乐。

***Mr** /ˈmɪstə; ˋmɪstɚ/ *n* 名【英】

美式：***Mr.***

a title for a man 先生

This is Mr Wilson. 这位是威尔逊先生。

注意 开头的字母必须用大写。

***Mrs** /ˈmɪsɪz; ˋmɪsɪz/ *n* 名【英】

美式：***Mrs.***

a title for a married woman 太太；夫人

Mrs Smith is a teacher. 史密斯太太是教师。

注意 开头的字母必须用大写。

比较 **Miss, Ms**

Ms /mɪz; mɪz/ *n* 名【英】

美式：***Ms.***

a title for a woman who is either married or single 女士

Ms Hall lives next to us. 哈尔女士住在我们隔壁。

注意 开头的字母必须用大写。

比较 **Miss, Mrs**

MTR /em tiː ˈɑː; ɛm ti ˋɑr/ *n* 名

the short form of **Mass Transit Railway** ☆Mass Transit Railway 的缩写

***much[1]** /mʌtʃ; mʌtʃ/ *adv* 副

more, most

to a high level …得多；更加

China is much bigger than Japan. 中国比日本大得多。

very much 非常；很

I love my puppy very much. 我非常喜欢我的小狗。

反义 **little[2]**

***much[2]** /mʌtʃ; mʌtʃ/ *adj* 形

more, most

a lot of 大量的；许多的

He does not spend much time on computer games. 他没有花很多时间玩电脑游戏。

M

用法 much 用于否定句或问句，与不可数名词一起使用，例如 much money、much time 等。

反义 little¹

比较 many¹

*much³ /mʌtʃ; mʌtʃ/ *pron* 代

a large amount of something 大量；许多

We don't know much about Mr Wood. 我们对伍德先生知道的并不多。

*mud /mʌd; mʌd/ *n* 名

无复数

soft wet earth 泥

There is mud all over the dog. 那只狗的身上沾满了泥。

muddy /ˈmʌdi; ˋmʌdɪ/ *adj* 形

muddier, muddiest

covered with mud 多泥的；沾满泥的

He took off his muddy shoes. 他把沾满泥的鞋子脱掉。

mug /mʌg; mʌg/ *n* 名

1. a large cup with straight sides and a handle 大杯

Chris loves to collect coffee mugs. 克里斯喜欢收藏咖啡杯。

2. the amount of a drink in a mug 一大杯（份量）

I drank a mug of milk this morning. 今天早上我喝了一大杯牛奶。

比较 cup

multiplication /ˌmʌltɪplɪˈkeɪʃn; ˌmʌltəpləˋkeʃən/ *n* 名

无复数

adding a number to itself a particular number of times 乘法

We have just learnt to do multiplication. 我们刚学了乘法。

multiply /ˈmʌltɪplaɪ; ˋmʌltəˌplaɪ/ *v* 动

multiplies, multiplying, multiplied, multiplied

to add a number to itself a particular number of times 乘；乘以

Five multiplied by eight equals forty. 5 乘以 8 等于 40。

*mum /mʌm; mʌm/, mummy /ˈmʌmi; ˋmʌmɪ/ *n* 名【英】

复数：***mummies*** │ 美式：***mom, mommy***

mother 妈妈

Mum, can I have some chocolates? 妈妈，我可以吃巧克力吗？

用法 mum 多用于口语，mummy 多用于儿语，mother 多用于比较正式的场合或书面语中。

比较 mother

murder¹ /ˈmɜːdə; ˋmɝdɚ/ *n* 名

the crime of killing someone on purpose 谋杀（罪）

The murder took place in the park. 那宗谋杀案发生在公园里。

murder² /ˈmɜːdə; ˋmɝdɚ/ *v* 动

to kill someone on purpose 谋杀；杀害

A man was murdered at home last night. 昨晚有一名男子在家中被杀。

murderer /ˈmɜːdərə; ˋmɝdərɚ/ *n* 名

a person who kills someone on purpose 凶手；谋杀犯

The police caught the murderer. 警察捉住了凶手。

muscle /ˈmʌsl; ˋmʌsl̩/ *n* 名

a part of your body under your skin that helps you to move 肌肉

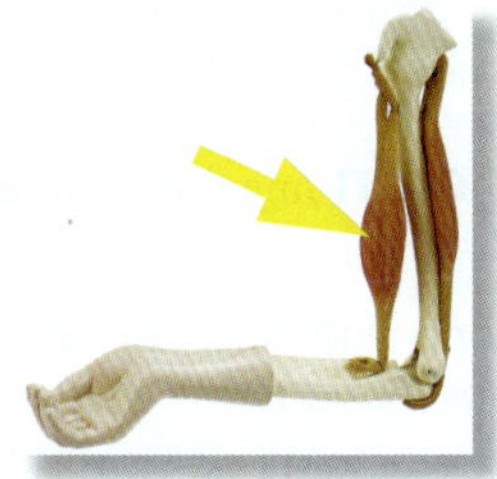

Running makes your leg muscles strong. 跑步使你的腿部肌肉结实。

*museum /mjuːˈziəm; mjuˋzɪəm/ *n* 名

a building where you can see objects about art, history or science 博物馆

We visited the art museum today. 我们今天参观了美术馆。

M

*mushroom /ˈmʌʃruːm; ˋmʌʃrum/ *n* 名

a small plant with a round top and a short stem 蘑菇

I had mushroom soup and bread for lunch. 我午餐喝了蘑菇汤，吃了面包。

*music /ˈmjuːzɪk; ˋmjuzɪk/ *n* 名

无复数

sounds made by people when they sing or play instruments 音乐

I love listening to pop music. 我爱听流行音乐。

用法 music 没有复数形式，如要说明音乐作品的数量，必须用量词，例如 a piece of music、two pieces of music 等。

musical /ˈmjuːzɪkl; ˋmjuzɪkḷ/ *adj* 形

of or about music 音乐的

Do you play any musical instrument? 你会弹什么乐器吗?

musician /mjuːˈzɪʃn; mjuˋzɪʃən/ *n* 名

someone who plays an instrument or writes music 音乐家

I want to be a musician. 我想成为音乐家。

***must** /məst; məst; *strong* 强读 mʌst; mʌst/ *v* 动

1. used when it is important or necessary for someone to do something 必须；一定要

   I must go home before 6 p.m. today. 我今天下午 6 点之前必须回家。

2. used to say that you think something is very likely or certain 一定；肯定

   My cat must be hungry now. 我的猫现在一定饿了。

mustn't /ˈmʌsnt; ˋmʌsṇt/

the short form of "**must not**" ☆must not 的缩写

You mustn't shout in here. 你不可以在这里大叫。

***my** /maɪ; maɪ/ *adj* 形

belonging to me 我的

Someone stole my watch. 有人偷了我的手表。

***myself** /maɪˈself; maɪˋsɛlf/ *pron* 代

the same person who is speaking 我自己

I made myself a fried egg. 我给自己煎了一只蛋。

mysterious /mɪˈstɪəriəs; mɪsˋtɪrɪəs/ *adj* 形

strange and difficult to explain 神秘的

They saw a mysterious object in the sky. Maybe it was a UFO. 他们看到天空上神秘的物体，可能是不明飞行物。

mystery /ˈmɪstəri; ˋmɪstərɪ/ *n* 名

复数：***mysteries***

something that is difficult to explain or understand 神秘的事；谜

I don't know where the money has gone — it's a mystery. 我不知道那些钱去了哪里，这是个谜。

M

***nail** /neɪl; nel/ *n* 名

1. a thin pointed piece of metal that is used to join things together or to hang things on 钉子

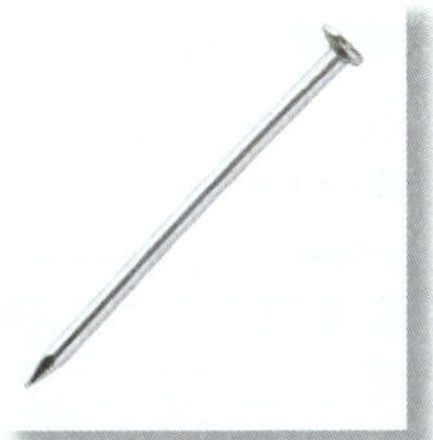

Jerry hit a nail into the wall. 杰瑞把一枚钉子钉入墙壁。

2. the hard part at the end of a finger or toe 指甲；趾甲

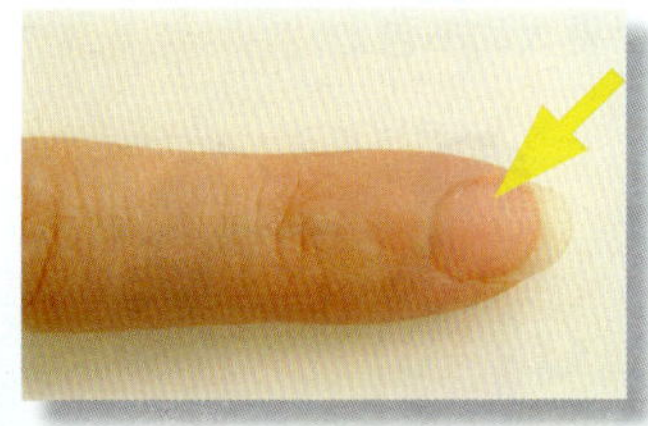

David, stop biting your nails! 大卫，别再咬指甲了！

***name[1]** /neɪm; nem/ *n* 名

what you call a person, place or thing 名字；姓名；名称

What's the name of your school? 你的学校叫什么名字?

注意 姓名中的姓是 family name, last name 或 surname，姓名中的名是 first name。

Daily conversation 日常会话

"What's your name?" "My name is Donald. You can call me Don." "你叫什么名字？""我叫 Donald。你可以叫我 Don。"

***name[2]** /neɪm; nem/ *v* 动

names, naming, named, named

to give a name to someone or something 取名；命名

They named their baby Joanna. 他们给宝宝取名为乔安娜。

nap /næp; næp/ *n* 名

a short sleep during the day 小睡

My grandmother has a nap every afternoon. 我的祖母每天下午都会小睡一会儿。

napkin /ˈnæpkɪn; ˋnæpkɪn/ *n* 名

a piece of cloth or paper used at meals to keep your clothes, mouth and hands clean 餐巾

He put a napkin on his lap. 他把餐巾放在大腿上。

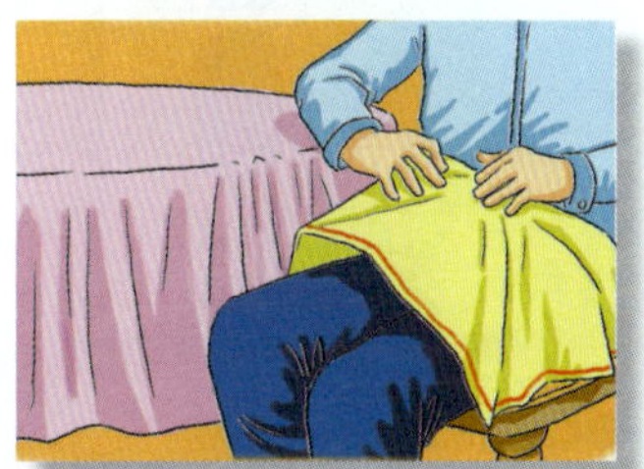

***narrow** /ˈnærəʊ; ˋnæro/ *adj* 形

narrower, narrowest

not far from side to side 狭窄的

This narrow path leads to the beach. 这条狭窄的小路通往沙滩。

反义 **broad, wide**

nasty /ˈnɑːsti; ˋnæstɪ/ *adj* 形

nastier, nastiest

1. very bad and not pleasant 糟糕的；令人讨厌的

   The food tastes nasty! 这食物很难吃！

2. not kind 不友善的；恶意的

   Don't be so nasty to your mother. 别对你妈妈那么凶。

nation /ˈneɪʃn; ˋneʃən/ *n* 名

a country and its people 国家；国民

The president will travel across the nation. 总统将周游全国。

***national** /ˈnæʃnəl; ˋnæʃənl̩/ *adj* 形

of the whole nation or a particular nation 国家的；全国的

Labour Day is a national holiday. 劳动节是国定假日。

nationality /ˌnæʃəˈnæləti; ˌnæʃəˋnælətɪ/ *n* 名

复数：***nationalities***

the country where someone has the right to live 国籍

Mr Clarke has Canadian nationality. 克拉克先生有加拿大国籍。

***natural** /ˈnætʃərəl; ˋnætʃərəl/ *adj* 形

1. not made by humans 天然的；自然的

   This chair is made of natural materials. 这张椅子是用天然材料制造的。

   反义 **man-made**

2. usual 平常的；正常的

   It is natural to feel nervous before an exam. 考试前感到紧张是正常的。

   同义 **normal**

***nature** /ˈneɪtʃə; ˋnetʃɚ/ *n* 名

无复数

everything in the world that is not made by humans 大自然；自然界

I like to watch films about nature. 我喜欢看关于大自然的影片。

***naughty** /ˈnɔːti; ˋnɔtɪ/ *adj* 形

naughtier, naughtiest

N

behaving badly 顽皮的；淘气的

The naughty boy kicked the cat. 那个顽皮的男童踢了猫一下。

反义 good

navy /ˈneɪvi; ˋnevɪ/ *n* 名

复数：*navies*

the people who fight at sea for a country 海军

My grandfather joined the navy when he was young. 我的爷爷年轻时加入了海军。

比较 air force, army

***near¹** /nɪə; nɪr/ *prep* 介

not far from 在…附近

The zoo is near the train station. 动物园在火车站附近。

同义 close²

***near²** /nɪə; nɪr/ *adv* 副

nearer, nearest

not far 在附近

Connie and Shirley live quite near. 康妮和雪莉住得很近。

反义 far¹

***near³** /nɪə; nɪr/ *adj* 形

nearer, nearest

not far 近的

The library is very near. 图书馆就在附近。

反义 far²

Asking for directions 问路

"Where is the nearest MTR station?" "It's just opposite the bus stop." "最近的地铁站在哪里？" "就在巴士站对面。"

nearby¹ /ˈnɪəbaɪ; ˋnɪrbaɪ/ *adj* 形

not far away 附近的

Jimmy goes to a nearby school. 吉米在附近的学校上学。

nearby² /ˈnɪəbaɪ; ˋnɪrbaɪ/ *adv* 副

not far away 在附近

Is there a hospital nearby? 附近有医院吗？

***nearly** /ˈnɪəli; ˋnɪrlɪ/ *adv* 副

almost 几乎；将近

I am nearly as tall as my mother. 我和妈妈几乎一样高。

***neat** /niːt; nit/ *adj* 形

neater, neatest

clean and tidy 整洁的；整齐的

Brian always keeps his room neat. 布莱恩一向把房间保持得很整洁。

***necessary** /ˈnesəsəri; ˋnɛsəˌsɛrɪ/ *adj* 形

if something is necessary, you need to do it or you must do it 必需的；必要的

Exercise is necessary for good health. 运动对健康是必要的。

反义 unnecessary

***neck** /nek; nɛk/ *n* 名

the part between your head and your shoulders 颈；脖子

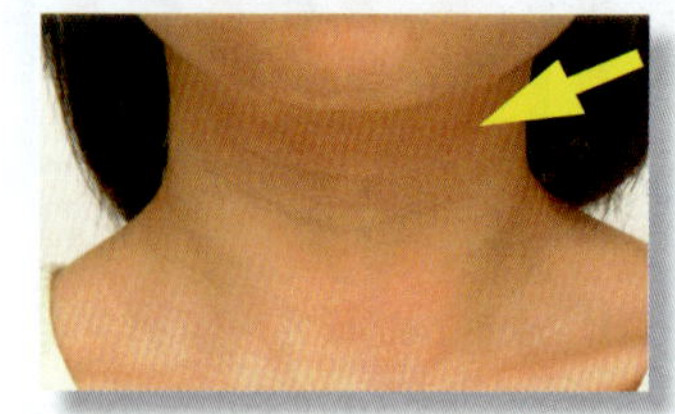

He put the scarf around his neck. 他把围巾围在脖子上。

necklace /ˈneklɪs; ˋnɛklɪs/ *n* 名

a piece of jewellery you wear around your neck 项链

Alice was wearing a beautiful necklace. 爱丽丝戴着一条美丽的项链。

***need¹** /niːd; nid/ *v* 动

if you need something, it is important for you to have it 需要

I need a bigger school bag. 我需要一个更大的书包。

don't need to do something/ needn't do something 不必做某事

You needn't feed the cat today. I've fed it. 你今天不用喂猫，我已经喂了。

need to do something 必须做某事

You need to attend the meeting. 你必须出席会议。

***need²** /niːd; nid/ *n* 名

a situation in which it is important for people to have someone or something 需要；需求

There is a big need for teachers. 对教师的需求很大。

***needle** /ˈniːdl; ˋnidl̩/ *n* 名

a small piece of pointed metal for sewing or injection 针；针头

I need a needle and thread to sew a button. 我需要针线来缝一颗钮扣。

needn't /ˈniːdnt; ˋnidn̩t/

the short form of "**need not**" ☆ need not 的缩写

You needn't come if you are busy. 如果你忙就不必来了。

needy /ˈniːdi; ˋnidɪ/ *adj* 形

needier, neediest

having little money or food 贫困的

How can we help needy families? 我们可以怎样帮助贫困家庭呢?

negative /ˈnegətɪv; ˋnɛgətɪv/ *adj* 形

1. meaning "no" 否定的；拒绝的
   He gave a negative reply. 他给了否定的回复。
2. a negative sentence or phrase has a word such as "no", "not", "nothing", etc（句子或短语）否定式的

***neighbour** /ˈneɪbə; ˋnebɚ/ *n* 名【英】

美式：***neighbor***

someone who lives next to you 邻居；邻人

Our new neighbours are very nice. 新来的邻居十分友善。

neighbourhood /ˈneɪbəhʊd; ˋnebɚˌhʊd/ *n* 名【英】

美式：***neighborhood***

an area of a city or town 附近地区

There is a new cinema in the neighbourhood. 这儿附近有一家新的电影院。

***neither[1]** /ˈnaɪðə; ˋniðɚ/ *pron* 代

not one or the other of two people or things 两者都不

Neither of the boys liked the film. 两个男孩都不喜欢那部电影。

另见 **either[1]**

Daily conversation 日常会话

"I can't swim." "Neither can I." "我不会游泳。" "我也不会。"

***neither[2]** /ˈnaɪðə; ˋniðɚ/ *conj* 连

neither ... nor ...

used to show two things that are not true 既不…也不…

My father neither gambles nor smokes. 我的爸爸既不赌博也不抽烟。

另见 **either[2]**

nephew /ˈnefjuː; ˋnɛfju/ *n* 名

the son of your brother or sister 侄子；外甥

Frank's nephew looks like him a lot. 法兰克的外甥很像他。

比较 **niece**

***nervous** /ˈnɜːvəs; ˋnɝvəs/ *adj* 形

feeling worried and scared 紧张的

Tony was very nervous when he saw the dentist. 托尼看牙医时很紧张。

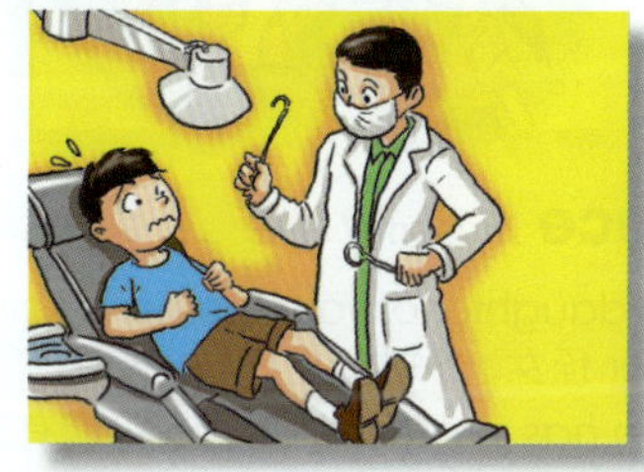

nervously /ˈnɜːvəsli; ˋnɝvəslɪ/ *adv* 副

in a worried way 紧张地

The little boy looked at him nervously. 那个小男孩紧张地看着他。

***nest** /nest; nɛst/ *n* 名

a home built by a bird or an insect 巢；窝

There are five eggs in the nest. 鸟巢里有 5 个蛋。

***net** /net; nɛt/ *n* 名

1. something made of strings tied together 网

   I kicked the ball into the net. 我把球踢进了网。
2. **the Net**【电脑】the Internet 互联网
   We can find a lot of information on the Net. 我们可以在互联网上找到大量信息。

注意 解作互联网时，必须用大写字母 N，并与 the 一起使用。

***never** /ˈnevə; ˋnɛvɚ/ *adv* 副

not at any time; not ever 不曾；从不

She never eats fish. 她从不吃鱼。

***new** /njuː; nu/ *adj* 形

newer, newest

not old or used 新的

My mother bought me a new pair of shoes. 妈妈给我买了一双新鞋子。

反义 **old**

***news** /njuːz; nuz/ *n* 名

无复数

information about things that have just happened 新闻；消息

We watched news about the war on TV. 我们在电视上看到关于这场战争的新闻报道。

注意 news 是不可数名词，如要表示一条、两条消息，用 a piece of news、two pieces of news 等。

***newspaper** /ˈnjuːsˌpeɪpə; ˋnuzˌpepɚ/ *n* 名

a number of large sheets of paper with news 报纸

N

Susan reads a free newspaper every day. 苏珊每天看一份免费的报纸。

同义 **paper**

newsstand /ˈnjuːzstænd; ˋnuzˌstænd/ *n* 名

a place on the street where you can buy newspapers and magazines 报摊；报刊亭

I bought a newspaper at a newsstand. 我在报摊买了一份报纸。

New Year /ˈnjuː jɪə; ˋnu jɪr/ *n* 名

无复数

the time when you celebrate the beginning of the year 新年

Happy New Year! 新年快乐！

***next**[1] /nekst; nɛkst/ *adj* 形

1. after this 下一个的；下次的

   Let's play football next Saturday. 我们下星期六踢足球吧。

2. nearest 最靠近的

   The library is in the next building. 图书馆在边上一座大楼里。

next door 隔壁

John lives next door. 约翰住在隔壁。

***next**[2] /nekst; nɛkst/ *adv* 副

after this 接着；之后

What should we do next? 我们接下来该怎么做?

next to 在…旁边

My cat is sleeping next to me. 我的猫在我旁边睡觉。

***nice** /naɪs; naɪs/ *adj* 形

nicer, nicest

1. good or pleasant 美好的；愉快的

   We had a nice holiday in Beijing. 我们在北京的假期过得很愉快。

2. kind and friendly 友善的；亲切的

   Sandra is nice to everyone. 珊德拉对每个人都友善。

同义 **friendly**

Greetings 问候

"Nice to meet you!" "Nice to meet you too!" "很高兴认识你！" "我也很高兴认识你！"

nickname /ˈnɪkneɪm; ˋnɪkˌnem/ *n* 名

a name given to someone that is not his or her real name 绰号；外号

His nickname is Polar Bear. 他的绰号是"北极熊"。

niece /niːs; nis/ *n* 名

the daughter of your brother or sister 侄女；外甥女

Sam has got three nieces. 山姆有三个侄女。

比较 **nephew**

***night** /naɪt; naɪt/ *n* 名

the time when it is dark and you go to bed 夜晚；晚间

I usually sleep for eight hours every night. 我通常每晚睡 8 小时。

all night (long) 通宵；整夜

I revised for the exam all night. 我为考试复习了一整夜。

the other night 几天前的一个夜里

There was a storm the other night. 几天前的一个夜里下起了暴风雨。

反义 **day**

nightingale /ˈnaɪtɪŋgeɪl; ˋnaɪtɪŋˌgel/ *n* 名

a small bird that sings beautifully at night 夜莺

I heard a nightingale sing last night. 昨晚我听到一只夜莺在唱歌。

nightmare /ˈnaɪtmeə; ˋnaɪtˌmɛr/ *n* 名

a dream that makes you afraid 噩梦

I had a nightmare last night. 我昨晚做了一场噩梦。

***nine** /naɪn; naɪn/ *num* 数

the number 9 九

We have nine lessons every day. 我们每天上 9 节课。

***nineteen** /ˌnaɪnˈtiːn; ˌnaɪnˋtin/ *num* 数

the number 19 十九

Ten plus nine equals nineteen. 10 加 9 等于 19。

nineteenth /ˌnaɪnˈtiːnθ; ˌnaɪnˋtinθ/ *ordinal num* 序数

19th in order 第十九(的)

It is David's nineteenth birthday today. 今天是大卫的 19 岁生日。

ninetieth /ˈnaɪntiəθ; ˋnaɪntɪəθ/ *ordinal num* 序数

90th in order 第九十(的)

Yesterday was my grandfather's ninetieth birthday. 昨天是祖父的九十大寿。

***ninety** /ˈnaɪnti; ˋnaɪntɪ/ *num* 数

the number 90 九十

My grandmother is nearly ninety years old. 我的祖母快 90 岁了。

ninth /naɪnθ; naɪnθ/ *ordinal num* 序数

9th in order 第九(的)

Mr Green's office is on the ninth floor. 格林先生的办公室在 9 楼。

注意 拼写中没有 e，不要写成 nineth。

***no[1]** /nəʊ; no/ *adv* 副

a word you use when you say that something is not true, or when you disagree or do not want something 不；不是(表示否定)

"Do you like cheese?" "No, I don't." "你喜欢吃奶酪吗？" "不，我不喜欢。"

反义 **yes**

Daily conversation 日常会话

no, thanks 不了，谢谢(表示拒绝)

"Would you like some coffee?" "No, thanks." "你要喝点咖啡吗？" "不了，谢谢。"

***no[2]** /nəʊ; no/ *adj* 形

not any; not one 没有；无

I have no money to buy shoes. 我没钱买鞋子。

***nobody** /ˈnəʊbədi; ˋnoˌbadɪ/, ***no one** /ˈnəʊ wʌn; ˋno wʌn/ *pron* 代

not one person 没有人

There is nobody in the classroom. 教室里没有人。

另见 **anybody, anyone**

***nod** /nɒd; nad/ *v* 动

nods, nodding, nodded, nodded

to move your head up and down to say yes or greet someone 点头(表示同意或打招呼)

They nodded at each other. 他们互相点头打招呼。

***noise** /nɔɪz; nɔɪz/ *n* 名

a loud and unpleasant sound 噪音；吵闹声

Our neighbours made a lot of noise at night. 我们的邻居在晚上发出很大的噪音。

比较 **sound[1]**

noisily /ˈnɔɪzɪli; ˋnɔɪzɪlɪ/ *adv* 副

in a way that makes a lot of noise 吵闹地

The children are playing noisily in the playground. 孩子们在操场上吵闹地玩耍。

反义 **quietly**

noisy /ˈnɔɪzi; ˋnɔɪzɪ/ *adj* 形

noisier, noisiest

making a lot of noise 吵闹的

It's very noisy in the restaurant. 这家餐馆十分吵闹。

反义 **quiet, silent**

***none** /nʌn; nʌn/ *pron* 代

not any; not one 没有一个；没有一点儿

None of them had any money. 他们都没有钱。

Daily conversation 日常会话

"Is there any milk left?" "No, there's none left." "还有牛奶吗？" "没有了，一点也没有。"

nonsense /ˈnɒnsəns; ˋnansɛns/ *n* 名

无复数

words that seem stupid because they are not true 废话；胡说

Don't talk nonsense! 不要胡说八道！

***noodles** /ˈnu:dlz; ˋnudl̩z/ *plural n* 复数名词

long, thin pieces of food made from flour, eggs and water 面条

I like to eat fried noodles. 我喜欢吃炒面。

***noon** /nu:n; nun/ *n* 名

无复数

12 o'clock in the middle of the day 中午；正午

Our lunch hour starts at noon. 我们的午餐时间从正午开始。

同义 **midday**

***nor** /nɔː; nɔr/ *conj* 连

neither ... nor ...

used to show two things that are not true 既不…也不…

My parrot neither eats nor drinks. Is it sick? 我的鹦鹉既不吃东西也不喝水，它是不是病了？

***normal** /ˈnɔːml; ˋnɔrml/ *adj* 形

usual 正常的；一般的

It is normal to feel tired after working hard all day. 辛苦工作一整天后感到疲劳是正常的。

同义 **natural**

north¹ /nɔːθ; nɔrθ/ *n* 名

无复数｜缩写：*N*

the direction that is opposite south 北方；北面

The wind is blowing from the north. 风从北方吹来。

north² /nɔːθ; nɔrθ/ *adj* 形

in the north or facing the north 北方的；北面的；向北的

We live in the north part of the city. 我们住在城市的北部。

north³ /nɔːθ; nɔrθ/ *adv* 副

towards the north 向北

The birds are flying north. 鸟儿向北飞行。

northern /ˈnɔːðən; ˋnɔrðən/ *adj* 形

in or from the north of a country or place 北方的；北部的

It is very cold in northern China. 中国北部非常寒冷。

***nose** /nəʊz; noz/ *n* 名

the part of your face you use to breathe and smell 鼻子

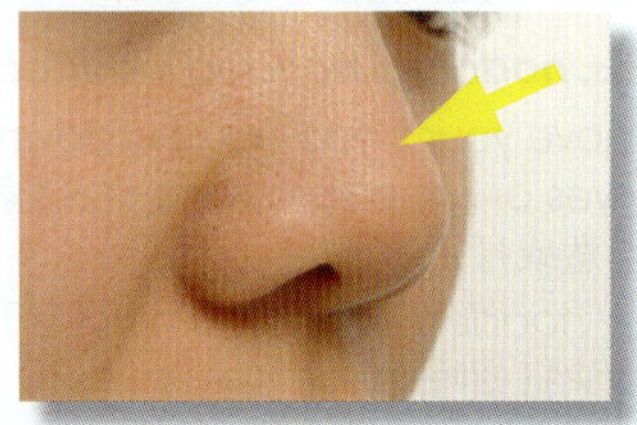

The clown has a big red nose. 小丑有个又大又红的鼻子。

***not** /nɒt; nɑt/ *adv* 副

a word you use to make a word or sentence have the opposite meaning 不；不是（表示相反）

She will not come. 她不会来。

not only ... but also ... 不仅…而且…

The weather is not only cold but also wet. 天气又冷又湿。

注意 在口语中，not 在 is、are、was、were、has、have、do、does 等动词后可缩写为 n't，例如 isn't 和 doesn't。而 cannot、shall not、will not 等词可缩写为 can't、shan't、won't 等。

Daily conversation 日常会话

not at all 别客气；没关系

"Thank you very much!" "Not at all." "非常谢谢您！""别客气。"

***note¹** /nəʊt; not/ *n* 名

1. a short letter 便条

   My mother left a note for me on the table. 我的妈妈在桌上给我留了张便条。
2. words that you write down to help you remember something 笔记

   I take notes during lessons. 我上课时会做笔记。
3. a sound in music or a symbol that shows the sound 音调；音符

   Dorothy can sing high notes. 多萝西能唱高音。
4. 【英】（美式：***bill***）a piece of paper money 纸币；钞票

   Sally took out a twenty-dollar note. 莎莉拿出一张 20 元纸币。

同义 **banknote, bank note**

***note²** /nəʊt; not/ *v* 动

notes, noting, noted, noted

to notice or pay attention to something 注意

Please note that there is no school on Tuesday. 请注意星期二不用上学。

note down 记下

She noted down my telephone number. 她记下了我的电话号码。

notebook /ˈnəʊtbʊk; ˋnotˌbʊk/ *n* 名

1. a book for writing notes in 笔记本

   I wrote down the new words in my notebook. 我把生词记在笔记本中。
2. 【电脑】a computer you can carry with you anywhere 笔记本电脑；手提电脑

   Mary carries a notebook when she is working. 玛丽工作时会带着笔记本电脑。

同义 **laptop**

N

notepad /ˈnəʊtpæd; ˋnotpæd/ *n* 名

sheets of paper held together for writing notes on 便条本；记事本

Lily wrote my address on her notepad. 莉莉在记事本上写下我的地址。

***nothing** /ˈnʌθɪŋ; ˋnʌθɪŋ/ *pron* 代

not anything 没有任何东西

There is nothing on the table. 桌子上什么都没有。

另见 **anything**

***notice[1]** /ˈnəʊtɪs; ˋnotɪs/ *n* 名

a short piece of writing that tells people something 告示；布告

The notice on the door said the shop was closed. 门上的告示写着商店已关门。

***notice[2]** /ˈnəʊtɪs; ˋnotɪs/ *v* 动

notices, noticing, noticed, noticed

to see or hear something 注意到；察觉

The teacher noticed that Robin was sleeping in class. 老师注意到罗宾在上课时睡觉。

noticeboard /ˈnəʊtɪsbɔːd; ˋnotɪsˌbɔrd/ *n* 名

a board on a wall that you can put notices on 告示牌；布告栏

There is a noticeboard next to the blackboard. 在黑板旁边有一块布告栏。

noun /naʊn; naʊn/ *n* 名

a word that is the name of a person, place or thing. In the sentence "The babies are drinking milk", "babies" and "milk" are nouns. 名词（在 The babies are drinking milk 这个句子中，babies 和 milk 都是名词。）

注意 英语中的名词一般分为可数与不可数名词，如在上例中，baby 是可数名词，milk 则是不可数名词。

novel /ˈnɒvl; ˋnɑvl̩/ *n* 名

a book that contains a long story 小说

Sophia loves reading novels. 苏菲亚喜欢看小说。

***November** /nəʊˈvembə; noˋvɛmbɚ/ *n* 名

缩写：***Nov.***

the eleventh month of the year 十一月

Our school trip is in November. 我们的学校旅行在 11 月。

注意 开头的字母必须用大写。

***now** /naʊ; naʊ/ *adv* 副

at the present time 现在

We are having dinner now. 我们正在吃晚饭。

from now on 从今以后

From now on I will work hard. 从今以后我会用功。

Daily conversation 日常会话

Now, ... 好了…（用于引起注意）

"Now, children, open your books at page 10." "好了，孩子们，把书翻到第 10 页。"

***nowadays** /ˈnaʊədeɪz; ˋnaʊəˌdez/ *adv* 副

at the present time 现今；目前

People seldom write letters nowadays. 现今很少有人写信了。

用法 nowadays 用于表示与过去相比不一样。

nowhere /ˈnəʊweə; ˋnoˌwɛr/ *adv* 副

not in or to any place 任何地方都不；无处

There was nowhere for me to put the books. 我找不到地方放这些书。

另见 **anywhere**

nuclear /ˈnjuːklɪə; ˋnuklɪr/ *adj* 形

using or producing a very powerful kind of energy 原子能的；核能的

Is nuclear energy safe? 核能是否安全呢？

***number** /ˈnʌmbə; ˋnʌmbɚ/ *n* 名

1. a sign or word that shows an amount or quantity 数；数字
   The teacher wrote down two numbers on the blackboard. 老师在黑板上写了两个数字。
2. a telephone number or a set of numbers that you use to show something（电话）号码；编号
   I'm afraid you've got the wrong number. 恐怕你是打错电话了。

a number of 一些；几个

A number of friends came to my birthday party. 有几个朋友参加了我的生日聚会。

另见 **附录**：Numbers 数字

***nurse[1]** /nɜːs; nɝs/ *n* 名

someone who looks after sick people in a hospital 护士

N

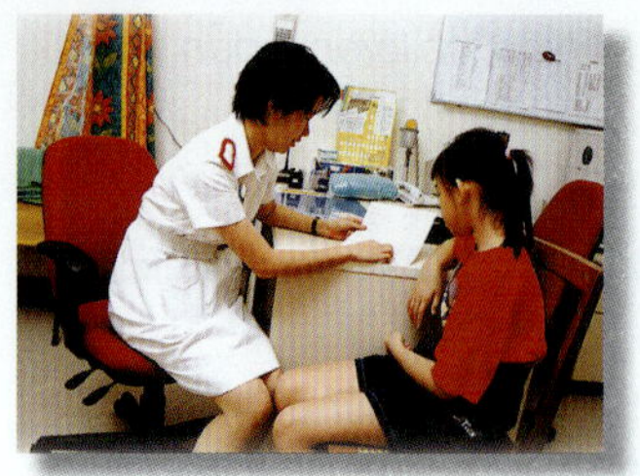

The nurse gave him an injection. 护士给他打了一针。

nurse² /nɜːs; nɝs/ *v* 动

nurses, nursing, nursed, nursed

to look after sick people 照料；护理

My mother nursed me when I had fever. 我发烧时，妈妈照料我。

nursery /ˈnɜːsəri; ˋnɝsərɪ/ *n* 名

复数：***nurseries***

a place where young children stay while their parents are working 托儿所

There are a lot of babies in the nursery. 托儿所里有很多婴儿。

nursery school /ˈnɜːsəri ˌskuːl; ˋnɝsərɪ ˏskul/ *n* 名

a school for very young children 幼儿园

I take my brother to a nursery school every day. 我每天带弟弟上幼儿园。

同义 **kindergarten**

***nut** /nʌt; nʌt/ *n* 名

a small fruit with a hard shell 坚果；果仁

I like chocolates with nuts. 我喜欢吃有果仁的巧克力。

nylon /ˈnaɪlɒn; ˋnaɪlɑn/ *n* 名

无复数

a strong material used to make clothes, ropes, etc 尼龙

This bag is made of nylon. 这个包是用尼龙做的。

N

oar /ɔ:; ɔr/ *n* 名

a long piece of wood with a flat end for rowing a boat 桨；橹

He was rowing the boat with the oars. 他用桨划着船。

比较 **paddle**[1]

oasis /əʊ'eɪsɪs; o`esɪs/ *n* 名

复数：***oases***

a place with water and plants in a desert（沙漠中的）绿洲

A camel is resting at the oasis. 一只骆驼在绿洲休息。

obedient /ə'bi:diənt; ə`bidɪənt/ *adj* 形

willing to do what someone tells you to do 服从的；听话的

Jason is an obedient child. 杰森是个听话的孩子。

反义 **disobedient**

***obey** /ə'beɪ; o`be/ *v* 动

to do what someone tells you to do 服从；遵守

My dog always obeys my orders. 我的狗总是听从我的命令。

object /'ɒbdʒekt; `ɑbdʒɪkt/ *n* 名

1. a thing 物件；物品
   What's that yellow object? 那个黄色的东西是什么？
2. a word that usually follows the verb in a sentence. In the sentence "They saw me", "me" is the object. 宾语（在 They saw me 这个句子中，me 是宾语。）

observe /əb'zɜ:v; əb`zɝv/ *v* 动

observes, observing, observed, observed

to watch something or someone carefully 观察；监视

The scientists are observing the monkey's behaviour. 科学家在观察那只猴子的行为。

obtain /əb'teɪn; əb`ten/ *v* 动

to get something 获得；得到

You have to obtain permission from the principal. 你必须取得校长的批准。

用法 obtain 是正式说法，口语多用 get，例如 He got an A in English（他英语得了个 A）。

occasion /ə'keɪʒn; ə`keʒən/ *n* 名

1. a time when something happens 时候；时刻
   We have met on several occasions. 我们见过几次面。
2. an important event 重要的活动
   I wear this suit only on special occasions. 在特别的日子我才会穿这套西装。

occupation /ˌɒkju'peɪʃn; ˌɑkjə`peʃən/ *n* 名

a job 职业；工作

"What's your occupation?" "I'm a nurse." "你的职业是什么？""我是护士。"

***occur** /ə'kɜ:; ə`kɝ/ *v* 动

occurs, occurring, occurred, occurred

to happen 发生

The accident occurred last night. 事故发生在昨晚。

***ocean** /'əʊʃn; `oʃən/ *n* 名

a very large sea 海洋

There are a lot of creatures in the ocean. 海洋中有很多生物。

***o'clock** /ə'klɒk; ə`klɑk/ *adv* 副

a word used to show the hour of the day …点钟

It's two o'clock now. 现在是两点钟。

用法 o'clock 只用于正点时刻，不带分钟，例如 1 点是 one o'clock，而 1 点 15 分是 a quarter past one（one 后不加 o'clock）。

另见 **附录**：Time 时间

O

***October** /ɒk'təʊbə; ɑk'tobɚ/ *n* 名

缩写：***Oct.***

the tenth month of the year 十月

Dolly's birthday is in October. 多莉的生日在 10 月。

注意 开头的字母必须用大写。

octopus /'ɒktəpəs; `ɑktəpəs/ *n* 名

复数：***octopuses***

a sea animal with a soft body and eight long arms 章鱼；八爪鱼

The fishermen caught a big octopus. 渔民捕了一只大章鱼。

odd /ɒd; ɑd/ *adj* 形

odder, oddest

1. strange and unusual 古怪的；不寻常的

   His behaviour is very odd. 他的行为很古怪。

同义 **strange**

2. an odd number is one that cannot be divided exactly by two 奇数的；单数的

   3, 5 and 7 are odd numbers. 3、5 和 7 是奇数。

反义 **even²**

***of** /əv; əv; *strong* 强读 ɒv; ɑv/ *prep* 介

1. used to show a relationship …的（表示关系）

   Bill is a friend of mine. 比尔是我的一位朋友。

2. forming a part of something …的一部分

   The legs of the chair are broken. 椅子的腿断了。

3. used to show what something is 关于…的

   Here is a photo of his son. 这是一张他儿子的照片。

4. used to show what is inside 含有…的

   Helen gave us a basket of apples. 海伦给了我们一篮苹果。

5. used to talk about amounts 表示数量

   We bought five kilograms of rice. 我们买了 5 公斤米。

6. used in dates 表示日期

   Today is the twentieth of July. 今天是 7 月 20 日。

***off¹** /ɒf; ɔf/ *prep* 介

1. not on something 落下

   He fell off the stairs. 他从楼梯上摔了下来。

2. out of a bus, train, etc 下（公共汽车、火车等）

   She got off the bus. 她下了公共汽车。

反义 **on¹**

***off²** /ɒf; ɔf/ *adv* 副

1. away from a place 离开

   He got into the car and drove off. 他上了车，开车走了。

2. not working or being used 关掉；不在使用

   She turned the lights off. 她把灯关掉了。

反义 **on²**

3. not on something 脱下

   Please take your shoes off. 请把鞋子脱下。

反义 **on²**

4. not at work or school 休假

   I will take three days off next week. 我下星期会休假三天。

***offer** /'ɒfə; `ɔfɚ/ *v* 动

to ask someone if they would like to have something（表示愿意）提供；给予

He offered me some tea. 他问我喝不喝茶。

***office** /'ɒfɪs; `ɔfɪs/ *n* 名

a place where people work 办公室

Nick works in an office. 尼克在办公室工作。

***officer** /'ɒfɪsə; `ɔfəsɚ/ *n* 名

someone who has an important job in the government, an organization, etc 官员；高级职员

Barry is a local government officer. 巴利是当地政府的官员。

***often** /'ɒfn; `ɔfən/ *adv* 副

many times or regularly 常常；经常

We often go swimming together. 我们经常一同去游泳。

反义 **seldom**

Daily conversation 日常会话

how often...? 多久…？

"How often do you go to the library?" "Once a week." "你多久去一次图书馆呢？""每星期一次。"

oh /əʊ; o/ *interj* 感叹

a word you say when you feel surprised, annoyed, etc 啊；噢；哎呀

Oh, I've got a postcard! 噢，我收到一张明信片！

Daily conversation 日常会话

oh, no! 哎呀，不好了！

"Oh, no! I've lost my phone." "Don't panic. Let's look for it." "哎呀，不好了！我的电话不见了。""别惊慌。我们找找看。"

***oil** /ɔil; ɔɪl/ *n* 名

无复数

1. a dark liquid from under the ground, used for making petrol 石油

   The price of oil is rising. 油价正在上升。

2. a thick liquid from plants or animals, used for cooking（食用的）油

She uses vegetable oil for cooking. 她用植物油来烧菜。

***OK[1], okay[1]** /ˌəʊ ˈkeɪ; ˏo ˋke/ *interj* 感叹

a word used to say you agree or ask someone if they agree with you 好；行（表示同意）；好吗；行吗（用于征求别人的同意）

"Shall we have lunch?" "Okay!" "我们吃午饭好吗？""好的！"

***OK[2], okay[2]** /ˌəʊ ˈkeɪ; ˏo ˋke/ *adj* 形

all right; good enough 好的；不错的

His idea is OK. 他的主意不错。

***old** /əʊld; old/ *adj* 形

older, oldest

1. not young 年老的

   Old people usually walk slowly. 老年人一般走路缓慢。

反义 **young**

2. used to show someone's age …岁的

   My brother is six years old. 我的弟弟6岁了。

3. not new 旧的

   They live in an old building. 他们住在一幢旧楼里。

反义 **new**

old-fashioned /əʊld ˈfæʃnd; old ˋfæʃənd/ *adj* 形

not modern 过时的；旧式的

This phone looks rather old-fashioned. 这个电话看起来相当过时。

Olympic Games /əˌlɪmpɪk ˈgeɪmz; oˌlɪmpɪk ˋgemz/ *plural n* 复数名词

也作：***Olympics***

a sports event held every four years. People from all over the world take part in it. 奥林匹克运动会；奥运会

China won a lot of medals in the last Olympic Games. 中国在上一届奥运会中赢得了很多奖牌。

omelette /ˈɒmlət; ˋɑmlət/ *n* 名

eggs cooked in a flat shape, sometimes with other food 煎蛋卷

I had a ham omelette for breakfast. 早餐我吃了火腿煎蛋卷。

***on[1]** /ɒn; ɑn/ *prep* 介

1. used to show the position of something 在…上

   There are pictures on the wall. 墙上有几幅画。

2. used to show the day or date when something happens 在（某一天）

   We have a music lesson on Monday. 我们在星期一上音乐课。

3. inside a bus, train, etc 上（公共汽车、火车等）

   I got on the bus to go home. 我乘上公共汽车回家。

反义 **off[1]**

***on[2]** /ɒn; ɑn/ *adv* 副词

1. without stopping 继续；向前

   Please read on. 请继续读下去。

2. working; being used 开着；运作中

   The lights are still on. 灯还亮着。

反义 **off[2]**

3. covering a part of your body 穿上；戴上

   It's cold outside. Put your coat on. 外面很冷。把大衣穿上吧。

反义 **off[2]**

O

***once** /wʌns; wʌns/ *adv* 副

1. one time 一次

   Ellen and her grandmother go shopping once a week. 艾伦和外婆每星期去购物一次。

2. at some time in the past 曾经

   My grandfather was once a teacher. 我的祖父曾经当过教师。

at once 立刻；马上

Get up at once! 马上起床！

once again 再一次

Let's sing the song once again. 我们再唱一遍这首歌吧。

once upon a time 从前（用于故事的开头）

Once upon a time, there was a prince who lived in a castle. 从前，有一个王子住在一座城堡里。

***one¹** /wʌn; wʌn/ *num* 数

the number 1 一

Let's count from one to one hundred. 我们从 1 数到 100 吧。

***one²** /wʌn; wʌn/ *pron* 代

someone or something that you have talked about 一个（指已提及的人或物）

There are five cups on the table. Which one is yours? 桌上有 5 只杯子。哪一只是你的？

one after another 接连地；一个接一个地

Traffic accidents occurred one after another. 交通意外接连发生。

one by one 一个一个地；逐一

The pupils went into the classroom one by one. 学生一个接一个走进课室。

one of 其中之一

One of her cats is sick. 她的猫有一只生病了。

***onion** /ˈʌnjən; ˋʌnjən/ *n* 名

a round vegetable with a strong smell and taste 洋葱

The cook is frying pork with onions. 厨师正在炒洋葱猪肉。

***only¹** /ˈəʊnli; ˋonlɪ/ *adv* 副

just; not more than 只；仅仅

I only have one sister. 我只有一个妹妹。

***only²** /ˈəʊnli; ˋonlɪ/ *adj* 形

used to say that there are no others 唯一的

Henry is the only child in his family. 亨利是家中的独生子。

***onto** /ˈɒntə, ˈɒntu; ˋɑntə, ˋɑntʊ/ *prep* 介

to a place 到…上

The leaves are falling onto the ground. 树叶落到地上。

onwards /ˈɒnwədz; ˋɑnwədz/ *adv* 副【英】

美式：*onward*

from ... onwards

starting at a particular time and continuing after that 从…起一直

From then onwards, he lived in Beijing. 从那时起他一直住在北京。

***open¹** /ˈəʊpən; ˋopən/ *adj* 形

1. not closed 开着的

   Keep the windows open. 把窗户开着。

   反义 **closed, shut²**

2. ready for business 开放的；营业的

   This shop is open at ten in the morning. 这家商店在上午 10 点开门营业。

   反义 **closed**

***open²** /ˈəʊpən; ˋopən/ *v* 动

1. to move things for someone or something to get in or out 开；打开

   Can you open the gate, please? 请你把大门打开好吗？

   反义 **close¹, shut¹**

2. to be ready for business 开始营业

   The new bakery will open next week. 新面包店将在下星期开始营业。

   反义 **close¹**

opera /ˈɒpərə; ˋɑpərə/ *n* 名

a musical play with songs 歌剧

She went to the theatre to see an opera. 她去剧院看了一场歌剧。

***operation** /ˌɒpəˈreɪʃn; ˌɑpəˋreʃən/ *n* 名

when a doctor cuts into someone's body to repair or remove a damaged part 手术

The patient is having an operation. 那个病人正在接受手术。

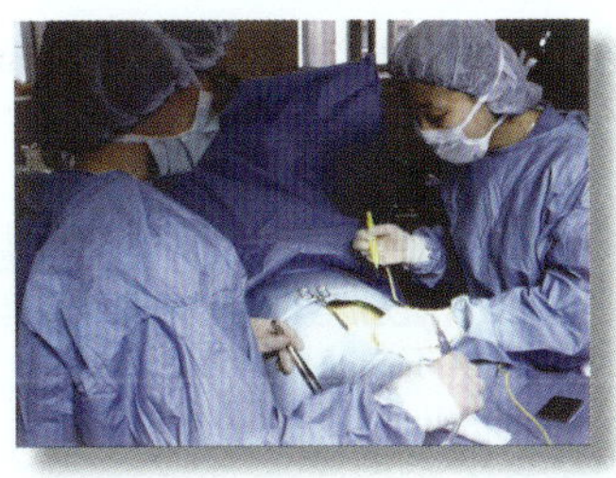

***opinion** /əˈpɪnjən; əˋpɪnjən/ *n* 名

what you think about something 意见；看法

Linda asked her teacher for his opinion. 琳达请老师给她意见。

***opportunity** /ˌɒpəˈtjuːnəti; ˌɑpəˋtunətɪ/ *n* 名

复数：*opportunities*

a time when you can do something 机会

Don't miss the opportunity! 不要错失机会！

同义 **chance**

***opposite[1]** /ˈɒpəzɪt; ˋɑpəzɪt/ *prep* 介

on the other side of something 在…对面

I sat opposite the girl. 我坐在那个女孩对面。

注意 opposite 之后不加 to。

Asking for directions 问路

"Where's the nearest bank?" "Go to the corner of the street and turn left. It's just opposite the cinema." "最近的银行在哪里？""走到街角向左转，就在电影院对面。"

opposite[2] /ˈɒpəzɪt; ˋɑpəzɪt/ *adj* 形

completely different 相反的

They went in opposite directions. 他们往反方向走了。

opposite[3] /ˈɒpəzɪt; ˋɑpəzɪt/ *n* 名

something that is completely different from something else 相反的事物

Louis is tall and strong, but I am just the opposite. 路易高大强壮，而我则恰恰相反。

***or** /ə; ɚ; *strong* 强读 ɔː; ɔr/ *conj* 连

a word used to give two or more choices 或；还是

Do you go to school by bus or by bike? 你是坐公共汽车还是骑自行车上学？

***oral** /ˈɔːrəl; ˋɔrəl/ *adj* 形

spoken 口头的；口语的

We had an English oral exam today. 我们今天考了英语口试。

***orange[1]** /ˈɒrɪndʒ; ˋɔrɪndʒ/ *n* 名

1. a round fruit with a thick skin 橙子；柑橘

   I had an orange after dinner. 晚饭后我吃了一个橙子。

2. the colour between red and yellow 橙色；橘黄色

   Orange is my favourite colour. 橙色是我最喜欢的颜色。

***orange[2]** /ˈɒrɪndʒ; ˋɔrɪndʒ/ *adj* 形

having the colour between red and yellow 橙色的；橘黄色的

This orange jacket is mine. 这件橙色外套是我的。

orangutang /ɔːˌræŋuːˈtæŋ; ɔˋræŋəˌtæŋ/ *n* 名

也作：*orang-utan*

an animal like a large monkey 猩猩

We saw two orangutangs in the zoo. 我们在动物园见到两只猩猩。

orchestra /ˈɔːkɪstrə; ˋɔrkɪstrə/ *n* 名

a large group of people who play music together 管弦乐团

Lily plays the cello in the orchestra. 莉莉在管弦乐团演奏大提琴。

***order[1]** /ˈɔːdə; ˋɔrdɚ/ *n* 名

1. （无复数）the way in which a group of things are arranged 次序；顺序

   These books are arranged in alphabetical order. 这些书是按字母顺序排列的。

2. something you are told to do 命令

   Go now! This is an order. 现在就去！这是命令。

3. when you ask a waiter for food or drinks in a restaurant 点菜

   May I take your order? 你要点菜吗？

in order to 为了

Sarah put on a sweater in order to keep warm. 莎拉穿上毛衣保暖。

out of order 出故障；失灵

The lift is out of order. 电梯坏了。

***order²** /ˈɔːdə; ˋɔrdɚ/ *v* 动

1. to tell someone to do something 命令

   "Don't move!" She ordered. "不要动！"她命令道。

2. to ask for something in a restaurant 点菜

   We ordered chicken and vegetables. 我们点了鸡肉和蔬菜。

ordinary /ˈɔːdənəri; ˋɔrdn̩ˌɛrɪ/ *adj* 形

normal or usual 平常的；普通的

This is just an ordinary restaurant. 这不过是一家普通的餐馆。

反义 **extraordinary**

organ /ˈɔːgən; ˋɔrgən/ *n* 名

1. a part of a person or an animal with a special function 器官

   The heart is a very important organ. 心脏是十分重要的器官。

2. a large musical instrument with a keyboard and pipes 管风琴

   He plays the organ in church every Sunday. 他每星期日在教堂里弹奏管风琴。

***organization** /ˌɔːgənaɪˈzeɪʃn; ˌɔrgənəˋzeʃən/ *n* 名

也作：***organisation***【英】

a group of people who meet and do things together 组织；机构

Kevin works for a big organization. 凯文在一家大型机构里工作。

***organize** /ˈɔːgənaɪz; ˋɔrgənˌaɪz/ *v* 动

organizes, organizing, organized, organized | 也作：***organise***【英】

to plan or arrange something carefully 组织；筹划

Our teacher organized a picnic for us. 老师为我们筹备了一次野餐。

orphan /ˈɔːfn; ˋɔrfən/ *n* 名

a child whose parents are dead 孤儿

He became an orphan after his parents were killed in a car crash. 他的父母在撞车事故中丧生后，他变成了孤儿。

***other¹** /ˈʌðə; ˋʌðɚ/ *adj* 形

1. not the same one 另一个的；其余的

   One shoe is dirty, but the other one is clean. 一只鞋子很脏，另一只却很干净。

2. different from this one 别的；其他的

   Do you have any other questions? 你们还有其他的问题吗？

the other day/night 前几天/晚

I met him the other day. 我几天前遇见过他。

***other²** /ˈʌðə; ˋʌðɚ/ *pron* 代

the other people or things 其他的（指人或物）

He was the only student in the classroom — all the others had gone home. 当时教室里只有他一个学生，其他所有人早已回家了。

otherwise /ˈʌðəwaɪz; ˋʌðɚˌwaɪz/ *adv* 副

if not 否则

You have to work harder, otherwise you will fail your exam. 你要用功点，否则考试会不及格。

***ought to** /ˈɔːt tə; ˋɔt tə/ *v* 动

should 应该

We ought to go home now. 我们现在应该回家了。

ounce /aʊns; aʊns/ *n* 名

缩写：***oz***

a unit of weight. There are 16 ounces in one pound. 盎司

The pork weighs five ounces. 这块猪肉重5盎司。

另见 **pound**

***our** /aʊə; aʊr/ *adj* 形

belonging to us 我们的

Our teachers are kind and helpful. 我们的老师都和蔼可亲，乐于助人。

ours /aʊəz; aʊrz/ *pron* 代

something that belongs to us 我们的（东西）

These bicycles are ours. 这些自行车是我们的。

ourselves /aʊəˈselvz; aʊrˋsɛlvz/ *pron* 代

the same people as the subject of the sentence 我们自己

We can see ourselves in the mirror. 我们可以在镜子里看到自己。

by ourselves 我们独自；我们独立

We solved the problem by ourselves. 我们独立解决了问题。

O

***out** /aʊt; aʊt/ *adv* 副

1. away from a place 出去；到外面
   She opened the door and went out. 她开门走出去了。

反义 **in²**

2. not at home or in the place where you work 不在家；不在工作的地方
   He's out but will be back soon. 他不在家，但很快会回来。

反义 **in²**

3. not shining 熄灭的
   The candles were out. 蜡烛熄灭了。

out of（从…里面）出来
She took a handkerchief out of her pocket. 她从口袋里拿出一块手帕。

outdoor /ˌaʊtˈdɔː; ˌaʊtˋdɔr/ *adj* 形

played or done outside a building 室外的；户外的
I like outdoor activities. 我喜欢户外活动。

反义 **indoor**

outdoors /ˌaʊtˈdɔːz; ˌaʊtˋdɔrz/ *adv* 副

outside a building 在室外；在户外
The children are playing outdoors. 孩子们在户外玩耍。

反义 **indoors**

outing /ˈaʊtɪŋ; ˋaʊtɪŋ/ *n* 名

a short trip for fun, usually in a group 短途旅游；远足
We went on an outing last weekend. 我们上周末去远足了。

outline /ˈaʊtlaɪn; ˋaʊtˌlaɪn/ *n* 名

a line showing the shape of something 轮廓；外形
James is drawing the outline of a cat. 詹姆斯在画一只猫的轮廓。

outlying /ˈaʊtˌlaɪ-ɪŋ; ˋaʊtˌlaɪ·ɪŋ/ *adj* 形

far from the main areas of a place 边远的；偏远的
Susan lives on an outlying island. 苏珊住在一个离岛上。

***outside¹** /aʊtˈsaɪd; aʊtˋsaɪd/ *n* 名

the part that is not inside 外面；外部
The outside of a watermelon is green, but the inside is red. 西瓜的外面是绿色的，但里面是红色的。

反义 **inside¹**

***outside²** /aʊtˈsaɪd; aʊtˋsaɪd/ *adv* 副

out of a building or place 在外面
It's very cold outside. 外面很冷。

反义 **inside²**

***outside³** /aʊtˈsaɪd; aʊtˋsaɪd/ *prep* 介

out of a building or place 在…的外面
We waited outside the cinema. 我们在电影院外面等候。

反义 **inside³**

outstanding /aʊtˈstændɪŋ; aʊtˋstændɪŋ/ *adj* 形

very good 杰出的；优秀的
She is an outstanding student. 她是个优秀的学生。

同义 **excellent**

outwards /ˈaʊtwədz; ˋaʊtwɚdz/ *adv* 副【英】

美式：***outward***

away from the middle 向外；往外
The door opens outwards. 这扇门向外开。

反义 **inwards**

***oval** /ˈəʊvl; ˋovl̩/ *n* 名

a shape like an egg 椭圆形；卵形

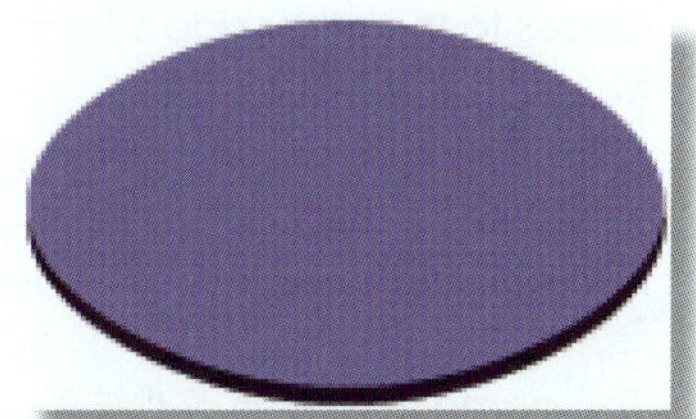

She drew an oval on the paper. 她在纸上画了一个椭圆形。

***oven** /ˈʌvn; ˋʌvən/ *n* 名

a piece of equipment for cooking or heating food 烤箱；烤炉

Bake the cake in the oven for an hour. 把蛋糕放入烤箱内烘一小时。

***over¹** /ˈəʊvə; ˋovɚ/ *prep* 介

1. from one side to the other side 从一边到另一边；越过

Let's jump over the stream. 我们跳过小溪吧。

2. above something 在…上方
   An eagle flew over the harbour. 一只鹰在海港上空飞过。

反义 **under¹**

3. on top of something 在…上面
   Put a blanket over his legs. 把毯子盖在他的腿上。

反义 **under¹**

4. more than 超过；以上
   The shoes cost over $500. 这双鞋子要 500 多元。

反义 **under¹**

***over²** /ˈəʊvə; ˋovɚ/ *adv* 副

1. down to a lying position 倒下
   He knocked the cup over. 他把杯子撞倒了。
2. across to the other side 到另一边；越过
   I saw Jenny and went over. 我见到珍妮便走了过去。
3. if something is over, it has ended 结束
   The game was over. 游戏结束了。

over and over (again) 一次又一次
He listened to the song over and over again. 那首歌他听了一遍又一遍。

Daily conversation 日常会话
over here/there 在这边/那边；在这里/那里
"Has anyone seen my glasses?" "They're over there!" "谁见过我的眼镜吗？""在那边！"

overcame /ˌəʊvəˈkeɪm; ˏovɚˋkem/ *v* 动

the past tense of **overcome**
☆overcome 的过去式

overcoat /ˈəʊvəkəʊt; ˋovɚkot/ *n* 名

a long warm coat 大衣
Put on your overcoat before going out. 外出前穿上大衣。

overcome /ˌəʊvəˈkʌm; ˏovɚˋkʌm/ *v* 动

overcomes, overcoming, overcame, overcome

to be able to control a feeling or problem that prevents you from doing something 控制；克服
You must overcome your fear. 你一定要克服恐惧。

overseas¹ /ˌəʊvəˈsiːz; ˏovɚˋsiz/ *adv* 副

in a foreign country 在海外；在国外
My cousins live overseas. 我的表兄弟在国外居住。

overseas² /ˈəʊvəsiːz; ˋovɚˏsiz/ *adj* 形

from a foreign country 海外的；国外的
She is an overseas student. 她是外国留学生。

overtake /ˌəʊvəˈteɪk; ˏovɚˋtek/ *v* 动

overtakes, overtaking, overtook, overtaken

to pass someone or something going in the same direction 超过；超越
The tortoise overtook the hare. 乌龟超过了兔子。

overtaken /ˌəʊvəˈteɪken; ˏovɚˋtekən/ *v* 动

the past participle of **overtake**
☆overtake 的过去分词

overtook /ˌəʊvəˈtʊk; ˏovɚˋtuk/ *v* 动

the past tense of **overtake**
☆overtake 的过去式

overweight /ˌəʊvəˈweɪt; ˏovɚˋwet/ *adj* 形

too heavy or too fat 超重的；太胖的
This boy is overweight. 这个男孩太胖了。

owe /əʊ; o/ *v* 动

owes, owing, owed, owed

1. to have to pay money back to someone who has lent you it 欠（钱）
   Charles owes me $100. 查理欠我 100 元。
2. to feel grateful to someone for something 感激
   I owe a lot to my teachers for the good results. 取得好成绩，我十分感激我的老师。

***owl** /aʊl; aul/ *n* 名

a bird that has large eyes and hunts at night 猫头鹰

Owls catch small animals at night. 猫头鹰在夜间捕捉小动物。

***own¹** /əʊn; on/ *adj* 形

belonging to you 自己的
Iris built her own house. 艾丽丝建造了自己的房子。

own² /əʊn; on/ *v* 动

if you own something, it belongs to you 拥有

My parents own this house. 我的父母拥有这所房子。

owner /ˈəʊnə; ˋonɚ/ *n* 名

the person that something belongs to 物主；拥有者

The man wants to see the owner of the shop. 这个男人要见店主。

***ox** /ɒks; ɑks/ *n* 名

复数：***oxen***

a large male cow used to work on farms 公牛

The ox is eating grass. 那头牛在吃草。

另见 **bull, cow**

oyster /ˈɔɪstə; ˋɔɪstɚ/ *n* 名

a sea animal that lives in a hard shell and makes pearls 生蚝；牡蛎

There is a pearl inside the oyster! 生蚝里有一颗珍珠！

oz

the short form of **ounce** ☆ ounce 的缩写

Pp

***pack**[1] /pæk; pæk/ *v* 动

to put things into a bag, box, etc 把…装箱；收拾行李

Jane packed her bags and left. 简收拾好行李后离开了。

反义 **unpack**

***pack**[2] /pæk; pæk/ *n* 名

a small container in which things are sold, usually made of paper 小包；小盒

Eve gave me a pack of gum. 伊芙给了我一包口香糖。

比较 **packet**

package /ˈpækɪdʒ; `pækɪdʒ/ *n* 名

something that is wrapped in paper or put in a box, then sent by mail 包裹

Alex sent me a package from New York. 亚历克斯从纽约给我寄来一个包裹。

用法 package 多用于美式英语，英式英语通常用 parcel。

***packet** /ˈpækɪt; `pækɪt/ *n* 名

a small container in which things are sold, usually made of paper, plastic or cardboard 小包；小盒

This box contains ten packets of biscuits. 这个盒子里有 10 包饼干。

比较 **pack**[2]

pad /pæd; pæd/ *n* 名

a small book for writing or drawing 便笺本

I always keep a pad of paper by the phone. 我一向在电话旁边放一本便笺本。

paddle[1] /ˈpædl; `pædḷ/ *n* 名

a piece of wood with a flat end that you use to make a small boat move through the water 短桨

The paddle dropped into the water. 短桨掉进水里了。

比较 **oar**

paddle[2] /ˈpædl; `pædḷ/ *v* 动

paddles, paddling, paddled, paddled

to move a small boat with a paddle 用短桨划（小船）

They paddled the boat to the beach. 他们把小船划到海滩。

比较 **row**[2]

***page** /peɪdʒ; pedʒ/ *n* 名

one side or both sides of a piece of paper in a book, newspaper, etc （书、报纸等的）一页；一版

A few pages of the book are missing. 这本书有几页不见了。

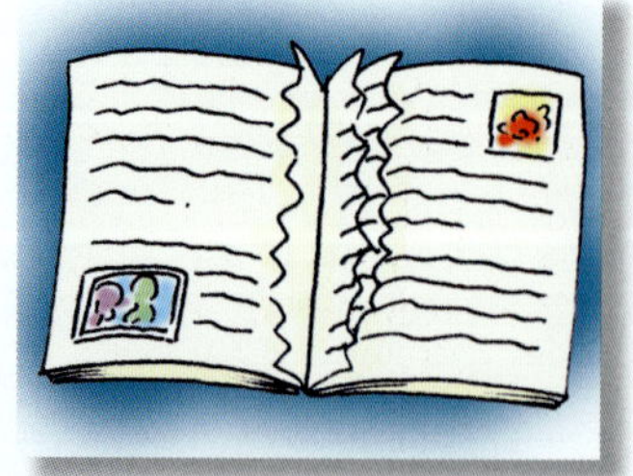

pagoda /pəˈgəʊdə; pə`godə/ *n* 名

a Buddhist building that has several floors（佛）塔

There is an old pagoda in the temple. 寺院里有座古老的佛塔。

paid /peɪd; ped/ *v* 动

the past tense and past participle of **pay** ☆pay 的过去式和过去分词

***pain** /peɪn; pen/ *n* 名

the feeling you have when you are hurt 痛；疼痛

I have a pain in my neck. 我脖子痛。

painful /ˈpeɪnfl; `penfəl/ *adj* 形

if part of your body is painful, you feel pain in it 疼痛的

My leg is still painful. 我的腿仍然很痛。

***paint**[1] /peɪnt; pent/ *n* 名

a liquid that you put on a wall, a picture, etc with a brush 油漆；颜料

The paint on the wall is wet. 墙上的油漆还未干。

***paint**[2] /peɪnt; pent/ *v* 动

1. to put paint on a surface to change its colour 给…上油漆

   They painted the wall white. 他们把墙壁漆成了白色。

2. to make a picture using paint （用颜料）绘画

   Amy loves painting flowers. 艾米喜欢画花。

比较 **draw**[1]

paintbrush /ˈpeɪntbrʌʃ; ˋpentˏbrʌʃ/ *n* 名

复数 : ***paintbrushes***

a brush that you use for painting 漆刷；画笔

Ellen cleaned her paintbrushes after painting her picture. 艾伦画完画后把画笔洗干净。

painter /ˈpeɪntə; ˋpentɚ/ *n* 名

1. someone who paints pictures 画家

   Picasso was a famous painter. 毕加索是著名画家。

2. someone whose job is painting walls, etc 油漆工

   We hired a painter to paint our house. 我们雇用了一名油漆工粉刷房子。

painting /ˈpeɪntɪŋ; ˋpentɪŋ/ *n* 名

a painted picture 绘画；油画

There is a large painting on the wall. 墙上挂着一幅很大的油画。

***pair** /peə; pɛr/ *n* 名

two things of the same kind that are used together 一双；一对

She was wearing a pair of red socks. 她穿着一双红色袜子。

in pairs 成对的

They are working in pairs to play the game. 他们两人一组玩这个游戏。

用法 a pair of 可以指两个一起使用的物件，例如 a pair of shoes（一双鞋子）、a pair of earrings（一对耳环）等，也可以指由两个部分连接的物件，例如 a pair of trousers（一条裤子）、a pair of scissors（一把剪刀）等。

pajamas /pəˈdʒɑːməz; pəˋdʒæməz/ *plural n* 复数名词【美】

英式 **pyjamas**

pal /pæl; pæl/ *n* 名

a friend 朋友

We've been pals for years. 我们是多年的好朋友了。

用法 一般用于口语中。

palace /ˈpæləs; ˋpælɪs/ *n* 名

a very large house where a king or queen lives 王宫；宫殿

Jessica visited a palace in Europe. 杰西卡参观了欧洲的一座王宫。

pale /peɪl; pel/ *adj* 形

paler, palest

1. having a skin colour that is very white 苍白的

   You look pale. Are you all right? 你的脸色很苍白。没事吧？

2. light in colour 浅色的

   Ted wore a pale blue jacket. 泰德穿了一件浅蓝色的外套。

palm /pɑːm; pam/ *n* 名

1. the inside surface of your hand that you hold things with 手掌；手心

   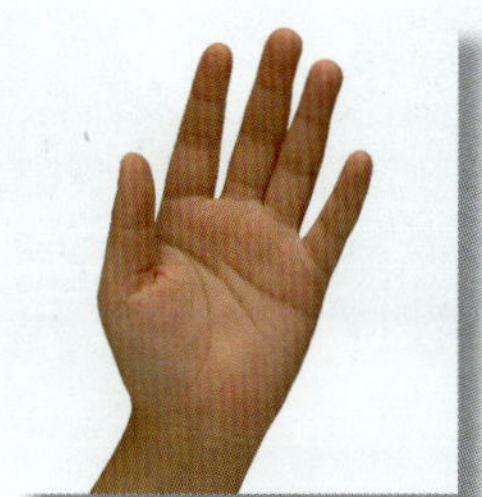

   She counted the coins in her palm. 她数了一下手心里的硬币。

2. （也作 : ***palm tree***）a tall tree with large leaves at the top 棕榈树

   There is a palm tree in the desert. 沙漠中有一棵棕榈树。

***pan** /pæn; pæn/ *n* 名

a round, metal container, usually with a long handle, used for cooking 平底锅

This pan is good for frying eggs. 这个平底锅用来煎蛋很好。

pancake /ˈpænkeɪk; ˋpænˏkek/ *n* 名

a thin, round cake that is cooked in a pan 薄饼

Tony likes to eat pancakes. 托尼喜欢吃薄饼。

***panda** /ˈpændə; ˋpændə/ *n* 名

a big, black and white animal that looks like a bear and lives in China 熊猫

I like pandas because they are cute. 我喜欢熊猫，因为它们很可爱。

P

panic /ˈpænɪk; ˋpænɪk/ *v* 动

panics, panicking, panicked, panicked

to suddenly feel frightened so that you cannot think clearly 惊慌；恐慌

I panicked when the fire broke out. 起火时我吓得手足无措。

pants /pænts; pænts/ *plural n* 复数名词

1. 【英】(美式：***underpants***) a piece of clothing that you wear under your trousers 内裤
   I change my pants every day. 我每天更换内裤。
2. 【美】裤子；长裤 英式 **trousers**

papaya /pəˈpaɪə; pəˋpaɪə/ *n* 名

a large, sweet, yellow and green fruit 木瓜

We had a nice papaya after dinner. 晚饭后我们吃了个美味的木瓜。

P

***paper** /ˈpeɪpə; ˋpepɚ/ *n* 名

1. (无复数) thin material used for writing on, wrapping things, etc 纸
   Don't waste paper! 不要浪费纸张！

用法 paper 是不可数名词，如要表示一张、两张纸，用 a piece/sheet of paper、two pieces/sheets of paper 等。

2. a newspaper 报纸
   My father reads a paper every morning. 我的爸爸每天早上看报纸。

parachute /ˈpærəʃuːt; ˋpærəˌʃut/ *n* 名

a thing that makes you fall slowly and safely to the ground from a plane 降落伞

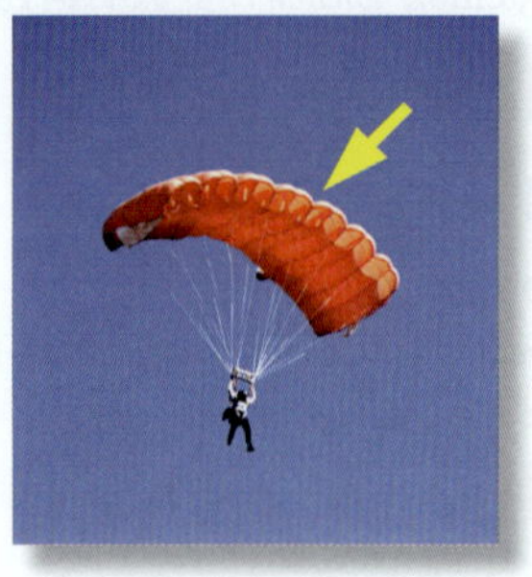

He put on a parachute and jumped out of the plane. 他穿上降落伞，从飞机上跳了下来。

parade /pəˈreɪd; pəˋred/ *n* 名

a celebration of a special day or event when people walk in a large group down the street (庆祝)游行

We went to the New Year parade. 我们参加了新年游行。

***paragraph** /ˈpærəgrɑːf; ˋpærəˌgræf/ *n* 名

a part of a piece of writing that starts on a new line (文章的)段落

The essay contains three paragraphs. 这篇文章分为三个段落。

parallel /ˈpærəlel; ˋpærəˌlɛl/ *adj* 形

if two lines are parallel, they are always at the same distance from each other 平行的

The two rows of trees are parallel to each other. 这两排树相互平行。

***parcel** /ˈpɑːsl; ˋparsl̩/ *n* 名

something that is wrapped in paper or put in a box, then sent by mail 包裹

This parcel was sent from Australia. 这个包裹是从澳洲寄来的。

用法 parcel 多用于英式英语，美式英语通常用 package。

***pardon** /ˈpɑːdn; ˋpardn̩/ *interj* 感叹

a word you use to ask someone to say something again because you did not hear it 对不起，你说什么？(请别人再说一遍)

Pardon? I didn't hear you. 对不起，我听不到你说什么。

***parent** /ˈpeərənt; ˋpɛrənt/ *n* 名

a father or mother 父亲；母亲

Parents should take care of their children. 父母应该照顾自己的子女。

***park¹** /pɑːk; park/ *n* 名

a public place that has grass or trees, where people can walk or relax 公园

We usually go for a walk in the park after dinner. 我们吃饭后通常去公园散步。

park² /pɑːk; park/ *v* 动

to leave a car somewhere for a

period of time 停放（汽车）
Paul parked his car near the bank. 保罗把汽车停在银行附近。

parking /'pɑ:kɪŋ; `parkɪŋ/ *n* 名

无复数

a space where you can leave a car 停车处；停车位
There is free parking at the hotel. 那家酒店有免费停车位。

***parrot** /'pærət; `pærət/ *n* 名

a bird which has bright and colourful feathers 鹦鹉

This parrot can say a lot of words. 这只鹦鹉会说很多单词。

***part** /pɑ:t; part/ *n* 名

1. a piece of something 部分
   The front part of the bus was damaged. 公共汽车的前部损坏了。
2. （无复数）some, but not all, of something（某物的）部分；局部
   I don't like this part of the story. 我不喜欢故事的这个部分。

***particular** /pə'tɪkjʊlə; pɚ`tɪkjəlɚ/ *adj* 形

this one and not any other 特定的；特指的
Are you looking for a particular book? 你在找某一本书吗？

***particularly** /pə'tɪkjʊləli; pɚ`tɪkjəlɚlɪ/ *adv* 副

more than usual; especially 特别；尤其
She was particularly happy that day. 她那天特别高兴。

***partner** /'pɑ:tnə; `partnɚ/ *n* 名

someone who does something with you 同伴；搭档
They are dancing partners. 他们是舞伴。

part-time /ˌpɑ:t 'taɪm; ˏpart `taɪm/ *adj* 形

working for only part of the day or week 兼职的
She found a part-time job. 她找到了一份兼职工作。

***party** /'pɑ:ti; `partɪ/ *n* 名

复数：*parties*

an occasion when people meet to enjoy themselves 聚会；派对

I will have my birthday party next week. 我将在下星期举行生日派对。

***pass¹** /pɑ:s; pæs/ *v* 动

passes, passing, passed, passed

1. to go past someone or something 经过；走过
   The car passed the flower shop. 汽车驶过那家花店。

比较 **past¹**

2. to give something to someone 递给；传递
   She passed a note to me. 她递了一张纸条给我。
3. to succeed in an examination or a test（考试）及格
   All of us passed the exam. 我们全部都通过考试了。

反义 **fail**

> **At a restaurant 餐厅里**
> *"Pass the pepper, please." "Here you are."* "请把胡椒粉递过来。""给你。"

pass² /pɑ:s; pæs/ *n* 名

复数：*passes*

a piece of paper that allows you to go somewhere 通行证
I showed my bus pass to the driver. 我向司机出示公共汽车乘车证。

passage /'pæsɪdʒ; `pæsɪdʒ/ *n* 名

1. a long, narrow way in a building that connects rooms 通道；走廊

P

Our room is at the end of the passage. 我们的房间在走廊的尽头。

2. a short part of a piece of writing （文章的）一段

   The teacher asked me to read this passage. 老师叫我把这一段读出来。

passenger /ˈpæsɪndʒə; ˋpæsṇdʒɚ/ *n* 名

someone who is travelling in a bus, train, plane, etc 乘客；旅客

Passengers should not eat or drink on a bus. 乘客不应在公共汽车上饮食。

passive /ˈpæsɪv; ˋpæsɪv/ *adj* 形

often not willing to do or change things 被动的；消极的

Some pupils in the class are very quiet and passive. 这个班上有些学生很文静，很被动。

反义 **active**

passport /ˈpɑːspɔːt; ˋpæsˌpɔrt/ *n* 名

a small book that shows who you are and allows you to go to another country 护照

You need a passport to travel to other countries. 要有护照才能到国外旅行。

password /ˈpɑːswɜːd; ˋpæsˌwɝd/ *n* 名

【电脑】the secret letters or numbers that you type to start using a computer or program 密码

Enter your user name and password. 输入你的用户名和密码。

***past¹** /pɑːst; pæst/ *prep* 介

1. up to and beyond something 经过；路过

   I walked past the post office. 我路过那家邮局。

比较 **pass¹**

2. later than a particular time （时间）超过；晚于

   It's ten past three. Let's have tea. 现在是 3 点 10 分，我们去吃下午茶吧。

***past²** /pɑːst; pæst/ *adj* 形

used about things that happened before now 过去的；以前的

I learned a lot from my past mistakes. 我从过去的错误中学到许多东西。

***past³** /pɑːst; pæst/ *n* 名

无复数

the time before now 过去；以前

In the past, this city was a fishing village. 这个城市过去是个渔村。

反义 **future**

pasta /ˈpæstə; ˋpɑstə/ *n* 名

无复数

an Italian food that is made from flour and water and has different shapes 意大利面

The pasta looks like shells. 这种意大利面很像贝壳。

paste /peɪst; pest/ *v* 动

pastes, pasting, pasted, pasted

1. to stick something to something else with glue 粘贴

   Our teacher pasted our drawings onto the board. 老师把我们的图画贴在板上。

2. 【电脑】to put something that you have cut or copied from a computer document in a new place 粘贴

   I paste the picture below the words. 我把图片粘贴在文字下面。

另见 **cut and paste**（见 **cut¹**）

pat /pæt; pæt/ *v* 动

pats, patting, patted, patted

to touch someone or something softly with your flat hand 轻拍

Diana patted the dog. 黛安娜轻轻拍了拍那条狗。

***path** /pɑːθ; pæθ/ *n* 名

a narrow road for people to walk on 小路；小径

We followed the path to the beach. 我们沿着这条小径走到海滩。

***patient¹** /ˈpeɪʃnt; ˋpeʃənt/ *n* 名

someone who is treated by a doctor 病人

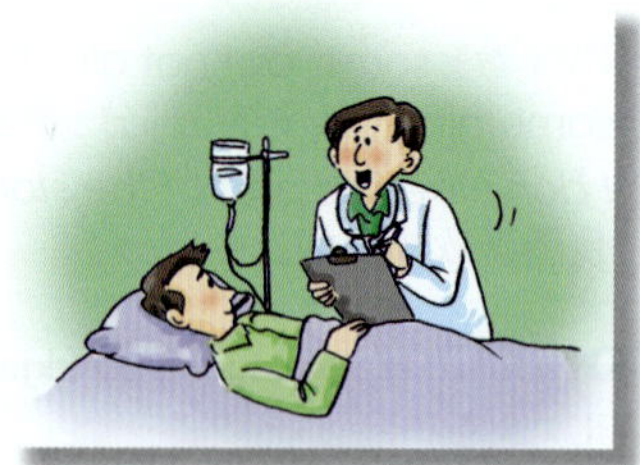

Several patients are waiting to see the doctor. 有几个病人正等候见医生。

***patient²** /ˈpeɪʃnt; ˋpeʃənt/ *adj* 形

able to wait for a long time or accept something difficult without feeling angry 有耐心的；忍耐的

P

You have to be patient and wait. 你得耐心等待。

反义 **impatient**

patiently /ˈpeɪʃntli; ˋpeʃəntlɪ/ *adv* 副

without feeling angry 耐心地；忍耐地

We waited patiently at the bus stop. 我们在公共汽车站耐心地等候。

反义 **impatiently**

patrol /pəˈtrəʊl; pəˋtrol/ *n* 名

when police, soldiers, etc go around a place to check that it is safe 巡逻；巡查

Police were on patrol in the street. 警方在街上巡逻。

***pattern** /ˈpætn; ˋpætən/ *n* 名

1. a regular design of shapes and colours 图案；花样

The cloth has a beautiful pattern. 这块布的图案很漂亮。

2. the regular way in which something happens or is done 模式

The murders seem to follow the same pattern. 这几宗谋杀案似乎都是同一个模式。

pavement /ˈpeɪvmənt; ˋpevmənt/ *n* 名【英】

美式：***sidewalk***

a path at the side of a road for people to walk on 人行道

You should not cycle on the pavement. 在人行道上不能骑自行车。

paw /pɔ:; pɔ/ *n* 名

the foot of an animal such as a cat, dog, or bear（动物的）爪

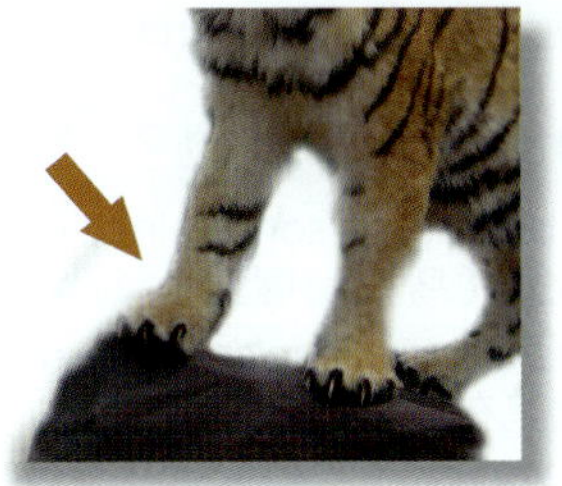

Tigers have very strong paws. 老虎的爪子很有力。

***pay** /peɪ; pe/ *v* 动

pays, paying, paid, paid

to give somebody money when you buy something 付款；支付

I paid ten dollars for the apples. 我付了 10 元买这些苹果。

pay attention 注意；留心

You must pay attention to the teacher. 你得专心听老师说的话。

PC /ˌpi: ˈsi:; ˌpi ˋsi/ *n* 名

the short form of **personal computer** ☆personal computer 的缩写

PE /ˌpi: ˈi:; ˌpi ˋi/ *n* 名

the short form of **physical education** ☆physical education 的缩写

***pea** /pi:; pi/ *n* 名

a small, round, green seed that you can eat 豌豆

I had a bowl of pea soup. 我喝了一碗豌豆汤。

peace /pi:s; pis/ *n* 名

无复数

1. a time when there is no war 和平

   After many years of war, the country finally had peace. 经过多年战争，这个国家最终得到了和平。

反义 **war**

2. a time when it is quiet and calm 平静；宁静

   I enjoy the peace of the countryside. 我享受郊外的宁静。

***peach** /pi:tʃ; pitʃ/ *n* 名

复数：***peaches***

a round, pink or yellow juicy fruit that has a soft skin 桃子

My grandmother loves to eat peaches. 我的祖母喜欢吃桃子。

P

peacock /ˈpi:kɒk; ˋpiˌkɑk/ *n* 名

a large male bird with long blue and green tail feathers 孔雀

The peacock is spreading its beautiful tail. 那只孔雀开屏了，十分美丽。

***peak** /pi:k; pik/ *n* 名

the top of a hill or mountain 山顶；

山峰

We could see the mountain peak from here. 我们从这儿可以看见山顶。

***peanut** /ˈpiːnʌt; ˋpiˏnʌt/ *n* 名

a small nut in a thin shell which grows under the ground 花生

Robert likes to eat peanuts when he watches TV. 罗伯特喜欢边看电视边吃花生。

peanut butter /ˌpiːnʌt ˈbʌtə; ˋpinʌt ˏbʌtɚ/ *n* 名

无复数

a soft food made from peanuts that you put on bread 花生酱

I like eating peanut butter sandwiches. 我喜欢吃花生酱三明治。

***pear** /peə; pɛr/ *n* 名

a sweet, juicy, green or yellow fruit 梨

She cut the pear into cubes. 她把梨切成小方块。

pearl /pɜːl; pɝl/ *n* 名

a round, white jewel that comes from an oyster 珍珠

Eliza was wearing a pearl necklace. 艾丽莎戴着一条珍珠项链。

peck /pek; pɛk/ *v* 动

if a bird pecks something, it bites it quickly（鸟）啄；啄食

The birds are pecking at the worms. 那些鸟在啄食虫儿。

pedal /ˈpedl; ˋpɛdḷ/ *n* 名

a part of a bicycle, car, etc that you push down with your foot 踏板

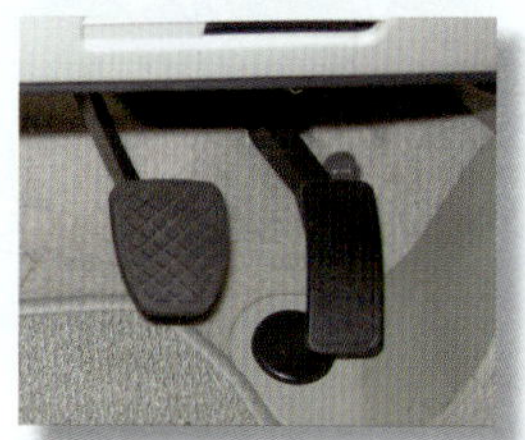

The bicycle pedal is broken. 那辆自行车的踏板坏了。

pedestrian /pəˈdestriən; pəˋdɛstrɪən/ *n* 名

someone who is walking in the street 行人

Two pedestrians were hit by the car. 两名行人被那辆汽车撞倒了。

pedestrian crossing 人行横道

It is safe to use the pedestrian crossings. 在人行横道上过马路很安全。

peel¹ /piːl; pil/ *n* 名

the skin of a fruit or vegetable（水果或蔬菜的）外皮

I took the peel off the orange. 我剥掉了橙子皮。

用法 peel 多指较厚的外皮，如橙皮、柠檬皮等。

peel² /piːl; pil/ *v* 动

to remove the skin of a fruit or vegetable 剥去；削去（水果或蔬菜）的皮

He peeled an apple. 他削了一只苹果。

peel off 剥落；脱落

The paint was peeling off the walls. 墙上的油漆正在剥落。

***pen** /pen; pɛn/ *n* 名

a thing you use to write with ink 笔；钢笔

Can I borrow your pen? 我可以借用你的笔吗?

***pencil** /ˈpensl; ˋpɛnsḷ/ *n* 名

a thing made of wood that you use for writing and drawing 铅笔

Jack drew a picture with a pencil. 杰克用铅笔画了一幅画。

pencil case 铅笔盒；铅笔袋

There are three pencils, a rubber and a ruler in my pencil case. 我的铅笔盒里有三支铅笔、一块橡皮和一把尺。

pencil sharpener 卷笔刀

Angela sharpened her pencils with a pencil sharpener. 安琪拉用卷笔刀削铅笔。

P

penguin /ˈpeŋgwɪn; ˋpɛŋgwɪn/ *n* 名

a large, black and white bird that lives in very cold places 企鹅

Penguins can swim but cannot fly. 企鹅只会游泳不会飞行。

peninsula /pəˈnɪnsjʊlə; pəˋnɪnsələ/ *n* 名

a piece of land that is almost completely surrounded by water 半岛

This is a map of the Kowloon Peninsula. 这是九龙半岛的地图。

***people** /ˈpiːpl; ˋpipl̩/ *plural n* 复数名词

men, women and children; the plural of person 人；人们（person 的复数形式）

A lot of people were at the meeting. 会议上有许多人。

***pepper** /ˈpepə; ˋpɛpə/ *n* 名

1. （无复数）a powder you use to give food a hot taste 胡椒粉
   Frank added pepper to his soup. 法兰克在汤里撒了胡椒粉。
2. a green, red or yellow vegetable that is almost empty inside 甜椒；灯笼椒

I cooked the beef with green peppers. 我用青椒烧牛肉。

***per** /pə; pɚ; *strong* 强读 pɜː; pɝ/ *prep* 介

for each 每；每一

The ticket is $50 per adult and $20 per child. 成人门票每位 50 元，儿童每位 20 元。

percent, per cent /pəˈsent; pɚˋsɛnt/ *n* 名

无复数

out of a hundred (%) 百分之…

Forty per cent of the workers are women. 工人中百分之四十是女性。

***perfect** /ˈpɜːfɪkt; ˋpɝfɪkt/ *adj* 形

without any mistakes; as good as possible 完美的；最佳的

Her English is perfect. 她的英语非常地道。

***perform** /pəˈfɔːm; pɚˋfɔrm/ *v* 动

1. to do something to entertain people 表演；演出
   The dancers will perform tonight. 舞蹈演员今晚会表演。

2. to do something such as a test, an experiment or a piece of work 做；执行
   The doctor performed some tests on him. 医生给他做了几个检验。

***performance** /pəˈfɔːməns; pɚˋfɔrməns/ *n* 名

1. a time when someone performs a play or a piece of music 表演；演出
   The performance will start at seven o'clock. 演出将于 7 点开始。
2. how well you do something 表现
   The team's performance in the match was really good. 这个队在比赛中的表现非常好。

***perhaps** /pəˈhæps; pɚˋhæps/ *adv* 副

used to say that something may be true, but you are not sure 可能；也许

Perhaps it will rain tomorrow. 明天可能会下雨。

同义 **maybe, possibly**

Daily conversation 日常会话
"Do you think Lily is angry with us?" "I don't know. Perhaps." "你觉得莉莉是在生我们的气吗？""我不知道，也许是吧。"

***period** /ˈpɪəriəd; ˋpɪrɪəd/ *n* 名

1. a length of time 一段时间；时期
   Simon lived in Canada for a long period of time. 西蒙在加拿大住了很长一段时间。
2. a lesson at school 一节（课）
   We have two periods of music every week. 我们每星期有两节音乐课。

同义 **lesson**

permission /pəˈmɪʃn; pɚˋmɪʃən/ *n* 名

无复数

allowing someone to do something 许可；允许

She got permission to leave school early. 她得到允许提早离开学校。

permit /pəˈmɪt; pɚˋmɪt/ *v* 动

permits, permitting, permitted, permitted

to allow someone to do something 准许；允许

Smoking is not permitted in the cinema. 电影院里不准吸烟。

用法 permit 用于较正式的场合，一般情况可用 allow 或 let。

P

***person** /ˈpɜːsn; ˋpɝsn̩/ *n* 名

复数：***people/persons***

a man, woman or child 人

Kim is an interesting person. 基姆是个有趣的人。

in person 亲自；亲身

You have to get your parcel in person. 你必须亲自领取包裹。

用法 person 的复数通常用 people，persons 是十分正式的用语。

***personal** /ˈpɜːsənəl; ˋpɝsn̩l/ *adj* 形

belonging to one person 个人的；私人的

Put your personal belongings in the locker. 把你的私人物品放在锁柜里。

personal computer /ˌpɜːsnəl kəmˈpjuːtə; ˌpɝsn̩l kəmˋpjutɚ/ *n* 名

缩写：***PC***

【电脑】a computer that is used by one person 个人电脑

I use a personal computer at home. 我在家里使用个人电脑。

pest /pest; pɛst/ *n* 名

an insect or a small animal that is harmful 害虫；有害小动物

The smell of food attracts pests. 食物的气味吸引害虫。

***pet** /pet; pɛt/ *n* 名

an animal you keep at home 宠物

Daniel has a dog as a pet. 丹尼尔养了一只狗作为宠物。

petal /ˈpetl; ˋpɛtl̩/ *n* 名

one of the coloured parts of a flower 花瓣

This flower has eight petals. 这种花有 8 片花瓣。

petrol /ˈpetrəl; ˋpɛtrəl/ *n* 名【英】

无复数｜美式：***gas***

a liquid used in a car to make its engine work 汽油

She had to put petrol in her car. 她的车子需要加油。

petrol station【英】加油站（美式：***gas station***）

Mr Roberts drove his car to the petrol station. 罗伯茨先生把车子驶去了加油站。

phone[1] /fəʊn; fon/ *n* 名

a machine you use to speak to someone in another place 电话

Can you answer the phone? 你接一下电话好吗？

同义 **telephone**[1]

on the phone 在通电话

She is on the phone right now. 她正在打电话。

phone[2] /fəʊn; fon/ *v* 动

phones, phoning, phoned, phoned

to speak to someone by phone 打电话

I will phone again later. 我过一会儿再打电话。

同义 **telephone**[2]

photo / ˈfəʊtəʊ; ˋfoto/ *n* 名

a photograph 照片；相片

I took a photo of the flower. 我给那朵花拍了一张照片。

用法 photo 多用于非正式的场合。

photocopier /ˈfəʊtəʊˌkɒpiə; ˋfotoˌkapɪɚ/ *n* 名

a machine that makes copies of documents 影印机；复印机

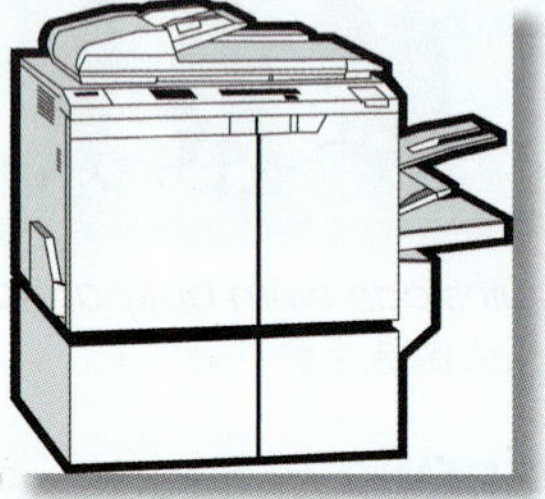

There are two photocopiers in the library. 图书馆里有两台影印机。

photocopy[1] /ˈfəʊtəʊˌkɒpi; ˋfotoˌkapɪ/ *n* 名

复数：***photocopies***

a copy of something that you make using a photocopier 影印本；复印件

Polly made a photocopy of the page. 波莉复印了这一页。

photocopy[2] /ˈfəʊtəʊˌkɒpi; ˋfotoˌkapɪ/ *v* 动

photocopies, photocopying, photocopied, photocopied

to make a copy of a document using a photocopier 影印；复印

He photocopied his identity card. 他复印了身份证。

***photograph** /ˈfəʊtəgrɑːf; ˋfotəˌgræf/ *n* 名

也作：***photo***

a picture made with a camera 照片；相片

The man's photograph was on the first page of the paper. 那男人的照片刊登在了报纸的头版上。

photographer /fəˈtɒgrəfə; fəˋtagrəfɚ/ *n* 名

someone who takes photographs,

usually as a job 照相者；摄影师

Joe is a photographer for a newspaper. 乔是一名报纸摄影师。

phrase /freɪz; frez/ *n* 名

a group of words that form part of a sentence, for example "in the morning" 片语；短语（指构成句子的词组，例如 in the morning）

***physical** /ˈfɪzɪkl; ˋfɪzɪkḷ/ *adj* 形

about your body, not your mind 身体的

You need to do more physical exercise. 你需要多锻炼身体。

physical education /ˌfɪzɪkl ˌedjʊˈkeɪʃn; ˏfɪzɪkḷ ˏɛdʒəˋkeʃən/ *n* 名

无复数 | 缩写：***PE***

a school subject in which sport and physical exercise are taught 体育（课）

We played football in the PE lesson today. 我们今天上体育课时踢足球。

pianist /ˈpiːənɪst; piˋænɪst/ *n* 名

someone who plays the piano 钢琴演奏者；钢琴家

He is a famous pianist. 他是一位著名钢琴家。

***piano** /piˈænəʊ; piˋæno/ *n* 名

a large musical instrument that you play by pressing a keyboard 钢琴

Julia is learning to play the piano. 朱莉娅在学弹钢琴。

***pick** /pɪk; pɪk/ *v* 动

1. to choose someone or something 选择；挑选

   He picked the best person to help him. 他选了最好的人来帮助他。

2. to take a flower or fruit from a plant or tree 采；摘

   The monkey is picking coconuts. 猴子正在摘椰子。

pick someone/something up 接某人；拾起某物

I'll pick you up at the airport at 3 p.m. 我下午 3 点来机场接你。

Matthew picked up the coins on the ground. 马修拾起地上的硬币。

pickpocket /ˈpɪkˌpɒkɪt; ˋpɪkˏpɑkɪt/ *n* 名

a person who steals things from your pocket 扒手

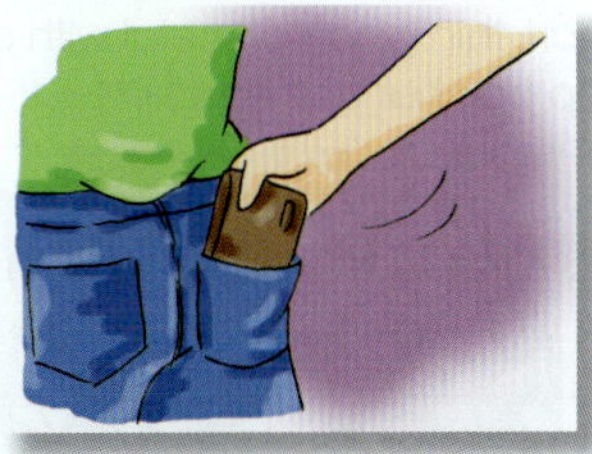

The policeman caught the pickpocket. 警察捉住了扒手。

***picnic** /ˈpɪknɪk; ˋpɪknɪk/ *n* 名

a meal that you eat outdoors 野餐

We had a picnic in the park. 我们在公园野餐。

***picture** /ˈpɪktʃə; ˋpɪktʃɚ/ *n* 名

a drawing, painting or photograph 图画；照片

I drew a picture of a lion. 我画了一幅狮子的图画。

This is a picture of my family. 这张是我家的全家福。

***pie** /paɪ; paɪ/ *n* 名

a baked dish with fruit, meat, etc 馅饼

Jimmy ate a piece of apple pie. 吉米吃了一块苹果馅饼。

比较 **tart**

P

***piece** /piːs; pis/ *n* 名

a part or bit of something 一片；一块；一件

He cut the cake into eight pieces. 他把蛋糕切成 8 块。

用法 a piece of 用于不可数名词之前，例如 a piece of bread（一

块面包）、a piece of paper（一张纸）、a piece of furniture（一件家具）等。

pier /pɪə; pɪr/ *n* 名

a place where boats can stop for people to get on or off 码头

The boat has left the pier. 小船已离开了码头。

***pig** /pɪg; pɪg/ *n* 名

a fat farm animal 猪

Farmers keep pigs for their meat. 农夫养猪以供食用。

***pigeon** /ˈpɪdʒən; ˋpɪdʒən/ *n* 名

a grey or white bird with short legs 鸽子

The man is feeding the pigeons. 那个男人在喂鸽子。

pile /paɪl; paɪl/ *n* 名

a number of things that have been put on top of each other 一堆；一叠

There is a pile of files on the desk. 书桌上有一堆文件夹。

pill /pɪl; pɪl/ *n* 名

a small, hard piece of medicine 药丸；药片

The doctor told me to take the pills before going to bed. 医生叫我睡前要服药。

同义 **tablet**

***pillow** /ˈpɪləʊ; ˋpɪlo/ *n* 名

a soft thing that you put your head on when you sleep 枕头

My pillow is made of cotton and is very comfortable. 我的枕头是棉花制成的，十分舒适。

***pilot** /ˈpaɪlət; ˋpaɪlət/ *n* 名

someone who controls a plane 飞行员；飞机驾驶员

The pilot said that the plane would land in five minutes. 飞行员说飞机将于5分钟后降落。

***pin[1]** /pɪn; pɪn/ *n* 名

a short, thin piece of metal with a sharp point at one end 别针；大头针

She fixed a flower to her coat with a pin. 她用别针把花朵固定在外套上。

pin[2] /pɪn; pɪn/ *v* 动

pins, pinning, pinned, pinned

to join or fasten things with a pin 把…别住；把…钉住

We pinned our pictures to the board. 我们把图画钉在板上。

***pineapple** /ˈpaɪnæpl; ˋpaɪnˌæpḷ/ *n* 名

a large, juicy, yellow fruit with a hard skin 菠萝；凤梨

I like pineapple juice. 我喜欢喝菠萝汁。

ping-pong /ˈpɪŋ pɒŋ; ˋpɪŋ pɑŋ/ *n* 名

无复数

a game that you play by hitting a small ball across a net on a table 乒乓球（运动）

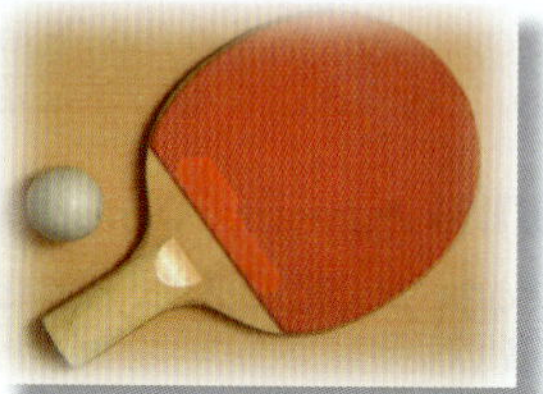

We played ping-pong after school. 我们放学后去打乒乓球。

同义 **table tennis**

***pink[1]** /pɪŋk; pɪŋk/ *adj* 形

pale red 粉红色的

Winnie is wearing a pink dress. 温妮穿着一条粉红色的连身裙。

***pink²** /pɪŋk; pɪŋk/ *n* 名

a pale red colour 粉红色

The wall was painted in pink. 墙壁被漆成了粉红色。

pip /pɪp; pɪp/ *n* 名

a small seed in a fruit such as an apple or orange（苹果或橙子的）果核

This orange has a lot of pips. 这个橙子有很多核。

pipe /paɪp; paɪp/ *n* 名

1. a tube through which a liquid or gas flows 管子；管道
   The water pipe has burst. 这根水管爆裂了。

2. a thing used for smoking 烟斗

Mr Brown is smoking a pipe. 布朗先生在抽烟斗。

pirate /ˈpaɪərət; ˋpaɪrət/ *n* 名

someone who attacks ships and steals things from them 海盗

The pirates stole all the jewellery from the ship. 海盗抢走了那艘船上所有的珠宝。

pity¹ /ˈpɪti; ˋpɪtɪ/ *n* 名

无复数

a sad feeling for someone who is unhappy, poor, etc 同情；怜悯

I feel pity for the family. 我很同情那家人。

Daily conversation 日常会话

What a pity 真遗憾；真可惜

"I can't go to your party." "What a pity!" "我不能参加你的聚会了。" "太可惜了！"

pity² /ˈpɪti; ˋpɪtɪ/ *v* 动

pities, pitying, pitied, pitied

to feel sad for someone who is unhappy, poor, etc 同情；可怜

Some people pitied the beggars and gave them money. 有些人同情那些乞丐，给他们钱。

***pizza** /ˈpiːtsə; ˋpitsə/ *n* 名

a flat, round piece of bread with tomatoes, meat, cheese, etc on top 意大利薄饼；披萨饼

We ordered a ham and cheese pizza. 我们点了一份火腿干酪披萨饼。

***place¹** /pleɪs; ples/ *n* 名

1. a particular building, town or country 地方；场所
   She has been to a lot of places over the world. 她去过世界上许多地方。
2. a particular area, point or position 地点；位置
   Put the books in the right place. 把这些书本放在适当的位置。

in place of someone/something 代替某人/某物

I went to the ceremony in place of my brother because he was ill. 弟弟病了，所以我代他出席典礼。

take place 发生；进行

The meeting will take place next Friday. 会议将于下星期五进行。

***place²** /pleɪs; ples/ *v* 动

places, placing, placed, placed

to put 放置

Mike placed the dishes in the cupboard. 迈克把碗碟放进碗橱里。

***plan¹** /plæn; plæn/ *n* 名

something you have decided to do 计划；打算

Do you have any plans for the long holidays? 这个长假你有什么打算吗?

***plan²** /plæn; plæn/ *v* 动

plans, planning, planned, planned

1. to think about something you want to do 计划；筹划
   They are planning their trip to Shanghai. 他们正在计划到上海的旅行。
2. to intend to do something 打算
   What are you planning to do after you leave school? 你打算毕业后干什么？

plane /pleɪn; plen/ *n* 名

a flying machine with wings 飞机

The plane from Thailand has just arrived. 来自泰国的飞机刚刚抵达。

同义 **aeroplane**

planet /ˈplænɪt; ˋplænɪt/ *n* 名

a large, round object in space that moves around a star 行星

Mercury is the closest planet to the sun. 水星是离太阳最近的行星。

***plant¹** /plɑːnt; plænt/ *n* 名

a living thing that grows in the soil 植物

Bobby grows some plants in his garden. 鲍比在花园里种了一些植物。

plant² /plɑːnt; plænt/ *v* 动

to put plants or seeds in the ground to grow 种植；栽种

Yesterday we learned how to plant flowers. 昨天我们学了怎样种花。

plaster /ˈplɑːstə; ˋplæstɚ/ *n* 名

a thin piece of material that you put on your skin to cover a wound 橡皮膏；胶布

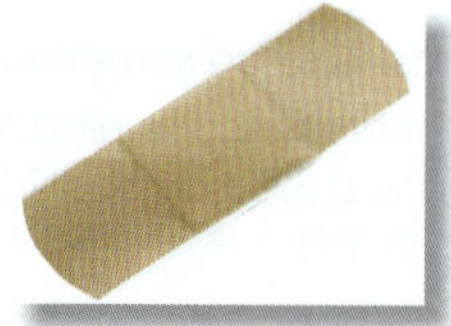

She put a plaster on my wound. 她在我的伤口上贴了橡皮膏。

***plastic¹** /ˈplæstɪk; ˋplæstɪk/ *n* 名

a light, strong material used for making bags, bottles, toys, etc 塑料；塑胶

This cup is made of plastic. 这个杯子是用塑料制的。

***plastic²** /ˈplæstɪk; ˋplæstɪk/ *adj* 形

made of plastic 塑料的；塑胶的

People should try to use fewer plastic bags. 人们应该尽量少用塑料袋。

***plate** /pleɪt; plet/ *n* 名

a flat, round dish for food 盘；碟

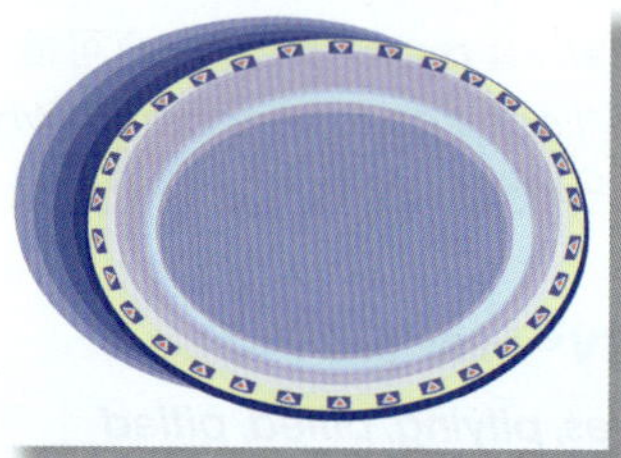

I put the potatoes on a plate. 我把马铃薯放在盘子上。

platform /ˈplætfɔːm; ˋplætˏfɔrm/ *n* 名

an area of a station where you get on and off trains 站台；月台

We are waiting on the platform. 我们在月台等着。

***play¹** /pleɪ; ple/ *v* 动

1. to do things that you enjoy 玩；玩耍

   The boys are playing outside. 那些男孩在外面玩耍。
2. to do a sport or take part in a game 参加（运动或比赛）

   Henry likes to play football. 亨利喜欢踢足球。
3. to make sounds on a musical instrument 演奏

   Christine is playing the violin. 克里斯汀在拉小提琴。
4. to make a CD, radio, etc produce sounds 播放

   I found the CD and played it. 我找到激光唱片，把它放来听。
5. to act in a play or film 扮演

   Laura plays a queen in the drama. 劳拉在剧中扮演一个女王。

***play²** /pleɪ; ple/ *n* 名

a story that you watch in a theatre 戏剧

We watched a play last night. 昨晚我们看了一出戏剧。

player /ˈpleɪə; ˋpleɚ/ *n* 名

someone who plays a game, sport or musical instrument 运动员；参赛者；（乐器）演奏者

He is a tennis player. 他是一名网球运动员。

***playground** /ˈpleɪgraʊnd; ˋpleˏgraʊnd/ *n* 名

a piece of ground for children to play on 操场；游乐场

The playground of our school is very big. 我们学校的操场很大。

pleasant /ˈpleznt; ˋplɛzn̩t/ *adj* 形

nice; enjoyable 令人愉快的；舒适的

I spent a pleasant day with my cousins. 我与表亲们度过了愉快的一天。

反义 **unpleasant**

***please¹** /pliːz; pliz/ *interj* 感叹

a word you say when you politely ask someone to do something 请（表示礼貌的请求）

Please bring your exercise book tomorrow. 明天请带你们的练习册。

Daily conversation 日常会话

"Would you like some more soup?" "Yes, please." "还要再喝些汤吗？""好的，谢谢。"

"Could you show me the way to the post office, please?" "Yes, of course." "请问你可以告诉我怎样去邮局吗？""当然可以。"

P

please² /pli:z; pliz/ *v* 动

pleases, pleasing, pleased, pleased

to try to make someone happy
取悦；讨好

Sally tried to please her father by being a good student. 莎莉为了讨好她爸爸试图做个好学生。

pleased /pli:zd; plizd/ *adj* 形

happy about something 高兴的；满意的

I was pleased that I had passed my exam. 我很高兴通过了考试。

同义 **contented, delighted**

Greetings 问候

"Pleased to meet you! I'm Connie." "Pleased to meet you too! I'm Ronald." "很高兴认识你！我是康妮。" "我也很高兴认识你！我是罗纳德。"

pleasure /ˈpleʒə; ˋplɛʒɚ/ *n* 名

无复数

a feeling of happiness that you get from doing something 愉快；快乐

I read for pleasure. 我看书消遣。

Daily conversation 日常会话

my pleasure 别客气（表示乐意为对方做事）

"Thank you for helping me!" "My pleasure." "谢谢你的帮忙！" "别客气。"

***plenty** /ˈplenti; ˋplɛntɪ/ *pron* 代

a lot; a large amount 充足；大量

We have plenty of time to get to the station. 我们有充足的时间去车站。

用法 plenty 常表示数量多过所需要的。

plough¹ /plaʊ; plau/ *n* 名

a piece of equipment for turning over soil before planting crops 犁

The farmer uses horses to pull the plough. 农夫用马来拖犁。

plough² /plaʊ; plau/ *v* 动

to turn over soil with a plough 犁地；耕地

The farmers plough the land before sowing seeds. 农夫在播种前先犁地。

***plug** /plʌg; plʌg/ *n* 名

1. something that stops water from flowing out 塞子

   He pulled out the bath plug to let the water run away. 他把浴缸塞子拔出来让水流走。

2. a thing that you use to connect a wire to the electricity 插头

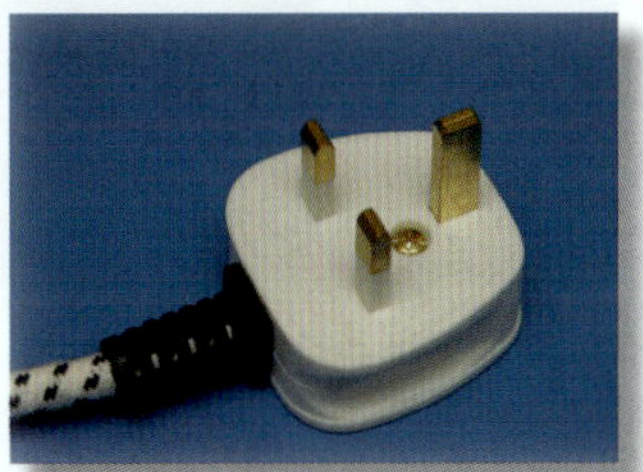

Don't touch the plug with wet hands! 不要用湿手碰插头！

plum /plʌm; plʌm/ *n* 名

a soft, round fruit with a smooth skin 李子；梅子

The plums are ripe. 这些李子熟了。

plural¹ /ˈplʊərəl; ˋplurəl/ *n* 名

the form of a word that shows more than one. For example, the plural of "potato" is "potatoes". 复数（形式）（例如 potato 的复数形式是 potatoes。）

另见 **singular¹**

plural² /ˈplʊərəl; ˋplurəl/ *adj* 形

a plural word is used when you talk or write about more than one thing, person, etc 复数的

另见 **singular²**

plus /plʌs; plʌs/ *prep* 介

used to show that one number is added to another number 加；加上

5 plus 6 equals 11. 5 加 6 等于 11。

反义 **minus**

***p.m.** /ˌpi: ˈem; ˌpi ˋɛm/ *n* 名

after midday 下午；午后

The shop closes at 9 p.m. 这家商店晚上 9 点关门。

另见 **a.m.**

***pocket** /ˈpɒkɪt; ˋpɑkɪt/ *n* 名

a small bag in your clothes for putting things in 衣袋；口袋

I have a handkerchief in my pocket. 我的口袋里有一条手帕。

pocket money /ˈpɒkɪt ˌmʌni; ˋpɑkɪt ˌmʌnɪ/ *n* 名

无复数
money that parents give to their children 零花钱；零用钱
How much pocket money do you get every month? 你每月有多少零用钱？

***poem** /ˈpəʊɪm; ˋpo·ɪm/ *n* 名
a piece of writing in short lines that rhyme 诗
The teacher read a poem to us. 老师给我们念了一首诗。

poet /ˈpəʊɪt; ˋpo·ɪt/ *n* 名
someone who writes poems 诗人
Burns was a famous poet. 彭斯是著名的诗人。

***point[1]** /pɔɪnt; pɔɪnt/ *n* 名
1. an idea or opinion 观点；论点
   I agree with your point. 我同意你的观点。
2. （无复数）the purpose or reason for doing something 目的；意图
   There is no point in telling him. 告诉他也没有用。
3. the exact position or place 地点；位置
   This corner is the point where the accident happened. 这个街角是事故发生的地点。
4. the sharp end of something（物件的）尖端
   Don't touch the point of the knife. 不要碰刀尖。
5. a number that you get in a game or competition 得分
   Our team lost by three points. 我们的队伍以三分之差输了。

***point[2]** /pɔɪnt; pɔɪnt/ *v* 动
to show where something is with your finger or an object 指；指向
Robin pointed to the building and said, "That's where I live." 罗宾指向那座大楼说："我就住在那里。"

pointed /ˈpɔɪntɪd; ˋpɔɪntɪd/ *adj* 形
having a sharp end 尖的
Susan has long pointed nails. 苏珊的指甲又长又尖。

poison /ˈpɔɪzn; ˋpɔɪzn̩/ *n* 名
something that can kill or harm you if you eat or drink it 毒药；毒物
This poison can kill rats. 这毒药能毒死老鼠。

poisonous /ˈpɔɪznəs; ˋpɔɪzn̩əs/ *adj* 形
containing poison 有毒的
These flowers are poisonous. 这些花有毒。

polar bear /ˌpəʊlə ˈbeə; ˌpolɚ ˋbɛr/ *n* 名
a large, white bear that lives near the North Pole 北极熊

The number of polar bears is decreasing. 北极熊的数量正在下降。

pole /pəʊl; pol/ *n* 名
1. a long, thin piece of wood or metal 柱；杆；竿
   The tent was supported by four poles. 帐篷由 4 根杆子支撑。
2. **the North/South Pole** the most northern or southern point on earth（地球的）北极/南极
   It is very cold at the South Pole. 南极非常寒冷。

***police** /pəˈliːs; pəˋlis/ *plural n* 复数名词
the people who protect your society and make sure that everyone obeys the law 警方
The police are searching for the murderer. 警方正在寻找凶手。

用法 police 后面用复数动词，例如上句不能说 The police is searching for the murderer。

***policeman** /pəˈliːsmən; pəˋlismən/ *n* 名
复数：*policemen*
a male member of the police 男警察
At last a policeman caught the thief. 一名警察终于抓住了窃贼。

police officer /pəˈliːs ˌɒfɪsə; pəˋlis ˌɔfəsɚ/ *n* 名
a member of the police 警察；警员
A police officer asked him for his ID card. 一名警察要求他出示身份证。

police station /pəˈliːs ˌsteɪʃn; pəˋlis ˌsteʃən/ *n* 名
a building where the police work 警察局；警署
The police station is at the end of the street. 警察局在街道的尽头。

***policewoman** /pəˈliːsˌwʊmən; pəˋlisˌwʊmən/ *n* 名
复数：*policewomen*
a female member of the police 女警察
There were fewer policewomen in the past. 以前女警察的人数比较少。

polish /ˈpɒlɪʃ; ˋpalɪʃ/ *v* 动
polishes, polishing, polished, polished
to make something smooth and shiny by rubbing it 擦亮；擦光
Mr Harris polished his shoes and put them on. 哈里斯先生把鞋子擦亮，然后穿上。

***polite** /pəˈlaɪt; pəˋlaɪt/ *adj* 形
politer, politest
not rude; having good manners 有礼貌的；客气的
Our neighbours are very polite. 我们的邻居很有礼貌。
反义 **impolite, rude**

politely /pəˈlaɪtli; pəˋlaɪtlɪ/
adv 副
in a polite way 有礼貌地；客气地
"Would you like something to drink?" Lily asked politely. "你要喝点什么吗？"莉莉有礼貌地问道。

***pollute** /pəˈluːt; pəˋlut/ *v* 动
pollutes, polluting, polluted, polluted
to make air, water, soil, etc dirty 污染
Smoking pollutes the air. 吸烟污染空气。

pollution /pəˈluːʃn; pəˋluʃən/ *n* 名
无复数
making air, water, soil, etc dirty 污染
Water pollution is getting serious. 水污染越来越严重。

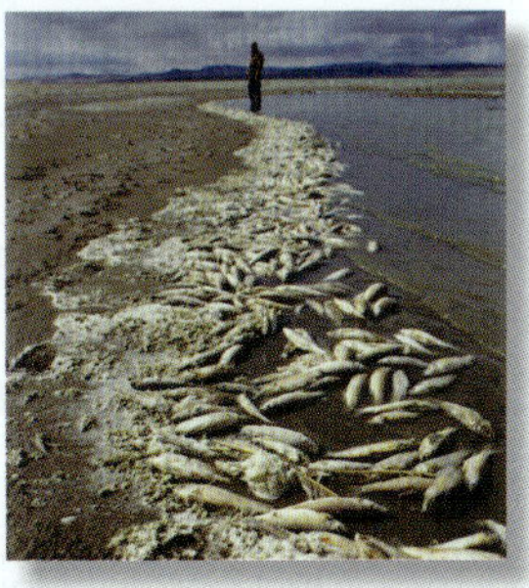

***pond** /pɒnd; pand/ *n* 名
a small area of water 池塘

There are some goldfish swimming in the pond. 有些金鱼在池塘里游来游去。

pony /ˈpəʊni; ˋponɪ/ *n* 名
复数：***ponies***
a small horse 小马

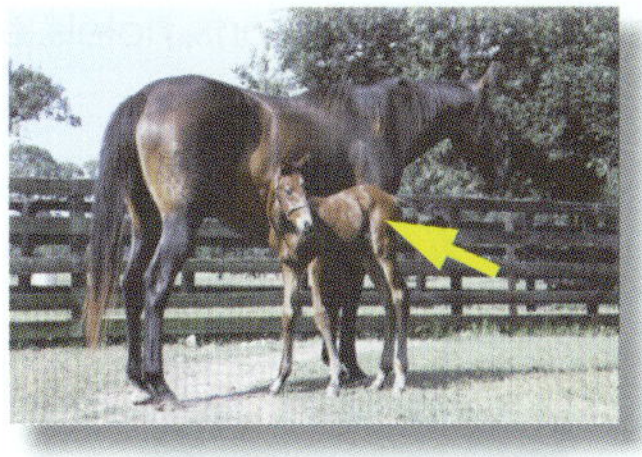

We rode on ponies at the farm. 我们在农场里骑小马。

ponytail /ˈpəʊniteɪl; ˋponɪˏtel/ *n* 名
a bunch of hair tied at the back of your head 马尾辫

Vanessa tied her hair in a ponytail. 瓦内萨把头发扎成马尾辫。

***pool** /puːl; pul/ *n* 名
a place that is built for people to swim in 游泳池

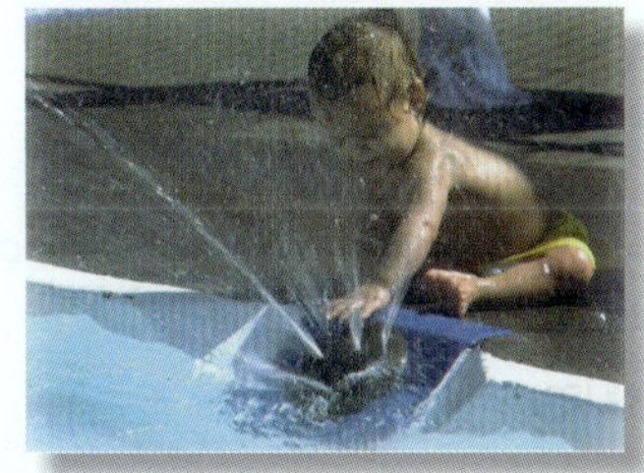

The children are learning to swim in the pool. 孩子们在游泳池里学游泳。
同义 **swimming pool**

***poor** /pɔː; pur/ *adj* 形
poorer, poorest
1. having very little money 贫穷的
   Her family was too poor to buy new clothes for her. 她家里太穷了，没有钱给她买新衣服。

反义 **rich, wealthy**

2. not good 差的；低劣的
   Paul is poor at writing. 保罗写作很差。
3. used to show that you feel sorry for someone 可怜的
   Poor child! She lost her way. 可怜的孩子！她迷了路。

the poor 穷人
The government should help the poor. 政府应该帮助穷人。

popcorn /ˈpɒpkɔːn; ˋpapˏkɔrn/ *n* 名
无复数
corn that is heated until it bursts, eaten with sugar or salt 爆米花

I often eat popcorn when I am watching a film. 我看电影时常常吃爆米花。

pop music /ˈpɒp ˌmjuːzɪk; ˋpap ˏmjuzɪk/ *n* 名
无复数
modern music that is popular with young people 流行音乐
Maria likes pop music. 玛丽亚喜爱流行音乐。

pop star /ˈpɒp stɑː; ˋpap star/ *n* 名
a famous singer who sings pop music 流行音乐歌星；流行音乐明星
The pop star is coming to Hong Kong for a show. 这位流行音乐歌星将要来香港演出。

***popular** /ˈpɒpjʊlə; ˋpapjələ/ *adj* 形
liked by a lot of people 受大众欢迎的；流行的

This song is very popular. 这首歌曲很流行。

***population** /ˌpɒpjuˈleɪʃn; ˏpɑpjəˋleʃən/ *n* 名

the number of people living in a place 人口

The population of this city is about one million. 这座城市的人口大约为 100 万。

***pork** /pɔːk; pɔrk/ *n* 名

无复数

meat from a pig 猪肉

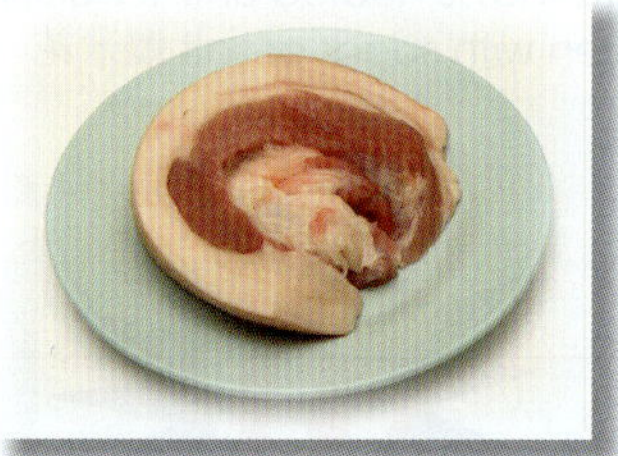

Terry likes roast pork. 泰瑞喜欢吃烤猪肉。

porridge /ˈpɒrɪdʒ; ˋpɔrɪdʒ/ *n* 名

无复数

a soft food made by boiling wheat or rice in milk or water 燕麦粥；麦片粥

We had porridge for breakfast. 我们早餐吃了麦片粥。

P

port /pɔːt; pɔrt/ *n* 名

a town or city with a harbour 港口城市

Shanghai is a busy port. 上海是座繁忙的港口城市。

porter /ˈpɔːtə; ˋpɔrtɚ/ *n* 名

someone who carries bags for other people at airports, hotels, etc 行李搬运工人

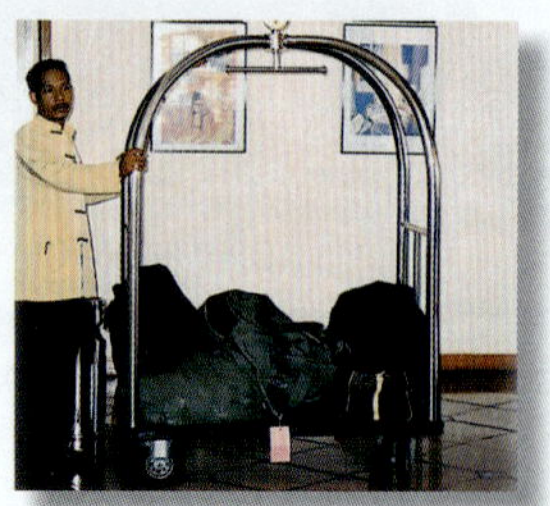

The porter carried the luggage for us. 行李搬运工帮我们搬行李。

***position** /pəˈzɪʃn; pəˋzɪʃən/ *n* 名

the place where someone or something is 位置

From my position I could see my car. 从我的位置可以看见我的汽车。

positive /ˈpɒzətɪv; ˋpɑzətɪv/ *adj* 形

showing that you agree with someone or something 赞同的；正面的

We received a positive answer. 我们收到了正面的回复。

***possible** /ˈpɒsəbl; ˋpɑsəbḷ/ *adj* 形

if something is possible, you can do it or it can happen 可能的

Is it possible to get there by bus? 坐公共汽车能否到达那里？

as soon as possible 尽快

I will return the book to you as soon as possible. 我会尽快把书还给你。

反义 **impossible**

possibly /ˈpɒsəbli; ˋpɑsəblɪ/ *adv* 副

used to say that something may be true, but you are not sure 可能；也许

It was possibly a mistake. 这也许是个错误。

同义 **maybe, perhaps**

Daily conversation 日常会话

"Are you coming with us tomorrow?" "Possibly. I'm not sure yet." "你明天会跟我们一起去吗？" "可能吧，我不太肯定。"

***post¹** /pəʊst; post/ *n* 名

1. 【英】(无复数 | 美式：***mail***) letters or parcels that you send or receive 邮件；信件
   Mrs Smith was opening her post. 史密斯太太在拆邮件。
2. a tall thick piece of wood or metal fixed in the ground 柱；杆
   Six posts support the roof. 6 根柱子支撑着屋顶。

***post²** /pəʊst; post/ *v* 动【英】

to send a letter or parcel 邮寄

I posted a Christmas card to Dolly. 我给多利寄了一张圣诞卡。

postbox /ˈpəʊstbɒks; ˋpostˏbɑks/ *n* 名【英】

复数：*postboxes* | **美式：*mailbox***

a large box in the street for you to post letters 邮箱；邮筒

The postbox is just opposite the bank. 那个邮箱就在银行对面。

***postcard** /ˈpəʊstkɑːd; ˋpostˏkard/ *n* 名

a card with a picture on one side that you can send by post without an envelope 明信片

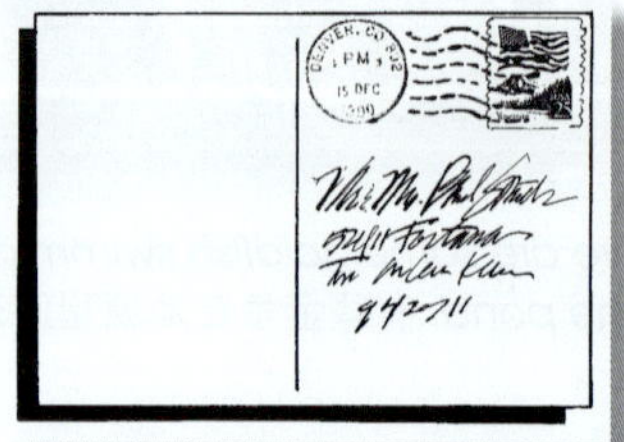

My aunt sent me a postcard from Malaysia. 阿姨从马来西亚给我寄了一张明信片。

***poster** /ˈpəʊstə; ˋpostɚ/ *n* 名

a large notice, picture, etc that is used as an advertisement or a decoration 海报

Louis hung the poster on the wall. 路易斯把海报挂在墙壁上。

postman /ˈpəʊstmən; ˋpostmən/ *n* 名【英】

复数：***postmen***

someone who collects and delivers letters and parcels 邮递员；邮差

The postman usually comes before noon. 邮差通常在正午前来。

post office /ˈpəʊst ˌɒfɪs; ˋpost ˌɔfɪs/ *n* 名

a place where you can buy stamps or send letters and parcels 邮局

I went to the post office to send a letter. 我去邮局寄了一封信。

***pot** /pɒt; pɑt/ *n* 名

a round container used for cooking or storing food 锅；罐

He cooked a chicken in a pot. 他用锅子煮了一只鸡。

***potato** /pəˈteɪtəʊ; pəˋteto/ *n* 名

复数：***potatoes***

a round white vegetable with a brown skin that grows under the ground 马铃薯；土豆

She added some potatoes to the soup. 她往汤里加了些马铃薯。

poultry /ˈpəʊltri; ˋpoltrɪ/ *plural n* 复数名词

birds that are kept for their eggs or meat 家禽

They keep chickens and other poultry. 他们养鸡和其他家禽。

pound /paʊnd; paʊnd/ *n* 名

缩写：***lb***

a unit of weight. There are 16 ounces in one pound. 磅

The baby weighs eight pounds. 这个婴儿重 8 磅。

另见 **ounce**

***pour** /pɔː; pɔr/ *v* 动

to make a liquid flow out of or into something 倒；注

He is pouring the milk into a glass. 他正把牛奶倒进玻璃杯。

***powder** /ˈpaʊdə; ˋpaʊdɚ/ *n* 名

something that is dry and in very small pieces like dust 粉；粉末

The medicine that the doctor gave me is a powder. 医生给我的药是一种粉末。

***power** /ˈpaʊə; ˋpaʊɚ/ *n* 名

无复数

1. the ability to control what people do 权力

   The king has a lot of power. 国王拥有很大的权力。

2. energy used to make something work 动力

   Wind power can produce electricity. 风力可以发电。

powerful /ˈpaʊəfl; ˋpaʊɚfəl/ *adj* 形

very strong; having a lot of power 强大的；力量大的

This machine has a powerful engine. 这台机器有一个强劲的发动机。

***practice** /ˈpræktɪs; ˋpræktɪs/ *n* 名

无复数

doing something many times in order to do it well 练习

It takes a lot of practice to learn a foreign language. 学习外语需要大量练习。

***practise** /ˈpræktɪs; ˋpræktɪs/ *v* 动

practises, practising, practised, practised

to do something many times in order to do it well 练习

Tracy practises her piano every day. 翠西每天练习弹钢琴。

praise /preɪz; prez/ *v* 动

praises, praising, praised, praised

to say nice things about someone or something 称赞；赞扬

My father praised me for my courage. 爸爸赞赏了我的勇气。

反义 **scold**

prawn /prɔːn; prɔn/ *n* 名

a small sea animal with a shell, a tail and ten legs 对虾；明虾

Prawns are my favourite seafood. 对虾是我最喜爱的海鲜。

pray /preɪ; pre/ *v* 动

to speak to God to ask for something or give thanks 祈祷；祷告

We prayed for the patients. 我们为病人祈祷。

prayer /preə; prɛr/ *n* 名

words that you say to God 祈祷文

The children said their prayers and went to bed. 孩子们做完祷告，上床睡觉。

precious /ˈpreʃəs; ˋprɛʃəs/ *adj* 形

valuable; very important or special 宝贵的；珍贵的

This photo album is very precious to me. 这本相册对我来说很珍贵。

prefect /ˈpriːfekt; ˋprifɛkt/ *n* 名【英】

a student who helps teachers to control other students 学长；级长；风纪员

The prefect told the students to be quiet. 学长叫那几个学生安静下来。

***prefer** /prɪˈfɜː; prɪˋfɝ/ *v* 动

prefers, preferring, preferred, preferred

to like one person or thing more than another 更喜欢；宁愿

He likes rice, but I prefer noodles. 他喜欢吃饭，但我更喜欢吃面。

prefer something to something 喜欢某事物多于另一事物

Maggie prefers tea to coffee. 玛姬喜欢喝茶多于咖啡。

***prepare** /prɪˈpeə; prɪˋpɛr/ *v* 动

prepares, preparing, prepared, prepared

to make something ready to be used 准备；预备

My mother is preparing breakfast for me. 我的妈妈正在给我准备早餐。

preposition /ˌprepəˈzɪʃn; ˏprɛpəˋzɪʃən/ *n* 名

a word used before a noun or pronoun to show time, place, etc. In the sentence "He fell down the stairs", "down" is a preposition. 介词；前置词（在 He fell down the stairs 这个句子中，down 是介词。）

***present[1]** /ˈpreznt; ˋprɛzn̩t/ *adj* 形

1. in a place or at a meeting or class 在场的；出席的

   She was not present at the meeting. 她没有出席会议。

反义 absent

2. happening or existing now 目前的；现在的

   He doesn't live here now. I don't know his present address. 他现在不住在这里了，我不知道他现在的住址。

***present[2]** /ˈpreznt; ˋprɛzn̩t/ *n* 名

something that you give to someone 礼物

I gave him a watch as a birthday present. 我给他送了一只手表作为生日礼物。

president /ˈprezɪdənt; ˋprɛzədənt/ *n* 名

1. （也作：***President***）the leader of some countries that do not have a king or queen 总统

   The President is going to visit the country next week. 总统将在下星期访问该国。

2. the head of a big company or organization 董事长；总裁；主席

   Mr Thompson is the president of the company. 汤普森先生是该公司的总裁。

***press** /pres; prɛs/ *v* 动

presses, pressing, pressed, pressed

to push something such as a button or switch 按；压

I pressed the bell and a man opened the door. 我按了门铃，一个男人开了门。

pretend /prɪˈtend; prɪˋtɛnd/ *v* 动

to make people believe that something is true when it is not 假装；装作

She is just pretending to be angry. 她只是装作愤怒而已。

P

***pretty** /ˈprɪti; ˋprɪtɪ/ *adj* 形

prettier, prettiest

nice to look at 漂亮的；好看的

You look very pretty in your dress. 你穿这条连衣裙看起来很漂亮。

同义 **beautiful**

反义 **ugly**

***prevent** /prɪˈvent; prɪˋvɛnt/ *v* 动

to stop something from happening 防止；阻止

Everyone should obey the traffic rules to prevent accidents. 人人都应该遵守交通规则以防止意外。

***price** /praɪs; praɪs/ *n* 名

the amount of money that you have to pay for something 价格；价钱

The price of food has increased. 食品的价格上涨了。

priest /priːst; prist/ *n* 名

someone whose job is to perform duties and ceremonies in religions 神父；牧师

The priests in the church are very kind. 教堂里的神父十分慈祥。

primary /ˈpraɪməri; ˋpraɪˌmɛrɪ/ *adj* 形

main; most important 主要的；首要的

The school's primary aim is to teach pupils to behave well. 学校的主要宗旨是教导学生守规矩。

primary school /ˈpraɪməri skuːl; ˋpraɪˌmɛrɪ skul/ *n* 名

a school for children between 6 and 11 years old 小学

I go to this primary school. 我上这所小学。

另见 **secondary school**

***prince** /prɪns; prɪns/ *n* 名

the son of a king or queen 王子

Jenny wants to marry a prince. 珍妮希望嫁给王子。

***princess** /ˌprɪnˈses; ˋprɪnsəs/ *n* 名

复数：***princesses***

the daughter of a king or queen 公主

The king has three beautiful princesses. 国王有三位美丽的公主。

***principal** /ˈprɪnsəpl; ˋprɪnsəpl̩/ *n* 名

the head of a school 校长

There will be a new principal at our school next year. 我们学校明年将有一位新校长。

***print** /prɪnt; prɪnt/ *v* 动

to make words or pictures on paper using a machine 印刷；打印

Can you print a copy for me? 你能帮我印一份副本吗？

printer /ˈprɪntə; ˋprɪntɚ/ *n* 名

a machine that prints things, usually from a computer 打印机

There is no ink in the printer. 打印机没有油墨了。

prison /ˈprɪzn; ˋprɪzn̩/ *n* 名

a place where people are kept as a punishment for a crime 监狱

He was in prison for three years. 他坐了三年牢。

同义 **jail**

prisoner /ˈprɪznə; ˋprɪzn̩ɚ/ *n* 名

a person who is kept in a prison 囚犯

A prisoner has escaped! 一名囚犯越狱了！

***private** /ˈpraɪvət; ˋpraɪvɪt/ *adj* 形

for only one person or group, not for everyone 私人的；个人的

This is a private pool. We cannot go in. 这是私人游泳池，我们不能进入。

反义 **public**

***prize** /praɪz; praɪz/ *n* 名

something that you win in a game, competition, etc 奖品

I won a prize in the competition. 我在比赛中赢了奖。

***probably** /ˈprɒbəbli; ˋprɑbəblɪ/ *adv* 副

used to say that something is likely to happen 很可能

He will probably go to London next month. 他下个月很可能去伦敦。

P

Daily conversation 日常会话
"Do you think they will win?" "Yes, probably." "你看他们会胜出吗？" "大概会吧。"

***problem** /ˈprɒbləm; ˋprɑbləm/ *n* 名

1. something that causes trouble for you 困难；问题
   We have some problems with our house. 我们的住宅有些问题。
2. a question 问题
   Jane solved the maths problem. 简解答了那道数学题。

Daily conversation 日常会话
no problem 没问题
"Can you help me carry the bag?" "Sure, no problem." "你可以帮我拿这个包吗？" "当然可以，没问题。"

process /ˈprəʊses; ˋprɑsɛs/ *n* 名

复数：*processes*

a set of actions that you take to get a result 过程

Learning a language is a slow process. 学习一种语言是一个漫长的过程。

***produce** /prəˈdjuːs; prəˋdus/ *v* 动

produces, producing, produced, produced

to make or grow something 生产；制造；出产

Japan produces a lot of cars. 日本生产大量汽车。

***product** /ˈprɒdʌkt; ˋprɑdʌkt/ *n* 名

something that is made or grown to be sold 产品；制品

This company sells its products on a website. 这家公司在网站上销售产品。

professor /prəˈfesə; prəˋfɛsɚ/ *n* 名

a teacher of the highest rank in a university 教授

Mr Wood is a mathematics professor. 伍德先生是一位数学教授。

***program** /ˈprəʊgræm; ˋprogræm/ *n* 名

1. 【电脑】a set of instructions that a computer follows 电脑程序；电脑程式
   They write programs for a big company. 他们为一家大公司编写电脑程序。
2. 【美】节目；节目表 英式 **programme**

***programme** /ˈprəʊgræm; ˋprogræm/ *n* 名【英】

美式：*program*

1. a show on television or radio （电视或电台）节目

   Which TV programme do you like most? 你最喜欢看哪个电视节目？
2. a plan of things that will be done to develop something 计划；方案
   There will be a training programme for the athletes. 运动员将有一个培训计划。

progress /ˈprəʊgres; ˋprɑgrɛs/ *n* 名

无复数

if you make progress, you get better at doing something 进步；进展

David has made good progress in English. 大卫的英语有很大的进步。

***project** /ˈprɒdʒekt; ˋprɑdʒɛkt/ *n* 名

a piece of schoolwork in which students collect information about something and write or talk about it 课题；专题；研究项目

We are doing a project on air pollution. 我们正在做一个有关空气污染的课题。

projector /prəˈdʒektə; prəˋdʒɛktɚ/ *n* 名

a piece of equipment that makes a film or picture appear on a screen 放映机；投影仪

There is a projector in each classroom. 每个教室都有一部投影仪。

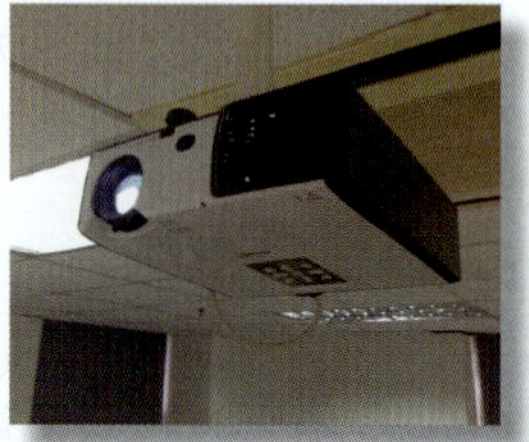

***promise**[1] /ˈprɒmɪs; ˋprɑmɪs/ *v* 动

promises, promising, promised, promised

to say that you will do something 承诺；答应

I promised to work harder. 我承诺会更加用功。

Daily conversation 日常会话
"I'll be back home by seven." "Promise?" "Yes! Don't worry." "我 7 点前会回家。" "你保证？" "是啊！放心吧。"

***promise**[2] /ˈprɒmɪs; ˋprɑmɪs/ *n* 名

something that you have said you will do 诺言

My mother made a promise to buy me a teddy bear. 我的妈妈答应给我买一只玩具熊。

break a promise 违背诺言

Chris broke his promise and did not help us. 克里斯不守诺言，没有帮我们。

keep a promise 遵守诺言

Uncle John kept his promise to take us to the amusement park. 约翰叔叔遵守诺言，带我们到游乐场。

pronoun /ˈprəʊnaʊn; ˋpronaʊn/ *n* 名

a word used instead of a noun. In the sentence "Judy saw her", "her" is a pronoun. 代词；代名词（在 Judy saw her 这个句子中，her 是个代词。）

pronounce /prəˈnaʊns; prəˋnaʊns/ *v* 动

pronounces, pronouncing, pronounced, pronounced

to make the sound of a word 发…的音

How do you pronounce this word? 这个词怎么念？

pronunciation /prəˌnʌnsiˈeɪʃn; prəˌnʌnsɪˋeʃən/ *n* 名

the way you make the sound of a word 发音

Mrs Martin teaches us English pronunciation. 马丁太太教我们英语发音。

proof /pruːf; pruf/ *n* 名

无复数

facts, things, etc which show that something is true 证明；证据

Mr Walker has proof that he was in another city yesterday. 沃克先生有证据证明他昨天在另一个城市。

proper /ˈprɒpə; ˋprapɚ/ *adj* 形

correct or suitable 正确的；恰当的

That is not the proper way to use the iron. 那不是正确使用熨斗的方法。

properly /ˈprɒpəli; ˋprapɚlɪ/ *adv* 副

correctly; in a suitable way 正确地；恰当地

Mr Johnson cannot hold chopsticks properly. 约翰逊先生不会拿筷子。

***property** /ˈprɒpəti; ˋprapɚtɪ/ *n* 名

无复数

something that someone owns 财产；财物

This house is their property. 这栋房子是他们的财产。

***protect** /prəˈtekt; prəˋtɛkt/ *v* 动

to keep someone or something safe 保护

The bird protected its eggs from its enemies. 那只鸟保护了自己的蛋，使其免受敌人侵害。

***proud** /praʊd; praʊd/ *adj* 形

prouder, proudest

1. feeling pleased about yourself or something you have 自豪的；引以为荣的

   She is proud of her son. 她为儿子感到自豪。

2. feeling that you are better than other people 自大的；骄傲的

   She was too proud to admit that she was wrong. 她太自大，不肯认错。

***prove** /pruːv; pruv/ *v* 动

proves, proving, proved, proved

to show that something is true 证明；证实

Darren proved that he could do the job well. 达伦证明了自己可以把工作做好。

***provide** /prəˈvaɪd; prəˋvaɪd/ *v* 动

provides, providing, provided, provided

to give something to someone 提供；供应

They provide food and clothes for the poor. 他们为穷人提供食物和衣服。

***public** /ˈpʌblɪk; ˋpʌblɪk/ *adj* 形

for everyone to use 公共的；公用的

I go to the public library once a week. 我每星期去一次公共图书馆。

反义 private

***pudding** /ˈpʊdɪŋ; ˋpʊdɪŋ/ *n* 名

a sweet food made with flour, milk, eggs, sugar, etc 布丁

I love mango pudding. 我喜欢吃芒果布丁。

***pull** /pʊl; pʊl/ *v* 动

1. to move someone or something towards you 拉；扯

   Stop pulling my hair! 不要再扯我的头发！

反义 push

2. to make something move along behind you 拖；牵引

   A horse is pulling the cart. 一匹马拖着那辆车。

pull the curtains 拉开/拉上窗帘

When I pulled the curtains open, I saw that it was raining. 我拉开窗帘时，看见正在下雨。

pullover /ˈpʊlˌəʊvə; ˋpʊlˌovɚ/ *n* 名

a piece of clothing made of wool that you wear on the top part of your body 套头毛衣

P

It was a cool evening so I put on a pullover. 晚上有点凉，所以我穿上套头毛衣。

同义 **sweater**

pump¹ /pʌmp; pʌmp/ *n* 名

a machine for moving water or air into or out of something 泵；抽水机；打气筒

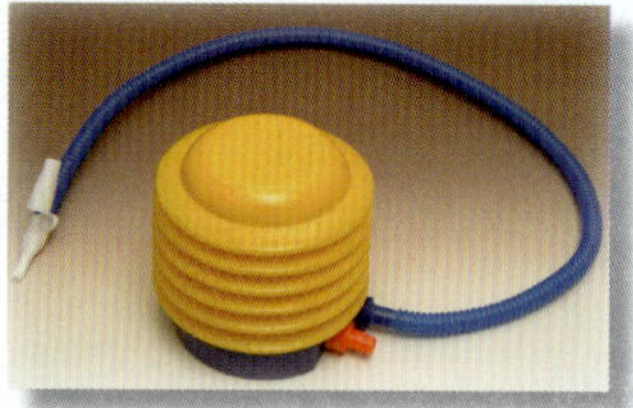

I put an air pump in the fish tank. 我在鱼缸中装了一个气泵。

pump² /pʌmp; pʌmp/ *v* 动

to move water or air into or out of something 抽水；打气

Paul pumped up the basketball. 保罗给篮球打了气。

***pumpkin** /ˈpʌmpkɪn; ˋpʌmpkɪn/ *n* 名

a large, round, orange vegetable that grows on the ground 南瓜

We had pumpkin soup tonight. 我们今晚喝了南瓜汤。

punch¹ /pʌntʃ; pʌntʃ/ *v* 动

punches, punching, punched, punched

to hit someone or something hard with your closed hand 用拳打

Robert was angry and punched me in the face. 罗伯特很愤怒，一拳打在我的脸上。

punch² /pʌntʃ; pʌntʃ/ *n* 名

复数：***punches***

a strong hit with your closed hand 拳打

I gave him a punch. 我打了他一拳。

***punctual** /ˈpʌŋktʃuəl; ˋpʌŋktʃʊəl/ *adj* 形

arriving at the right time 准时的；守时的

She is always punctual. 她一向守时。

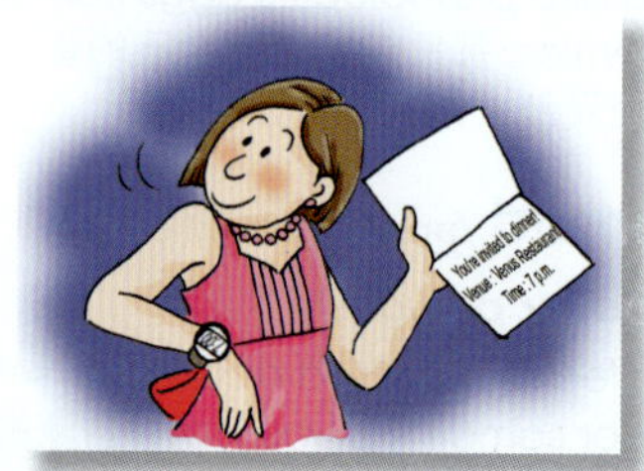

反义 **late¹**

***punctuation** /ˌpʌŋktʃuˈeɪʃn; ˏpʌŋktʃʊˋeʃən/ *n* 名

无复数

signs used in writing that divide sentences or parts of sentences, for example (,) (!) (?) or (:) 标点符号

另见 **附录**：Punctuation 标点符号

***punish** /ˈpʌnɪʃ; ˋpʌnɪʃ/ *v* 动

punishes, punishing, punished, punished

to do something unpleasant to someone because they have done something wrong 处罚；惩罚

The students were punished for cheating in the exam. 那些学生因为考试作弊而受到处罚。

punishment /ˈpʌnɪʃmənt; ˋpʌnɪʃmənt/ *n* 名

something that is done to punish someone 处罚；惩罚

His punishment was five years in prison. 他的惩罚是入狱5年。

***pupil** /ˈpjuːpl; ˋpjupl/ *n* 名

a child who is studying at a school （小）学生；学童

Our school has 700 pupils. 我们的学校有700名学生。

注意 pupil 一般指小学生，中学生或大学生是 student。

puppet /ˈpʌpɪt; ˋpʌpɪt/ *n* 名

a toy like a person or an animal that you can move by pulling strings or putting your hand inside it（牵线或布袋）木偶

Connie is playing with a puppet. 康妮在玩木偶。

***puppy** /ˈpʌpi; ˋpʌpɪ/ *n* 名

复数：***puppies***

a young dog 小狗

These puppies are lovely. 这些小狗很可爱。

pure /pjʊə; pjʊr/ *adj* 形

purer, purest

not mixed with anything else 纯的；纯净的

The water in the stream is pure. 那条溪流的水很纯净。

***purple[1]** /ˈpɜːpl; ˋpɝpl̩/ *adj* 形

having the colour of blue mixed with red 紫色的

Her handbag is purple. 她的手袋是紫色的。

***purple[2]** /ˈpɜːpl; ˋpɝpl̩/ *n* 名

the colour that is made by mixing blue and red 紫色

Purple was the colour of kings and queens. 从前紫色是帝王专用的颜色。

***purpose** /ˈpɜːpəs; ˋpɝpəs/ *n* 名

a reason for doing something or what something is used for 目的；意图

The purpose of an advertisement is to sell something. 广告的目的是推销。

on purpose 故意

I didn't do that on purpose. 我不是故意那样做的。

purr /pɜː; pɝ/ *v* 动

if a cat purrs, it makes a sound that shows it is happy（猫高兴时）发出呜呜声

The cat is purring. 那只猫在呜呜地叫。

***purse** /pɜːs; pɝs/ *n* 名

a small bag that women use to keep money（女性用的）钱包

I have only a few coins in my purse. 我的钱包里只有几个硬币。

另见 **wallet**

***push** /pʊʃ; pʊʃ/ *v* 动

pushes, pushing, pushed, pushed

1. to move someone or something forward or away from you 推

   She is pushing the trolley. 她推着手推车。

反义 **pull**

2. to press a button, switch, etc to make something work or stop 按下（按钮、开关等）

   I pushed the button for the ground floor. 我按了到底层的按钮。

***put** /pʊt; pʊt/ *v* 动

puts, putting, put, put

to move something to a place 放；放置

I put the book on the bookcase. 我把书放在书架上。

put something away 把…收拾起来；把…放回原处

Put away all your toys. 把你所有的玩具收拾好。

put something off 推迟；延迟

We have to put off our trip until next year. 我们只得把旅行延期到明年。

put something on 穿上；戴上（衣物）

I put on my coat and went out. 我穿上外套出去了。

put something out 扑灭；熄灭

The firefighters put out the fire quickly. 消防员迅速把火扑灭了。

同义 **place[2]**

***puzzle** /ˈpʌzl; ˋpʌzl̩/ *n* 名

1. a toy with a lot of small pieces that you have to fit together 拼图玩具

   The puzzle has 1000 pieces. 这幅拼图有 1000 块。

2. something that is difficult to understand or explain 谜；难题

   The meaning of the picture is a puzzle. 这幅画的含义是个谜。

puzzled /ˈpʌzəld; ˋpʌzl̩d/ *adj* 形

unable to understand something 迷惑的；困惑的

He looked puzzled when I asked him the question. 我向他提出问题时，他看起来很迷惑。

***pyjamas** /pəˈdʒɑːməz; pəˋdʒæməz/ *plural n* 复数名词【英】

美式：***pajamas***

a loose shirt and trousers that you

P

wear in bed 睡衣裤

I put on my pyjamas and went to bed. 我穿上睡衣上床睡觉。

pyramid /ˈpɪrəmɪd; ˋpɪrəmɪd/

n 名

a building or shape that has a square bottom and a pointed top 金字塔；锥体

We visited the pyramids in Egypt. 我们在埃及参观了金字塔。

P

quack /kwæk; kwæk/ *v* 动

to make the sound that a duck makes（鸭子）发出嘎嘎声

The duck is quacking. 这只鸭子在嘎嘎叫。

*__quality__ /ˈkwɒləti; ˋkwɑlətɪ/ *n* 名

无复数

how good or bad something is 质量；品质

We did not have our PE lesson today because the air quality was poor. 我们今天没有上体育课，因为空气质量很差。

quantity /ˈkwɒntəti; ˋkwɑntətɪ/ *n* 名

复数：*quantities*

an amount of something 数量

The fishermen caught a large quantity of fish yesterday. 那些渔民昨天捕获了很多鱼。

quarrel[1] /ˈkwɒrəl; ˋkwɔrəl/ *n* 名

an angry argument 争吵；吵架

They had a quarrel last night and they are still angry with each other now. 他们昨夜争吵，今天仍在生对方的气。

*__quarrel[2]__ /ˈkwɒrəl; ˋkwɔrəl/ *v* 动

quarrels, quarrelling, quarrelled, quarrelled

to argue about something 争吵；吵架

My brother and I often quarrelled when we were small. 我和哥哥在小时候经常吵架。

quarrel about something 为某事争吵

Lily and Mike are quarrelling about toys. 莉莉和迈克正在为玩具争吵。

quarrel with someone 与某人争吵

They never quarrel with each other. 他们从来不吵架。

*__quarter__ /ˈkwɔːtə; ˋkwɔrtɚ/ *n* 名

one of the four equal parts of something 四分之一

A quarter of one hundred is twenty-five. 100 的四分之一是 25。

a quarter past …点过 15 分钟

It's a quarter past six. 现在是 6 点 15 分。

a quarter to 差 15 分钟到…点

It's a quarter to ten. 现在是 9 点 45 分。

quay /kiː; ki/ *n* 名

a place where boats unload 码头

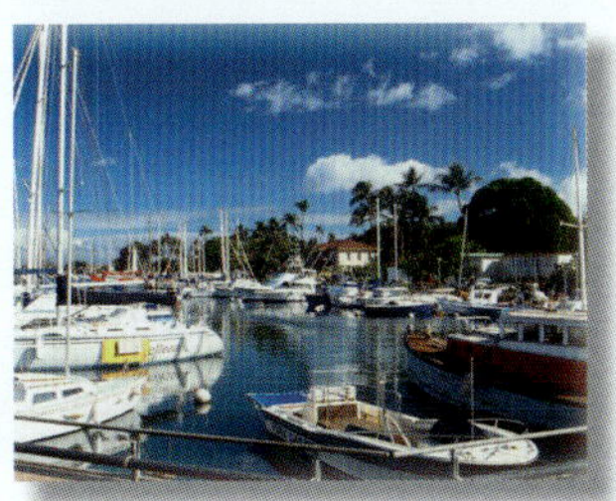

Some old men were fishing on the quay. 一些老人在码头边垂钓。

注意 发音和 key 相同。

*__queen__ /kwiːn; kwin/ *n* 名

a woman who rules a country or is married to a king 女王；王后

The queen lives in the palace. 女王住在王宫里。

另见 king

*__question[1]__ /ˈkwestʃən; ˋkwɛstʃən/ *n* 名

a sentence or phrase that you use to ask for information 问题

Can you answer this question? 你能回答这个问题吗？

*__question[2]__ /ˈkwestʃən; ˋkwɛstʃən/ *v* 动

to ask someone questions 询问；审问

The police were questioning the suspect. 警察盘问那个嫌疑犯。

question mark /ˈkwestʃən ˌmɑːk; ˋkwɛstʃən ˌmɑrk/ *n* 名

the sign you use at the end of a question (?) 问号

另见 **附录**：Punctuation 标点符号

*__queue__ /kjuː; kju/ *n* 名【英】

美式：*line*

a line of people waiting for something or a line of cars waiting to move（人或车等候的）队；行列

There was a long queue at the shop. 商店外排着一条长队。

*__quick__ /kwɪk; kwɪk/ *adj* 形

quicker, quickest

Q

taking a short time 快速的；匆匆的
There was not much time so we just had a quick meal. 时间不多，我们只能匆匆吃些东西。

反义 **slow**

*quickly /'kwɪkli; `kwɪklɪ/ *adv* 副

fast 很快地；迅速地
We walked quickly across the road. 我们迅速穿过马路。

反义 **slowly**

*quiet /'kwaɪət; `kwaɪət/ *adj* 形

quieter, quietest

not making a lot of noise; not noisy or loud 安静的；轻声的

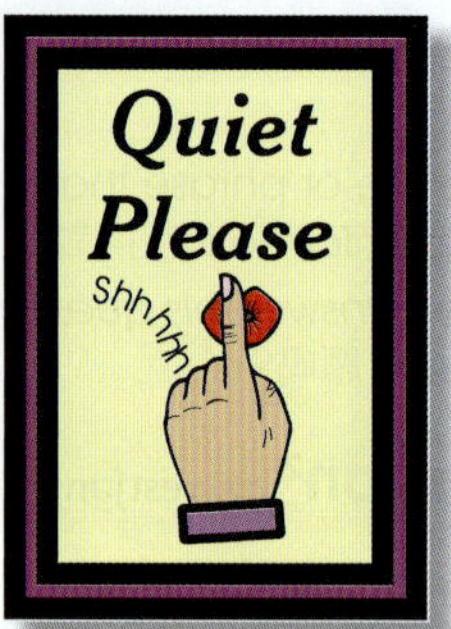

We should keep quiet in the library. 我们在图书馆里应该保持安静。

同义 **silent**

反义 **noisy**

Q

Daily conversation 日常会话
be quiet! 别吵！小声点！
"Be quiet! Grandma's sleeping." "OK." "小声点！外婆在睡觉。""好的。"

quietly /'kwaɪətli; `kwaɪətlɪ/ *adv* 副

in a quiet way 静静地
Can you speak quietly? 你说话可以轻一点吗?

反义 **noisily**

quilt /kwɪlt; kwɪlt/ *n* 名

a thick warm cover for a bed 被子

The cat hid itself in the quilt. 猫躲进被子里去了。

*quite /kwaɪt; kwaɪt/ *adv* 副

1. fairly or very 相当；很
   Today is quite warm. 今天相当暖和。
2. 【英】completely 完全；十分
   You are quite right. 你非常对。

quite a lot 非常多
There are quite a lot of people on the street. 街道上的人非常多。

Daily conversation 日常会话
I'm not quite sure 我不太清楚
"Do you know how to use this camera?" "Sorry, I'm not quite sure." "你会用这台相机吗？""很抱歉，我不太清楚。"

*quiz /kwɪz; kwɪz/ *n* 名

复数：***quizzes***

1. a game or competition where you answer questions 问答比赛
   My sister likes doing quizzes. 我的姐姐喜欢参加问答比赛。
2. a short test that a teacher gives to students 小测验
   Our teacher gave us a quiz today. 今天老师让我们做了一个小测验。

quiz show 问答比赛节目
We took part in the TV quiz show. 我们参加了电视问答比赛节目。

quotation marks /kwəʊ'teɪʃn ˌmɑːks; kwo`teʃən ˏmarks/ *plural n* 复数名词

a pair of signs you use to show what someone said or wrote (" " or ' ') 引号

同义 **inverted commas**

另见 附录：Punctuation 标点符号

quote /kwəʊt; kwot/ *v* 动

quotes, quoting, quoted, quoted

to repeat exactly what someone said or wrote 引述；引用
He quoted a sentence from the book in his composition. 他在作文中引用了书中的一句话。

***rabbit** /ˈræbɪt; ˋræbət/ *n* 名

a small animal with soft fur and long ears 兔

She keeps a rabbit as a pet. 她养了一只兔子做宠物。

***race**[1] /reɪs; res/ *n* 名

1. a competition to see who is the fastest and finishes first 竞赛；比赛

   He won the bicycle race. 他在自行车比赛中胜出了。

2. a group of people who have the same skin colour, type of face etc, and come from the same area of the world 种族

   People of different races live in this city. 这个城市里住着不同种族的人。

race[2] /reɪs; res/ *v* 动

races, racing, raced, raced

to try to go faster than someone or something 参加比赛；（和…）比赛

I raced my sister to the end of the path. 我和姐姐比赛跑到小路的尽头。

***racket** /ˈrækɪt; ˋrækət/ *n* 名

a piece of sports equipment that you use to hit a ball in tennis, badminton, etc 球拍

This tennis racket is very good. 这个网球球拍很好。

radar /ˈreɪdɑː; ˋredɑr/ *n* 名

无复数

a piece of equipment used to find the position and movement of things such as planes 雷达

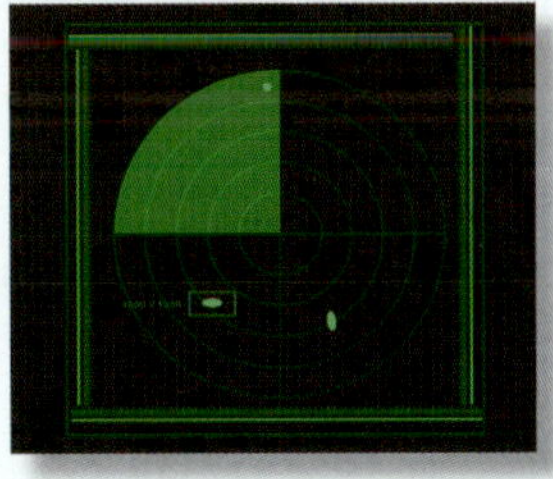

Radar shows the position of the typhoon. 雷达显示了台风的位置。

***radio** /ˈreɪdiəʊ; ˋredɪˌo/ *n* 名

1. a piece of equipment that you use to listen to programmes such as news and music 收音机

   I turned off the radio before I went to bed. 我睡觉前关掉了收音机。

2. （无复数）programmes that you listen to using a radio 无线电广播节目；电台节目

   My mother listens to the radio every morning. 妈妈每天早上都收听广播节目。

rail /reɪl; rel/ *n* 名

1. a long bar around or along something to stop you from falling 扶手；栏杆

   My grandmother held onto the rail and walked up the stairs. 我的外婆抓着栏杆走上楼梯。

2. one of the two long metal bars on the ground for trains to move along 铁轨

   Don't walk on the rails! 不要走在铁轨上！

3. （无复数）the railway system 铁路系统

   I usually go to Guangzhou by rail. 我通常乘火车去广州。

***railway** /ˈreɪlweɪ; ˋrelˌwe/ *n* 名

【英】

美式：***railroad***

1. a track for trains 铁路

   The dog ran across the railway. 那条狗跑过了铁路。

2. （无复数）a train system 铁路系统

   The railway connects all the major cities. 铁路系统连接了所有主要城市。

railway station 火车站

There is a railway station next to the museum. 博物馆旁边有个火车站。

***rain¹** /reɪn; ren/ *n* 名

无复数

water falling from clouds in the sky 雨

The rain stopped before noon. 中午前雨停了。

***rain²** /reɪn; ren/ *v* 动

if it rains, water falls from clouds in the sky 下雨

It rained yesterday so we cancelled the picnic. 昨天下雨，所以我们取消了野餐。

用法 若要说“下雨了”，句子应用 it 开头。中文可以说“天下雨了”，但英文不能写作 The sky is raining。

***rainbow** /ˈreɪnbəʊ; ˋrenˏbo/ *n* 名

a curve of different colours that you see in the sky when the sun shines through rain 彩虹

I saw a rainbow in the sky. 我看到了天上的彩虹。

R

***raincoat** /ˈreɪnkəʊt; ˋrenkot/ *n* 名

something that you wear when it rains to keep you dry 雨衣

It was raining so I put on my raincoat. 天下雨了，所以我穿上雨衣。

rainwater /ˈreɪnwɔːtə; ˋrenˏwɔtɚ/ *n* 名

无复数

water that falls as rain 雨水

Rainwater isn't clean enough to drink. 雨水不干净，不适宜喝。

***rainy** /ˈreɪni; ˋrenɪ/ *adj* 形

rainier, rainiest

having a lot of rain 多雨的

We do not like rainy days. 我们不喜欢雨天。

***raise** /reɪz; rez/ *v* 动

raises, raising, raised, raised

1. to lift or move something to a higher position 举起

   Paul raised his hand to ask a question. 保罗举手发问。

2. to increase an amount, number, etc 增加；提高

   They have raised the price of books. 他们把书价提高了。

用法 raise 后面必须加宾语，即要指明某物或某事。

比较 **rise**

raisin /ˈreɪzn; ˋreznˌ/ *n* 名

a dried grape 葡萄干

I've put raisins on the cake. 我在蛋糕上放了葡萄干。

ran /ræn; ræn/ *v* 动

the past tense of **run** ☆run 的过去式

rang /ræŋ; ræŋ/ *v* 动

the past tense of **ring²** ☆ring² 的过去式

***range¹** /reɪndʒ; rendʒ/ *n* 名

a group of different things of the same type 一系列

The school holds a range of activities for students. 这间学校给学生举办各式各样的活动。

range² /reɪndʒ; rendʒ/ *v* 动

ranges, ranging, ranged, ranged

to be between two numbers, two amounts, etc 在…范围内

The age of the students in this class ranges from 10 to 12. 这个班学生的年龄在 10 至 12 岁之间。

rank /ræŋk; ræŋk/ *n* 名

the position that someone has in an organization or a society 等级

He rose to the rank of chairperson in the company. 他晋升为公司的主席。

rap /ræp; ræp/ *n* 名

无复数

a type of music in which words are spoken but not sung 说唱乐

He is a rap star. 他是说唱乐歌星。

rare /reə; rɛr/ *adj* 形

rarer, rarest

unusual; not happening very often 稀有的；罕有的

Blue roses are rare. 蓝色的玫瑰很稀有。

反义 **common**

***rat** /ræt; ræt/ *n* 名

an animal like a big mouse 大老鼠

Rats are dirty animals. 大老鼠是肮脏的动物。

用法 rat 指体形较大的老鼠，mouse 指体形较小的老鼠。

比较 **mouse**

***rather** /ˈrɑːðə; ˋræðɚ/ *adv* 副

quite; a little 相当；有些

This book is rather interesting. 这本书相当有趣。

would rather ... (than) 宁可；宁愿

She would rather go home than play with us. 她宁愿回家也不愿跟我们玩。

raw /rɔː; rɔ/ *adj* 形

not cooked 生的；未煮熟的

The Japanese like eating raw fish. 日本人喜欢吃生鱼。

***reach** /riːtʃ; ritʃ/ *v* 动

reaches, reaching, reached, reached

1. to arrive at a place 到达

   We reached the airport at four o'clock. 我们4点到达机场。

2. to stretch your arm towards something because you want to touch or take it 伸手去碰；伸手去取

   Oliver reached into his bag to get his wallet. 奥立弗伸手到袋子里掏钱包。

reach out 伸手

She reached out to the soap bubbles. 她伸手去碰肥皂泡。

***read** /riːd; rid/ *v* 动

reads, reading, read, read

1. to look at words and understand them 阅读；看懂

   He is reading a letter. 他正在看信。

2. to say the words in a book, magazine, etc so that other people can hear them 朗读；读出

   I read the poem in class. 我在课堂上朗读了这首诗。

read someone something 给某人朗读某物

My parents read me a story every night when I was a kid. 我小时候，父母每晚会给我讲故事。

read something out 宣读；宣布

The principal read out the results of the football match. 校长宣布了足球比赛的结果。

注意 read 的过去式和过去分词发音和 red 相同。

***reader** /ˈriːdə; ˋridɚ/ *n* 名

1. a person who reads a book, newspaper, etc 读者

   Lily is a fast reader. 莉莉是个看书很快的人。

2. an easy book that is used to help children to learn to read 读本；简易读物

   I like the pictures in the reader. 我喜欢读本里的图画。

***ready** /ˈredi; ˋrɛdɪ/ *adj* 形

1. if someone is ready, he or she is prepared to do something 准备好（做某事）的

   I am ready to leave. 我已准备好离开。

2. if something is ready, it is prepared and can be used immediately 准备好的；已完成的

   Breakfast is ready. 早餐已经准备好了。

***real** /rɪəl; ˋriəl/ *adj* 形

true, not false 真的

The statue looks just like a real monkey. 这座雕像很像真的猴子。

***realize** /ˈrɪəlaɪz; ˋriəˌlaɪz/ *v* 动

realizes, realizing, realized, realized

也作：***realise***【英】

to know and understand something 领悟；觉察

The boy finally realized his mistake. 那个男孩终于知道自己错在哪里了。

注意 通常不会用进行式。

***really** /ˈrɪəli; ˋriəlɪ/ *adv* 副

1. very or very much 非常

   It is really cold today. 今天非常冷。

2. used when saying what is true 真正；实际上

   Is she really your sister? 她真是你的姐姐吗？

Daily conversation 日常会话

Really? 真的吗？（表示感兴趣或惊讶）

"I've got full marks in all subjects." "Really?" "我所有科目都考了满分。" "真的吗？"

Not really 不是；不尽然（表示不同意）

"Do you want to go to the party?" "Not really." "你想参加派对吗？" "不太想。"

***reason** /ˈriːzn; ˋrizn̩/ *n* 名

why you do something or why something happens 理由；原因

James gave the reason for being late. 詹姆斯说出了迟到的原因。

同义 **cause**[1]

***receive** /riˈsiːv; rɪˋsiv/ *v* 动

receives, receiving, received, received

to get or be given something 收到；接到

I received a birthday present from my aunt. 我收到阿姨给我的生日礼物。

用法 常用于书面语，口语多用 get，例如 I got a birthday present.

反义 **give**

***recent** /ˈriːsnt; ˋrisn̩t/ *adj* 形

happening or beginning a short time ago 最近的；近来的

I need a recent photo for the passport. 我申请护照需要一张近照。

***recently** /ˈriːsntli; ˋrisn̩tlɪ/ *adv* 副

not a long time ago 最近；近来

I haven't seen Mr Wilson recently. 我近来没有见过威尔逊先生。

R

***recess** /ri'ses; `risɛs/ *n* 名【美】**无复数**

英式 **break²**

recipe /'resəpi; `rɛsəpɪ/ *n* 名

a list of things you need to do to make food 食谱；烹饪法

This is a recipe for cookies. 这是一份小甜饼的食谱。

recite /ri'saɪt; rɪ`saɪt/ *v* 动

recites, reciting, recited, recited

to say a piece of writing that you have learnt 背诵；朗诵

Shirley is reciting a poem to us. 雪莉正在给我们朗诵一首诗。

***recognize** /'rekəgnaɪz; `rɛkəg͵naɪz/ *v* 动

recognizes, recognizing, recognized, recognized

也作：*recognise*【英】

to know someone or something when you see or hear them again 认出；认得

Alan still recognized Olivia although he had not seen her for 10 years. 虽然艾伦已经10年没见过奥莉维亚，但仍然认得出她。

***recommend** /ˌrekə'mend; ͵rɛkə`mɛnd/ *v* 动

to tell someone that someone else or something is good for them 推荐；介绍

Our teacher recommended an English book to us. 老师向我们推荐了一本英文书。

***record¹** /'rekɔ:d; `rɛkɚd/ *n* 名

1. information that you keep for future use 记录；记载

   Sally has kept a record of the books she has read. 莎莉记录了所有看过的书。

2. the best result（最佳）纪录

   Henry won the race and broke the school record. 亨利赢了冠军，并打破了学校的纪录。

***record²** /ri'kɔ:d; rɪ`kɔrd/ *v* 动

to write something down or store words, sounds or pictures for future use 记录；录音；录影

Lily recorded the songs on a CD. 莉莉把歌曲录制在光碟里。

recover /ri'kʌvə; rɪ`kʌvɚ/ *v* 动

to become healthy again after an illness or injury 康复；痊愈

Ann was ill last week but she has recovered now. 安上星期生病，但现在已经康复了。

***rectangle** /'rektæŋgl; `rɛktæŋgl̩/ *n* 名

a shape with four angles of 90° and four straight sides, two of which are usually longer than the other two 长方形

Please count the number of rectangles in the picture. 请数出图中有多少个长方形。

***recycle** /ˌri:'saɪkl; ri`saɪkl̩/ *v* 动

recycles, recycling, recycled, recycled

to make something new from something that has been used 回收利用；循环再用

We should recycle cans, bottles and paper. 我们应该把金属罐、瓶子和纸张回收利用。

recycling bin 回收箱

There are three recycling bins at the playground. 操场内有三个回收箱。

***red¹** /red; rɛd/ *adj* 形

redder, reddest

having the colour of blood 红色的

She bought a red purse. 她买了一个红色钱包。

***red²** /red; rɛd/ *n* 名

the colour of blood 红色

Please circle the mistakes in red. 请把错误处用红色圈出来。

***reduce** /ri'dju:s; rɪ`dus/ *v* 动

reduces, reducing, reduced, reduced

to make something smaller or less in size, amount, etc 缩小；减少；降低

The bakery reduced the price of cake. 那家面包店的蛋糕降价了。

***refer** /ri'fɜ:; rɪ`fɝ/ *v* 动

refers, referring, referred, referred

refer to someone or something

1. to mention someone or something 提及；提到（某人或某物）

   In the book he never refers to his family. 他在书中从没提及家人。

2. to find information in a book,

R

map, etc 参考；查看

Jenny referred to the story book while she was telling the story. 珍妮看着故事书讲故事。

referee /ˌrefəˈriː; ˌrɛfəˋri/ *n* 名

someone who makes sure that sports players follow rules 裁判员

The referee gave the player a yellow card. 裁判员给了那位球员一张黄牌。

***reflect** /riˈflekt; rɪˋflɛkt/ *v* 动

to show the image of someone or something on the surface of water, glass or a mirror 照出（影像）；反映

Her face was reflected in the mirror. 她的脸映照在镜子里。

***refrigerator** /riˈfrɪdʒəreɪtə; rɪˋfrɪdʒəˌretɚ/ *n* 名

a machine that keeps food and drinks cold 冰箱

I put the milk in the refrigerator. 我把牛奶放在冰箱里。

同义 **fridge**

另见 **freezer**

***refuse** /riˈfjuːz; rɪˋfjuz/ *v* 动

refuses, refusing, refused, refused

to say that you will not do something or accept something 拒绝；不肯

I asked her to help me but she refused. 我请她帮忙，但是她拒绝了。

反义 **accept**

***region** /ˈriːdʒən; ˋridʒən/ *n* 名

a large area 地区；地带

Some birds live in very cold regions. 有些鸟在很寒冷的地区生息。

regular /ˈregjʊlə; ˋrɛgjələ/ *adj* 形

1. happening or doing something over and over again at the same time or in the same way 定期的；有规律的

   The class club holds regular meetings. 班会定期开会。

2. happening or doing something often 经常的

   Regular exercise is good for health. 经常做运动对健康有益。

3. normal; not too big or too small 普通的；一般的；标准的

   The regular opening hours of the restaurant are 8 a.m. to 10 p.m. 这间餐厅正常的营业时间是从上午 8 点到晚上 10 点。

***rehearsal** /riˈhɜːsl; rɪˋhɝsl/ *n* 名

a time when a person or group practises for a public performance 排练；排演

We will have three more rehearsals before the performance. 在表演之前，我们会再排练三次。

***relationship** /riˈleɪʃnʃɪp; rɪˋleʃənˌʃɪp/ *n* 名

the way in which two people, groups, etc behave towards each other 关系

I have a good relationship with my classmates. 我和同学的关系良好。

***relative** /ˈrelətɪv; ˋrɛlətɪv/ *n* 名

someone in your family 亲戚

I had dinner with some relatives last night. 我昨晚和几个亲戚吃晚餐。

***relax** /riˈlæks; rɪˋlæks/ *v* 动

relaxes, relaxing, relaxed, relaxed

to rest and become calm, so that you do not feel worried about anything 轻松；放松

Take a break and relax. 休息一会，放松一下。

Daily conversation 日常会话

"I'm really worried about my exams." "Relax! You'll be OK." "我真的很为考试担心。""放松些！你会考好的。"

religion /riˈlɪdʒən; rɪˋlɪdʒən/ *n* 名

1. （无复数）believing in one or more gods 宗教信仰

   We have freedom of religion. 我们有宗教信仰自由。

2. a system of believing in one or more gods（一种）宗教

   People of different religions live in the city. 这个城市的居民信奉不同的宗教。

***remain** /riˈmeɪn; rɪˋmen/ *v* 动

1. to be in the same condition 保持；还是（某状态）

   The water in the pot remains cool. 壶中的水保持清凉。

2. to continue to exist after the rest has been taken away or used 留下；剩下

   Few houses remained after the fire. 火灾后房屋所剩无几。

remark /riˈmɑːk; rɪˋmark/ *n* 名

something that you say or write to give your opinion about something 评论；评语；意见

My teacher made some remarks about my drawing. 老师对我的画给出了一些评语。

R

remarkable /ri'mɑːkəbl; rɪ`mɑrkəbḷ/ *adj* 形

unusual or surprising 不寻常的；出色的

Her singing was remarkable. 她唱得非常出色。

*__remember__ /ri'membə; rɪ`mɛmbɚ/ *v* 动

to keep an image or idea in your mind; to not forget something 记得；记住

He cannot remember my name. 他记不起我的名字。

用法 不用进行式，例如我们不说 I am remembering her，而说 I remember her（我记得她）。

反义 forget

*__remind__ /ri'maɪnd; rɪ`maɪnd/ *v* 动

to make someone remember something 提醒；使（某人）记起

Please remind me to feed the fish. 请提醒我喂鱼。

remind someone of something 使（某人）想起某事

This song reminds me of Christmas. 这首歌使我想起圣诞节。

remote control /rɪˌməʊt kən'trəʊl; rɪˌmote kən`trol/ *n* 名

a piece of equipment that you use to control something from a distance 遥控器

I can't find the remote control. 我找不到遥控器。

R

*__remove__ /ri'muːv; rɪ`muv/ *v* 动

removes, removing, removed, removed

to take something away from a place 搬走；移走；去掉

I removed everything from the desk. 我移走了书桌上的所有东西。

*__rent__¹ /rent; rɛnt/ *n* 名

the money you pay to live in or use a room, car, etc 租金

He pays the rent every month. 他每个月缴付租金。

*__rent__² /rent; rɛnt/ *v* 动

to pay for the use of something that belongs to someone else, such as a room, car, etc 租用

We have rented the flat for one year. 我们租住这套公寓一年了。

*__repair__ /ri'peə; rɪ`pɛr/ *v* 动

to make something be in good condition again, after it has been broken or damaged 修理；修补

My father repaired the broken chair. 我的爸爸把破烂的椅子修好了。

*__repeat__ /ri'piːt; rɪ`pit/ *v* 动

to say or do something again 重说；重做

We should not repeat the same mistake. 我们不应重复犯同一错误。

In the classroom 在教室里

"Can you repeat the answer?" "OK." "你可以再说一次答案吗？" "可以。"

*__replace__ /ri'pleɪs; rɪ`ples/ *v* 动

replaces, replacing, replaced, replaced

1. if you replace something that has been broken, damaged, etc, you get a new one 取代；替换

   I replaced the old TV with a new one. 我换了新电视机。

2. to put something back in its place 把…放回原处

   I replaced the books on the shelf. 我把书放回架子上。

*__reply__¹ /ri'plaɪ; rɪ`plaɪ/ *v* 动

replies, replying, replied, replied

to say or write something to answer someone 回答；答复

I sent him an email but he did not reply. 我给他发了电邮，但他没有回复。

reply to something 回答；答复

Yesterday he replied to my letter. 昨天他给我回了信。

同义 answer¹

反义 ask

*__reply__² /ri'plaɪ; rɪ`plaɪ/ *n* 名

复数：***replies***

something that you say or write as an answer to someone or something 回答；答复

I am writing a reply to the email. 我在回复电子邮件。

同义 answer²

*__report__¹ /ri'pɔːt; rɪ`pɔrt/ *n* 名

1. something that someone writes about a situation or event 报告；报道

   This is a report of the car accident. 这是一篇关于那起车祸的报道。

2. 【英】（美式：***report card***）something that a teacher writes about a student's work at school 学生成绩报告单；成绩单

   I got my report on Parents' Day. 我在家长日拿到了成绩单。

*__report__² /ri'pɔːt; rɪ`pɔrt/ *v* 动

1. to give information about an event in a newspaper, on the television or radio 报道

   The fire was reported in the newspaper. 报纸报道了那场火灾。

2. to tell someone about an accident or about something bad that someone has done 举报；报告；投诉

   I reported the robbery to the police. 我向警察举报了抢劫案。

***reporter** /ri'pɔːtə; rɪ`pɔrtɚ/ *n* 名

someone who gets information about news events and reports them for newspapers, television or radio 记者；新闻报道员

My sister is a reporter for a newspaper. 我的姐姐是一名记者，为一家报社工作。

***represent** /ˌrepri'zent; ˏrɛprɪ`zɛnt/ *v* 动

1. to act or speak for someone or something 代表

   Sally represented our class in the singing contest. 莎莉代表我们班参加歌唱比赛。

2. to be a sign or example of something 象征；表示

   Red represents good luck for the Chinese. 红色对中国人来说象征着幸运。

representative /ˌrepri'zentətiv; ˏrɛprɪ`zɛntətɪv/ *n* 名

a person who represents someone or something 代表

Ross and Lily are the representatives of our class. 罗斯和莉莉是我们班里的代表。

reptile /'reptail; `rɛptḷ/ *n* 名

an animal that has cold blood and lays eggs, such as a snake or a tortoise 爬行动物；爬虫类

Some people keep reptiles as pets. 有些人把爬行动物当宠物。

***require** /ri'kwaiə; rɪ`kwaɪr/ *v* 动

requires, requiring, required, required

to need something 需要

The orphans require our care. 孤儿需要我们的关心。

用法 常用于书面语，口语多用 need，例如：They need our care（他们需要我们的关心）。

***rescue** /'reskjuː; `rɛskju/ *v* 动

rescues, rescuing, rescued, rescued

to save someone or something from danger 拯救

They rescued the sailors from the sinking ship. 他们把那些海员从正在下沉的船中救了出来。

同义 **save**

reservoir /'rezəvwaː; `rɛzɚˏvwar/ *n* 名

a place where water is stored for people to use 水库；水塘

The reservoir collects rainwater. 水库收集雨水。

***respect** /ri'spekt; rɪ`spɛkt/ *v* 动

to admire someone or something and treat them in a way that shows you think they are good 尊重；敬重

I respect my parents. 我尊重我的父母。

用法 不用进行式。

***responsible** /ri'spɒnsəbl; rɪ`spansəbḷ/ *adj* 形

if you are responsible for doing something, it is your duty to do it 负责的；负有责任的

We are responsible for organizing the party. 我们负责筹备派对。

***rest**[1] /rest; rɛst/ *n* 名

1. a time when you can relax or sleep 休息

   Tony has caught a cold and needs a good rest. 托尼得了感冒，需要好好休息。

2. **the rest** the part of something that is left 其余的人或东西；剩余部分

   I will do the rest of my homework tomorrow. 我明天会完成余下的功课。

have/take a rest 休息一下

You look tired. Why don't you take a rest? 你看来很累，怎么不休息一下？

rest[2] /rest; rɛst/ *v* 动

to stop working and sit down to relax or sleep 休息

Sam is resting on the sofa. 山姆坐在沙发上休息。

restart /ˌriː'staːt; ri`start/ *v* 动

to start something again 重新启动

I restarted the computer. 我重启了电脑。

***restaurant** /'restərɒnt; `rɛstərənt/ *n* 名

a place where you can buy and eat a meal 餐厅；餐馆

We had dinner in my favourite restaurant. 我们在我最喜爱的餐厅吃了晚饭。

***result** /ri'zʌlt; rɪ`zʌlt/ *n* 名

1. something that happens because of something else 结果
   Her success was the result of hard work. 她取得成功，是她努力的成果。
2. 【英】the mark you get in an examination 成绩
   We will get our exam results next week. 我们下星期会收到考试成绩。

retired /ri'taɪəd; rɪ`taɪrd/ *adj* 形

a retired person has stopped working, usually because he or she is getting old 退休的

My uncle is a retired teacher. 我的叔叔是一位退休教师。

***return[1]** /ri'tɜːn; rɪ`tɝn/ *v* 动

1. to come or go back to a place again 回来；回去
   Mark has just returned from the USA. 马克刚从美国回来。
2. to bring, give, put or take something back 归还；送还
   I returned the books to the library. 我把书还给了图书馆。

用法 return 不与 back 同用，例如不能说 I returned the books back to the library。

return[2] /ri'tɜːn; rɪ`tɝn/ *n* 名

无复数

when someone comes back or goes to a place where he or she was before 回来；回去

She is waiting for her daughter's return. 她在等待女儿归来。

***revise** /ri'vaɪz; rɪ`vaɪz/ *v* 动

revises, revising, revised, revised

to study something again for an examination 温习；复习

My exams begin tomorrow. I have to revise today. 明天开始考试，我今天必须温习。

revise for 温习以准备（考试或测验）

We are revising for the mathematics examination. 我们在温习功课以准备数学考试。

***revision** /ri'vɪʒn; rɪ`vɪʒən/ *n* 名

无复数

studying something that you have learnt before, usually for an examination 温习；复习

Linda has done enough revision for the test. 琳达对测验准备充足。

reward[1] /ri'wɔːd; rɪ`wɔrd/ *n* 名

something given to someone because of good work or actions 奖赏；报酬

I wanted to give him a reward for his good work. 他工作做得好，所以我想奖励他。

reward[2] /ri'wɔːd; rɪ`wɔrd/ *v* 动

to give a present or money to someone who has done something good 奖赏；酬谢

The teacher rewarded Paul for his hard work. 保罗用功读书，所以老师奖励他。

rhinoceros /raɪ'nɒsərəs; raɪ`nɑsərəs/ *n* 名

复数：***rhinoceros/rhinoceroses*** ｜ 也作：***rhino***

a large animal that has very thick skin and one or two horns 犀牛

Rhinoceroses live in Africa and South East Asia. 犀牛住在非洲和东南亚地区。

***rhyme[1]** /raɪm; raɪm/ *n* 名

1. a word that ends with the same sound as another word 同韵词；押韵词
   "Bell" and "well" are rhymes. bell 和 well 是同韵词。
2. a short poem or song in which the last word in each line ends with the same sound as the last word in another line 押韵短诗；童谣
   The girls were singing rhymes. 那些女孩在唱童谣。

rhyme[2] /raɪm; raɪm/ *v* 动

rhymes, rhyming, rhymed, rhymed

if one word rhymes with the other word, they end with the same sound 押韵

"You" rhymes with "two". you 跟 two 押韵。

rhythm /'rɪðəm; `rɪðəm/ *n* 名

a regular pattern of sounds in music 节奏；韵律

Candy likes music with a fast rhythm. 坎蒂喜爱节奏快的音乐。

***ribbon** /'rɪbən; `rɪbən/ *n* 名

a narrow piece of material that you use to tie things up 丝带；缎带

I tied a ribbon round the present. 我给这份礼物系了一条丝带。

***rice** /raɪs; raɪs/ *n* 名

无复数

small white or brown grains you cook to eat 米；饭

Ben ate two bowls of rice. 本吃了两

R

碗饭。

***rich** /rɪtʃ; rɪtʃ/ *adj* 形

richer, richest

having a lot of money or property 富有的；有钱的

His family is very rich. 他家很有钱。

the rich 富人；有钱人

The rich should help the poor. 富人应该帮助穷人。

同义 **wealthy**

反义 **poor**

***riddle** /ˈrɪdl; ˋrɪdl/ *n* 名

a difficult question which is asked in a game and has a funny answer 谜语

The boy is trying to solve the riddle. 那个男孩正在猜谜语。

***ride¹** /raɪd; raɪd/ *v* 动

rides, riding, rode, ridden

to travel on a bicycle or an animal such as a horse, or in a bus, car, etc 骑；乘

My mother and I enjoy riding a bicycle. 妈妈和我都喜欢骑自行车。

ride² /raɪd; raɪd/ *n* 名

a journey on a bicycle or an animal such as a horse, or in a bus, car, etc 骑自行车；骑马；乘车

I had my first ride on a horse yesterday. 我昨天第一次骑马。

***right¹** /raɪt; raɪt/ *adj* 形

1. correct or true 对的；正确的

   The answers are right. 这些答案都正确。

反义 **incorrect, wrong¹**

2. on the opposite of left 右边的；右方的

   Robin raised his right hand. 罗宾举起右手。

反义 **left³**

Daily conversation 日常会话

that's right 对；没错

"Is this your school bag?" "That's right." "这是你的书包吗？""没错。"

***right²** /raɪt; raɪt/ *n* 名

1. something that you are allowed to do or have 权利

   Everyone has the right to education. 人人都有受教育的权利。

2. （无复数）what is fair and good 对；正确

   We must learn the difference between right and wrong. 我们必须学会分辨是非。

反义 **wrong³**

3. （无复数）the opposite of left 右边；右方

   The zoo is on the right of the road. 动物园在路的右边。

反义 **left²**

Asking for directions 问路

"How do you get to the park?" "Walk along the road and you'll see it. It's on your right." "公园该怎么去呢？" "沿着这条街往前走，你就会见到了。公园就在你的右边。"

***right³** /raɪt; raɪt/ *adv* 副

1. correctly 正确地

   Sally spelt every word right. 莎莉正确地拼写出每个词。

反义 **wrong²**

2. towards the right side 向右

   Turn right and you will see the bookshop. 向右一拐你就会见到书店。

反义 **left⁴**

3. immediately 马上；立刻

   Please wait for a moment. She will be right back. 请等一会儿。她马上就回来。

right away/now 马上；立刻

Please come here right away. 请马上来这里。

right click【电脑】按鼠标右键

Right click and you'll see a menu on the screen. 按鼠标右键，你就会在电脑屏幕上见到菜单。

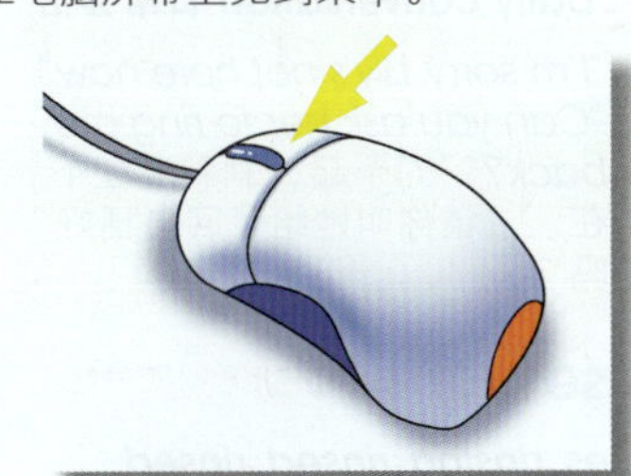

R

ring[1] /rɪŋ; rɪŋ/ *n* 名

1. a piece of jewellery that you wear on your finger 戒指

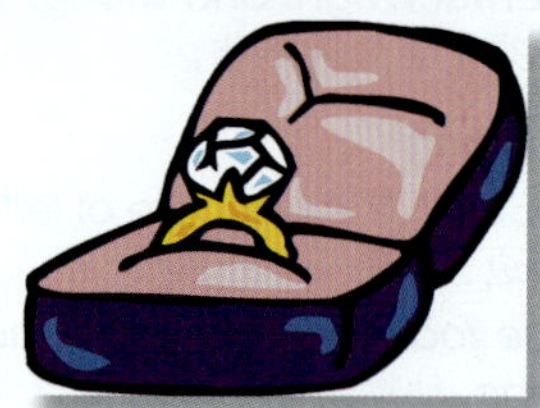

Michelle has a beautiful diamond ring. 米歇尔有一枚漂亮的钻石戒指。

2. something in the shape of a circle 环；圈

We stood in a ring around our teacher. 我们围着老师站成一圈。

3. the sound of a bell 铃声；钟声

I heard a ring at the door. 我听见门铃响。

Daily conversation 日常会话

give someone a ring 给某人打电话

"Can I give you a ring tonight?" "No problem." "我今晚可以给你打电话吗？""没问题。"

ring[2] /rɪŋ; rɪŋ/ *v* 动

rings, ringing, rang, rung

1. to make the sound of a bell 发出铃声

The telephone is ringing. 电话在响。

2. to telephone someone（给…）打电话

Winnie rang me yesterday. 威妮昨天打电话给我。

用法 ring 后面接宾语，不用加上 to。

Daily conversation 日常会话

"I'm sorry. Lily's not here now." "Can you ask her to ring me back?" "对不起，莉莉现在不在。""请你叫她给我回电话好吗？"

rinse /rɪns; rɪns/ *v* 动

rinses, rinsing, rinsed, rinsed

to wash something with clean water to remove dirt, soap, etc 冲洗

Henry rinsed the apple under the tap. 亨利用自来水冲洗苹果。

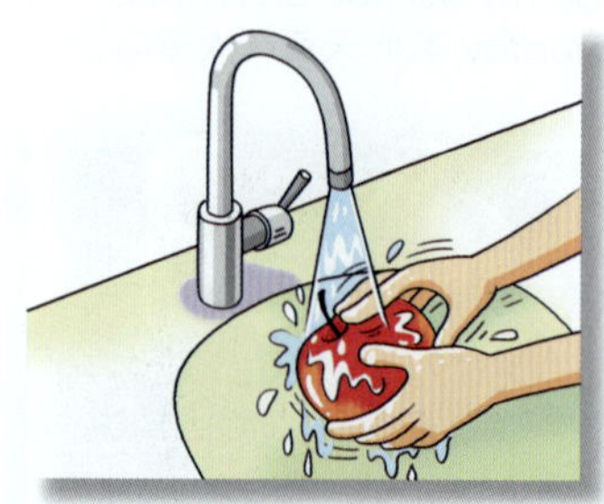

ripe /raɪp; raɪp/ *adj* 形

riper, ripest

if fruit or crops are ripe, they are ready to eat 成熟的

The mangoes aren't ripe yet. 那些芒果还没熟。

***rise** /raɪz; raɪz/ *v* 动

rises, rising, rose, risen

1. to move upwards 上升；升起

The balloon is rising in the air. 气球正飘上天空。

2. to increase in number, amount, etc 增加；上升

The price of books has risen. 图书的价格上涨了。

3. if the sun or the moon rises, it appears in the sky（太阳、月亮）升起

The sun rises in the east. 太阳从东边升起。

用法 不能在 rise 后面加宾语，例如不能说 They rose the price of books。

比较 **raise**

risen /ˈrɪzn; ˋrɪzn̩/ *v* 动

the past participle of **rise** ☆ rise 的过去分词

***risk**[1] /rɪsk; rɪsk/ *n* 名

a chance that something bad may happen 危险；风险

Smoking can increase the risk of cancer. 吸烟会增加患癌症的风险。

同义 **danger**

risk[2] /rɪsk; rɪsk/ *v* 动

to put someone or something in a dangerous situation 冒险

The firefighter risked his life to save the girl. 消防员冒着生命危险拯救那女孩。

***river** /ˈrɪvə; ˋrɪvɚ/ *n* 名

a long line of water flowing into the sea 河；江

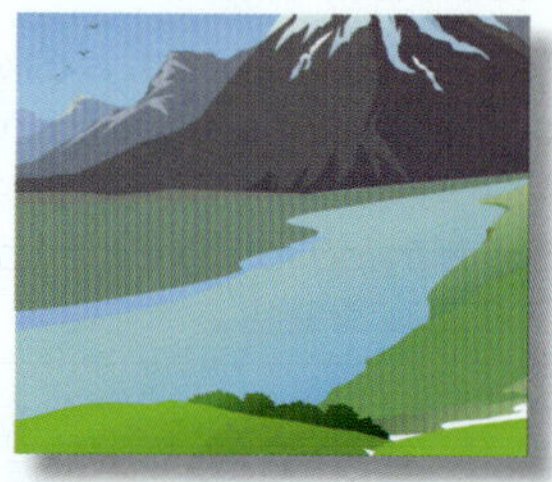

There are a lot of fish in the river. 河里有很多鱼。

***road** /rəʊd; rod/ *n* 名

a way that vehicles and people use to go from one place to another place 路；道路

My school is on a quiet road. 我的学校在一条宁静的路上。

***roar**[1] /rɔː; rɔr/ *v* 动

to make a loud deep noise like a lion 咆哮；吼叫

The lion is roaring. 狮子在咆哮。

roar[2] /rɔː; rɔr/ *n* 名

a loud deep noise 咆哮声；吼叫声

We heard the roar of a lion. 我们听到狮子的吼叫声。

***roast¹** /rəʊst; rost/ *v* 动

to cook something without water in an oven or over a fire 烤

My brother roasted some potatoes. 哥哥烤了一些马铃薯。

***roast²** /rəʊst; rost/ *adj* 形

cooked without water in an oven or over a fire 烤制的

Joan likes roast chicken. 琼喜欢吃烤鸡。

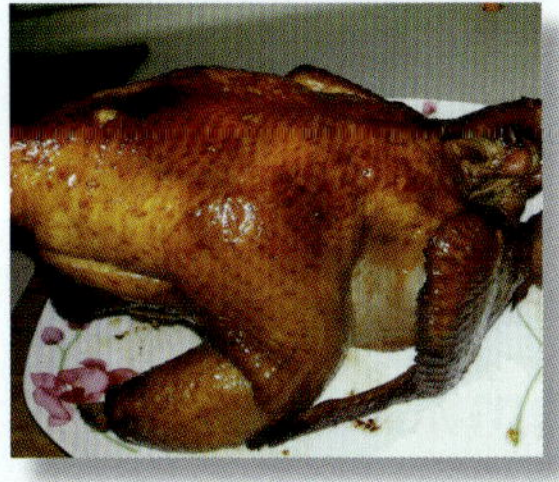

***rob** /rɒb; rɑb/ *v* 动

robs, robbing, robbed, robbed

to steal something from a person or a place 抢劫；打劫

Three men robbed the bank. 三名男子抢劫了银行。

用法 rob 用于指抢劫人或机构，steal 用于指偷钱或其他物品。

比较 **steal**

***robber** /ˈrɒbə; ˋrɑbɚ/ *n* 名

someone who steals something from a person or a place 强盗；盗贼

Before the robber could escape the police arrested him. 盗贼还没来得及逃走就被警察抓住了。

robbery /ˈrɒbəri; ˋrɑbərɪ/ *n* 名

复数：***robberies***

the crime of stealing something from a person or a place 抢劫

There was a robbery at the shop. 这家商店发生了抢劫案。

***robot** /ˈrəʊbɒt; ˋrobɑt/ *n* 名

a machine that is controlled by a computer and can do some of the work of a person 机器人

The cars are built by robots in a factory. 这些汽车是由工厂里的机器人制造的。

***rock** /rɒk; rɑk/ *n* 名

a big stone 大石块

There are a lot of rocks on the beach. 海滩上有许多大石块。

***rocket** /ˈrɒkɪt; ˋrɑkɪt/ *n* 名

a vehicle that is like a big tube and is used to carry things into space 火箭

The rocket will carry a satellite into space. 这支火箭将携带人造卫星进入太空。

另见 **spaceship**

rod /rɒd; rɑd/ *n* 名

a straight thin pole or stick 杆；竿；棒

I caught a fish with a fishing rod. 我用钓竿钓到了一条鱼。

rode /rəʊd; rod/ *v* 动

the past tense of **ride¹** ☆ride¹ 的过去式

***role** /rəʊl; rol/ *n* 名

a character in a drama, play or film 角色

Sophia played the role of the fairy in the play. 索菲亚在戏剧中扮演小仙子。

***role-play** /ˈrəʊl pleɪ; ˋrol ple/ *n* 名

an exercise in which you try to behave like someone else in a particular situation 角色扮演

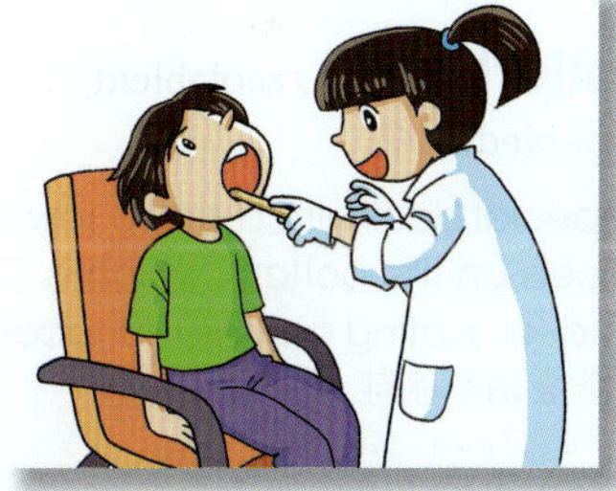

We did role-plays in class today. 我们今天上课时玩角色扮演。

***roll¹** /rəʊl; rol/ *v* 动

1. to move by turning over and over 滚动

   The ball rolled down the hill. 球从小山上滚下来。

2. （也作：***roll up***）to make something into the shape of a ball or tube 卷

   Ross rolled up the newspaper.

R

罗斯把报纸卷了起来。

roll something into a ball/tube
把某物弄成球形/筒形
The cook rolled the dough into small balls. 厨师把面团搓成小丸子。

***roll²** /rəʊl; rol/ *n* 名

something made into the shape of a ball or tube 卷

Mike is making sushi rolls. 迈克在做寿司卷。

roll-call /ˈrəʊl kɔːl; ˋrol kɔl/ *n* 名

the reading of a list of names to check who is present and who is absent 点名
Our teacher takes the roll-call every morning. 老师每天早上点名。

Rollerblade /ˈrəʊləbleɪd; ˋrolɚˌbled/ *n* 名

a special boot with a single row of wheels on the bottom, which is used for skating on hard surfaces 直排滚轴旱冰鞋

I put on my Rollerblades and started skating. 我穿上直排滚轴旱冰鞋溜起冰来。

注意 Rollerblade 是商标名称，一般以大写开头。

roller coaster /ˈrəʊlə ˌkəʊstə; ˋrolɚ ˏkostɚ/ *n* 名

a special small train in an amusement park which makes sudden big turns and which you ride on for fun（游乐园中的）过山车

We like riding on a roller coaster.
我们喜欢坐过山车。

roller skate /ˈrəʊlə skeɪt; ˋrolɚ sket/ *n* 名

a special boot with four wheels on the bottom, which is used for skating on hard surfaces 四轮旱冰鞋；滚轴溜冰鞋

I enjoy going fast on roller skates.
我爱穿上滚轴溜冰鞋快速滑行。

roller-skating /ˈrəʊlə ˌskeɪtɪŋ; ˋrolɚ ˏsketɪŋ/ *n* 名

无复数

the sport of moving over hard surfaces on roller skates 滑旱冰；滚轴溜冰
Let's go roller-skating this afternoon.
我们今天下午去滑旱冰吧。

romantic /rəʊˈmæntɪk; roˋmæntɪk/ *adj* 形

showing or describing love 浪漫的；爱情的
I watched a romantic film last night.
我昨晚看了一部爱情电影。

***roof** /ruːf; ruf/ *n* 名

the top part of a building, vehicle, etc 屋顶；顶部

There is a hole on the roof. 屋顶上有一个洞。

***room** /ruːm; rum/ *n* 名

1. a part of a building that has its own walls and a door 房间
   The room is large and comfortable. 这个房间又大又舒适。
2. （无复数）empty space for someone or something 空间；空位
   There is no room at home for a piano. 家里没有空间放钢琴。

***root** /ruːt; rut/ *n* 名

the part of a plant which grows under the ground 根

Tree roots get water from the soil.
树的根部吸收泥土中的水分。

注意 发音和 route 相同。

***rope** /rəʊp; rop/ *n* 名

a very thick strong string which is made by twisting a lot of thin strings together 粗绳

He tied the cow with a rope. 他用一根绳把牛绑起来。

比较 **string, thread**

***rose[1]** /rəʊz; roz/ *n* 名

a flower which has thorns on its stem and a sweet smell 玫瑰花

There are a lot of roses in the garden. 花园里有很多玫瑰花。

rose[2] /rəʊz; roz/ *v* 动

the past tense of **rise** ☆rise 的过去式

***rotten** /ˈrɒtn; ˋrɑtn̩/ *adj* 形

if something is rotten, it has gone bad and cannot be eaten or used 腐烂的；变质的

He threw away the rotten apple. 他把烂苹果扔掉了。

***rough** /rʌf; rʌf/ *adj* 形

rougher, roughest

1. not smooth 粗糙的；不平的

   My grandfather has very rough hands. 爷爷的双手很粗糙。

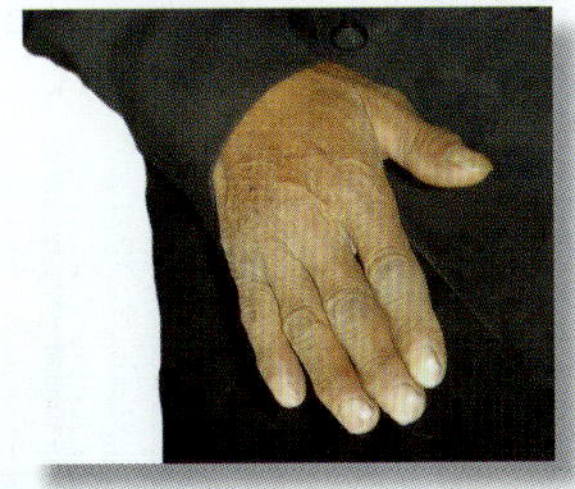

反义 **smooth, soft**

2. not exact 粗略的；概略的

   I made a rough drawing of the car. 我画了一幅汽车的草图。

3. with strong wind and big waves 风浪大的

   The ship sank in rough seas. 船在风高浪急的海中沉没了。

反义 **calm**

roughly /ˈrʌfli; ˋrʌflɪ/ *adv* 副

about 大约；大概

Roughly half of the pupils are boys. 大约一半学生是男孩。

***round[1]** /raʊnd; raund/ *adj* 形

having the shape of a circle or ball 圆的；圆形的

The clock is round. 这只钟是圆形的。

***round[2]** /raʊnd; raund/ *adv* 副

也作：***around***

1. moving in a circle 环绕；围绕

   The children danced round happily. 那些孩子围成一圈开心地跳舞。

2. on all sides of someone or something 周围；四周

   The students gathered round to watch the experiment. 那些学生围成一圈看实验。

3. moving to face the opposite direction 转过头

   Colin turned round and spoke to me. 科林转过头来跟我说话。

round and round 不停地转

The wheel is turning round and round. 那个轮子不停地转。

round[3] /raʊnd; raund/ *prep* 介

也作：***around***

1. in a circle 环绕；围绕

   The earth goes round the sun. 地球围绕太阳运行。

2. on all sides of someone or something 周围；四周

   We sat round the table. 我们围着桌子坐。

3. in or to many places or parts of something 到处；四处

   The teacher showed the new students round the school. 老师带新来的学生参观了学校。

roundabout /ˈraʊndəbaʊt; ˋraundəˏbaut/ *n* 名【英】

1. （美式：***merry-go-round***）a round structure which children push around while others are standing or sitting on it 旋转台

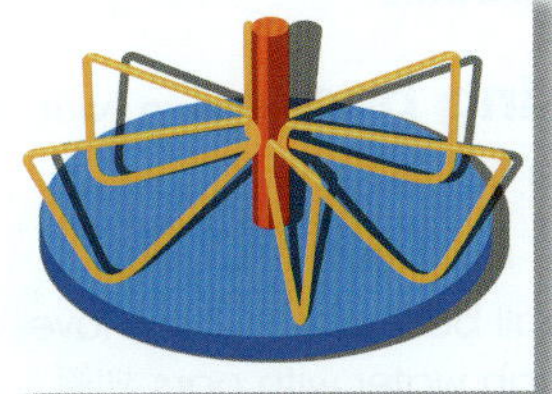

   There is a roundabout in the playground. 游乐场里有个旋转台。

2. a big machine with model animals or vehicles which children can ride on while it turns round and round 旋转木马

   We went for a ride on the roundabout in the amusement park. 我们在游乐园乘坐旋转木马。

同义 **merry-go-round**

route /ruːt; rut/ *n* 名

a way from one place to another 路线；路径

Which is the best route to the train station? 到火车站的最佳路线怎么走?

注意 发音和 root 相同。

row[1] /rəʊ; ro/ *n* 名

a line of people or things next to each other 一排；一列；一行

The children stood in a row. 孩子站成了一排。

R

row² /rəʊ; ro/ *v* 动

to make a boat move through water with oars 划（船）

They are rowing a boat in the lake. 他们在湖中划船。

比较 **paddle²**

rowing boat /ˈrəʊɪŋ bəʊt; ˋroɪŋ bot/ *n* 名【英】

美式：***row boat***

a small boat which you move through water with oars 划艇

We crossed the river on a rowing boat. 我们坐划艇过河。

***royal** /ˈrɔɪəl; ˋrɔɪəl/ *adj* 形

of or belonging to a king or queen 王室的；皇家的

The royal family lives in the palace. 王室住在王宫里。

***rub** /rʌb; rʌb/ *v* 动

rubs, rubbing, rubbed, rubbed

to press something against another thing and move it backwards and forwards 擦；摩擦

Lily rubbed her hands to keep warm. 莉莉摩擦双手取暖。

***rubber** /ˈrʌbə; ˋrʌbɚ/ *n* 名

1. （无复数）a soft material used to make tyres, balls, etc 橡胶

   We wear rubber boots on rainy days. 我们雨天穿胶靴。

2. 【英】（美式：***eraser***）something you use to remove pencil marks from paper 橡皮擦

   I put two pencils and a rubber in my pencil case. 我在笔盒里放了两支铅笔和一块橡皮擦。

rubber band /ˌrʌbə ˈbænd; ˏrʌbɚ ˋbænd/ *n* 名

a thin ring of rubber that you use to hold things together 橡皮圈；橡皮筋

The teacher put a rubber band round the pile of exercise books. 老师用橡皮圈捆着练习册。

***rubbish** /ˈrʌbɪʃ; ˋrʌbɪʃ/ *n* 名

无复数

things that you do not want and throw away 垃圾；废物

Throw the rubbish in the bin. 把垃圾扔在垃圾箱里。

rubbish bin 垃圾箱

There is a rubbish bin in the kitchen. 厨房里有一个垃圾箱。

同义 **litter**

***rude** /ruːd; rud/ *adj* 形

ruder, rudest

behaving in a way that is not polite 粗鲁的；无礼的

We should not be rude to our parents. 我们不应该对父母无礼。

反义 **polite**

rudely /ˈruːdli; ˋrudlɪ/ *adv* 副

in a rude way 粗鲁地；无礼地

May never speaks rudely. 梅从不会粗鲁地说话。

rug /rʌg; rʌg/ *n* 名

a piece of thick material that covers part of the floor 小地毯

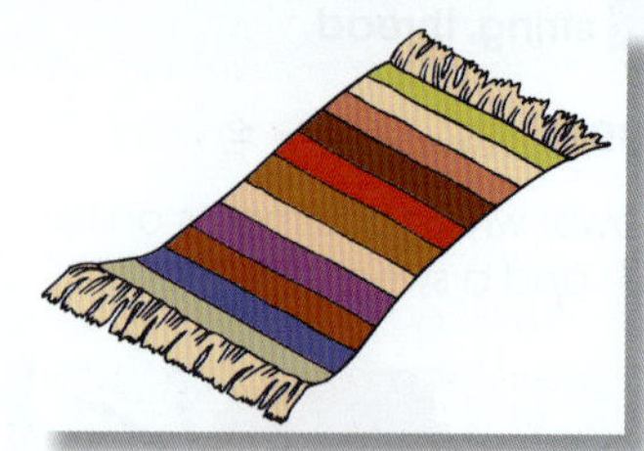

My dog likes to sleep on the rug. 我的狗喜欢睡在小地毯上。

比较 **carpet**

***rule¹** /ruːl; rul/ *n* 名

something that tells you what you must or must not do in a game, school, organization, etc 规则；规定

Students should obey school rules. 学生必须遵守校规。

rule² /ruːl; rul/ *v* 动

rules, ruling, ruled, ruled

to control a country 统治；控制

The king ruled the country for 30 years. 国王统治了这个国家 30 年。

***ruler** /ˈruːlə; ˋrulɚ/ *n* 名

1. a person who controls a country 统治者

   The king was a good ruler. 国王是个英明的统治者。

2. a thing you use to draw straight lines or measure things 尺

   I drew a line with a ruler. 我用一把尺画了一条线。

***run** /rʌn; rʌn/ *v* 动

runs, running, ran, run

R

1. to move quickly by moving your legs faster than walking 跑；奔跑
   Students should not run in the corridor. 学生不得在走廊奔跑。
2. to be in charge of an activity, company, country, etc 经营；管理
   My aunt runs a flower shop. 我的阿姨经营一家花店。
3. to go from a place to another place at regular times 定时行驶
   Buses between the hotel and the airport run every 15 minutes. 从酒店到机场的公共汽车每 15 分钟一班。

run after someone or something 追逐

The policeman is running after the thief. 警员正在追赶小偷。

run into someone or something （开车）撞到；碰见（某人）

The car ran into a big tree. 汽车撞到了一棵大树。

I ran into Mrs Green this morning. 我今早偶然遇见格林太太。

run out of something 用尽；用完

Hurry up! We are running out of time. 快点！时间快到了。

rung /rʌŋ; rʌŋ/ *v* 动

the past participle of **ring**[2] ☆ring[2] 的过去分词

runner /ˈrʌnə; ˋrʌnɚ/ *n* 名

a person who runs, especially in a race 跑步者；赛跑者

There were eight runners in the race. 参加赛跑的人有 8 个。

runway /ˈrʌnweɪ; ˋrʌnˏwe/ *n* 名

a long narrow part of ground where planes land and take off 飞机跑道

The plane landed on the runway. 飞机降落在跑道上。

***rush** /rʌʃ; rʌʃ/ *v* 动

rushes, rushing, rushed, rushed

to move or do something very quickly 赶快；匆忙

Mark rushed to catch the bus. 马克急忙地赶乘公共汽车。

同义 **hurry**[1]

rusty /ˈrʌsti; ˋrʌstɪ/ *adj* 形

rustier, rustiest

covered with a red or brown substance that forms on some metals when they get wet 生锈的

The school gate is rusty. 学校大门生了锈。

R

sack /sæk; sæk/ *n* 名

a large bag made of strong cloth, paper or plastic 麻袋；粗布袋；厚纸袋

He put the watermelons into a sack. 他把西瓜放进麻袋里。

***sad** /sæd; sæd/ *adj* 形

sadder, saddest

unhappy 伤心的；难过的

She was sad when her puppy ran away. 她的小狗跑掉了，她很伤心。

反义 **happy**

sadly /ˈsædli; ˋsædlɪ/ *adv* 副

in a sad way 伤心地；悲伤地

She looked at the poor child sadly. 她伤心地看着那个可怜的小孩。

***safe**[1] /seɪf; sef/ *adj* 形

safer, safest

not dangerous 安全的

It is not safe to go out alone at night. 晚上独自外出并不安全。

反义 **dangerous**

safe[2] /seɪf; sef/ *n* 名

a strong metal box with a lock that you use to keep valuable things 保险箱

My mother keeps her jewellery in the safe. 我的妈妈把首饰存放在保险箱里。

safely /ˈseɪfli; ˋseflɪ/ *adv* 副

in a safe way 安全地

The plane arrived safely in New York. 飞机安全抵达纽约。

反义 **dangerously**

safety /ˈseɪfti; ˋseftɪ/ *n* 名

无复数

being safe from danger or harm 安全

It is important to learn about road safety. 学会注意道路安全是很重要的。

反义 **danger**

said /sed; sɛd/ *v* 动

the past tense and past participle of **say** ☆say 的过去式和过去分词

***sail**[1] /seɪl; sel/ *v* 动

to travel on water in a boat or ship（乘船）航行

We sailed across the ocean. 我们乘船横渡海洋。

sail[2] /seɪl; sel/ *n* 名

a large piece of cloth fixed to a boat for the wind to move it 帆

The sails waved in the wind. 帆在风中摇动。

sailor /ˈseɪlə; ˋselɚ/ *n* 名

someone who works on a ship 水手；海员

There are twenty sailors on the ship. 船上有 20 名水手。

***salad** /ˈsæləd; ˋsæləd/ *n* 名

a mixture of vegetables or fruit that have not been cooked 色拉；沙拉

Betsy made a fruit salad. 贝特西做了水果沙拉。

salary /ˈsæləri; ˋsælərɪ/ *n* 名

复数：*salaries*

money that you get every month for your job（按月领取的）薪水；薪金

The workers are asking for a salary increase. 员工正要求加薪。

比较 **wage**

***sale** /seɪl; sel/ *n* 名

1. selling something 出售；销售
   The sale of guns is illegal. 出售枪械是非法的。
2. a time when a shop sells things at lower prices than usual 大减价
   Jennifer bought two pairs of shoes in a sale. 詹妮弗在大减价时买了两双鞋子。

S

for sale 待售；供出售

This house is for sale. 这座房子在出售。

salesman /ˈseɪlzmən; ˋselzmən/ *n* 名

复数：***salesmen***

a man who sells things for a company 男推销员；男售货员

The salesman showed me some mobile phones. 售货员拿了几只手机给我看。

另见 **saleswoman**

salesperson /ˈseɪlz pɜːsn; ˋselzˏpɝsn/ *n* 名

复数：***salespeople***

a person who sells things for a company 推销员；售货员

The salesperson sold three cars today. 那个推销员今天卖了三辆汽车。

saleswoman /ˈseɪlzˌwʊmən; ˋselzˏwʊmən/ *n* 名

复数：***saleswomen***

a woman who sells things for a company 女推销员；女售货员

She asked the saleswoman for help. 她叫了售货员来帮忙。

另见 **salesman**

salmon /ˈsæmən; ˋsæmən/ *n* 名

复数：***salmon***

a large fish with silver skin 鲑鱼；三文鱼

We ordered salmon for dinner. 我们晚餐点了三文鱼。

salon /ˈsælɒn; səˋlɑn/ *n* 名

a shop where you can get a haircut, etc 发廊；美容院

Mary goes to the hair salon once a month. 玛丽每个月去一次发廊。

***salt** /sɔːlt; sɔlt/ *n* 名

无复数

something white that you put on food to make it taste better 盐

Don't put too much salt in the soup. 不要在汤里放太多盐。

salty /ˈsɔːlti; ˋsɔltɪ/ *adj* 形

saltier, saltiest

having salt or the taste of salt 含盐的；咸的

The chicken was too salty. 那些鸡肉太咸了。

***same**[1] /seɪm; sem/ *adj* 形

not another one; not different 同一个的；相同的

Tina and Irene go to the same school. 蒂娜和艾琳上同一所学校。

at the same time 同时

Don't eat and talk at the same time. 不要一边吃饭一边说话。

用法 same 一般与 the 同用。

反义 **different**

***same**[2] /seɪm; sem/ *pron* 代

if two or more people or things are the same, they are exactly like each other 一样；同样

These kittens look the same to me. 在我看来这些小猫长得一模一样。

the same as ... 和…一样

Your school bag is the same as mine. 你的书包和我的一模一样。

Daily conversation 日常会话

(and the) same to you 你也一样（用以回应问候）

"Have a nice weekend!" "Thanks, and the same to you!" "周末愉快！""谢谢，愿你也周末愉快！"

sampan /ˈsæmpæn; ˋsæmpæn/ *n* 名

a small boat with a flat bottom 舢舨

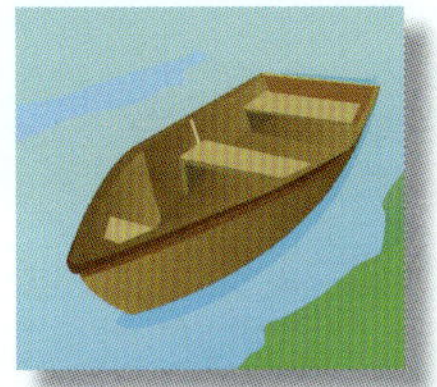

Chris went fishing in a sampan. 克里斯坐舢舨去钓鱼。

***sand** /sænd; sænd/ *n* 名

无复数

very small pieces of rock on beaches and in deserts 沙

The beach is covered with beautiful white sand. 海滩遍布美丽的白沙。

sandal /ˈsændl; ˋsændl̩/ *n* 名

a light shoe with leather bands that you wear in warm weather 凉鞋

I often wear sandals in summer. 夏天我常常穿凉鞋。

比较 **slipper**

sandcastle /ˈsændˌkɑːsl; ˋsændˏkæsl̩/ *n* 名

a small model of a castle that you make with sand on a beach（在沙滩上堆成的）沙堡

Daisy made a sandcastle on the beach. 黛西在沙滩上堆了一个沙堡。

***sandwich** /ˈsænwɪdʒ; ˋsændwɪtʃ/ *n* 名

复数：***sandwiches***

two pieces of bread with meat, cheese, etc between them 三明治；三文治

S

I ate a ham sandwich. 我吃了一个火腿三明治。

sandy /ˈsændi; ˋsændɪ/ *adj* 形

sandier, sandiest

containing sand 含沙的；多沙的

My shoes are all sandy! 我的鞋子全是沙子！

sang /sæŋ; sæŋ/ *v* 动

the past tense of **sing**☆sing 的过去式

sank /sæŋk; sæŋk/ *v* 动

the past tense of **sink²**☆sink² 的过去式

Santa Claus /ˈsæntə klɔːz; ˋsæntɪ ˌklɔz/ *n* 名

也作：***Santa***

an old man who wears red clothes and has a long white beard. Some children believe that he brings presents to them at Christmas. 圣诞老人

I dreamt about Santa Claus last night. 昨晚我梦见圣诞老人了。

注意 开头的 S 和 C 必须用大写。

同义 **Father Christmas**

S

sashimi /sæˈʃiːmi; saˋʃimɪ/ *n* 名

无复数

a Japanese food made of small pieces of fish that have not been cooked 生鱼片；刺身（一种日本食物）

I like eating sashimi with soy sauce. 吃生鱼片时我喜欢蘸些酱油。

sat /sæt; sæt/ *v* 动

the past tense and past participle of **sit**☆sit 的过去式和过去分词

satay /ˈsæteɪ; ˋsɑte/ *n* 名

无复数

a kind of food that has meat on sticks and is eaten with a sauce 沙嗲烤肉；沙嗲串烧

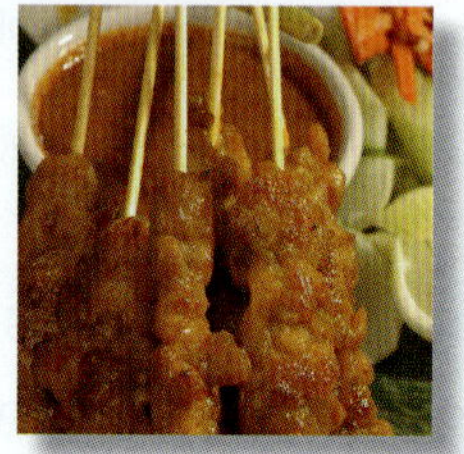

She makes very good satay. 她做的沙嗲烤肉很好吃。

satellite /ˈsætəlaɪt; ˋsætḷˌaɪt/ *n* 名

a machine that is sent into space and used to send signals from one place to another 人造卫星

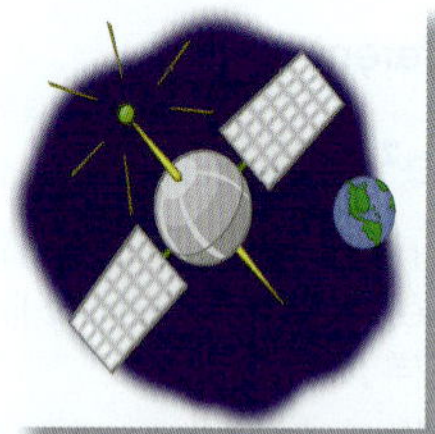

This programme came from Japan by satellite. 这个节目是通过人造卫星从日本转播的。

satisfactory /ˌsætɪsˈfæktəri; ˌsætɪsˋfæktərɪ/ *adj* 形

good enough 令人满意的

His exam results are satisfactory. 他的考试成绩令人满意。

***Saturday** /ˈsætədeɪ; ˋsætəde/ *n* 名

缩写：***Sat.***

the day between Friday and Sunday 星期六

We went hiking last Saturday. 上星期六我们去徒步了。

注意 开头的字母必须用大写。

***sauce** /sɔːs; sɔs/ *n* 名

a thick liquid that gives food a nice taste 调味汁；酱汁

She ate pasta with tomato sauce. 她吃了拌番茄酱的意大利面条。

saucepan /ˈsɔːspən; ˋsɔsˌpæn/ *n* 名

a deep, round pan with a handle that you use for cooking（有柄的）深平底锅

He cooked noodles in a saucepan. 他用深平底锅煮面。

saucer /ˈsɔːsə; ˋsɔsɚ/ *n* 名

a small plate that you put under a cup 茶碟；茶托

I broke the saucer. 我打碎了茶碟。

***sausage** /ˈsɒsɪdʒ; ˋsɔsɪdʒ/ *n* 名

meat in a long, thin shape 香肠

Paul loves to eat pork sausages. 保罗爱吃猪肉香肠。

***save** /seɪv; sev/ *v* 动

saves, saving, saved, saved

1. to make someone or something safe from danger 救；拯救

The firefighters saved a girl from the fire. 消防员从大火中救出一名女孩。

同义 **rescue**

2. （也作：***save up***）to keep money so that you can use it later 储蓄

Donald saved $100 for a model car. 唐纳德为买模型车攒了 100 元。

3. 【电脑】to keep the work that you have done on a computer 储存；存盘

Save the file before you close it. 先把文档保存好再把它关闭。

savings /'seɪvɪŋz; `sevɪŋz/ *plural n* 复数名词

money that you have saved, especially in a bank 存款；积蓄

I put all my savings in the bank. 我把所有存款放在银行里。

saw[1] /sɔ:; sɔ/ *v* 动

the past tense of **see**☆see 的过去式

saw[2] /sɔ:; sɔ/ *n* 名

a tool with sharp points for cutting wood 锯

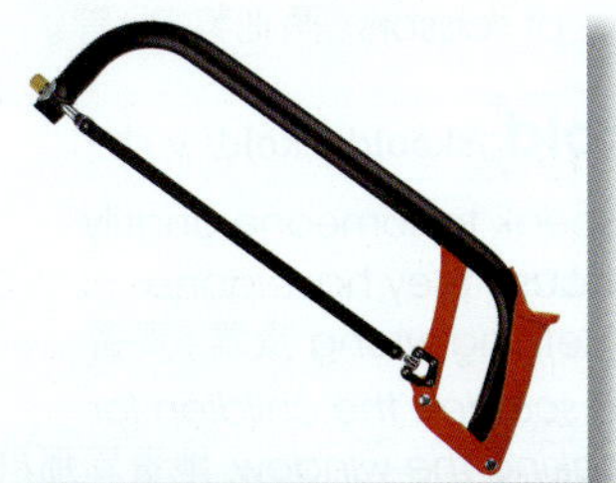

He cut the branch off with a saw. 他用锯子把树枝锯断。

saw[3] /sɔ:; sɔ/ *v* 动

saws, sawing, sawed, sawn

to cut something with a saw 锯；锯开

He sawed the wood into two pieces. 他把木头锯成两截。

***say** /seɪ; se/ *v* 动

says, saying, said, said

to speak or tell someone something 说；讲

"I'm very hungry!" he said. "我饿极了！"他说。

I don't understand what you said. 我不明白你说的话。

用法 say 不以人作受词，例如不可以说 He said me something，要说 He said something to me。

Daily conversation 日常会话

let's say 假设；假如

"Let's say you have a lot of money — what would you do?" "I would buy a house." "假设你有很多钱，你会做什么呢？""我会买一所房子。"

scales /skeɪlz; skelz/ *plural n* 复数名词【英】

美式：***scale***

a machine for weighing people or things 秤；磅秤

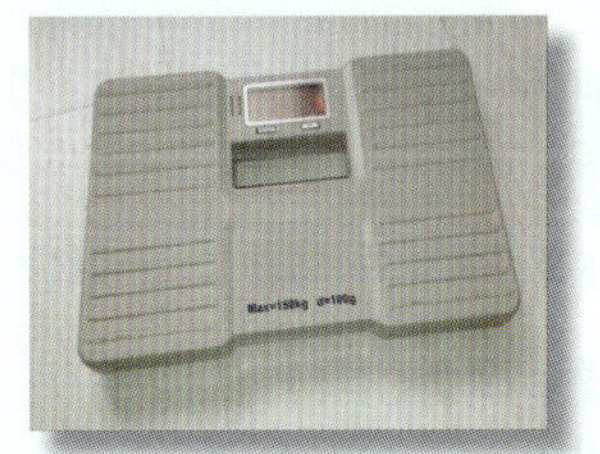

We put the scales in the bathroom. 我们把磅秤放在浴室里。

scan /skæn; skæn/ *v* 动

scans, scanning, scanned, scanned

【电脑】to copy pictures or words from paper onto a computer using a machine 扫描

Terry scanned the photo into his computer. 泰瑞把相片扫描到电脑里。

scanner /'skænə; `skænɚ/ *n* 名

【电脑】a machine that copies pictures or words from paper onto a computer 扫描仪；扫描器

The quality of this scanner is very good. 这部扫描仪的质量很好。

scar /skɑ:; skɑr/ *n* 名

a mark left on your skin after you have had a cut or wound 伤疤；疤痕

There is a scar on his face. 他的脸上有一道疤痕。

scare /skeə; skɛr/ *v* 动

scares, scaring, scared, scared

to make someone feel afraid 使害怕；惊吓

The snake scared me. 那条蛇把我吓坏了。

scare away/off 把…吓跑

Don't scare the birds away! 不要把鸟儿吓走！

同义 **frighten**

scarecrow /'skeəkrəʊ; `skɛr͵kro/ *n* 名

a thing that looks like a person and is put in a field to make birds go away 稻草人

S

The farmer put a scarecrow in the field. 农夫在田里放了一个稻草人。

***scared** /skeəd; skɛrd/ *adj* 形

feeling afraid 害怕的；感到惊慌的

When he saw the dog, he was scared. 他看见那只狗，感到害怕。

scared of something 害怕某物

Lily is scared of cockroaches. 莉莉害怕蟑螂。

***scarf** /skɑːf; skɑrf/ *n* 名

复数：*scarfs/scarves*

a piece of cloth that you wear around your neck, head or shoulders 围巾；头巾

Mrs White wore a silk scarf today. 怀特太太今天戴了一条丝巾。

***scene** /siːn; sin/ *n* 名

1. the things you see in a place 景色；景象

It was a beautiful scene and I took a photograph. 那儿景色秀丽，我拍了一张照片。

2. （无复数）the place where something bad happens 现场；发生地点

The firefighters arrived at the scene of the accident quickly. 消防员迅速到达事故现场。

3. a short part of a play or film（戏剧中的）一场；（电影中的）场面

This film has a lot of violent scenes. 这出电影有不少暴力的场面。

***school** /skuːl; skul/ *n* 名

a place where children go to learn 学校

Albert goes to school on foot. 阿尔伯特步行上学。

before/after school 上学前/放学后

I'll see you after school. 放学后见吧。

用法 指"上学"时，school 前不加 the 或 a，例如 She goes to school by bus（她乘公共汽车上学）；如指"这所学校"时则要加 the 或 this，例如 I go to this school（我上这所学校）。

schoolboy /ˈskuːlbɔɪ; ˋskulˏbɔɪ/ *n* 名

a boy who goes to school 男学生

The schoolboys were playing hide-and-seek. 那些男生在玩捉迷藏。

schoolgirl /ˈskuːlɡɜːl; ˋskulˏɡɝl/ *n* 名

a girl who goes to school 女学生

When my mother was a schoolgirl, she didn't have a computer. 我的妈妈还是个学生的时候，她并没有电脑。

schoolwork /ˈskuːlwɜːk; ˋskulˏwɝk/ *n* 名

无复数

work that you do at school or for school 课堂作业；功课

There is a lot of schoolwork this week. 这个星期的作业很多。

比较 **homework**

***science** /ˈsaɪəns; ˋsaɪəns/ *n* 名

无复数

the knowledge about the natural world that you learn by testing and proving facts 科学

We studied about electricity in our science lesson. 我们上科学课时学过电力。

scientist /ˈsaɪəntɪst; ˋsaɪəntɪst/ *n* 名

someone who studies science 科学家

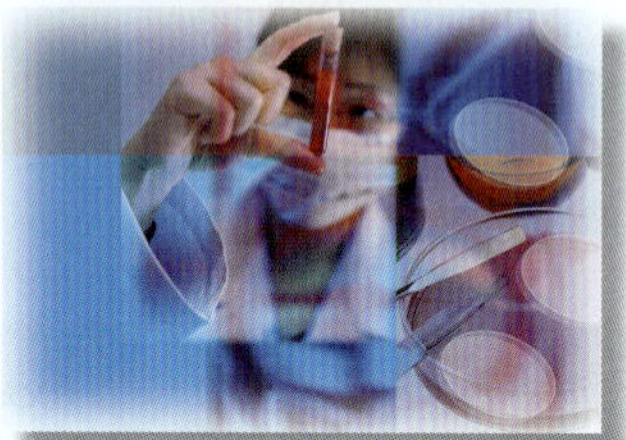

Newton was a great scientist. 牛顿是个伟大的科学家。

***scissors** /ˈsɪzəz; ˋsɪzɚz/ *plural n* 复数名词

a tool with two sharp parts, used for cutting things 剪刀

Cut the paper in half with scissors. 用剪刀把纸剪成两半。

用法 不能说 a scissors 或 two scissors，要说 a pair of scissors（一把剪刀）、two pairs of scissors（两把剪刀）等。

scold /skəʊld; skold/ *v* 动

to speak to someone angrily because they have done something wrong 责骂；责备

She scolded the children for breaking the window. 她责骂那群孩子打破了窗户。

反义 **praise**

***score[1]** /skɔː; skɔr/ *n* 名

the number of points that you get

S

in a game or test（比赛的）得分；（考试的）分数

The final score of the match is 4-2. 比赛的最后比分是 4 比 2。

score² /skɔː; skɔr/ *v* 动

scores, scoring, scored, scored

to get points in a game or test（比赛或考试中）得（分）

I scored 80% in my English exam. 我的英文考试得了 80 分。

scout /skaʊt; skaʊt/ *n* 名

也作：***boy scout/Boy Scout***

a member of a club for boys 男童子军

The scouts learn a lot of skills such as cooking and first aid. 男童子军学习许多技能，例如烹饪和急救。

另见 **guide¹**

scratch¹ /skrætʃ; skrætʃ/ *v* 动

scratches, scratching, scratched, scratched

1. to make a cut or mark on something with a sharp thing 抓伤；划破

   The cat is scratching the floor. 那只猫在抓地板。

2. to rub your skin with your nails because it is itching 搔；挠（以止痒）

   Mum scratched my back for me. 妈妈帮我挠了挠背。

scratch² /skrætʃ; skrætʃ/ *n* 名

复数：***scratches***

a cut or mark that is made by something sharp 抓痕；划痕

There is a scratch on his car. 他的车上有一道划痕。

***scream¹** /skriːm; skrim/ *v* 动

to give a loud high cry, because you are frightened, excited, etc 尖叫

She screamed when she heard a bang. 她听到砰的一声，尖叫起来。

scream² /skriːm; skrim/ *n* 名

a loud high cry 尖叫声

We heard a loud scream downstairs. 我们听见楼下传来响亮的尖叫声。

screen /skriːn; skrin/ *n* 名

the flat part of a television, computer, etc on which you see pictures or information（电视机或电脑等的）屏幕；荧光屏

Sitting too close to the TV screen is bad for your eyes. 电视屏幕离太近对眼睛不好。

screw /skruː; skru/ *n* 名

a small pointed piece of metal that you use to fix things together 螺丝钉

The chair has lost a screw. 这张椅子丢了一个螺丝钉。

screwdriver /ˈskruːˌdraɪvə; ˋskruˏdraɪvɚ/ *n* 名

a tool for turning screws 螺丝刀；螺丝起子

This screwdriver is good for these screws. 这把螺丝刀用来拧这些螺丝钉正合适。

***sea** /siː; si/ *n* 名

the water on the earth's surface 海；海洋

She lives by the sea. 她住在海边。

比较 **land¹**

***seafood** /ˈsiːfuːd; ˋsiˏfud/ *n* 名

无复数

fish and other sea animals that you can eat 海鲜；海味

S

My favourite seafood is crab. 螃蟹是我最喜爱吃的海鲜。

seagull /ˈsiːɡʌl; ˋsiˏɡʌl/ *n* 名

也作：***gull***

a grey and white bird with long wings that lives near the sea 海鸥

A seagull is resting on a rock. 一只海鸥在岩石上歇息。

seahorse /ˈsiːhɔːs; ˋsiˏhɔrs/ *n* 名

a small fish with a head that looks like a horse's head 海马

I found a seahorse when I was picking up shells. 我在拣贝壳时发现了一只海马。

seal /siːl; sil/ *n* 名

a large sea animal that eats fish and lives in and near the sea 海豹

A seal is lying on the beach. 一只海豹在海滩上躺着。

sea lion /ˈsiː ˌlaɪən; ˋsi ˌlaɪən/ *n* 名

a large type of seal 海狮

A sea lion is feeding its baby. 一只海狮在喂它的宝宝。

***search** /sɜːtʃ; sɝtʃ/ *v* 动

searches, searching, searched, searched

1. to look carefully because you want to find someone or something 寻找；搜索

   The police are searching for the missing child. 警方在寻找失踪的小孩。

2. 【电脑】to use a computer to find information（用电脑）搜索；检索

   We searched the Web for information about the concert. 我们在网上搜索了有关那个音乐会的信息。

seashore /ˈsiːʃɔː; ˋsiˏʃɔr/ *n* 名

the seashore the land along the edge of the sea 海岸；海滨

They are walking along the seashore. 他们沿着海滨散步。

seasick /ˈsiːsɪk; ˋsiˏsɪk/ *adj* 形

feeling sick when you are travelling on a boat or ship 晕船的

Lenny felt seasick on the ferry. 兰尼在渡轮上感到晕船。

seaside /ˈsiːsaɪd; ˋsiˏsaɪd/ *n* 名【英】

the seaside an area near the sea where people go to enjoy themselves 海边；海滨

We spent a day at the seaside. 我们在海边过了一天。

***season** /ˈsiːzn; ˋsizn̩/ *n* 名

one of the four periods of the year 季节

Autumn is my favourite season. 秋季是我最喜爱的季节。

***seat** /siːt; sit/ *n* 名

a place where you can sit 座位

There are forty seats in the classroom. 教室里有 40 个座位。

have/take a seat 坐下；就座

Please take a seat. 请就座。

seat belt（交通工具座位上的）安全带

Nora, fasten your seat belt! 诺拉，系好安全带！

seaweed /ˈsiːwiːd; ˋsiˏwid/ *n* 名

无复数

a plant that grows in the sea 海藻；海草

Some kinds of seaweed can be used to make sushi. 某些种类的海藻可用来做寿司。

***second¹** /ˈsekənd; ˋsɛkənd/

ordinal num 序数

number two in order, after the first one 第二（的）

This is my second visit to Singapore. 这是我第二次游览新加坡。

***second²** /ˈsekənd; ˋsɛkənd/

adv 副

next after the first one 第二；其次

Gilbert came second in the race. 吉尔伯特在赛跑中得了第二名。

***second[3]** /ˈsekənd; ˋsɛkənd/
n 名

a unit of time. There are 60 seconds in a minute. 秒

She swam across the pool in 50 seconds. 她用了 50 秒游到泳池的对面。

in a second 一会儿；片刻

I'll be back in a second. 我一会儿就回来。

> **Daily conversation 日常会话**
>
> **just a second** 等一等
>
> *"Can you help me lift this box?" "OK. Just a second."* "你能帮我抬起这个箱子吗？""好，等一下。"

secondary school
/ˈsekəndəri ˌskuːl; ˋsɛkəndɛrɪ ˏskul/
n 名

a school for children between 11 and 16 or 18 years old 中学

My sister is at secondary school. 我的姐姐在上中学。

另见 primary school

***secret[1]** /ˈsiːkrət; ˋsikrɪt/ *n* 名

something that only a few people know about 秘密

Can you keep a secret? 你能保守秘密吗？

secret[2] /ˈsiːkrət; ˋsikrɪt/ *adj* 形

if something is secret, only a few people know about it 秘密的

The dog hid the bone in a secret place. 那条狗把骨头藏在秘密的地方。

***secretary** /ˈsekrətəri; ˋsɛkrəˏtɛrɪ/
n 名

复数：***secretaries***

someone who types letters, answers telephone calls, etc in an office 秘书

Kylie is a secretary in a big company. 凯莉在一家大公司当秘书。

***section** /ˈsekʃn; ˋsɛkʃən/
n 名

a part of something 部分

One section of the road was closed. 这条公路有一段封闭了。

***see** /siː; si/ *v* 动

sees, seeing, saw, seen

1. to notice someone or something by using your eyes 看见；看到

   You can see the hill from here. 从这里可以见到那座山。
2. to watch a film, television programme, etc 观看（电影、电视节目等）

   We went to see a French film last night. 昨晚我们去看了一部法国电影。
3. to understand something 明白；理解

   I can see why you are angry. 我明白你为什么生气。
4. to meet or visit someone 会见；探访

   I'll see you outside the cinema at 6 o'clock. 我 6 点钟在电影院外和你见面。
5. to try to find out something 查看；弄清楚

   Try on the skirt to see if it fits. 试穿这条裙子看看是否合身。

see someone off（到机场、车站等）给…送行

We saw Nick off at the airport. 我们到机场给尼克送行。

> **Daily conversation 日常会话**
>
> **I see** 我知道了；我明白了
>
> *"Just click here to save the file." "Oh, I see."* "只要点击这儿就可以保存文件了。""噢，知道了。"
>
> **see you** 再见
>
> *"I have to go now." "OK. See you later."* "我要走了。""好的。回头见。"

***seed[1]** /siːd; sid/ *n* 名

a small hard thing that grows into a plant 种子

He planted the seeds in the field. 他把种子播在田里。

seed[2] /siːd; sid/ *v* 动

to take away seeds from fruit or vegetables 给（蔬果）去核

She seeded the watermelon. 她把西瓜去了籽。

***seem** /siːm; sim/ *v* 动

to appear to be 好像；似乎

Catherine seemed to be unhappy. 凯瑟琳好像不开心。

It seems no one knows the answer. 看来没有人知道答案。

seen /siːn; sin/ *v* 动

the past participle of **see** ☆see 的过去分词

***seesaw** /ˈsiːsɔː; ˋsiˏsɔ/ *n* 名

a long piece of wood that children sit on each end and move up and down 跷跷板

Let's play on the seesaw. 我们玩跷跷板吧。

***seldom** /ˈseldəm; ˋsɛldəm/
adv 副

not often 很少；不常

He seldom goes to the market. 他很少上市场。

反义 often

S

select /sə'lekt; sə`lɛkt/ *v* 动

to choose 选择；挑选

The coach selected Jerry as the captain. 教练选了杰瑞当队长。

***selfish** /'selfɪʃ; `sɛlfɪʃ/ *adj* 形

caring only about yourself and not about other people 自私的

Barry is selfish. He won't give up his seat. 巴瑞很自私，不会让座给别人。

反义 **unselfish**

***sell** /sel; sɛl/ *v* 动

sells, selling, sold, sold

to give something to someone and get money from them for it 卖；出售

He sold his bicycle to me. 他把他的自行车卖给我。

That shop sells ice cream. 那家商店出售冰淇淋。

反义 **buy**

semicolon /ˌsemi'kəulən; `sɛməˌkolən/ *n* 名

the sign you use to separate different parts of a sentence or list (;) 分号

另见 附录：Punctuation 标点符号

***send** /send; sɛnd/ *v* 动

sends, sending, sent, sent

to make something or someone go to a place 发出；送出；寄出；派遣

Bob sent me a parcel from Japan. 鲍勃从日本给我寄来了一个包裹。

The thief was sent to prison. 那个小偷被送进了监狱。

send for someone/something 请某人来；请人送来某物

Someone's fainted. Send for a doctor quickly! 有人晕倒了，快些叫医生来！

***sense**[1] /sens; sɛns/ *n* 名

1. （无复数）the ability to understand something 判断力；理智

   Terence has a really good sense of direction. 泰伦斯的方向感非常好。
2. a feeling about something 感觉

   I had the sense that John was lying. 我感觉到约翰在说谎。
3. one of the five natural abilities to see, hear, smell, taste and touch 感官

   Dogs have a strong sense of smell. 狗的嗅觉很强。

sense[2] /sens; sɛns/ *v* 动

senses, sensing, sensed, sensed

to feel or know something that is not said 感觉到；意识到

We sensed danger when we walked into the cave. 我们走进洞穴后感到有危险。

sensible /'sensəbl; `sɛnsəbḷ/ *adj* 形

1. if you are sensible, you are able to make good decisions 有判断力的

   I trust her because she is a sensible girl. 她是个有判断力的女孩，所以我信任她。
2. if something is sensible, it is a good idea 合理的；明智的

   The teacher gave me some sensible advice. 老师给了我一些明智的建议。

sent /sent; sɛnt/ *v* 动

the past tense and past participle of **send**☆send 的过去式和过去分词

***sentence** /'sentəns; `sɛntəns/ *n* 名

a group of words that starts with a capital letter and usually ends with a full stop 句子

Answer the questions in complete sentences. 用完整的句子作答。

separate[1] /'seprət; `sɛpərɪt/ *adj* 形

1. not joined to something else 分开的；独立的

   They work in separate offices. 他们在独立的办公室工作。
2. different 不同的

   I put the fish in separate jars. 我把鱼放在不同的瓶子里。

separate[2] /'sepəreɪt; `sɛpəˌret/ *v* 动

separates, separating, separated, separated

1. to divide people or things 使分开；使分离

   The teacher separated the class into five groups. 老师把全班分成5组。
2. to be between two things 隔开

   This river separates the two cities. 这条河把两个城市隔开。

***September** /sep'tembə; sɛp`tɛmbɚ/ *n* 名

缩写：*Sept.*

the ninth month of the year 九月

The new school year begins in September. 新学年在9月开始。

注意 开头的字母必须用大写。

***serious** /'sɪəriəs; `sɪrɪəs/ *adj* 形

1. very bad or dangerous 严重的；危急的

   The old man has a serious illness. 那个老人患了重病。
2. not funny or joking 认真的

S

Are you serious about selling the house? 你真的要把房子买掉吗？

3. if someone is serious, they are quiet and do not often laugh 严肃的

   He looks very serious. 他看起来非常严肃。

servant /'sɜːvnt; `sɝvənt/ *n* 名

a person who works for someone in their house 仆人；佣人

The rich woman has four servants. 那个富有的女人有 4 个佣人。

***serve** /sɜːv; sɝv/ *v* 动

serves, serving, served, served

1. to give someone food or drinks, for example in a restaurant 端上（食物或饮料）

   The waiter served breakfast to us. 服务员把早餐端给我们。

2. to help the customers in a shop 接待；为（顾客）服务

   Michelle is serving a customer in the shop. 米歇尔正在店内招呼一名顾客。

***service** /'sɜːvɪs; `sɝvɪs/ *n* 名

1. （无复数）the work that you do for someone in a restaurant, shop, etc 服务；接待

   The food is quite good in this restaurant, but the service is poor. 这家餐馆的食物不错，但服务不好。

2. a system or an organization that provides something for everyone in a country 公共服务系统；公共事业机构

   Bernard works for the police service. 伯纳德在警察部门工作。

in service/out of service 可供使用/不能使用

The lift is out of service. 电梯暂停使用。

***set[1]** /set; sɛt/ *v* 动

sets, setting, set, set

1. to put something somewhere carefully 放置

   My sister set the vase down on the table. 我的姐姐把花瓶放到桌上。

2. to decide what something should be 确定；安排

   Amy and Tony have set a date for their wedding. 艾米和托尼已定了婚礼的日期。

3. when the sun sets, it goes down in the sky（太阳）落下

   We watched the sun slowly set. 我们看着夕阳缓缓落下。

set an example 树立榜样

The monitor sets a good example to the rest of the class. 班长给班上其他同学树立了良好的榜样。

set fire to something/set something on fire 放火；点燃

They set fire to the house. 他们放火焚烧房子。

set off/out 出发；启程

We set out early for Beijing. 我们一早出发到北京去。

set the table 摆好餐具（准备开饭）

Would you please set the table for dinner? 请你摆好餐具准备吃饭好吗？

***set[2]** /set; sɛt/ *n* 名

1. a group of things that belong together 一套；一组（同类的东西）

   He brought us tea in a beautiful set of cups. 他用一套精美的杯子沏茶给我们。

2. a television or radio 电视机；收音机

   There is a television set in the bedroom. 卧室里有一台电视机。

settle /'setl; `sɛtl̩/ *v* 动

settles, settling, settled, settled

to go and live in a place for a long time 定居

They are going to settle in Australia. 他们将到澳洲定居。

settle down 安静下来

Class, please settle down. 同学们，请安静。

***seven** /'sevn; `sɛvən/ *num* 数

the number 7 七

I read seven books last month. 上个月我看了 7 本书。

***seventeen** /ˌsevn'tiːn; ˏsɛvən`tin/ *num* 数

the number 17 十七

There are seventeen boys in our class. 我们这个班有 17 个男生。

seventeenth /ˌsevn'tiːnθ; ˏsɛvən`tinθ/ *ordinal num* 序数

17th in order 第十七（的）

Aunt Janet will come back on the seventeenth of July. 珍尼特阿姨将在 7 月 17 日回来。

seventh /'sevnθ; `sɛvənθ/ *ordinal num* 序数

7th in order 第七（的）

Mrs Davis lives on the seventh floor. 戴维斯太太住在 7 楼。

seventieth /'sevntiəθ; `sɛvəntɪəθ/ *ordinal num* 序数

70th in order 第七十（的）

My grandmother just had her

S

seventieth birthday. 外婆刚刚过了 70 岁生日。

***seventy** /ˈsevnti; ˋsɛvəntɪ/ *num* 数

the number 70 七十

More than seventy people took part in the race. 超过 70 人参加了这项赛跑。

***several** /ˈsevrəl; ˋsɛvərəl/ *adj* 形

more than two, but not a lot 几个；一些

Several parents are waiting outside the school. 几个家长在学校门外等候。

***sew** /səʊ; so/ *v* 动

sews, sewing, sewed, sewn/sewed

to make or repair clothes with a needle and thread 缝制；缝补

I sewed a button on my shirt. 我给衬衫钉了一粒钮扣。

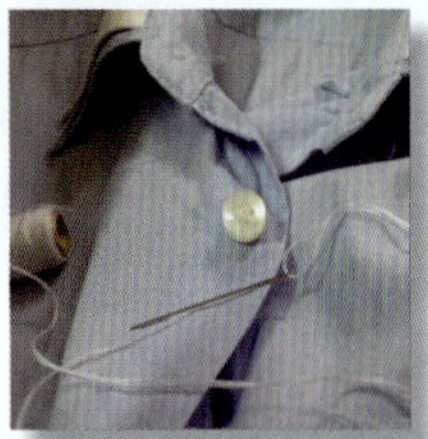

sewing machine /ˈsəʊɪŋ məˌʃiːn; ˋsoɪŋ məˌʃin/ *n* 名

a machine for sewing things 缝纫机

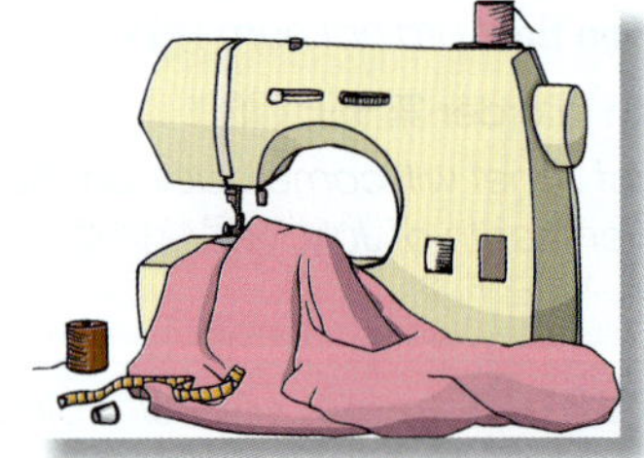

She sewed a skirt on her sewing machine. 她用缝纫机缝了一条裙子。

***sex** /seks; sɛks/ *n* 名

无复数

the fact of being male or female 性别

What sex is your dog? 你的狗是公的还是母的?

shade /ʃeɪd; ʃed/ *n* 名

无复数

an area that is cool and dark because the light of the sun cannot reach it 荫；阴凉处

Nick sat in the shade of a tree. 尼克坐在树荫下。

shadow /ˈʃædəʊ; ˋʃædo/ *n* 名

a dark shape that forms on a surface when a person or thing is between the light and the surface 影子

Gloria is looking at her own shadow. 歌洛莉亚看着自己的影子。

***shake** /ʃeɪk; ʃek/ *v* 动

shakes, shaking, shook, shaken

to move or make something move quickly from side to side or up and down 摇动；抖动

He is shaking the bottle. 他在摇瓶子。

shake hands 握手

They shook hands with each other. 他们互相握手。

shake your head 摇头（表示不、反对等）

I asked her if she would like an apple, and she shook her head. 我问她吃不吃苹果，她摇摇头。

shaken /ˈʃeɪkən; ˋʃekən/ *v* 动

the past participle of **shake** ☆shake 的过去分词

***shall** /ʃl; ʃəl; *strong* 强读 ʃæl; ʃæl/ *v* 动

should

1. **I/we shall** used to say what you are going to do 我/我们将要

   We shall be in Spain next month. 下个月我们要去西班牙。

用法 这是用于正式场合的英式英语。

2. **shall I/we...?** used in questions for making a suggestion or asking for someone's opinion 我/我们…好吗?（用于提议或征求意见）

   Shall I get you some water? 要不要给你倒点水？

   What shall we do now? 我们现在干什么好呢？

shallow /ˈʃæləʊ; ˋʃælo/ *adj* 形

shallower, shallowest

measuring a short way down to the bottom 浅的

That river is shallow. 那条河很浅。

反义 deep

shampoo /ʃæmˈpuː; ʃæmˋpu/ *n* 名

a special liquid for washing your hair 洗发水

This shampoo is good for my hair. 这种洗发水适合我的头发。

shan't /ʃɑːnt; ʃænt/【英】

the short form of "**shall not**" ☆shall not 的缩写

We shan't stay here for long. 我们不会在这儿逗留太久。

S

***shape¹** /ʃeɪp; ʃep/ *n* 名

the form of something 形状

These mooncakes have different shapes. 这些月饼有不同的形状。

shape² /ʃeɪp; ʃep/ *v* 动

shapes, shaping, shaped, shaped

to make something into a particular form 把…做成某种形状

Janet shaped the clay into balls. 珍尼特把黏土搓成球状。

***share¹** /ʃeə; ʃɛr/ *v* 动

shares, sharing, shared, shared

1. to have or use something with someone else 共享；共用

   My brother and I share a bedroom. 我和哥哥共用一个卧室。

2. to divide something between two or more people 分配；均分

   My sister and I shared the chocolate. 我和姐姐分吃了巧克力。

***share²** /ʃeə; ʃɛr/ *n* 名

a part of something that has been divided（分得的）一份

Everyone did a share of the work. 每个人都完成了一份工作。

***shark** /ʃɑːk; ʃɑrk/ *n* 名

a large sea fish with very sharp teeth 鲨鱼

Some sharks may attack people. 有些鲨鱼可能袭击人。

***sharp** /ʃɑːp; ʃɑrp/ *adj* 形

sharper, sharpest

having a thin edge or point that can cut things easily 锋利的；尖的

This knife is very sharp. 这把刀很锋利。

I need a sharp pencil to draw lines. 我需要一支尖的铅笔来画线。

反义 **blunt**

sharpen /ˈʃɑːpən; ˋʃɑrpən/ *v* 动

to make something sharp 削尖；磨尖

I sharpened all my pencils. 我把所有的铅笔都削尖了。

sharpener /ˈʃɑːpnə; ˋʃɑrpənə/ *n* 名

a tool that you use to make a knife or pencil sharp 磨刀器；卷笔刀

She borrowed my pencil sharpener. 她借了我的卷笔刀。

shave /ʃeɪv; ʃev/ *v* 动

shaves, shaving, shaved, shaved

to cut off hair from the skin, usually on your face 刮（胡子）；刮（脸）

My father shaves every morning. 我的爸爸每天早上刮胡子。

***she** /ʃi; ʃɪ; *strong* 强读 ʃiː; ʃi/ *pron* 代

a woman, girl or female animal that has already been mentioned or is known about 她

This is Eva. She is my cousin. 这是伊娃。她是我的表妹。

she'd /ʃid; ʃɪd; *strong* 强读 ʃiːd; ʃid/

1. the short form of "**she had**" ☆she had 的缩写

   He said she'd left before three. 他说她 3 点前已经离开了。

2. the short form of "**she would**" ☆she would 的缩写

   She'd love to come if you invite her. 如果你邀请她，她很乐意来。

***sheep** /ʃiːp; ʃip/ *n* 名

复数：***sheep***

a farm animal that you keep for its meat and wool 羊；绵羊

These sheep produce very soft wool. 这些绵羊的羊毛很柔软。

sheet /ʃiːt; ʃit/ *n* 名

1. a large piece of thin cloth that you put on a bed 床单；被单

   I'm helping my father to change the sheets. 我在帮爸爸换床单。

2. a piece of paper 一张（纸）

   I need a clean sheet of paper. 我需要一张白纸。

***shelf** /ʃelf; ʃɛlf/ *n* 名

复数：***shelves***

a flat board fixed to a wall or in a cupboard for putting things on 架子；搁板

She put the cups and saucers on the shelf. 她把杯子和茶碟放在架子上。

she'll /ʃil; ʃɪl; *strong* 强读 ʃiːl; ʃil/

the short form of "**she will**" ☆she will 的缩写

She'll come to our party. 她会来参加我们的聚会。

***shell** /ʃel; ʃɛl/ *n* 名

the hard outside part of a nut, an egg or some animals（坚果、蛋或某些动物的）壳

I collected a lot of shells on the beach. 我在海滩上拾到很多贝壳。

shelter[1] /ˈʃeltə; ˋʃɛltɚ/ *n* 名

1. a place that keeps someone safe from bad weather or danger 遮蔽处；避难处

   We waited for the bus in the bus shelter. 我们在公共汽车站的候车亭等车。
2. （无复数）protection from bad weather or danger 遮蔽；庇护

   We took shelter from the rain under a tree. 我们在树下避雨。

shelter[2] /ˈʃeltə; ˋʃɛltɚ/ *v* 动

to keep someone safe from bad weather or danger 躲避；掩蔽

They went under a tree to shelter from the storm. 他们走到树下躲避暴风雨。

she's /ʃiz; ʃɪz; *strong* 强读 ʃiːz; ʃiz/

1. the short form of "**she is**" ☆she is 的缩写

   She's busy now. 她正忙着。
2. the short form of "**she has**" ☆she has 的缩写

   She's seen a doctor. 她已经看了医生。

S

***shine** /ʃaɪn; ʃaɪn/ *v* 动

shines, shining, shone, shone

1. to give out light 发光

   The sun was shining. 阳光普照。
2. to look bright 发亮

   Her eyes were shining with joy. 她的眼里闪耀着喜悦的光芒。

shiny /ˈʃaɪni; ˋʃaɪnɪ/ *adj* 形

shinier, shiniest

smooth and bright 光滑的；闪光的

Richard's shoes are always shiny. 理查德的鞋子总是亮闪闪的。

***ship** /ʃɪp; ʃɪp/ *n* 名

a large boat that carries people or things 船

A lot of ships come to the harbour every day. 每天许多船只来到这个海港。

***shirt** /ʃɜːt; ʃɝt/ *n* 名

a piece of clothing with a collar and buttons that you wear on the upper body 衬衫；恤衫

He wore a white shirt and a blue tie. 他穿了一件白色衬衫，系了一条蓝色领带。

另见 **T-shirt**

shiver /ˈʃɪvə; ˋʃɪvɚ/ *v* 动

to shake because you are cold or afraid 颤抖；发抖

She was shivering because it was very cold. 天气非常寒冷，她冻得直发抖。

同义 **tremble**

shock[1] /ʃɒk; ʃɑk/ *n* 名

a strong feeling of surprise when something bad suddenly happens 震惊

He got a shock when he heard the news. 他听到那个消息时大吃一惊。

shock[2] /ʃɒk; ʃɑk/ *v* 动

to make someone feel very surprised and upset 使震惊

I was shocked to hear that she died. 听到她死了，我感到震惊。

***shoe** /ʃuː; ʃu/ *n* 名

something that you wear on your foot 鞋

Please take off your shoes before you come in. 进来前请脱掉鞋子。

shoelace /ˈʃuːleɪs; ˋʃuˌles/ *n* 名

a thin piece of string used to tie a shoe 鞋带

Your shoelaces are undone. 你的鞋带松开了。

shone /ʃɒn; ʃon/ *v* 动

the past tense and past participle of **shine** ☆shine 的过去式和过去分词

shook /ʃʊk; ʃʊk/ *v* 动

the past tense of **shake** ☆shake 的过去式

shoot /ʃu:t; ʃut/ *v* 动

shoots, shooting, shot, shot

1. to injure or kill someone with a gun, an arrow, etc 射击；射杀
   The policeman shot the robber in the arm. 警察射中了劫匪的手臂。
2. to kick or throw a ball towards the place where you can score a goal or point 射门；投篮

Kenneth shot from the middle of the field. 肯尼思在中场射门。

***shop[1]** /ʃɒp; ʃap/ *n* 名【英】

美式：***store***

a place where you buy things 商店；店铺

We bought a rabbit in a pet shop. 我们在宠物店买了一只兔子。

shop[2] /ʃɒp; ʃap/ *v* 动

shops, shopping, shopped, shopped

to go to shops to buy things（去商店）买东西；购物

My mother often shops in this street. 我的妈妈经常在这条街购物。

go shopping 逛商店购物

Lily went shopping with her friends. 莉莉和朋友们去商店购物了。

shoplifting /ˈʃɒpˌlɪftɪŋ; ˋʃapˌlɪftɪŋ/ *n* 名

无复数

the crime of stealing things from a shop 在商店行窃；店铺盗窃

He was arrested for shoplifting. 他因在商店行窃被拘捕了。

shopping centre /ˈʃɒpɪŋ ˌsentə; ˋʃapɪŋ ˏsentɚ/ *n* 名【英】

美式：***shopping center***

a group of shops together in one area, usually in a large building 购物中心；商场

I went to the new shopping centre to buy a computer. 我去了新的购物中心买电脑。

同义 **mall, shopping mall**

shopping mall /ˈʃɒpɪŋ mɔ:l; ˋʃapɪŋ mɔl/ *n* 名

另见 **mall, shopping centre**

shore /ʃɔ:; ʃɔr/ *n* 名

the land along the edge of the sea, a lake, etc（海、湖等的）岸；滨

They went fishing on the shore of the lake. 他们去湖滨钓鱼。

***short** /ʃɔ:t; ʃɔrt/ *adj* 形

shorter, shortest

1. measuring a small length or distance（长度或距离）短的
   Amanda has short hair. 阿曼达有一头短发。

   反义 **long[1]**
2. lasting a small amount of time（时间）短的；短暂的
   We only stayed there for a short time. 我们只在那里逗留了很短的时间。

   反义 **long[1]**
3. not tall 矮的
   Roger is a short fat boy. 罗杰是个矮胖的男孩。

   反义 **tall**

shorten /ˈʃɔ:tn; ˋʃɔrtn̩/ *v* 动

to make something shorter 改短；缩短

He shortened the piece of wood with a saw. 他用锯子把木块锯短了。

***shorts** /ʃɔ:ts; ʃɔrts/ *plural n* 复数名词

trousers that end at or above the knees 短裤

I wear shorts when I go running. 我去跑步时会穿短裤。

注意 如要表示一条、两条短裤，用 a pair of shorts、two pairs of shorts 等。

shot[1] /ʃɒt; ʃat/ *n* 名

firing a gun or the sound that a gun makes 开枪；枪声

He took a shot at the bear. 他向那只熊开了枪。

I heard two shots outside. 我听到外面传来两声枪响。

S

shot² /ʃɒt; ʃɑt/ *v* 动

the past tense and past participle of **shoot** ☆shoot 的过去式和过去分词

***should** /ʃəd; ʃəd *strong* 强读 ʃʊd; ʃʊd/ *v* 动

1. used to say what is the right thing to do 应该
   You should have enough sleep every day. 你每天都应该有充足的睡眠。

同义 **ought to**

Daily conversation 日常会话
"What should I do?" "I think you should tell your parents." "我该怎么做呢？""我认为你应该告诉你的父母。"

2. the past tense of **shall** ☆shall 的过去式

***shoulder** /ˈʃəʊldə; ˋʃoldɚ/ *n* 名

the part of your body between your neck and the top of your arm 肩膀

He was carrying a bag on his shoulder. 他肩上扛着一个包。

shouldn't /ˈʃʊdnt; ˋʃʊdn̩t/

the short form of "**should not**" ☆should not 的缩写

You shouldn't hit him. 你不应该打他。

***shout¹** /ʃaʊt; ʃaʊt/ *v* 动

to say something in a loud voice 喊叫；呼喊

You don't need to shout. I can hear you. 你不用大声喊叫，我听得见。

shout² /ʃaʊt; ʃaʊt/ *n* 名

a loud cry 喊叫（声）；呼叫（声）

She heard a shout and looked back. 她听见一声大叫，回头去看。

***show¹** /ʃəʊ; ʃo/ *v* 动

shows, showing, showed, shown

1. to let someone see something 给…看；出示
   Please show me your tickets. 请出示你们的票。

2. to make something clear by giving facts or information 表明；显示
   The X-ray showed that his arm was broken. X 光显示他的手臂断了。
3. to tell someone how to do something by letting them see you do it（通过演示）解释；说明
   Sarah showed me how to make a cheese cake. 莎拉教我怎样做干酪蛋糕。

show off 炫耀；卖弄

Norman likes to show off in front of others. 诺曼喜欢在别人面前炫耀。

***show²** /ʃəʊ; ʃo/ *n* 名

1. a performance in a theatre 演出；表演
   We went to a show last night. 昨晚我们去看演出了。
2. a programme on television or the radio（电视或广播）节目
   There is a new show on television tomorrow night. 明天晚上会有一个新的电视节目。

***shower** /ˈʃaʊə; ˋʃaʊɚ/ *n* 名

1. a piece of equipment that sends out water and you stand under to wash yourself 淋浴器；花洒
   Our bathroom has a shower but no bath. 我们的浴室有淋浴器，但没有浴缸。
2. when you wash yourself under the shower 淋浴
   He's having a shower. 他在淋浴。

3. a short period of rain 阵雨
   There may be some showers today. 今天可能会有几场阵雨。

shown /ʃəʊn; ʃon/ *v* 动

the past participle of **show¹** ☆show¹ 的过去分词

shrimp /ʃrɪmp; ʃrɪmp/ *n* 名

复数：***shrimp/shrimps***

a small sea animal with a shell and ten legs 虾；小虾

Bob likes fried rice with shrimps. 鲍勃喜欢吃虾炒饭。

***shut¹** /ʃʌt; ʃʌt/ *v* 动

shuts, shutting, shut, shut

to close 关闭

He shut the windows. 他关上了窗。

shut down 关闭；使停止运作

Shut down the computer before you leave. 离开前要关掉电脑。

同义 **close¹**

反义 **open²**

Daily conversation 日常会话
shut up! 闭嘴！住口！
"Shut up! You're talking too much." "闭嘴！你说得太多了。"

注意 这是比较粗鲁的说法，较礼貌的用语是 be quiet。

***shut²** /ʃʌt; ʃʌt/ *adj* 形

not open 关闭的；闭着的

She kept her eyes shut. 她让眼睛闭着。

同义 **closed**

反义 **open**[1]

***shy** /ʃaɪ; ʃaɪ/ *adj* 形

shyer, shyest

nervous or afraid to be with other people 害羞的；羞怯的

Elsie is too shy to talk to others. 埃尔西太害羞，不敢跟别人说话。

***sick** /sɪk; sɪk/ *adj* 形

not feeling well 生病的

Jessica was sick and didn't go to school. 杰西卡病了，没有去上学。

feel sick 反胃；作呕

The bad smell made me feel sick. 那种臭味让我想吐。

同义 **ill, unwell**

反义 **well**[1]

***side** /saɪd; saɪd/ *n* 名

1. one of the two parts that something is divided into（某物的）一边；一面

   There is a bus on the right side of the road. 马路的右边有一辆公共汽车。
2. a position just next to someone or something 侧边；旁边

   Her dog was walking by her side. 她的狗在她身边走。
3. the part of something that is away from the middle 边；边缘

   He parked his car at the side of the road. 他把车子停在路边。
4. a part of something that is not the top, bottom, front or back 侧面

   There are windows on each side of the house. 房子的两侧都有窗户。
5. one of the two surfaces of a thin object（扁平物体的）一面

   I wrote on both sides of the paper. 我在纸的两面写字。
6. the part of your body from the top of your arm to the top of your leg 身体的侧边

   Jack lay on his side. 杰克侧身躺着。

side by side 并排地；肩并肩地

Eve and I sat side by side. 我和伊芙并排坐着。

sidewalk /ˈsaɪdwɔːk; ˋsaɪdˏwɔk/ *n* 名【美】

英式 **pavement**

sigh /saɪ; saɪ/ *v* 动

to breathe in and out with a long sound, because you are bored, sad, tired, etc 叹气；叹息

She sighed when she saw that she had missed the last train. 她看到已经错过了最后一班列车，叹了口气。

sight /saɪt; saɪt/ *n* 名

无复数

the ability to see 视力

My grandmother's sight isn't very good. 祖母的视力不佳。

***sightseeing** /ˈsaɪtˌsiːɪŋ; ˋsaɪtˏsiɪŋ/ *n* 名

无复数

the activity of visiting famous or interesting places 游览；观光

They went sightseeing in Europe last month. 他们上个月到欧洲游览。

sign[1] /saɪn; saɪn/ *n* 名

1. a notice which gives information about something 标志；告示

   What does this road sign mean? 这个路标是什么意思？

2. a picture, shape, etc that has a special meaning 符号

   The sign "+" means "plus". "+"这个符号是"加"的意思。

***sign**[2] /saɪn; saɪn/ *v* 动

to write your name on something 签名；签字

He finished the letter and signed it. 他写完信就签了名。

***signal** /ˈsɪgnl; ˋsɪgnl̩/ *n* 名

an action, movement or sound that gives you information about something or tells you to do something 信号

The policeman gave a signal for the car to stop. 警察示意那辆汽车停下来。

***signature** /ˈsɪgnətʃə; ˋsɪgnətʃɚ/ *n* 名

your name written by yourself in a special way, especially on a letter or cheque 签名

The bank will make sure that the signature on the cheque is correct. 银行将确认支票上的签名是正确的。

S

***silence** /ˈsaɪləns; ˋsaɪləns/ *n* 名

无复数

a situation in which there is no sound

or no one is speaking 无声；寂静
They read in silence. 他们静静地看书。

***silent** /'saɪlənt; `saɪlənt/ *adj* 形
not speaking or without any sound 寂静的；沉默的
The streets are silent at night. 晚上的街道寂静无声。
同义 **quiet**
反义 **noisy**

***silk** /sɪlk; sɪlk/ *n* 名
无复数
a smooth and light cloth 丝绸

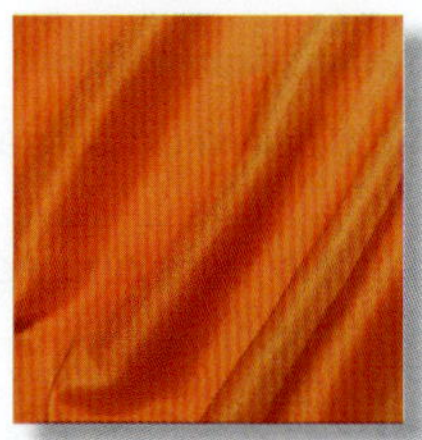

Mary likes silk dresses. 玛丽喜欢丝绸裙子。

***silly** /'sɪli; `sɪlɪ/ *adj* 形
sillier, silliest
foolish or stupid 傻的；愚蠢的
Everyone makes silly mistakes sometimes. 每个人有时都会犯一些愚蠢的错误。
反义 **clever, smart**

***silver[1]** /'sɪlvə; `sɪlvɚ/ *n* 名
无复数
a white grey metal that is valuable and is used to make coins, jewellery, etc 银
This medal is made of silver. 这块奖章是银制的。

S

***silver[2]** /'sɪlvə; `sɪlvɚ/ *adj* 形
made of silver or having the colour of silver 银的；银色的
She wore a silver ring. 她戴着一枚银戒指。

***similar** /'sɪmələ; `sɪmələ/ *adj* 形
alike but not exactly the same 近似的；相似的
Sally and I have similar hobbies. 莎莉和我有相似的爱好。
反义 **different**

***simple** /'sɪmpl; `sɪmpl/ *adj* 形
simpler, simplest
1. easy to do or understand 容易的；简单的
   This is a simple question. 这是一个简单的问题。

   反义 **difficult, hard[1]**
2. not having a lot of decoration 简单的；朴素的
   The dress is simple but I like it. 虽然这条裙子很简单，但我喜欢。

***simply** /'sɪmpli; `sɪmplɪ/ *adv* 副
1. just; only 仅仅；只不过
   She was late for school, simply because she didn't hear her alarm clock. 她上学迟到了，只是因为她没听见闹钟。
2. in a simple way 简单地
   Can you explain it simply? 你可以简单地解释一下吗？

***since[1]** /sɪns; sɪns/ *prep* 介
from a point of time or event in the past until now 自从…以来；自从…之后
She has worked in this company since 1999. 她自 1999 年起便在这个公司里工作。
用法 与现在完成式或过去完成式一起使用。

***since[2]** /sɪns; sɪns/ *conj* 连
1. from a point of time or event in the past until now 自从…以来；自从…之后
   I have not seen Oscar since he left the school. 自从奥斯卡离校之后，我就没有再见过他。

   用法 与现在完成式或过去完成式一起使用。
2. because 因为；由于
   Since I finished my homework quickly, I had time to watch TV. 因为我很快就做完功课了，所以有时间看电视。

***since[3]** /sɪns; sɪns/ *adv* 副
from a point of time or event in the past until now 自从…以来；自从…之后
Emily moved to Australia last year and has lived there since. 埃米莉去年到了澳洲之后，就一直住在那儿。
用法 与现在完成式或过去完成式共用。

sincere /sɪn'sɪə; sɪn`sɪr/ *adj* 形
honest and showing true feelings 诚实的；真诚的
Paul is a sincere friend. 保罗是个真诚的朋友。

***sincerely** /sɪn'sɪəli; sɪn`sɪrlɪ/ *adv* 副
in a sincere way 诚实地；真诚地
I sincerely hope that you will be happy. 我由衷地希望你快乐。
Yours sincerely 敬上；谨启（信末写于签名前的用语，只用于以某人名字开头的信件）
She wrote "Yours sincerely" and signed the letter. 她写了"敬上"，然后在信上签名。

***sing** /sɪŋ; sɪŋ/ *v* 动
sings, singing, sang, sung
1. to make music with your voice 唱歌
   My sister sang three songs at the concert. 姐姐在音乐会唱了三首歌。
2. to make high sounds that sound

like music 鸣唱
The birds are singing in the trees. 鸟儿在树上鸣叫。

singer /ˈsɪŋə; ˋsɪŋɚ/ *n* 名
someone who sings 歌手；歌唱家
She is my favourite singer. 她是我最喜欢的歌手。

singing /ˈsɪŋɪŋ; ˋsɪŋɪŋ/ *n* 名
无复数
the activity of making music with your voice 唱歌
She took part in the singing competition. 她参加了歌唱比赛。

***single** /ˈsɪŋgl; ˋsɪŋgl̩/ *adj* 形
1. only one 单一的；唯一的
   My sister is a baby and can't say a single word. 我的妹妹还是个婴儿，一个字也不会说。
2. not married 单身的；未婚的
   He is single and lives with his parents. 他未婚，与父母同住。

反义 **married**

***singular**[1] /ˈsɪŋgjʊlə; ˋsɪŋgjəlɚ/ *n* 名
the form of a word that shows only one thing, person, etc. For example, the singular of "children" is "child". 单数（形式）（例如 children 的单数形式是 child。）

另见 **plural**[1]

***singular**[2] /ˈsɪŋgjʊlə; ˋsɪŋgjəlɚ/ *adj* 形
a singular word is used to talk or write about only one thing, person, etc 单数的

另见 **plural**[2]

***sink**[1] /sɪŋk; sɪŋk/ *n* 名
a large open container in a kitchen or bathroom that you use for washing dishes, your hands, etc 洗涤槽；洗脸盆

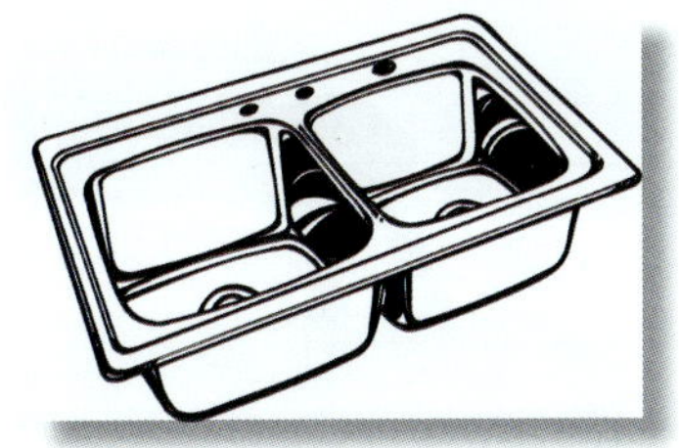

He washed the dishes in the sink. 他在洗涤槽洗碗碟。

***sink**[2] /sɪŋk; sɪŋk/ *v* 动
sinks, sinking, sank, sunk
1. to go down below the surface of water, mud, etc 下沉；沉没
   The stone sank to the bottom of the pond. 石头下沉到池底。

反义 **float**

2. to fall or move to a lower position 下沉；下降
   The sun was sinking behind the hills. 太阳渐渐沉到山后。

sir /sə; sɚ; *strong* 强读 sɜː; sɝ/ *n* 名
1. a polite way of speaking to or writing to a man whose name you do not know 先生
   Sir, you've dropped your key. 先生，您丢了钥匙。

用法 对男子的尊称。

另见 **madam**

2. 【英】a word that children use at school when they speak to or talk about a male teacher （男性）老师
   Sir, I'm sorry I haven't brought my textbooks. 老师，很抱歉，我忘了带课本。

用法 常用于口语。

另见 **Miss**

***sister** /ˈsɪstə; ˋsɪstɚ/ *n* 名
a girl or woman who has the same parents as you 姐姐；妹妹；姐妹
I have two sisters. 我有两个姐妹。

***sit** /sɪt; sɪt/ *v* 动
sits, sitting, sat, sat
to rest on your bottom 坐
My father is sitting in front of the computer. 我的爸爸正坐在电脑前。

反义 **stand**

sit down 坐下
Please come over and sit down. 请过来这边坐。

site /saɪt; saɪt/ *n* 名
a place where something was, is or will be built 地点；建筑工地

This is the site of the new library. 这是建新图书馆的工地。

sitting room /ˈsɪtɪŋ ruːm; ˋsɪtɪŋ ˏrum/ *n* 名
a room in a house where you sit and relax 客厅；起居室
She is watching TV in the sitting room. 她正在客厅里看电视。

同义 **living room**

另见 **附录**：Inside a flat 住所里

***situation** /ˌsɪtʃuˈeɪʃn; ˏsɪtʃuˋeʃən/ *n* 名
all the conditions and events at a particular place and time 情况；环境
Firefighters work in dangerous situations. 消防员在危险的环境中工作。

***six** /sɪks; sɪks/ *num* 数
the number 6 六
An ant has six legs. 蚂蚁有 6 条腿。

***sixteen** /sɪkˈstiːn; sɪksˋtin/ *num* 数
the number 16 十六

S

This book has sixteen pages. 这本书有 16 页。

sixteenth /sɪkˈstiːnθ; sɪkˋstinθ/ *ordinal num* 序数

16th in order 第十六(的)

The school picnic day is on the sixteenth of this month. 本月 16 日是学校的野餐日。

sixth /sɪksθ; sɪksθ/ *ordinal num* 序数

6th in order 第六(的)

Ann's sister celebrated her sixth birthday yesterday. 安的妹妹昨天庆祝了 6 岁生日。

sixtieth /ˈsɪkstiəθ; ˋsɪkstɪɪθ/ *ordinal num* 序数

60th in order 第六十(的)

My father's company is on the sixtieth floor of this building. 爸爸的公司在这栋大楼的 60 楼。

***sixty** /ˈsɪksti; ˋsɪkstɪ/ *num* 数

the number 60 六十

There are sixty minutes in an hour. 一小时有 60 分钟。

***size** /saɪz; saɪz/ *n* 名

how big or small someone or something is 大小；尺寸；尺码

I baked some cookies in different sizes. 我烤了不同大小的甜饼干。

skate¹ /skeɪt; sket/ *n* 名

a special boot which you wear to move on ice or hard surfaces 溜冰鞋；旱冰鞋

You can borrow a pair of skates at the counter. 你可以到柜台借一双溜冰鞋。

比较 **ski¹**

***skate²** /skeɪt; sket/ *v* 动

skates, skating, skated, skated

to move on skates 溜冰；滑旱冰

She is skating on the ice. 她在溜冰。

比较 **ski²**

***skating** /ˈskeɪtɪŋ; ˋsketɪŋ/ *n* 名

无复数

the sport of moving on ice or hard surfaces on skates 溜冰；滑旱冰

Lily went skating with her friends yesterday. 莉莉昨天和朋友去溜冰。

比较 **skiing**

skeleton /ˈskelɪtən; ˋskɛlətn̩/ *n* 名

the structure that consists of all the bones in a person or animal 骨骼；骨架

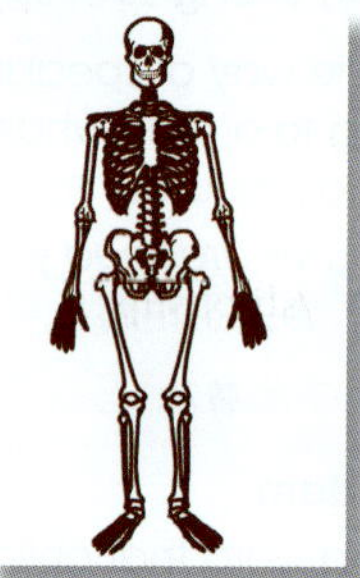

The skeleton supports our body. 骨骼支撑我们的身体。

ski¹ /skiː; ski/ *n* 名

one of a pair of long narrow pieces of wood, metal, etc that are fastened to your boots and are used for moving on the snow 滑雪板

I put on skis and glided over the snow. 我穿上滑雪板在雪上滑行。

比较 **skate¹**

ski² /skiː; ski/ *v* 动

skis, skiing, skied, skied

to move on skis 滑雪

Roger is skiing down the hill. 罗杰正滑雪下山。

比较 **skate²**

skid /skɪd; skɪd/ *v* 动

skids, skidding, skidded, skidded

to slide along a wet or very smooth surface 滑行；打滑

The car skidded on the wet road. 汽车在湿滑的路上打滑。

***skiing** /ˈskiːɪŋ; ˋskiɪŋ/ *n* 名

无复数

the sport of moving on the snow wearing skis 滑雪(运动)

They went skiing in Korea last week. 他们上星期去了韩国滑雪。

比较 **skating**

skilful /ˈskɪlfl; ˋskɪlfəl/ *adj* 形

good at doing something, especially something that needs practice 熟练的；技术好的

She is a skilful driver. 她是个技术好的司机。

***skill** /skɪl; skɪl/ *n* 名

an ability to do something well 技能；技巧

It is important to have good language skills. 拥有良好的语言技巧是很重要的。

***skin** /skɪn; skɪn/ *n* 名

1. (无复数) the thing that covers a person's or animal's body (人的)皮肤；(动物的)皮

   The baby has soft skin. 宝宝有柔嫩的皮肤。

2. the outside part of some fruits

and vegetables（水果、蔬菜的）外皮；果皮

Don't step on the banana skin! 别踩在香蕉皮上！

skinny /ˈskɪni; ˋskɪnɪ/ *adj* 形

skinnier, skinniest

very thin 极瘦的；皮包骨的

She doesn't eat much and is skinny. 她吃得不多，极为消瘦。

用法 skinny 常带贬义。

反义 **fat**

比较 **slim, thin**

***skip** /skɪp; skɪp/ *v* 动

skips, skipping, skipped, skipped

1. to move forwards by jumping in small steps 蹦跳地走

   Ross skipped along the path. 罗斯沿着小径蹦蹦跳跳地走。

2. to jump over a rope as you swing it over your head and under your feet 跳绳

   The girls are skipping in the playground. 女孩们在操场上跳绳。

skipping rope /ˈskɪpɪŋ ˌrəʊp; ˌskɪpɪŋ ˋrop/ *n* 名

a piece of rope with handles that you swing to jump over 跳绳

Three children jumped over the skipping rope together. 三个孩子一起跳一条绳。

***skirt** /skɜːt; skɝt/ *n* 名

a piece of clothing for girls and women that hangs from the waist 半腰裙；裙子

Sally is wearing a new skirt. 莎莉穿着新裙子。

比较 **dress[1]**

***sky** /skaɪ; skaɪ/ *n* 名

复数：***skies***

the space above the earth where the sun, moon, stars, etc appear 天空

The sky was blue and clear. 天空晴朗蔚蓝。

用法 常与 the 一起使用，即 the sky。

***sleep[1]** /sliːp; slip/ *v* 动

sleeps, sleeping, slept, slept

to rest with your eyes closed 睡；睡觉

I slept well last night. 我昨晚睡得很好。

***sleep[2]** /sliːp; slip/ *n* 名

无复数

when you close your eyes and rest 睡；睡觉

I am very tired and need to get some sleep. 我很累，需要睡一会。

go to sleep 睡觉；入睡

I always go to sleep at 10 p.m. 我总是在晚上 10 点睡觉。

***sleepy** /ˈsliːpi; ˋslipɪ/ *adj* 形

sleepier, sleepiest

tired and wanting to sleep 困倦的；想睡的

The medicine made him sleepy. 这种药物使他昏昏欲睡。

***sleeve** /sliːv; sliv/ *n* 名

the part of a piece of clothing that covers some or all of your arm 衣袖

My brother is wearing a shirt with short sleeves. 我的哥哥穿着一件短袖衬衫。

sleigh /sleɪ; sle/ *n* 名

a vehicle with no wheels that is pulled by animals and is used to travel over snow 雪橇

Santa Claus travels in a sleigh and gives presents to children. 圣诞老人坐雪橇给孩子们送礼物。

slept /slept; slɛpt/ *v* 动

the past tense and past participle of **sleep[1]** ☆sleep[1] 的过去式和过去分词

***slice** /slaɪs; slaɪs/ *n* 名

a thin piece that is cut from a larger piece 一片

She cut the pizza into eight slices. 她把比萨饼切成 8 块。

slid /slɪd; slɪd/ *v* 动

the past tense and past participle of **slide[1]** ☆slide[1] 的过去式和过去分词

***slide[1]** /slaɪd; slaɪd/ *v* 动

slides, sliding, slid, slid

to move smoothly over a surface or to make something move in this way（使）滑行；（使）滑动

He slid the pencil across the desk. 他把铅笔滑过桌子。

S

***slide²** /slaɪd; slaɪd/ *n* 名

a structure for children to climb up and slide down 滑梯

Henry came down the slide. 亨利从滑梯滑下来。

slim /slɪm; slɪm/ *adj* 形

slimmer, slimmest

thin in a good-looking way 苗条的

Candy is very slim. 坎蒂很苗条。

用法 slim 带有赞美的含义。

反义 **fat**

比较 **skinny, thin**

slip¹ /slɪp; slɪp/ *v* 动

slips, slipping, slipped, slipped

to slide a short distance by accident and fall or nearly fall 滑倒

Paul slipped on the wet floor. 保罗在湿地板上滑倒了。

slip² /slɪp; slɪp/ *n* 名

a small piece of paper 纸条

I wrote the phone number on a slip of paper. 我在纸条上写下电话号码。

reply slip 回执

Please return the reply slip next Monday. 请于下星期一把回执交回。

***slipper** /ˈslɪpə; ˋslɪpɚ/ *n* 名

a light soft shoe that you wear indoors 拖鞋

He took off his shoes and put on slippers. 他脱去鞋子穿上拖鞋。

比较 **sandal**

slope /sləʊp; slop/ *n* 名

a side of a hill or mountain 山坡；斜坡

A rock is rolling down the slope. 一块岩石正从斜坡上滚下来。

***slow** /sləʊ; slo/ *adj* 形

slower, slowest

1. not moving quickly; taking a long time 慢的；迟缓的

   The tram is slower than the bus. 电车比巴士慢。

反义 **fast¹, quick**

2. if a clock or watch is slow, it shows a time that is earlier that the real time（钟、表）偏慢的

   The clock is three minutes slow. 这只钟慢了 3 分钟。

反义 **fast¹**

***slowly** /ˈsləʊli; ˋslolɪ/ *adv* 副

in a slow way 慢慢地；缓慢地

My grandmother always walks slowly. 我的祖母总是慢慢地走路。

反义 **fast², quickly**

***small** /smɔːl; smɔl/ *adj* 形

smaller, smallest

1. little in amount or size or few in number 小的

   He has small eyes. 他的眼睛很小。

同义 **little¹**

反义 **big, large**

2. very young 幼小的；年幼的

   We have been friends since we were small. 我们从小就是朋友。

***smart** /smɑːt; smɑrt/ *adj* 形

smarter, smartest

1. clever 聪明的；机灵的

   Vivian is a smart girl. 维维安是个聪明的女孩。

反义 **silly, stupid**

2. a smart person wears neat and attractive clothes and looks tidy 整洁的；漂亮的

   Colin looked smart in his new coat today. 科林今天穿了一件新外套，看起来很漂亮。

smart card 智能卡

I bought a sandwich with my smart card. 我用智能卡买了一份三明治。

***smell¹** /smel; smɛl/ *v* 动

smells, smelling, smelt/smelled, smelt/smelled

1. to notice or recognize a smell 闻出；闻到

   I can smell something burning! 我闻到有什么东西烧焦了！

比较 **sniff**

用法 不用进行式，常与 can 和 could 一起使用。

2. to have a particular smell 有某种气味

   The flowers smell nice. 这些花闻起来很香。

3. to have a bad smell 发出臭气

   Something in the room smells. 房间里有什么东西发臭了。

用法 不用进行式。

***smell²** /smel; smɛl/ *n* 名

1. something that you notice using your nose 气味；气息

   I like the smell of flowers. 我很喜欢花的香气。

S

2. a bad smell 臭味
The smell comes from the litter bin. 阵阵臭气从垃圾箱传来。

***smelly** /ˈsmeli; ˋsmɛlɪ/ *adj* 形
smellier, smelliest
having a bad smell 有臭味的
The socks are smelly. 这些袜子很臭。

***smile¹** /smaɪl; smaɪl/ *v* 动
smiles, smiling, smiled, smiled
to make the corners of your mouth turn upwards because you are happy 微笑
The baby is smiling at me. 那个婴儿在对着我笑。
另见 **grin¹, laugh**

smile² /smaɪl; smaɪl/ *n* 名
the expression on your face when you are happy 微笑；笑容
She has a smile on her face. 她面带笑容。
另见 **grin², laughter**

smiley /ˈsmaɪli; ˋsmaɪlɪ/ *n* 名
a symbol used in writing, email, etc, to show that you are happy 微笑符号

I put a smiley at the end of the email. 我在电子邮件的结尾加了一个微笑符号。

***smoke¹** /sməʊk; smok/ *n* 名
无复数
the cloud of white, grey or black gas that comes from something burning 烟
Smoke was coming out of the chimney. 烟从烟囱里冒出来。

***smoke²** /sməʊk; smok/ *v* 动
smokes, smoking, smoked, smoked
to breathe in smoke from a cigarette or pipe 吸烟；抽烟
We should not smoke because it is bad for our health. 我们不应吸烟，因为吸烟危害健康。

smoked /sməʊkt; smokt/ *adj* 形
smoked fish or meat has been hung in smoke and has a special flavour 烟熏的
I like smoked salmon. 我喜欢烟熏三文鱼。

smoking /ˈsməʊkɪŋ; ˋsmokɪŋ/ *n* 名
无复数
the activity of breathing in smoke from a cigarette or pipe 吸烟；抽烟
Smoking is bad for your health. 吸烟有害健康。

***smooth** /smuːð; smuð/ *adj* 形
smoother, smoothest
if a surface is smooth, it does not have holes or rough places 光滑的；平坦的
These eggs have smooth shells. 这些鸡蛋的壳很光滑。

同义 **soft**
反义 **rough**

***snack** /snæk; snæk/ *n* 名
a small amount of food that you eat between main meals 小吃；点心
We ate snacks while we were watching the film. 我们边看电影边吃零食。
snack bar 小吃店
Let's get some sweets at the snack bar. 我们在小吃店买些糖果吧。

***snail** /sneɪl; snel/ *n* 名
a small animal that has a hard shell on its back and moves very slowly 蜗牛
After the rain a lot of snails came out. 雨后许多蜗牛爬出来。

***snake** /sneɪk; snek/ *n* 名
a thin animal with a long body and no legs 蛇

There is a snake in the tree. 树上有一条蛇。

***sneeze** /sniːz; sniz/ *v* 动
sneezes, sneezing, sneezed, sneezed
if you sneeze, you suddenly make air come out of your nose with a loud noise 打喷嚏
The flowers make me sneeze. 那些花朵令我打喷嚏。

sniff /snɪf; snɪf/ *v* 动

1. to breathe air in through your nose noisily, for example when you have a cold 抽鼻子
   I can't stop sniffing because I have got a cold. 我患了感冒，所以不停地抽鼻子。
2. to smell something by breathing air in your nose 嗅；闻
   The dog sniffed my bag. 那条狗嗅了嗅我的袋子。

比较 **smell**[1]

***snore** /snɔː; snɔr/ *v* 动

snores, snoring, snored, snored

to breathe noisily while you are asleep 打鼾

Did I snore last night? 我昨晚有没有打鼾?

***snow**[1] /snəʊ; sno/ *n* 名

无复数

soft white pieces of frozen water that fall from the sky in cold weather 雪；雪花

The mountains were covered in snow. 山峰盖满了雪。

***snow**[2] /snəʊ; sno/ *v* 动

if it snows, snow falls from the sky 下雪

It sometimes snows in winter in Beijing. 北京的冬天有时会下雪。

***snowman** /ˈsnəʊmæn; ˋsnoˌmæn/ *n* 名

复数：*snowmen*

a model of a person made of snow 雪人

The children are making a snowman. 那些孩子正在堆雪人。

***so**[1] /səʊ; so/ *adv* 副

1. very; to a high level 这么；如此（用于强调）
   Annie is so tall. 安妮长得真高。
2. also; in the same way 也；同样
   Nancy loves drawing and so do I. 南茜喜欢画画，我也喜欢。

and so on 等等

The shop sells books, magazines and so on. 这家店铺出售书籍、杂志等等。

or so 大约；左右

That watch costs $500 or so. 那只手表要 500 元左右。

so ... that ... 如此…，以致…

Chris was so tired that he went to bed early. 克里斯很累，所以很早便睡觉了。

Daily conversation 日常会话

"Is John coming to the party?" "I don't think so." "约翰来聚会吗？""我想他不会来了。"

"Is Amy coming?" "I hope so." "艾米来吗？""我希望她来。"

***so**[2] /səʊ; so/ *conj* 连

for this reason; therefore 因此；所以

It was raining so she took an umbrella. 下雨了，所以她拿了雨伞。

so (that) 为了；以便

Can you speak up so that we can hear you? 你可以说大声一点让我们听见吗?

***soap** /səʊp; sop/ *n* 名

无复数

something you use with water for washing 肥皂

I washed my hands with soap. 我用肥皂洗了手。

用法 soap 是不可数名词，若要表示数量，可说 a bar of soap（一块肥皂）、two bars of soap（两块肥皂）等。

***society** /səˈsaɪəti; səˋsaɪətɪ/ *n* 名

复数：*societies*

1. （无复数）people who live together and share the same laws, traditions, etc 社会
   The effects of computers on modern society are huge. 电脑对现代社会的影响非常大。
2. an organization or a club 社团；协会
   I joined the drama society at school last year. 我去年加入了学校的剧社。

***sock** /sɒk; sak/ *n* 名

a soft piece of clothing that you wear on your foot 短袜

He wore a pair of grey socks. 他穿了一双灰袜。

socket /ˈsɒkɪt; ˋsakɪt/ *n* 名

a place in a wall where you connect a piece of equipment to electricity（电源）插座

I connected the radio to the socket. 我把收音机的插头插入插座。

S

***sofa** /'səʊfə; `sofə/ *n* 名

a long, soft seat for two or more people to sit on 长沙发

We watched TV on the sofa. 我们坐在沙发上看电视。

***soft** /sɒft; sɔft/ *adj* 形

softer, softest

1. not hard or firm 软的；柔软的

   I need a soft pillow. 我需要一个柔软的枕头。

反义 hard[1]

2. smooth 柔滑的；细嫩的

   Her baby has soft skin. 她宝宝的皮肤很柔滑。

反义 rough

3. quiet and gentle 轻柔的；柔和的

   Lynn has a soft voice. 琳的嗓音很柔和。

反义 loud

soft drink /'sɒft drɪŋk; `sɔft drɪŋk/ *n* 名

a cold drink with no alcohol in it （不含酒精的）软饮料；汽水

The shop sells soft drinks and snacks. 这家店铺出售汽水和小吃。

softly /'sɒftli; `sɔftlɪ/ *adv* 副

in a quiet and gentle way 轻轻地；轻柔地

She spoke softly to the baby. 她对着宝宝轻声地说话。

software /'sɒftweə; `sɔft,wɛr/ *n* 名

无复数

【电脑】the programs used on a computer 软件

The fault was caused by a problem with the software. 这个故障是由软件问题引起的。

比较 hardware

***soil** /sɔɪl; sɔɪl/ *n* 名

the earth in which plants grow 土壤；泥土

Rice grows well in this soil. 稻米在这种土壤里生长良好。

sold /səʊld; sold/ *v* 动

the past tense and past participle of **sell** ☆sell 的过去式和过去分词

soldier /'səʊldʒə; `soldʒɚ/ *n* 名

someone in the army 军人；士兵

A lot of soldiers died in the battle. 许多士兵在那场战役中阵亡。

solid[1] /'sɒlɪd; `sɑlɪd/ *adj* 形

hard or firm, and not a liquid or gas 坚硬的；固体的

The baby has started to eat solid food. 这个婴儿已经开始吃固体食物了。

solid[2] /'sɒlɪd; `sɑlɪd/ *n* 名

something like wood, which is hard and is not a liquid or gas 固体

Water is a liquid and ice is a solid. 水是液体，冰是固体。

***solution** /sə'lu:ʃn; sə`luʃən/ *n* 名

an answer to a problem or question 解决办法；答案

We have to find a solution to the problem. 我们得寻找解决问题的办法。

solve /sɒlv; sɑlv/ *v* 动

solves, solving, solved, solved

to find an answer to a problem or question 解决；解答

Tom is trying to solve the maths problems. 汤姆正在努力解答数学题。

***some[1]** /səm; səm; *strong* 强读 sʌm; sʌm/ *adj* 形

1. a number of; an amount of 一些；若干

   He gave me some stamps. 他给了我一些邮票。

   Do you want some tea? 你想喝点茶吗？

用法 some 用于疑问句时，表示预计对方会作出肯定回答，例如 Would you like some drinks?（你想喝点什么吗？）；any 则用于不知道对方会如何回答的疑问句中，例如 Do you have any money?（你有没有钱？）。

比较 any[1]

2. a particular number of, but not all 有些；一部分

   Some birds can swim. 有些鸟类会游泳。

***some[2]** /səm; səm; *strong* 强读 sʌm; sʌm/ *pron* 代

a number of people or things; an amount of something 一些；若干（人或物）

Some of the boys are quiet. 这群男孩中有些很沉静。

I'm making coffee. Would you like some? 我在煮咖啡，你要喝点吗？

比较 any[2]

***somebody** /'sʌmbɒdi; `sʌm,badɪ/, **someone** /'sʌmwʌn; `sʌm,wʌn/ *pron* 代

a person who is not known or mentioned 某人；有人

I saw someone at the door. 我见到门口有人。

somersault /ˈsʌməsɔːlt; ˋsʌmɚˌsɔlt/ *n* 名

a movement in which your feet turn over your head and touch the ground 筋斗；滚翻

Jimmy did two somersaults. 吉米翻了两个筋斗。

***something** /ˈsʌmθɪŋ; ˋsʌmθɪŋ/ *pron* 代

a thing that is not known or mentioned 某物；某事

There's something in the cup. 杯子里有什么东西。

She told me something about Vincent. 她跟我说了些关于文森特的事。

 **Daily conversation 日常会话**

something like that 大约如此

"How much is this doll?" "Fifty dollars, something like that." "这个玩具娃娃要多少钱？" "大约 50 元吧。"

***sometimes** /ˈsʌmtaɪmz; ˋsʌmˌtaɪmz/ *adv* 副

on some occasions, but not always 有时；间或

Sometimes we go fishing by the river. 有时我们会到河边钓鱼。

somewhere /ˈsʌmweə; ˋsʌmˌwɛr/ *adv* 副

in, at or to a place 在某处；到某处

The book is somewhere in this room but I can't find it. 这本书在这个房间的某个地方，但我找不到它。

***son** /sʌn; sʌn/ *n* 名

a male child 儿子

Her son was born in 2005. 她的儿子在 2005 年出生。

另见 **daughter**

***song** /sɒŋ; sɔŋ/ *n* 名

a piece of music with words that you sing 歌曲

Let's sing a song. 我们来唱首歌吧。

***soon** /suːn; sun/ *adv* 副

sooner, soonest

in a short time from now 很快；不久

Shirley is going to London soon. 雪莉很快要去伦敦了。

as soon as 一…就…

The baby cried as soon as his mother left. 妈妈一走开宝宝就哭了。

sooner or later 迟早；总有一天

Your parents will know it sooner or later. 你的父母迟早会知道的。

sore /sɔː; sɔr/ *adj* 形

if a part of your body is sore, it is painful 疼痛的

I've got a sore throat. 我喉咙痛。

***sorry** /ˈsɒri; ˋsɑrɪ/ *adj* 形

sorrier, sorriest

used to tell someone that you feel bad about something you have done 对不起；抱歉（用于道歉）

I'm sorry. I've lost your number. 对不起，我弄丢了你的电话号码。

be/feel sorry for someone 为某人感到难过；同情某人

Alan's cat has died. I feel sorry for him. 艾伦的猫死了，我为他感到难过。

Daily conversation 日常会话

"Let's go swimming." "Sorry, I can't go. I have a test tomorrow." "我们去游泳吧。" "对不起，我不能去。我明天有考试。"

***sort** /sɔːt; sɔrt/ *n* 名

a type of person or thing 种类；类型

What sort of music do you like? 你喜欢哪种音乐呢?

sort of 有点；有几分

You look sort of like my brother. 你看上去有几分像我弟弟。

用法 sort of 用于非正式的场合。

同义 **kind[1], type[1]**

***sound[1]** /saʊnd; saʊnd/ *n* 名

something that you hear 声音；响声

I heard the sound of a car behind me. 我听到背后的汽车声。

比较 **noise**

sound[2] /saʊnd; saʊnd/ *v* 动

to seem good, bad, etc from what you have heard or been told 听起来；似乎

The film sounds very interesting. 这部电影似乎很有趣。

***soup** /suːp; sup/ *n* 名

a hot liquid food that has meat, vegetables, etc 汤

We ordered two bowls of soup. 我们叫了两碗汤。

***sour** /saʊə; saʊr/ *adj* 形

having a strong taste like a lemon 酸的；有酸味的

These oranges are very sour. 这些橙子很酸。

***source** /sɔːs; sɔrs/ *n* 名

where something comes from 来源；出处

This website is a useful source of information. 这个网站是有用的资料来源。

south¹ /saʊθ; saʊθ/ *n* 名

无复数｜缩写：*S*

the direction that is opposite north 南方；南面

A typhoon is coming from the south. 一个台风从南面而来。

south² /saʊθ; saʊθ/ *adj* 形

in the south or facing the south 南方的；南面的；向南的

My uncle lives on the south coast. 我的叔叔住在南海岸。

south³ /saʊθ; saʊθ/ *adv* 副

towards the south 向南

This house faces south. 这所房子朝南。

southern /ˈsʌðən; ˋsʌðɚn/ *adj* 形

in or from the south of a country or place 南方的；南部的

We visited southern Italy last summer. 我们去年夏天到意大利南部游览。

souvenir /ˌsuːvəˈnɪə; ˏsuvəˋnɪr/ *n* 名

something that you keep to help you remember a place or an event 纪念品；纪念物

This beer mug is a souvenir of our trip to Germany. 这个大啤酒杯是我们去德国旅行的纪念品。

sow /səʊ; so/ *v* 动

sows, sowing, sowed, sown/sowed

to put seeds in the ground 播(种)

The farmers sowed the seeds in early spring. 农夫在初春时播了种。

sown /səʊn; son/ *v* 动

the past participle of **sow** ☆sow 的过去分词

soya bean /ˈsɔɪə biːn; ˋsɔɪə ˏbin/ *n* 名【英】

美式：*soybean*

a bean that is used as a food 大豆；黄豆

A lot of dishes can be made from soya beans. 用黄豆可以烹调许多菜肴。

soy sauce /ˌsɔɪ ˈsɔːs; ˋsɔɪ ˏsɔs/ *n* 名

无复数｜也作：*soya sauce*【英】

a dark brown sauce made from soya beans 酱油；豉油

The Chinese often cook with soy sauce. 中国人常常用酱油烧菜。

***space** /speɪs; spes/ *n* 名

1. an empty area 空位；空间
   There is a parking space at the corner of the street. 街角有一个停车位。
   There is no space for a desk in my room. 我的房间没有地方放书桌。
2. (无复数) the area outside the earth where the stars and planets are 太空

China has sent people into space. 中国已经把人送上太空了。

spaceship /ˈspeɪsˌʃɪp; ˋspesˌʃɪp/ *n* 名

a vehicle that travels in space 宇宙飞船；太空船

A spaceship landed on the moon. 一艘太空船在月球登陆。

另见 **rocket**

spade /speɪd; sped/ *n* 名

a tool with a long handle that you use for digging 铲子；铁锹

He dug a hole with a spade. 他用铲子挖了一个洞。

spaghetti /spəˈgeti; spəˋgɛtɪ/ *n* 名

无复数

a kind of pasta in long thin pieces 意大利面条；意大利粉

I had spaghetti for lunch. 我午餐吃了意大利面。

S

spare /speə; spɛr/ *adj* 形

for later use; extra 备用的；额外的

He keeps a spare tyre in his car. 他在车内存放了一个备用轮胎。

spare time 空闲时间

Oliver plays table tennis in his spare time. 奥立弗在空余时间打乒乓球。

spat /spæt; spæt/ *v* 动

the past tense and past participle of **spit** ☆spit 的过去式和过去分词

***speak** /spi:k; spik/ *v* 动

speaks, speaking, spoke, spoken

1. to say something or talk to someone about something 说话；谈话
   The baby is learning to speak. 宝宝在牙牙学语。
   He's spoken to his teacher about it. 那件事他和老师谈过了。
2. to be able to talk in a particular language 会说；会讲（某种语言）
   Miss Miller speaks English and Spanish. 米勒小姐会说英语和西班牙语。

Daily conversation 日常会话

speak up 大声说

"Could you speak up, please? We can't hear you." "OK, sorry." "请你说大声一点好吗？我们听不见你的话。" "好的。对不起。"

speaker /ˈspi:kə; ˋspikɚ/ *n* 名

1. someone who talks about something to a group of people 演讲者；发言人
   Joseph is a good public speaker. 约瑟夫擅长在公开场合演讲。
2. someone who speaks a particular language 讲某种语言的人
   There are some French speakers in Canada. 在加拿大有一些讲法语的人。
3. the part of a radio, computer, etc where the sound comes out 扬声器；喇叭
   I connected the speakers to my computer. 我给电脑接上喇叭。

***special** /ˈspeʃl; ˋspɛʃəl/ *adj* 形

different from others, usually better or more important 特别的；特殊的

Tomorrow is a special day for Daisy because she's going to Japan. 明天对黛西而言是一个特别的日子，因为她要去日本了。

specially /ˈspeʃli; ˋspɛʃəlɪ/ *adv* 副

for a particular purpose 特意；专门地

Barbara made a cake specially for her husband. 芭芭拉特意为丈夫做了一个蛋糕。

sped /sped; spɛd/ *v* 动

the past tense and past participle of **speed²** ☆speed² 的过去式和过去分词

***speech** /spi:tʃ; spitʃ/ *n* 名

复数：***speeches***

a talk that someone gives to a group of people 演讲；演说

The principal gave a speech in the hall. 校长在礼堂里发表了演说。

***speed¹** /spi:d; spid/ *n* 名

how fast something moves 速度

He was driving at a speed of 70 kilometres per hour. 他当时以每小时70公里的速度行驶。

speed² /spi:d; spid/ *v* 动

speeds, speeding, sped/speeded, sped/speeded

to move quickly 快速移动

The driver sped away after the accident. 发生事故后司机很快驾车走了。

speed up 加速

There's not much time left. We need to speed up. 时间不多了，我们得加速。

speedboat /ˈspi:dbəʊt; ˋspidˌbot/ *n* 名

a small boat that goes very fast 快艇

We went to the island on a speedboat. 我们乘快艇到那个岛上去。

***spell¹** /spel; spɛl/ *v* 动

spells, spelling, spelt/spelled, spelt/spelled

to say or write the letters of a word 拼写；拼出

How do you spell your name? 你的名字怎么拼呢?

spell² /spel; spɛl/ *n* 名

a group of words that make magic happen 符咒；咒语

The witch said a magic spell and the frog became a prince. 女巫念了魔咒，青蛙就变成了王子。

spelling /ˈspelɪŋ; ˋspɛlɪŋ/ *n* 名

the correct way you spell a word 拼法

You can find British and American spellings in the dictionary. 英式和美式拼法都可以在词典内找到。

spelt /spelt; spɛlt/ *v* 动

the past tense and past participle of **spell¹** ☆spell¹ 的过去式和过去分词

***spend** /spend; spɛnd/ *v* 动

spends, spending, spent, spent

1. to use money to pay for something 花（钱）；花费
   I spent $120 on my new dress.

S

我花了 120 元买新连衣裙。

2. to use time doing something 花（时间）；度过
We spent a month in London. 我们在伦敦过了一个月。
I spent half an hour reading. 我花了半小时看书。

spent /spent; spɛnt/ *v* 动
the past tense and past participle of **spend**☆spend 的过去式和过去分词

***spicy** /ˈspaɪsi; ˋspaɪsɪ/ *adj* 形
spicier, spiciest
having a strong, hot taste 辛辣的
Samuel likes spicy food. 塞缪尔喜欢吃辣的食物。
同义 hot

***spider** /ˈspaɪdə; ˋspaɪdɚ/ *n* 名
a small animal that has eight legs and makes webs to catch insects 蜘蛛

The spider caught a fly. 那只蜘蛛捉了一只苍蝇。

spill /spɪl; spɪl/ *v* 动
spills, spilling, spilt/spilled, spilt/spilled
if a liquid spills, or if you spill it, it flows over the edge of a container （使）溢出；（使）洒出
Water is spilling out of the bath. 水正从浴缸里溢出来。

He spilt tea on my shirt. 他把茶洒到我的衬衫上了。

spilt /spɪlt; spɪlt/ *v* 动
the past tense and past participle of **spill**☆spill 的过去式和过去分词

spirit /ˈspɪrɪt; ˋspɪrɪt/ *n* 名
1. a person's mind, thoughts and feelings 精神；心灵
I will always remember his kind spirit. 我将永远怀念他的慈爱精神。
2. **spirits** the way you are feeling 心境；情绪
We were in high spirits during the match. 比赛期间我们情绪高昂。

spit /spɪt; spɪt/ *v* 动
spits, spitting, spat, spat
to push liquid or food out of your mouth 吐（痰、口水、食物等）
Don't spit on the floor! 不要在地上吐痰！
The baby spat the milk out. 宝宝把奶吐了出来。

splash /splæʃ; splæʃ/ *v* 动
splashes, splashing, splashed, splashed
if a liquid splashes, or if you splash it, it falls on or hits something（使）溅；泼（到…上）
The waves splashed against the shore. 波浪拍打着岸边。
She splashed water on my face. 她往我脸上泼水。

spoil /spɔɪl; spɔɪl/ *v* 动
spoils, spoiling, spoiled/spoilt, spoiled/spoilt
to damage or have a bad effect on something good 破坏；糟蹋
Their quarrel spoiled the party. 他们的争吵破坏了聚会。

spoilt /spɔɪlt; spɔɪlt/ *v* 动
the past tense and past participle of **spoil**☆spoil 的过去式和过去分词

spoke /spəʊk; spok/ *v* 动
the past tense of **speak**☆speak 的过去式

spoken[1] /ˈspəʊkən; ˋspokən/ *v* 动
the past participle of **speak**☆speak 的过去分词

spoken[2] /ˈspəʊkən; ˋspokən/ *adj* 形
using language that you speak 口语的
In spoken English, "dad" is used more than "father". 在英语口语中，dad 较 father 更常用。

sponge /spʌndʒ; spʌndʒ/ *n* 名
a soft thing full of small holes that you use for washing 海绵

I cleaned off the dirt with a sponge. 我用海绵清洗了污垢。

***spoon** /spuːn; spun/ *n* 名
a tool that has a handle and a round end, used for eating or stirring food 汤匙；调羹
Angela tasted the soup with a spoon. 安琪拉用汤匙尝了尝汤的味道。

spoonful /ˈspuːnfʊl; ˋspunˌfʊl/ *n* 名
the amount that a spoon holds 一匙的量
He put a spoonful of sugar in his coffee. 他在咖啡里放了一匙糖。

***sport** /spɔːt; sport/ *n* 名
a game or an activity that you do by using your body, for example football or running 体育运动
Basketball is a popular sport. 篮球是一项受大众喜爱的运动。

用法 作体育运动的总称时，sport 没有复数形式，例如 He is good at sport（他很擅长体育运动）。指某项体育运动时，sport 则有复数形式，例如 Tennis and swimming are his favourite sports（网球和游泳是他最喜爱的体育运动）。

sports centre /ˈspɔːts ˌsentə; ˋspɔrts ˏsɛntɚ/ *n* 名【英】

美式：***sports center***

a building where you can play sports 体育运动中心；体育馆

We play badminton at the sports centre every Saturday. 我们每周六在体育馆打羽毛球。

spot /spɒt; spɑt/ *n* 名

1. a small, round area that is different from the rest of a surface 点；斑点
   Jonathan has a white dog with black spots. 乔纳森养了一条有黑色斑点的白狗。
2. a small dirty mark on something 污迹
   There is a mud spot on her jacket. 她的外套上有一点泥污。

3. a place 地点；地方
   This is a nice spot for a picnic. 这里是野餐的好地点。

spray[1] /spreɪ; spre/ *v* 动

to make liquid come out of something in small drops 喷；喷洒

Someone sprayed red paint on the wall. 有人在墙上喷了红漆。

spray[2] /spreɪ; spre/ *n* 名

liquid that you spray 喷雾液体；喷剂

I tried a new hair spray. 我试用了新的喷发定型剂。

***spread** /spred; sprɛd/ *v* 动

spreads, spreading, spread, spread

1. to open something so that it covers a flat surface 展开；摊开
   Philip spread the map out on the table. 菲利普在桌子上摊开了地图。
2. to affect a larger area or more people 扩散；蔓延
   The cancer has spread to other parts of her body. 癌症已经扩散到她身体的其他部位。
3. to tell a lot of people about something 散播；散布
   He was spreading lies about her. 他到处散播关于她的谎言。
4. to put a soft substance onto a surface 涂；敷
   She spread peanut butter on the bread. 她在面包上涂了花生酱。

***spring** /sprɪŋ; sprɪŋ/ *n* 名

the season between winter and summer 春天；春季

You can see a lot of beautiful flowers in spring. 春天可以见到许多美丽的花。

***square**[1] /skweə; skwɛr/ *n* 名

1. a shape with four straight sides of the same length and four angles of 90° 正方形；四方形
   This cloth has a pattern of blue and white squares. 这种布有蓝白正方形图案。
2. an outdoor area in a town, with buildings around it 广场
   A choir is singing in the square. 一队合唱团在广场上演唱。

***square**[2] /skweə; skwɛr/ *adj* 形

having the shape of a square 正方形的；四方形的

There are two square windows in this room. 这个房间有两扇正方形的窗户。

squash /skwɒʃ; skwɑʃ/ *n* 名

无复数

1. a game played by two people who hit a small ball against the four walls of a court 壁球

   Frank and I play squash once a month. 我和法兰克每个月打一次壁球。
2. 【英】a drink made from fruit juice, sugar and water 果汁饮料
   She drank a glass of lemon squash. 她喝了一杯柠檬汁饮料。

squeeze /skwiːz; skwiz/ *v* 动

squeezes, squeezing, squeezed, squeezed

to press something hard, usually with your fingers 挤；压；捏

Ivy cut an orange and squeezed the juice into a bowl. 艾薇切开橙子，把橙汁挤进碗里。

S

squid /skwɪd; skwɪd/ *n* 名

复数：***squid/squids***

a sea animal with a long soft body and ten arms 枪乌贼；鱿鱼

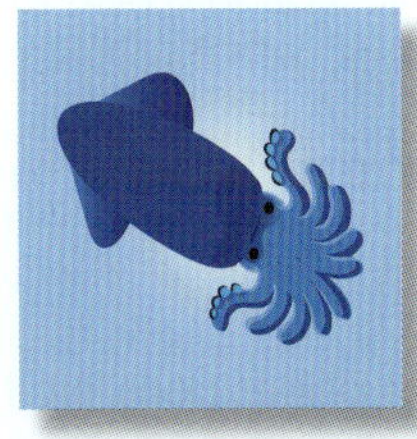

The fishermen caught a lot of squid in a net. 渔民用网捞到了许多鱿鱼。

squirrel /ˈskwɪrəl; ˋskwɝəl/ *n* 名

a small animal with a long thick tail that lives in trees and eats nuts 松鼠

The squirrel is eating a nut. 这只松鼠在吃坚果。

stadium /ˈsteɪdiəm; ˋstedɪəm/ *n* 名

复数：***stadiums/stadia***

a large place that has seats around it and is used for sports events, concerts, etc 运动场；体育场

We watched a football match at the stadium. 我们在运动场看了一场足球赛。

***staff** /stɑːf; stæf/ *n* 名

the group of people who work for a school, a company, etc 全体职员；员工

Our school has a staff of forty. 我们的学校有 40 名教职员。

用法 staff 指全体员工，如指一名员工可以说 a member of staff。

***stage** /steɪdʒ; stedʒ/ *n* 名

1. a period in a long event 阶段；时期

   We've come to the final stage of the plan. 我们已经到了这个计划的最后阶段。

2. an area in a theatre where actors, etc stand and perform 舞台

   Catherine is dancing on the stage. 凯瑟琳在舞台上跳舞。

***stairs** /steəz; stɛrz/ *plural n* 复数名词

a set of steps that go from one floor to another floor 楼梯

Paul ran up the stairs. 保罗跑上楼梯。

stall /stɔːl; stɔl/ *n* 名

a table or small shop, usually outdoors, where you sell things 货摊；摊位

There are several food stalls in this street. 这条街道上有几个食品摊位。

***stamp**[1] /stæmp; stæmp/ *n* 名

a small piece of paper that you put on an envelope or a parcel before you post it 邮票

I forgot to put a stamp on the letter before I sent it. 我忘了贴邮票便把信寄出了。

***stamp**[2] /stæmp; stæmp/ *v* 动

to put your foot down hard on the ground 跺（脚）；用力踩

Glen saw the cockroach and stamped on it. 格伦见到蟑螂，一脚踩下去。

***stand** /stænd; stænd/ *v* 动

stands, standing, stood, stood

1. to be on your feet 站；站立

   He stood under the tree. 他站在树下。

反义 **sit**

2. （也作：***stand up***）to get up onto your feet from a low position 站起来；起立

   All the pupils stood up when the teacher came in. 老师进来时，所有学生站了起来。

3. to be in a particular place 位于

   The castle stands on the top of the hill. 城堡位于山顶上。

stand for 是…的缩写；代表

VIP stands for "very important person". VIP 是 very important person（重要人物）的缩写。

stapler /ˈsteɪplə; ˋsteplɚ/ *n* 名

a tool that you use to fasten pieces of paper together 订书器

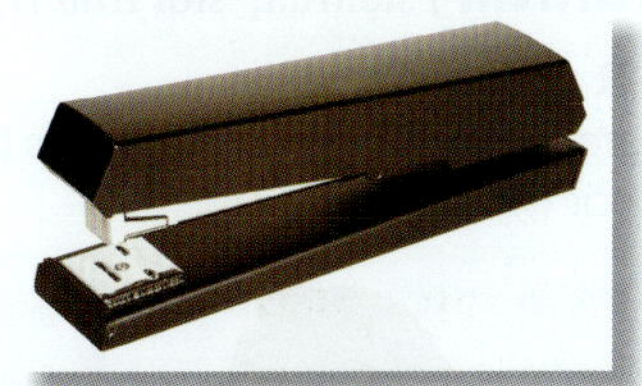

I fastened the notes with a stapler. 我用订书器把笔记订在一起。

***star** /stɑː; stɑr/ *n* 名

1. a small point of light that you can see in the sky at night 星

S

We looked at the stars in the sky. 我们看着天空中的星星。

2. a famous actor, singer, etc 明星

Rebecca wants to be a film star. 丽贝卡想成为电影明星。

stare /steə; stɛr/ *v* 动

stares, staring, stared, stared

to look at someone or something for a long time 盯着看；凝视

It is not polite to stare at others. 盯着别人是不礼貌的。

starfish /ˈstɑːˌfɪʃ; ˋstarˏfɪʃ/ *n* 名

复数：*starfish*

a sea animal that has five arms and looks like a star 海星

We saw a starfish on the bottom of the sea. 我们在海底见到一只海星。

starfruit /ˈstɑːfruːt; ˋstarˏfrut/ *n* 名

复数：*starfruit*

a green or yellow fruit that looks like a star 杨桃

These starfruit are from Malaysia. 这些杨桃来自马来西亚。

***start**[1] /stɑːt; start/ *v* 动

to begin 开始

The race starts at 2 p.m. 赛跑在下午 2 点开始。

start doing something 开始做某事

The baby started crying. 宝宝哭了起来。

start to do something 开始做某事

It started to rain. 开始下雨了。

反义 **end[2], finish**

***start**[2] /stɑːt; start/ *n* 名

the beginning of something 开头；开端

We missed the start of the concert. 我们错过了音乐会的开头。

starve /stɑːv; starv/ *v* 动

starves, starving, starved, starved

to be ill or die because you do not have enough food 挨饿；饿死

In this country, a lot of children are starving. 在这个国家，许多儿童在挨饿。

state /steɪt; stet/ *n* 名

1. the condition that someone or something is in 状态；状况

   The house was in a bad state. 那所房子破旧不堪。

2. （也作：***State***）one of the parts that some countries are divided into 州

   There are fifty states in the US. 美国有 50 个州。

***station** /ˈsteɪʃn; ˋsteʃən/ *n* 名

1. a place or building where a train or bus stops and you can get on or off 车站

   The train has arrived at the station. 火车到站了。

2. a building or place for some special work 站；所；局

   The fire station is next to the hospital. 消防局在医院的旁边。

stationery /ˈsteɪʃənri; ˋsteʃənˏɛrɪ/ *n* 名

无复数

things like paper, pens, etc that you use for writing 文具

He keeps all the stationery in the drawer. 他把所有文具放在抽屉里。

statue /ˈstætʃuː; ˋstætʃu/ *n* 名

a large object in the shape of a person or an animal that is made of stone, metal, etc 雕像；塑像

There is a statue of the writer in the park. 公园里有这位作家的一座雕像。

***stay** /steɪ; ste/ *v* 动

1. to continue to be in the same place, job, school, etc 停留；逗留

   Rose stayed in her room all day. 罗丝整天待在房间里。

2. to continue to be in a particular state 保持；继续是

   Albert swims every day to stay healthy. 阿尔伯特每天游泳来保持健康。

3. to live in a place for a short time 暂住；留宿

   My aunt is coming to stay with us for a few days. 我的阿姨要来我家住几天。

stay in 待在家里

I feel tired. Let's stay in tonight. 我有点累，我们今晚待在家吧。

stay out 待在外面

She stayed out all night. 她整晚没回家。

steady /ˈstedi; ˋstɛdɪ/ *adj* 形

steadier, steadiest

1. not moving or shaking 稳固的；不摇晃的
   He held the ladder steady while I climbed it. 他扶稳梯子，让我爬上去。
2. continuing in a regular way over a period of time 稳定的；持续的
   Derek has made steady progress over the past years. 德里克过去几年取得持续的进步。

steak /steɪk; stek/ *n* 名

a thick, flat piece of beef or fish 牛排；鱼排

He had steak and vegetables for dinner. 他晚餐吃了牛排和蔬菜。

*steal /stiːl; stil/ *v* 动

steals, stealing, stole, stolen

to take something that is not yours, without asking for it 偷；窃取

Someone stole my watch. 有人偷了我的手表。

用法 steal 用于指偷钱或其他物品。

比较 rob

steam[1] /stiːm; stim/ *n* 名

无复数

the gas that water becomes when it boils 蒸汽；水蒸气

Steam came out from the pot. 蒸汽从锅子里冒出来。

steam[2] /stiːm; stim/ *v* 动

to cook something in steam 蒸

Nancy is steaming a fish. 南茜在蒸鱼。

steel /stiːl; stil/ *n* 名

无复数

a strong, hard metal used to make knives, etc 钢；钢铁

These knives and forks are made of steel. 这些刀叉是钢制的。

steep /stiːp; stip/ *adj* 形

steeper, steepest

a steep road, hill, etc goes up or down at a large angle（路、山等）陡峭的

This road is too steep to walk on. 这条路太陡了，难以行走。

反义 flat[1]

stem /stem; stɛm/ *n* 名

the long, thin part of a plant, from which leaves or flowers grow 茎；梗

A rose has thorns on its stem. 玫瑰的茎有刺。

*step[1] /step; stɛp/ *n* 名

1. a movement of your foot that you make when you are walking 脚步
   Nick took a step back to let her pass. 尼克后退了一步，让她走过去。
2. a flat part of a set of stairs that you put your foot on 梯级；台阶
   He walked down some steps to the garden. 他走下几级台阶来到花园。

*step[2] /step; stɛp/ *v* 动

steps, stepping, stepped, stepped

to raise your foot and put it down in front of the other 迈步；跨步

She stepped forward to see what happened. 她向前走去，看发生了什么事。

stepfather /ˈstepfɑːðə; ˋstɛpˌfaðɚ/ *n* 名

a man who is married to your mother but is not your father 继父

His stepfather is a businessman. 他的继父是个商人。

stepmother /ˈstepmʌðə; ˋstɛpˌmʌðɚ/ *n* 名

a woman who is married to your father but is not your mother 继母

Ann's stepmother treats her like her own daughter. 安的继母把她当作亲生女对待。

*stick[1] /stɪk; stɪk/ *v* 动

sticks, sticking, stuck, stuck

1. to fix one thing to another with glue, tape, etc 黏；贴
   He stuck a poster on the wall. 他在墙上贴了一张海报。

S

2. to push a sharp thing into something 刺；插
   Kylie stuck a few candles in the birthday cake. 凯莉在生日蛋糕上插了几支蜡烛。

***stick²** /stɪk; stɪk/ *n* 名

1. a thin piece of wood that has fallen from a tree 枝条；柴枝
   The children used sticks to draw pictures on the sand. 孩子们用枝条在沙上画画。

2. a long, thin piece of wood or metal that has a special use（有特殊用途的）棍；条
   The old man walked with a stick. 那个老人拄着拐杖走路。

sticker /ˈstɪkə; ˋstɪkɚ/ *n* 名

a small piece of paper with a picture, words, etc on it that you can stick onto something 粘贴标签；贴纸
Ada likes to put stickers on her books. 艾达喜欢在书上粘贴纸。

比较 **label**

sticky /ˈstɪki; ˋstɪkɪ/ *adj* 形

stickier, stickiest

having something that sticks to surfaces 黏的；黏性的
These sweets are so sticky. 这些糖果很粘牙。

***still¹** /stɪl; stɪl/ *adv* 副

1. used to say that something has not changed and is continuing 仍然；还
   He's still busy now. 他现在仍然很忙。
2. used to say that something is true even if it is not expected 虽然如此；然而
   Liza was ill, but she still went to school. 丽莎生病了，但还是去上学了。

still² /stɪl; stɪl/ *adj* 形

not moving 静止的；不动的
The child just can't stay still. 这个孩子就是不能静下来。

sting¹ /stɪŋ; stɪŋ/ *v* 动

stings, stinging, stung, stung

if an insect or a plant stings you, it hurts you by making a very small hole in your skin 刺；蜇；叮
I was stung by a bee. 我被蜜蜂蜇了。

sting² /stɪŋ; stɪŋ/ *n* 名

a wound made when an insect or a plant stings you 刺伤处；蜇痛处
He's got a bee sting on his leg. 他的腿上被蜜蜂蜇了一下。

***stir** /stɜː; stɝ/ *v* 动

stirs, stirring, stirred, stirred

to mix something by moving a spoon around in it 搅；搅拌
She poured milk into her coffee and stirred it. 她把牛奶倒进咖啡里，然后搅匀。

stocking /ˈstɒkɪŋ; ˋstɑkɪŋ/ *n* 名

a thin piece of clothing that fits closely over a woman's foot and leg（女式）长筒袜
Miranda was wearing a pair of silk stockings. 米兰达穿着一双长筒丝袜。

stole /stəʊl; stol/ *v* 动

the past tense of **steal** ☆steal 的过去式

stolen /ˈstəʊlən; ˋstolən/ *v* 动

the past participle of **steal** ☆steal 的过去分词

***stomach** /ˈstʌmək; ˋstʌmək/ *n* 名

the part of your body where food goes after you eat it 胃
My stomach hurt because I ate too much. 我吃得过多，所以胃痛。

stomachache, stomach ache /ˈstʌmək-eɪk; ˋstʌmək͵ek/ *n* 名

pain in your stomach 胃痛
She's got a terrible stomachache. 她胃痛得要命。

***stone** /stəʊn; ston/ *n* 名

1. （无复数）a hard, solid material in the ground 石头；石料
   Their house is built of stone. 他们的房子是用石头建造的。
2. a small piece of rock 石块；石子

We threw stones into the river. 我们往河里掷石子。

stood /stʊd; stʊd/ *v* 动

the past tense and past participle of **stand** ☆stand 的过去式和过去分词

stool /stuːl; stul/ *n* 名

a seat with three or four legs but without anything to support your back or arms 凳子
He went to the bar and sat on a stool. 他走进酒吧，坐在凳子上。

***stop¹** /stɒp; stɑp/ *v* 动

stops, stopping, stopped, stopped

1. to not continue moving or doing

S

something 停止；停下

The bus stopped outside the hotel. 公共汽车在酒店外面停下来。

The rain stopped in the afternoon. 雨在下午停了。

2. to make someone or something not move or not do something 使停止；使终止

A policeman stopped his car. 一名警察拦住了他的车。

stop doing something 停止做某事

The baby stopped crying. 婴儿不哭了。

stop someone (from) doing something 阻止某人做某事

They stopped Tom from going in. 他们不让汤姆进去。

***stop[2]** /stɒp; stɑp/ *n* 名

a place where a bus or train stops and you can get on or off 车站

Let's get off at the next stop. 我们在下一站下车吧。

***store[1]** /stɔː; stɔr/ *n* 名【美】

英式 **shop[1]**

store[2] /stɔː; stɔr/ *v* 动

stores, storing, stored, stored

1. to put things in a place and keep them there until you need them 贮藏；储存

She stored her old clothes in the boxes. 她把旧衣服存放在箱子里。

2. 【电脑】to keep information on a computer 储存（信息）

I stored the photos on my computer. 我把照片储存在电脑里。

storey /ˈstɔːri; ˋstɔrɪ/ *n* 名【英】

美式：***story***

a floor of a building（建筑物的）层

This building has thirty storeys. 这座大楼有 30 层。

***storm** /stɔːm; stɔrm/ *n* 名

a time of bad weather with strong winds and heavy rain 暴风雨

There was a big storm last night. 昨晚下了一场狂风暴雨。

stormy /ˈstɔːmi; ˋstɔrmɪ/ *adj* 形

stormier, stormiest

with strong winds and heavy rain 有暴风雨的

It was a stormy night. 那是一个风雨交加的夜晚。

***story** /ˈstɔːri; ˋstɔrɪ/ *n* 名

复数：***stories***

1. something you say or write about events or people that can be real or not real 故事

He told us a story about dragons. 他给我们讲了一个关于龙的故事。

2. 【美】（建筑物的）层 英式 **storey**

storybook /ˈstɔːribʊk; ˋstɔrɪˌbʊk/ *n* 名

a book of stories for children 故事书

Dad reads me a storybook every night. 爸爸每晚为我读一本故事书。

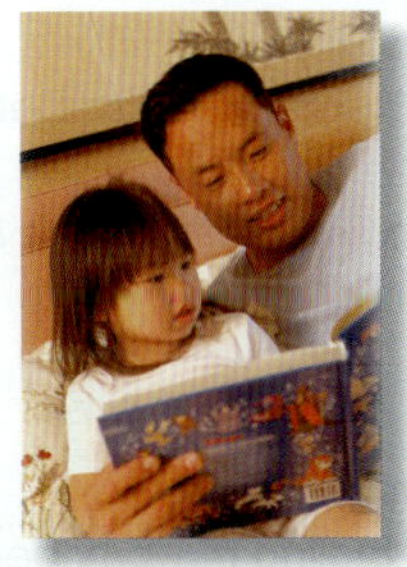

stove /stəʊv; stov/ *n* 名

a thing you use for cooking 厨灶；炉具

She cooked a pot of soup on the stove. 她在炉上煮了一锅汤。

***straight[1]** /streɪt; stret/ *adj* 形

straighter, straightest

1. not curved 直的

The road is straight. 这条路是笔直的。

反义 **crooked**

2. not leaning to one side 端正的；平直的

The picture is not straight. 那幅画挂得不正。

***straight[2]** /streɪt; stret/ *adv* 副

straighter, straightest

1. in a straight line 径直地；成直线地

The dog is coming straight at me. 那只狗向我直走过来。

2. in a vertical position 挺直地；平正地

The scouts stood straight. 童子军们站得笔直。

3. immediately 立即；直接

I went straight home after school. 我放学后直接回家了。

Asking for directions 问路

"Where is the park, please?" "Go straight down the road and you'll find it." "请问公园在哪里？""沿着这条路一直走你就会见到了。"

***strange** /streɪndʒ; strendʒ/ *adj* 形

stranger, strangest

S

1. not usual or normal 奇怪的；不寻常的

   Max often wears strange clothes. 麦克斯常常穿奇装异服。

同义 odd

2. not known to you 陌生的

   Mum taught me not to speak to strange people. 妈妈教我不要和陌生人说话。

stranger /'streɪndʒə; `strendʒɚ/ *n* 名

someone that you do not know 陌生人

Never open the door to strangers. 千万不要给陌生人开门。

straw /strɔ:; strɔ/ *n* 名

1. （无复数）the dried stems of wheat or other plants 麦秆；稻草

   The cat slept on a straw mat. 那只猫睡在草垫上。

2. a thin tube of plastic or paper that you use for drinking（喝饮料用的）吸管

   He drank the juice through a straw. 他用吸管喝果汁。

***strawberry** /'strɔ:bəri; `strɔˌbɛrɪ/ *n* 名

复数：*strawberries*

a small, soft, red fruit with yellow seeds on its surface 草莓

We picked a lot of strawberries. 我们摘了许多草莓。

stray /streɪ; stre/ *adj* 形

a stray animal is lost and has no home（动物）走失的；流浪的

There is a stray dog at the door. 门外有一只流浪狗。

stream /stri:m; strim/ *n* 名

a small river 小河；小溪

A stream flows through the field. 一条小河流经田地。

***street** /stri:t; strit/ *n* 名

a road in a town or city with buildings on it 街；街道

He walked along the street. 他沿着街道走。

strength /streŋθ; strɛŋθ/ *n* 名

无复数

the power and energy to move heavy things 力气；力量

They pushed the car with all their strength. 他们用尽全力推车。

strengthen /'streŋθn; `strɛŋθən/ *v* 动

to make someone or something stronger 增强；加强

Swimming strengthens the body. 游泳增强体魄。

stress /stres; strɛs/ *n* 名

复数：*stresses*

a strong feeling of worry because of problems in your life 压力

I've been under a lot of stress at school recently. 最近我在学校的压力很大。

stretch /stretʃ; strɛtʃ/ *v* 动

stretches, stretching, stretched, stretched

1. to make something longer or bigger by pulling it 拉长；使伸展

   Stretch the clothes before hanging them to dry. 把衣服拉直再晾起来。

2. if something stretches, it becomes longer or bigger when you pull it 伸展

   These trousers can stretch. 这条裤子可以伸缩。

strict /strɪkt; strɪkt/ *adj* 形

stricter, strictest

a strict person makes sure that people obey the rules and behave well 严格的；严厉的

Tina's parents are very strict with her. 蒂娜的父母对她很严格。

***string** /strɪŋ; strɪŋ/ *n* 名

1. a strong thread used for tying things 细绳；带子

   Jonathan tied the box with a piece of string. 乔纳森用一根细绳把盒子捆好。

比较 rope, thread

2. a thin piece of wire that is used on a musical instrument to produce sounds（乐器的）弦

   A guitar has six strings. 吉他有 6 根弦。

stripe /straɪp; straɪp/ *n* 名

a long, thin line of colour 条纹

His new trousers have red and white stripes. 他的新裤子上有红白条纹。

striped /straɪpt; straɪpt/ *adj* 形

having stripes 有条纹的

Kevin wore a blue and white striped shirt. 凯文穿了一件蓝白条纹的衬衫。

stroke /strəʊk; strok/ *n* 名

a sudden illness in the brain that

may make you unable to move or speak 中风
He had a stroke and was taken to hospital. 他中风了，被送进医院。

***strong** /strɒŋ; strɔŋ/ *adj* 形

stronger, strongest

1. having a lot of power or force 强壮的；力气大的
   He has strong arms. 他有强壮的手臂。

2. not easily broken or damaged 坚固的；结实的
   This kind of glass is very strong. 这种玻璃非常坚固。
3. if you have a strong feeling, opinion, etc, you are very serious about it（情感、看法等）强烈的；坚定的
   He has strong opinions about the law. 他对这条法律有强烈看法。
4. having a taste or smell that you can tell easily（味道或气味）浓烈的；强烈的
   I like strong tea. 我喜欢浓茶。

strongly /ˈstrɒŋli; ˋstrɔŋlɪ/ *adv* 副

if you feel or believe something strongly, you are very serious about it 强烈地；坚定地
Henry is strongly against the idea. 亨利强烈反对这个主意。

structure /ˈstrʌktʃə; ˋstrʌktʃɚ/ *n* 名

the way in which the parts of something are put together 结构
The structure of this machine is simple. 这台机器的结构很简单。

struggle /ˈstrʌgl; ˋstrʌgl̩/ *v* 动

struggles, struggling, struggled, struggled

1. to try to do something very difficult 奋斗；拼搏
   They were struggling in bad conditions. 他们在恶劣的环境下挣扎。
2. to fight someone who is attacking you 搏斗
   Ann got hurt when she struggled with the robber. 安和劫匪搏斗时受伤了。

stuck[1] /stʌk; stʌk/ *v* 动

the past tense and past participle of **stick[1]** ☆stick[1] 的过去式和过去分词

stuck[2] /stʌk; stʌk/ *adj* 形

difficult or unable to move 卡住的
The key was stuck in the lock. 钥匙被卡在锁里。

用法 不能用于名词前。

***student** /ˈstjuːdnt; ˋstudn̩t/ *n* 名

someone who studies at a school or university 学生
Arthur is a student at the University of Tokyo. 亚瑟是东京大学的学生。

注意 student 一般指中学生或大学生，小学生是 pupil。

studio /ˈstjuːdiəʊ; ˋstudɪˌo/ *n* 名

1. a room where television or radio programmes are made 演播室；录音室；播音室
   We visited a TV studio today. 我们今天参观了电视演播室。
2. a room where a painter or photographer works（画家或摄影师的）工作室
   Judy works in an art studio. 朱迪在一间画室里工作。

***study[1]** /ˈstʌdi; ˋstʌdɪ/ *n* 名

复数：***studies***

1. a piece of work that you do to find out more about something 研究
   The study shows that most children do not have good eating habits. 这项研究显示大多数儿童没有良好的饮食习惯。
2. **studies** the work you do when you are a student 学业
   Desmond spends a lot of time on his studies. 德斯蒙德花很多时间在学业上。

***study[2]** /ˈstʌdi; ˋstʌdɪ/ *v* 动

studies, studying, studied, studied

to learn about a subject 学习；攻读
Nora is studying Japanese. 诺拉在学习日语。

stuff /stʌf; stʌf/ *n* 名

无复数

a material of any kind 东西；物品
What's that black stuff on the ground? 地上那黑色的东西是什么？

用法 stuff 表示不知道物件的名称或它的名称不重要。

stung /stʌŋ; stʌŋ/ *v* 动

the past tense and past participle of **sting[1]** ☆sting[1] 的过去式和过去分词

***stupid** /ˈstjuːpɪd; ˋstupɪd/ *adj* 形

not clever 愚蠢的；笨的
She made a stupid mistake. 她犯了一个愚蠢的错误。

同义 **foolish, silly**

反义 **clever, smart**

***style** /staɪl; staɪl/ *n* 名

1. a way of doing something 风格；作风
   I like his style of singing. 我喜欢他唱歌的风格。
2. a particular design of something 款式；式样
   Janice has her hair cut in a new style. 贾尼斯剪了个新发型。

S

***subject** /ˈsʌbdʒɪkt; ˋsʌbdʒɪkt/ *n* 名

1. something that you study at school 学科；科目
English is my favourite subject. 英文是我最喜爱的科目。
2. something that you talk or write about 话题；主题
Let's change the subject. 我们换个话题吧。
3. a word that usually comes before the verb in a sentence. In the sentence "Peter kicked the ball", "Peter" is the subject. 主语；主词（在 Peter kicked the ball 这个句子中，Peter 是主语。）

submarine /ˌsʌbməˈriːn; ˋsʌbmərin/ *n* 名

a ship that can travel under water 潜水艇

The submarine went to the bottom of the sea. 潜水艇潜到了海底。

substance /ˈsʌbstəns; ˋsʌbstəns/ *n* 名

a particular type of solid, liquid or gas 物质
There are some harmful substances in cigarettes. 香烟含有害物质。

subtract /səbˈtrækt; səbˋtrækt/ *v* 动

to take one number away from another number 减去
If you subtract 2 from 10, you get 8. 10 减去 2 等于 8。

subtraction /səbˈtrækʃn; səbˋtrækʃən/ *n* 名

无复数
taking one number away from another number 减；减法
The kids are learning to do subtraction. 小孩们正在学减法。

subway /ˈsʌbweɪ; ˋsʌbˌwe/ *n* 名

1. 【英】a path for people to walk under a road or railway 地下人行道；地下通道
I went through the subway to the other side of the street. 我走过地下通道到街道的另一面去。
2. 【美】地铁 英式 **underground**[3]

succeed /səkˈsiːd; səkˋsid/ *v* 动

to do what you tried to do 成功；做成
Paul succeeded in breaking the swimming record. 保罗成功打破了游泳纪录。

反义 **fail**

***success** /səkˈses; səkˋsɛs/ *n* 名

无复数
the fact that you have done what you tried to do 成功；成就
He tried hard to find a job, but without success. 他努力尝试找工作，但没有成功。

***successful** /səkˈsesfl; səkˋsɛsfəl/ *adj* 形

having done what you tried to do 成功的；有成效的
His business is very successful. 他的生意做得很成功。

反义 **unsuccessful**

successfully /səkˈsesfəli; səkˋsɛsfəlɪ/ *adv* 副

in a successful way 成功地；顺利地
Eva successfully finished the work. 伊娃顺利完成了工作。

***such** /sʌtʃ; sʌtʃ/ *adj* 形

1. like the person or thing that you have mentioned 这种；这类（指已提及的人或事物）
Don't play with matches — such things are dangerous! 不要玩火柴，这类东西很危险！
2. used to make what you say stronger 这样；如此（用于强调）
This is such a beautiful dress. 这件连衣裙真漂亮。

such as 例如
He likes all kinds of sports, such as badminton and football. 他喜爱各种各样的运动，例如羽毛球和足球。

suck /sʌk; sʌk/ *v* 动

to hold something in your mouth and pull on it with your tongue and lips 吮；啜
The baby is sucking its thumb. 这个婴儿在吮自己的大拇指。

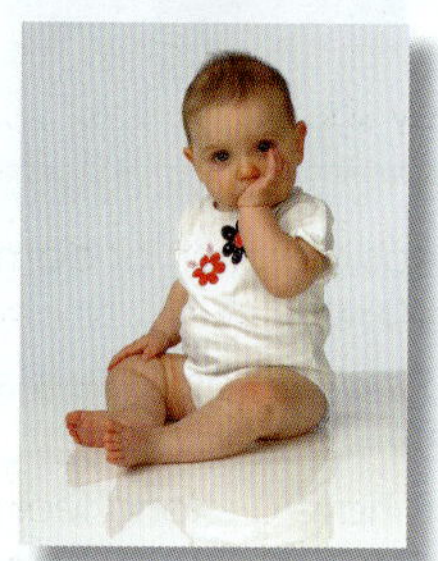

sudden /ˈsʌdn; ˋsʌdn̩/ *adj* 形

happening quickly or without being expected 突然的；忽然的
There was a sudden shower and we all got wet. 突然下了一阵雨，我们都给淋湿了。

***suddenly** /ˈsʌdnli; ˋsʌdn̩lɪ/ *adv* 副

quickly and without being expected 突然；忽然
I suddenly heard a scream. 我突然听到一声尖叫。

反义 **gradually**

***sugar** /ˈʃʊgə; ˋʃʊgɚ/ *n* 名

无复数
a substance that is used to make food and drinks sweet 糖；食用糖
I put some sugar in my tea. 我往茶里放了点糖。

S

sugarcane, sugar cane /ˈʃʊɡəkeɪn; ˋʃʊɡɚˏken/ *n* 名

无复数

a tall plant that is used to make sugar 甘蔗

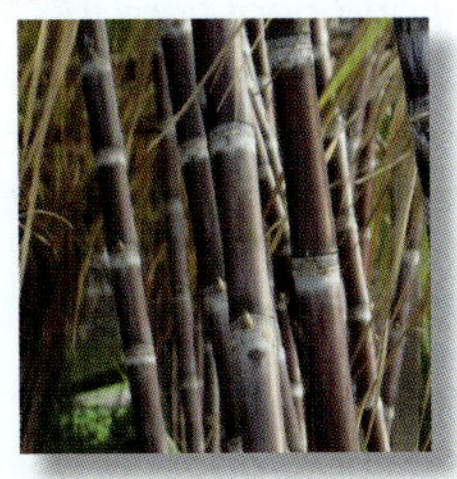

I like to drink sugarcane juice on hot days. 在炎热的日子我喜欢喝甘蔗汁。

***suggest** /səˈdʒest; səɡˋdʒɛst/ *v* 动

to tell someone your ideas about what they should do 建议；提议

George suggested that we should take a taxi. 乔治提议我们乘出租车。

Polly suggested going to the museum. 波莉提议去博物馆。

suggestion /səˈdʒestʃən; səɡˋdʒɛstʃən/ *n* 名

an idea or a plan that someone suggests 建议；提议

Lily made a good suggestion. 莉莉给的建议不错。

***suit**[1] /suːt; sut/ *n* 名

a jacket and trousers, or a jacket and skirt, that you wear together 一套衣服；套装；西装

Dad usually wears a suit to go to work. 爸爸通常穿西装上班。

suit[2] /suːt; sut/ *v* 动

to make someone look good 使…显得漂亮

This hat suits me. 我戴这顶帽子很好看。

***suitable** /ˈsuːtəbl; ˋsutəbl̩/ *adj* 形

right for someone or something 合适的；适宜的

This film is suitable for everyone. 这部电影适合所有人观看。

suitcase /ˈsuːtkeɪs; ˋsutˏkes/ *n* 名

a large case with a handle, used for carrying clothes and other things when you travel（旅行用的）手提箱

She packed her suitcase quickly. 她很快装好了手提箱。

sum /sʌm; sʌm/ *n* 名

1. an amount of money 金额
   I've saved a small sum of money. 我存了一小笔钱。
2. the number that you get by adding two or more numbers（加法的）和
   The sum of 9 and 12 is 21. 9 和 12 的和是 21。

summary /ˈsʌməri; ˋsʌmərɪ/ *n* 名

复数：*summaries*

a short piece of writing that gives the main ideas of something 总结；摘要

Ivan is writing a summary of the report. 伊万在写一份报告摘要。

***summer** /ˈsʌmə; ˋsʌmɚ/ *n* 名

the season between spring and autumn 夏天；夏季

We are going to Thailand this summer. 今年夏天我们将会去泰国。

***sun** /sʌn; sʌn/ *n* 名

无复数

1. （**也作：*Sun***）the large round object in the sky that gives light and heat 太阳

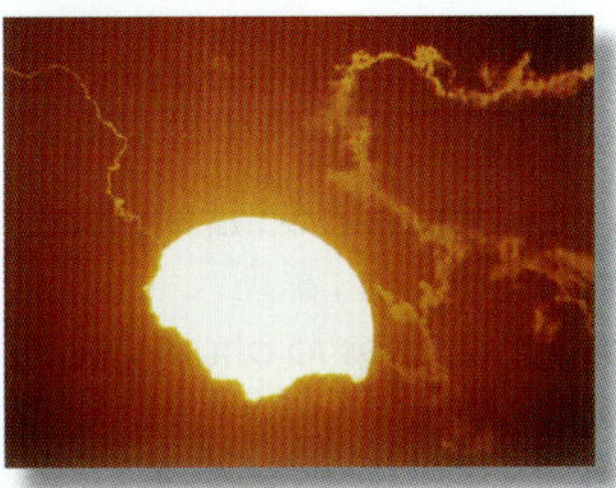

   The sun sets in the west. 太阳在西边落下。
2. the light and heat from the sun 阳光；日光
   Too much sun is bad for the skin. 晒过多太阳对皮肤不好。

sunbathe /ˈsʌnbeɪð; ˋsʌnˏbeð/ *v* 动

sunbathes, sunbathing, sunbathed, sunbathed

to lie in the sun to make your skin brown 晒太阳；沐日光浴

We are sunbathing on the beach. 我们在海滩上晒太阳。

sundae /ˈsʌndeɪ; ˋsʌnde/ *n* 名

a sweet dish of ice cream with fruit, nuts, etc on top 圣代冰淇淋；新地

S

Mary likes strawberry sundaes. 玛丽喜欢吃草莓圣代冰淇淋。

***Sunday** /'sʌndeɪ; `sʌnde/ *n* 名

缩写：***Sun.***

the day between Saturday and Monday 星期日；星期天

Mrs Moore goes to church every Sunday. 摩尔太太每个星期天去教堂。

注意 开头的字母必须用大写。

sunflower /'sʌnˌflaʊə; `sʌnˌflaʊɚ/ *n* 名

a tall plant with large yellow flowers 向日葵

I saw a lot of sunflowers in the garden. 我在花园里看到许多向日葵。

sung /sʌŋ; sʌŋ/ *v* 动

the past participle of **sing** ☆ sing 的过去分词

***sunglasses** /'sʌnˌglɑːsɪz; `sʌnˌglæsɪz/ *plural n* 复数名词

dark glasses that you wear to protect your eyes from the sun 太阳眼镜；墨镜

She put on her sunglasses and went out. 她戴上太阳眼镜后出门了。

用法 若要表示数量，不能说 a sunglasses 或 two sunglasses，要说 a pair of sunglasses（一副太阳眼镜）、two pairs of sunglasses（两副太阳眼镜）等。

sunk /sʌŋk; sʌŋk/ *v* 动

the past participle of **sink[2]** ☆ sink[2] 的过去分词

***sunlight** /'sʌnlaɪt; `sʌnˌlaɪt/ *n* 名

无复数

the light from the sun 阳光；日光

The morning sunlight came in through the windows. 早晨的阳光从窗户射进来。

比较 moonlight

sunny /'sʌni; `sʌnɪ/ *adj* 形

sunnier, sunniest

having a lot of sunlight 阳光充足的

If it's sunny tomorrow, we'll go for a barbecue. 如果明天天晴，我们就去烧烤。

sunrise /'sʌnraɪz; `sʌnˌraɪz/ *n* 名

无复数

the time in the morning when the sun goes up 日出（时分）；黎明

We got up before sunrise. 我们在日出前就起床了。

sunset /'sʌnset; `sʌnˌsɛt/ *n* 名

无复数

the time in the evening when the sun goes down 日落（时分）；黄昏

The farmers finish work at sunset. 农夫日落而息。

sunshade /'sʌnʃeɪd; `sʌnˌʃed/ *n* 名

a thing like an umbrella that you use to protect yourself from the sun 太阳伞

They sat under a sunshade. 他们坐在太阳伞下。

sunshine /'sʌnʃaɪn; `sʌnˌʃaɪn/ *n* 名

无复数

the light and heat from the sun 阳光；日光

We are enjoying the afternoon sunshine. 我们在享受午后的阳光。

super[1] /'suːpə; `supɚ/ *adj* 形

extremely good 极好的；了不起的

Hilary is a super cook! 希拉里是个出色的厨师！

同义 wonderful

super[2] /'suːpə; `supɚ/ *adv* 副

extremely 极；非常

Terence is super handsome! 泰伦斯帅极了！

用法 只用于口语中。

***supermarket** /'suːpəˌmɑːkɪt; `supɚˌmarkɪt/ *n* 名

a large shop that sells food and other things for your home 超级市场

You can buy this shampoo in any supermarket. 在各家超市都可以买到这种洗发水。

***supper** /'sʌpə; `sʌpɚ/ *n* 名

the meal that you eat in the evening 晚饭；晚餐

Have you had supper? 你吃过晚饭了吗？

supply /sə'plaɪ; sə`plaɪ/ *v* 动

supplies, supplying, supplied, supplied

to provide people with what they need 供应；供给

This company supplies electricity to the city. 这家公司为该城市供电。

***support[1]** /sə'pɔːt; sə`pɔrt/ *v* 动

1. to say that you agree with someone or something 支持；拥护

He supports the plan to build a new airport. 他支持建造新机场的计划。

2. to provide money for someone to live 供养；抚养

   She supports her family by doing three jobs. 她做三份工作来供养家人。

3. to keep something in a particular position, or prevent it from falling 支撑

   This table is supported by four legs. 这张桌子由四只脚支撑。

***support²** /sə'pɔːt; sə`pɔrt/ *n* 名

无复数

help that you give to someone or something 支持；帮助

My parents always give me a lot of support. 我的父母总给予我很多支持。

***sure** /ʃɔː; ʃʊr/ *adj* 形

surer, surest

knowing that something is true or correct 肯定的；确信的

I am sure that everything will be all right. 我肯定一切都会好的。

make sure (that) 弄清楚；确保

Make sure you turn off the lights. 你要确定把灯关了。

Can you make sure you'll get there on time? 你可以确保准时到达那里吗？

同义 certain

surf /sɜːf; sɝf/ *v* 动

1. to ride on waves using a special board 冲浪；滑浪

   It is dangerous to surf during a storm. 在暴风雨中冲浪是很危险的。

2. **surf the Internet/Net** to look for information on the Internet 浏览互联网

   You can use this mobile phone to surf the Net. 你可以用这部手机上网。

***surface** /'sɜːfɪs; `sɝfɪs/ *n* 名

the outside or top part of something 表面；外层

The surface of the road is smooth. 这条路的表面很平坦。

surname /'sɜːneɪm; `sɝˌnem/ *n* 名

your family name 姓；姓氏

Her surname is Williams. 她的姓是威廉姆斯。

同义 last name

另见 first name

***surprise¹** /sə'praɪz; sɚ`praɪz/ *n* 名

1. something that is not expected 意想不到的事

   Please don't tell him — we're having a surprise party for him. 请不要告诉他，我们准备给他一个惊喜派对。

2. （无复数）the feeling you have when something unexpected happens 惊奇；惊讶

   She looked at him in surprise. 她惊讶地看着他。

surprise² /sə'praɪz; sɚ`praɪz/ *v* 动

surprises, surprising, surprised, surprised

to do something that someone does not expect 使惊奇；使感到意外

The ending of the film surprised us. 电影的结局令我们感到意外。

***surprised** /sə'praɪzd; sɚ`praɪzd/ *adj* 形

feeling surprise because something that you did not expect has happened 惊奇的；惊讶的

Molly looked surprised when Eric gave her flowers. 埃里克送花给莫莉的时候，她显得很惊讶。

用法 surprised 用来形容人。

比较 surprising

surprising /sə'praɪzɪŋ; sɚ`praɪzɪŋ/ *adj* 形

causing surprise 使人惊奇的；出人意料的

I heard a surprising thing yesterday. 昨天我听到一件令人惊奇的事。

用法 surprising 用来形容事物。

比较 surprised

surround /sə'raʊnd; sə`raʊnd/ *v* 动

to be or go all around someone or something 围绕；包围

The singer was surrounded by her fans. 那名歌手被歌迷团团围住。

survey /'sɜːveɪ; `sɝve/ *n* 名

a set of questions that you ask a lot of people to find out what they think about something or what they usually do 调查

We did a survey on sleeping habits. 我们做了一个关于睡眠习惯的调查。

survive /sə'vaɪv; sɚ`vaɪv/ *v* 动

survives, surviving, survived, survived

to continue to live after an accident, war, etc 幸存；活下来

Ten people died in the plane crash and fifty people survived. 这场空难中 10 人死亡，50 人生还。

sushi /'suːʃi; `suʃɪ/ *n* 名

无复数

a kind of Japanese food made of cooked rice, raw fish, etc 寿司

We had sushi in a Japanese restaurant. 我们在一家日本餐厅吃了寿司。

suspect¹ /sə'spekt; sə`spɛkt/ *v* 动

to think that something is true, usually something bad 怀疑（常指坏事）

I suspected that Bill was lying. 我怀疑比尔在说谎。

suspect² /'sʌspekt; `sʌspɛkt/ *n* 名

someone who you think has done something wrong, usually a crime 嫌疑犯；可疑分子

The police caught two murder suspects. 警方抓了两个杀人嫌疑犯。

***swallow** /'swɒləʊ; `swalo/ *v* 动

to make food or drink go down your throat 吞下；咽下

She drank some water and swallowed the pills. 她喝了些水，把药丸吞了下去。

swam /swæm; swæm/ *v* 动

the past tense of **swim¹** ☆swim¹ 的过去式

swan /swɒn; swan/ *n* 名

a large, white bird with a long neck 天鹅

There is a swan in the lake. 湖里有一只天鹅。

sweat¹ /swet; swɛt/ *v* 动

if you sweat, liquid comes out through your skin 出汗；冒汗

I sweat a lot when I run. 我跑步时大汗淋漓。

sweat² /swet; swɛt/ *n* 名

无复数

liquid that comes out through your skin 汗；汗水

He wiped his sweat with a towel. 他用毛巾把汗擦干。

sweater /'swetə; `swɛtɚ/ *n* 名

a piece of clothing made of wool or cotton that you wear on the top part of your body 套头衫；毛衣

Put on your sweater if you feel cold. 你觉得冷就穿上毛衣吧。

同义 **pullover**

sweatshirt /'swet-ʃɜ:t; `swɛtʃɝt/ *n* 名

a soft, thick piece of clothing with long sleeves that you usually wear for sports 长袖运动衫

I often wear a sweatshirt when I go cycling. 我骑自行车时常穿运动衫。

***sweep** /swi:p; swip/ *v* 动

sweeps, sweeping, swept, swept

to clean the floor using a brush 打扫；清扫

He sweeps the floor every day. 他天天打扫地板。

***sweet¹** /swi:t; swit/ *adj* 形

sweeter, sweetest

1. having a taste like sugar 甜的
   This chocolate is too sweet for me. 我觉得这种巧克力太甜了。
2. kind and gentle 和蔼的；温柔的
   Fanny has a sweet smile. 范妮的笑容很甜美。

***sweet²** /swi:t; swit/ *n* 名【英】

美式：***candy***

a sweet food made from sugar or chocolate 糖果

Eating too many sweets is bad for your teeth. 吃太多糖果对牙齿不好。

sweetcorn /'swi:tkɔ:n; `switkɔrn/ *n* 名【英】

无复数 | 美式：***corn***

the yellow seeds of a plant that you can eat 甜玉米

This sweetcorn soup tastes good. 这道甜玉米汤味道很好。

sweet potato /ˌswi:t pə'teɪtəʊ; ˌswit pə`teto/ *n* 名

复数：***sweet potatoes***

a vegetable that looks like a red potato and tastes sweet 番薯；甘薯

He chopped the sweet potatoes into pieces. 他把番薯切成块。

swept /swept; swɛpt/ *v* 动

the past tense and past participle of **sweep** ☆sweep 的过去式和过去分词

***swim[1]** /swɪm; swɪm/ *v* 动

swims, swimming, swam, swum

to move through water using your arms and legs 游泳；游水

They swam across the river. 他们游到了河对岸。

swim[2] /swɪm; swɪm/ *n* 名

a period of time when you swim 游泳

Let's go for a swim. 我们去游泳吧。

swimmer /ˈswɪmə; ˋswɪmə/ *n* 名

someone who swims 游泳者

Frank is a good swimmer. 法兰克擅长游泳。

swimming /ˈswɪmɪŋ; ˋswɪmɪŋ/ *n* 名

无复数

the sport of moving through water using your arms and legs 游泳（运动）

Swimming is a good way to keep fit. 游泳是保持身体健康的好方法。

***swimming pool** /ˈswɪmɪŋ puːl; ˋswɪmɪŋ pul/ *n* 名

a place that is built for people to swim in 游泳池

The swimming pool is very crowded during summer. 夏天期间游泳池挤满了人。

同义 **pool**

swimming trunks /ˈswɪmɪŋ trʌŋks; ˋswɪmɪŋ trʌŋks/ *plural n* 复数名词

a piece of clothing that boys and men wear for swimming（男式）游泳裤

Jack changed into his swimming trunks and jumped into the pool. 杰克换上游泳裤，跳进游泳池里。

用法 若要表示数量，不能说 a swimming trunks 或 two swimming trunks，要说 a pair of swimming trunks（一条游泳裤）、two pairs of swimming trunks（两条游泳裤）等。

swimsuit /ˈswɪmsuːt; ˋswɪmˌsut/ *n* 名

a piece of clothing that girls and women wear for swimming（女式）游泳衣

I prefer swimsuits with lighter colours. 我较喜欢颜色浅一点的游泳衣。

***swing[1]** /swɪŋ; swɪŋ/ *v* 动

swings, swinging, swung, swung

to move backwards and forwards or from side to side, or to make something do this 摇摆；摆动

Brenda is swinging her handbag. 布兰达把手提包摆来摆去。

***swing[2]** /swɪŋ; swɪŋ/ *n* 名

a seat that hangs from ropes or chains for children to play on 秋千

Tom loves playing on the swing. 汤姆喜欢荡秋千。

***switch[1]** /swɪtʃ; swɪtʃ/ *v* 动

switches, switching, switched, switched

to change from one thing to another 转换；转变

This channel is boring. Can I switch to another one? 这个频道很无聊，我可以换个频道吗？

switch off 关掉（机器等）

I switched my computer off. 我把电脑关掉了。

switch on 打开（机器等）

He switched on the radio. 他打开了收音机。

switch[2] /swɪtʃ; swɪtʃ/ *n* 名

复数：*switches*

a thing that you press to make a machine, a light, etc start or stop working（机器等的）开关

Where's the light switch? 电灯开关在哪里？

sword /sɔːd; sɔrd/ *n* 名

a weapon like a long knife that you use for fighting 剑；长刀

In the past, people fought with swords. 古时人们用刀剑搏斗。

S

swum /swʌm; swʌm/ *v* 动

the past participle of **swim**[1] ☆swim[1] 的过去分词

swung /swʌŋ; swʌŋ/ *v* 动

the past tense and past participle of **swing**[1] ☆swing[1] 的过去式和过去分词

syllable /ˈsɪləbl; ˋsɪləbl̩/ *n* 名

a part of a word that has one vowel sound. For example, "body" has two syllables. 音节（如 body 一词有两个音节）

symbol /ˈsɪmbl; ˋsɪmbl̩/ *n* 名

1. a picture, shape, etc that has a particular meaning 象征
   The dove is a symbol of peace.
   鸽子是和平的象征。
2. a sign, letter, etc that represents something 符号
   The symbol for "dollar" is "$".
   $ 是"元"的符号。

***system** /ˈsɪstəm; ˋsɪstəm/ *n* 名

a group of things or parts that work together 系统
The railway system in Hong Kong is very good. 香港的铁路系统很完善。

S

***table** /ˈteɪbl; ˋtebl̩/ *n* 名

1. a piece of furniture with a flat top and legs 桌子

The child put his toys on the table. 那个小孩把他的玩具放在桌子上。

另见 **desk**

2. a list of information that is arranged in rows and columns 表；表格
   This table shows the weather for the week. 这张表显示了一周的天气。

tablecloth /ˈteɪblklɒθ; ˋtebl̩ˌklɔθ/ *n* 名

a cloth that covers a table 桌布
He put a clean tablecloth on the table. 他把干净的桌布铺在桌子上。

tablespoon /ˈteɪblspuːn; ˋtebl̩ˌspun/ *n* 名

1. a large spoon for serving food 大汤匙
   A tablespoon is bigger than a teaspoon. 大汤匙比茶匙大。
2. the amount that a tablespoon can hold 一汤匙（的份量）
   Add two tablespoons of sugar into the flour. 把两汤匙的糖加入面粉里。

tablet /ˈtæblət; ˋtæblɪt/ *n* 名

a small, hard piece of medicine that you swallow 药片；药丸

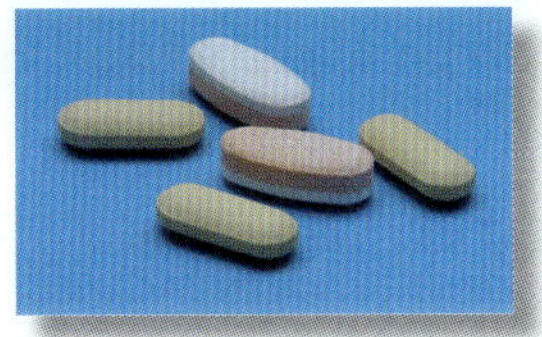

I took two tablets because I had a headache. 我头痛，吃了两片药。

同义 **pill**

tablet computer /ˈtæblət kəmˈpjuːtə; ˋtæblɪt kəmˋpjutɚ/ *n* 名

【电脑】a small computer that is a little larger than a mobile phone and that you can carry around easily 平板电脑

The tablet computer is very light. 平板电脑很轻。

table tennis /ˈteɪbl ˌtenɪs; ˋtebl̩ ˌtenɪs/ *n* 名

无复数

a game that you play by hitting a small ball across a net on a table 乒乓球（运动）
We often play table tennis after school. 我们放学后常常打乒乓球。

同义 **ping-pong**

tadpole /ˈtædpəʊl; ˋtædˌpol/ *n* 名

a small black animal that will grow into a frog 蝌蚪

There are some tadpoles in the pond. 池塘里有一些蝌蚪。

tael /teɪl; tel/ *n* 名

a Chinese unit of weight 两（中国重量单位）
This ring weighs a tael, or about 37.8 grams. 这只戒指重一两，即大约 37.8 克。

注意 发音和 tail 相同。

另见 **catty**

***tail** /teɪl; tel/ *n* 名

the long thin part of an animal's body at its back 尾巴

The dog is chasing its tail. 那只狗在追自己的尾巴。

注意 发音和 tale 相同。

***tailor** /ˈteɪlə; ˋtelɚ/ *n* 名

someone who makes clothes 裁缝
The tailor is making a dress for me. 裁缝正在为我缝制连衣裙。

***take** /teɪk; tek/ *v* 动

takes, taking, took, taken

1. to carry or hold something 拿着
   Let me take your school bag. 让我帮你拿书包吧。
2. to move something from one

place to another 拿走；携带
It's raining. Take an umbrella with you. 下雨了，带把雨伞吧。

3. to go with someone from one place to another 带；带领
   Roger took me to the library. 罗杰带我去了图书馆。
4. to travel in a vehicle 乘坐
   I took a bus to the zoo. 我坐公共汽车去了动物园。
5. to need a particular amount of time 需要花（一段时间）
   It took him three hours to repair the car. 他花了三小时修理汽车。
6. to swallow a medicine 服（药）
   Amanda took some medicine for her cold. 阿曼达吃了些治感冒的药。
7. used with nouns to say someone does something 做；进行（与名词连用）
   He took a look at the magazine. 他看了看杂志。

take away 拿走；带走
Ted took away my book. 泰德拿走了我的书。

take down 写下；记下
I took down his address. 我写下了他的地址。

take off（飞机）起飞
The plane will take off at midnight. 飞机将在午夜起飞。

take part in something 参加；参与
Michael took part in the race. 迈克尔参加了赛跑比赛。

take something off 脱下（衣物）
He took his shoes off before he entered the room. 他把鞋子脱下然后进入房间。

T

takeaway /ˈteɪkəweɪ; ˋtekəˏwe/ *n* 名【英】

美式：*takeout*

a meal that you buy from a shop or restaurant but eat somewhere else 外卖食品
We had a takeaway last night. 我们昨晚吃了外卖食品。

taken /ˈteɪkən; ˋtekən/ *v* 动

the past participle of **take** ☆take 的过去分词

takeout /ˈteɪkaʊt; ˋtekaʊt/ *n* 名【美】

英式 **takeaway**

tale /teɪl; tel/ *n* 名

a story about things that are not real（虚构的）故事
My mother told me a tale about dragons. 我的妈妈给我讲了一个关于龙的故事。

注意 发音和 tail 相同。

talent /ˈtælənt; ˋtælənt/ *n* 名

a special ability to do something very well 天赋；才华
Lilian has a talent for music. 莉莲有音乐才华。

talented /ˈtæləntɪd; ˋtæləntɪd/ *adj* 形

having a special ability to do something very well 有天赋的
He is a talented painter. 他是天赋很高的画家。

***talk[1]** /tɔːk; tɔk/ *v* 动

to speak to someone 说话；谈话
The teacher is talking to Alice. 老师正跟爱丽丝交谈。

talk about something 谈论
They were talking about their pets. 他们在谈论宠物。

***talk[2]** /tɔːk; tɔk/ *n* 名

1. when two or more people talk about something 谈话；交谈
   I'd like to have a talk with you. 我想跟你谈一谈。
2. speaking to a group of people about a particular subject 演讲
   A policeman came to the school and gave a talk about his work. 一位警察来学校做了一次有关自己工作的演讲。

***talkative** /ˈtɔːkətɪv; ˋtɔkətɪv/ *adj* 形

someone who is talkative likes to talk a lot 爱说话的
The children are very talkative. 这些孩子很爱说话。

***tall** /tɔːl; tɔl/ *adj* 形

taller, tallest

higher than other people or things 高的；高大的
This tree is very tall. 这棵树长得很高。

用法 可用来形容人、建筑物、树木等。

反义 **short**

比较 **high**

Daily conversation 日常会话

How tall...? …有多高？
"How tall are you?" "I'm 160 centimetres tall." "你有多高？" "我有 160 公分高。"

tame /teɪm; tem/ *adj* 形

tamer, tamest

if an animal is tame, it has been trained to obey people（动物）驯服的
These are tame elephants. 这些大象已被驯服。

反义 **wild**

tank /tæŋk; tæŋk/ *n* 名

1. a container for holding liquid or gas 箱；缸
   I put some small stones in the fish tank. 我在鱼缸里放了一些小石头。
2. a heavy vehicle that has guns on it 坦克车

The tanks attacked the city. 坦克车向这座城市发动攻击。

***tap[1]** /tæp; tæp/ *n* 名

1. something that you turn to get water from a pipe 水龙头

I turned on the tap to wash my hands. 我开了水龙头洗手。

2. hitting someone or something lightly 轻拍；轻敲
   I heard a tap at the door. 我听到有人在敲门。

tap[2] /tæp; tæp/ *v* 动

taps, tapping, tapped, tapped

to hit someone or something lightly 轻拍；轻敲

Vivian tapped Ross on his shoulder. 维维安轻拍罗斯的肩膀。

***tape** /teɪp; tep/ *n* 名

无复数

a long narrow piece of sticky material used to stick things together 胶带；胶纸

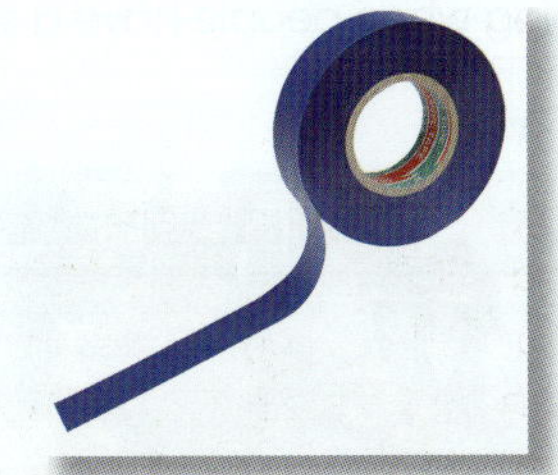
He stuck the photo to the wall with tape. 他用胶带把照片贴在墙上。

target /ˈtɑːgɪt; ˋtɑrgɪt/ *n* 名

1. something that you are trying to achieve 目标
   His target is to play in the school team. 他的目标是加入校队。
2. something that you try to hit with a gun, an arrow, etc（射击）目标；靶子
   He fired and hit the target. 他开枪打中了目标。

***tart** /tɑːt; tɑrt/ *n* 名

a pie without a top, usually with something sweet in it 甜馅饼

I baked a strawberry tart yesterday. 我昨天烤了一个草莓馅饼。

比较 **pie**

***task** /tɑːsk; tæsk/ *n* 名

a piece of work that someone has to do 任务；工作

His first task was to sweep the floor. 他要做的第一件事是扫地。

***taste[1]** /teɪst; test/ *n* 名

1. the flavour of a food or drink in your mouth 味道
   The ice cream has a very nice taste. 这个冰淇淋味道很好。
2. something that someone likes 品位；爱好
   They have different tastes in clothes. 她们的服装品位很不同。

***taste[2]** /teɪst; test/ *v* 动

tastes, tasting, tasted, tasted

1. to have a particular flavour 有…的味道
   The juice tastes sweet. 这种果汁很甜。
2. to eat or drink a little of something to see what it is like 尝；品尝
   She is tasting the soup. 她在尝汤的味道。

***tasty** /ˈteɪsti; ˋtestɪ/ *adj* 形

tastier, tastiest

having a good taste 美味的；可口的

The cake is tasty. 这个蛋糕很美味。

同义 **delicious**

taught /tɔːt; tɔt/ *v* 动

the past tense and past participle of **teach** ☆teach 的过去式和过去分词

***taxi** /ˈtæksi; ˋtæksɪ/ *n* 名

a car with a driver that you pay to take you somewhere 计程车；出租车；的士

We took a taxi to the airport. 我们乘出租车去机场。

taxi stand 计程车站；出租车站；的士站

There was a long queue at the taxi stand. 出租车站排了长队。

T

***tea** /tiː; ti/ *n* 名

1. （无复数）a drink made by adding hot water onto dried leaves 茶
   Mrs Harris likes to drink tea. 哈里斯太太喜欢喝茶。
2. 【英】a small meal in the afternoon 下午茶
   I had tea with my friends yesterday. 我昨天和朋友吃了下午茶。

***teach** /tiːtʃ; titʃ/ *v* 动

teaches, teaching, taught, taught

1. to give lessons in a school, university, etc 教；讲课

   Mr Wang teaches us Putonghua. 王老师教我们普通话。
2. to show someone how to do something 教（某人做某事）
   My father taught me how to swim. 我的爸爸教我游泳。

teach someone a lesson 给某人一个教训
She decided to teach the boy a lesson and made him clear up all the mess. 她决定给那个男孩一个教训，要他收拾所有凌乱不堪的地方。

***teacher** /ˈtiːtʃə; ˋtitʃɚ/ *n* 名

someone who teaches, especially in a school 教师；老师
She is an English teacher. 她是一位英语老师。

***team** /tiːm; tim/ *n* 名

1. a group of people who play a sport or game together against another group（运动或游戏的）队
   Our football team won yesterday. 我们的足球队昨天赢了。
2. a group of people who work together to do a particular job 工作队；工作组
   A team of workers cleaned the house. 一队工人把房子打扫干净了。

teamwork /ˈtiːmwɜːk; ˋtimˏwɝk/ *n* 名

无复数
when people work well together as a team 合作；协作
With good teamwork, we finished the job on time. 良好的团队合作使我们按时完成了工作。

***teapot** /ˈtiːpɒt; ˋtiˏpɑt/ *n* 名

a container with a handle that you use to make and serve tea 茶壶

He poured hot water into the teapot to make tea. 他把热水倒进茶壶里泡茶。

***tear¹** /tɪə; tɪr/ *n* 名

a drop of water from your eye when you cry 眼泪；泪水
Tears rolled down her cheeks. 眼泪沿她的脸颊流了下来。

tear² /teə; tɛr/ *v* 动

tears, tearing, tore, torn

to damage something by pulling it hard 撕破；撕碎
I tore the piece of paper in half. 我把纸撕成两半。

tear down 拆除（建筑物）
Workers were tearing down the old building. 工人把旧大厦拆除。

tear up 撕碎
We tore up the old posters. 我们把旧海报撕碎了。

tease /tiːz; tiz/ *v* 动

teases, teasing, teased, teased

to laugh at someone or make jokes about them 取笑；戏弄
They teased Sarah about her small eyes. 他们取笑莎拉的小眼睛。

teaspoon /ˈtiːspuːn; ˋtiˏspun/ *n* 名

1. a small spoon that is used especially for mixing sugar or milk in tea, coffee, etc 茶匙
   He is stirring his coffee with a teaspoon. 他用茶匙搅拌咖啡。
2. the amount that a teaspoon can hold 一茶匙（的份量）
   She added a teaspoon of honey in her tea. 她在茶里加了一茶匙蜂蜜。

teatime /ˈtiːtaɪm; ˋtitaɪm/ *n* 名【英】

无复数
a time in the late afternoon or early evening when people have a small meal 下午茶时间

We had cake at teatime. 我们在下午茶时间吃了蛋糕。

***technology** /tek'nɒlədʒi; tɛk`nɑlədʒɪ/ *n* 名

复数：***technologies***

new machines, equipment and the use of science in industry to create new things or to solve problems 科技；技术

Modern technology has improved our life. 现代科技改善了我们的生活。

teddy bear /'tedi beə; `tɛdɪ bɛr/ *n* 名

也作：***teddy***

a soft toy that looks like a bear 玩具熊

She put the teddy bear on her bed. 她把玩具熊放在床上。

teenager /'ti:neɪdʒə; `tin͵edʒɚ/ *n* 名

a young person between 13 and 19 years old（13 至 19 岁的）青少年

This TV programme is for teenagers. 这档电视节目是给青少年观看的。

teeth /ti:θ; tiθ/ *n* 名

the plural of **tooth** ☆tooth 的复数形式

***telephone[1]** /'telɪfəʊn; `tɛlə͵fon/ *n* 名

a machine you use to speak to someone in another place 电话

The telephone rang while I was taking a bath. 当我洗澡时，电话响了起来。

be on the telephone 讲电话

She's on the telephone. 她在讲电话。

make a telephone call 打电话

I need to make a telephone call. 我得打个电话。

同义 **phone[1]**

***telephone[2]** /'telɪfəʊn; `tɛlə͵fon/ *v* 动

telephones, telephoning, telephoned, telephoned

to speak to someone using a telephone 打电话

I telephoned him yesterday. 我昨天给他打了电话。

用法 作动词用时，telephone 是正式的说法。

同义 **phone[2]**

telescope /'telɪskəʊp; `tɛlə͵skop/ *n* 名

a long round piece of equipment that you use to look at things that are far away 望远镜

We can see the stars clearly through a telescope. 我们用望远镜可清楚地看到星星。

***television** /'telɪ͵vɪʒn; `tɛlə͵vɪʒən/ *n* 名

1. a machine with a screen on which you can watch programmes 电视机

He turned off the television before he went to bed. 他睡觉前把电视机关掉。

同义 **TV**

2. （无复数）programmes that you watch on a television 电视节目

I watched television after I finished my homework. 我完成作业后看电视 。

同义 **TV**

***tell** /tel; tɛl/ *v* 动

tells, telling, told, told

1. to give someone information about something by speaking or writing 告诉；说；讲

   She told me the news. 她把这个消息告诉了我。

   This book tells you how to make a cake. 这本书教人如何做蛋糕。

   The teacher told a story in class. 老师上课时讲了一个故事。

2. to say that someone should do something 劝告；吩咐

   The teacher told the students to keep quiet. 老师叫学生保持安静。

tell someone off 斥责某人

Chris told his brother off for breaking the vase. 克里斯责备弟弟，因为他打破了花瓶。

Daily conversation 日常会话

tell me 告诉我（用于发问）

"Tell me, do you like the new dress?" "Yes. It looks nice." "告诉我，你喜欢这条新裙子吗？" "我喜欢，它很好看。"

temper /'tempə; `tɛmpɚ/ *n* 名

how someone feels, especially when they are angry 脾气；心情

You should learn to control your temper. 你得学会控制自己的脾气。

lose your temper 发脾气

The teacher lost his temper because the students were very naughty. 那些学生太顽皮，所以老师大发脾气。

***temperature** /ˈtemprətʃə; ˋtɛmprətʃɚ/ *n* 名

how hot or cold something is 温度；气温；体温

The temperature is 28 degrees. 气温是 28 度。

have a temperature 发烧

He had a temperature, so he went to see a doctor. 他发烧了，所以去看医生。

take someone's temperature 替某人量体温

The nurse took my temperature. 护士替我量体温。

***temple** /ˈtempl; ˋtɛmpl̩/ *n* 名

a building where you go to pray 庙宇；寺院

Mr Brown visited several temples when he went to China. 布朗先生去中国时到过几座寺庙。

***ten** /ten; tɛn/ *num* 数

the number 10 十

Five plus five equals ten. 5 加 5 等于 10。

***tennis** /ˈtenɪs; ˋtɛnɪs/ *n* 名

无复数

a game in which you hit a ball with a racket over a net 网球（运动）

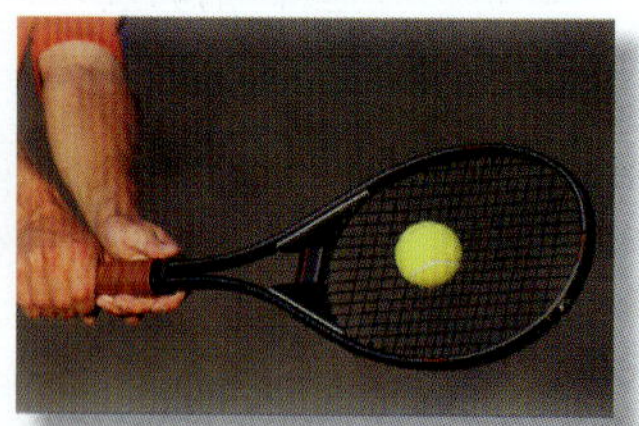

They play tennis every Sunday. 他们每个星期天都打网球。

tense[1] /tens; tɛns/ *adj* 形

feeling nervous or worried, and unable to relax 紧张的；焦虑的

Paul felt tense before the exam. 保罗在考试前感到紧张。

***tense[2]** /tens; tɛns/ *n* 名

the form of a verb that shows when something happens, for example "I play" and "I'm playing" are present tenses; "I played" and "I was playing" are past tenses.（动词的）时态（用于表示某事于何时发生，例如 I play 和 I am playing 是现在时态，I played 和 I was playing 是过去时态。）

另见 **附录**：Irregular verbs 不规则动词

tent /tent; tɛnt/ *n* 名

a shelter that is made of thick cloth and is used outdoors 帐篷

We stayed in the tent on the grass. 我们在草地上的帐篷里留宿。

tenth /tenθ; tɛnθ/ *ordinal num* 序数

10th in order 第十（的）

This is his tenth year at the football club. 这是他在足球俱乐部的第十年。

***term** /tɜːm; tɝm/ *n* 名

a part of the school year 学期

The new school term begins in September. 新学期在 9 月开始。

terminal /ˈtɜːmɪnl; ˋtɝmənl̩/ *n* 名

a place or building where people wait to get onto buses, planes or ships（公共汽车、飞机或轮船的）总站；终点站

We reached the bus terminal at 10 a.m. 我们在上午 10 点到达公共汽车总站。

***terrible** /ˈterəbl; ˋtɛrəbl̩/ *adj* 形

very bad or unpleasant 糟糕的；可怕的

His cooking is terrible. 他的厨艺很差劲。

同义 **horrible**

terrify /ˈterəfaɪ; ˋtɛrəˌfaɪ/ *v* 动

terrifies, terrifying, terrified, terrified

to make someone very frightened 使惊恐；吓怕

The fierce dog terrified me! 那条凶恶的狗让我害怕！

territory /ˈterətəri; ˋtɛrəˌtorɪ/ *n* 名

复数：***territories***

land that belongs to a particular country 领土

Hong Kong is Chinese territory. 香港是中国的领土。

terror /ˈterə; ˋtɛrɚ/ *n* 名

无复数

very strong fear 惊恐；恐惧

Colin screamed in terror when he saw the spider on his bed. 科林看见床上的蜘蛛时，吓得尖叫起来。

***test[1]** /test; tɛst/ *n* 名

1. a set of questions that measures someone's knowledge or skill 测验

   All of us passed the English test. 我们全都通过了英文测验。

2. a process to see if something works properly or if someone is healthy 测试；检验；身体检查

   The scientists did a test on the

new medicine. 科学家测试了这种新的药物。

test² /test; tɛst/ *v* 动

1. to find out what someone knows about something by asking them questions 测验；考验
   This exercise tests your knowledge of tenses. 这个练习考验你对时态的知识。
2. to use or check something to see if it works well 测试；检验
   The worker is testing the machine. 工人在测试机器。

text /tekst; tɛkst/ *n* 名

无复数

words or writing 文字

This storybook has a lot of pictures but very little text. 这本故事书有很多图画，只有很少文字。

***textbook** /ˈtekstbʊk; ˋtɛkstˌbuk/ *n* 名

a book about a subject that students use at school 教科书；课本

The pictures in my English textbook are beautiful. 我英文课本中的插图很漂亮。

text message /ˈtekst ˌmesɪdʒ; ˋtɛkst ˌmɛsɪdʒ/ *n* 名

a written message that is sent or received using a mobile phone（手机的）短信

I added a smiley in the text message. 我在短信里加了一个微笑符号。

***than** /ðən; ðən; *strong* 强读 ðæn; ðæn/ *conj* 连

a word that you use when you compare people or things 比（用于比较人或事物）

Harry is taller than me. 哈利比我高。

***thank** /θæŋk; θæŋk/ *v* 动

to tell someone that you are grateful for what they did or gave you 感谢

She thanked me for helping her. 她感谢我帮助她。

> **Daily conversation 日常会话**
> **thank you** 谢谢你
> *"Thank you very much!" "You're welcome."* "非常感谢你！" "不用客气。"

***thanks** /θæŋks; θæŋks/ *interj* 感叹

used to tell someone that you are grateful for what they did or gave you 感谢；谢谢

Thanks a lot for the ice cream! 谢谢你请我吃冰淇淋！

> **Daily conversation 日常会话**
> **no thanks** 不，谢谢
> *"Would you like some cake?" "No thanks."* "你想吃一点蛋糕吗？" "不吃了，谢谢。"

***that¹** /ðæt; ðæt/ *adj* 形

复数：*those*

1. used to talk about someone or something that you can see, but is not close enough to touch 那；那个（指较远的人或事物）
   How much is that dress? 那条连衣裙多少钱？
2. used to talk about someone or something that has already been mentioned 那；那个（指已提及的人或事物）
   I was at school at that time. 那个时候我在学校。

***that²** /ðæt; ðæt/ *pron* 代

1. （**复数：*those***）the one that you can see, but is not close enough to touch 那；那个（指较远的人或事物）
   That's an interesting book. 那本书很有趣。
2. （**复数：*those***）the one that has already been mentioned 那；那个（指已提及的人或事物）
   I had a bath and after that I went to bed. 我洗了个澡，然后去睡觉了。
3. a word you use instead of "which" or "who"（用于引导子句，代替 which 或 who）
   The film that we watched last night was wonderful. 我们昨晚看的那部电影很精彩。

***that³** /ðət; ðət; *strong* 强读 ðæt; ðæt/ *conj* 连

used to join two parts of a sentence（用于连接句子的两个部分）

Nicholas told me that he sold his bicycle. 尼古拉斯告诉我他卖了他的自行车。

***the** /ðə; ðə; 元音前读作 ði; ðɪ; *strong* 强读 ðiː; ði/ *art* 冠

1. used before a noun when you are talking about a particular person or thing（用于名词前，指特定的人或事物）
   I met the girl again. 我再次遇上那个女孩。
   There are two pens. I'll choose the red one. 有两支笔，我会选红色那 支。

> **用法** the 用于指已提及、已知道或唯一存在的人或事物。

2. used before the names of some countries, oceans, rivers, etc（用于某些国家、海洋、河流等的名称前）
   Jonathan lives in the US. 乔纳森在美国居住。
3. used before a singular noun to talk about people or things in general（用于单数名词前，泛指人或事物）
   The tiger is a dangerous animal. 老虎是危险的动物。
4. used before a particular date（用于某日期前）

T

Our party was on the fifth of August. 我们的聚会在 8 月 5 日。

比较 **a, an**

另见 **article**

***theatre** /ˈθɪətə; ˋθɪətɚ/ *n* 名【英】

美式：***theater***

a building where you watch plays 剧院；剧场

We were watching a play at the theatre. 我们在剧院看戏。

theft /θeft; θɛft/ *n* 名

1. （无复数）the crime of stealing something 盗窃罪；偷窃罪

A man was arrested for theft. 一名男子因盗窃被拘捕。

2. when someone steals something 盗窃；偷窃

There was a theft in the shop. 这家商店里发生了一起偷窃案。

***their** /ðə; ðɚ; *strong* 强读 ðeə; ðɛr/ *adj* 形

belonging to the people, animals or things that have already been mentioned 他们的；她们的；它们的；它们的

The children are playing with their toys. 孩子们在玩他们的玩具。

***theirs** /ðeəz; ðɛrz/ *pron* 代

used to refer to something that belongs to the people, animals or things that have already been mentioned 他们的；她们的；它们的；它们的（东西）

This house is theirs. 这所房子是他们的。

***them** /ðəm; ðəm; *strong* 强读 ðem; ðɛm/ *pron* 代

a word used for the people, animals or things that have already been mentioned 他们；她们；它们；它们

We haven't seen them for a few years. 我们有几年没见过他们了。

***theme** /θiːm; θim/ *n* 名

the main subject or idea in a book, film, etc 主题；题目

The theme of the film is peace. 这部电影的主题是和平。

theme park 主题公园

We visit the theme park every year. 我们每年都会游览那个主题公园。

***themselves** /ðəmˈselvz; ðəmˋsɛlvz/ *pron* 代

the same people, animals or things that the sentence is about 他们自己；她们自己；它们自己

The dogs warmed themselves in the sun. 那些狗在阳光下取暖。

by themselves 他们独自；她们独自；它们独自

They painted the wall by themselves. 他们自己粉刷了墙壁。

***then** /ðen; ðɛn/ *adv* 副

1. at that time 那时；当时

   The weather was bad then. 当时天气很恶劣。

2. after that; next 然后；接着

   We had lunch and then went shopping. 我们吃了午饭，然后去买了东西。

3. if that is true 那么

   If it rains tomorrow, then we'll stay at home. 如果明天下雨，那么我们就待在家里。

***there¹** /ðeə; ðɛr/ *adv* 副

in, at or to that place 在那里；到那里

Put the books there. 把书本放在那里。

Who's that woman over there? 那边那个女人是谁?

比较 **here**

***there²** /ðeə; ðɛr/ *pron* 代

there is/are, etc used to say that someone or something exists or something happens 有（表示某人或事物存在或某事发生）

There are three birds in the sky. 天空中有三只鸟。

Is there a hospital nearby? 附近有医院吗?

***therefore** /ˈðeəfɔː; ˋðɛrˏfɔr/ *adv* 副

for that reason 所以；因此

This bag is light and therefore easy to carry. 这个包很轻，所以容易携带。

thermometer /θəˈmɒmɪtə; θɚˋmamətɚ/ *n* 名

a piece of equipment that measures temperature 温度计；寒暑表

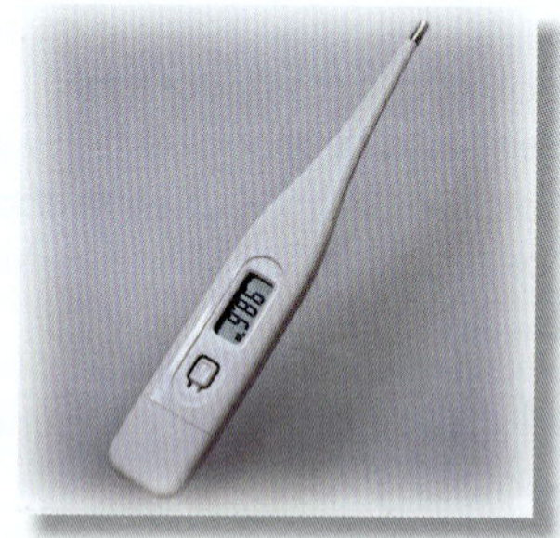

The nurse put a thermometer in my mouth. 护士把温度计放进我的嘴里。

these¹ /ðiːz; ðiz/ *adj* 形

the plural of **this¹** ☆this¹ 的复数形式

these² /ðiːz; ðiz/ *pron* 代

the plural of **this²** ☆this² 的复数形式

***they** /ðeɪ; ðe/ *pron* 代

the people, animals or things that have already been mentioned 他们；她们；它们

"Have you seen my socks?" "They are under the chair." "你见过我的袜子吗？""它们在椅子下面。"

they'd /ðeɪd; ðed/

1. the short form of "**they had**" ☆they had 的缩写

   They'd already left when I arrived. 我到达的时候，他们已经离开了。
2. the short form of "**they would**" ☆they would 的缩写

   They said they'd come before six. 他们说在 6 点前会来。

they'll /ðeɪl; ðel/

the short form of "**they will**" ☆they will 的缩写

They'll go to Korea next month. 他们下个月会去韩国。

they're /ˈðeɪə; ðer/

the short form of "**they are**" ☆they are 的缩写

They're from India. 他们是印度人。

they've /ðeɪv; ðev/

the short form of "**they have**" ☆they have 的缩写

They've gone home. 他们已经回家了。

***thick** /θɪk; θɪk/ *adj* 形

thicker, thickest

1. having a large distance between two opposite surfaces or sides 厚的；粗的

   This book is very thick. 这本书很厚。

反义 thin

2. growing very close together 稠密的；茂密的

   There is a thick forest behind the mountain. 山背后有一座茂密的森林。

同义 dense

3. difficult to see through 浓密的；混浊的

   Thick smoke was coming out of the chimney. 浓烟从烟囱里冒出来。
4. a thick liquid does not flow easily（液体）稠的；浓的

   The soup is a bit thick. 这碗汤有点稠。

反义 thin

thickness /ˈθɪknəs; ˋθɪknɪs/ *n* 名

how thick something is 厚；厚度

The thickness of this board is 20 mm. 这块木板的厚度是 20 毫米。

***thief** /θiːf; θif/ *n* 名

复数：*thieves*

someone who steals things 小偷；贼

The thieves stole the jewellery and drove away. 窃贼偷了珠宝后，开车走了。

thigh /θaɪ; θaɪ/ *n* 名

the top part of your leg 大腿

I have a bruise on my thigh. 我的大腿有一处淤伤。

***thin** /θɪn; θɪn/ *adj* 形

thinner, thinnest

1. having a small distance between two opposite surfaces or sides 薄的；细的

   She cut the bread into thin slices. 她把面包切成薄片。

反义 thick

2. if a person is thin, he or she does not weigh much 瘦的

   Alan ate little so he got thin. 艾伦吃得很少，所以变瘦了。

用法 有时含贬义。

反义 fat

比较 slim, skinny

3. a thin liquid flows very easily（液体）稀的；淡的

   The soup is too thin and tastes bad. 这碗汤太稀了，味道不好。

反义 thick

***thing** /θɪŋ; θɪŋ/ *n* 名

1. an object 物品；东西

   She loves all sweet things. 她喜爱任何甜的东西。
2. something that happens; what someone says or does 事情；事件

   A strange thing happened last night. 昨晚发生了一件奇怪的事。

   I have a lot of things to do tomorrow. 明天我有很多事情要做。

***think** /θɪŋk; θɪŋk/ *v* 动

thinks, thinking, thought, thought

1. to have an opinion or to believe something 认为；以为

   I think the story is interesting. 我认为这个故事很有趣。
2. to use your mind to imagine or remember something, or to solve a problem 想；思考

   Think carefully before you make a decision. 作出决定前要先仔细考虑。

Daily conversation 日常会话

"Let's watch a movie. What do you think?" "That's great!" "我们去看电影吧，怎么样？""好极了！"

third /θɜːd; θɝd/ *ordinal num* 序数

3rd in order 第三（的）

This is the third book I have read this month. 这是我这个月内看的第三本书。

T

***thirsty** /ˈθɜːsti; ˋθɝstɪ/ *adj* 形

thirstier, thirstiest

wanting to drink something 口渴的

I felt hot and thirsty. 我感到又热又渴。

比较 **hungry**

***thirteen** /ˌθɜːˈtiːn; ˏθɝˋtin/ *num* 数

the number 13 十三

Laura went to secondary school when she was thirteen. 劳拉 13 岁时上中学。

thirteenth /ˌθɜːˈtiːnθ; ˏθɝˋtinθ/ *ordinal num* 序数

13th in order 第十三(的)

Our holiday started on the thirteenth of February. 我们的假期从 2 月 13 日开始。

thirtieth /ˈθɜːtiəθ; ˋθɝtɪɪθ/ *ordinal num* 序数

30th in order 第三十(的)

Today is his thirtieth birthday. 今天是他的 30 岁生日。

***thirty** /ˈθɜːti; ˋθɝtɪ/ *num* 数

the number 30 三十

Thirty people attended the meeting. 30 人参加了会议。

***this[1]** /ðɪs; ðɪs/ *adj* 形

复数: ***these***

1. used to talk about someone or something that is near you 这；这个(指较近的人或事物)
   This pen is my birthday present. 这支笔是我的生日礼物。
2. used to talk about someone or something that has just been mentioned 这；这个(指刚提及的人或事物)
   This question is difficult to answer. 这个问题很难回答。
3. used to talk about a time that is close to the present time 这；这个(指接近现在的时间)
   We're going to Stephen's home this weekend. 这个周末我们将到史蒂芬的家里。

***this[2]** /ðɪs; ðɪs/ *pron* 代

复数: ***these***

1. the one that is near to you 这；这个(指较近的人或事物)
   How much is this? 这个多少钱？
2. the one that has just been mentioned 这；这个(指刚提及的人或事物)
   This is the funniest story I've ever heard. 这是我听过最有趣的故事。

Greetings 问候

this is ... 这是…(用于介绍某人)

"Jason, this is my sister, Isabel." "杰森，这是我的妹妹伊莎贝尔。"

thorn /θɔːn; θɔrn/ *n* 名

a sharp, pointed part on the stem of a plant (植物茎上的)刺

I scratched my hand on a rose thorn. 我的手给玫瑰的刺划伤了。

those[1] /ðəʊz; ðoz/ *adj* 形

the plural of **that[1]** ☆that[1] 的复数形式

those[2] /ðəʊz; ðoz/ *pron* 代

the plural of **that[2]** ☆that[2] 的复数形式

***though** /ðəʊ; ðo/ *conj* 连

even if; even so 虽然；尽管

Though Kevin was injured, he still took part in the race. 尽管凯文受了伤，但他仍然参加比赛。

注意 though 和 but 不可出现在同一句子中。

同义 **although**

***thought[1]** /θɔːt; θɔt/ *n* 名

something that you think of or remember 思想；想法

The thought of failing the exam made her worried. 想到考试不及格，她就感到担忧。

thought[2] /θɔːt; θɔt/ *v* 动

the past tense and past participle of **think** ☆think 的过去式和过去分词

***thousand** /ˈθaʊznd; ˋθaʊzn̩d/ *num* 数

the number 1000 一千

This computer costs five thousand dollars. 这部电脑要 5000 元。

用法 如要说出具体数目，如 2000，thousand 不作复数，后面不加 of，应写成 two thousand; 如要说"数千"，thousand 便要用复数，后面常接 of，例如 thousands of dollars。

thousandth /ˈθaʊznθ; ˋθaʊzn̩dθ/ *ordinal num* 序数

1000th in order 第一千(的)

Dennis was the thousandth customer of the shop and won a free gift. 丹尼斯是该店的第一千个顾客，获得了一份免费礼品。

***thread** /θred; θrɛd/ *n* 名

a long, thin string of cotton, silk, etc that you use for sewing (缝衣用的)线

Have you got a needle and thread? 你有没有针线？

比较 **rope, string**

***three** /θriː; θri/ *num* 数

the number 3 三

T

Agnes is three years older than me. 阿格尼斯大我三岁。

threw /θruː; θru/ *v* 动

the past tense of **throw** ☆throw 的过去式

***throat** /θrəʊt; θrot/ *n* 名

the part at the back of your mouth where you swallow food 咽喉；喉咙

She couldn't sing because she had a sore throat. 她喉咙痛，所以不能唱歌。

clear your throat（说话前）清嗓子

The speaker cleared his throat before the speech. 演讲者在演说前先清了清嗓子。

***through[1]** /θruː; θru/ *prep* 介

1. from one side or end of something to the other 从一边到另一边；穿过
   He walked through the corridor. 他从走廊的一端走到另一端。
   The river flows through the forest. 这条河流经森林。
2. by way of 通过；透过
   Sunlight came in through the window. 阳光透过窗户射进来。
3. from the beginning to the end 从头到尾；自始至终
   The baby cried through the night. 宝宝哭了整个夜晚。

***through[2]** /θruː; θru/ *adv* 副

1. from one side or end of something to the other 从一边到另一边；穿过
   This bridge is too narrow for cars to go through. 这道桥太狭窄，汽车开不过去。
2. from the beginning to the end 从头到尾；自始至终
   Read the passage through before you answer the questions. 回答问题前，先把文章从头到尾读一遍。

***throughout** /θruː'aʊt; θru`aʊt/ *prep* 介

1. in every part of a place 遍及；在…各处
   There are fast food shops throughout the city. 这个城市到处都是快餐店。
2. during the whole period of time 从头到尾；自始至终
   It rained throughout the week. 整个星期都在下雨。

***throw** /θrəʊ; θro/ *v* 动

throws, throwing, threw, thrown

to make something move quickly through the air by pushing it out of your hand 投；抛；掷；扔

Bob threw a bone and his dog caught it. 鲍勃抛出骨头，他的狗接住了。

throw something away 扔掉；抛弃

She threw away the rubbish. 她把垃圾扔掉了。

thrown /θrəʊn; θron/ *v* 动

the past participle of **throw** ☆throw 的过去分词

***thumb** /θʌm; θʌm/ *n* 名

the short, thick finger on the side of your hand（大）拇指

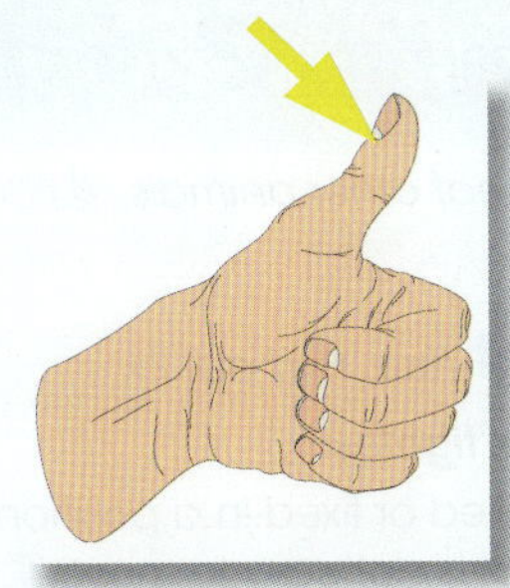

Babies often suck their thumbs. 婴儿经常吮自己的大拇指。

***thunder** /'θʌndə; `θʌndɚ/ *n* 名

无复数

the loud noise that you hear during a storm 雷声

I was woken by thunder last night. 昨夜我被雷声吵醒了。

比较 **lightning**

thunderstorm /'θʌndəstɔːm; `θʌndɚˌstɔrm/ *n* 名

a storm with thunder and lightning 雷雨；雷暴

We stayed at home during the thunderstorm. 在雷暴期间，我们待在家里。

***Thursday** /'θɜːzdi; `θɝzdɪ/ *n* 名

缩写：*Thurs./Thur.*

the day between Wednesday and Friday 星期四

Oscar has piano lessons every Thursday. 奥斯卡每星期四上钢琴课。

注意 开头的字母必须用大写。

***thus** /ðʌs; ðʌs/ *adv* 副

as a result of something 因此；因而

The chairman could not attend the meeting. Thus, it was cancelled. 主席不能出席会议，因此会议取消了。

用法 thus 用于正式场合，在一般场合用 so。

***tick[1]** /tɪk; tɪk/ *n* 名【英】

a mark that shows something is correct or has been done（√）钩号

The teacher put a tick next to the correct answer. 老师在正确的答案旁打了钩。

***tick[2]** /tɪk; tɪk/ *v* 动【英】

to put a tick on or next to something 给…打钩

Tick the things you want on the list. 在清单上把你想要的东西打上钩。

***ticket** /'tɪkɪt; `tɪkɪt/ *n* 名

a small piece of paper that shows

T

you have paid to travel on a vehicle, watch a film, etc（乘交通工具、看电影等的）票；入场券
I bought two tickets for the concert. 我买了两张音乐会的票。

tide /taɪd; taɪd/ *n* 名
the daily rising and falling of the sea 海潮；潮汐
The tide carried the boat away. 海潮把小船冲走了。

tidily /ˈtaɪdɪli; ˋtaɪdɪlɪ/ *adv* 副
in a tidy way 整洁地；整齐地
Put the toys away tidily. 把玩具整齐地放好。

***tidy**[1] /ˈtaɪdi; ˋtaɪdɪ/ *adj* 形
tidier, tidiest
neat; with everything in the right place 整洁的；整齐的
Matthew keeps his desk very tidy. 马修把办公桌保持得很整洁。

反义 **untidy**

***tidy**[2] /ˈtaɪdi; ˋtaɪdɪ/ *v* 动
tidies, tidying, tidied, tidied
也作：***tidy up***
to make a place look tidy 整理；收拾
We tidied up our house before our friends came. 我们在朋友来到前把房子收拾干净了。

***tie**[1] /taɪ; taɪ/ *v* 动
ties, tying, tied, tied
1. to fasten something with a piece of string, rope, etc 捆；扎；绑；系
   He tied the dog to a tree with a rope. 他用一根绳子把狗系在树上。

反义 **untie**

2. to make a knot in a piece of string, rope, etc 把（绳子等）打结；系上
   Philip tied his shoelaces. 菲利普把鞋带系好。

反义 **untie**

tie someone/something up 捆绑某人/某物
The kidnappers tied him up and took him away. 绑匪把他捆绑起来并把他带走。

***tie**[2] /taɪ; taɪ/ *n* 名
a long, narrow piece of cloth that a man wears around his neck 领带
Bruce wore a black tie today. 布鲁斯今天打了一条黑色的领带。

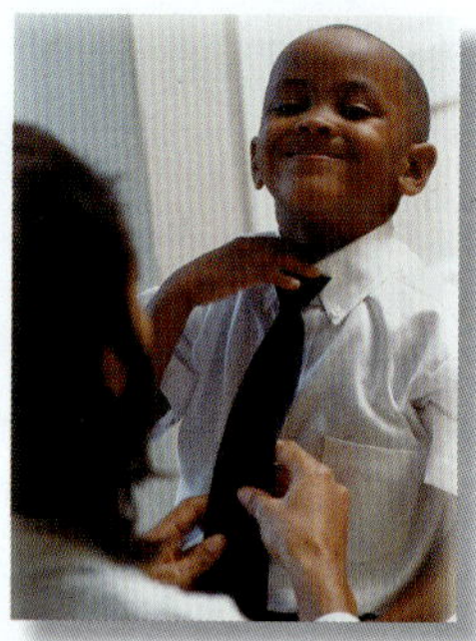

***tiger** /ˈtaɪgə; ˋtaɪgɚ/ *n* 名
a large wild animal that has yellow fur with black lines 老虎

Tigers eat other animals. 老虎吃其他动物。

***tight** /taɪt; taɪt/ *adj* 形
tighter, tightest
1. pulled or fixed in a position that is not easy to move 紧的；牢固的
   The lid of the bottle is too tight. I can't open it. 这个瓶盖太紧了，我打不开。
2. fitting closely 紧身的；贴身的
   This jacket's too tight — can I have a bigger size? 这件外套太紧了，可以给我一件尺码大一点的吗？

反义 **loose**

tighten /ˈtaɪtn; ˋtaɪtn̩/ *v* 动
to become tight or make something tight 变紧；拉紧；拧紧
She tightened the screw. 她把螺丝钉拧紧。

反义 **loosen**

tightly /ˈtaɪtli; ˋtaɪtlɪ/ *adv* 副
in a tight way 紧紧地；牢固地
She held the baby tightly in her arms. 她把婴儿紧紧地抱在怀中。

till[1] /tɪl; tɪl/ *prep* 介
until 直到（…为止）
We watched TV till midnight. 我们看电视看到午夜。

till[2] /tɪl; tɪl/ *conj* 连
until 直到
Let's wait till he comes back. 我们等到他回来吧。

***time** /taɪm; taɪm/ *n* 名
1. （无复数）the thing that you measure in minutes, hours, days, etc 时间
   I am sorry I don't have much time to talk with you. 抱歉，我没有太多时间跟你谈话。

2. （无复数）a particular minute or hour of the day 时间；钟点

T

"What time is it?" "It's three o'clock." "几点了？" "3 点。"

3. （无复数）an amount of time 一段时间

It took me a long time to learn swimming. 我学游泳花了许多时间。

4. an occasion when something happens 次；回

We've been to Thailand four times. 我们到过泰国 4 次。

all the time 一直；经常

The kids just keep running around the house all the time. 孩子们整天就在房子里跑来跑去。

from time to time 有时；偶尔

They go camping from time to time. 他们偶尔会去露营。

in time 及时

I got on the last bus just in time. 我刚好赶上最后一班公共汽车。

on time 准时

Make sure you get there on time. 你一定要准时到达那里。

Daily conversation 日常会话

have a good time 玩得开心；过得愉快

"Did you have a good time at the party?" "Yes!" "你在派对上玩得开心吗？" "很开心！"

time's up 时间到（比赛、考试等结束时的用语）

"Time's up! Put down your pens." "时间到了！立即停下笔。"

times /taɪmz; taɪmz/ *prep* 介

multiplied by 乘；乘以

Three times two equals six. 3 乘 2 等于 6。

*timetable /ˈtaɪmˌteɪbl; ˋtaɪmˏtebl/ *n* 名【英】

美式：***schedule***

a list of times when something happens 时间表；时刻表

We get a new timetable at the beginning of a school year. 我们在学期初会收到一份新的时间表。

*tin /tɪn; tɪn/ *n* 名【英】

a metal container in which food or drink is sold or stored 罐；罐头

She added a tin of tomatoes to the soup. 她往汤里加了一罐番茄。

tin opener 开罐器；罐头刀

He opened the tins with a tin opener. 他用罐头刀开了罐头。

tinned /tɪnd; tɪnd/ *adj* 形【英】

sold in a tin 罐装的

This tinned fruit can be kept for one year. 这种罐头水果可以存放一年。

*tiny /ˈtaɪni; ˋtaɪnɪ/ *adj* 形

tinier, tiniest

very small 极小的；微小的

The baby's fingers are tiny. 宝宝的手指很纤小。

反义 **enormous, huge**

tip /tɪp; tɪp/ *n* 名

1. the pointed end of something 尖端；末端

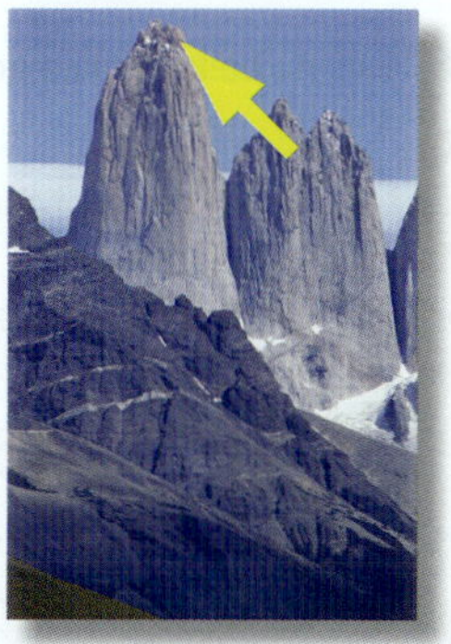

There is dirt on the tip of your nose. 你的鼻尖上有点污垢。

2. a small amount of money that you give to a waiter, taxi driver, etc 小费

He gave the waitress a tip. 他给了女服务员小费。

3. a useful piece of advice 实用的提示

He gave me some tips on how to learn English. 他给了我一些如何学习英语的实用提示。

*tired /ˈtaɪəd; taɪrd/ *adj* 形

feeling that you want to sleep or rest 疲倦的；累的

I felt tired after working all day. 工作了一整天后，我感到很累。

be tired of something 对某事感到厌倦

I'm very tired of her complaints. 我对她的抱怨感到厌烦极了。

用法 tired 用来形容人的感觉。

比较 **tiring**

tiring /ˈtaɪrɪŋ; ˋtaɪrɪŋ/ *adj* 形

making you feel tired 令人疲劳的；累人的

This job is really tiring. 这项工作十分累人。

用法 tiring 用来形容事物。

比较 **tired**

*tissue /ˈtɪʃuː; ˋtɪʃu/ *n* 名

a thin piece of soft paper for cleaning your nose, wiping up liquid, etc 纸巾；面巾纸

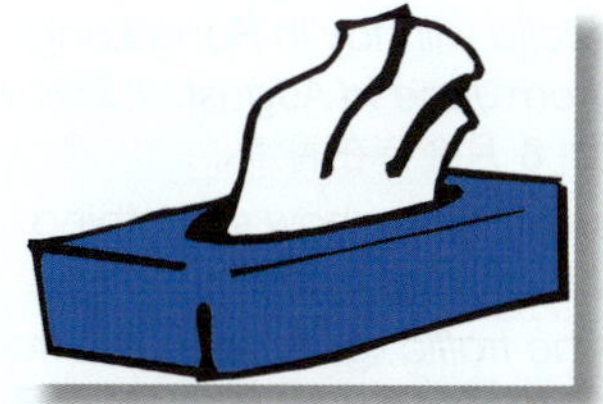

Leslie wiped his nose with a tissue. 莱斯利用纸巾擦了擦鼻子。

*title /ˈtaɪtl; ˋtaɪtl̩/ *n* 名

the name of a book, painting, film, etc（书、画、电影等的）名称；标题

The title of this storybook is

T

"Cinderella". 这本故事书的书名是《灰姑娘》。

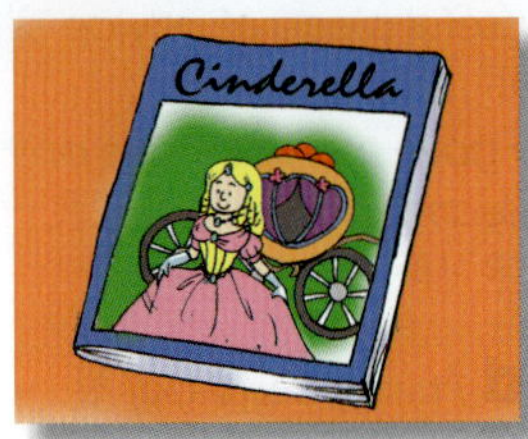

***to¹** /tə; tə; *strong* 强读 tuː; tu/

used before the basic form of a verb to show an action, a purpose, a result, etc（用于动词原形前，表示动作、目的、结果等）

I want to sleep. 我想睡觉。

He opened the window to let some air in. 他打开了窗，让空气流通一下。

***to²** /tə; tə; *strong* 强读 tuː; tu/ *prep* 介

1. used to say where someone or something goes 向；朝；到
   She went to the market. 她去了市场。
2. used to say who receives something 给
   Daisy gave a book to me. 黛西给了我一本书。
3. as far as 达到
   The price of apples rose to $5 each. 苹果的价格升到每个 5 元。
4. until 直到
   Stella will stay in Hong Kong from June to August. 史黛拉 6 月到 8 月会待在香港。
5. used to say how something changes（表示变化）
   The traffic lights changed from green to red. 交通信号灯由绿色变成了红色。
6. used to say how many minutes there are before the next hour 差…分钟（到整点）
   It's five minutes to one. 差 5 分钟就到 1 点了。

toast /təʊst; tost/ *n* 名

无复数

bread that has been heated until it is brown 烤面包片；吐司；多士

I had toast with butter for breakfast. 我早餐吃了黄油吐司。

用法 若要表示数量，不能说 a toast、two toasts，要说 a piece/slice of toast（一块 / 片吐司）、two pieces/slices of toast（两块 / 片吐司）等。

toaster /ˈtəʊstə; ˋtostɚ/ *n* 名

a machine for making toast 烤面包机；吐司炉；多士炉

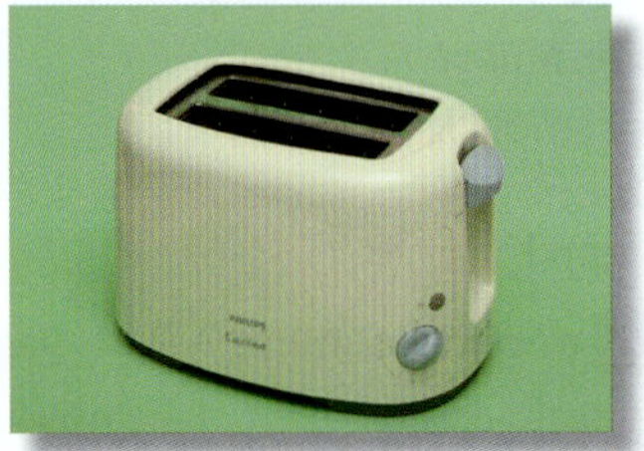

You can put two slices of bread in this toaster each time. 这个烤面包机每次可以放两片面包。

tobacco /təˈbækəʊ; təˋbæko/ *n* 名

无复数

the dried leaves of a plant that are used for smoking 烟叶；烟草

The tobacco trade has decreased in recent years. 近年来烟草贸易减少了。

***today¹** /təˈdeɪ; təˋde/ *adv* 副

on this day 在今天

It's sunny today. 今天天气晴朗。

***today²** /təˈdeɪ; təˋde/ *n* 名

无复数

this day 今天

Today is Monday. 今天是星期一。

***toe** /təʊ; to/ *n* 名

one of the five parts at the end of your foot 脚趾

I hurt my toe when I was playing football. 我踢足球时弄伤了脚趾。

toffee /ˈtɒfi; ˋtɑfɪ/ *n* 名

a hard, brown, sticky sweet 太妃糖

Grandma gave me a box of toffees. 奶奶给了我一盒太妃糖。

***together** /təˈgeðə; təˋgɛðɚ/ *adv* 副

1. with each other 一起；共同
   Annie and Kitty go to school together. 安妮和吉蒂一起上学。
2. if you put things together, you join them into one thing 结合起来
   Mix the flour and water together. 把面粉和水拌在一起。

***toilet** /ˈtɔɪlət; ˋtɔɪlɪt/ *n* 名

1. a large bowl that you sit on to clear waste from your body 抽水马桶

   Don't forget to flush the toilet. 别忘了冲厕所。
2. 【英】（美式：**bathroom**）a room with a toilet 厕所；洗手间
   There are public toilets in the mall. 商场内有公共厕所。

go to the toilet 上厕所

May I go to the toilet, please? 请问我可以去洗手间吗？

T

told /təʊld; told/ *v* 动

the past tense and past participle of **tell** ☆tell 的过去式和过去分词

***tomato** /təˈmɑːtəʊ; təˋmeto/ *n* 名

复数：***tomatoes***

a round, soft, red fruit that is a vegetable 番茄；西红柿

These tomatoes are fresh. 这些番茄很新鲜。

tomb /tuːm; tum/ *n* 名

a place where a dead person is buried 坟墓

We visited an old tomb in Egypt. 我们在埃及参观了一个古老的坟墓。

***tomorrow[1]** /təˈmɒrəʊ; təˋmɔro/ *adv* 副

on the day after today 在明天

We're having a party tomorrow. 我们明天有个聚会。

***tomorrow[2]** /təˈmɒrəʊ; təˋmɔro/ *n* 名

无复数

the day after today 明天

Tomorrow is my birthday. 明天是我的生日。

tone /təʊn; ton/ *n* 名

the way your voice sounds, which shows how you are feeling 语气；腔调

Maureen always speaks in a friendly tone. 莫琳说话的语气总是很友善。

***tongue** /tʌŋ; tʌŋ/ *n* 名

the soft part in your mouth that you use for tasting and speaking 舌；舌头

The taste of the chilli was still on my tongue. 辣椒的味道仍留在我的舌头上。

***tonight[1]** /təˈnaɪt; təˋnaɪt/ *adv* 副

on this evening or night 在今晚

Are you free tonight? 你今晚有空吗？

***tonight[2]** /təˈnaɪt; təˋnaɪt/ *n* 名

无复数

this evening or night 今晚

Tonight will be cloudy. 今晚会多云。

tonne /tʌn; tʌn/ *n* 名

复数：***tonnes/tonne***

a unit of weight. There are 1000 kilograms in a tonne. 公吨

The car weighs two tonnes. 这辆汽车重两公吨。

***too** /tuː; tu/ *adv* 副

1. more than what you need or want 太；过于

   The music is too loud. 音乐声太响了。

2. also 也；同样

   I like mangoes, and I like pears too. 我喜欢吃芒果，也喜欢吃梨。

用法 too 的这个用法一般用于句尾。

took /tʊk; tuk/ *v* 动

the past tense of **take** ☆take 的过去式

***tool** /tuːl; tul/ *n* 名

something that you hold in your hand to do a job 工具

I need a tool to dig the soil. 我需要一件挖泥的工具。

***tooth** /tuːθ; tuθ/ *n* 名

复数：***teeth***

one of the hard, white things in your mouth that you use for biting food 牙齿

I brush my teeth every morning and night. 我每天早晚都刷牙。

toothache /ˈtuːθ-eɪk; ˋtuθˌek/ *n* 名

a pain in a tooth 牙痛

I've got a terrible toothache. 我牙痛得很厉害。

***toothbrush** /ˈtuːθbrʌʃ; ˋtuθˌbrʌʃ/ *n* 名

复数：***toothbrushes***

a small brush for cleaning your teeth 牙刷

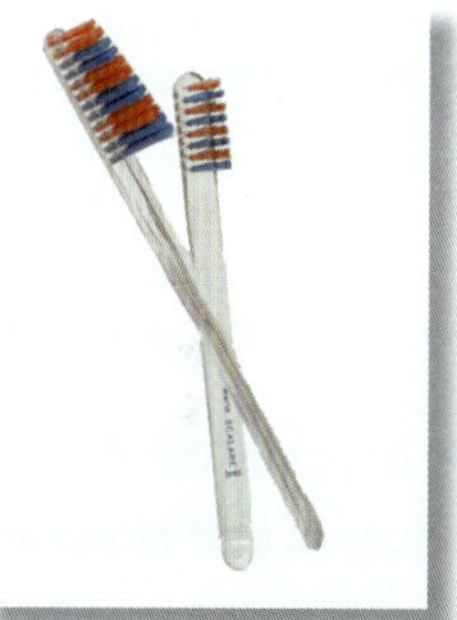

Maggie changes her toothbrush every three months. 玛姬每三个月换一次牙刷。

toothpaste /ˈtuːθpeɪst; ˋtuθˌpest/ *n* 名

无复数

something that you put on a toothbrush to clean your teeth 牙膏

Don't drop toothpaste on the floor. 不要把牙膏掉在地板上。

toothpick /ˈtuːθpɪk; ˋtuθˌpɪk/ *n* 名

a small piece of wood for taking out pieces of food from between your teeth 牙签

T

Please pass me the toothpicks. 请把牙签递给我。

***top¹** /tɒp; tɑp/ *n* 名

1. the highest part of something 顶部；顶端
   They climbed to the top of the mountain. 他们攀上了山顶。

反义 **bottom**

2. the lid or cover of something （物品的）盖；帽
   I've lost the top of this pen. 我丢了这支笔的笔帽。

from top to bottom 彻底地
I cleaned my bedroom from top to bottom. 我把卧室彻底打扫干净。

***top²** /tɒp; tɑp/ *adj* 形

at the highest part of something 顶端的；最高的
Amy and her family live on the top floor. 艾米一家住在顶层。

topic /ˈtɒpɪk; ˋtɑpɪk/ *n* 名

a subject that you talk or write about 话题；题目
The topic of the discussion is food safety. 讨论的题目是食品安全。

torch /tɔːtʃ; tɔrtʃ/ *n* 名【英】

复数：***torches***
a small electric lamp that you can carry 手电筒
Jack turned on his torch and saw some bats flying around. 杰克打开手电筒，见到一些蝙蝠飞来飞去。

tore /tɔː; tɔr/ *v* 动

the past tense of **tear²** ☆tear² 的过去式

torn /tɔːn; tɔrn/ *v* 动

the past participle of **tear²** ☆tear² 的过去分词

***tortoise** /ˈtɔːtəs; ˋtɔrtəs/ *n* 名

an animal with a hard, round shell that lives on land and moves slowly 龟；陆龟

A tortoise usually has a long life. 龟一般很长寿。

比较 **turtle**

***total¹** /ˈtəʊtl; ˋtotl̩/ *adj* 形

1. including everyone or everything 总共的；全部的
   The total cost of making the film is ten million dollars. 制作这部电影的总成本是 1000 万元。
2. complete 完全的；彻底的
   There was total silence in the classroom. 教室里一片寂静。

total² /ˈtəʊtl; ˋtotl̩/ *n* 名

the final amount you have when you add everything together 总数；总额
A total of twenty computers were stolen. 总共有 20 部电脑失窃了。

***touch¹** /tʌtʃ; tʌtʃ/ *v* 动

touches, touching, touched, touched
to put your hand or finger on someone or something 触摸；碰
Don't touch the broken glass! 不要碰碎玻璃！

touch² /tʌtʃ; tʌtʃ/ *n* 名

复数：***touches***
the action of touching someone or something 触摸；碰
I felt a gentle touch on my shoulder. 我感到有人轻轻碰了一下我的肩膀。

get in touch 联系
I'll get in touch with you soon. 我很快会与你联系。

keep/stay in touch 保持联系
Edith and I have still kept in touch since we left school. 我和伊迪丝自离校后仍然保持联系。

touch screen /ˈtʌtʃ skriːn; ˋtʌtʃ skrin/ *n* 名

【电脑】a type of computer screen that you touch to tell the computer what to do 触控式屏幕；触摸屏

This tablet computer has a touch screen. 这个平板电脑有触摸屏 。

tough /tʌf; tʌf/ *adj* 形

tougher, toughest

1. difficult 困难的；棘手的
   Her family has had a tough time recently. 她家最近的日子很难熬。
2. a tough person is strong and brave 坚强的；顽强的
   Victoria is a tough woman — she takes care of her three children by herself. 维多利亚是个坚强的女人，她自己照顾她的三个孩子。
3. tough food is difficult to cut and eat（食物）难切开的；咬不动的
   This steak is too tough to chew. 这块牛排老得咬不动。

***tour** /tʊə; tʊr/ *n* 名

a journey during which you visit several places 旅游；旅行
We went on a tour of Bangkok. 我们去了曼谷旅游。

T

tour guide 导游
The tour guide took us to an art gallery. 导游带我们参观一家美术馆。

***tourist** /ˈtʊərɪst; ˋtʊrɪst/ *n* 名
someone who visits a place on holiday 游客

This temple attracts a lot of tourists. 这座庙宇吸引了大批游客。

***towards** /təˈwɔːdz; tɔrdz/ *prep* 介【英】
美式：***toward***
1. in the direction of 向着；朝着
   She walked towards the garden. 她朝花园走去。
2. near a time or place 接近（某时间或地点）
   We're planning a trip towards the end of July. 我们打算将 7 月底去旅行。

***towel** /ˈtaʊəl; ˋtaʊəl/ *n* 名
a piece of cloth for drying things 毛巾
Paul dried his hair with a towel. 保罗用毛巾擦干头发。

tower /ˈtaʊə; ˋtaʊɚ/ *n* 名
a tall, narrow building or part of a building such as a church 塔；塔楼

You can see the whole town from the top of the tower. 从塔顶可以看到整个城镇。
bell/clock tower 钟楼
The old clock tower is an important building in this city. 这座古老的钟楼是该城市的一个重要建筑。

***town** /taʊn; taʊn/ *n* 名
a place that has many houses, shops, etc. A town is larger than a village but smaller than a city. 城镇；市镇
He grew up in a small town. 他在一个小镇上长大。

***toy** /tɔɪ; tɔɪ/ *n* 名
a thing for children to play with 玩具
This teddy bear is her new toy. 这个玩具熊是她的新玩具。

track /træk; træk/ *n* 名
1. a narrow, rough path（路面不平的）小道；小径
   They walked along the track to the forest. 他们沿着小径走到森林。
2. a path with a special surface for racing 跑道；赛道
   All runners gathered at the tracks. 所有赛跑选手在跑道上集合。
3. the two metal lines that a train runs on（火车的）轨道；铁轨
   The train went off the track. 火车出轨了。

tracksuit /ˈtræksuːt; ˋtrækˌsut/ *n* 名【英】
a loose jacket and trousers you wear for sport 运动服

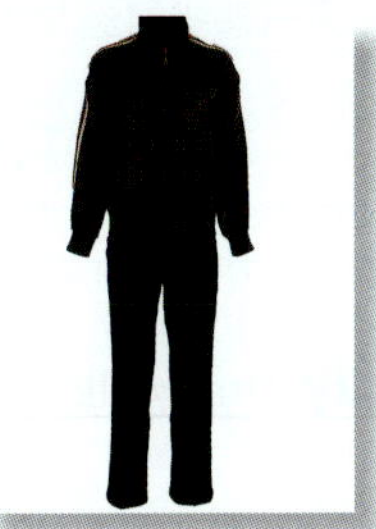

Edward went jogging in his tracksuit. 爱德华穿上运动服去慢跑了。

***trade** /treɪd; tred/ *n* 名
无复数
buying and selling things 买卖；贸易；交易
There is a lot of trade between the two countries. 两国之间有许多贸易往来。

tradition /trəˈdɪʃn; trəˋdɪʃən/ *n* 名
a way of doing something that has existed for a long time 传统
Dragon boat racing is a Chinese tradition. 赛龙舟是中国的传统。

***traditional** /trəˈdɪʃnəl; trəˋdɪʃənl̩/ *adj* 形
belonging to the traditions of a country or group of people 传统的
It's traditional to eat mooncakes at the Mid-Autumn Festival. 传统上中秋节要吃月饼。

***traffic** /ˈtræfɪk; ˋtræfɪk/ *n* 名
无复数
the vehicles that move along a road 交通
There was heavy traffic on the highway. 公路上交通繁忙。
traffic jam 交通阻塞；塞车

There are often traffic jams in bad

T

weather. 天气恶劣时经常出现交通阻塞。

traffic lights 交通信号灯；红绿灯

Stop when the traffic lights turn red. 交通信号灯转为红灯时要停下。

tragedy /ˈtrædʒədi; ˋtrædʒədɪ/ *n* 名

复数：***tragedies***

a play with a sad ending 悲剧

Hamlet *is a tragedy by Shakespeare.*《哈姆雷特》是莎士比亚的悲剧。

另见 **comedy**

***train[1]** /treɪn; tren/ *n* 名

a long vehicle that travels along a railway 火车

Bill goes to work by train. 比尔乘火车上班。

***train[2]** /treɪn; tren/ *v* 动

to teach a person or an animal how to do something 培训；训练

Thomas trained his dog to catch balls. 托马斯训练他的狗接球。

trainer /ˈtreɪnə; ˋtrenɚ/ *n* 名

1. someone who teaches people or animals how to do something 教练员；驯兽师

   Jerry is an animal trainer at a zoo. 杰瑞是动物园的驯兽师。

2. 【英】a type of shoe that you wear for sport 运动鞋

   These trainers are good for running. 这双运动鞋适合跑步时穿。

***training** /ˈtreɪnɪŋ; ˋtrenɪŋ/ *n* 名

无复数

the activity of learning the skills for a job 培训；训练

All the lifeguards have received special training. 所有救生员都受过特殊训练。

***tram** /træm; træm/ *n* 名

an electric vehicle that travels along metal tracks（有轨）电车

She went home by tram. 她乘电车回家了。

***transport[1]** /ˈtrænspɔːt; ˋtrænspɔrt/ *n* 名

无复数

a system or a kind of vehicle that you use for going from one place to another 交通运输系统；交通工具

Most people in the city go to work by public transport. 城里大多数人乘公共交通工具上班。

transport[2] /trænˈspɔːt; trænˋspɔrt/ *v* 动

to carry goods or people from one place to another in a vehicle 运输；运送

The parcels were transported by plane. 这些包裹是空运的。

trap[1] /træp; træp/ *n* 名

something that you use to catch animals（捕捉动物的）夹子；罗网；陷阱

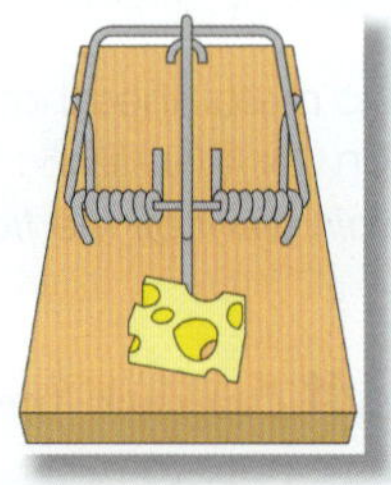

We put a trap there to catch mice. 我们在那里放置捕鼠夹来抓老鼠。

trap[2] /træp; træp/ *v* 动

traps, trapping, trapped, trapped

to catch an animal in a trap（用罗网等）捕捉（动物）

The hunters trapped the bear. 猎人捕获了那只熊。

***travel** /ˈtrævl; ˋtrævl̩/ *v* 动

travels, travelling, travelled, travelled

1. to go from one place to another 旅行；出行

   He travels abroad every year. 他每年都去国外旅行。

   She travels to work by metro. 她乘地铁上班。

2. to move at a particular speed（以某速度）行进

   The train was travelling at a high speed. 火车以高速行驶。

traveller /ˈtrævlə; ˋtrævlɚ/ *n* 名【英】

美式：***traveler***

a person who is travelling or travels a lot 旅客；经常旅行的人

A lot of travellers were at the airport. 机场里有许多旅客。

tray /treɪ; tre/ *n* 名

a flat piece of plastic, wood, etc for carrying things 托盘；盘子

The waitress was carrying a tray of drinks. 女服务员端着一托盘的饮料。

treasure /ˈtreʒə; ˋtrɛʒɚ/ *n* 名

无复数

valuable things such as gold, silver, etc, usually hidden in a place 金银财宝；宝藏

They found the treasure inside the cave. 他们在地洞里面发现了宝藏。

***treat¹** /triːt; trit/ *v* 动

1. to behave towards someone in a particular way 对待；看待
   Rose treats her cats very well. 罗丝对她的猫很好。
2. to try to cure an illness or injury 治疗；医治
   The doctor treated the patients. 医生医治了病人。
3. to buy or do something special for someone 款待；招待
   Mrs Green treated us to dinner. 格林太太请我们吃晚饭。

treat² /triːt; trit/ *n* 名

something special that you give someone or do for them 款待；招待
My parents took me to dinner as a birthday treat. 爸爸妈妈带我去吃晚饭过生日。

Daily conversation 日常会话
"Let's go out for tea. It's my treat." "我们出去喝茶吧。我请客。"

***tree** /triː; tri/ *n* 名

a tall plant with branches and leaves 树；树木
Monkeys like to climb trees. 猴子喜欢爬树。

tremble /'trembl; `trɛmbl̩/ *v* 动

trembles, trembling, trembled, trembled

to shake because you are afraid, excited, etc 发抖；颤抖
Maria trembled with fear when the robber pointed a gun at her back. 强盗用枪指着玛莉亚的背，吓得她浑身发抖。

同义 shiver

***triangle** /'traɪæŋgl; `traɪˌæŋgl̩/ *n* 名

a shape with three straight sides and three angles 三角形

Samantha cut the sandwiches into triangles. 萨曼莎把三明治切成三角形。

trick /trɪk; trɪk/ *n* 名

1. something that you do to cheat someone 骗局；诡计
   I think what he said was a trick. 我认为他的话是诡计。
2. something that you do to make other people laugh at someone 恶作剧
   He always plays tricks on me. 他老是捉弄我。

tricycle /'traɪsɪkl; `traɪsɪkl̩/ *n* 名

a bicycle with three wheels 三轮脚踏车

This tricycle is good for young children. 这辆三轮脚踏车适合幼童骑。

tried /traɪd; traɪd/ *v* 动

the past tense and past participle of **try** ☆try 的过去式和过去分词

***trip** /trɪp; trɪp/ *n* 名

a journey to a place 旅行；旅游
Louis made a short trip to Suzhou with his friends. 路易斯和朋友去了苏州旅游。

用法 trip 常指短途旅行。

trolley /'trɒli; `trɑlɪ/ *n* 名【英】

美式：***cart***

a small vehicle with wheels that you use for carrying things 手推车

She put all the food in the shopping trolley. 她把所有食品放进购物手推车内。

***trouble** /'trʌbl; `trʌbl̩/ *n* 名

problems or difficulties 麻烦；问题；困难
He's having trouble with his computer. 他的电脑有问题。
She told me her troubles at school. 她告诉我她在学校的烦恼。

be in trouble 在困境中
The company has been in trouble since the new manager came. 新经理上任以来，公司一直处于困境中。

get into trouble 惹麻烦
You will get into trouble if you tell anyone about this. 如果你对其他人提及此事，就会惹麻烦。

T

***trousers** /'traʊzəz; `traʊzɚz/ *plural n* 复数名词【英】

美式：***pants***

a piece of clothing for your legs 裤子

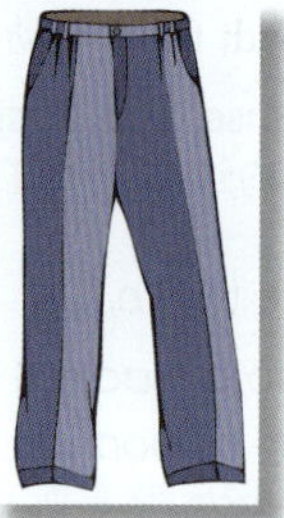

These trousers are too tight. 这条裤子太紧了。

用法 表示一条裤子、两条裤子，用 a pair of trousers、two pairs of trousers 等。

***truck** /trʌk; trʌk/ *n* 名

a big vehicle for carrying things 货车；卡车

They put the boxes on the truck and drove away. 他们把箱子搬上货车开走了。

同义 **lorry**

***true** /truː; tru/ *adj* 形

correct or real 真的；真实的

That's a true story. 那是一个真实的故事。

come true（梦想或愿望）实现；成真

Her dream of having her own toy shop finally came true. 她想拥有一家玩具店的梦想终于实现了。

T

trumpet /ˈtrʌmpɪt; ˋtrʌmpɪt/ *n* 名

a musical instrument that you blow into 小号；喇叭

Daniel can play the trumpet. 丹尼尔会吹小号。

trunk /trʌŋk; trʌŋk/ *n* 名

1. the thick main stem of a tree 树干

The tree trunk is three metres tall. 这根树干有 3 米高。

2. the long nose of an elephant 象鼻

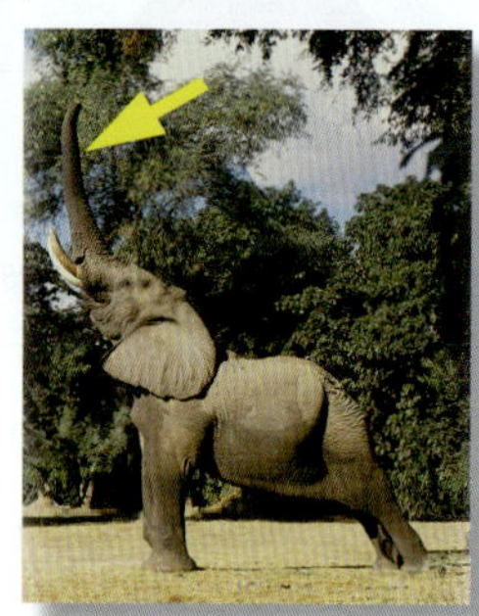

The elephant picked up the ball with its trunk. 大象用鼻子把球卷起来。

***trust** /trʌst; trʌst/ *v* 动

to believe that someone is good or honest 信任；相信

She lied to me. I don't trust her any more. 她曾经向我撒谎，我不再信任她了。

truth /truːθ; truθ/ *n* 名

无复数

the true facts about something 事实；真相

I'm not sure if he's telling the truth. 我不能确定他说的是不是实话。

反义 **lie**[3]

***try** /traɪ; traɪ/ *v* 动

tries, trying, tried, tried

1. to make an effort to do something 尝试；试图；设法
   The firefighter is trying to save the girl. 消防员正设法拯救那个女孩。

2. to use or test something to see if you like it 试；试用；试验
   I've tried the new chocolate and it tastes really good. 我尝过这种新巧克力，味道好极了。

try something on 试穿（衣物）

I tried the shirt on but it was too small. 我试穿了这件衬衫，但它太小了。

***T-shirt** /ˈtiː ʃɜːt; ˋti ʃɝt/ *n* 名

也作：***tee-shirt***

a shirt with short sleeves and no collar 短袖汗衫；T 恤衫

Gordon was wearing a red T-shirt. 戈登穿着一件红色 T 恤衫。

另见 **shirt**

tube /tjuːb; tub/ *n* 名

1. a hollow pipe made of glass, metal, rubber, etc 管；管子
   Air gets into the fish tank through the tube. 空气通过这条管子进入鱼缸。

2. a soft, narrow container 软管
   I need a new tube of toothpaste. 我需要一管新牙膏。

***Tuesday** /ˈtju:zdeɪ; ˋtuzde/ *n* 名

缩写：***Tues./Tue.***

the day between Monday and Wednesday 星期二

He visited his grandmother last Tuesday. 他上星期二去探望外婆。

注意 开头的字母必须用大写。

tug-of-war /ˌtʌg əv ˈwɔ:; ˏtʌg əv ˋwɔr/ *n* 名

无复数

a competition in which two teams pull against each other at opposite ends of a rope 拔河（比赛）

We had a tug-of-war at the end of sports day. 我们在运动会结束时进行了一场拔河比赛。

tuna /ˈtju:nə; ˋtunə/ *n* 名

复数：***tuna/tunas***

a large sea fish that you can eat 金枪鱼；吞拿鱼

I had a tuna sandwich for lunch. 我午餐吃了金枪鱼三明治。

tune /tju:n; tun/ *n* 名

a number of musical notes that are nice to listen to 调子；曲调

She played a beautiful tune on the piano. 她用钢琴弹奏出一段优美的曲子。

***tunnel** /ˈtʌnl; ˋtʌnl̩/ *n* 名

a long hole under the ground for cars or trains to go through 隧道；地道

A lot of cars go through this tunnel in the early morning. 清晨有许多车辆穿越这条隧道。

turkey /ˈtɜ:ki; ˋtɝkɪ/ *n* 名

a bird that looks like a large chicken, or the meat from it. You often eat turkey at Christmas. 火鸡；火鸡肉

Celia roasted a turkey in the oven. 西莉亚在烤箱里烤了一只火鸡。

***turn[1]** /tɜ:n; tɝn/ *v* 动

1. to move around or make something move around in a circle（使）转动；旋转
   The wheels were turning quickly. 轮子在急速旋转。
   Gary turned the key and opened the door. 加里转动钥匙，打开了门。
2. to change direction, or make something change direction （使）转向
   Turn right at the end of the street. 到了街口向右拐。
3. to move your body so that you are looking in a different direction 转身
   Jenny turned around and saw Helen. 珍妮转过身来看见海伦。
4. to move a page in a book or magazine so that you can see the next page 翻（书、杂志）

   Class, please turn to page 15 of your book. 同学们，请翻到书的第 15 页。
5. to become different 变成；成为
   The weather turned cold last night. 昨晚天气转凉了。

turn down 把（音量、温度等）调低

Can you turn down the TV? I'm doing homework. 你可以把电视机的音量调低吗？我正在做功课。

turn off 关掉（机器等）

He turned off the lights and went to bed. 他关灯后睡觉去了。

turn on 打开（机器等）

She turned on the electric fan. 她开了电风扇。

turn up 把（音量、温度等）调高

I can't hear the radio. Can you turn it up? 我听不见收音机，请你把音量调高好吗？

***turn[2]** /tɜ:n; tɝn/ *n* 名

1. a change in the direction that you are moving 转向；转弯
   Make a left turn at the corner of the street. 在街角向左拐。
2. the time when you can or should do something, not anyone else 轮到的机会
   It's your turn to wash the dishes. 轮到你洗碗了。

take turns 轮流；依次

The children took turns on the swing. 孩子们轮流荡秋千。

***turtle** /ˈtɜ:tl; ˋtɝtl̩/ *n* 名

an animal with a hard, round shell that lives mainly in the sea 海龟

Turtles lay eggs on beaches. 海龟在沙滩上生蛋。

比较 **tortoise**

T

tusk /tʌsk; tʌsk/ *n* 名

one of the two long teeth that grow outside the mouth of some animals such as elephants（象等动物的）长牙

Elephants use their tusks to dig for food. 象用长牙来挖食物。

tutor /ˈtjuːtə; ˋtutɚ/ *n* 名

someone who teaches one student or a small group of students 家庭教师；私人教师

My mother hired a private tutor for me. 妈妈帮我雇用了一位私人教师。

***TV** /ˌtiː ˈviː; ˌti ˋvi/ *n* 名

television 电视机；电视节目

We are going to buy a new TV. 我们会买一部新电视机。

He was watching TV all night. 他整夜都在看电视节目。

twelfth /twelfθ; twɛlfθ/ *ordinal num* 序数

12th in order 第十二（的）

We'll leave on the twelfth of May. 我们将在 5 月 12 日走。

***twelve** /twelv; twɛlv/ *num* 数

the number 12 十二

I cut the cake into twelve pieces. 我把蛋糕切成 12 块。

T

twentieth /ˈtwentiəθ; ˋtwɛntɪɪθ/ *ordinal num* 序数

20th in order 第二十（的）

Computers first appeared in the twentieth century. 电脑在 20 世纪首次出现。

***twenty** /ˈtwenti; ˋtwɛntɪ/ *num* 数

the number 20 二十

Mr Davis and his wife were married twenty years ago. 戴维斯先生和太太 20 年前结的婚。

***twice** /twaɪs; twaɪs/ *adv* 副

two times 两次

I brush my teeth twice a day. 我每天刷牙两次。

***twin** /twɪn; twɪn/ *n* 名

one of two children who have the same mother and are born at the same time 孪生儿；双胞胎

My brother and I are twins. 我和弟弟是双胞胎。

twinkle /ˈtwɪŋkl; ˋtwɪŋkl̩/ *v* 动

twinkles, twinkling, twinkled, twinkled

if a star or light twinkles, it shines and changes quickly from being bright to dark 闪烁；闪耀

Look at the stars twinkling in the sky. 看看天空中闪烁的星星。

twist /twɪst; twɪst/ *v* 动

to bend or turn something and change its shape 扭；拧

He twisted the balloon into the shape of a rabbit. 他把气球扭成兔子的形状。

***two** /tuː; tu/ *num* 数

the number 2 二

Patrick has lived in Paris for two years. 帕特里克在巴黎已经住了两年。

tying /ˈtaɪ-ɪŋ; ˋtaɪ-ɪŋ/ *v* 动

the present participle of **tie**[1] ☆tie[1] 的现在分词

***type**[1] /taɪp; taɪp/ *n* 名

a group of people or things that are similar to each other 种类；类型

What type of shoes do you like? 你喜欢哪一种鞋?

同义 **kind**[1], **sort**

***type**[2] /taɪp; taɪp/ *v* 动

types, typing, typed, typed

to write something using a computer 打字

I'm typing a letter. 我在打一封信。

typhoon /ˌtaɪˈfuːn; taɪˋfun/ *n* 名

a violent storm with very strong winds 台风

A few trees fell down during the typhoon. 台风期间有几棵树倒了。

tyre /ˈtaɪə; taɪr/ *n* 名【英】

美式：***tire***

a thick rubber ring that is filled with air and put round the wheel of a car, bicycle, etc 轮胎

Raymond pumped up the bicycle tyres. 雷蒙德给自行车的轮胎打了气。

UFO /ˌjuː ef ˈəʊ, ˈjuːfəʊ; ˌju ɛf ˋo, ˋjuˏfo/ *n* 名

a strange object in the sky that some people believe comes from another world 不明飞行物（Unidentified Flying Object 的缩写）

They have taken photos of UFOs. 他们曾经拍下不明飞行物的相片。

同义 **flying saucer**

***ugly** /ˈʌgli; ˋʌglɪ/ *adj* 形

uglier, ugliest

not good to look at 丑陋的；难看的

The duckling is uglier than others. 这只小鸭比其他小鸭难看。

反义 **beautiful, good-looking, handsome, pretty**

***umbrella** /ʌmˈbrelə; ʌmˋbrɛlə/ *n* 名

a thing that you use to protect yourself from the rain or sun 伞；雨伞

It's starting to rain. Take an umbrella with you. 开始下雨了，带上雨伞吧。

unable /ʌnˈeɪbl; ʌnˋebl̩/ *adj* 形

if you are unable to do something, you cannot do it 不能（做…）的；不会…的

He was unable to walk after the accident. 事故后他不能走路。

反义 **able**

***uncle** /ˈʌŋkl; ˋʌŋkl̩/ *n* 名

the brother of your mother or father, or the husband of your aunt 舅舅；叔叔；伯伯；姑夫；姨夫

Uncle John is a doctor. 约翰叔叔是一名医生。

uncomfortable /ʌnˈkʌmftəbl; ʌnˋkʌmfɚtəbl̩/ *adj* 形

1. not nice to sit on, lie on or wear 不舒服的；不舒适的
   I couldn't sleep because the bed was very uncomfortable. 这张床太不舒服了，我睡不着觉。

反义 **comfortable**

2. embarrassed or worried 不自在的；不安的
   Winnie felt uncomfortable about speaking in front of the class. 在班上的同学面前说话，威妮感到不自在。

反义 **comfortable**

***under[1]** /ˈʌndə; ˋʌndɚ/ *prep* 介

1. below something 在…下面
   The ball is under the table. 球在桌子下面。

反义 **over[1]**

2. covered by something 在…底下
   She wore a sweater under her coat. 她在外衣里面穿了一件毛衣。

反义 **over[1]**

3. less than 低于；少于
   This toy is suitable for children under eight. 这种玩具适合 8 岁以下的儿童。

反义 **over[1]**

***under[2]** /ˈʌndə; ˋʌndɚ/ *adv* 副

below something 在下面

The bridge was too low for ships to sail under. 这座桥太矮，轮船不能从下面驶过。

underground[1] /ˌʌndəˈgraʊnd; ˌʌndɚˋgraʊnd/ *adj* 形

under the surface of the ground 地下的

They're digging an underground passage. 他们在挖一条地下通道。

underground[2] /ˌʌndəˈgraʊnd; ˌʌndɚˋgraʊnd/ *adv* 副

under the surface of the ground 在地下

One part of the river flows underground. 这条河的一段流经地下。

underground[3] /ˈʌndəgraʊnd; ˋʌndɚˏgraʊnd/ *n* 名【英】

美式：***subway***

a railway system under the ground 地下铁路；地铁

Julian goes to work by underground. 朱利安乘地铁上班。

***underline** /ˌʌndəˈlaɪn; ˌʌndɚˋlaɪn/ *v* 动

underlines, underlining, underlined, underlined

to draw a line under a word or words 在（词语）下面划线

Please underline your name. 请在你的名字下划线。

Theresa Wong

U

underneath[1] /ˌʌndəˈniːθ; ˏʌndɚˋniθ/ *prep* 介

under or below something 在…下面；在…底下

I found a coin underneath the leaves. 我发现树叶底下有一枚钱币。

underneath[2] /ˌʌndəˈniːθ; ˏʌndɚˋniθ/ *adv* 副

under or below something 在下面；在底下

He was wearing a jacket with a blue shirt underneath. 他穿了一件外套，里面是一件蓝色衬衫。

*__understand__ /ˌʌndəˈstænd; ˏʌndɚˋstænd/ *v* 动

understands, understanding, understood, understood

1. to know the meaning of something or why something happens 懂得；理解
   The dictionary helps me understand these words. 这本词典帮助我理解这些单词。
2. to know how someone feels 了解；明白
   Laura thought that her parents didn't understand her. 劳拉认为她的父母并不了解她。

用法 不用进行式。

U

understood /ˌʌndəˈstʊd; ˏʌndɚˋstʊd/ *v* 动

the past tense and past participle of **understand** ☆understand 的过去式和过去分词

underwear /ˈʌndəweə; ˋʌndɚˏwɛr/ *n* 名

无复数

clothes that you wear under other clothes 内衣

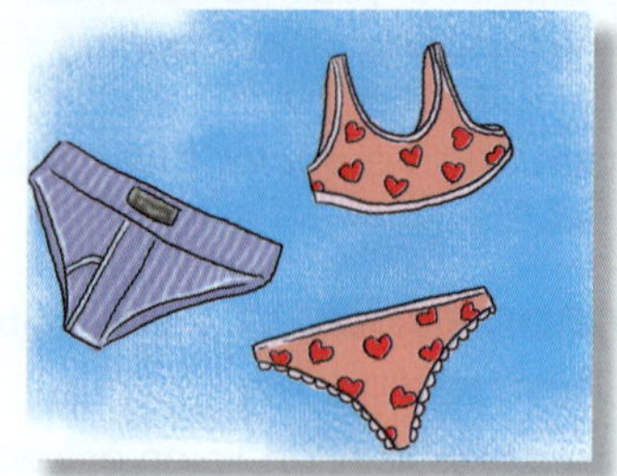

I change my underwear every day. 我天天更换内衣。

undid /ʌnˈdɪd; ʌnˋdɪd/ *v* 动

the past tense of **undo** ☆undo 的过去式

undo /ʌnˈduː; ʌnˋdu/ *v* 动

undoes, undoing, undid, undone

to open something that is tied or wrapped 解开；打开

He undid the buttons on his jacket. 他解开了外套的钮扣。

undone /ʌnˈdʌn; ʌnˋdʌn/ *v* 动

the past participle of **undo** ☆undo 的过去分词

undress /ʌnˈdres; ʌnˋdrɛs/ *v* 动

undresses, undressing, undressed, undressed

to take your clothes off, or take someone's clothes off 脱去（…）的衣服

I undressed and had a bath. 我脱掉衣服，然后洗澡。

uneasy /ʌnˈiːzi; ʌnˋizɪ/ *adj* 形

worried because you think something bad may happen 不安的；忧虑的

Albert felt uneasy about the exam results. 阿尔伯特为考试成绩感到不安。

unexpected /ˌʌnɪkˈspektɪd; ˏʌnɪkˋspɛktɪd/ *adj* 形

if something is unexpected, it is surprising because you did not expect it 想不到的；意外的

The ending of the story was unexpected. 故事的结尾真出人意料。

unfair /ˌʌnˈfeə; ʌnˋfɛr/ *adj* 形

not treating people in the same way 不公平的

My brother can go out to play, but I have to stay home. It's so unfair! 哥哥可以出去玩，我却要待在家中。太不公平了！

反义 fair

unfold /ʌnˈfəʊld; ʌnˋfold/ *v* 动

to open something that has been folded 打开；展开

Sophia is unfolding a map on the table. 索菲亚在桌子上打开地图。

unfriendly /ʌnˈfrendli; ʌnˋfrɛndlɪ/ *adj* 形

unfriendlier, unfriendliest

not kind or helpful to someone 不友善的；冷漠的

They are very unfriendly to their neighbours. 他们对邻居很不友善。

反义 **friendly, nice**

unhappily /ʌnˈhæpɪli; ʌnˋhæpɪlɪ/ *adv* 副

in an unhappy way 不高兴地；不快乐地

She sighed unhappily and left the room. 她不高兴地叹了口气，然后离开了房间。

反义 **happily**

unhappy /ʌnˈhæpi; ʌnˋhæpɪ/ *adj* 形

unhappier, unhappiest

not happy; sad 不高兴的；不快乐的

Leslie was unhappy because he lost his school bag. 莱斯利丢了书包，很不高兴。

反义 **happy**

unhealthy /ʌnˈhelθi; ʌnˋhɛlθɪ/ *adj* 形

unhealthier, unhealthiest

not in good health; making you ill 不健康的；损害健康的

It is unhealthy to drink too much beer. 喝太多啤酒对身体不好。

反义 **healthy**

unhelpful /ʌnˈhelpfl; ʌnˋhɛlpfəl/ *adj* 形

not willing to help 不愿帮忙的

The salesman was rude and unhelpful. 那个售货员既无礼又不肯帮忙。

反义 **helpful**

Unidentified Flying Object /ˌʌnaɪdentɪfaɪd ˌflaɪ-ɪŋ ˈɒbdʒɪkt; ˏʌnaɪdɛntɪfaɪd ˏflaɪ-ɪŋ ˋɑbdʒɪkt/ *n* 名

另见 **UFO**

***uniform** /ˈjuːnɪfɔːm; ˋjunəˏfɔrm/ *n* 名

a type of clothing that you wear for a job or at school 制服；校服

Claire always keeps her school uniform clean. 克莱尔总是把校服保持得干干净净。

unimportant /ˌʌnɪmˈpɔːtnt; ˏʌnɪmˋpɔrtn̩t/ *adj* 形

not important 不重要的；无足轻重的

Please tell me the main points, not the unimportant details. 请告诉我要点，而不是无关紧要的细节。

反义 **important**

unique /juˈniːk; juˋnik/ *adj* 形

if something is unique, it is the only one of its kind 唯一的；独一无二的

The designer wants his products to be unique. 这位设计师希望自己的作品与众不同。

unit /ˈjuːnɪt; ˋjunɪt/ *n* 名

1. an amount of something that is used to show measurements （计量用的）单位

   The gram is a unit of weight. 克是重量单位。

2. a part of a textbook or course （课本或课程的）单元

   This grammar book has ten units. 这本语法书有 10 个单元。

universe /ˈjuːnɪvɜːs; ˋjunəˏvɝs/ *n* 名

无复数

the universe all the stars and planets in space 宇宙

Scientists study the universe in various ways. 科学家使用各种各样的方法来研究宇宙。

***university** /ˌjuːnɪˈvɜːsəti; ˏjunəˋvɝsətɪ/ *n* 名

复数：*universities*

a place where you study subjects at a high level after secondary school 大学

Gloria is going to university next year. 格洛里亚明年上大学。

unkind /ˌʌnˈkaɪnd; ʌnˋkaɪnd/ *adj* 形

not friendly or nice to other people 不仁慈的；不友善的

Tony was unkind to his classmates. 托尼对他的同学不友善。

同义 **cruel**

反义 **kind**[2]

***unless** /ənˈles; ənˋlɛs/ *conj* 连

used to say that something will happen if something else does not happen 除非

You will fail the exam unless you work harder. 你要是不用功一点，考试就会不及格。

unlike /ˌʌnˈlaɪk; ʌnˋlaɪk/ *prep* 介

U

different from another person or thing 不像；和…不同
Unlike his brother, George is very lazy. 乔治很懒惰，和他的哥哥不同。

unload /ʌn'ləʊd; ʌn`lod/ *v* 动
to take things off a vehicle 把（货物）卸下
The workers are unloading the lorry. 工人们正在把卡车上的货物卸下。

反义 load[2]

unlock /ʌn'lɒk; ʌn`lɑk/ *v* 动
to open a door, a box, etc with a key 开…的锁

He unlocked the door and went in. 他打开门锁走了进去。

反义 lock[2]

unlucky /ʌn'lʌki; ʌn`lʌkɪ/ *adj* 形
unluckier, unluckiest
having bad luck 不幸的；倒霉的
I was so unlucky that I lost two umbrellas in a month. 我一个月内丢了两把雨伞，真倒霉。

反义 lucky

unnecessary /ʌn'nesəsəri; ʌn`nɛsəˌsɛrɪ/ *adj* 形
not needed; more than what you need 不必要的；多余的
It is unnecessary to worry about the exam if you have prepared well for it. 你如果准备充足，就不必为考试担忧。

反义 necessary

unpack /ʌn'pæk; ʌn`pæk/ *v* 动
to take things out of a bag, box, etc 从（包、箱等）取出物品

He unpacked his suitcase when he got to the hotel. 他到了酒店后，把手提箱里的东西拿了出来。

反义 pack[1]

unpleasant /ʌn'pleznt; ʌn`plɛznt/ *adj* 形
not nice or enjoyable 令人不愉快的；令人难受的
There was an unpleasant smell from the kitchen. 厨房传来一股难闻的气味。

反义 pleasant

unselfish /ʌn'selfɪʃ; ʌn`sɛlfɪʃ/ *adj* 形
caring about other people and not just yourself 不自私的；无私的
Paula is unselfish. She always cares more about other people than herself. 波拉为人不自私，她总是为他人着想多于为自己着想。

反义 selfish

unsuccessful /ˌʌnsək'sesfl; ˌʌnsək`sɛsfəl/ *adj* 形
not having done what you tried to do 不成功的；失败的
The police made several unsuccessful attempts to catch the murderer. 警方几次设法捉拿凶手都失败了。

反义 successful

untidy /ʌn'taɪdi; ʌn`taɪdɪ/ *adj* 形
untidier, untidiest
not neat 不整洁的；凌乱的
David's room is so untidy! 大卫的房间太乱了！

反义 tidy[1]

untie /ʌn'taɪ; ʌn`taɪ/ *v* 动
unties, untying, untied, untied
to open something that is tied 解开；打开
I untied the parcel. 我解开了包裹。

反义 tie[1]

***until**[1] /ən'tɪl; ən`tɪl/ *prep* 介
也作：***till***
up to a particular time 直到（…为止）
The restaurant is open until 11 p.m. 这家餐馆营业至晚上 11 点。

U

***until²** /ən'tɪl; ən`tɪl/ *conj* 连

也作：***till***

up to a particular time that 直到

We waited until the rain stopped. 我们一直等到雨停。

untying /ʌn'taɪ-ɪŋ; ʌn`taɪ-ɪŋ/ *v* 动

the present participle of **untie** ☆untie 的现在分词

unusual /ʌn'juːʒuəl; ʌn`juʒuəl/ *adj* 形

different from what is usual or normal 不平常的；异常的

She has an unusual name that I've never heard of before. 她的名字很特别，我以前从未听过。

unwell /ʌn'wel; ʌn`wɛl/ *adj* 形

ill 生病的；不舒服的

Linda has been unwell since last week. 琳达从上星期起就一直生病。

同义 **sick**

反义 **well¹**

unwrap /ʌn'ræp; ʌn`ræp/ *v* 动

unwraps, unwrapping, unwrapped, unwrapped

to remove the paper, plastic, etc that covers something 拆开…的包装

Judy unwrapped her birthday gifts. 朱迪把生日礼物拆开了。

反义 **wrap**

***up¹** /ʌp; ʌp/ *adv* 副

1. to or in a higher place or position 由下而上地；在高处

   The lift is going up. 电梯正向上升。

   We hung the pictures up on the wall. 我们把图画挂在墙上。

反义 **down¹**

2. to or at a higher amount or level 上升；增多

   The food prices have gone up. 食物价格上升了。

反义 **down¹**

3. not in bed 起床

   Adam, it's time to get up! 亚当，该起床了！

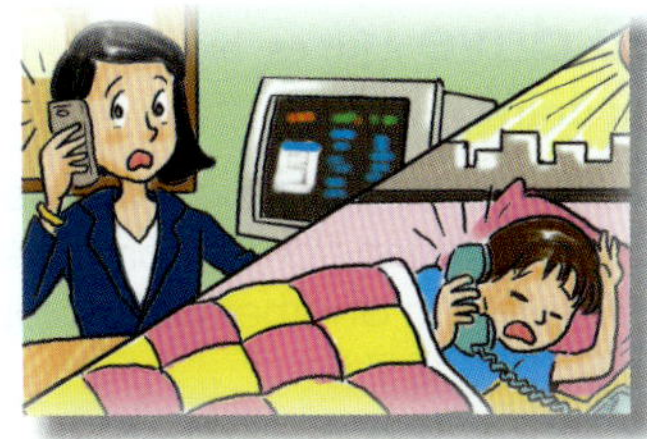

up to something 多达（某数量或数目）；直到（某时刻）

The room can hold up to 50 people. 这个房间最多可容纳 50 人。

Up to now we have received no complaints from customers. 到目前为止，我们没收到顾客的投诉。

Daily conversation 日常会话

it's up to ... 由…决定

"Shall we have sushi or noodles?" "It's up to you." "我们吃寿司还是面条好呢？" "你决定吧。"

***up²** /ʌp; ʌp/ *prep* 介

1. to or in a higher place or position 向上；在（较高位置）

   He climbed up the ladder. 他爬上了梯子。

反义 **down²**

2. to or in a place that is further along something 沿着；在…的较远处

   I walked up the street to the station. 我沿着街道向车站走去。

反义 **down²**

upload /ˌʌp'ləʊd; `ʌpˌlod/ *v* 动

【电脑】to move information or programs from your computer, phone, etc onto the Internet 上传（数据或程序）

She uploaded the video to the website. 她把视频上传到这个网站。

反义 **download**

***upon** /ə'pɒn; ə`pɑn/ *prep* 介

on 在…上

He placed the books upon the shelf. 他把书本放在架上。

用法 upon 和 on 同义，但只用于较正式的场合以及一些短语中，例如 once upon a time（从前）。

upper /'ʌpə; `ʌpɚ/ *adj* 形

in a higher position than something else（位置）较高的；上面的

I like to sit on the upper deck when I take the tram. 我乘电车时喜欢坐在上层。

用法 只用于名词前。

***upset** /ˌʌp'set; ʌp`sɛt/ *adj* 形

unhappy because something bad has happened 不快的；苦恼的

She was upset because he didn't trust her. 他不信任她，使她感到不快。

upside down /ˌʌpsaɪd 'daʊn; `ʌpˌsaɪd `daʊn/ *adj* 形

with the top at the bottom and the bottom at the top 倒置的；上下颠倒的

The picture is upside down. 这幅图画挂倒了。

***upstairs** /ˌʌpˈsteəz; ˌʌpˋsterz/ *adv* 副

on or to a higher floor of a building 在楼上；向楼上

Mr Jackson lives upstairs. 杰克逊先生住在楼上。

反义 **downstairs**

upwards /ˈʌpwədz; ˋʌpwɚdz/ *adv* 副【英】

美式：***upward***

towards a higher position 向上；朝上

The kite began to fly upwards. 风筝开始向上飞。

urgent /ˈɜːdʒənt; ˋɝdʒənt/ *adj* 形

if something is urgent, it is very important and you need to do it or do something about it immediately 紧急的；迫切的

He sent me an urgent message. 他给我发了一条紧急信息。

U

urgently /ˈɜːdʒəntli; ˋɝdʒəntlɪ/ *adv* 副

in an urgent way 紧急地；迫切地

I need help urgently. 我急需帮忙。

***us** /əs, əs; *strong* 强读 ʌs; ʌs/ *pron* 代

the person who is speaking and one or more other people 我们

She invited us to her home. 她邀请我们到她家里。

注意 let（让）与 us 同用时会缩写成 let's，例如 Let's play football（我们去踢足球吧）。

USB drive /ˌjuː es ˈbiː draɪv; ˌju ɛs ˋbi draɪv/ *n* 名

【电脑】a small thing that you use to store information from a computer and move it to another computer 随身碟；USB 记忆体

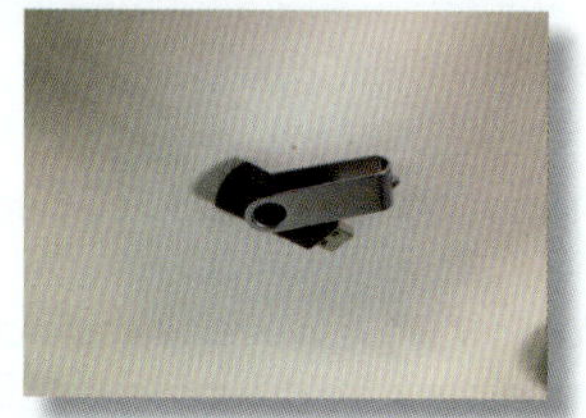

I saved my homework on a USB drive. 我把功课储存在 USB 记忆体内。

***use[1]** /juːz; ˋjuz/ *v* 动

uses, using, used, used

1. to do something with a tool, method, etc 用；使用（某工具、方法等）

   I used a knife to cut the apples. 我用刀来切苹果。

2. to say or write a particular word or phrase 使用；应用（某词语或短语）

   We use the word "duckling" to say a young duck. 我们用 duckling 这个单词来说小鸭。

use up 用完；耗尽

She used up the shampoo. 她把洗发水用完了。

***use[2]** /juːs; jus/ *n* 名

a purpose that something is used for 用途；用处

A computer has many uses. 电脑有许多用途。

it's no use (doing something)（做某事）没有用

It's no use talking to her — she never listens to others. 跟她谈也没有用，她从不听别人的意见。

used[1] /juːst; just/ *adj* 形

be/get used to (doing) something

if you are used to or get used to something, you have seen it or done it many times so that it does not surprise you 习惯于（做）某事

She's not used to driving her new car yet. 她还未习惯驾驶她的新车。

I soon got used to the cold weather in the city. 我很快习惯了这个城市寒冷的天气。

比较 **used to**

used[2] /juːzd; juzd/ *adj* 形

having been used; not new 用过的；旧的

Wayne bought a used car because it was much cheaper than a new car. 韦恩买了一辆二手车，因为它比新车便宜得多。

用法 常用于名词前。

used to /ˈjuːst tuː, ˋjust tu/ *v* 动

if something used to happen, it happened often in the past but does not happen now 过去经常发生；曾经

Mr Brown used to live in Germany. 布朗先生过去住在德国。

用法 used to 的否定式是 didn't use to 或 used not to，例如 Amy didn't use to like cats/Amy used not to like cats（艾米以前不喜欢猫）。

比较 **used[1]**

***useful** /ˈjuːsfl; ˋjusfəl/ *adj* 形

if something is useful, it can help you to do or get what you want 有用的；有帮助的

This knife is very useful. 这把刀很有用。

反义 **useless**

useless /ˈjuːsləs; ˋjuslɪs/ *adj* 形

having no use 无用的；无效的

This chair is useless — one of its legs is broken. 这张椅子没有用了，它的一只脚断了。

反义 **useful**

***user** /ˈjuːzə; ˋjuzɚ/ *n* 名

a person who uses something 使用者；用户

These lockers are for library users. 这些寄物柜是给图书馆用户使用的。

usual /ˈjuːʒuəl; ˋjuʒʊəl/ *adj* 形

happening most of the time or in most situations 通常的；惯常的

We met at the usual place. 我们在老地方见面。

as usual 像往常一样；照常

Robert came first in the race, as usual. 罗伯特像往常一样在赛跑比赛中又得了第一名。

***usually** /ˈjuːʒuəli; ˋjuʒʊəlɪ/ *adv* 副

most of the time; in most situations 通常地；惯常地

He usually gets up at seven o'clock. 他通常 7 点起床。

U

vacation /və'keɪʃn; ve`keʃən/ *n* 名【美】

英式 **holiday**

vacuum cleaner /'vækjuəm ˌkliːnə; `vækjuəm ˏklinə/ *n* 名

a machine that takes dirt from the floor 真空吸尘器

She is cleaning the floor with a vacuum cleaner. 她在用吸尘器清洁地板。

valley /'væli; `vælɪ/ *n* 名

an area of low land between hills or mountains 山谷

There is a river running through the valley. 有一条河流经山谷。

valuable /'væljuəbl; `væljuəbḷ/ *adj* 形

worth a lot of money 贵重的；值钱的

He gave her a valuable watch. 他送给她一只贵重的手表。

***value** /'væljuː; `vælju/ *n* 名

the amount of money that something is worth 价值

The value of the diamond ring has increased a lot. 这枚钻石戒指的价值上升了不少。

vampire /'væmpaɪə; `væmpaɪr/ *n* 名

in stories, a dead person who bites people's necks and drinks their blood 吸血鬼

Nicholas played the role of the vampire in the drama. 尼古拉斯在这出戏剧里扮演吸血鬼。

***van** /væn; væn/ *n* 名

a vehicle, smaller than a truck, that you use for carrying goods 小型货车

Steven delivers parcels by van. 史蒂芬驾驶小型货车运送包裹。

vanilla /və'nɪlə; və`nɪlə/ *n* 名

无复数

something used to give a sweet taste to ice cream and other types of food 香草精

My favourite flavour of ice cream is vanilla. 我最喜爱吃香草味的冰淇淋。

***variety** /və'raɪəti; və`raɪətɪ/ *n* 名

复数：***varieties***

a variety of a lot of different types of things or people 各种各样的

The shop sells a variety of sweets. 这家商店售卖各种各样的糖果。

variety show 综艺节目

My family enjoys watching variety shows on TV. 我的家人喜欢看电视综艺节目。

***various** /'veəriəs; `vɛrɪəs/ *adj* 形

several different 各种各样的

There are various ways to do this job. 做这项工作的方法有很多。

***vase** /vɑːz; ves/ *n* 名

a container for holding flowers 花瓶

The cat broke the vase. 猫打破了花瓶。

***vegetable** /'vedʒtəbl; `vɛdʒtəbḷ/ *n* 名

a plant such as a cabbage, carrot, tomato, etc that you eat 蔬菜

V

It is good to eat a lot of vegetables. 多吃蔬菜是好的。

vehicle /ˈviːɪkl; ˋviɪkl̩/ *n* 名

a machine with wheels that carries people or things from one place to another 交通工具；车辆

Several vehicles crashed in the accident. 事故中有几辆汽车相撞。

verb /vɜːb; vɝb/ *n* 名

a word that tells you what someone does or what happens. In the sentences "He is a singer" and "He sang a song", "is" and "sang" are verbs. 动词（在 He is a singer 和 He sang a song 两个句子中，is 和 sang 是动词。）

verse /vɜːs; vɝs/ *n* 名

a set of lines that forms one part of a song or poem（歌曲或诗的）一节

Let's read the last verse again. 我们再来朗读最后一节吧。

vertical /ˈvɜːtɪkl; ˋvɝtɪkl̩/ *adj* 形

standing or pointing straight up 垂直的；直立的

His T-shirt has green and orange vertical stripes. 他的T恤衫有橙绿相间的直条纹。

反义 **horizontal**

***very** /ˈveri; ˋvɛrɪ/ *adv* 副

a word you use to make another word stronger 很；非常

Flora is very pretty. 弗罗拉很漂亮。

用法 very 主要用来强调形容词和副词。如要强调动词，用 very much，例如 We miss you very much（我们很想念你）。very 不能和比较级形容词一起使用，要用 much，例如 These trousers are much longer（这条裤子长多了）。

Daily conversation 日常会话

"Is the salad good?" "Yes, very good." "这个沙拉好吃吗？""非常好吃。"

"Was the film good?" "Not very." "这部电影好看吗？""不太好看。"

vest /vest; vɛst/ *n* 名【英】

a piece of clothing that you wear under other clothes on the top part of your body 内衣背心；汗衫

He wore a vest under his shirt. 他在衬衫里面穿了一件背心。

vet /vet; vɛt/ *n* 名

a doctor for sick animals 兽医

She took her dog to the vet. 她带狗去看兽医。

victim /ˈvɪktɪm; ˋvɪktɪm/ *n* 名

someone who has been hurt or killed because of a crime, an accident, etc 受害者；罹难者

She was the victim of the murder. 她是那件谋杀案的受害者。

victory /ˈvɪktəri; ˋvɪktərɪ/ *n* 名

复数：***victories***

when you win a game, competition, war, etc 胜利

The team won their first victory in today's match. 这个队在今天的比赛中获得了首次胜利。

***video** /ˈvɪdiəʊ; ˋvɪdɪ͵o/ *n* 名

a film, television programme, or an event that has been recorded 录影；录像

I saw the video on the Internet. 我在互联网上看到这段录像。

video game /ˈvɪdiəʊ ˌgeɪm; ˋvɪdɪo ͵gem/ *n* 名

a game that you play by pressing buttons to move pictures on a computer or television screen 电子游戏

My mother doesn't allow me to play video games when I have exams. 当我要考试时，妈妈不许我玩电子游戏。

***view** /vjuː; vju/ *n* 名

1. what you can see from a particular place 风景；景色

   The view from the peak is beautiful. 从山顶看到的景色很美。

2. your opinion about something 看法；意见

   What's your view on this plan? 你对这个计划有什么看法？

***village** /ˈvɪlɪdʒ; ˋvɪlɪdʒ/ *n* 名

a small place in the countryside where people live 乡村；村庄

Shanghai was once a fishing village. 上海曾经是一个渔村。

V

villager /ˈvɪlɪdʒə; ˋvɪlɪdʒɚ/ *n* 名

someone who lives in a village 村民

More and more villagers move to the city to work. 越来越多的村民迁移到城里工作。

villain /ˈvɪlən; ˋvɪlən/ *n* 名

the main bad character in a story, film, etc（故事、电影等的）反派主角；坏人

He became famous after playing villains in several films. 他因在好几部电影中饰演坏人的角色而闻名。

vinegar /ˈvɪnɪgə; ˋvɪnɪgɚ/ *n* 名

无复数

a liquid with a sour taste that you put in some food 醋

Would you like some vinegar in your noodles? 你的面里要加点醋吗?

violence /ˈvaɪələns; ˋvaɪələns/ *n* 名

无复数

when a person intends to hurt or kill other people 暴力

There is too much violence on television these days. 如今电视上有太多暴力镜头。

violent /ˈvaɪələnt; ˋvaɪələnt/ *adj* 形

a violent action, event or person is likely to hurt or kill other people 暴力的；凶暴的

He was drunk and became violent. 他喝醉了，变得凶神恶煞。

***violin** /ˌvaɪəˈlɪn; ˏvaɪəˋlɪn/ *n* 名

a musical instrument with strings that you hold under your chin and play by pulling a stick 小提琴

Michael can play the violin. 迈克尔会拉小提琴。

virus /ˈvaɪərəs; ˋvaɪrəs/ *n* 名

复数：***viruses***

1. a very small living thing that causes diseases 病毒

   The flu virus was spreading quickly around the town. 流感病毒在城镇周围迅速传播。

2. 【电脑】a computer program that can destroy information on a computer 电脑病毒

   This software will find viruses and remove them. 这个软件能找出电脑病毒并把它们移除。

visible /ˈvɪzəbl; ˋvɪzəbl̩/ *adj* 形

able to be seen 看得见的；可见的

The hill was visible from far away. 从远处可以见到这座山。

反义 **invisible**

***visit**[1] /ˈvɪzɪt; ˋvɪzɪt/ *v* 动

to go and spend time in a place or with someone 游览；参观；探访

We visited the Space Museum last month. 上个月我们参观了太空馆。

Stanley went to Toronto to visit his relatives. 斯坦利到多伦多探访亲戚。

***visit**[2] /ˈvɪzɪt; ˋvɪzɪt/ *n* 名

when you visit a place or person 游览；参观；探访

When was your last visit to the dentist? 你上一次去看牙医是什么时候?

visitor /ˈvɪzɪtə; ˋvɪzɪtɚ/ *n* 名

someone who visits a place or person 参观者；访客

The art gallery attracts thousands of visitors every month. 这座美术馆每个月都吸引成千上万的游客。

vitamin /ˈvɪtəmɪn; ˋvaɪtəmɪn/ *n* 名

something found in food that you need for good health 维生素；维他命

Oranges contain a lot of vitamin C. 橙子含有大量维生素 C。

vocabulary /vəˈkæbjʊləri; vəˋkæbjəˏlɛrɪ/ *n* 名

复数：***vocabularies***

all the words that someone knows or uses 词汇；词汇量

Paula has a good vocabulary. 波拉的词汇量很丰富。

***voice** /vɔɪs; vɔɪs/ *n* 名

the sound that you make when you speak or sing 嗓音；（说话或唱歌的）声音

She spoke in a soft voice. 她轻声地说话。

volcano /vɒlˈkeɪnəʊ; vɑlˋkeno/ *n* 名

复数：***volcanoes/volcanos***

a mountain with a large hole at the top where hot liquid rock, steam, etc sometimes come out 火山

Mount Fuji is a volcano in Japan. 富士山是日本的一座火山。

***volleyball** /ˈvɒlibɔːl; ˋvɑlɪˏbɔl/ *n* 名

1. （无复数）a game in which two

V

teams hit a ball over a net with their hands and try not to let it touch the ground 排球（运动）

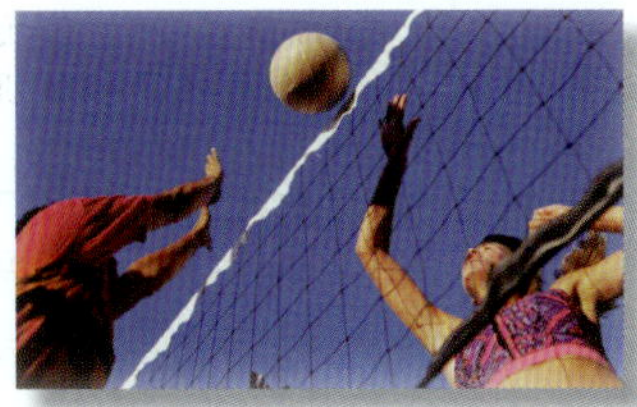

The girls played volleyball after school. 女孩们放学后打排球。

2. the ball used in a game of volleyball 排球

   He hit the volleyball with his wrist. 他用手腕打排球。

volume /ˈvɒljuːm; ˋvɑljəm/ *n* 名

1. the amount of space that something fills, or the amount of space in a container 容量；体积

   The volume of this bottle is two litres. 这个瓶子的容量是两升。

2. （无复数） the amount of sound that a television, radio, etc produces 音量

   Could you please turn the volume down? 请你把音量调低好吗？

volunteer[1] /ˌvɒlənˈtɪə; ˏvɑlənˋtɪr/ *n* 名

someone who does work without getting money 志愿者；义务工作者

The volunteers helped to clean up old people's homes. 这群志愿者帮忙收拾老人的住所。

volunteer[2] /ˌvɒlənˈtɪə; ˏvɑlənˋtɪr/ *v* 动

to offer to do something that you do not have to do 自愿（做某事）

Ted volunteered to help the poor. 泰德自愿帮助穷人。

vomit /ˈvɒmɪt; ˋvɑmɪt/ *v* 动

if you vomit, food comes up from your stomach and comes out of your mouth 呕吐

The drunken man vomited all over the floor. 那个醉酒的人吐得满地都是。

***vote** /vəʊt; vot/ *v* 动

votes, voting, voted, voted

to choose someone or something by putting up your hand or marking a piece of paper 投票；表决

All members of the committee have voted. 委员会的所有成员已经投票了。

vowel /ˈvaʊəl; ˋvaʊəl/ *n* 名

a letter or the sound of a letter that is not a consonant. In English the vowels are "a", "e", "i", "o", and "u". 元音字母；母音字母；元音；母音（英语的元音字母为 a, e, i, o 和 u）

另见 书末的发音表

比较 **consonant**

voyage /ˈvɔɪ·ɪdʒ; ˋvɔɪ·ɪdʒ/ *n* 名

a long journey by sea or in space （海上或太空的）航行

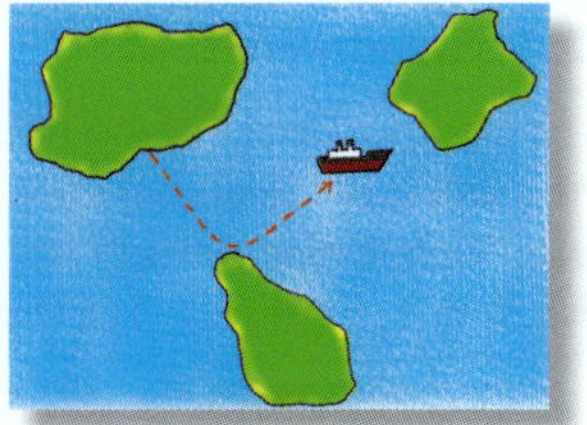

The Titanic sank during its first voyage. 泰坦尼克号第一次航行就沉没了。

wafer /ˈweɪfə; ˋwefɚ/ *n* 名

a very thin biscuit 威化饼干；薄脆饼

Lisa likes to eat wafers with ice cream. 丽莎喜欢吃威化饼干拌冰淇淋。

wage /weɪdʒ; wedʒ/ *n* 名

money that you get every day or week for your job（按日或周领取的）工资

He earns a daily wage of $250. 他的工资是每日 250 元。

比较 **salary**

waist /weɪst; west/ *n* 名

the narrow part around the middle of your body 腰；腰部

Mandy wore a belt around her waist. 曼迪在腰上束了一条皮带。

***wait**[1] /weɪt; wet/ *v* 动

to stay somewhere until someone comes or something happens 等候；等待

A few people were waiting for the bus. 有些人在等公共汽车。

Daily conversation 日常会话

wait a moment 等一下

"May I speak to Miss Taylor?" "Wait a moment, please." "请问泰勒小姐在吗？" "请等一下。"

wait[2] /weɪt; wet/ *n* 名

a period of time when you wait 等待的时间

We had a long wait before she came. 我们等了很久她才到。

***waiter** /ˈweɪtə; ˋwetɚ/ *n* 名

a man who serves food or drinks to people in a restaurant 男服务员；男侍应生

The waiter brought us two glasses of water. 服务员给我们拿来两杯水。

***waitress** /ˈweɪtrəs; ˋwetrɪs/ *n* 名

复数：***waitresses***

a woman who serves food or drinks to people in a restaurant 女服务员；女侍应生

They asked the waitress for the bill. 他们请服务员拿账单来。

***wake** /weɪk; wek/ *v* 动

wakes, waking, woke, woken

也作：***wake up***

1. to stop sleeping 醒来；睡醒

   I usually wake up at 7 a.m. 我通常早上 7 点钟醒来。

2. to make someone stop sleeping 唤醒；弄醒

   Can you wake me up at six o'clock tomorrow? 你明天 6 点钟叫醒我好吗？

***walk**[1] /wɔːk; wɔk/ *v* 动

to move forward by putting one foot in front of the other 走；行走；步行

Peter often walks to school. 彼得常常步行上学。

***walk**[2] /wɔːk; wɔk/ *n* 名

a journey by walking 步行；散步

Let's go for a walk after dinner. 我们吃完饭去散散步吧。

***wall** /wɔːl; wɔl/ *n* 名

1. one of the sides of a room or building 墙壁

   She hung the picture on the wall. 她把图画挂在墙上。

2. a structure made of stone or brick that surrounds an area or divides one area from the other 围墙

   A cat jumped down from the wall. 一只猫从墙上跳了下来。

***wallet** /ˈwɒlɪt; ˋwalɪt/ *n* 名

a small flat case for you to carry paper money 钱包；皮夹子

I put the banknotes in my wallet. 我把钞票放进钱包里。

另见 **purse**

wallpaper /ˈwɔːlˌpeɪpə; ˋwɔlˏpepɚ/ *n* 名

无复数

paper that you stick onto the walls of a room 墙纸

The wallpaper in our bedroom is peeling off. 我们卧室的墙纸正在剥落。

wand /wɒnd; wɑnd/ *n* 名

a thin stick that you hold in your hand to do magic tricks 魔杖；魔棒

She waved her wand and a bird flew out of the box. 她挥一挥魔杖，一只鸟从箱子里飞出来。

wander /ˈwɒndə; ˋwɑndɚ/ *v* 动

to walk slowly around a place without a purpose 闲逛；漫步

We were just wandering around the mall. 我们只是在商场里闲逛。

***want** /wɒnt; wɑnt/ *v* 动

to wish that you could have or do something 想要

Ida wants a doll for her birthday. 艾达生日想要一个玩具娃娃。

I want to sleep now. 我想睡觉了。

***war** /wɔː; wɔr/ *n* 名

a time when there is fighting between two or more countries 战争

The war between the two countries lasted five years. 这两个国家的战争持续了 5 年。

反义 **peace**

比较 **battle**

ward /wɔːd; wɔrd/ *n* 名

a room in a hospital where patients stay 病房

Two nurses are working in the children's ward. 两名护士在儿科病房工作。

warden /ˈwɔːdn; ˋwɔrdn̩/ *n* 名

a person who is in charge of a building or place 管理员；看守人

Darren is the warden of a home for old people. 达伦是一所养老院的管理员。

***wardrobe** /ˈwɔːdrəʊb; ˋwɔrdˏrob/ *n* 名

a large cupboard for hanging clothes 衣柜；衣橱

I hung the coats in the wardrobe. 我把大衣挂在衣柜里。

warehouse /ˈweəhaʊs; ˋwɛrˏhaʊs/ *n* 名

a large building for storing goods 仓库；货仓

The warehouse is full of boxes. 货仓里满是箱子。

***warm**[1] /wɔːm; wɔrm/ *adj* 形

warmer, warmest

1. a little hot 温暖的；暖和的

   I enjoy having a warm bath. 我喜欢洗温水浴。

反义 **cool**

2. able to keep in heat 保暖的；御寒的

   This sweater is very warm. 这件毛衣很保暖。

warm[2] /wɔːm; wɔrm/ *v* 动

to make someone or something warm 使温暖；使暖和

They sat by the fire to warm their hands. 他们坐在炉火旁暖手。

warm up (使)变暖；热身

I put the sandwiches in the oven to warm them up. 我把三明治放在烤箱里热一热。

The swimmers were warming up before the competition. 游泳选手在比赛前先做热身运动。

warm-up /ˈwɔːm ʌp; ˋwɔrm ʌp/ *n* 名

a set of exercises that you do to prepare your body for sport 热身运动

We did a ten-minute warm-up before running. 我们跑步前做了 10 分钟热身运动。

***warn** /wɔːn; wɔrn/ *v* 动

to tell someone that something bad or dangerous may happen 警告；提醒

She warned him not to drive too fast. 她提醒他开车不要太快。

warning /ˈwɔːnɪŋ; ˋwɔrnɪŋ/ *n* 名

something that tells you that something bad or dangerous may happen 警告；警示

There is a health warning on cigarette packets. 香烟盒上有健康警示。

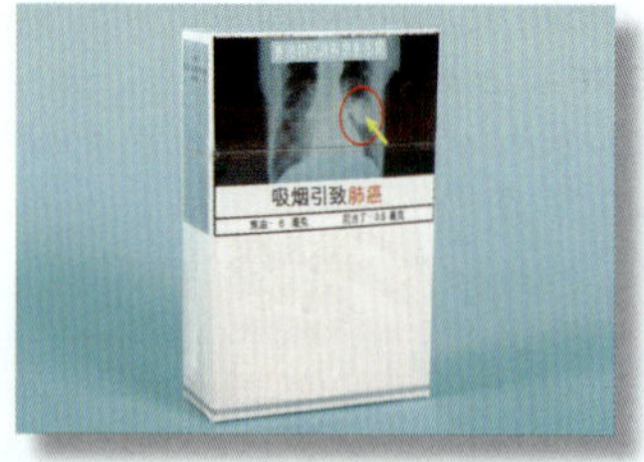

was /wəz; wəz; *strong* 强读 wɒz; wɑz/ *v* 动

the past tense of **be**, used with "I", "he", "she" and "it" ☆be 的过去式，与 I、he、she 和 it 一起使用

I was tired. 我累了。

Why was he angry? 他为什么生气了？

***wash** /wɒʃ; wɑʃ/ *v* 动

washes, washing, washed, washed

to clean something with water and soap 洗；洗涤

Wash your hands before eating. 进食前要洗手。

get washed 洗澡

He got washed and went to bed. 他洗过澡就去睡觉了。

wash up【英】洗碗碟

Jimmy, it's your turn to wash up. 吉米，轮到你洗碗碟了。

washbasin /ˈwɒʃbeɪsn; ˋwɑʃˌbesn̩/ *n* 名

a large bowl fixed to a wall for washing your hands and face 洗脸盆

We put a mirror above the washbasin. 我们在洗脸盆上面装了一块镜子。

washing /ˈwɒʃɪŋ; ˋwɑʃɪŋ/ *n* 名【英】

无复数

clothes that are going to be washed, or that have just been washed 待洗的衣服；刚洗好的衣服

Would you hang the washing out? 你把洗好的衣服晾出去好吗？

washing machine 洗衣机

This washing machine is quiet and washes clothes very well. 这部洗衣机很安静，把衣服洗得很干净。

washing powder【英】洗衣粉

This washing powder is good for washing wool. 这种洗衣粉适用于羊毛衣物。

washroom /ˈwɒʃrʊm; ˋwɑʃˌrum/ *n* 名【美】

a toilet in a public building 厕所；洗手间

There are washrooms on each floor of the mall. 商场每层都有洗手间。

wasn't /ˈwɒznt; ˋwɑznt/

the short form of "**was not**" ☆was not 的缩写

I wasn't at home then. 我那时不在家。

***waste¹** /weɪst; west/ *v* 动

wastes, wasting, wasted, wasted

to use too much of something or to use it in the wrong way 浪费

Don't waste food. 不要浪费食物。

***waste²** /weɪst; west/ *n* 名

无复数

1. when you use too much of something or when you use something in the wrong way 浪费
   Listening to his speech was just a waste of time. 听他的演讲简直是浪费时间。
2. things that are left after you have done something 废弃物；废料
   It is a good habit to recycle waste. 将废物回收利用是好习惯。

wastepaper basket /ˌweɪstˈpeɪpə ˌbɑːskɪt; ˋwestˌpepɚ ˌbæskɪt/ *n* 名【英】

美式：***wastebasket***

a small container in which you put paper or other things that you do not want 废纸篓

She threw the letter into the wastepaper basket. 她把信扔进废纸篓里。

***watch¹** /wɒtʃ; wɑtʃ/ *v* 动

watches, watching, watched, watched

1. to look at something for a period of time and pay attention to it 观看；注视
   Watch me do it. Then try to do it yourself. 看我怎么做。然后尝试自己做。
   We watched a film about war. 我们看了一部关于战争的影片。
2. to take care of someone or something for a short time（短时间）照看；照管
   Could you watch my baby while I go to the toilet? 我去洗手间时，你可以帮我照看一下宝宝吗？

watch out 注意；当心

Watch out! There's a car coming. 当心！有辆车正开过来。

***watch²** /wɒtʃ; wɑtʃ/ *n* 名

复数：***watches***

a small clock that you wear on your wrist 表；手表

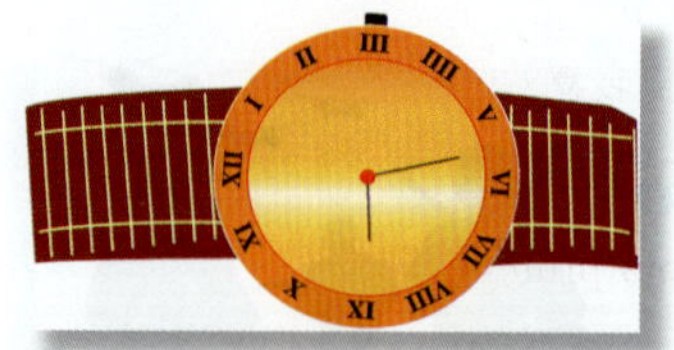

He kept looking at his watch. 他不停地看手表。

***water[1]** /ˈwɔːtə; ˋwɔtɚ/ *n* 名

无复数

the clear liquid that falls as rain and is used for drinking, washing, etc 水

I drink a lot of water every day. 我每天喝很多水。

water[2] /ˈwɔːtə; ˋwɔtɚ/ *v* 动

to pour water on plants, land, etc 给…浇水；灌溉

Samuel is watering the plants in the garden. 塞缪尔在花园里给植物浇水。

waterfall /ˈwɔːtəfɔːl; ˋwɔtɚˏfɔl/ *n* 名

a place where a river or stream falls down from a high place 瀑布

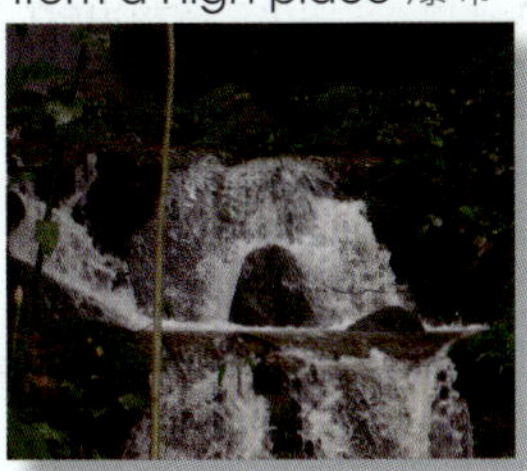

We stood and watched the beautiful waterfall for a long time. 我们站着看美丽的瀑布，看了很久。

***watermelon** /ˈwɔːtəˌmelən; ˋwɔtɚˏmɛlən/ *n* 名

a large, round fruit with thick, green skin and black seeds 西瓜

I like to eat watermelons in summer. 夏天我喜欢吃西瓜。

waterproof /ˈwɔːtəpruːf; ˋwɔtɚˋpruf/ *adj* 形

if something is waterproof, it does not allow water to go through 防水的；不透水的

I wear waterproof boots on rainy days. 雨天我会穿防水靴。

water skiing, waterskiing /ˈwɔːtə ˌskiːɪŋ; ˋwɔtɚ ˏskiɪŋ/ *n* 名

无复数

a sport in which you ski over water while you are pulled by a boat 滑水（运动）

The coach taught us how to do water skiing safely. 教练教我们怎样安全地玩滑水。

***wave[1]** /weɪv; wev/ *n* 名

a line of raised water that moves across the surface of the sea 海浪；波浪

High waves were hitting the shore. 巨浪拍打着海岸。

***wave[2]** /weɪv; wev/ *v* 动

waves, waving, waved, waved

1. to raise your arm and move your hand from side to side 挥手

   Molly is waving to me from the tram. 莫莉在电车上向我挥手。

2. if you wave something, or if it waves, it moves from side to side 挥动；摇晃

   The leaves waved in the wind. 树叶在风中飘扬。

   The guide is waving a flag. 导游挥动着旗子。

wave goodbye 挥手道别

We waved goodbye to each other. 我们互相挥手道别。

wax /wæks; wæks/ *n* 名

无复数

a material that you use to make candles, crayons, etc 蜡

Some wax dripped down on the table. 有些蜡滴在了桌子上。

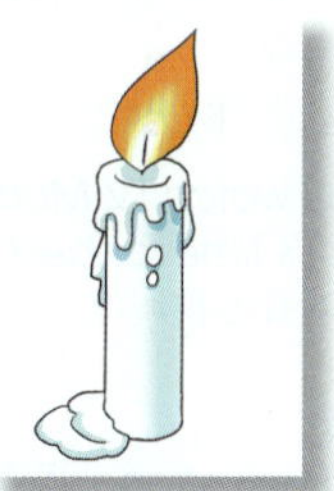

***way** /weɪ; we/ *n* 名

1. a road or path that you take to go to a place（去某处的）路

   He showed us the way to the school. 他给我们指了到学校的路。

2. a particular direction 方向

   Which way is south? 哪边是南？

3. a distance or a length of time 距离；时段

   It's a long way to the airport from here. 这里离机场很远。

4. how you do something 方法；方式

   You can do it in your own way. 你可以按照自己的方法去做。

give way (to something) 给…让道；让…先行

The taxi driver gave way to the ambulance. 出租车司机让救护车先行。

in a ... way 以…方式

She spoke in a friendly way. 她说话的态度很友善。

on the way 在途中；在路上

I posted a letter on the way home. 我在回家的路上寄了封信。

> **Daily conversation 日常会话**
>
> **by the way** 顺便说；附带说
>
> *"Did you go to the library?" "Yes, by the way, I met Fiona there."* "你去过图书馆吗？""是的，顺便说一句，我在那里遇到了菲欧娜。"
>
> **no way!** 不行！
>
> *"Can I watch TV, Mum?" "No way! It's time for bed."* "妈妈，我可以看电视吗？""不行！该睡觉了。"

***we** /wi; wɪ; *strong* 强读 wiː; wi/ *pron* 代

the person who is speaking and one or more other people 我们

We are friends. 我们是朋友。

***weak** /wiːk; wik/ *adj* 形

weaker, weakest

1. not strong 虚弱的；无力的

   He hadn't eaten anything all day and he was feeling weak with hunger. 他整天没吃东西，因饥饿而感到虚弱。

2. not able to support a lot of weight; likely to break 不牢固的；易损坏的

   The legs of this chair are weak. 这张椅子的脚不牢固。

3. not good at something 不擅长的；差的

   I am good at written English but my spoken English is weak. 我擅长英语写作，但英语口语很差。

wealthy /ˈwelθi; ˋwɛlθɪ/ *adj* 形

wealthier, wealthiest

having a lot of money or property 富有的；富裕的

Simon's family is very wealthy. 西蒙的家庭很富裕。

同义 **rich**

反义 **poor**

weapon /ˈwepən; ˋwɛpən/ *n* 名

something that you use to attack someone, for example a gun or knife 武器

The police were searching the house for weapons. 警方在屋里搜寻武器。

***wear** /weə; wɛr/ *v* 动

wears, wearing, wore, worn

to have clothes, shoes or jewellery on your body 穿；戴

He was wearing a new jacket. 他穿着一件新外套。

She wore a pair of earrings. 她戴了一对耳环。

***weather** /ˈweðə; ˋwɛðɚ/ *n* 名

无复数

the temperature and other conditions such as sun, rain and wind 天气

The weather will turn cold tomorrow morning. 明早天气会转冷。

the weather forecast 天气预报

We watched the weather forecast before going out. 我们外出前先看天气预报。

用法 weather 指某地区短时间内的天气状况。

> **Daily conversation 日常会话**
>
> *"What's the weather like today?" "It's sunny."* "今天的天气怎么样？""天气晴朗。"

web /web; wɛb/ *n* 名

1. a net of thin threads made by a spider 蜘蛛网

   I found a spider's web in the corner. 我在墙角发现了蜘蛛网。

2. **the Web**【电脑】the system that connects computers around the world so that you can find information on the Internet 万维网

   He spent two hours on the Web. 他花了两小时上网。

注意 解作万维网时，必须用大写字母 W,并与 the 一起使用。

同义 **the World Wide Web**（见 **World Wide Web**）

webcam /ˈwebkæm; ˋwɛbkæm/ *n* 名

【电脑】a video camera that records something and shows it on a website 网络摄影机；网络摄像头

I chat with friends in Canada using the webcam. 我用网络摄像头和加拿大的朋友聊天。

***website** /ˈwebsaɪt; ˋwɛbsaɪt/ *n* 名

【电脑】a place on the Internet where you can find information about something 网站

For details, please visit our website. 详情请浏览我们的网站。

we'd /wid, wɪd; *strong* 强读 wiːd; wid/

1. the short form of "**we had**" ☆we

W

had 的缩写
We'd already finished the work. 我们已经完成了工作。

2. the short form of "**we would**" ☆we would 的缩写
We'd like sandwiches and orange juice. 我们要三明治和橙汁。

***wedding** /ˈwedɪŋ; ˋwɛdɪŋ/ *n* 名

a ceremony in which a man and a woman get married 婚礼

I was invited to Wendy and John's wedding. 我获邀参加温迪和约翰的婚礼。

***Wednesday** /ˈwenzdeɪ; ˋwɛnzde/ *n* 名

缩写：***Wed./Weds.***

the day between Tuesday and Thursday 星期三

This programme is on Wednesdays. 这个节目逢星期三播出。

注意 开头的字母必须用大写。

***week** /wiːk; wik/ *n* 名

a period of seven days 星期；周

I go swimming once a week. 我每星期去游一次泳。

Daily conversation 日常会话

"What day of the week is it?" "Friday." "今天是星期几？" "星期五。"

weekday /ˈwiːkdeɪ; ˋwikˌde/ *n* 名

any day of the week except Saturday and Sunday 工作日（星期一到星期五的任何一天）

My parents are usually very busy on weekdays. 我的父母工作日通常都很忙。

***weekend** /ˌwiːkˈend; ˋwikˌɛnd/ *n* 名

Saturday and Sunday 周末

I saw a good film last weekend. 我上个周末看了一部很好的电影。

Daily conversation 日常会话

"What are you doing this weekend?" "I'm going to visit the Space Museum." "你这个周末做什么呢？" "我打算去参观太空馆。"

weekly¹ /ˈwiːkli; ˋwiklɪ/ *adj* 形

happening once a week 每周（一次）的

This weekly magazine is $20. 这本周刊要 20 元。

weekly² /ˈwiːkli; ˋwiklɪ/ *adv* 副

once a week 每周（一次）

These workers are paid weekly. 这些工人是每周领工资的。

weep /wiːp; wip/ *v* 动

weeps, weeping, wept, wept

to cry a lot 哭泣

Fanny wept when she lost her doll. 芬妮丢了玩具娃娃，哭了起来。

weigh /weɪ; we/ *v* 动

1. to have a particular weight 重量为…
This parcel weighs two kilograms. 这个包裹重 2 公斤。

2. to measure how heavy someone or something is 称…的重量
I weigh myself every month. 我每个月都称体重。

weight /weɪt; wet/ *n* 名

how heavy someone or something is 重量

The weight of this bag of rice is five kilograms. 这包米的重量是 5 公斤。

lose weight 减轻体重

George is trying to lose some weight for health reasons. 乔治为了健康正努力减肥。

put on weight 增加体重

Mary has put on a lot of weight this year. 今年玛丽的体重增加了不少。

***welcome¹** /ˈwelkəm; ˋwɛlkəm/ *adj* 形

if you are welcome in a place, people are happy to see you there 受欢迎的

You are always welcome here. 这里随时欢迎你。

Daily conversation 日常会话

you're welcome 别客气；不用谢

"Thanks for the present." "You're welcome." "谢谢你的礼物。" "别客气。"

***welcome²** /ˈwelkəm; ˋwɛlkəm/ *v* 动

welcomes, welcoming, welcomed, welcomed

to say hello in a friendly way to someone who has just arrived 迎接；欢迎

Please welcome our guest today, Mr Roberts. 请欢迎我们今天的嘉宾罗伯茨先生。

***welcome³** /ˈwelkəm; ˋwɛlkəm/ *interj* 感叹

a word used to greet someone who has just arrived 欢迎

Welcome to Hong Kong! 欢迎来到香港！

W

we'll /wil, wɪl; *strong* 强读 wi:l; wil/

the short form of "**we will**" or "**we shall**" ☆we will 或 we shall 的缩写

We'll see you tomorrow. 我们明天见。

***well¹** /wel; wɛl/ *adj* 形

better, best

healthy 健康的

I hope you'll get well soon. 我希望你早日康复。

反义 ill, sick, unwell

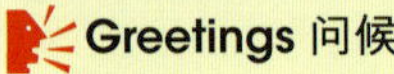

Greetings 问候

"How are you?" "Very well, thank you." "你好吗？""很好，谢谢。"

***well²** /wel; wɛl/ *adv* 副

better, best

1. in a good way 很好地；顺利地
   Henry speaks English very well. 亨利的英语说得很好。

反义 badly

2. completely 完全地；彻底地
   She knows the place quite well. 她很熟悉这个地方。

as well (as someone/something)

（除…之外）也；还

He swept the floor, and washed the clothes as well. 他打扫了地板，还洗了衣服。

There were local people as well as tourists. 有本地人，也有游客。

Daily conversation 日常会话

well done 做得好

"We've won the match!" "Well done!" "我们赢了比赛！""做得好！"

***well³** /wel; wɛl/ *interj* 感叹

a word that you use when you start speaking 嗯；唔（用于停顿后开始说话）

"Who is he?" "Well, let me see, I've met him before." "他是谁？""嗯，让我想想，我以前见过他的。"

well⁴ /wel; wɛl/ *n* 名

a deep hole in the ground from which water or oil is taken 井

The villagers get water from this well. 村民从这口井取水。

well-known /ˌwel ˈnəʊn; ˏwɛl ˋnon/ *adj* 形

known by a lot of people 著名的；闻名的

She is a well-known actress. 她是一位著名的演员。

went /went; wɛnt/ *v* 动

the past tense of **go** ☆go 的过去式

wept /wept; wɛpt/ *v* 动

the past tense and past participle of **weep** ☆weep 的过去式和过去分词

we're /wiə, wɪə; *strong* 强读 wi:ə; wiɚ/

the short form of "**we are**" ☆we are 的缩写

We're going to leave. 我们要走了。

were /wə; wɚ; *strong* 强读 wɜ:; wɝ/ *v* 动

the past tense of **be**, used with "you", "we" and "they" ☆be 的过去式，与 you、we 和 they 一起使用

They were born in Beijing. 他们生于北京。

We were walking home. 我们正在走回家。

weren't /wɜ:nt; wɝnt/

the short form of "**were not**" ☆were not 的缩写

The children weren't at school. 孩子们不在学校里。

west¹ /west; wɛst/ *n* 名

无复数 | 缩写：*W*

the direction in which the sun goes down 西方；西面

The sun sets in the west. 太阳从西方落下。

west² /west; wɛst/ *adj* 形

in the west or facing the west 西方的；西面的；向西的

Andrew lives on the west coast. 安德鲁住在西海岸。

west³ /west; wɛst/ *adv* 副

towards the west 向西

The bedroom faces west. 这个卧室朝西。

western /ˈwestən; ˋwɛstɚn/ *adj* 形

in or from the west of a country or place 西方的；西部的

California is a western state of the United States. 加利福尼亚是美国西部的一个州。

***wet** /wet; wɛt/ *adj* 形

wetter, wettest

1. covered with or full of water or another liquid 湿的；潮湿的
   Be careful! The floor is wet. 小心！地面湿了。

同义 damp

反义 dry¹

2. rainy 多雨的；下雨的

W

It's a wet day. 今天下雨。

wetland /'wetlænd; `wɛtlənd/ *n* 名

an area of land that is covered with shallow water and plants 湿地

A lot of birds live in the wetlands. 许多鸟类在湿地栖息。

we've /wiv, wɪv; *strong* 强读 wi:v; wiv/

the short form of "**we have**" ☆we have 的缩写

We've just had lunch. 我们刚吃了午饭。

whale /weɪl; wel/ *n* 名

a very large animal that looks like a fish and lives in the sea 鲸

It is a good place to watch whales. 那儿是看鲸的好地点。

***what¹** /wɒt; wɑt/ *pron* 代

1. used in questions to ask for information 什么

   What was he doing? 他在做什么？

   What is your name? 你叫什么名字？

2. used to talk about something that is not known 什么（用于谈论不知道的事）

   She asked me what happened. 她问我发生了什么事。

3. the thing which …的东西；…的事情

   I don't believe what he said. 我不相信他说的话。

Daily conversation 日常会话

what about ...? …怎么样？（用于提议）

"What about going to the cinema?" "Very good!" "去看电影怎么样？""好极了！"

what ... for? …有什么用处？

"What's this tool for?" "It's for cutting metal." "这个工具用来干什么？""用来切割金属。"

***what²** /wɒt; wɑt/ *adj* 形

1. used in questions to ask for information 什么（的）

   What time is it? 现在几点了？

   What colour is your car? 你的汽车是什么颜色的？

2. used at the beginning of a sentence to say how you feel 多么；真

   What a good idea! 多好的主意！

***whatever¹** /wɒt'evə; wɑt`ɛvɚ/ *pron* 代

1. anything or everything 任何…的事物

   You can take whatever you want. 你想要什么就拿什么。

2. no matter what 无论什么；不管什么

   Whatever happens, I won't give up. 无论发生什么事，我都不会放弃。

***whatever²** /wɒt'evə; wɑt`ɛvɚ/ *adj* 形

any or every 任何；一切

He answered whatever questions we asked. 我们问什么问题，他都回答了。

wheat /wi:t; wit/ *n* 名

无复数

a plant that produces grains for making flour 小麦

Wheat is the main crop of this country. 小麦是这个国家的主要农作物。

***wheel** /wi:l; wil/ *n* 名

one of the round things under a car, bus, etc that turns when it moves 车轮；轮子

He was pulling a suitcase with wheels. 他拖着一个有轮子的手提箱。

wheelchair /'wi:ltʃeə; `wil͵tʃɛr/ *n* 名

a chair with large wheels used by people who cannot walk 轮椅

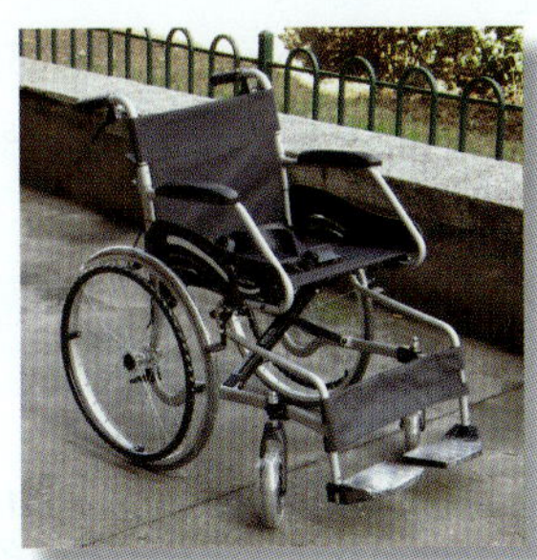

He was in a wheelchair for a month after the accident. 发生事故后，他坐了一个月轮椅。

***when¹** /wen; wɛn/ *adv* 副

at what time 什么时候

When will you come back? 你什么时候会回来?

She asked me when I arrived. 她问我什么时候到达。

Daily conversation 日常会话

"When is your birthday?" "The second of October." "你是哪天生日？""10 月 2 日。"

***when²** /wen; wɛn/ *conj* 连

1. at or during the time that 在…

时；当…时
I lived in the countryside when I was a child. 我小时候住在乡村。
2. after 在…后
I'll tell you when I have finished. 我做完以后会通知你。

whenever /wen'evə; wɛn`ɛvɚ/ *conj* 连
1. at any time 任何时候
You can phone me whenever you like. 你喜欢什么时候给我打电话就打吧。
2. every time 每当；每次
Whenever I see a cat, I want to hug it. 我每次见到猫都想抱一下。

***where**[1] /weə; wɛr/ *adv* 副
in or to which place 在哪里；到哪里
Where are you going? 你要去哪里?
A man asked me where the hospital was. 一个男人问我医院在哪里。

***where**[2] /weə; wɛr/ *conj* 连
used to talk about a particular place 在…的地方
That is the shop where I bought the new dress. 那就是我买新连衣裙的商店。

wherever /weər'evə; wɛr`ɛvɚ/ *conj* 连
1. in any place 在任何地方；无论在哪里
You can take a seat wherever you like. 你想坐哪儿就坐哪儿。
2. in every place 在各个地方；处处
My puppy follows me wherever I go. 我走到哪里小狗都会跟着我。

***whether** /'weðə; `wɛðɚ/ *conj* 连
used when you talk about a choice or something that is not certain 是否(表示选择或对某事不确定)
I'm thinking whether to stay or not. 我在想着要不要留下。
She asked me whether the story was true. 她问我这个故事是否是真的。

***which**[1] /wɪtʃ; wɪtʃ/ *adj* 形
used to ask or talk about one or more people or things when there is a choice 哪一个；哪些
Which book did you read? 你看了哪本书?
I'm not sure which one he wants. 我不确定他想要哪一个。

***which**[2] /wɪtʃ; wɪtʃ/ *pron* 代
1. used to ask or talk about one or more people or things when there is a choice 哪一个；哪些
Which do you like more, football or volleyball? 你比较喜爱足球还是排球？
2. used to say what thing you are talking about, or to give more information about something …的那个；…的那些
I found the pen which I lost two days ago. 我找回了两天前丢失的笔。
We had dinner in the restaurant, which served very good food. 我们在那家餐馆吃了晚饭，那儿的饭菜很好。

***while**[1] /waɪl; waɪl/ *conj* 连
1. during the time that something is happening 在…的时候
The door bell rang while I was having a bath. 我在洗澡的时候，门铃响了。
2. all the time that something is happening 在…的过程中
Don't speak while you are eating. 吃东西时不要说话。

***while**[2] /waɪl; waɪl/ *n* 名
无复数
a while a period of time 一会儿
He came back after a while. 过了一会儿他回来了。

whisker /'wɪskə; `wɪskɚ/ *n* 名
one of the long hairs that grow near the mouth of a cat, mouse, etc (猫、鼠等的)须

The cat has long and white whiskers. 那只猫的胡子又长又白。

whisper /'wɪspə; `wɪspɚ/ *v* 动
to speak very quietly 低声说；耳语

She was whispering, so I couldn't hear what she was saying. 她说话声音很小，所以我听不见她说了什么。

whistle[1] /'wɪsl; `wɪsl̩/ *n* 名
a small thing that you blow to make a high sound 哨子

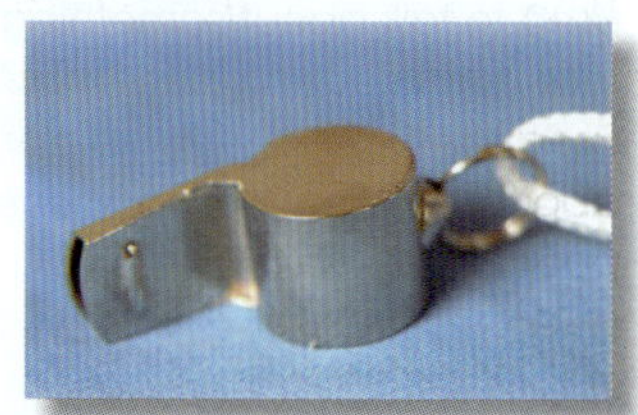

W

The policeman blew his whistle to stop the cars. 警察吹响哨子拦下汽车。

whistle² /ˈwɪsl; ˋwɪsḷ/ *v* 动

whistles, whistling, whistled, whistled

1. to make a high sound by blowing air out through your lips 吹口哨

   He whistled on his way home. 他在回家的路上吹着哨子。

2. to make a high sound by blowing into a whistle 吹哨子

   The referee whistled and the match began. 裁判员吹响哨子，比赛开始了。

***white¹** /wait; waɪt/ *adj* 形

whiter, whitest

having the colour of milk 白色的

Jimmy is wearing a white shirt. 吉米穿着白色的衬衫。

***white²** /wait; waɪt/ *n* 名

1. the colour of milk 白色

   Her favourite colour is white. 她最喜爱的颜色是白色。

2. the part of an egg that surrounds the yolk and turns white when you cook it 蛋白

   This cake contains egg whites, not egg yolks. 这个蛋糕只含蛋白，不含蛋黄。

另见 **yolk**

***who** /hu:; hu/ *pron* 代

1. used in questions to ask about a person or a group of people 谁(用于问句)

   Who is she? 她是谁？

   Who switched off the TV? 谁关掉了电视？

2. used to give more information about a person or a group of people …的人(用于补充有关某人的资料)

   The man who is wearing glasses is Nick. 戴眼镜的那个男人是尼克。

who'd /hu:d; hud/

1. the short form of "**who had**" ☆who had 的缩写

   Ann asked who'd seen her watch. 安问谁见过她的手表。

2. the short form of "**who would**" ☆who would 的缩写

   Chris wanted to know who'd be going to the party. 克里斯想知道谁会去派对。

***whole¹** /həʊl; hol/ *adj* 形

complete; having no parts missing 全部的；整个的

Ben ate the whole cake. 本吃了一整个蛋糕。

注意 发音和 hole 相同。

whole² /həʊl; hol/ *n* 名

1. **the whole of something** the total amount; all of something 全部；整个

   I spent the whole of the morning doing my revision. 我整个早上都在复习。

2. **on the whole** in general 大体上；总的来说

   On the whole, I think the story is interesting. 大体上，我觉得这个故事很有趣。

注意 发音和 hole 相同。

***whom** /hu:m; hum/ *pron* 代

who 谁；…的人

He was one of the people to whom I wrote. 他是我写信联系的人之一。

用法 whom 用在非常正式的场合，在一般情况下常用 who。

who's /hu:z; huz/

1. the short form of "**who is**" ☆who is 的缩写

   Who's that girl? 那个女孩是谁？

2. the short form of "**who has**" ☆who has 的缩写

   Who's seen Colin? 谁见过科林？

***whose** /hu:z; huz/ *pron* 代

1. used in questions to ask who something belongs to 谁的(用于提问)

   Whose book is this? 这本书是谁的？

2. used to show the relationship between someone and something or to give more information about a person or a thing 那个人的…；那一个的…(用于表示某人与某物之间的关系或补充资料)

   This is the man whose money was stolen. 就是这个男人，他的钱被偷了。

***why** /waɪ; waɪ/ *adv* 副

used to ask for or talk about a reason 为什么

Why are you so unhappy? 你为什么那么不高兴?

That is why I came late. 那就是我迟到的原因。

Daily conversation 日常会话

why don't you...? 你怎么不…？(用于建议)

"Why don't you go with us?" "I have to study for a test." "你为什么不跟我们一起去呢？" "我要温习功课准备考试。"

why not...? 为什么不…？

"Why not have a rest?"
"OK, let's have a rest." "为什么不休息一下？" "好的，休息一会吧。"

***wicked** /ˈwɪkɪd; ˋwɪkɪd/ *adj* 形

very bad 极坏的；邪恶的

The wicked wizard turned the prince

into a frog. 邪恶的巫师把王子变成了一只青蛙。

***wide** /waɪd; waɪd/ *adj* 形

wider, widest

1. having a long distance from one side to the other side 宽的；宽阔的

   This river is very wide. 这条河流很宽阔。

同义 **broad**

反义 **narrow**

2. used to say how long the distance of something from one side to the other is 有…宽的

   This swimming pool is 25 metres wide. 这个游泳池宽 25 米。

width /wɪdθ; wɪdθ/ *n* 名

the distance from one side of something to the other 宽度

The width of the bridge is about 2 metres. 这座桥的宽度约为 2 米。

***wife** /waɪf; waɪf/ *n* 名

复数：***wives***

the woman that a man is married to 妻子；太太

Terry met his wife five years ago. 泰瑞 5 年前认识了他的太太。

另见 **husband**

Wi-Fi, wi-fi /ˈwaɪ faɪ; ˋwaɪ faɪ/ *n* 名

无复数

【电脑】a way of connecting computers, mobile phones, etc to each other and to the Internet without using wires 无线区域网路

There is a free Wi-Fi service here. 这里提供免费的无线上网服务。

wig /wɪg; wɪg/ *n* 名

a cover for the head that looks like hair 假发

The actor is wearing a wig. 那个演员戴着假发。

***wild** /waɪld; waɪld/ *adj* 形

wilder, wildest

living or growing in natural conditions, not controlled by people 野生的

Wild flowers grew in the field. 野花在田野生长。

反义 **tame**

wildlife /ˈwaɪldlaɪf; ˋwaɪldˏlaɪf/ *n* 名

无复数

animals and plants that grow in natural conditions 野生生物；野生动植物

The TV programme is about wildlife. 这档电视节目是关于野生生物的。

***will** /wɪl; wɪl/ *v* 动

would

1. used to say that something is going to happen 将会；将要

   Annie will be ten years old next month. 安妮下个月就 10 岁了。

2. used in questions to ask someone to do something 请…好吗（用于请求某人做某事）

   Will you help me, please? 请你帮我个忙，好吗？

willing /ˈwɪlɪŋ; ˋwɪlɪŋ/ *adj* 形

wanting to do something that someone has asked you to 愿意的；乐意的

Mike is always willing to help. 迈克总是乐于助人。

***win** /wɪn; wɪn/ *v* 动

wins, winning, won, won

1. to be the first or best in a competition, game, etc 赢；获胜

   She won the race. 她赢了这场赛跑。

反义 **lose**

2. to get a prize in a competition or game 赢得；获得（奖品）

   Colin won a gold medal in the singing contest. 科林在歌唱比赛中得了一块金牌。

***wind[1]** /wɪnd; wɪnd/ *n* 名

air that moves strongly or quickly 风

The wind is strong today. 今天风很大。

wind[2] /waɪnd; waɪnd/ *v* 动

winds, winding, wound, wound

1. to turn or twist something around another 缠；绕

   He wound a string round his thumb. 他把线缠在大拇指上。

2. （也作：***wind up***）to turn a particular part of a machine several times to make it work 转动；给…上发条

   She winds the clock every day. 她每天都给钟上发条。

***window** /ˈwɪndəʊ; ˋwɪndo/ *n* 名

a space in the wall of a building, car, etc usually covered with glass, which lets light and air in 窗户

Please open the window. 请打开窗户。

W

windsurfing /ˈwɪndˌsɜːfɪŋ; ˋwɪndˌsɝfɪŋ/ *n* 名

无复数

a sport in which you move across water on a board with a sail 帆板运动；滑浪风帆（运动）

Windsurfing is a sport for people of all ages. 滑浪风帆是老少咸宜的运动。

***windy** /ˈwɪndi; ˋwɪndɪ/ *adj* 形

windier, windiest

with a lot of wind 多风的；风大的

It's very windy outside. 外面风很大。

***wine** /waɪn; waɪn/ *n* 名

a drink which is made from grapes and contains alcohol 酒；葡萄酒

Mr White likes to drink wine. 怀特先生喜欢喝葡萄酒。

***wing** /wɪŋ; wɪŋ/ *n* 名

a part of the body of a bird, insect, plane, etc that is used for flying 翼；翅膀

The butterfly has colourful wings. 这只蝴蝶有色彩鲜艳的翅膀。

***winner** /ˈwɪnə; ˋwɪnɚ/ *n* 名

someone who wins a competition or game 获胜者；得奖者

Who's the winner of the dancing contest? 谁是舞蹈比赛的获胜者？

***winter** /ˈwɪntə; ˋwɪntɚ/ *n* 名

the season between autumn and spring 冬天；冬季

It often snows here in winter. 冬天这儿常常下雪。

***wipe** /waɪp; waɪp/ *v* 动

wipes, wiping, wiped, wiped

to clean or dry something by using a cloth or your hand 抹；擦；揩

I wiped my hands on the towel. 我用毛巾擦了擦手。

wipe something from/off something 抹去；擦去

Please wipe the crumbs off the table. 请把桌子上的面包屑擦掉 。

***wire** /waɪə; waɪr/ *n* 名

1. a piece of thin metal thread 金属线；金属丝

   They built a wire fence around the garden. 他们在花园的四周架起铁丝网。

2. a piece of thin metal thread that is used to send and receive electricity 电线

The wire connects the scanner to the computer. 电线把扫描仪连接到电脑。

high wire（马戏团的）高空钢索

A clown is walking on the high wire. 小丑在走高空钢索。

wireless /ˈwaɪələs; ˋwaɪrlɪs/ *adj* 形

not using wires 无线的

The singer is using a wireless microphone. 那个歌手在用无线麦克风。

***wise** /waɪz; waɪz/ *adj* 形

wiser, wisest

able to give good advice and make good decisions 明智的；有智慧的

In the story, the king is kind and wise. 故事里的国王既仁慈又有智慧。

***wish[1]** /wɪʃ; wɪʃ/ *v* 动

wishes, wishing, wished, wished

1. to want to do something 想做；希望做（某事）

   I wish to see him. 我希望见见他。

2. to want something to happen or to be true although you know it cannot happen or will probably not happen 想；希望（不可能或不大可能发生的事情）

   I wish I could fly. 我希望我会飞。

用法 对于不可能或难以实现的愿望，wish 后所接的动词必须用过去式，所以上句不能说成 I wish I can fly。

比较 **hope[1]**

wish someone luck/a happy New Year, etc 祝某人好运/新年快乐等

I wish you a happy Christmas. 我祝你圣诞快乐。

***wish²** /wɪʃ; wɪʃ/ *n* 名

复数：***wishes***

something that you want to have or to happen 愿望

She closed her eyes and made a wish. 她闭上眼睛，许了一个愿。

(with) best wishes 祝福您（用于书信的结尾）

She wrote "Best wishes" before her signature. 她写上"祝福您"然后签名。

witch /wɪtʃ; wɪtʃ/ *n* 名

复数：***witches***

a woman who is believed to have magic powers and who usually uses them to do bad things 女巫；巫婆

The witch turned people into stone. 巫婆把人变成了石头。

另见 **wizard**

***with** /wɪð; wɪð/ *prep* 介

1. having or carrying something 有；带有
   I like storybooks with pictures. 我喜欢有插图的故事书。
   It is raining now. Bring an umbrella with you. 外面正在下雨，记得带雨伞。
2. a word used to say that people or things are in the same place 跟；和；与…一起
   I went shopping with my mother. 我和妈妈一起去购物了。
3. using something 用
   I opened the door with a key. 我用钥匙开了门。
4. because of 由于；因为
   They cheered with joy. 他们开心得欢呼起来。

***within** /wɪð'ɪn; wɪð`ɪn/ *prep* 介

1. before the end of a particular period of time（时间）在…之内；不超过
   I finished my homework within an hour. 我在一个小时内完成了功课。
2. inside a place or not further than a particular distance from someone or something（范围）在…之内；（距离）不到
   The kids can play only within the house. 小孩只可以在屋内玩耍。
   The school is within 200 metres of my home. 学校与我家距离不到 200 米。

***without** /wɪð'aʊt; wɪð`aʊt/ *prep* 介

1. not having, doing or using something 没有；不做；不使用
   My grandmother cannot read without her glasses. 我的祖母没有眼镜就不能阅读。
   He came in without knocking. 他没敲门就进来了。
2. not being with someone 不与…一起
   John's wife went home without him. 约翰的妻子没有和他一起回家。

***witness¹** /'wɪtnəs; `wɪtnɪs/ *n* 名

复数：***witnesses***

someone who sees something happen 证人

Two witnesses saw the car accident. 两个证人目击了车祸。

witness² /'wɪtnəs; `wɪtnɪs/ *v* 动

witnesses, witnessing, witnessed, witnessed

to see something happen 目击

She witnessed the robbery. 她目击了抢劫案。

wizard /'wɪzəd; `wɪzəd/ *n* 名

a man who is believed to have magic powers and who usually uses them to do bad things 巫师

In the story, the wizard has a dragon. 在这故事里，巫师养了一条龙。

另见 **witch**

wok /wɒk; wɑk/ *n* 名

a pan with a round bottom that is used in Chinese cooking（中国烹饪使用的）铁锅

He is cooking with a wok. 他正在用铁锅烧菜。

woke /wəʊk; wok/ *v* 动

the past tense of **wake**☆wake 的过去式

woken /'wəʊkən; `wokən/ *v* 动

the past participle of **wake**☆wake 的过去分词

***wolf** /wʊlf; wʊlf/ *n* 名

复数：***wolves***

a wild animal like a big dog 狼

A wolf is running after a goat. 一只狼在追赶一头山羊。

***woman** /ˈwʊmən; ˋwʊmən/ *n* 名

复数：***women***

an adult female person 女人；妇女

A woman is crossing the road. 一个女人正在过马路。

won /wʌn; wʌn/ *v* 动

the past tense and past participle of **win** ☆win 的过去式和过去分词

注意 发音和 one 相同。

wonder /ˈwʌndə; ˋwʌndɚ/ *v* 动

to think about something and try to guess what is true, what will happen, etc 想知道；想弄明白

I wonder where my ruler is. 我想知道我的尺在哪里。

Daily conversation 日常会话

I wonder if 请问可否（用于礼貌地提出要求）

"I wonder if I could use your telephone." "Sure." "请问可不可以用你的电话？" "可以。"

***wonderful** /ˈwʌndəfl; ˋwʌndɚfəl/ *adj* 形

very good, beautiful or happy 极好的；奇妙的；精彩的

It's a wonderful idea! 这是个极好的主意！

同义 super[1]

won't /wəʊnt; wont/

the short form of "**will not**" ☆will not 的缩写

They won't give up. 他们不会放弃。

wonton /ˌwɒnˈtɒn; ˏwɑːnˋtɑːn/ *n* 名

无复数

a Chinese food wrapped in dough that has meat, seafood, etc inside 馄饨；云吞

I like to eat wonton noodles. 我喜欢吃云吞面。

***wood** /wʊd; wʊd/ *n* 名

1. （无复数）a hard substance from trees, which is used for making things 木；木材
   This house is made of wood. 这幢房子是用木头建的。
2. （也作：***the woods***）a small forest 树林
   Birds are singing in the woods. 鸟儿在林中歌唱。

***wooden** /ˈwʊdn; ˋwʊdn̩/ *adj* 形

made of wood 木制的

I had a wooden horse at home when I was young. 我小时候家里有一只木马。

***wool** /wʊl; wʊl/ *n* 名

无复数

the soft hair of a sheep, or the material made from it 羊毛；毛线

My cat likes to play with a ball of wool. 我的猫喜欢玩毛线球。

***woollen** /ˈwʊlən; ˋwʊlən/ *adj* 形【英】

美式：***woolen***

made of wool 羊毛的

The woollen coat keeps me warm. 这件羊毛大衣让我很暖和 。

用法 只用于名词前。

***word** /wɜːd; wɝd/ *n* 名

a group of letters which has a particular meaning 词；字

What does this word mean? 这个词是什么意思？

Daily conversation 日常会话

have a word with someone 和某人谈一谈

"Can I have a word with you after school?" "Sure." "我可以放学后跟你聊聊吗？" "好的。"

wore /wɔː; wɔr/ *v* 动

the past tense of **wear** ☆wear 的过去式

***work[1]** /wɜːk; wɝk/ *v* 动

1. to have a job, especially to earn money 工作；做事
   Her father works at a bank. 她的父亲在银行工作。
2. to spend time doing something 做事；干活
   He is working on his essay. 他正在写一篇文章。
3. to do something or move correctly 操作；运转
   My computer isn't working. 我的电脑坏了。

work something out 计算；想出；解决

Colin worked out the answer quickly. 科林很快算出了答案。

*work² /wɜːk; wɝk/ *n* 名

无复数

1. a job which you do to earn money 工作
   My brother is looking for work. 我的哥哥正在找工作。
2. something that you have to do in your job or at school 工作；功课
   Our teachers gave us a lot of work to do today. 老师今天给我们布置了很多作业。
3. the place where you do your job 工作地点
   My father is at work. 爸爸在上班。

*workbook /ˈwɜːkbʊk; ˋwɝkbʊk/ *n* 名

a book that contains problems and exercises for students 练习册；作业本

Please pass your workbooks to the front. 请把练习册传到前面。

*worker /ˈwɜːkə; ˋwɝkɚ/ *n* 名

a person who does a job to earn money 工人；职员

Most customers of this shop are office workers. 这家商店的大部分顾客都是办公室职员。

workman /ˈwɜːkmən; ˋwɝkmən/ *n* 名

复数：*workmen*

a man who works with his hands or with machines 工匠；工人

The workmen are digging up the road. 工人正在挖路。

*worksheet /ˈwɜːkʃiːt; ˋwɝkˌʃit/ *n* 名

a piece of paper that contains problems and exercises for students 工作表

I have to do a worksheet about verbs. 我得做一张关于动词的表。

*world /wɜːld; wɝld/ *n* 名

无复数

the world the earth and everything on it 世界

This is the tallest building in the world. 这是世界上最高的大楼。

all over the world 世界各地

People from all over the world visit Beijing. 世界各地的人都到北京观光。

World Wide Web /ˌwɜːld waɪd ˈweb; ˌwɝld waɪd ˋwɛb / *n* 名

无复数 | 缩写：*WWW*

the World Wide Web【电脑】the system that connects computers around the world so that you can find information on the Internet 万维网

I often search for information on the World Wide Web. 我经常在万维网上查资料。

注意 三个 W 字母必须用大写，并与 the 一起使用。

同义 **the Web**（见 **web**）

*worm /wɜːm; wɝm/ *n* 名

a long thin creature with no bones or legs and often lives in the soil 虫子

Look! There are worms in the apple! 看！苹果里有虫子！

worn /wɔːn; wɔrn/ *v* 动

the past participle of **wear** ✰wear 的过去分词

*worried¹ /ˈwʌrid; ˋwɝɪd/ *adj* 形

feeling unhappy because you think something bad may happen 忧虑的；担心的

I'm worried about you. 我担心你。

worried² /ˈwʌrid; ˋwɝɪd/ *v* 动

the past tense and past participle of **worry** ✰worry 的过去式和过去分词

worries /ˈwʌriz; ˋwɝɪz/ *v* 动

a form of **worry** ✰worry 的另一种现在式，与主语 he、she 和 it 一起使用

*worry /ˈwʌri; ˋwɝɪ/ *v* 动

worries, worrying, worried, worried

to feel that something bad may happen 担心；忧虑

Don't worry about the examination. 别担心考试。

worse¹ /wɜːs; wɝs/ *adj* 形（*bad* 的比较级）

1. more bad 更坏的；更糟糕的；更差的
   His school results are getting worse. 他的学习成绩越来越差了。

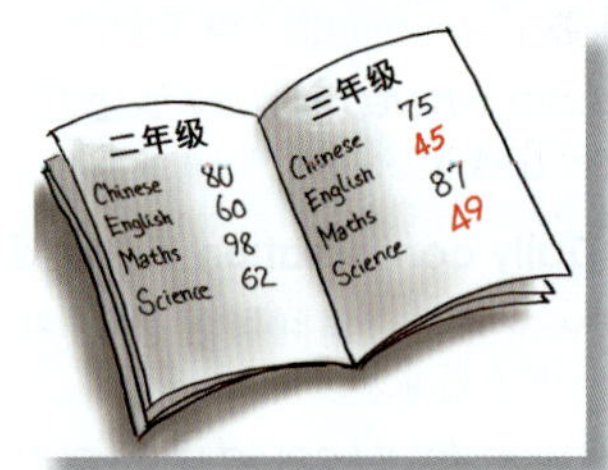

反义 **better¹**

2. more ill 健康转差的
   The medicines seemed to make her worse. 她吃了那些药似乎病得更重了。

反义 **better¹**

worse² /wɜːs; wɝs/ *adv* 副（*badly* 的比较级）

in a worse way 更坏地；更糟糕地；更差地

He sings even worse than I do. 他唱得比我还差。

反义 **better²**

worship /ˈwɜːʃɪp; ˋwɝʃəp/ *v* 动

worships, worshipping, worshipped, worshipped

to pray and show respect to God or a god 崇拜；敬仰

We worship God. 我们信奉上帝。

worst[1] /wɜːst; wɝst/ *adj* 形（*bad* 的最高级）

worse than anything else or anyone else 最坏的；最糟糕的；最差的

This is the worst film I've ever seen. 这是我看过最差劲的电影。

反义 **best[1]**

worst[2] /wɜːst; wɝst/ *adv* 副（*badly* 的最高级）

in a way that is worse than any other 最坏地；最糟糕地；最差地

Tom sings the worst in our class. 在我们班中，汤姆的歌唱得最差。

反义 **best[2]**

worst[3] /wɜːst; wɝst/ *n* 名

无复数

someone or something that is worse than any other 最差的人或物

All these books are bad, but this one is the worst. 所有这些书都很糟糕，但这本是最差的。

反义 **best[3]**

worth /wɜːθ; wɝθ/ *prep* 介

1. having a value in money 值…钱

   This ring is worth $20,000. 这枚戒指价值 2 万元。

2. **be worth (doing) something** used to say that you think something is interesting, useful, etc 值得做

   This book is worth reading. 这本书值得一看。

***would** /wəd; wəd; *strong* 强读 wʊd; wʊd/ *v* 动

1. the past tense of **will** ☆will 的过去式
2. used to talk about a possible situation that you imagine or want to happen 会（用于想象或希望发生的情况）

   If I knew the answer, I would tell you. 如果我知道答案，我会告诉你。

Daily conversation 日常会话

would like 想要

"Would you like a drink?" "Yes, I'd like a cup of tea." "你要喝点什么吗？""好的，我想要一杯茶。"

would rather 宁可；宁愿

"Let's go for a walk after dinner." "I'd rather stay at home". "吃完饭后去散步好吗？""我宁愿留在家里。"

would you ...? 请你…好吗？（礼貌地询问对方时用）

"Would you close the door, please?" "No problem." "请你把门关上好吗？""没问题。"

wouldn't /ˈwʊdnt; ˋwʊdn̩t/

the short form of "**would not**" ☆would not 的缩写

She wouldn't answer my question. 她不愿意回答我的问题。

wound[1] /waʊnd; waʊnd/ *v* 动

the past tense and past participle of **wind[2]** ☆wind[2] 的过去式和过去分词

wound[2] /wuːnd; wund/ *v* 动

to hurt someone 伤害

Five people were wounded in the accident. 事故中有 5 个人受了伤。

wound[3] /wuːnd; wund/ *n* 名

a cut or injury to part of your body 伤口；伤

He had a wound on his arm. 他的手臂受了伤。

***wrap** /ræp; ræp/ *v* 动

wraps, wrapping, wrapped, wrapped

to cover or surround something with paper or other materials 包；裹

I wrapped the present in paper. 我用纸包好礼物。

反义 **unwrap**

wreck /rek; rɛk/ *n* 名

a car, plane, etc that has been badly damaged（车、飞机等的）残骸

The firefighter pulled the driver from the wreck. 消防员把司机从失事的车辆中拉了出来。

***wrinkle** /ˈrɪŋkl; ˋrɪŋkl̩/ *n* 名

a line on the skin that you get when you are old 皱纹

My grandfather has wrinkles on his face. 爷爷的脸上有皱纹。

wrist /rɪst; rɪst/ *n* 名

the part of your body between your arm and your hand 手腕

He hurt his wrist when he fell over. 他跌倒时弄伤了手腕。

***write** /raɪt; raɪt/ *v* 动

writes, writing, wrote, written

1. to make letters or words with a pen, pencil, etc 写字；书写

We learn to read and write at school. 我们在学校学习读书写字。

2. to create a book, poem, etc 写作

   I wrote a poem about the sea. 我写了一首关于海洋的诗。

3. to send someone a letter or an email 写信；写电邮

   He writes to me every month. 他每个月都给我写信。

write something down 记下；写下

I wrote down her telephone number. 我记下了她的电话号码。

***writer** /ˈraɪtə; ˋraɪtɚ/ *n* 名

someone who writes books, stories, etc 作家；作者

He is a writer of children's stories. 他是儿童故事作家。

writing /ˈraɪtɪŋ; ˋraɪtɪŋ/ *n* 名

无复数

1. words that have been written or printed 文字

   The T-shirt has some Chinese writing on it. 这件T恤衫上印有一些中文字。

2. the activity of writing something 写作

   Candy likes writing and she wants to be a writer. 坎蒂喜爱写作，她希望当一个作家。

written¹ /ˈrɪtn; ˋrɪtn̩/ *v* 动

the past participle of **write** ☆ write 的过去分词

written² /ˈrɪtn; ˋrɪtn̩/ *adj* 形

using writing or expressed in writing 书面的

I will take the written exam next week. 我下星期要参加笔试。

***wrong¹** /rɒŋ; rɔŋ/ *adj* 形

1. not right 错误的；不对的

   Your answer is wrong. 你的答案错了。

同义 incorrect

反义 correct¹, right¹

2. not in a proper or good condition 有问题的；有毛病的

   The printer isn't working. There must be something wrong. 打印机没有反应，一定是哪里出问题了。

   You look pale. What's wrong with you? 你看起来很苍白。哪里不舒服？

wrong² /rɒŋ; rɔŋ/ *adv* 副

not in the correct way 错误地；不正确地

He has spelled my name wrong. 他拼错了我的名字。

反义 right³

go wrong 弄错；出问题

I don't know what went wrong. 我不知道什么出了错。

Daily conversation 日常会话

don't get me wrong 请不要误会我

"You don't like my cooking, do you?" "Yes, I like it. Don't get me wrong." "你不喜欢我做的饭菜吗？""请别误会，我很喜欢。"

wrong³ /rɒŋ; rɔŋ/ *n* 名

无复数

something that is bad 坏事

My parents always teach me the difference between right and wrong. 我父母时常教导我分清是非。

反义 right²

wrote /rəʊt; rot/ *v* 动

the past tense of **write** ☆ write 的过去式

WWW

the short form of **World Wide Web** ☆ World Wide Web 的缩写

Xmas /'krɪsməs; `krɪsməs/ *n* 名

无复数

the short form of **Christmas**

☆Christmas 的缩写

注意 Xmas 是非正式的写法。

X-ray /'eks reɪ; `ɛks `re/ *n* 名

a photograph of the inside of your body which is taken with a special light ☆X 光片

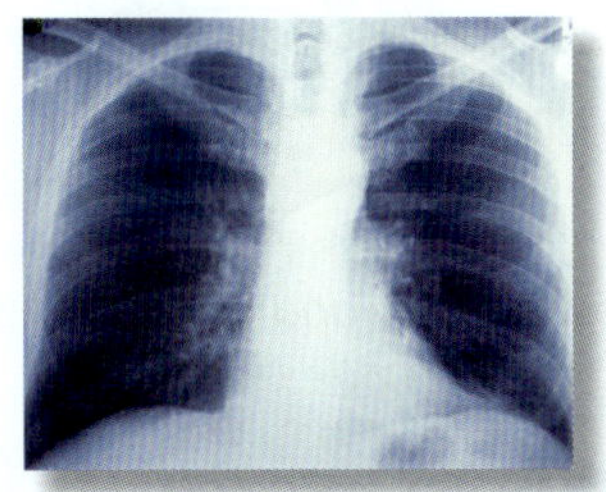

The X-ray showed that his lungs are fine. X 光片显示他的肺部正常。

xylophone /'zaɪləfəʊn; `zaɪlə͵fon/ *n* 名

a musical instrument that you play by hitting metal or wooden parts 木琴

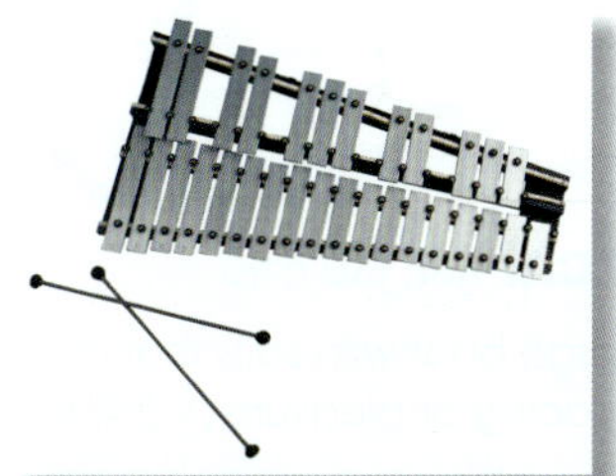

A xylophone produces lovely sounds. 木琴发出美妙的乐声。

yacht /jɒt; jɑt/ *n* 名

a large boat with sails that is used for racing or pleasure 大型帆船；游艇

They went sailing on a yacht. 他们坐游艇出海。

yam /jæm; jæm/ *n* 名

1. the long thick root of a plant that is eaten as a vegetable 薯蓣；山药
   The cook added some yams into the soup. 厨师在汤里放了一些山药。
2. 【美】a sweet potato 番薯；山芋

The roast yam tasted good. 烤番薯很美味。

***yawn** /jɔːn; jɔn/ *v* 动

to open your mouth wide and take a lot of air into the lungs because you are tired or bored 打呵欠

She felt sleepy and yawned. 她困了，打了个呵欠。

***yeah** /jeə; jɛə/ *adv* 副

yes 是；对

"Are you coming with us?" "Yeah." "你跟我们一起来吗？" "是呀。"

用法 用于口语或非正式的场合。

***year** /jɪə; jɪr/ *n* 名

1. a period of time that is equal to 12 months 年；岁
   Grandpa is 70 years old. 祖父 70 岁了。
2. a period of time from 1 January to 31 December 历年
   I went to Switzerland last year. 我去年去了瑞士。

all year round 全年

The North Pole is cold all year round. 北极全年寒冷。

yearly[1] /ˈjɪəli; ˋjɪrlɪ/ *adj* 形

happening every year or once a year 每年的；一年一次的

The school holds a yearly concert in July. 学校在每年 7 月都会举办音乐会。

yearly[2] /ˈjɪəli; ˋjɪrlɪ/ *adv* 副

once a year 每年

We have a picnic twice yearly. 我们每年去野餐两次。

***yell** /jel; jɛl/ *v* 动

to shout or say something very loudly 叫喊

He yelled for help. 他大声呼救。

yell at someone 对某人大喊大叫

Don't yell at your parents! 别对父母大喊大叫！

***yellow[1]** /ˈjeləʊ; ˋjɛlo/ *adj* 形

having the colour of a lemon or the middle part of an egg 黄色的

Look at those yellow flowers! 看那些黄色的花！

***yellow[2]** /ˈjeləʊ; ˋjɛlo/ *n* 名

the colour of a lemon or the middle part of an egg 黄色

"Do you like yellow?" "Yes, I do." "你喜欢黄色吗？" "喜欢。"

***yes** /jes; jɛs/ *adv* 副

used as an answer to say that something is true or that you agree with something 对；是；好的

"Did he steal your handbag?" "Yes, he did." "是不是他偷了你的手提包？" "是的。"

反义 no[1]

***yesterday[1]** /ˈjestədi; ˋjɛstədɪ/ *adv* 副

on or during the day before today 昨天

It rained a lot yesterday. 昨天下了很多雨。

***yesterday²** /ˈjestədi; ˋjɛstɚdɪ/ *n* 名

无复数

the day before today 昨天

Yesterday was Henry's birthday. 昨天是亨利的生日。

***yet** /jet; jɛt/ *adv* 副

used in questions and negative sentences when asking or saying if something has happened（用于疑问句和否定句）已经；还不；还没

Has the teacher come yet? 老师来了没有?

She hasn't phoned me yet. 她还没有打电话给我。

Daily conversation 日常会话

not yet 还没有（用于否定句）

"Are they here yet?" "No, not yet." "他们已经来了吗？""还没有。"

yoga /ˈjəʊgə; ˋjogə/ *n* 名

无复数

exercises that help you relax your body and mind 瑜伽

Susan goes to a yoga class every Sunday. 苏珊每个星期天都上瑜伽课。

***yoghurt** /ˈjɒgət; ˋjogɚt/ *n* 名

也作：***yogurt***

a thick liquid food that is made from milk 酸奶；奶酪

Sally likes to eat yoghurt. 莎莉喜欢吃酸奶。

yolk /jəʊk; jok/ *n* 名

the yellow part in the middle of an egg 蛋黄

We need two egg yolks to make the dessert. 我们做餐后甜点要用两个蛋黄。

另见 white²

***you** /jə; jʊ; *strong* 强读 juː; ju/ *pron* 代

the person or people someone is speaking or writing to 你（们）

You are my best friend. 你是我最好的朋友。

you'd /jəd; jʊd; *strong* 强读 juːd; jud/

1. the short form of "**you had**" ☆you had 的缩写

   You'd left when I got there. 我到那儿的时候，你已经走了。

2. the short form of "**you would**" ☆you would 的缩写

   I thought you'd still be there. 我以为你还在那儿。

you'll /jəl; jʊl; *strong* 强读 juːl; jul/

the short form of "**you will**" ☆you will 的缩写

You'll be late if you don't go now. 你现在还不走就会迟到了。

***young** /jʌŋ; jʌŋ/ *adj* 形

younger, youngest

not having lived or existed for a long time 年轻的；年幼的

Young children like to play this game. 小孩都爱玩这个游戏。

反义 old

***your** /jə; jɚ; *strong* 强读 jɔː; jur/ *adj* 形

belonging to you 你（们）的

I like your new jacket. 我喜欢你的新外套。

you're /jə; jɚ; *strong* 强读 jɔː; jur/

the short form of "**you are**" ☆you are 的缩写

You're right! 你是对的！

***yours** /jɔːz; jurz/ *pron* 代

1. used to refer to something that belongs to the person or people someone is speaking or writing to 你的（东西）；你们的（东西）

   This is my book, not yours. 这是我的书，不是你的。

2. **Yours** used at the end of a letter（用于书信的结尾）你的

   Lily wrote "Yours" before she signed the letter. 莉莉在签名前写上 Yours。

用法 Yours 用于非正式书信的结尾。除了 Yours 之外，还可以用 Best wishes（祝好）。

***yourself** /jɔːˈself; jurˋsɛlf/ *pron* 代

复数：***yourselves***

the same person that someone is speaking or writing to 你自己

Did you do all the work yourself? 你自己干了所有的活吗?

youth /juːθ; juθ/ *n* 名

无复数

the period of time when someone is young 年轻时期；青年时期

He was a famous singer in his youth. 他年轻时是一个出名的歌手。

you've /juːv; juv/

the short form of "**you have**" ✫ you have 的缩写

You've grown taller than me. 你长得比我高了。

yo-yo /ˈjəʊ jəʊ; ˋjo jo/

n 名

a toy that goes up and down a string that you hold around your finger 溜溜球

We are playing with our yo-yos. 我们在玩溜溜球。

yummy /ˈjʌmi; ˋjʌmɪ/ *adj* 形

tasting very good 好吃的；美味的

The fried chicken is yummy! 炸鸡真好吃！

用法 常用于口语中。

***zebra** /ˈziːbrə; ˋzibrə/ *n* 名

a wild animal that looks like a horse but has black and white lines on its body 斑马

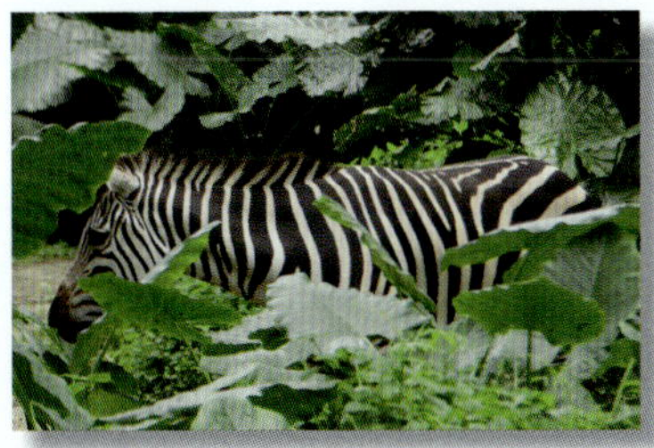

I saw zebras when I went to Africa last year. 我去年在非洲旅行时见到了斑马。

***zebra crossing** /ˌziːbrə ˈkrɒsɪŋ; ˏzibrə ˋkrɔsɪŋ/ *n* 名

a place on a road painted with black and white lines where people can cross the road safely 斑马线

We crossed the road at the zebra crossing. 我们从斑马线上过马路。

***zero** /ˈzɪərəʊ; ˋzɪro/ *num* 数

复数 : ***zeros/zeroes***

the number 0 零

He got zero in the test. 他在测验中得了零分。

zigzag /ˈzɪgzæg; ˋzɪgzæg/ *n* 名

a line that looks like a number of Z's joined together ☆Z 字形；之字形

The kids are running in zigzags in the playground. 小孩子在操场里之字形跑。

zip¹ /zɪp; zɪp/ *n* 名【英】

美式 : ***zipper***

a thing with two rows of small plastic or metal pieces that can be joined together to fasten clothes, bags, etc 拉链

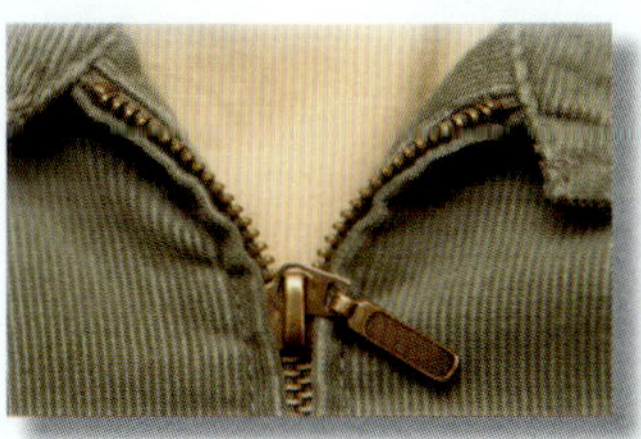

The zip was stuck and he couldn't open the bag. 拉链卡住了，他打不开袋子。

do up/undo the zip 拉上/拉开拉链

It is cold outside. Do up the zip of your jacket. 外面很冷，拉上外套的拉链吧。

zip² /zɪp; zɪp/ *v* 动

zips, zipping, zipped, zipped

zip up to fasten something with a zip 拉上拉链

Can you help me to zip up my bag, please? 你可以帮我拉上袋子的拉链吗?

zip file /ˈzɪp faɪl; ˋzɪp faɪl/ *n* 名

【电脑】a computer document that has been made smaller so that you can store and move it easily 压缩文件

I sent the zip file to Vivian through email. 我用电子邮件给薇薇安发了压缩文件。

***zoo** /zuː; zu/ *n* 名

a place where you can see different kinds of animals 动物园

We went to the zoo yesterday. 我们昨天去了动物园。

English alphabet 英文字母表

正楷

Aa Bb Cc Dd Ee Ff

Gg Hh Ii Jj Kk Ll Mm Nn Oo

Pp Qq Rr Ss Tt Uu Vv Ww

Xx Yy Zz

草书

Aa Bb Cc Dd Ee

Ff Gg Hh Ii Jj Kk Ll Mm

Nn Oo Pp Qq Rr Ss Tt Uu

Vv Ww Xx Yy Zz

Dates 日期

Days of the week 星期

全拼	缩写	中文
Sunday	Sun.	星期日
Monday	Mon.	星期一
Tuesday	Tues./Tue.	星期二
Wednesday	Wed./Weds.	星期三
Thursday	Thurs./Thur.	星期四
Friday	Fri.	星期五
Saturday	Sat.	星期六

Months of the year 月份

全拼	缩写	中文	全拼	缩写	中文
January	Jan.	一月	July	Jul.	七月
February	Feb.	二月	August	Aug.	八月
March	Mar.	三月	September	Sept.	九月
April	Apr.	四月	October	Oct.	十月
May	May	五月	November	Nov.	十一月
June	Jun.	六月	December	Dec.	十二月

月份有单数和复数形式，而写日期时必须用单数形式。计算有多少个二月（或其他月份），才用复数形式，如 The past two Februaries were very cold（前两年的二月很寒冷）。

Writing and saying the date 日期的写法和读法

<table>
<tr><th></th><th>英式英语</th><th>美式英语</th></tr>
<tr><td>日期的写法</td><td>一般的次序是日月年
1 August 2012 或 1st August 2012
1 Aug. 2012 或 1st Aug. 2012
1-8-2012 或 1-8-12
1/8/2012
1/8/12</td><td>一般的次序是月日年
August 1, 2012 或 August 1st, 2012
Aug. 1, 2012 或 Aug. 1st, 2012
8-1-2012 或 8-1-12
8/1/2012
8/1/12</td></tr>
<tr><td>日、月的读法</td><td>先说日，后说月，例如 2 月 1 日读作 the first of February。</td><td>先说月，后说日，例如 2 月 1 日读作 February the first。</td></tr>
<tr><td>年份的读法</td><td colspan="2">英语中一般把年份分成两半来说，英式英语和美式英语没有差别，例如：
1997 年分成 19 和 97 两半，读作 nineteen ninety-seven
2012 年分成 20 和 12 两半，读作 twenty twelve
2016 年分成 20 和 16 两半，读作 twenty sixteen
2000 年则直接说成 the year two thousand。</td></tr>
</table>

Time 时间

Units of time 时间单位

1 minute 分钟	= 60 seconds
1 hour 小时	= 60 minutes
1 day 日	= 24 hours
1 week 星期	= 7 days

1 fortnight 两周	= 2 weeks
1 month 月	= 28 to 31 days
1 year 年	= 12 months
1 century 世纪	= 100 years

Times of the day 一天里的时间

morning	上午；早上
noon/midday	中午；正午
afternoon	下午
evening	傍晚；晚上（日落至睡觉前的一段时间）
night	夜晚；晚间（日落后至次日日出前的一段时间）
midnight	午夜

Saying the time 时间的读法

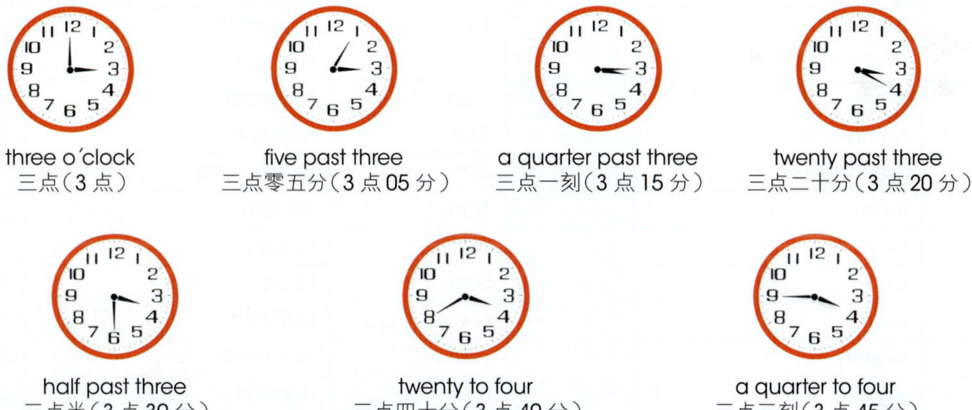

three o'clock
三点（3 点）

five past three
三点零五分（3 点 05 分）

a quarter past three
三点一刻（3 点 15 分）

twenty past three
三点二十分（3 点 20 分）

half past three
三点半（3 点 30 分）

twenty to four
三点四十分（3 点 40 分）

a quarter to four
三点三刻（3 点 45 分）

表示上午的时间：使用 **a.m.** 或 **in the morning**
8 a.m./8 o'clock in the morning 上午 8 点
9:20 a.m./twenty past nine in the morning 上午 9 点 20 分

表示下午的时间：使用 **p.m.** 或 **in the afternoon/in the evening/at night**
2 p.m./2 o'clock in the afternoon 下午 2 点
6:30 p.m./half past six in the evening 下午 6 点 30 分
10:45 p.m./a quarter to eleven at night 晚上 10 点 45 分

Numbers 数字

基数			序数		
0	zero	零			
1	one	一	1st	first	第一
2	two	二	2nd	second	第二
3	three	三	3rd	third	第三
4	four	四	4th	fourth	第四
5	five	五	5th	fifth	第五
6	six	六	6th	sixth	第六
7	seven	七	7th	seventh	第七
8	eight	八	8th	eighth	第八
9	nine	九	9th	ninth	第九
10	ten	十	10th	tenth	第十
11	eleven	十一	11th	eleventh	第十一
12	twelve	十二	12th	twelfth	第十二
13	thirteen	十三	13th	thirteenth	第十三
14	fourteen	十四	14th	fourteenth	第十四
15	fifteen	十五	15th	fifteenth	第十五
16	sixteen	十六	16th	sixteenth	第十六
17	seventeen	十七	17th	seventeenth	第十七
18	eighteen	十八	18th	eighteenth	第十八
19	nineteen	十九	19th	nineteenth	第十九
20	twenty	二十	20th	twentieth	第二十
21	twenty-one	二十一	21st	twenty-first	第二十一
29	twenty-nine	二十九	29th	twenty-ninth	第二十九
30	thirty	三十	30th	thirtieth	第三十
40	forty	四十	40th	fortieth	第四十
50	fifty	五十	50th	fiftieth	第五十
60	sixty	六十	60th	sixtieth	第六十
70	seventy	七十	70th	seventieth	第七十
80	eighty	八十	80th	eightieth	第八十
90	ninety	九十	90th	ninetieth	第九十
100	one hundred	一百	100th	one hundredth	第一百
101	one hundred and one	一百零一	101st	one hundred and first	第一百零一
500	five hundred	五百	500th	five hundredth	第五百
1000	one thousand	一千	1000th	one thousandth	第一千
10,000	ten thousand	一万	10,000th	ten thousandth	第一万
100,000	one hundred thousand	十万	100,000th	one hundred thousandth	第十万
1,000,000	one million	一百万	1,000,000th	one millionth	第一百万

Fractions 分数

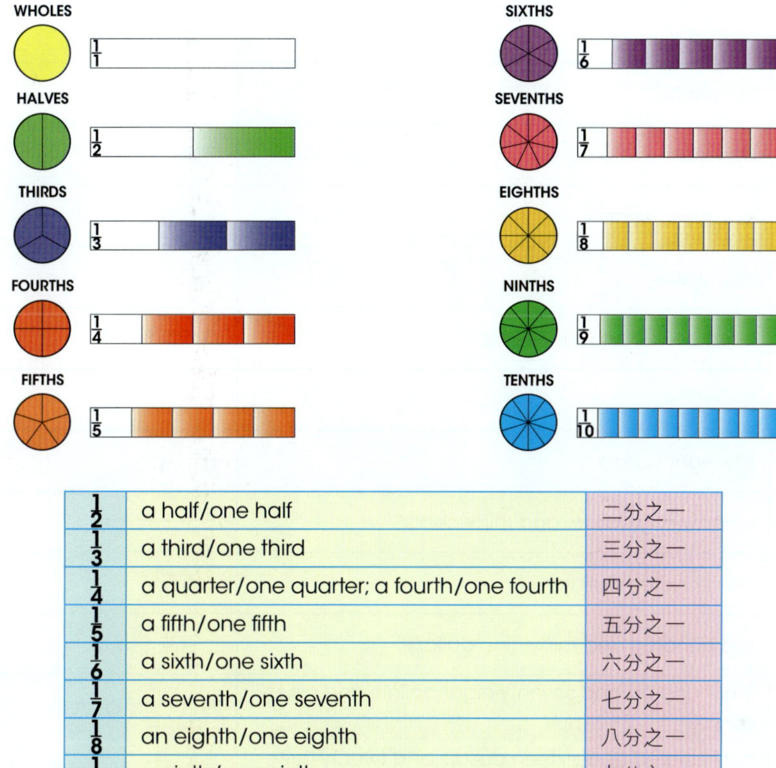

$\frac{1}{2}$	a half/one half	二分之一
$\frac{1}{3}$	a third/one third	三分之一
$\frac{1}{4}$	a quarter/one quarter; a fourth/one fourth	四分之一
$\frac{1}{5}$	a fifth/one fifth	五分之一
$\frac{1}{6}$	a sixth/one sixth	六分之一
$\frac{1}{7}$	a seventh/one seventh	七分之一
$\frac{1}{8}$	an eighth/one eighth	八分之一
$\frac{1}{9}$	a ninth/one ninth	九分之一
$\frac{1}{10}$	a tenth/one tenth	十分之一

$\frac{3}{4}$	three quarters/three fourths	四分之三
$6\frac{1}{2}$	six and a half	六又二分之一
$12\frac{3}{5}$	twelve and three fifths	十二又五分之三

Decimals 小数

0.1	(zero) point one	零点一
0.15	(zero) point one five	零点一五
0.165	(zero) point one six five	零点一六五
0.2	(zero) point two	零点二
0.5	(zero) point five	零点五
5.4	five point four	五点四
12.32	twelve point three two	十二点三二
26.871	twenty-six point eight seven one	二十六点八七一

Talking about money 金钱的表达方法

$0.01	one cent	一分
$0.1	ten cents	一角
$0.5	fifty cents	五角
$0.75	seventy-five cents	七角五分
$1	one dollar	一元
$8.6	eight dollars and sixty cents	八元六角
$10	ten dollars	十元
$58	fifty-eight dollars	五十八元
$71.3	seventy-one dollars and thirty cents	七十一元三角
$100	one hundred dollars	一百元
$239	two hundred and thirty-nine dollars	二百三十九元
$478.9	four hundred and seventy-eight dollars and ninety cents	四百七十八元九角
$516.23	five hundred and sixteen dollars and twenty-three cents	五百一十六元二角三分
$1000	one thousand dollars	一千元
$3642	three thousand six hundred and forty-two dollars	三千六百四十二元
$6275.8	six thousand two hundred and seventy-five dollars and eighty cents	六千二百七十五元八角
$10,000	ten thousand dollars	一万元
$30,000	thirty thousand dollars	三万元
$150,000	one hundred and fifty thousand dollars	十五万元
$876,543.21	eight hundred seventy-six thousand five hundred and forty-three dollars and twenty-one cents	八十七万六千五百四十三元二角一分
$1,000,000	one million dollars	一百万元
$4,000,000	four million dollars	四百万元
$60,000,000	sixty million dollars	六千万元

Weights and measures 度量单位

Length 长度
公制
1 cm (centimetre) 厘米 = **10 mm** (millimetres) 毫米
1 m (metre) 米 = **100 cm** (centimetres) 厘米
1 km (kilometre) 公里; 千米 = **1000 m** (metres) 米

英制
1 foot 英尺 = **12 inches** 英寸
1 yard 码 = **3 feet** 英尺
1 mile 英里 = **1760 yards** 码

Weight 重量
公制
1 kg (kilogram) 公斤; 千克 = **1000 g** (grams) 克

英制
1 lb (pound) 磅 = **16 oz** (ounces) 盎司

Capacity 容量
1 l (litre) 升 = **1000 ml** (millilitres) 毫升

Temperature 温度
°C (Celsius) 摄氏度
°F (Fahrenheit) 华氏度
冰点是 0°C 或 32°F。水的沸点是 100°C 或 212°F。

Directions 方向

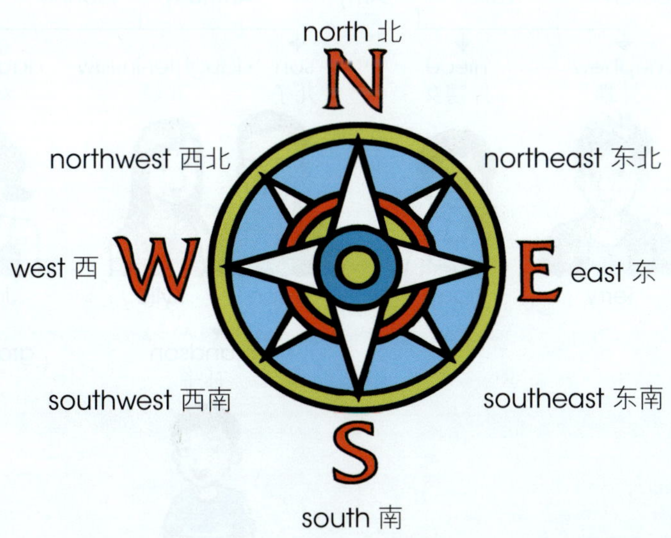

Family tree 家庭关系

All the people shown here are **Anthony**'s relatives.
以下这些人是安东尼的亲戚。

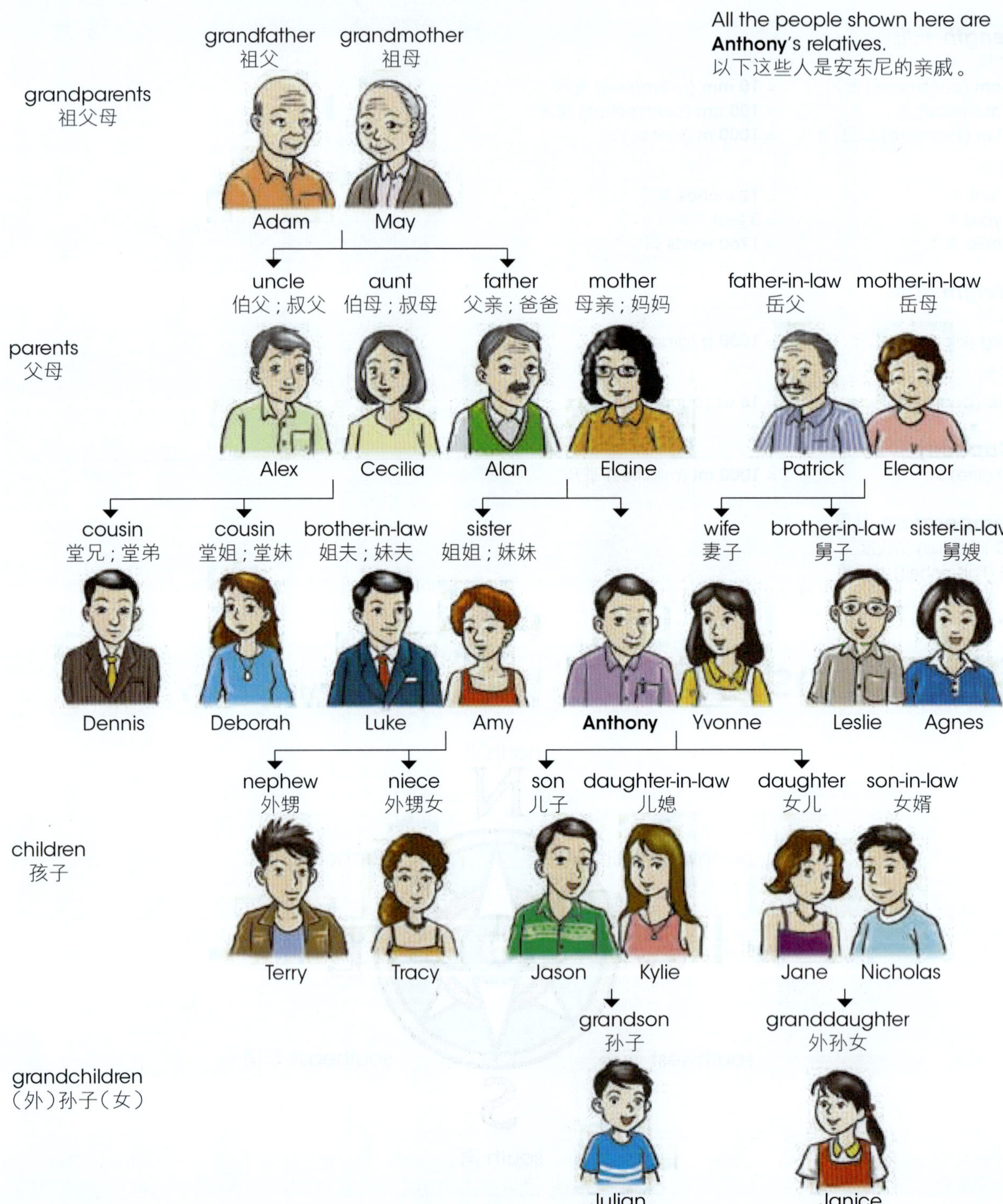

Parts of the body 身体部位

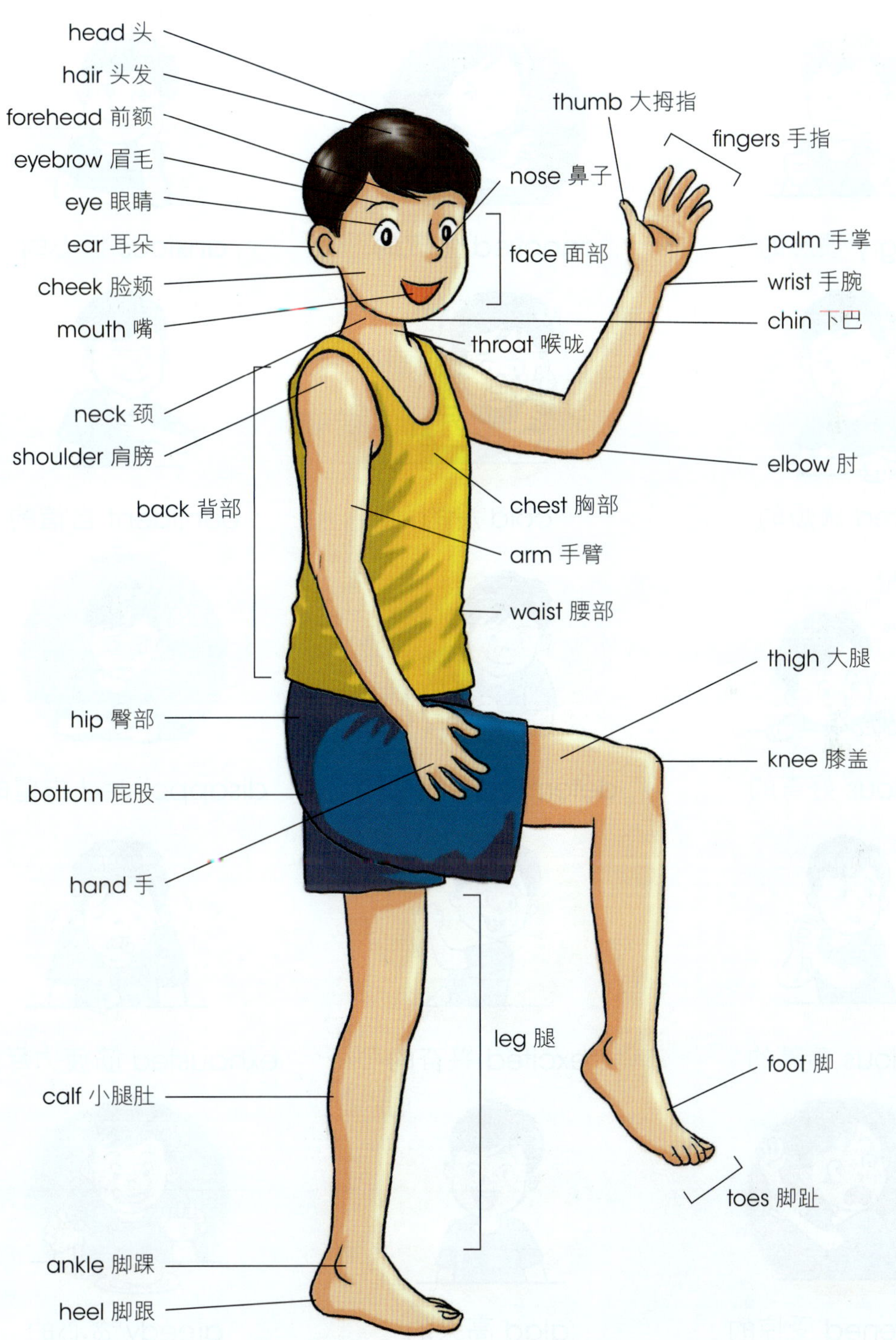

Adjectives of feelings 表达感觉的形容词

angry 愤怒的

annoyed 生气的

anxious 担心的

bored 厌烦的

cold 冷的

confident 自信的

curious 好奇的

determined 坚决的

disappointed 失望的

envious 羡慕的

excited 兴奋的

exhausted 筋疲力尽的

frightened 受惊的

glad 高兴的

greedy 贪心的

guilty 内疚的

happy 快乐的

hot 热的

interested 感兴趣的

jealous 嫉妒的

lonely 孤独的

miserable 悲惨的

painful 疼痛的

proud 自豪的

sad 伤心的

shocked 感到震惊的

shy 害羞的

sleepy 困倦的

surprised 惊奇的

worried 忧虑的

Verbs of movement 动作动词

Inside a flat 住所里：living room 客厅

Inside a flat 住所里：bedroom 卧室

Inside a flat 住所里：bathroom 浴室

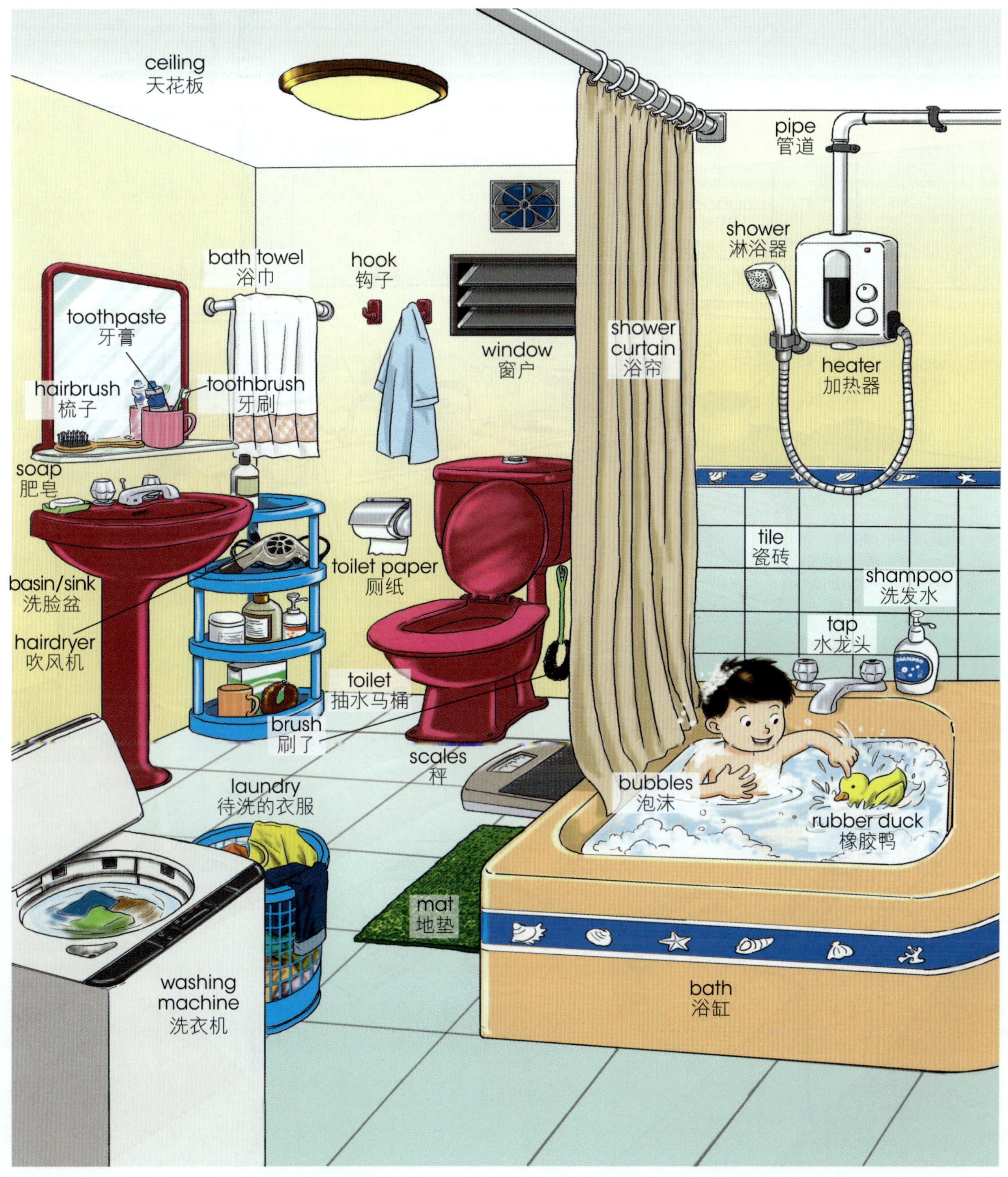

Inside a flat 住所里：kitchen 厨房

In a classroom 教室里

The computer world 电脑世界

Countries and people 国家和民族

Afghanistan 阿富汗
Argentina 阿根廷
Australia 澳大利亚，澳洲
Austria 奥地利
Bangladesh 孟加拉国
Belgium 比利时
Brazil 巴西
Brunei 文莱
Bulgaria 保加利亚
Cambodia 柬埔寨
Canada 加拿大
Chile 智利
China 中国
Colombia 哥伦比亚
Croatia 克罗地亚
Cuba 古巴
Czech Republic 捷克共和国
Denmark 丹麦
Egypt 埃及
Ethiopia 埃塞俄比亚
Finland 芬兰
France 法国
Germany 德国
Greece 希腊
Hungary 匈牙利
Iceland 冰岛
India 印度
Indonesia 印度尼西亚，印尼
Iran 伊朗
Iraq 伊拉克
Irish Republic 爱尔兰共和国
Israel 以色列
Italy 意大利
Jamaica 牙买加
Japan 日本
Kenya 肯尼亚
Korea, North 朝鲜
Korea, South 韩国
Kuwait 科威特
Libya 利比亚
Luxembourg（也作 Luxemburg）卢森堡
Malaysia 马来西亚
Maldives 马尔代夫
Mexico 墨西哥
Mongolia 蒙古
Morocco 摩洛哥
Myanmar 缅甸（旧称 Burma）
Nepal 尼泊尔
Netherlands, the 荷兰（也作 Holland）

Afghan 阿富汗人
Argentinian 阿根廷人
Australian 澳洲人
Austrian 奥地利人
Bangladeshi 孟加拉人
Belgian 比利时人
Brazilian 巴西人
Bruneian 文莱人
Bulgarian 保加利亚人
Cambodian 柬埔寨人
Canadian 加拿大人
Chilean 智利人
Chinese 中国人
Colombian 哥伦比亚人
Croatian 克罗地亚人
Cuban 古巴人
Czech 捷克人
Dane 丹麦人
Egyptian 埃及人
Ethiopian 埃塞俄比亚人
Finn 芬兰人
French 法国人
German 德国人
Greek 希腊人
Hungarian 匈牙利人
Icelander 冰岛人
Indian 印度人
Indonesian 印尼人
Iranian 伊朗人
Iraqi 伊拉克人
Irish 爱尔兰人
Israeli 以色列人
Italian 意大利人
Jamaican 牙买加人
Japanese 日本人
Kenyan 肯尼亚人
North Korean 朝鲜人
South Korean 韩国人
Kuwaiti 科威特人
Libyan 利比亚人
Luxembourger 卢森堡人
Malaysian 马来西亚人
Maldivian 马尔代夫人
Mexican 墨西哥人
Mongolian/Mongol 蒙古人
Moroccan 摩洛哥人
Burmese 缅甸人
Nepalese 尼泊尔人
Dutch 荷兰人

New Zealand 新西兰，纽西兰
Nigeria 尼日利亚
Norway 挪威
Pakistan 巴基斯坦
Peru 秘鲁
Philippines, the 菲律宾
Poland 波兰
Portugal 葡萄牙
Romania 罗马尼亚
Russia 俄罗斯
Saudi Arabia 沙特阿拉伯
Serbia 塞尔维亚
Singapore 新加坡
South Africa 南非
Spain 西班牙
Sri Lanka 斯里兰卡
Sudan 苏丹
Sweden 瑞典
Switzerland 瑞士
Thailand 泰国
Turkey 土耳其
Ukraine 乌克兰
United Kingdom, the 联合王国，英国
United States, the 美利坚合众国，美国
Vietnam 越南

New Zealander 新西兰人，纽西兰人
Nigerian 尼日利亚人
Norwegian 挪威人
Pakistani 巴基斯坦人
Peruvian 秘鲁人
Filipino 菲律宾人
Pole 波兰人
Portuguese 葡萄牙人
Romanian 罗马尼亚人
Russian 俄罗斯人
Saudi (Arabian) 沙特阿拉伯人
Serbian/Serb 塞尔维亚人
Singaporean 新加坡人
South African 南非人
Spaniard 西班牙人
Sri Lankan 斯里兰卡人
Sudanese 苏丹人
Swede 瑞典人
Swiss 瑞士人
Thai 泰国人
Turk 土耳其人
Ukrainian 乌克兰人
British 英国人
American 美国人
Vietnamese 越南人

Cities of the world 世界城市

Amsterdam 阿姆斯特丹
Athens 雅典
Auckland 奥克兰
Baghdad 巴格达
Bangkok 曼谷
Beijing 北京
Berlin 柏林
Boston 波士顿
Brisbane 布里斯本
Cairo 开罗
Chicago 芝加哥
Dublin 都柏林
Frankfurt 法兰克福
Geneva 日内瓦
Guangzhou 广州
Hanoi 河内

Ho Chi Minh City 胡志明市
Hong Kong 香港
Jakarta 雅加达
Jerusalem 耶路撒冷
Johannesburg 约翰内斯堡
Kuala Lumpur 吉隆坡
Lisbon 里斯本
London 伦敦
Los Angeles 洛杉矶
Macau（也作 Macao）澳门
Madrid 马德里
Manila 马尼拉
Melbourne 墨尔本
Montreal 蒙特利尔
Moscow 莫斯科
Mumbai 孟买

New Delhi 新德里
New York 纽约
Paris 巴黎
Rome 罗马
San Francisco 旧金山
Seattle 西雅图
Seoul 首尔
Shanghai 上海
Sydney 悉尼
Taipei 台北
Tokyo 东京
Toronto 多伦多
Vancouver 温哥华
Vienna 维也纳
Washington 华盛顿
Zurich 苏黎世

Punctuation 标点符号

apostrophe （'）撇号

- used to show that one or more letters have been left out of a word 表示某些字母的省略 *(don't = do not)*
- used with "s" to show that a thing belongs to someone 与 s 连用表示所有格 *(Paul's pencil/the students' books)*

brackets （ ）括号

used to separate extra information that may be helpful but not really necessary 用以分隔句中的附加信息 *(One of the winners (Peter) is my brother.)*

colon （:）冒号

used before giving examples 用以引出下文各项 *(I like all kinds of sports: swimming, table tennis, basketball and volleyball.)*

comma （,）逗号

used to show a short stop in a sentence 用在句子中表示稍作停顿 *(My sister likes reading, but she reads storybooks only.)*

dash （—）破折号

used to give extra information 用于补充说明 *(For her birthday, Lily got a computer — a modern tablet computer.)*

exclamation mark （!）感叹号

used when you are excited, angry or surprised about something 用于表示兴奋、愤怒或惊讶等强烈感情 *(That's great!/ "I'm very hungry!" she cried.)*

full stop （.）句号

- used to end a sentence 用于表示句子完结 *(I like dancing.)*
- used in abbreviations 用于缩写中 *(Dec./p.m.)*

hyphen （-）连字符

used to join two or more words to form a new word 用以把两个或以上单词组合成另一个词 *(thirty-five/ merry-go-round)*

question mark （?）问号

used at the end of a question 用于问句末尾 *(Where's my school bag?)*

quotation marks/inverted commas （" " 或 ' '）引号

- used to show what someone said or wrote 用以标示直接引语 *("Why are you crying?" she asked.)*
- used to show the title of an article, poem, etc 用以标明文章、诗歌等的名称 *(I was reading the poem "Night".)*

semicolon （;）分号

used to separate different parts of a sentence 用以分隔句子中的不同部分 *(The car is expensive; the bicycle is cheap.)*

Verbs 动词变位

The verbs in the brackets are used with "he", "she", "it" or other singular nouns. 括号内的动词与 he、she、it 或其他单数名词一起使用。

To save space we include only one Chinese translation of each verb. 限于篇幅，每个动词只附带一个中文释义。

present tense 现在式	present participle 现在分词	past tense 过去式	past participle 过去分词
accuse (accuses) 指责	accusing	accused	accused
ache (aches) 疼痛	aching	ached	ached
achieve (achieves) 做成	achieving	achieved	achieved
admire (admires) 仰慕	admiring	admired	admired
admit (admits) 承认	admitting	admitted	admitted
advertise (advertises) 登广告	advertising	advertised	advertised
advise (advises) 劝告	advising	advised	advised
agree (agrees) 同意	agreeing	agreed	agreed
amuse (amuses) 使人发笑	amusing	amused	amused
apologize (apologizes) 道歉	apologizing	apologized	apologized
apply (applies) 申请	applying	applied	applied
argue (argues) 争论	arguing	argued	argued
arrange (arranges) 排列	arranging	arranged	arranged
arrive (arrives) 到达	arriving	arrived	arrived
bake (bakes) 烘	baking	baked	baked
be (am/is/are) 是	being	was/were	been
beat (beats) 打败	beating	beat	beaten
become (becomes) 变成	becoming	became	become
beg (begs) 恳求	begging	begged	begged
begin (begins) 开始	beginning	began	begun
behave (behaves) 表现	behaving	behaved	behaved

believe (believes) 信	believing	believed	believed
bend (bends) 弄弯	bending	bent	bent
bite (bites) 咬	biting	bit	bitten
blame (blames) 责怪	blaming	blamed	blamed
bleed (bleeds) 流血	bleeding	bled	bled
blow (blows) 吹	blowing	blew	blown
bounce (bounces) 弹跳	bouncing	bounced	bounced
break (breaks) 打碎	breaking	broke	broken
breathe (breathes) 呼吸	breathing	breathed	breathed
bring (brings) 带来	bringing	brought	brought
browse (browses) 浏览	browsing	browsed	browsed
brush (brushes) 刷	brushing	brushed	brushed
build (builds) 建筑	building	built	built
burn (burns) 燃烧	burning	burnt/burned	burnt/burned
burst (bursts) 破裂	bursting	burst	burst
bury (buries) 埋藏	burying	buried	buried
buy (buys) 购买	buying	bought	bought
cancel (cancels) 取消	cancelling	cancelled	cancelled
capture (captures) 俘虏	capturing	captured	captured
care (cares) 关心	caring	cared	cared
carry (carries) 携带	carrying	carried	carried
catch (catches) 捕捉	catching	caught	caught
cause (causes) 导致	causing	caused	caused
celebrate (celebrates) 庆祝	celebrating	celebrated	celebrated
change (changes) 改变	changing	changed	changed
charge (charges) 收费	charging	charged	charged
chase (chases) 追赶	chasing	chased	chased
chat (chats) 闲谈	chatting	chatted	chatted
chime (chimes) 鸣响	chiming	chimed	chimed
choose (chooses) 选择	choosing	chose	chosen

chop (chops) 砍	chopping	chopped	chopped
circle (circles) 圈出	circling	circled	circled
clap (claps) 拍手	clapping	clapped	clapped
close (closes) 关闭	closing	closed	closed
combine (combines) 结合	combining	combined	combined
come (comes) 来	coming	came	come
communicate (communicates) 沟通	communicating	communicated	communicated
compare (compares) 比较	comparing	compared	compared
compete (competes) 比赛	competing	competed	competed
complete (completes) 完成	completing	completed	completed
continue (continues) 持续	continuing	continued	continued
control (controls) 控制	controlling	controlled	controlled
cooperate (cooperates) 合作	cooperating	cooperated	cooperated
copy (copies) 抄	copying	copied	copied
cost (costs) 价值	costing	cost	cost
crash (crashes) 相撞	crashing	crashed	crashed
create (creates) 创造	creating	created	created
cross (crosses) 横过	crossing	crossed	crossed
crush (crushes) 压	crushing	crushed	crushed
cry (cries) 哭	crying	cried	cried
cure (cures) 医治	curing	cured	cured
cut (cuts) 切	cutting	cut	cut
cycle (cycles) 骑自行车	cycling	cycled	cycled
damage (damages) 损坏	damaging	damaged	damaged
dance (dances) 跳舞	dancing	danced	danced
dare (dares) 敢	daring	dared	dared
decide (decides) 决定	deciding	decided	decided
decorate (decorates) 装修	decorating	decorated	decorated
decrease (decreases) 减少	decreasing	decreased	decreased
delete (deletes) 删除	deleting	deleted	deleted

demonstrate (demonstrates) 示范	demonstrating	demonstrated	demonstrated
deny (denies) 否认	denying	denied	denied
describe (describes) 形容	describing	described	described
deserve (deserves) 该得	deserving	deserved	deserved
dial (dials) 拨电话	dialling	dialled	dialled
dice (dices) 切粒	dicing	diced	diced
die (dies) 死	dying	died	died
dig (digs) 挖	digging	dug	dug
disagree (disagrees) 不同意	disagreeing	disagreed	disagreed
discuss (discusses) 讨论	discussing	discussed	discussed
dislike (dislikes) 不喜欢	disliking	disliked	disliked
dismiss (dismisses) 解散	dismissing	dismissed	dismissed
dive (dives) 跳水	diving	dived	dived
divide (divides) 分开	dividing	divided	divided
do (does) 做	doing	did	done
donate (donates) 捐赠	donating	donated	donated
double (doubles) 使加倍	doubling	doubled	doubled
doze (dozes) 打瞌睡	dozing	dozed	dozed
drag (drags) 拖	dragging	dragged	dragged
draw (draws) 画	drawing	drew	drawn
dream (dreams) 做梦	dreaming	dreamt/dreamed	dreamt/dreamed
dress (dresses) 穿衣服	dressing	dressed	dressed
drink (drinks) 喝	drinking	drank	drunk
drip (drips) 滴下	dripping	dripped	dripped
drive (drives) 驾驶	driving	drove	driven
drop (drops) 跌下	dropping	dropped	dropped
dry (dries) 弄干	drying	dried	dried
dye (dyes) 染	dyeing	dyed	dyed
eat (eats) 吃	eating	ate	eaten
educate (educates) 教育	educating	educated	educated

emigrate (emigrates) 移居	emigrating	emigrated	emigrated
empty (empties) 倒空	emptying	emptied	emptied
encourage (encourages) 鼓励	encouraging	encouraged	encouraged
enlarge (enlarges) 扩大	enlarging	enlarged	enlarged
equal (equals) 等于	equalling	equalled	equalled
escape (escapes) 逃走	escaping	escaped	escaped
examine (examines) 检查	examining	examined	examined
exchange (exchanges) 交换	exchanging	exchanged	exchanged
excuse (excuses) 原谅	excusing	excused	excused
exercise (exercises) 做运动	exercising	exercised	exercised
explode (explodes) 爆炸	exploding	exploded	exploded
explore (explores) 探索	exploring	explored	explored
express (expresses) 表达	expressing	expressed	expressed
face (faces) 面向	facing	faced	faced
fade (fades) 褪色	fading	faded	faded
fall (falls) 落下	falling	fell	fallen
fancy (fancies) 想要	fancying	fancied	fancied
feed (feeds) 喂	feeding	fed	fed
feel (feels) 觉得	feeling	felt	felt
fetch (fetches) 拿来	fetching	fetched	fetched
fight (fights) 打架	fighting	fought	fought
find (finds) 找到	finding	found	found
finish (finishes) 完成	finishing	finished	finished
fire (fires) 射击	firing	fired	fired
fish (fishes) 钓鱼	fishing	fished	fished
fit (fits) 合身	fitting	fitted	fitted
fix (fixes) 修理	fixing	fixed	fixed
flap (flaps) 振翼	flapping	flapped	flapped
flash (flashes) 发出闪光	flashing	flashed	flashed
flush (flushes) 脸红	flushing	flushed	flushed

fly (flies) 飞	flying	flew	flown
forbid (forbids) 禁止	forbidding	forbade	forbidden
force (forces) 强迫	forcing	forced	forced
forget (forgets) 忘记	forgetting	forgot	forgotten
forgive (forgives) 原谅	forgiving	forgave	forgiven
free (frees) 释放	freeing	freed	freed
freeze (freezes) 结冰	freezing	froze	frozen
fry (fries) 煎	frying	fried	fried
gamble (gambles) 赌博	gambling	gambled	gambled
get (gets) 取得	getting	got	got
giggle (giggles) 傻笑	giggling	giggled	giggled
give (gives) 给	giving	gave	given
glide (glides) 滑行	gliding	glided	glided
go (goes) 去	going	went	gone
grab (grabs) 抓住	grabbing	grabbed	grabbed
grin (grins) 露齿而笑	grinning	grinned	grinned
grip (grips) 紧握	gripping	gripped	gripped
grow (grows) 成长	growing	grew	grown
grumble (grumbles) 抱怨	grumbling	grumbled	grumbled
guess (guesses) 猜想	guessing	guessed	guessed
guide (guides) 带路	guiding	guided	guided
handle (handles) 触	handling	handled	handled
hang (hangs) 挂	hanging	hung	hung
hate (hates) 憎恨	hating	hated	hated
have (has) 有	having	had	had
hear (hears) 听见	hearing	heard	heard
hide (hides) 躲藏	hiding	hid	hidden
hire (hires) 租用	hiring	hired	hired
hiss (hisses) 发出嘶嘶声	hissing	hissed	hissed
hit (hits) 打	hitting	hit	hit

hold (holds) 拿住	holding	held	held
hop (hops) 单脚跳	hopping	hopped	hopped
hope (hopes) 希望	hoping	hoped	hoped
hug (hugs) 拥抱	hugging	hugged	hugged
hurry (hurries) 赶快	hurrying	hurried	hurried
hurt (hurts) 弄伤	hurting	hurt	hurt
ignore (ignores) 不理会	ignoring	ignored	ignored
imagine (imagines) 想象	imagining	imagined	imagined
improve (improves) 进步	improving	improved	improved
include (includes) 包括	including	included	included
increase (increases) 增加	increasing	increased	increased
influence (influences) 影响	influencing	influenced	influenced
injure (injures) 伤害	injuring	injured	injured
input (inputs) 输入	inputting	input/inputted	input/inputted
inspire (inspires) 启发	inspiring	inspired	inspired
introduce (introduces) 介绍	introducing	introduced	introduced
invade (invades) 侵略	invading	invaded	invaded
investigate (investigates) 调查	investigating	investigated	investigated
invite (invites) 邀请	inviting	invited	invited
itch (itches) 发痒	itching	itched	itched
jog (jogs) 慢跑	jogging	jogged	jogged
joke (jokes) 说笑话	joking	joked	joked
keep (keeps) 保留	keeping	kept	kept
kidnap (kidnaps) 绑架	kidnapping	kidnapped	kidnapped
kiss (kisses) 吻	kissing	kissed	kissed
kneel (kneels) 跪下	kneeling	knelt	knelt
knit (knits) 编织	knitting	knitted/knit	knitted/knit
know (knows) 知道	knowing	knew	known
lay (lays) 放置	laying	laid	laid
lead (leads) 带领	leading	led	led

lean (leans) 屈身	leaning	leaned/leant	leaned/leant
leap (leaps) 跳	leaping	leaped/leapt	leaped/leapt
learn (learns) 学习	learning	learned/learnt	learned/learnt
leave (leaves) 离开	leaving	left	left
lend (lends) 借出	lending	lent	lent
let (lets) 让	letting	let	let
lie (lies) 躺卧	lying	lay	lain
lie (lies) 说谎	lying	lied	lied
light (lights) 点火	lighting	lighted/lit	lighted/lit
like (likes) 喜欢	liking	liked	liked
live (lives) 居住	living	lived	lived
log (logs) 登入/登出	logging	logged	logged
lose (loses) 遗失	losing	lost	lost
love (loves) 爱	loving	loved	loved
make (makes) 做	making	made	made
manage (manages) 管理	managing	managed	managed
manufacture (manufactures) 制造	manufacturing	manufactured	manufactured
march (marches) 齐步行走	marching	marched	marched
marry (marries) 结婚	marrying	married	married
match (matches) 配对	matching	matched	matched
mean (means) 意思是	meaning	meant	meant
measure (measures) 度量	measuring	measured	measured
meet (meets) 会面	meeting	met	met
misbehave (misbehaves) 行为不端	misbehaving	misbehaved	misbehaved
miss (misses) 怀念	missing	missed	missed
mix (mixes) 混合	mixing	mixed	mixed
move (moves) 移动	moving	moved	moved
multiply (multiplies) 乘	multiplying	multiplied	multiplied
name (names) 取名	naming	named	named

nod (nods) 点头	nodding	nodded	nodded
note (notes) 注意	noting	noted	noted
notice (notices) 注意到	noticing	noticed	noticed
nurse (nurses) 照料	nursing	nursed	nursed
observe (observes) 观察	observing	observed	observed
occur (occurs) 发生	occurring	occurred	occurred
organize (organizes) 组织	organizing	organized	organized
overcome (overcomes) 克服	overcoming	overcame	overcome
overtake (overtakes) 超过	overtaking	overtook	overtaken
owe (owes) 欠	owing	owed	owed
paddle (paddles) 用短桨划	paddling	paddled	paddled
panic (panics) 惊慌	panicking	panicked	panicked
pass (passes) 经过	passing	passed	passed
paste (pastes) 黏贴	pasting	pasted	pasted
pat (pats) 轻拍	patting	patted	patted
pay (pays) 付款	paying	paid	paid
permit (permits) 准许	permitting	permitted	permitted
phone (phones) 打电话	phoning	phoned	phoned
photocopy (photocopies) 影印	photocopying	photocopied	photocopied
pin (pins) 把…别住	pinning	pinned	pinned
pity (pities) 同情	pitying	pitied	pitied
place (places) 放置	placing	placed	placed
plan (plans) 计划	planning	planned	planned
please (pleases) 取悦	pleasing	pleased	pleased
polish (polishes) 擦亮	polishing	polished	polished
pollute (pollutes) 污染	polluting	polluted	polluted
practise (practises) 练习	practising	practised	practised
praise (praises) 称赞	praising	praised	praised
prefer (prefers) 更喜欢	preferring	preferred	preferred
prepare (prepares) 准备	preparing	prepared	prepared

press (presses) 按	pressing	pressed	pressed
produce (produces) 生产	producing	produced	produced
promise (promises) 承诺	promising	promised	promised
pronounce (pronounces) 发…的音	pronouncing	pronounced	pronounced
prove (proves) 证明	proving	proved	proved
provide (provides) 提供	providing	provided	provided
punch (punches) 用拳打	punching	punched	punched
punish (punishes) 处罚	punishing	punished	punished
push (pushes) 推	pushing	pushed	pushed
put (puts) 放	putting	put	put
quarrel (quarrels) 争吵	quarrelling	quarrelled	quarrelled
quote (quotes) 引述	quoting	quoted	quoted
race (races) 参加比赛	racing	raced	raced
raise (raises) 举起	raising	raised	raised
range (ranges) 在…范围内	ranging	ranged	ranged
reach (reaches) 到达	reaching	reached	reached
read (reads) 阅读	reading	read	read
realize (realizes) 领悟	realizing	realized	realized
receive (receives) 收到	receiving	received	received
recite (recites) 背诵	reciting	recited	recited
recognize (recognizes) 认出	recognizing	recognized	recognized
recycle (recycles) 回收利用	recycling	recycled	recycled
reduce (reduces) 缩小	reducing	reduced	reduced
refer (refers) 提及	referring	referred	referred
refuse (refuses) 拒绝	refusing	refused	refused
relax (relaxes) 轻松	relaxing	relaxed	relaxed
remove (removes) 搬走	removing	removed	removed
replace (replaces) 取代	replacing	replaced	replaced
reply (replies) 回答	replying	replied	replied
require (requires) 需要	requiring	required	required

rescue (rescues) 拯救	rescuing	rescued	rescued
revise (revises) 复习	revising	revised	revised
rhyme (rhymes) 押韵	rhyming	rhymed	rhymed
ride (rides) 骑	riding	rode	ridden
ring (rings) 发出铃声	ringing	rang	rung
rinse (rinses) 冲洗	rinsing	rinsed	rinsed
rise (rises) 上升	rising	rose	risen
rob (robs) 抢劫	robbing	robbed	robbed
rub (rubs) 擦	rubbing	rubbed	rubbed
rule (rules) 统治	ruling	ruled	ruled
run (runs) 跑	running	ran	run
rush (rushes) 赶快	rushing	rushed	rushed
save (saves) 救	saving	saved	saved
saw (saws) 锯	sawing	sawed	sawn
say (says) 说	saying	said	said
scan (scans) 扫描	scanning	scanned	scanned
scare (scares) 使害怕	scaring	scared	scared
score (scores) 得分	scoring	scored	scored
scratch (scratches) 抓伤	scratching	scratched	scratched
search (searches) 寻找	searching	searched	searched
see (sees) 看见	seeing	saw	seen
sell (sells) 卖	selling	sold	sold
send (sends) 发出	sending	sent	sent
sense (senses) 感觉到	sensing	sensed	sensed
separate (separates) 使分开	separating	separated	separated
serve (serves) 端上	serving	served	served
set (sets) 放置	setting	set	set
settle (settles) 定居	settling	settled	settled
sew (sews) 缝制	sewing	sewed	sewn/sewed
shake (shakes) 摇动	shaking	shook	shaken

shape (shapes) 把…做成某种形状	shaping	shaped	shaped
share (shares) 共享	sharing	shared	shared
shave (shaves) 剃	shaving	shaved	shaved
shine (shines) 发光	shining	shone	shone
shoot (shoots) 射击	shooting	shot	shot
shop (shops) 买东西	shopping	shopped	shopped
show (shows) 给…看	showing	showed	shown
shut (shuts) 关闭	shutting	shut	shut
sing (sings) 唱歌	singing	sang	sung
sink (sinks) 下沉	sinking	sank	sunk
sit (sits) 坐	sitting	sat	sat
skate (skates) 溜冰	skating	skated	skated
skid (skids) 滑行	skidding	skidded	skidded
skip (skips) 蹦跳地走	skipping	skipped	skipped
sleep (sleeps) 睡	sleeping	slept	slept
slide (slides) 滑行	sliding	slid	slid
slip (slips) 滑倒	slipping	slipped	slipped
smell (smells) 闻出	smelling	smelt/smelled	smelt/smelled
smile (smiles) 微笑	smiling	smiled	smiled
smoke (smokes) 吸烟	smoking	smoked	smoked
sneeze (sneezes) 打喷嚏	sneezing	sneezed	sneezed
snore (snores) 打鼻鼾	snoring	snored	snored
solve (solves) 解决	solving	solved	solved
sow (sows) 播种	sowing	sowed	sown/sowed
speak (speaks) 说话	speaking	spoke	spoken
speed (speeds) 快速移动	speeding	sped/speeded	sped/speeded
spell (spells) 拼写	spelling	spelt/spelled	spelt/spelled
spend (spends) 花费	spending	spent	spent
spill (spills) 溢出	spilling	spilt/spilled	spilt/spilled

spit (spits) 吐	spitting	spat	spat
splash (splashes) 溅	splashing	splashed	splashed
spoil (spoils) 破坏	spoiling	spoiled/spoilt	spoiled/spoilt
spread (spreads) 展开	spreading	spread	spread
squeeze (squeezes) 挤	squeezing	squeezed	squeezed
stand (stands) 站	standing	stood	stood
stare (stares) 盯着看	staring	stared	stared
starve (starves) 挨饿	starving	starved	starved
steal (steals) 偷	stealing	stole	stolen
step (steps) 迈步	stepping	stepped	stepped
stick (sticks) 黏	sticking	stuck	stuck
sting (stings) 刺	stinging	stung	stung
stir (stirs) 搅	stirring	stirred	stirred
stop (stops) 停止	stopping	stopped	stopped
store (stores) 贮藏	storing	stored	stored
stretch (stretches) 拉长	stretching	stretched	stretched
struggle (struggles) 奋斗	struggling	struggled	struggled
study (studies) 学习	studying	studied	studied
sunbathe (sunbathes) 晒太阳	sunbathing	sunbathed	sunbathed
supply (supplies) 供应	supplying	supplied	supplied
surprise (surprises) 使惊奇	surprising	surprised	surprised
survive (survives) 幸存	surviving	survived	survived
sweep (sweeps) 打扫	sweeping	swept	swept
swim (swims) 游泳	swimming	swam	swum
swing (swings) 摇摆	swinging	swung	swung
switch (switches) 转换	switching	switched	switched
take (takes) 拿着	taking	took	taken
tap (taps) 轻拍	tapping	tapped	tapped
taste (tastes) 尝	tasting	tasted	tasted
teach (teaches) 教	teaching	taught	taught

tear (tears) 撕破	tearing	tore	torn
tease (teases) 取笑	teasing	teased	teased
telephone (telephones) 打电话	telephoning	telephoned	telephoned
tell (tells) 告诉	telling	told	told
terrify (terrifies) 使惊恐	terrifying	terrified	terrified
think (thinks) 认为	thinking	thought	thought
throw (throws) 投	throwing	threw	thrown
tidy (tidies) 整理	tidying	tidied	tidied
tie (ties) 捆	tying	tied	tied
touch (touches) 触摸	touching	touched	touched
trap (traps) 捕捉	trapping	trapped	trapped
travel (travels) 旅行	travelling	travelled	travelled
tremble (trembles) 发抖	trembling	trembled	trembled
try (tries) 尝试	trying	tried	tried
twinkle (twinkles) 闪烁	twinkling	twinkled	twinkled
type (types) 打字	typing	typed	typed
underline (underlines) 在（词语）下面划线	underlining	underlined	underlined
understand (understands) 懂得	understanding	understood	understood
undo (undoes) 解开	undoing	undid	undone
undress (undresses) 脱衣服	undressing	undressed	undressed
untie (unties) 解开	untying	untied	untied
unwrap (unwraps) 拆开	unwrapping	unwrapped	unwrapped
use (uses) 用	using	used	used
vote (votes) 投票	voting	voted	voted
wake (wakes) 醒来	waking	woke	woken
wash (washes) 洗	washing	washed	washed
waste (wastes) 浪费	wasting	wasted	wasted
watch (watches) 观看	watching	watched	watched
wave (waves) 挥手	waving	waved	waved
wear (wears) 穿	wearing	wore	worn

weep (weeps) 哭泣	weeping	wept	wept
welcome (welcomes) 迎接	welcoming	welcomed	welcomed
whistle (whistles) 吹口哨	whistling	whistled	whistled
win (wins) 赢	winning	won	won
wind (winds) 缠	winding	wound	wound
wipe (wipes) 抹	wiping	wiped	wiped
wish (wishes) 想做	wishing	wished	wished
witness (witnesses) 目击	witnessing	witnessed	witnessed
worry (worries) 担心	worrying	worried	worried
worship (worships) 崇拜	worshipping	worshipped	worshipped
wrap (wraps) 包	wrapping	wrapped	wrapped
write (writes) 写字	writing	wrote	written
zip (zips) 拉上拉链	zipping	zipped	zipped